The Essential Study Companion *for* Every Disciple

David C. Cook Bible Lesson Commentary

NIV

David Ⓒ Cook®

transforming lives together

DAVID C. COOK'S NIV BIBLE LESSON COMMENTARY 2009–2010
Published by David C. Cook
4050 Lee Vance View
Colorado Springs, CO 80918 U.S.A.

David C. Cook Distribution Canada
55 Woodslee Avenue, Paris, Ontario, Canada N3L 3E5

David C. Cook U.K., Kingsway Communications
Eastbourne, East Sussex BN23 6NT, England

David C. Cook and the graphic circle C logo
are registered trademarks of Cook Communications Ministries.

Scripture quotations are taken from the *Holy Bible, New International Version®*.
NIV®. Copyright © 1973, 1978, 1984 by International Bible Society.
Used by permission of Zondervan. All rights reserved.

Lessons based on *International Sunday School Lessons: The International Bible Lessons for
Christian Teaching*, © 2005 by the Committee on the Uniform Series.

ISBN 978-1-4347-6754-7

© 2009 David C. Cook

Written and edited by Dan Lioy, PhD
The Team: John Blase, Doug Schmidt, Amy Kiechlin, and Jack Campbell
Cover Design: Amy Kiechlin
Cover Photo: iStockphoto

Printed in the United States of America
First Edition 2009

1 2 3 4 5 6 7 8 9 10

020409

David C. Cook Bible Lesson Commentary

The New Covenant Community

Unit I: Leaders in the Covenant Community

Unit II: An Open Invitation to Covenant Living

Unit III: The New Covenant Community

Christ, the Fulfillment

Unit I: The Promised Birth Fulfilled

Unit II: Evidences of Jesus as Messiah

Unit III: Testimonies to Jesus as Messiah

Teachings on Community

Christian Commitment in Today's World

A Word to the Teacher

Several years ago at a well-known college, one of the students told the dean that Christians would make better grades than the unbelievers just because they were Christians. This person's claim embarrassed a lot of his fellow believers, who knew very well that some of the unsaved were smarter than they were and got better grades.

The Bible clearly teaches that the Holy Spirit can supply believers with divine wisdom. But does the Spirit's presence guarantee an "A" in biology if believers don't study? No. Every Christian student must work hard, pray faithfully, and trust God for the results. The Spirit does not produce an "A," but He will give unusual peace and courage.

The Spirit's teaching brings Jesus to our hearts and minds. And if we learn Jesus, as well as biology (or any other subject), then we are being faithful disciples. In fact, that is the primary objective for us and the students we teach, not making the dean's list.

As we undertake the important task of leading class members into a deeper and clearer understanding of Scripture, let us be motivated by the fact that our hearts and minds are battlegrounds for truth. The classic struggle is waged when we hear the Gospel and decide it's either foolishness or the greatest news we have ever encountered. So much of our secular education tells us it's foolishness. We have the awesome task to teach otherwise.

As we work our way through a new year's worth of lessons, let us be invigorated by the realization that the battle never stops to affirm the truth of the Gospel. We can turn to the Spirit for inspiration and strength to remind our fellow believers how to build on their faith.

From week to week, let the class members know that their faith is not an irrational leap in the dark. Take time to assure them that Jesus really lived and died for us. Don't hesitate to stress that He ascended into heaven, sent the Holy Spirit to teach us, and will one day come again. May God richly bless you as you share the riches of His truth with your students!

Your fellow learner at the feet of the Master Teacher,
Dan Lioy

Using *David C. Cook's NIV Bible Lesson Commentary* with Materials from Other Publishers

Sunday school materials from the following denominations and publishers follow International Sunday School Lesson outlines (sometimes known as Uniform Series). Because *David C. Cook's NIV Bible Lesson Commentary* (formerly *Peloubet's*) follows the same outlines, you can use the *Commentary* as an excellent teacher resource to supplement the materials from these publishing houses.

NONDENOMINATIONAL:
>   Standard Publishing: *Adult*
>   Urban Ministries
>   Echoes Teacher's Commentary (Cook Communications Ministries): *Adult*

DENOMINATIONAL:
>   Advent Christian General Conference: *Adult*
>   American Baptist (Judson Press): *Adult*
>   United Holy Church of America: *Adult*
>   Church of God in Christ (Church of God in Christ Publishing House): *Adult*
>   Church of Christ Holiness: *Adult*
>   Church of God (Warner Press): *Adult*
>   Church of God by Faith: *Adult*
>   National Baptist Convention of America *(Boyd): All ages*
>   National Primitive Baptist Convention: *Adult*
>   Progressive National Baptist Convention: *Adult*
>   Presbyterian Church (U.S.A.) (Bible Discovery Series—Presbyterian Publishing House or P.R.E.M.): *Adult*
>   Union Gospel Press: *All ages*
>   United Holy Church of America: *Adult*
>   United Methodist (Cokesbury): *All ages*

Joshua: A Leader for the People

DEVOTIONAL READING

1 Timothy 2:1-6

DAILY BIBLE READINGS

Monday August 31
1 Timothy 2:1-6 Pray for Leaders

Tuesday September 1
Exodus 24:12-18 Training as a Leader

Wednesday September 2
Numbers 11:24-29 Misplaced Zeal

Thursday September 3
Numbers 32:6-13 Following without Reserve

Friday September 4
Numbers 27:15-23 Commissioned to Lead

Saturday September 5
Deuteronomy 34:1-9 Ready to Lead

Sunday September 6
Joshua 1:1-11, 16-17 A Leader Led by God

Scripture

Background Scripture: *Joshua 1*
Scripture Lesson: *Joshua 1:1-11, 16-17*
Key Verse: *"Have I not commanded you? Be strong and courageous. Do not be terrified; do not be discouraged, for the LORD your God will be with you wherever you go."* Joshua 1:9.
Scripture Lesson for Children: *Joshua 1:1-11*
Key Verse for Children: *"Be strong and courageous . . . for the LORD your God will be with you wherever you go."* Joshua 1:9.

Lesson Aim

To stress the importance of remaining obedient to the Lord, knowing that He is ever present to watch over and empower His people.

Lesson Setting

Time: *1406 B.C.*
Place: *Plains of Moab*

Lesson Outline

Joshua: A Leader for the People

   I. The Commission of Joshua: Joshua 1:1-9
      A. *The Lord's Empowerment of Joshua: vss. 1-5*
      B. *The Lord's Command to Be Courageous: vss. 6-9*
  II. The Compliance of the People: Joshua 1:10-11, 16-17
      A. *The Divine Plan: vss. 10-11*
      B. *The People's Obedience: vss. 16-17*

Introduction for Adults

Topic: *Leadership Strong and Courageous*

Though John Wesley stands as a giant in the history of the church, Charles Wesley is not hidden in his brother's shadow. Charles' evangelical ministry stirred the souls of thousands of people of his time, and many of his hymns have thrilled the hearts of millions of Christians since the eighteenth century. "Hark, the Herald Angels Sing" and "Christ the Lord Is Risen Today" are just two of his songs that will be an eternal blessing to God's people.

"He exercised a distinctive ministry," states Christian historian, A. Skevington Wood, "as an evangelist, a counselor, and a shepherd of souls. . . . It is, however, as a composer of Christian hymns that Charles Wesley is now mostly remembered." Indeed, Charles' music has inspired countless people to follow the Savior as their leader and encourage others to do the same.

Introduction for Youth

Topic: *Courageous Leadership under Fire*

Alexandra Hernandez is a prevention program coordinator at Youth Leadership Institute (YLI) in San Francisco, California. In 1984, when she was nine years old, she came to the United States from her native country, Nicaragua. In a press release from YLI, Hernandez shared that in her adolescence she "started . . . organizing young people around the issues that affected them in their community." Gradually, this kind of work became for her "more than a job. It became a mission."

Reflecting on herself and those whom she serves at YLI, Hernandez makes the following observation: "It's important to be grounded in who you are, to take pride in where you come from and what you represent, and then to share that." She believes her "role in life" is to "give something back." As Christians, we must be grounded in our faith in Christ, following Him as our Lord as we share with others the miracle He has done in our lives. Our role in life is to give back to Him the honor and glory He deserves.

Concepts for Children

Topic: *A Brave Leader Is Chosen*

1. God chose Joshua as Israel's new leader.
2. God promised to be with Joshua in the same way that God was with Moses.
3. God commanded Joshua to be strong and brave in obeying God's law.
4. God promised to give Joshua strength to lead the Israelites into the promised land.
5. God also promises to be with us and to strengthen us, especially as we serve Him.

Lesson Commentary

I. THE COMMISSION OF JOSHUA: JOSHUA 1:1-9

A. The Lord's Empowerment of Joshua: vss. 1-5

After the death of Moses the servant of the LORD, the LORD said to Joshua son of Nun, Moses' aide: "Moses my servant is dead. Now then, you and all these people, get ready to cross the Jordan River into the land I am about to give to them—to the Israelites. I will give you every place where you set your foot, as I promised Moses. Your territory will extend from the desert to Lebanon, and from the great river, the Euphrates—all the Hittite country—to the Great Sea on the west. No one will be able to stand up against you all the days of your life. As I was with Moses, so I will be with you; I will never leave you nor forsake you."

Joshua 1:1 picks up where Deuteronomy 34:5 left off—with the death of Moses, the Lord's servant. The Lord directed Joshua (through what means remains unknown) to prepare the people to cross the Jordan and enter the land God had promised to the descendants of Abraham (Josh. 1:2; see Gen. 12:7; 13:15; 15:18; 50:24; Exod. 23:31; Deut. 1:7-8). The Israelites must have known they were embarking upon a formidable task. Camped on the plains of Moab, the Israelites probably suspected their fierce Canaanite foes were expecting an Israelite attack. One could not blame God's people if they had shied away from attacking fortified cities defended by well-trained and well-equipped warriors. But, unlike their Israelite forefathers, this new generation believed God would be faithful to His promise. In response to the Lord's call and Joshua's leadership, the people prepared to overcome all the obstacles and enter the promised land.

The Lord's promise to Joshua was similar to the one He had made earlier to Moses (see Deut. 11:24-25). God pledged to the new Israelite leader that He would give the Hebrews all the regions through which they walked during their military campaign in Canaan (Josh. 1:3). This would bring to completion the work initiated by Moses. The main emphasis is on the fact that the land was God's gift to the Israelites. Still, the land would be theirs only as they would appropriate it.

The land promised to Joshua was broader than what was actually conquered under his leadership. Verse 4 says the territory would stretch from the wilderness in the south to Lebanon in the north. Moreover, the nation would control all the land from the Euphrates River in the east (including all of Syria, that is, the "Hittite country") to the Mediterranean Sea in the west. However, the land conquered by the Israelites under Joshua only stretched from Dan in the north to Beersheba in the south (see Gen. 15:18; Num. 34:3-12; Deut. 34:1-4).

The Israelites' inability to gain control of all the promised land was not due to God's negligence, but rather to the people's failure to keep their part of the covenant. Even though the region was given to them, certain conditions had to be met by the new tenants. The early Israelites' disobedience and halfhearted devotion to God prevented them from conquering the entire area, at least not until

King Solomon extended Israel's borders to their farthest reaches in the tenth century B.C. (see Judg. 2:1-4, 20-23; 1 Kings 4:21, 24). Although decisive battles were won under Joshua, the Israelite general intended for the tribes to take the rest of the land on their own initiative. When Joshua died and the Israelites entered into the period of the judges, their spiritual infidelity kept them on the defensive and squelched their attempts to take all that God had given to them.

The Lord promised that throughout Joshua's life, no one would be able to resist his efforts to conquer Canaan. God's abiding presence was the key to the Israelites' military success. Indeed, just as God had promised Moses His constant presence, so He pledged to comfort and encourage Joshua in the same way. The Lord declared that He would never abandon or forsake Israel's general (Josh. 1:5). God wanted Joshua to be assured of this, especially as he led the people into Canaan and ongoing combat.

B. The Lord's Command to Be Courageous: vss. 6-9

"Be strong and courageous, because you will lead these people to inherit the land I swore to their fore-fathers to give them. Be strong and very courageous. Be careful to obey all the law my servant Moses gave you; do not turn from it to the right or to the left, that you may be successful wherever you go. Do not let this Book of the Law depart from your mouth; meditate on it day and night, so that you may be careful to do everything written in it. Then you will be prosperous and successful. Have I not command-ed you? Be strong and courageous. Do not be terrified; do not be discouraged, for the LORD your God will be with you wherever you go."

Shortly before his death, Moses commissioned Joshua a second time in the sight of all Israel. His words to Joshua recorded in Deuteronomy 31:7-8 parallel those of the Lord found in Joshua 1:5-6. The Israelites' newly appointed general was to be "strong and courageous," for God, the divine King, had summoned Joshua to lead the people into the land promised to their ancestors (namely, Abraham, Isaac, and Jacob). In addition, Joshua was to strictly obey the law the Lord had given to Moses at Mount Sinai. If Joshua heeded the divine injunctions, God would guarantee his success. These pledges set the tone for the entire Book of Joshua and provide the context in which all the events recorded in the rest of the book were to occur. Moreover, in the account of Israel's history after the Exodus, Joshua's obedience is often contrasted with the nation's disobedience.

Joshua was commanded six times to be strong and courageous: once by Moses (Deut. 31:7), four times by the Lord (Deut. 31:23; Josh. 1:6-7, 9), and once by the people of Israel (Josh. 1:18). Undeniably, strength and courage would be essential assets for Joshua. Now that Moses was dead, the full burden of leading the Israelites was on Joshua's shoulders. It was an intimidating position to be in, for he was following in the footsteps of Moses, the man "whom the Lord knew face to face (see Deut. 34:10-12). In spite of Moses' position before the Lord, however, there were still times when the Israelites challenged his authority as their intercessor and advocate. Joshua witnessed those instances when the Hebrews showed disrespect for Moses and Joshua had no real assurance that the people would treat him any better.

Strength and courage were also vital because, for the most part, the people's greatest enemies while wandering in the wilderness had been the elements of nature. Now they were about to face some of the cruelest and most ruthless warriors in the region. The Israelites were out-manned and out-equipped by the inhabitants they were about to attack. Thus God's people could not afford to have a timid leader. There is no indication in Scripture that Joshua ever hesitated to take on any challenge God gave him. Even so, the courageous Joshua needed to know that God would be with him, at least in part because of the odds against the nation he was leading.

The "law" (Josh. 1:7) Moses gave to Joshua probably comprised most of the Book of Deuteronomy (see Deut. 31:24-26; Josh. 8:34-35; 23:6; 24:26). In fact, Joshua might have had the original manuscripts of the Pentateuch (the first five books of the Bible) at his disposal. The many parallels between the books of Deuteronomy and Joshua lead specialists to conclude that the author of Joshua was quite familiar with the contents of Deuteronomy. As far as the nation's obedience to God's law was concerned, there was to be no deviation. The phrase "to the right or to the left" implied that the Hebrews were to strictly obey the commandment. They were to walk the fine line of obedience.

Both a promise and a condition for the fulfillment of that pledge are included in verse 8. Joshua's not allowing the "Book of the Law" (vs. 8) to leave his lips meant that he should remember, rehearse, and obey the teaching Moses had passed on to him. God also directed Joshua to "meditate" on the law. The Hebrew verb for "meditate" implies a barely audible muttering of the words recorded in Scripture while studying them or reflecting upon them. Such a practice assured that Joshua would be thinking about what he read as he repeated the words to himself. Nonetheless, God would not consider knowledge of the law to be enough. The Lord also demanded obedience. So the practice of Joshua repeating the law as he meditated on it also served to remind him to carefully obey all that was "written in it."

To focus one's mind on God's Word "day and night" does not mean one has to live the life of a hermit. Certainly this was not true of Joshua. God intended him to fulfill this command even as he was in the process of conquering the land. Consequently, Joshua was to keep God's law in mind as he entered into each battle. After all, God was fulfilling through Joshua what He had promised to Abraham. If Joshua kept the commandments and the history of his ancestors in mind as he led the people, he would be more likely to obey God's will and less likely to repeat the mistakes of previous generations. Since God had denied Moses entrance into the promised land because of his disobedience, Joshua could be sure that the Lord would not make an exception for him.

God's admonition to Joshua to "be strong and courageous" (vs. 9) was more than just a word of encouragement; it was a command. The promise of the Lord's presence would be enough for Joshua to act bravely in spite of any fear or insecurity that might have remained after the death of Moses, his leader and mentor of 40 years. Evidently, any trembling or hesitation on Joshua's part would cause the courage of the people to waver. Therefore, Joshua had to be a rock of bravery and faithfulness, especially if the Israelites were to succeed.

II. THE COMPLIANCE OF THE PEOPLE: JOSHUA 1:10-11, 16-17

A. The Divine Plan: vss. 10-11

So Joshua ordered the officers of the people: "Go through the camp and tell the people, 'Get your supplies ready. Three days from now you will cross the Jordan here to go in and take possession of the land the **LORD** *your God is giving you for your own.'"*

Joshua dedicated himself to following the command God had given him (Josh. 1:2). He summoned his officers (vs. 10), those whom Moses evidently appointed before his death (see Exod. 18:21; Deut. 1:15). Joshua directed his subordinates to prepare the people for the start of the military campaign into Canaan (vs. 11). Initially, Joshua anticipated that it would be no more than three days before the Israelites began the process of crossing the Jordan River as a prelude to entering and seizing the promised land.

Joshua 2:22 and 3:1-2 indicate that the subsequent chain of events took longer to play out than Joshua thought. One possible reason for this is that in his enthusiasm, Joshua was a bit optimistic about how quickly the Hebrews could prepare to move into Canaan. A second option is that in 1:11, he used a common figure of speech that meant the people were to set out on their journey a few days later. A third alternative is that "three days" denotes a ritual period before the onset of the military operation (see Gen. 40:13, 19-20; Exod. 3:18; 19:11; Hos. 6:2). In any case, Joshua apparently did not meet any resistance from his subordinates. Being secure in God's promises, he passed on his confidence and enthusiasm to the people.

Through a well-organized chain of command, the instruction to prepare to cross the Jordan River quickly filtered throughout the Israelites' encampment. Their first order was to begin collecting supplies. Even though the people were about to launch a long and difficult military campaign, they would not be able to depend upon a miraculous provision of manna from heaven. Once the Israelites had established a toehold in Canaan, they would have to depend upon the fruit of the land for sustenance (see Josh. 5:12). Because the Israelites were entering Canaan during the harvest season, they realized that there would be ample food for everyone. In the meantime, however, they were to collect, prepare, and stockpile provisions to take with them as they advanced into enemy territory. They did not include manna in their supplies because it would not keep for more than a day.

B. The People's Obedience: vss. 16-17

Then they answered Joshua, "Whatever you have commanded us we will do, and wherever you send us we will go. Just as we fully obeyed Moses, so we will obey you. Only may the LORD your God be with you as he was with Moses."

After Joshua addressed the officials of all the Israelite tribes, he turned his attention to the Transjordan tribes—the two and a half tribes whose inheritance would lie east of the Jordan River (Josh. 1:12-15). Moses had granted these tribes their request to settle this land (see Num. 32). The Transjordan tribes vowed to heed whatever he "commanded" (Josh. 1:16). Wherever the Israelite general dispatched them, they pledged to go. In the same way they had "fully obeyed Moses" (vs. 17), they likewise promised to heed Joshua's orders. By and large, what the Transjordan tribes pledged reflected the sentiments of the entire nation of Israel at that time. This implies that Joshua achieved the unity for which he was hoping.

It is ironic, however, that the people promised to obey Joshua just as much as they had obeyed Moses. Given their history of rebellion against Moses' leadership, this might have caused Joshua a lot of concern. On numerous occasions recorded throughout books of the Pentateuch, the Israelites are shown to have failed to obey Moses and to have been severely disciplined as a result. Joshua himself had spent the last four decades in the wilderness because an earlier generation of Israelites refused to enter the promised land.

Given the character of Joshua, however, he probably accepted the people's vow without question. This is the first indication we are given that the Israelites fully recognized Joshua's leadership. Moses had taken great pains to let the people know that Joshua was to succeed him. Also, if the Israelites were going to capture the land of promise, Joshua needed their undivided loyalty. In pledging their commitment to Joshua, the people implied that they would stand behind him as long as the Lord stood behind him. More to the point, the Israelites pledge of commitment was also a prayer that God would grant Joshua His abiding and sustaining presence.

The people of Israel concluded their affirmation of Joshua with an oath. Whoever rebelled against Joshua and his commands was to be put to death (vs. 18). Now that the Israelites were launching a military campaign against the Canaanites, strict discipline was required. The execution of Achan (Joshua 7:24-25) would later demonstrate the people's willingness to keep their word in this matter. Much like the effect of the deaths of Ananias and Sapphira on the early Christians (see Acts 5:1-11), such a shocking demonstration of God's holiness would have squelched any desire the Hebrews may have had to rebel. Consequently, rebellion never became the kind of problem within the Israelite ranks that it had been during Moses' leadership. Apart from periods of overconfidence that momentarily distracted Joshua, the Israelite general kept his eyes on the Lord and successfully prepared the people of Israel to conquer Canaan.

Discussion Questions

1. What was the basis for Joshua being courageous in leading the Israelites in their conquest of Canaan?
2. What was the reason for God directing Joshua to heed the commandments recorded in the law?
3. How did the Israelites respond to Joshua's leadership?
4. How can we focus our minds on God's Word "day and night" without becoming hermits?
5. How can we develop the kind of unshakable faith Joshua needed to carry out God's plan for the Israelites?

Contemporary Application

Someone has said that people today lack heroes, or that they follow the wrong kinds of popular music and film stars. The Bible is full of heroes, or role models, like Joshua. He accepted a dangerous mission—leading the chosen people to conquer and settle the promised land—because he knew God personally.

As an expression of our obedience, the Lord asks us to step out in faith with new, godly behaviors—for instance, reaching to others in need, being kind to a difficult peer, going the extra mile for a friend, and maintaining our integrity while making decisions, even in the face of opposition. Sometimes God prompts us with gentle nudges and on other occasions through the direct words of a friend. We might try to pretend that we are unaware of God's leading. Or, in contrast, we can recognize how much better off we would be if we took the risk of remaining obedient to the Lord. We can do so, for we know that He is ever present to watch over and empower us to do His will.

Joshua understood this truth. Admittedly, not many people today will be attracted to him as a hero, that is, unless they are convinced that the way of faith, courage, and obedience is much more satisfying than other options they might choose. They need to see this kind of robust faith in the lives of other Christians.

In this week's lesson, we find not only a courageous leader, but also brave followers. The key was an unshakable confidence in God's presence, power, and provision. Saved adults face a similar, seemingly impossible assignment when they choose to obey the Redeemer. Moral decisions are tough, and sometimes they stumble. Nonetheless, they need encouragement and guidance to keep growing in their faith. Like Joshua, they need to be exhorted not to allow the Scriptures to "depart from their mouth," to obey His Word, and to cling to God's promise to be with His people wherever they go.

Gideon: A Deliverer for the People

DEVOTIONAL READING

1 Corinthians 1:26-31

DAILY BIBLE READINGS

Monday September 7
1 Corinthians 1:26-31 The Standards of God's Choice

Tuesday September 8
Judges 6:4-10 Crying for Help

Wednesday September 9
Judges 6:14-24 Seeking Proof of Favor

Thursday September 10
Judges 6:25-27 Cautious Obedience

Friday September 11
Judges 7:2-8 Thinning the Ranks

Saturday September 12
Judges 7:9-15 Assured for the Task

Sunday September 13
Judges 6:1-3, 7-14 Go and Deliver

Scripture

Background Scripture: *Judges 6—8*
Scripture Lesson: *Judges 6:1-3, 7-14*
Key Verse: *The LORD turned to him and said, "Go in the strength you have and save Israel out of Midian's hand. Am I not sending you?"* Judges 6:14.
Scripture Lesson for Children: *Judges 6:1-3, 11-14; 7:19-21*
Key Verses for Children: *The LORD . . . said, "Go in the strength you have . . . Am I not sending you?"* Judges 6:14.

Lesson Aim

To follow Gideon's determination and faith in God.

Lesson Setting

Time: *1162 B.C.*
Place: *Central Canaan*

Lesson Outline

Gideon: A Deliverer for the People

   I. The Scourge of the Midianites: Judges 6:1-3
      A. The Consequence of Disobedience: vs. 1
      B. The Crushing Weight of Oppression: vss. 2-3
  II. The Divine Appointment of Gideon: Judges 6:7-14
      A. The Israelite Plea for Help: vs. 7
      B. The Lord's Response: vss. 8-10
      C. The Arrival of the Lord's Angel: vs. 11
      D. The Lord's Command to Gideon: vss. 12-14

Introduction for Adults

Topic: *An Unexpected Leader*

There was an encourager named Elizabeth Fry who lived in England between 1780 and 1845, when conditions for those in prisons were appallingly bad. With the help of a London clergyman's wife and 10 Quaker women, Fry formed the Association for the Improvement of the Female Prisoners in Newgate.

The Association's first task was to convince the inmates that they had not come to condemn, but to bring comfort and relief. Fry and others provided clothing, bedding, instruction in orderliness and cleanliness, and lessons from the Bible. The results were so spectacularly successful that leaders from other countries came to visit Newgate and to consult with Fry. She was also asked to travel abroad to study conditions in other prisons and to make suggestions for improvements.

Elizabeth Fry is known today as a pioneer in prison reform, but this concern led her to ever-widening activities for the homeless, for the unemployed, and for underprivileged children. Tasks that seemed far too heavy for one woman to carry she took upon herself. She had chosen to be a follower of Jesus Christ, and to her this meant to help the captive and the poor.

Introduction for Youth

Topic: *Confident Leadership beyond Doubt*

The death of Florence Griffith Joyner on September 21, 1998, removed one of the most positive role models for young girls. "FloJo" had been an Olympic gold medalist in the 1988 Seoul games in the 100 and 200 meters and a relay team. Known for her dazzling fingernails and speed, she devoted large amounts of time and resources to helping children—especially those in devastated neighbor-hoods—find and use their own talents.

"FloJo" never backed away from taking on big responsibilities such as her youth work. The commitment in time was huge. However, she willingly gave of her time and energy. Like "FloJo," God wants us never to hesitate from taking on a big responsibility as well. He can empower us to give large amounts of our time and energy to the cause of helping others in need.

Concepts for Children

Topic: *A Helpful Leader Is Chosen*

1. Because the Israelites disobeyed, God allowed their enemies to harm them for seven years.
2. The Israelites lived in caves to protect themselves.
3. An angel of God appeared to Gideon while he was working.
4. Gideon was commanded to go in God's power and rescue the Israelites from their enemy.
5. God can give us the power to obey Him and be kind to those around us.

Lesson Commentary

I. THE SCOURGE OF THE MIDIANITES: JUDGES 6:1-3

A. The Consequence of Disobedience: vs. 1

Again the Israelites did evil in the eyes of the LORD, and for seven years he gave them into the hands of the Midianites.

The accounts recorded in the Book of Judges reflect a theological interpretation of history. For instance, a cyclical pattern of disobedience, oppression, repentance, and deliverance can clearly be seen in its pages. The narratives in the book underscore the truth that disregard for God brought oppression and that a broken spirit brought deliverance. Judges has both a historical and a religious purpose. The former is to provide glimpses of Israel's history from the death of Joshua to the beginning of the monarchy—a period of significant transition. The religious purpose of Judges is to underscore the Lord's discipline of the Israelites when their hearts turned to pagan deities. God allowed His people to be oppressed by several enemies because they worshiped a host of idols.

We see this dynamic at work in the account of Gideon. Like their predecessors, a new generation of Israelites was guilty of practicing idolatry. Judges 6:1 refers to this as God's people doing what was "evil" in His sight, which denotes attitudes and actions that were odious to the Lord. After the Israelites settled in Canaan, they were constantly tempted to compromise the monotheism of their ancestors. (Monotheism is the belief in a single supreme being.) Most of the Canaanites were polytheistic, believing that many gods coexisted peacefully as long as each was given its proper due. Later in their history, various groups of Hebrews tried to blend their faith with that of the Canaanites, and later on, with that of their captors; but this process—called syncretism—failed miserably.

The Lord refuses to coexist with any other object of worship. Consequently, because of the Israelites' apostasy, God allowed His people to be dominated and oppressed by the Midianites for seven years. Genesis 25:2 and 4 indicate that the Midianites were descendants of Abraham and Keturah. Be that as it may, the Midianites were never considered a part of the covenant people and never treated Israel with hospitality. The Midianites existed as Bedouins (or tribal nomads) in the desert and did not acknowledge any boundaries. The land of Midian was located principally in northwest Arabia, though the Midianites roamed throughout portions of northern Sinai, the Negev, and the southern Transjordan region.

Scripture reveals that Jacob's son, Joseph, was sold by his brothers to some Midianite traders (Gen. 37:28, 36). Years later, when Moses fled from the pharaoh of Egypt, he found shelter with Jethro, a priest of Midian (Exod. 2:15-16). When Israel was in the Transjordan and preparing to enter Palestine, the elders of Midian and the Moabites tried to hire Balaam to curse God's people (Num. 22:4-7). Some Midianite women were evidently involved in leading the Israelites into apostasy

(25:6). Five Midianite kings and their men were slain by the Israelites (31:7-8).

B. The Crushing Weight of Oppression: vss. 2-3

Because the power of Midian was so oppressive, the Israelites prepared shelters for themselves in moun-
tain clefts, caves and strongholds.Whenever the Israelites planted their crops, the Midianites,
Amalekites and other eastern peoples invaded the country.

The Hebrew of Judges 6:2 literally says "the hand of Midian was strong against
Israel." By this is meant the Israelites were overwhelmed by this new foe. They so
oppressed God's people that they were forced to evacuate the low-lying regions of
their homeland and seek shelter in the upland areas, namely, in the clefts of mountains, caves, and other naturally occurring places of refuge. The Hebrew noun *min-*
harah, which is rendered "shelters," only occurs here in the Old Testament. It has
been variously translated as "hiding places," "dens," and "secret storage places."

Evidently, the Midianites were not strong enough to oppress the Israelites alone.
Thus, they banded with the Amalekites and other semi-nomadic peoples from the
desert region east of Moab and Ammon to conduct raids against Israel (vs. 3). The
Amalekites were descended from Amalek, the son of Eliphaz and the grandson of
Esau (Gen. 36:12, 16). The Amalekites became a tribal people who lived in the
Negev and the Sinai peninsula.

During times of harvest, the Midianite coalition would move into the Jezreel
Valley from the Transjordan region, camp in the land, then attack the farms of the
Israelites and devour their crops. The marauders left virtually nothing for the
Israelites to eat, taking sheep, cattle, and even donkeys (vs. 4). The enemy raids
extended as far south as Gaza, a city that was located about three miles inland from
the Mediterranean Sea. This town was located on a major military and trade route
to Egypt. There were numerous wells around Gaza, and the plain surrounding the
city was quite fertile. Like hordes of locusts coming in and stripping a land bare,
the invaders swarmed throughout southern Canaan with their livestock and tents
(see Joel 1:5-7). A seemingly countless number of Midianite men and camels devastated the area (Judg. 6:5). (In the arid desert, the camel provided an ideal means
of swift and reliable transportation.)

II. THE DIVINE APPOINTMENT OF GIDEON: JUDGES 6:7-14

A. The Israelite Plea for Help: vs. 7

When the Israelites cried to the LORD because of Midian.

The Midianite coalition's repeated and sustained raids weakened the economic
strength of the Israelites (see the covenant curses recorded in Deut. 28:30-33, 38-
43). Eventually, they became so poor that they finally cried out to the Lord for help
and relief from their oppressors (Judg. 6:6-7). A four-step cycle keeps repeating
itself in Judges. First, Israel would wander from God and follow the idols of
Canaan. Second, God would raise up an oppressor to discipline His wayward

people. Eventually, the Israelites would repent and cry out to God. Finally, the Lord would raise up a deliverer, one of the judges (see 3:9, 15; 4:3-7). Each time the Israelites went through this cycle, they seemed to sink even deeper into spiritual darkness than the time before.

B. The Lord's Response: vss. 8-10

He sent them a prophet, who said, "This is what the LORD, the God of Israel, says: I brought you up out of Egypt, out of the land of slavery. I snatched you from the power of Egypt and from the hand of all your oppressors. I drove them from before you and gave you their land. I said to you, 'I am the LORD your God; do not worship the gods of the Amorites, in whose land you live.' But you have not listened to me."

Unlike previous episodes, in the circumstance involving the Midianites, the Lord did not immediately appoint a judge to deliver them. Instead, He first dispatched an unnamed prophet to speak directly to His people (Judg. 6:8). In the Old Testament era, God's spokespersons typically would observe what was taking place around them and deliver a divine message for that situation. Often, the prophecy was a reminder to the people and their leaders that they should change their ways and obey the Lord. For instance, the prophet whom God sent to His people during the Midianite crisis reminded the Israelites of the great things God had done for them. This included freeing them from slavery in Egypt, driving out the powerful Canaanite nations, and giving the Israelites the land of Canaan (vs. 9).

"LORD" (vs. 10) renders the four Hebrew letters making up the divine name, *YHWH* (or Yahweh). This special name for the covenant-keeping God of Israel emphasizes His eternal existence, supreme power, and active involvement in human history. In short, He is the ever-present, ever-living God (see Exod. 3:13-14). "God" (Judg. 6:10) renders the noun *'elohim*. Despite its plural form, it is consistently used in the Old Testament as a singular term. *Elohim* portrays the Lord as the one, true, and unique God. The totality of Scripture leaves the impression that He is unique in His being or essence, the fountain and source of all things, and the one who unifies all the forces of time and eternity.

The prophet's exhortation to the Israelites to remain true to the Lord and to His law have Exodus 20:1-6 and Deuteronomy 5:6-11 as the theological backdrop. In these verses, God said that because He had made His covenant with them, He should be their ultimate focus. He would not abide by anything else that vied for their worship and adoration. The Lord also commanded that idols were not to be made like anything in the sky (such as the sun, moon, stars, and birds), or on the earth (animals), or in the waters below (fish, crocodiles, and other sea life). The Lord explained that making idols was forbidden because He is a jealous God. He is zealous to ensure that His people's devotion is rendered exclusively to Him—just as in a relationship between a husband and wife.

Because God upheld His covenant with Israel, He expected His people to do the same (Judg. 6:10). Tragically, as the Lord's prophet declared, they had not done so. Instead, in violation of the Lord's commands, they worshiped the gods of the Amorites. By venerating and serving pagan deities, the Israelites showed how ungrateful they were for the Lord's past provision. The Amorites originally migrated from northwest Mesopotamia into Syria and Canaan. They eventually established a kingdom in the Transjordan region that extended from the Arnon River to the Jabbok River. The Amorites venerated such deities as Dagon (a grain god), Hadad (a storm god), Anath (a goddess of war and love), and Amurru (a storm god). For some reason, these pagan deities had a strong appeal to the Israelites. Perhaps smaller "gods" seemed easier to appease, and ultimately control, than the all-powerful God of Israel.

C. The Arrival of the Lord's Angel: vs. 11

The angel of the LORD *came and sat down under the oak in Ophrah that belonged to Joash the Abiezrite, where his son Gideon was threshing wheat in a winepress to keep it from the Midianites.*

Judges 6:11 says that the "angel of the Lord" arrived and sat down under a prominent oak (or sacred terebinth) tree in Ophrah. Some think that the appearances of the Lord's angel were theophanies, or manifestations of God in visible form. Since the angel of the Lord seems never to have appeared after Jesus' incarnation, some think this special messenger of God was a preincarnate manifestation of Christ. Another possibility is that the angel was the Lord's personal emissary. As such, the messenger operated in God's authority, spoke on His behalf, and bore His credentials.

The exact location of Ophrah remains unknown, though scholars generally think the town was located west of the Jordan River in the northern portion of Manasseh's territory (perhaps in the Jezreel Valley). Joash, who was a descendant of Abiezer (or Iezer), owned property in Ophrah. Abiezer was a descendant of Joseph and a leader of one of the clans of Manasseh that settled west of the Jordan River (see Num. 26:30; Josh. 17:1-2).

The Lord's emissary saw Gideon, the son of Joash, using an unconventional method of threshing wheat. He was separating the grain from the chaff while standing in a winepress. In ancient times, a winepress was a pit hacked out of rock or dug out of the ground. The inner walls of the pit were usually coated with plaster. Grapes were first placed in a large upper chamber and trampled. The juice would then flow through a duct or channel into a smaller lower chamber. There the juice would begin to ferment.

Gideon threshed grain in a winepress to stay out of the sight of the Midianites. In that era, harvested grain was normally spread out in the open on a hard level surface called a threshing floor. Oxen were often used to separate the kernels of grain from the worthless shells (chaff), which were then blown away by the wind. If Gideon had adopted this more conventional method, the Midianites would have spotted him and seized his grain. Although the winepress was a secure location, the space was confining, which made Gideon's task more difficult. This illustrates the extreme measures the Israelites adopted to hide their food from the marauders.

D. The Lord's Command to Gideon: vss. 12-14

When the angel of the LORD appeared to Gideon, he said, "The LORD is with you, mighty warrior." "But sir," Gideon replied, "if the LORD is with us, why has all this happened to us? Where are all his wonders that our fathers told us about when they said, 'Did not the LORD bring us up out of Egypt?' But now the LORD has abandoned us and put us into the hand of Midian." The LORD turned to him and said, "Go in the strength you have and save Israel out of Midian's hand. Am I not sending you?"

God was aware of His people's dilemma, and that's why He dispatched His heavenly emissary to Gideon with this message: "The LORD is with you, mighty warrior" (Judg. 6:12). Commentators suggest as many as three reasons why the Lord referred to him in that manner. First, the phase translated "mighty warrior" may have referred to Gideon's future bravery in accepting God's challenge to confront the Midianites. Expressed differently, the Lord anticipated what Gideon would accomplish.

Another possibility is that while the Hebrew phrase is often applied to fighting men (see Josh. 1:14; 10:7), the phrase is also applied to prominent men of wealth, such as Boaz (Ruth 2:1). The biblical text tells us that Gideon had at least 10 servants (Judg. 6:27), which indicates that he could possibly be thought of as a person of standing in the community. Thus, perhaps the Lord's address was in keeping with Gideon's social position. A third, less likely, option is that God was displaying humor by calling Gideon a "mighty warrior" (vs. 12), especially since he was hiding from the enemy.

Gideon learned that the Lord had appointed him to free Israel from the Midianites and would ensure victory over the enemy. But Gideon found it hard to believe that God was truly with His people. Gideon's doubts were fueled by the deplorable situation he and the rest of the Israelites were enduring. He was familiar with the great miracles the Lord performed to rescue His people from slavery in Egypt. Gideon, however, could not find any evidence that God was still willing to work in that way. As a matter of fact, Gideon believed the Lord had deserted His people and allowed the Midianites to defeat them (vs. 13).

The Lord's emissary did not debate the matter. Instead, he turned to Gideon and said that God had given him the strength to deliver the Israelites from their oppressors. Gideon was told to carry out this important task, for the Lord commissioned him to do so (vs. 14). In response, Gideon asked how he could possibly rescue the Israelites. Though Gideon no longer thought that freeing God's people was impossible, he felt he was not the right person for the job. Gideon not only believed his clan was the feeblest among all of Manasseh, but also that he was the least important member in his family (vs. 15).

Gideon's lack of status among his people was not an obstacle for the Lord. He is able to use anyone to accomplish His will. This truth is evident in God's response to Gideon. The Lord not only promised to be with him, but also that through him, the Midianites would surely be struck down (vs. 16; see Isa. 9:4; 10:26). Slowly, Gideon's reluctance diminished, especially as he recognized the supernatural character of his visitor. Though the Lord's reassurance of victory reduced Gideon's fears, he persisted in asking for evidence that God was truly with him every step of the way (Judg. 6:17-23, 36-40).

Discussion Questions

1. How did the Israelites respond to the Midianite oppression?
2. How extensive was the damage done by the Midianite coalition to Israel?
3. What did the Lord's prophet declare to the Israelites?
4. How does God using Gideon despite his doubts encourage us today?
5. How can we be prepared for faith-challenging events that come our way?

Contemporary Application

We love Gideon's account because it reminds us so much of ourselves. We would like to be brave, but we are scared. We wish we had plans for great victories, but our dreams seem so small. We would like to attempt great things for God, but our resources seem so limited. We would like to step out in faith, but we need strong assurances.

Despite our weak faith, God continually comes to our aid. He does not delight in our strength, but in our willingness to love and obey Him. God is with us, even when our enemies seem so overwhelming. God does not abandon us, even when we fail Him (2 Tim. 2:11-13). In fact, He promises never to forsake us (Heb. 13:5).

Each time our faith is challenged, we are faced with choices. For instance, will we trust the Lord to the point that we choose to obey without doubting? Will we let go of our fears of what others might think of us? Will we remember God's track record of faithfulness to us? We must choose to step over each stumbling block of hesitation and remember that God provides the strength and resources to meet each challenge.

Based on this week's Scripture lesson text, here are some key lessons from Gideon's life. God calls us to serve Him in the midst of our present obedience. Also, as we are faithful, He gives us more responsibility. God expands and uses the abilities He has already built into us. In fact, He uses us despite our limitations and failures. As Paul said in 1 Corinthians 15:58, we should stand firm in our faith and let nothing move us, for we know that our "labor in the Lord is not in vain."

Ezra: A Priest for the People

DEVOTIONAL READING

Psalm 32:1-5

DAILY BIBLE READINGS

Monday September 14
*Psalm 32:1-5 Confession
and Forgiveness*

Tuesday September 15
*Ezra 7:1-6 Skilled in the
Law of Moses*

Wednesday September 16
*Ezra 7:7-10 A Heart Set on
Study*

Thursday September 17
*Ezra 7:25-28 Guided by
God's Hand*

Friday September 18
*Ezra 8:21-23 Seeking God's
Protection*

Saturday September 19
*Nehemiah 8:1-12 Hearing
the Law of God*

Sunday September 20
*Ezra 9:5-11, 15 A Fervent
Prayer for the People*

Scripture

Background Scripture: *Ezra 9*
Scripture Lesson: *Ezra 9:5-11, 15*
Key Verse: *"O my God, I am too ashamed and disgraced to
lift up my face to you, my God, because our sins are higher
than our heads and our guilt has reached to the heavens."*
Ezra 9:6.
Scripture Lesson for Children: *Ezra 7:1-10*
Key Verse for Children: *Ezra had devoted himself to study
and observance of the Law of the LORD, and to teaching its
decrees and laws in Israel. Ezra 7:10.*

Lesson Aim

To recognize that doing what God wants may require
radical changes in our lifestyles.

Lesson Setting

Time: *458 B.C.*
Place: *Jerusalem*

Lesson Outline

Ezra: A Priest for the People
  I. The Reality of Sin: Ezra 9:5-9
      A. *Ezra's Consternation: vs. 5*
      B. *Ezra's Confession of Sin: vss. 6-7*
      C. *Ezra's Recognition of God's Goodness: vss. 8-9*
  II. The Consequences of Sin: Ezra 9:10-11, 15
      A. *Ezra's Acknowledgement of His People's
         Disobedience: vss. 10-11*
      B. *Ezra's Pleas for God's Mercy: vs. 15*

Introduction for Adults

Topic: *Getting Back on Course*

Ezra's encounter with sin in his faith community finds numerous parallels today. He discovered many, including civic and religious leaders, who had violated God's will. On a more positive note, Ezra discovered the power of remorse, confession, and repentance at work among God's people. The scribe found members of the faith community who were willing to acknowledge and renounce their sins. Beyond that, they accepted considerable hardship in order to make things right.

Confession, repentance, restoration—these are the steps to getting back on course spiritually when we sin. No one is exempt, for everyone has sinned. Perhaps it has not been openly or flagrantly, but we have all broken God's laws and have fallen far short of His glory. That's why we need courageous spiritual leaders who are willing to identify with sinful people. The Holy Spirit honors these leaders, especially when they confront people with the requirements of God's holiness.

Introduction for Youth

Topic: *Faithful Leadership Calls for Obedience*

One day, as I was casually walking through a shopping mall, I suddenly heard a mother scream to her disobedient child, "I'm telling you for the last time!" The child needed to know that heeding her mother's warning was the wisest decision to make.

In ancient Judah, the Lord's spokepersons kept issuing warnings, but God's people ignored them. Despite many years of hearing the prophets' declarations, the people refused to repent. In the end, they experienced sorrow and loss for their disobedience.

God's warning to us is clear. If we disobey Him, He will discipline us. The good news, of course, is that when we turn away from our sins and seek to obey God, we will be eternally blessed. Just as He did for the Jews who returned to their homeland from exile, so today He also gives us the strength to do His will.

Concepts for Children

Topic: *A Teaching Leader Is Chosen*

1. The king said Ezra could lead some Jews back to Jerusalem.
2. The king's announcement resulted from God praising Ezra.
3. Ezra was willing to give up his important job in the king's court in order to return to Jerusalem to teach God's Word to the Israelites.
4. Ezra devoted himself to study God's Word.
5. God also wants us to spend time reading the Bible.

Lesson Commentary

I. THE REALITY OF SIN: EZRA 9:5-9

A. Ezra's Consternation: vs. 5

Then, at the evening sacrifice, I rose from my self-abasement, with my tunic and cloak torn, and fell on my knees with my hands spread out to the LORD my God.

Ezra arrived in Jerusalem on August 4, 458 B.C. (see 7:8-9). While he was tying up the loose ends of delivering the gifts and goods he brought and settling his fellow travelers, a delegation of Jewish leaders came to the scribe with a problem they felt needed urgent attention. It was the ninth month (see 10:9), which corresponds roughly to December. Ezra had been in Jerusalem only about four months. He learned that all the people of Israel were entangled in this problem, but it was the involvement of the priests and Levites that posed the greatest danger (9:1). These men had intermarried with some of the idolatrous women of the land. This moral compromise threatened the spiritual purity of Israel. Those who brought the problem to Ezra spun out a list of names of nations reminiscent of the peoples in the land when Joshua conquered it (see Josh. 9:1; 24:11).

Only the Ammonites, Moabites, and Egyptians still existed in Ezra's day. The archaic names reminded everyone that the threat of intermarriage with idolaters was an ancient one that had gotten Israel into serious spiritual trouble since the days of the conquest under Joshua (Ezra 9:2; see Exod. 34:11-16; Deut. 7:1-4). The informants admitted that the leadership class had led the way in this abomination. Evidently, they wanted Ezra to use his imperial mandate to enforce a prohibition against such intermarriages. Later, from 440–430 B.C., Malachi preached against returned exiles who divorced Jewish wives to marry foreign women (see Mal. 2:10-16). Ancient rabbis took this to mean that many Jewish wives had aged prematurely from the rigors of the return and the rebuilding, and their husbands preferred more attractive local women. It may also be that many unmarried men had accepted the challenge of returning to Jerusalem and later could find only local brides. Still others may have married idolaters for economic advantage.

In any event, the prohibitions against intermarriage with surrounding nations are expressed not in racial terms but in religious ones. Converts to faith in Israel's God from among the nations were not stigmatized. Spiritual purity was the issue. Ezra did not react to the report by exercising his imperial power. Instead, he went into mourning. Tearing garments was a typical Jewish method of displaying grief (Ezra 9:3; see Gen. 37:29, 34; Esth. 4:1). Ezra's pulling out his hair and beard is unparalleled in the Bible, though others shaved their head in grief (see Job 1:20; Amos 8:10). Ezra's grief exceeded normal bounds, and he sat where he was, immobilized with appalling sorrow, anger, and dread (Ezra 9:4). The Hebrew verb *shamem*, which is rendered "appalled," vividly suggests trembling, paleness, and stunned senses.

Apparently, Ezra received the news and reacted in grief to it in front of the temple. Everyone else who felt the same dread about the future gathered around the priest-scholar to mourn with him. The sense of the passage is that Ezra sat appalled for some time before the evening sacrifice at 3:00 P.M. In the routine of the Jewish day, the evening sacrifice was a recognized time for prayer and confession (Ezra 9:5; see Acts 3:1). Ezra roused himself from his display of self-abasement (which included his tunic and robe being torn) to stand, face the temple (see Ezra 10:1), and fall on his knees with hands upraised to God in heaven. The scribe confessed the sins of Israel out loud in the temple courtyard in the presence of all the trembling worshipers.

Ancient Hebrews expressed their sorrow visibly and audibly. Wearing sackcloth of dark goat or camel hair (Jer. 6:26; Isa. 32:11), lying in dirt or ashes, and putting them in one's hair (Job 2:12; Ezek. 27:30), tearing one's own clothing (2 Sam. 1:11; 3:31), wailing and weeping aloud (Ezek. 27:30-32), and even lacerating one's body (Jer. 16:6; 41:5) in violation of the law of God (Lev. 19:28) marked occasions of deep distress. Men typically shaved their hair or beards to symbolize loss (2 Sam. 10:4; Isa. 15:2; Ezek. 7:18). In contrast, full hair and beard represented vigor and prosperity. A Phoenician carving on a sarcophagus older than the time of Ezra shows professional female mourners tearing at their hair. Ezra is the only man whom the Bible tells us spontaneously tore at his hair. Evidently, his sorrow was so intense that he could not wait for a razor. By contrast, when Nehemiah was later confronted with similar sin, he tore out the offenders' hair (Neh. 13:25).

B. Ezra's Confession of Sin: vss. 6-7

And prayed: "O my God, I am too ashamed and disgraced to lift up my face to you, my God, because our sins are higher than our heads and our guilt has reached to the heavens. From the days of our forefathers until now, our guilt has been great. Because of our sins, we and our kings and our priests have been subjected to the sword and captivity, to pillage and humiliation at the hand of foreign kings, as it is today."

The typical Jewish posture of prayer was to raise one's face to heaven, the acknowledged dwelling place of God; but Ezra felt unworthy to do so. The Hebrew verb rendered "ashamed" (Ezra 9:6) refers to a sense of guilt connected with wrongdoing. The verb translated "disgraced" literally denotes a reddening of the face as a sign of embarrassment. Succinctly put, Ezra was ashamed in relation to God and disgraced in relation to his fellow Jews. In the spirit of Nehemiah and Daniel, two others who confessed the sins of their people, Ezra corporately identified himself with the sinners around him (9:6; see Neh. 1:5-11; Dan. 9:4-19).

The scribe used graphic terms to describe the predicament facing the returned exiles. "Sins" (Ezra 9:6) translates a Hebrew noun that is used in the Old Testament to refer to perversity, depravity, and iniquity. "Guilt" renders a noun that denotes a range of trespasses and offenses. The parallel sentence structure conveys the sense of iniquities being piled head-high and transgressions reaching to heaven. Ezra feared that the community of reestablished Jews had fallen right back into the pattern of rebellion that had resulted in the Babylonian captivity and left their predecessors a subject people in the Persian Empire.

Ezra did not equivocate when he noted that, since the earliest days of Israel, the "guilt" (vs. 7) connected with their offenses had been huge. The scribe acknowledged that, as a result of their iniquities, the people of God had experienced His wrath. Along with ordinary citizens, Israel's monarchs and priests had also been brutalized by pagan rulers and dragged away into "captivity." The Lord did not spare anyone in the promised land from being slaughtered, plundered, and humiliated with exile. The sense of total disgrace continued to be felt right up to the time of Ezra.

C. Ezra's Recognition of God's Goodness: vss. 8-9

"But now, for a brief moment, the LORD our God has been gracious in leaving us a remnant and giving us a firm place in his sanctuary, and so our God gives light to our eyes and a little relief in our bondage. Though we are slaves, our God has not deserted us in our bondage. He has shown us kindness in the sight of the kings of Persia: He has granted us new life to rebuild the house of our God and repair its ruins, and he has given us a wall of protection in Judah and Jerusalem."

Ezra recognized the precarious existence of the Jewish homeland and its temple. It was because of the Lord's mercy that He allowed His people to return to their homeland for what seemed up to that point to be a relatively short period of time (especially when compared to Israel's long history). The Hebrew noun rendered "gracious" (Ezra 9:8) refers to the undeserved favor and compassion of God. The priest-scholar connected the latter to the divine preservation of a Jewish "remnant." This word renders a Hebrew noun that literally refers to a group that has escaped or been delivered from a protracted, distressing situation. Perhaps one of the most enduring concepts in Scripture is that of the remnant—a faithful minority that survives a judgment or catastrophe.

The miracle of the Jews' return to their homeland was followed by their rebuilding of the temple in Jerusalem. Ezra literally referred to the situation as being given a "tent peg in [God's] holy place." The imagery recalls the practice of nomads, who used short, cylindrical pieces of wood and metal to secure their tents in the ground where they established camp. Moreover, the scribe affirmed that God gave "light" to the eyes of His people. The Hebrew literally says "cause our eyes to shine." This figure of speech refers to individuals being revived and enlightened. Metaphorically speaking, "light" denoted the mystery of the Lord's glorious presence among His people. It also symbolized the provision of His goodness and blessing on the remnant.

In all these ways, God graced the returnees with a "little relief" in their time of servitude to foreign taskmasters. The Hebrew noun translated "relief" can also be rendered "sustenance." Just as the Lord had provided manna for the generation of Israelites who wandered for four decades in the wilderness, so, too, centuries later, He provided for the Jews living in Jerusalem and Judea. Even though they languished in bondage under the Persians, God had not forsaken His people in their time of servitude.

Indeed, the Lord had extended "kindness" (vs. 9) to the remnant. *Checed* is the underlying Hebrew noun and refers to the favorable way in which the emperors of Persia had treated the Jewish exiles. Through the gracious intervention of God, their existence as a nation was given "new life." This was particularly evident in the Persian kings authorizing the returnees to restore the Jerusalem temple and raise up its ruins. In a figurative sense, the Lord had acted as a "wall of protection" around the tiny enclave of Jews living in the holy city and throughout Judah.

II. THE CONSEQUENCES OF SIN: EZRA 9:10-11, 15

A. Ezra's Acknowledgement of His People's Disobedience: vss. 10-11

"But now, O our God, what can we say after this? For we have disregarded the commands you gave through your servants the prophets when you said: 'The land you are entering to possess is a land polluted by the corruption of its peoples. By their detestable practices they have filled it with their impurity from one end to the other.'"

Before the destruction of Jerusalem by the Babylonians, many people of Judah did not believe that God would destroy His own temple and His holy city until it actually happened. They continued in their worship of pagan deities. The prophets repeatedly pointed out that the people's unfaithfulness would bring judgment, and it did, namely, their 70-year exile in Babylon. The rejection of the prophets proved the people's unfaithfulness. Though the Lord's representatives occasionally foretold future events, their primary responsibility was calling the nation to obey God in the present. They spoke to Israel's leaders and, through them, to all the people.

Tragically, the entire nation was guilty of stubbornly refusing to follow the Lord's will. And because God is just in everything He does, He had no other choice but to pour out on His wayward people the judgment solemnly threatened in the Mosaic law (see Deut. 28:15-68). God had given His people a very simple choice—obey Him and be blessed or disobey Him and suffer terrible curses. Because Israel had chosen the latter course, the people were dispersed and Jerusalem fell (Dan. 9:12). These horrible calamities were meant to bring God's people back to Him.

In light of all the ways the Lord had been good to His people (Ezra 9:8-9), it was amazing that the returnees had sinned against God by intermarrying with pagans (vs. 10). The law of Moses forbade intermarriage between Israelites and the various nations inhabiting Canaan at the time of the Conquest (Deut. 7:1-3). Further, the law forbade the presence of Ammonites, Moabites, and their descendants in the sanctuary of God (Deut. 23:3). The prohibition seems to have been against marriage with foreign women committed to idolatry, not foreign women who had identified with the God of Israel (Deut. 7:4). Marriage with converts to faith in the Lord was not unlawful and may explain the lengthy interview process preceding the divorces reported in Ezra 10.

Understandably, Ezra was horrified that his fellow Jews would even think about violating the Mosaic law. The prophets had written over and over about the moral pollution of Canaan (9:11; see Deut. 9:4; 18:9-13; 1 Kings 14:22-24). The priest-scholar referred to one oracle deriding how the promised land prior to the Conquest had been sullied by the unholy practices of the local residents (see Lev. 18:25; Deut. 7:3; 18:9; 2 Kings 21:16). "Polluted" (Ezra 9:11) translates a Hebrew noun that refers to what is unclean or impure. "Corruption" also renders the same noun and denotes the sinful and wicked ways of Canaan's inhabitants. "Detestable practices" translates a noun that refers to behavior that is morally abhorrent. "Impurity" renders a noun that points to filthy, disgusting actions, which the prophets said filled the land from one end to the other.

B. Ezra's Pleas for God's Mercy: vs. 15

"O LORD, God of Israel, you are righteous! We are left this day as a remnant. Here we are before you in our guilt, though because of it not one of us can stand in your presence."

Because of the degeneracy of the Canaanite people at the time of the Conquest, Israel was forbidden to intermarry with them or form other intimate alliances (Ezra 9:12). Prosperity in the homeland had always depended in part on not being entangled with foreign people and their idols. The Assyrian and Babylonian conquests in 722 and 586 B.C. occurred because Israel had flagrantly and persistently rebelled against the law of God (vs. 13). Ezra insisted that the Lord's punishment had not been commensurate with Israel's crime; in other words, He had gone easy on them. Now the remnant—the proof of God's mercy—was once again trying His patience by intermarrying with foreigners whose religious practices the Lord abhorred (vs. 14).

Ezra feared the Lord might justifiably destroy the remnant for their ungrateful, repeated disobedience. Accordingly, the scribe concluded his prayer of confession by acknowledging the covenant faithfulness of God. The Hebrew noun translated "righteous" (vs. 15) points to the Lord's holy character, just conduct, and upright judgments. In contrast, Ezra referred to the returnees as standing before God in their "guilt" (see vs. 6). The scribe did not so much as request forgiveness or petition the Lord in any way. He only admitted their unworthiness to stand before His holy presence.

Ezra may have felt his mission to teach the law of God to the Jewish exiles had ended before it began. Instead of founding a school, he faced a spiritual emergency that threatened the future of the remnant. He responded to it as a priest leading his people in repentance. He wailed in the temple courtyard as he prayed (10:1). Repeatedly he stood and then prostrated himself in abject remorse.

Astoundingly, the multitude of men, women, and children who gathered around Ezra in the temple joined him in repentant wailing. Then a spokesman for the people approached Ezra to confirm the report that the nation had sinned through intermarriage and to insist that it was not too late to remedy the situation by means of a specific measure (vs. 10.2). In response to the heartfelt repentance of Ezra, a plan emerged from the people of the remnant. They had already recognized their sinfulness; and Ezra's public display of grief gave them a rallying point around which to express their spiritual concerns.

Discussion Questions

1. Why had Ezra been sitting in a posture of mourning?
2. What sorts of sins did Ezra refer to as he prayed?
3. Why had the Lord preserved a remnant of His people?
4. How had God shown His unfailing love to His people through the Persian monarchs?
5. In what ways has God demonstrated His mercy and grace to you?

Contemporary Application

In this week's lesson, the sin of intermarriage with foreign women was only the tip of the problem. What really demanded the extreme measures of Ezra's religious reforms was the danger of transgressing the first commandment in the Decalogue, namely, to have "no other gods" (Exod. 20:3) besides the Lord. Anyone who violated or enticed others to violate this injunction was to be stoned to death (see Deut. 13:6-10).

Ezra knew from Israel's history what could happen if the Jews began marrying people who worshiped other gods. Such a practice would probably lead to the Jews' mixing the worship of the true God with their pagan wives' false gods. This is precisely the sin that Solomon—Israel's wisest monarch—fell into, and it eventually brought the Lord's judgment on his dynasty (see 1 Kings 11:1-13).

Obedience to God's will results from an inner decision and a personal commitment. Admittedly, our personal commitment is under continual pressure from outside forces. Daily exposure to those who are living to please themselves can strike hard at our desire to follow the Lord wholeheartedly. Moreover, being surrounded by those whose lives reflect a disregard for God's will can tempt us to compromise. One way we can win the spiritual battle is by altering any aspects of our lifestyle that are compromising to God's will, as revealed in His Word.

Regardless of our age—whether younger or older—it is never too late to deal with the presence of sin in our lives. The prospect of having to renounce ungodly deeds might not be appealing to us. But it is necessary, especially if spiritual health is to be restored to us and encouraged among our peers in church.

Nehemiah: A Motivator for the People

DEVOTIONAL READING

Isaiah 62:1-7

DAILY BIBLE READINGS

Monday September 21
Isaiah 62:1-7 Hope for God's Vindication

Tuesday September 22
Nehemiah 1:1-4 Mourning over Jerusalem

Wednesday September 23
Nehemiah 1:5-11 Confession and Petition to God

Thursday September 24
Nehemiah 2:1-4 Identifying the Problem

Friday September 25
Nehemiah 2:6-10 Preparing for the Task

Saturday September 26
Nehemiah 4:15-23 Dealing with Opposition

Sunday September 27
Nehemiah 2:5, 11-20 Rallying Support

Scripture

Background Scripture: *Nehemiah 2*
Scripture Lesson: *Nehemiah 2:5, 11-20*
Key Verse: *I also told them about the gracious hand of my God upon me and what the king had said to me. They replied, "Let us start rebuilding." So they began this good work.* Nehemiah 2:18.
Scripture Lesson for Children: *Nehemiah 2:1-8*
Key Verse for Children: *[Nehemiah] sat down and wept. For some days, I mourned and fasted and prayed before the God of heaven.* Nehemiah 1:4.

Lesson Aim

To realize that if God's work is to get done, sometimes we must be bold and take the lead.

Lesson Setting

Time: *446–445 B.C.*
Place: *Susa and Jerusalem*

Lesson Outline

Nehemiah: A Motivator for the People

I. Nehemiah's Visit to Jerusalem: Nehemiah 2:5, 11-12
    A. *Nehemiah's Explanation to the King: vs. 5*
    B. *Nehemiah's Initial Preparations: vss. 11-12*
II. Nehemiah's Inspection of the Wall: Nehemiah 2:13-20
    A. *The First Part of the Nighttime Inspection: vss. 13-14*
    B. *The Second Part of the Nighttime Inspection: vss. 15-16*
    C. *The Summons to Rebuild the Wall: vss. 17-18*
    D. *The Stern Response to Opposition: vss. 19-20*

Introduction for Adults

Topic: *Overcoming Problems*

A veteran of many years in the U.S. Navy chaplains' corps retired. Instead of looking for a comfortable place where he could relax and take it easy, he chose a run-down church in a tough urban neighborhood. When his friends asked him why, he said, "It was the toughest thing I could find to do."

That's the attitude with which we must be open to God's leading. Regardless of our age and circumstances, we need the Holy Spirit's guidance—as well as courage and faith—to follow the Lord and overcome the challenges we face. The thrill of living for God is always there when we offer ourselves for His service.

Introduction for Youth

Topic: *Strategic Leadership for Accomplishment*

A sports headline in *USA Today* read, "Coale Resuscitates Oklahoma." In 1996, Sherry Coale was hired to coach the University of Oklahoma women's basketball team. She appeared an unlikely choice since she was a high school English teacher who was eight months pregnant with her second child and had no college coaching experience. She came into her interview with a 12-page plan to revitalize the program and a contagious excitement that convinced the search committee she was the person for the coaching job.

During Coale's first year, the team went 7-22 and drew less than 100 fans a game. In 2000, her Sooner team made the Sweet Sixteen for a second consecutive year, and set school attendance records, peaking with over 11,000 fans for a NCAA second-round tournament game against Stanford. Coale says, "When people talk about turning things around, I'm always taken aback. I had all the tools. I landed in a fabulous place."

As Christians, we can be sure that God has gifted us with all the tools we need to accomplish His plan for our lives. These take the form of spiritual gifts and natural talents that work together to enable us to glorify God and serve one another.

Concepts for Children

Topic: *A Praying Leader Is Chosen*

1. While Nehemiah was performing his duties, the king saw that he was sad.
2. Nehemiah asked for permission to go to Jerusalem and rebuild the city.
3. The king said Nehemiah could rebuild Jerusalem's wall and gates.
4. The king also gave Nehemiah whatever he needed to do his job.
5. Like Nehemiah, God will give us the strength to do His will.

Lesson Commentary

I. NEHEMIAH'S VISIT TO JERUSALEM: NEHEMIAH 2:5, 11-12

A. Nehemiah's Explanation to the King: vs. 5

And I answered the king, "If it pleases the king and if your servant has found favor in his sight, let him send me to the city in Judah where my fathers are buried so that I can rebuild it."

Nehemiah learned that, even though the returned exiles had been in Jerusalem for a number of years, the city's walls remained in disrepair. This circumstance left the inhabitants vulnerable and without any defense (Neh. 1). After hearing about this deplorable circumstance, Nehemiah took the bold step of going to the court of the Persian monarch and asking for permission to travel to Jerusalem.

Artaxerxes' blunt "What is it you want?" (2:4) may have been more than the cup-bearer hoped for so early in the conversation. In the space of a deep breath, Nehemiah's heart reached for God's hand even as his mouth started forming the words of his petition to the emperor. Perhaps he asked for wisdom about what to say and that God would grant him favor in his earthly master's sight. Nehemiah knew he needed the "LORD, God of heaven, the great and awesome God" (1:5) to shape Artaxerxes' attitude toward the project and toward himself as a petitioner.

In the exchange between Artaxerxes I and Nehemiah, the emperor was brusque and demanding, while the courtier was formal and deferential. This is evident by the usage of such phrases as "if it pleases the king" (2:5) and "if your servant has found favor in your sight." In a master stroke of diplomacy, Nehemiah did not specifically mention Jerusalem by name but always tied the city to himself and his family. Neither did he waste the emperor's time with wishful generalities.

B. Nehemiah's Initial Preparations: vss. 11-12

I went to Jerusalem, and after staying there three days I set out during the night with a few men. I had not told anyone what my God had put in my heart to do for Jerusalem. There were no mounts with me except the one I was riding on.

Artaxerxes I gave permission to Nehemiah by asking how long it would take him to get to Judah and when he would be back (Neh. 2:6). Although Nehemiah may have anticipated a brief leave of absence from service in the imperial court, his actual stay in Jerusalem lasted 12 years (5:14; 13:6). Artaxerxes I was moved by Nehemiah's sincerity and perhaps by reasoning that the prosperity of Judah would benefit the king.

Nonetheless, the monarch's favorable response was also a remarkable example of the power of prayer. Earlier, when the trouble had arisen over the first efforts to rebuild Jerusalem, Artaxerxes I himself had issued the decree that ended the exiles' efforts to completely restore their city (Ezra 4:17-23). Nehemiah's faith in God and boldness to approach the king had effectively reversed that decree, an outcome that was highly out of the ordinary in a culture in which governmental policies were rarely repealed (see Esth. 1:19; 8:8; Dan. 6:8, 12, 15).

Because the king was amenable to dispatching Nehemiah, the cupbearer asked for official documents to present to the governors assigned in the Trans-Euphrates region of the empire (Neh. 2:7). The papers Nehemiah requested would authorize whatever his rebuilding efforts required. In this situation, he would need permission to travel freely through various territories without any complications. Nehemiah also needed an escort to safeguard his journey. He requested a letter to Asaph (the keeper of the monarch's royal park or nature preserve) giving him access to the required building supplies he needed to restore Jerusalem. These included timber to make beams for the gates of the citadel on the north side of the temple, to construct the city wall, and to build a palace for the governor to live.

While Nehemiah's words and actions suggest his careful thought and planning, he nevertheless acknowledged that the gracious hand of God upon him led to the king granting these requests (vs. 8). The Lord also made Nehemiah's journey to Jerusalem successful. He presented documents authorizing his mission to the governing authorities in Trans-Euphrates (vs. 9). His status was enhanced by the presence of an imperial escort, which included "army officers and cavalry."

Ominously, Nehemiah introduced into his narrative two characters who were upset that he had arrived to promote the welfare of the Jews (vs. 10). Sanballat's name was Babylonian; he was likely named after Sin, the moon god. He was probably from Upper or Lower Beth Horon, two villages about 12 miles northwest of Jerusalem on the main road to the Mediterranean coast. He was the governor of Samaria and a leader of the Samarian opposition. Tobiah was a Jewish name meaning "The Lord Is Good." He was probably a cosmopolitan Jew living in and controlling the territory associated with Ammon east of the Jordan River (vs. 10). These two men would be Nehemiah's bitter enemies for years to come.

A papyrus document dated about 40 years after the time of Nehemiah identifies Sanballat as the governor of Samaria. The letter concerns Sanballat's adult sons, suggesting that he was elderly at the time. Other archaeological finds pertaining to Samaria in the time between the Old and New Testaments connect the name Sanballat (perhaps a grandson) with the movement that produced the Samaritan religion and temple. Tobiah's ancestors may have been powerful landowners in the vicinity of Ammon with influence at Jerusalem as early as the eighth century B.C.

After contacting the officials of the satrapy of Trans-Euphrates, Nehemiah went on to Jerusalem (vs. 11). As Ezra had done before him (see Ezra 8:32), Nehemiah rested three days before initiating any activity. For the time being, he did not tell anyone the plans God had put in his heart for the restoration of Jerusalem (Neh. 2:12). Perhaps the greatest challenge the governor faced was transmitting his conviction that rebuilding the city's walls at this time was God's idea—not the fantasy of a government official who would go home in a while and leave the locals to live with the trouble he had stirred up.

To help him inspect the Jerusalem wall, Nehemiah took only a few trusted associates, possibly some local residents who were familiar with the city and its challenging topography. The governor exercised a fair bit of caution as he and his escort set out to examine the walls at night, perhaps by moonlight. To make the clandestine operation even less detectable, Nehemiah decided to forgo the usage of any pack animals, that is, except for the donkey or mule on which he rode. Perhaps the mount helped to minimize the possibility of any mishap, especially as the newly appointed governor traversed over unfamiliar terrain.

II. NEHEMIAH'S INSPECTION OF THE WALL: NEHEMIAH 2:13-20

A. The First Part of the Nighttime Inspection: vss. 13-14

By night I went out through the Valley Gate toward the Jackal Well and the Dung Gate, examining the walls of Jerusalem, which had been broken down, and its gates, which had been destroyed by fire. Then I moved on toward the Fountain Gate and the King's Pool, but there was not enough room for my mount to get through.

Nehemiah surveyed the most damaged portions of whatever remained of the city walls. The inspection party began at the ruins of the "Valley Gate" (Neh. 2:13), which was located near the southwest corner of the wall of Jerusalem. The entrance overlooked the Valley of Hinnom. During the time of King Uzziah (or Azariah; 792–740 B.C.), the towers for the Valley Gate were built (see 2 Chron. 26:9). As Nehemiah made his way south, he went past the "Jackal Well" (Neh. 2:13; also called the "Dragon's Well" and the "Serpent's Well"). This was a spring located in the Valley of Hinnom. Evidently, the well was a favorite haunt for jackals (nocturnal predators and scavengers who were most active at dawn and dusk). The governor also passed by the "Dung Gate" (also called the "Potsherd Gate"; see Jer. 19:2). Undoubtedly, this was the spot where residents exited the city before heading to a commonly-used site to dump their refuse. It is estimated that the distance between the Valley Gate and Dung Gate was about 500 yards.

After rounding the southern side of Jerusalem, Nehemiah turned north up the Kidron Valley along the eastern wall (Neh. 2:14). Here the inspection party passed by the ruins of the "Fountain Gate" (also called the "Gate of the Spring" and the "Gate of the Well"). According to 3:15, this entrance was near a set of stairs that descended from the "City of David." Likewise, Nehemiah examined the "King's Pool" (2:14; possibly the "Pool of Siloam" mentioned in 3:15), a reservoir that some think was built during Hezekiah's reign (715–686 B.C.; see 2 Kings 20:20; Isa. 8:6; 22:9, 11).

The governor discovered that the hillside from Jerusalem into the Kidron Valley was steep. Moreover, he saw that the old wall of Jerusalem had been far down the hill and a system of terraces that supported buildings had been anchored against that wall. When the old wall was destroyed, the terraces had also crumbled. Since the slope along the east side of Jerusalem was choked with rubble that even a nimble pack animal could not negotiate in the moonlight, Nehemiah had to dismount and continue on foot.

B. The Second Part of the Nighttime Inspection: vss. 15-16

So I went up the valley by night, examining the wall. Finally, I turned back and reentered through the Valley Gate. The officials did not know where I had gone or what I was doing, because as yet I had said nothing to the Jews or the priests or nobles or officials or any others who would be doing the work.

Although it was still dark, Nehemiah decided to head north up the Kidron Valley to further inspect the ruins of the eastern wall. This side would be the most daunting section to rebuild. Much of the rest of the wall stood on relatively level ground. The inspection party made their way for an unspecified distance before they finally turned back. This involved retracing their steps over the rocks, rounding the southern point of Jerusalem, and reentering the Valley Gate to the southwest (Neh. 2:15). Why Nehemiah opted not to inspect the northern wall remains a matter of conjecture. One theory is that little or none of that portion of the structure remained intact. Another hypothesis is that the governor believed he could examine this part of the city without arousing any suspicion during the daylight hours.

In any case, neither Persian officials nor Jewish leaders (including the priests, nobles, officers, and the rest of the workers) were informed about Nehemiah's investigation before it occurred (vs. 16). As an outsider, the governor wanted to be able to give the leaders of Jerusalem an informed account of what needed to be done when he disclosed his mission. He knew there were enemies all around. Thus, it was imperative that he keep his plans a secret until they were fixed in his mind. Only when his strategy was formulated would he disclose it to the residents of Jerusalem.

C. The Summons to Rebuild the Wall: vss. 17-18

Then I said to them, "You see the trouble we are in: Jerusalem lies in ruins, and its gates have been burned with fire. Come, let us rebuild the wall of Jerusalem, and we will no longer be in disgrace." I also told them about the gracious hand of my God upon me and what the king had said to me. They replied, "Let us start rebuilding." So they began this good work.

When the time was right, Nehemiah gathered everyone and surprised them. First, he outlined the problem and then suggested the solution. For about 150 years, much of the city lay in ruins, with only a broken-down wall and charred timbers for gates. The solution was to rebuild Jerusalem's wall and remove the residents' feeling of disgrace and defeat (Neh. 2:17). In Old Testament times, the condition of a city's wall indicated its power and prosperity. Since the wall was the primary means of defense against an enemy, the quality of its construction and maintenance reflected the financial condition and vulnerability of the city's inhabitants.

Nehemiah challenged the people to rebuild the wall and thus restore the standing of the Jewish community in the holy city. As his clincher, the governor shared the amazing account of God's intervention with Artaxerxes I to secure official sanction for this task (vs. 18). In the books of Ezra and Nehemiah, the concept of "the hand of the Lord my God" (see Ezra 7:6, 28; 8:31) or "the gracious hand of my God" (see 7:9; 8:18, 22; Neh. 2:8, 18) explains the influencing force behind everything that happens. Emperors, nations, and the people of God are all tools in that gracious hand.

The vision and decisiveness of Nehemiah were what the remnant had needed to get started. In point of fact, the response of the priests, nobles, officials, and ordinary people was profoundly united. This is seen in Nehemiah 2:18, which literally says, "Arise! Let us rebuild!" The Hebrew text also idiomatically says that the Jews "strengthened their hands." This meant they readied themselves to begin the enormous rebuilding project. By calling it "good," they affirmed not only that undertaking the task was worthwhile, but also that it pleased the Lord. This remained true, regardless of whatever short-term sacrifices had to be made to ensure the success of the operation.

D. The Stern Response to Opposition: vss. 19-20

But when Sanballat the Horonite, Tobiah the Ammonite official and Geshem the Arab heard about it, they mocked and ridiculed us. "What is this you are doing?" they asked. "Are you rebelling against the king?" I answered them by saying, "The God of heaven will give us success. We his servants will start rebuilding, but as for you, you have no share in Jerusalem or any claim or historic right to it."

Opposed to the gracious hand of God were three potent human enemies (Neh. 2:19; see vs. 10). The company of Sanballat and Tobiah was joined by Geshem the Arab. Ancient sources reveal that Geshem led an assortment of Arab tribes that controlled the deserts south of Judah from Egypt to the Arabian peninsula. He was more powerful than Sanballat and Tobiah combined, but his hostility to the Jews appears to have been less intense. Sanballat to the north, Tobiah to the east, and Geshem to the south forged a hostile boundary around Judah.

Together the threesome launched a campaign of ridicule and mockery against the small Jewish community. Their initial charge was the old standby: rebellion against the emperor (see Ezra 4:11-16). Nehemiah shrugged off Sanballat, Tobiah, and Geshem as though they were minor annoyances (Neh. 2:20). He was used to dealing with the real political heavyweights of Persia; comparatively speaking, these men were lightweights.

On the other hand, Nehemiah looked at the situation in Jerusalem through a theological lens. Because the God of heaven wanted the walls built, He would ensure the success of His people. Nehemiah declared that he and the Jews were the servants of the Lord by terms of a covenant. In contrast, Sanballat, Tobiah, and Geshem had no covenant status. Since Jerusalem belonged to God and His people, the blustering nations around them had no share, legal right, or historic claim to the Lord's plan for the holy city.

Discussion Questions

1. What was the nature of the plan that Nehemiah brought before the king of Persia?
2. Why did Nehemiah decide to inspect the remains of the Jerusalem wall at night, rather than during the day?
3. Why was it necessary at one point along the route for Nehemiah to dismount from the animal on which he rode?
4. Why did Nehemiah think it was unacceptable for the wall and gates of Jerusalem to lie in ruins?
5. If you were Nehemiah, how would you motivate your peers to accept the challenge to begin the rebuilding project?

Contemporary Application

"Racers, start your engines!" With that announcement, the crowd roared and the race car drivers zoomed down the speedway. But before the event started, highly skilled engineers, mechanics, and drivers had spent many hours and lots of money in preparation.

How foolish it is to start a road race without adequate equipment and trained drivers. Yet sometimes that's how we try to get ahead in our spiritual lives. We think we know how to run the race of faith. We think we can jump in at any time and succeed with little preparation and effort. But we are incorrect. We cannot start and finish unless we trust in God and obey His Word.

Nehemiah did not start his rebuilding project without first going to God in prayer. Nehemiah knew God's promises, and he knew about the presence of sin in his life. Nehemiah also knew the importance of God's name and honor. Only then was the governor ready to start doing great work for the Lord.

There are times when we might think that our options are closed, especially when we reach a certain age. Another possibility is that we might feel closed in by confining circumstances. Nonetheless, if we are willing to serve God, He will give us the courage and ability to start new ministries and other ventures, despite what might appear to be overwhelming obstacles.

Prayer will be crucial to our success in life, especially when it feels uncertain. Admittedly, in a day of rapid change, we might at times find ourselves feeling too impatient to pray. Consider this: though Nehemiah was a man of action, he still saw the importance of undergirding his life with prayer. He did not act rashly, either. Instead, he prayed for four months before taking action. Clearly, a major contributor to his success was his willingness to pray at length.

Looking for Jesus

Scripture

Background Scripture: *Mark 1:35-45*

Scripture Lesson: *Mark 1:35-45*

Key Verse: *When [the disciples] found [Jesus], they exclaimed: "Everyone is looking for you!"* Mark 1:37.

Scripture Lesson for Children: *Mark 1:35-45*

Key Verse for Children: *Jesus reached out his hand and touched the [leper].* Mark 1:41.

Lesson Aim

To understand that Jesus is uniquely able to help the afflicted.

Lesson Setting

Time: *About A.D. 26*

Place: *Galilee*

Lesson Outline

Looking for Jesus

  I. Jesus' Preaching throughout Galilee: Mark 1:35-39
    A. *Jesus' Growing Popularity: vss. 35-37*
    B. *Jesus' Itinerant Ministry: vss. 38-39*
  II. Jesus Healing a Person with Leprosy: Mark 1:40-45
    A. *The Request Made by the Leper: vs. 40*
    B. *The Savior's Healing of the Leper: vss. 41-42*
    C. *The Savior's Stern Warning to the Leper: vss. 43-44*
    D. *The Presence of Increasingly Large Crowds: vs. 45*

Introduction for Adults

Topic: *In Search of a Leader*

According to its organizational press release, the Barna Research Group, during the first two decades of its existence, sought to provide "current, accurate and reliable information . . . to ministries in order to facilitate strategic decision-making." Then, in 2005, George Barna redirected the focus of the organization. Instead of "emphasizing the provision of information to ministry leaders," he and his team adopted the role of "creating resources and relationships that facilitate kingdom advancement."

As a result of these major decisions, the organization today sees itself undertaking a "new ministry that . . . seeks to move forward in ways that will enhance the health of the Church more dramatically." Commendably, they also strive to be "dependent upon the Holy Spirit's ability to guide and work" through them.

Introduction for Youth

Topic: *Searching for True Treasure*

In 2004, *National Treasure* was released by Walt Disney Pictures. According to the producers, the movie features a "treasure hunter" named Benjamin Franklin Gates, who is in "hot pursuit of a mythical treasure that has been passed down for centuries." In an early scene, the audience encounters Benjamin as a "preteen boy rummaging through his grandfather's attic." When the grandfather finds the boy there, he "sits the lad down, tells him he's probably old enough now to hear the family story."

Benjamin learns about a "vast, unimaginable treasure that was amassed by the ancient Egyptian and Roman empires, and which the Knights Templar found in Jerusalem during the Crusades." What unfolds next is a treasure hunt, in which the characters follow a litany of clues. It turns out these are rather contrived. Even the plot tends to be rather farcical.

When it comes to the Gospel, its eternal treasures are not hidden; nor do they require searching to be found. The Lord Jesus came to earth to proclaim the Good News and urge everyone to freely and openly receive by faith the gracious offer of salvation. Nothing could be more real or down to earth!

Concepts for Children

Topic: *A Leper Is Touched*

1. Because of Jesus' ministry and message, people looked for Him.
2. Jesus responds to the needs of people, including someone with a skin disease, such as a leper.
3. Jesus can meet all our physical and spiritual needs.
4. The man with leprosy whom Jesus healed joyously told others what Jesus had done.
5. People may become followers of Jesus after we have told them about Him.

Lesson Commentary

I. JESUS' PREACHING THROUGHOUT GALILEE: MARK 1:35-39

A. Jesus' Growing Popularity: vss. 35-37

Very early in the morning, while it was still dark, Jesus got up, left the house and went off to a solitary place, where he prayed. Simon and his companions went to look for him, and when they found him, they exclaimed: "Everyone is looking for you!"

Mark 1:21-28 spotlights an episode in which Jesus expelled a demon from a man in attendance at a synagogue service in Capernaum. Then, after leaving the synagogue, Jesus walked with James and John to the home of Peter and Andrew to eat a Sabbath meal, which was customarily served at that time (vs. 29). Part of the reason for this visit was the illness of Peter's mother-in-law. She was lying down in bed, being sick with a high-grade fever (vs. 30; see Luke 4:38). In that day, a fever was considered to be an illness itself, rather than a symptom of many kinds of illness.

We don't know precisely what was wrong with Peter's mother-in-law, but Jesus knew what to do. He went over to her bedside and ordered the fever to go away (vs. 39). Here the woman's malady is personified as an entity that held her captive and that Jesus rebuked and cast out by the power of His command. Next, He took Peter's mother-in-law by the hand and gently helped her up. In the process, Jesus healed her. With her fever now gone, the grateful host prepared an evening meal for her guests (Mark 1:31).

Later that Saturday evening, many local people came to Jesus, bringing the sick and the demon-possessed (vs. 32). The widespread occurrence of the latter might have been due to the presence of pagan occult practices in Galilee. According to Jewish law, now that the Sabbath was over (having ended at sunset), the people could travel and carry a burden. The crowd was so large that it looked as though the entire town had turned out (vs. 33). Jesus healed the sick and drove out demons (vs. 34). Here we see a distinction made between healing and exorcism, which implies that Jesus was dealing with two separate issues—one physical and the other spiritual in nature.

The Savior would not allow the demons to identify Him, for they knew He was the Messiah (vs. 34; see Luke 4:41). After all, He did not need the testimony of the demonic world to establish His credibility. He also did not want unclean spirits to give people the false impression that He had any political aspirations to liberate Israel from their Gentile taskmasters. It would be incorrect to assume from Jesus' growing popularity that He was widely received as the promised Messiah of the Jews. Most of those who came to Him at this stage were not seeking Him because they appreciated who He is. Some just wanted to be healed, while most of the rest were curiosity seekers. Jesus was calling them to His eternal kingdom, but they were chiefly interested in a comfortable existence within the kingdoms of this world.

Jesus knew the value of renewing His spiritual vitality. That's why, before daybreak the next morning, He got up, left the home of Peter and Andrew (see 1:29), went out to an isolated place, and spent time in prayer (vs. 35). The Greek adjective rendered "solitary" refers to a locale that is remote, uninhabited, and (in some cases) desolate. The verb rendered "prayed" suggests that the Son brought an assortment of supplications and entreaties to the Father.

The demands of Jesus' ministry were already pressing upon Him, so it made sense for Him to commune alone with the heavenly Father. Perhaps the Son focused on the holiness of the Father, the advent of His kingdom, and the fulfillment of His will throughout creation. Jesus possibly also entreated the Lord to provide the disciples with sufficient food to eat, strength to endure temptation, and protection from all forms of evil (see Matt. 6:9-13; Luke 11:2-4).

Meanwhile, crowds of people started searching everywhere for Jesus (see Luke 4:42). After Peter and his colleagues got up and noticed that Jesus had left the house, they decided to join the others in tracking Him down (Mark 1:36). The Greek verb translated "went to look for" conveys the idea of earnestly pursuing and hunting down something. In the case of the disciples, when they found Jesus, they interrupted His prayer, exclaiming, "Everyone is looking for you!" (vs. 37). Indeed, when the people finally found the Messiah, they implored Him not to leave them. Perhaps reflecting a superficial and shallow mind-set, they just wanted Him to perform more miracles on their behalf and bring some relief to their temporal existence (see John 6:26).

Evidently, Peter and his colleagues did not understand why Jesus would ignore the call of the crowd, even for prayer. Undoubtedly, the disciples assumed the success of the Redeemer's mission required approval from the masses; but Jesus knew better. The success of His mission necessitated approval from the Father. The Gospel of John reveals that many people believed in Jesus because they saw the miraculous signs He performed. Despite that, the Messiah would not entrust Himself to them, for He understood the fickleness of human nature. No one had to tell Him what people were like, for He already knew (2:23-25). Later in His earthly ministry, many of His aspiring disciples would turn away and desert the Savior (6:66).

B. Jesus' Itinerant Ministry: vss. 38-39

Jesus replied, "Let us go somewhere else—to the nearby villages—so I can preach there also. That is why I have come." So he traveled throughout Galilee, preaching in their synagogues and driving out demons.

Despite the pressure from the crowds and the insistence of the disciples, Jesus never wavered from His redemptive mission. He knew that the Father had sent Him to declare the good news of the divine kingdom in a variety of towns in Judea and Galilee (see Luke 4:43). Thus, in response to the disciples, Jesus stated that it was imperative for them to travel elsewhere, particularly the "nearby villages" (Mark 1:38).

"Preach" translates a Greek verb that refers to a herald declaring a message of considerable importance. In this case, Jesus was "proclaiming the good news of God" (vs. 14). The Savior's mission also included confronting people with the truth that the promised Kingdom was at hand (vs. 15). For this reason, Jesus did not want to see the Gospel confined to one place. Consequently, the Messiah traveled throughout the region of Galilee.

Galilee was the Roman province of northern Palestine. Galilee extended from Mount Hermon in the north to Mount Carmel in the south and lay between the Mediterranean Sea and the Jordan River. Unlike Judea, Galilee remained under the rule of the Herods during the first half of the first century (see Acts 12:1-2). Herod the Great depopulated Judea by resettling Jews in new or rebuilt cities in Samaria and Galilee. Galilee, meaning "circuit," "district," or "cylinder," was surrounded and heavily influenced by Gentiles. Jews to the south derided its mixed population by literally calling it "Galilee [circle] of the Gentiles [nations]" (Isa. 9:1; Matt. 4:15). Galilee was known for its prosperous fishing industry and fertile lands. It also benefitted from trade as a crossroads between Egypt to the south and Damascus to the north.

As Jesus made His way from town to town, He preached in the synagogues and expelled demons from their victims (Mark 1:39). These are just some of the signs Jesus performed in the presence of His disciples. Also, while the four Gospels do not record every miracle, what they do report is intended to convince everyone to believe that Jesus is the Messiah, the Son of God, and thereby have life in His name (John 20:30-31).

The word *synagogue* means "assembly," coming from a Greek verb that means "to bring together." The Jews probably established synagogues during the Exile. The Babylonians had destroyed Jerusalem and its temple and deported most of the inhabitants of Judah. In order for the Jews to preserve their religious teachings and practices, they established synagogues as local places for worship and instruction. Most communities where Jews lived had at least one synagogue, and some had two or more. According to tradition, the Jewish leaders in a community were to establish a synagogue if at least 10 Jewish men lived in the town.

In New Testament times, Jews would meet in the synagogue principally on the Sabbath. During the worship service, men sat on one side and women on the other. The participants would recite the Shema (a confession of faith in the oneness of God, based on Deuteronomy 6:4-9), prayers, and readings from the Law and the Prophets. A speaker would deliver a message and then give a benediction (Luke 4:16-21). The elders of the town selected laymen to oversee the care of the building and the property, to supervise the public worship, to choose people to read Scripture and pray, and to invite visitors to address the congregation. An attendant would hand the sacred scrolls to the reader during the service. After the reader finished, the attendant would return the scrolls to a chest mounted on a wall.

As Jesus taught and preached in the towns of Galilee, John the Baptizer heard in

45

prison what the Savior was doing. John decided to send some of his disciples to ask whether Jesus was the promised Messiah of Israel. Jesus directed these emissaries from John to report what they had seen and heard. This included Jesus proclaiming the Good News to the poor and performing many miracles of healing and exorcism (Matt. 11:1-5; Luke 7:18-22). Jesus' point seems to be that since He was fulfilling prophecies about the Messiah (see Isa. 61:1-2), He must be the Messiah.

II. Jesus Healing a Person with Leprosy: Mark 1:40-45

A. The Request Made by the Leper: vs. 40

A man with leprosy came to him and begged him on his knees, "If you are willing, you can make me clean."

In the Gospel of Mark's continuing presentation of the Good News (see 1:1), we next find Jesus encountering a leper (evidently somewhere outside of the nearest town). This man had heard of Jesus' power, but evidently knew little about His compassion. The leper came to the Savior, knelt in front of Him, and begged Him for help. The leper reasoned that if Jesus was willing to do so, He could cleanse the leper of his affliction (vs. 40). The wording of the Greek text indicates that the leper was not presuming that Jesus would heal him, only that the Messiah had the power to do so.

Lepros is the adjective translated "leprosy" and refers to several types of inflammatory skin diseases. Judging by the excitement that followed the healing (vs. 45), the leper who approached Jesus was probably suffering from true leprosy (Hansen's disease), not just a mild skin ailment. Old Testament laws covered how to treat people with many skin diseases like leprosy (Lev. 13:1-46; 14:1-32). Nonetheless, what we label as leprosy was distinct from other skin diseases because some rabbis taught that it was a punishment for sin. To them, leprosy was the visible sign of inward corruption. The Jews feared leprosy, not only because it was disfiguring, but also because lepers were treated as outcasts. Lepers lived in communities outside the city gates and were not allowed contact with others.

B. The Savior's Healing of the Leper: vss. 41-42

Filled with compassion, Jesus reached out his hand and touched the man. "I am willing," he said. "Be clean!" Immediately the leprosy left him and he was cured.

"Filled with compassion" (Mark 1:41) translates the reading found in many manuscripts of the Greek New Testament. A smaller number of other manuscripts, however, contain a reading that could be translated "moved with anger." It's not hard to imagine that Jesus simultaneously felt a mixture of pity and indignation. For instance, He might have been upset by the leper's apparent doubt over the Savior's desire to heal him (vs. 40). As well, Jesus could have felt sorry for the man's intolerable condition. In either case, there's no uncertainty about the Messiah's response. He was willing and able to heal the leper. Thus, Jesus stretched out His hand, touched the leper, and made him clean.

The man probably had not been touched by a nonleper in months or even years. Religious law declared that a person became "unclean" (that is, ceremonially polluted) by touching a leper. Jesus could have healed the leper without touching him, but He did touch him, instantly healing him (vs. 42). Here we see that Jesus' compassion ignored ritual defilement. As He was with the crowds in Capernaum (see vss. 21-28), Jesus was moved by kindness at the sight of suffering and willingly removed its cause.

C. The Savior's Stern Warning to the Leper: vss. 43-44

Jesus sent him away at once with a strong warning: "See that you don't tell this to anyone. But go, show yourself to the priest and offer the sacrifices that Moses commanded for your cleansing, as a testimony to them."

Jesus did not waste any time sending the former leper on his way. The Greek verb rendered "strong warning" (Mark 1:43) is derived from a term that literally means "to snort with anger." It underscores how sternly Jesus admonished the man He had healed to tell no one about the miracle. In the time of Jesus, the Jews wanted freedom from Rome. Expectations ran high that God would raise up a warrior-prince who would throw off the yoke of pagan rule and usher in a Jewish kingdom of worldwide proportions. John 6:15 and Acts 1:6 show traces of this hope among the people. This explains why Jesus was careful not to give false impressions about the exact nature of His messiahship (see John 18:33-37). He saw His destiny in terms of service to God and sacrificial suffering (see Mark 8:31; 9:31; 10:33-34; Luke 24:45-46).

Jesus, reflecting the protocol of the day, told the former leper to go to a priest, let him examine the once-afflicted body area, and verify that a genuine healing had occurred. Jesus also directed the man to take along the offering required in the Mosaic law for those who had been cleansed from leprosy (Mark 1:44; see Lev. 13:6, 13, 17, 23; 14:2-32; Luke 5:14). Not only would such verification fulfill a requirement of the Mosaic law, but also it would testify to the religious establishment of Jesus' authority and His respect for the law. The last part of Mark 1:44 could also be rendered "as an indictment against them" or "as proof to the people" (see 13:9). In this case, the sight of a fully healed leper would attest to the religious leaders that Jesus is the Messiah, for the Jews believed only God could cure such a disease (see 2 Kings 5:1-7). Thus, the authorities' eventual rejection of Him would cast them in a guilty light before God.

D. The Presence of Increasingly Large Crowds: vs. 45

Instead he went out and began to talk freely, spreading the news. As a result, Jesus could no longer enter a town openly but stayed outside in lonely places. Yet the people still came to him from everywhere.

The former leper may have obeyed the priestly verification part of Jesus' orders, but he did not heed the Lord's command to remain silent. Instead, the man left Jesus' presence and began to announce publicly what Jesus had done. The former leper's declaration resulted in the news about Jesus spreading far and wide. In turn, this led to large crowds swarming around Jesus wherever He went. The presence of so many miracle seekers (along with the intensifying opposition of the religious leaders) hindered Jesus' ability to publicly enter a town or synagogue anywhere in Galilee. Instead, He had to confine Himself to "lonely places" (Mark 1:45), that is, secluded, remote areas. Even then, the people were so desperate that they kept coming to Him from everywhere to be healed.

Discussion Questions

1. Why did Jesus chose to pray when it was very early in the morning?
2. Why did Peter and his colleagues feel compelled to search for Jesus?
3. What did Jesus say was His reason for coming to earth?
4. How did Jesus respond to the leper's request to be healed?
5. If you were the healed leper, how do you think you would have expressed your gratitude for what the Savior had done for you?

Contemporary Application

"It's a miracle I passed that test yesterday." "It would take a miracle to get that man away from the television." "I use this miracle product for a healthy and beautiful garden."

It's amazing how many seemingly "miraculous" events happen every day. One would think we were people who believed wholeheartedly in the possibility of miracles. But that doesn't seem to be true. Many people find it easier to wrestle the facts every which way just so they can reach explanations that deny the miraculous.

Consider a well-known religious leader's comments during a radio interview. "I believe that everything in the Bible is absolutely true," he declared. "Well, given everything we know about science today," the host replied, "how do you reconcile that view with such things as the Virgin Birth described in the New Testament?"

"Well," the minister said carefully, "when I said 'absolutely true,' I didn't mean 'absolutely factual.' We need to look beyond the Bible's fables and parables to see the intent behind them." In other words, he was saying, "Don't be naïve. We all know that it is physically impossible for a virgin to conceive a child."

While nice and neat, such a view denies Jesus' ability to break through "everything we know about science today" and enter our world in supernatural ways. As in the incident involving the leper, the Savior changes lives—by repairing broken families, healing physical and emotional illnesses, and guiding us in unforeseeable ways.

Recognizing Jesus

Scripture

Background Scripture: *Mark 5:1-20*
Scripture Lesson: *Mark 5:1-13, 18-20*
Key Verse: *Jesus did not let him, but said, "Go home to your family and tell them how much the Lord has done for you, and how he has had mercy on you."* Mark 5:19.
Scripture Lesson for Children: *Mark 5:1-13, 18-20*
Key Verse for Children: *When he saw Jesus from a distance, he ran and fell on his knees in front of him.* Mark 5:6.

Lesson Aim

To affirm the power of Jesus to bring about needed spiritual and physical healing in our lives.

Lesson Setting

Time: *About A.D. 29*
Place: *Region of the Gerasenes*

Lesson Outline

Recognizing Jesus
  I. The Messiah's Authority over Demons: Mark 5:1-13
    A. *The Journey Across the Lake: vs. 1*
    B. *The Appearance of a Demon-Possessed Man: vss. 2-5*
    C. *The Shouts Uttered by the Man: vss. 6-8*
    D. *The Question Asked by Jesus: vss. 9-10*
    E. *The Expulsion of the Demons: vss. 11-13*
  II. The Good News of God's Mercy: Mark 5:18-20
    A. *The Healed Man's Request: vs. 18*
    B. *The Savior's Admonition: vss. 19-20*

Introduction for Adults

Topic: *Restored to Wholeness*

We should be thankful that Jesus heals us, as sinners, to spiritual wholeness, for otherwise none of us would be saved. Yet once we become Christians and settle down among the nice people in church, we often forget that Jesus wants to touch the lives of all people with His reconciling power. Sometimes those whom He calls embarrass us, and we feel uncomfortable in their presence. We don't approve of the way they look and the things they do. Would we ever sit down to dinner with people like them?

The church's hardest task is to expand its vision to unlikely candidates for salvation and fellowship. Once our lives get cleaned up, we don't want to get dirty again. But if we refuse to reach sinners like Jesus did, then the church becomes a holier-than-thou club. It fails to fulfill its divine mission. Perhaps once in a while we need to put a banner behind the pulpit that says JESUS HEALS SINNERS TO SPIRITUAL WHOLENESS.

Introduction for Youth

Topic: *The Treasure of True Freedom*

Max Lucado tells the story of Anibal, who sat in a Brazilian jail cell. He had been convicted of murder. The man he'd killed was a drug dealer, but murder was murder, and Anibal was sentenced to prison for life. He ended up a bitter man, resisting all attempts to help him. A mutual friend took Lucado to visit Anibal in prison. He tried to help Anibal see his need for God's grace. The first step to receiving it was admitting his sin. But Anibal felt little interest in asking anyone for forgiveness.

"Do you want to go to heaven?" "Sure." "Are you ready?" Anibal knew he wasn't and continued to think about his future. "All right, I'll become a Christian, but . . . don't expect me to change the way I live."

Anibal lived in a prison with bars of steel, but worse, his own stubbornness and pride kept him from knowing freedom. If he could have humbly confessed his sin and received Jesus' life-transforming forgiveness, he would have escaped the most deadly prison of all.

Concepts for Children

Topic: *Caring for Outsiders*

1. Jesus says "yes" to anyone who comes to Him for help.
2. Jesus takes time to reach out to people who need Him.
3. Jesus has the ability to help all sorts of people who need Him.
4. People who experience the healing touch of Jesus also want to become His followers.
5. We know that Jesus is with us no matter how hard life seems at times.

Lesson Commentary

I. THE MESSIAH'S AUTHORITY OVER DEMONS: MARK 5:1-13

A. The Journey Across the Lake: vs. 1

They went across the lake to the region of the Gerasenes.

Jesus had been ministering with His disciples in the region of Galilee when He decided to go to the east side of a lake called the Sea of Galilee (Mark 4:35). Eventually, Jesus and His followers reached the other side of the lake. After disembarking from the boat in which all of them had ridden, the group found themselves in the "region of the Gerasenes" (5:1). The exact wording of the Greek text is debated among specialists. While some manuscripts read "Gerasenes," other variants include "Gadarenes" and "Gergesenes." These differences in spelling could be due to variations in the way inhabitants throughout the surrounding area referred to the locale (see Matt. 8:28; Luke 8:26).

As one of the 10 cities of the Decapolis, Gerasa was a prominent city in the region, being located about 35 miles southeast of the Sea of Galilee. Excavations of the city have included ruins of the temple of Artemis, a triumphal arch, a forum with a street lined with columns, and a stairway leading to a pagan temple. Additionally, there were cavern tombs (caves in limestone rocks) where people lived among the dead. For instance, the demon-possessed man mentioned in Mark 5:2 had been driven away from normal society. Also, in the vicinity was a reasonably steep slope not far from the shore of the lake. This may be the steep hillside over which the herd of swine plunged (vs. 13).

B. The Appearance of a Demon-Possessed Man: vss. 2-5

When Jesus got out of the boat, a man with an evil spirit came from the tombs to meet him. This man lived in the tombs, and no one could bind him any more, not even with a chain. For he had often been chained hand and foot, but he tore the chains apart and broke the irons on his feet. No one was strong enough to subdue him. Night and day among the tombs and in the hills he would cry out and cut himself with stones.

Perhaps not long after the Savior and His followers exited the boat, they encountered two men who were demon-possessed (see Matt. 8:28). Evidently, one of the two was more outspoken, and this explains why Mark 5:2 and Luke 8:27 focus particular attention on him. Mark 5:2 says he had "an evil spirit." The Greek adjective rendered "evil" can also be translated "unclean," "impure," or "foul." According to verse 9, the man was inhabited by a demonic cohort self-described as "legion." The Greek noun is of Latin origin and denotes a Roman regiment. In the time of Jesus, the composition would have been over 6,000 infantry, more than 100 cavalry, and an accompaniment of auxiliaries. In a figurative sense, "legion" suggests a great multitude of unspecified numbers. With so many demons inhabiting the man, it is hard to imagine the horrific oppression he had to endure.

How can we explain demon possession? Let's draw a comparison to the fact that Jesus lives in all believers. We know that some people manifest His presence to a far greater degree. We recognize more Spirit-filled believers, but also observe other Christians who live just barely inside the door of the Kingdom. On the other side, Satan has power over all non-believers, but also in varying degrees. A key difference between God's people and Satan's people is that all people whom the Savior controls still maintain their own identity and will. In contrast, one whom Satan truly possesses loses, at least at times, the ability to think, speak, or act independently.

The person described in verses 1-20 illustrates this tragedy. As this man did, demon-possessed people today are often said to possess superhuman powers of insight or physical strength. Yet, as powerful as Satan and all his forces may be, they must ultimately yield to God's power, which is far greater. The demons may have rebelled against Him, but they still recognize His absolute authority. In this regard, we are wise to avoid two opposite errors. On the one hand, we are fools if we live as if Satan does not exist. On the other hand, if we pay too much attention to the forces of evil, we may forget the One who still rules the world.

The man's condition was so severe that he sought refuge among nearby burial caves (vs. 3). Villagers tried to secure chains to his wrists and shackles to his feet. But he was so strong that he always snapped the chains and smashed the shackles. Moreover, no person had enough strength to subdue and control him (vs. 4). Beyond that, the cadre of demons so tormented their victim that throughout the night and day he would wander among the tombs and throughout the surrounding hills. He could be heard howling in distress and slashing himself with jagged stones (vs. 5). His actions were so mournful and self-destructive that they inspired fear in all who came near him.

C. The Shouts Uttered by the Man: vss. 6-8

When he saw Jesus from a distance, he ran and fell on his knees in front of him. He shouted at the top of his voice, "What do you want with me, Jesus, Son of the Most High God? Swear to God that you won't torture me!" For Jesus had said to him, "Come out of this man, you evil spirit!"

In Acts 10:36-38, Peter summoned up for the household of Cornelius the essence of the earthly ministry of the Lord Jesus. The Father sent the Son (who is the Lord of all) to herald the good news of peace. After John baptized the Redeemer, He ministered first in Galilee and then throughout the province of Judea. He was empowered by the Holy Spirit to perform deeds of mercy, which included healing people of their infirmities and expelling demons from those who were oppressed by them. The tormented man described in Mark 5:3-5 is a prime example.

This wretch was still some distance away from Jesus when he spotted the Messiah. Whether out of a sense of desperation or prompted by the cohort of demons (or both), the man ran to the Savior and fell on his knees in front of Jesus (vs. 6).

When the evil spirits realized they were in the presence of the "Son of God" (Matt. 8:29), they used their victim as a mouthpiece to let out a bone-chilling shriek. The question appearing in Mark 5:7 is literally rendered "What [is it] to me and you?" This idiomatic expression might be paraphrased as "Why are you bothering me?" Clearly, the demons wanted Jesus to leave them alone, and they personally addressed Him by name in a failed attempt to gain control over Him. In that day, it was popularly believed that knowing and declaring the name of others (whether a person or spirit) gave one authority over them.

The evil entities first referred to the divine Messiah as "Jesus," which is the Greek transliteration of the Hebrew name *Joshua*, which means "Yahweh saves." The implication is that the Father chose, appointed, and empowered His Son to save people from their sins (see Matt 1:21; Luke 1:30-33). The demons also referred to the Redeemer as the "Son of the Most High God" (Mark 5:7; see Luke 8:28). The phrase rendered "Most High" (see Gen. 14:18-19; Num. 24:16; Dan. 3:26) spotlights Yahweh's exaltation and absolute right to lordship over the creation (including any perceived rivals, such as pagan gods and goddesses). A key emphasis implicit in the phrase "Son of God" (Matt. 8:29) is Jesus' divinity. The title indicates that He is to be identified with the Father and considered fully and absolutely equal to Him (see John 5:18; 10:30, 36).

The New Testament also applied "Son of God" as a messianic title to the Lord Jesus (see Rom. 1:4; Rev. 2:18). The phrase emphasizes the special and intimate relationship that exists between the first and second persons of the Trinity (see Matt 16:16; Luke 1:35). Indeed, Jesus is the one and only Son of the Father (see John 3:16, 18; 1 John 4:9). As such, Jesus is the extraordinary object of the Father's love and co-equal with the Father and the Spirit. Hebrews 1:5 and 5:5 quote Psalm 2:7 in connection with the Messiah being the Son of God. Most likely, the Israelites applied this verse to the descendants of David, whom they crowned king. However, Psalm 2:7 ultimately refers to the Savior. This is made clear in Acts 13:33. When God raised Jesus from the dead, He conferred great dignity on Him by declaring Him to be His Son (something that had been true of Jesus for all eternity).

In an ironic twist, the host of demons invoked God's name as a form of protection. The Greek text can be literally rendered "I adjure you as God." More specifically, they implored Jesus for mercy. The Greek verb rendered "torture" (Mark 5:7) can also be translated "harass," "torment," or "vex." Apparently, the evil spirits discerned that they were in the presence of their Lord and Judge (see John 5:26-27; Rom. 2:16; Phil. 2:9-11). They feared that His presence signaled the arrival of the appointed time in which they would face their judgment (see Matt. 8:29). Mark 5:8 adds a parenthetical note explaining that Jesus had already commanded the demonic cohort to leave their victim. In contrast with the convoluted and elaborate routines performed by exorcists of the day, the Son's authoritative command was all that was needed to cast out any evil spirit from its human host.

D. The Question Asked by Jesus: vss. 9-10

Then Jesus asked him, "What is your name?" "My name is Legion," he replied, "for we are many." And he begged Jesus again and again not to send them out of the area.

In today's society, a person's name frequently is just a set of words by which they are known, referred to, and addressed. The situation was considerably different in Bible times. Someone's name often captured the essence of a person's character and mission in life. With respect to the demon-possessed man, when Jesus asked him to identify himself, his alien occupants forced him to reply, "My name is Legion" (Mark 5:9). The explanation given for the peculiar name is that a horde of evil entities were living in their human host.

The mob of demons especially feared the prospect of being cast into the "Abyss" (Luke 8:31). The latter renders the Greek noun *abussos*, which can also be translated the "bottomless pit" or the "immeasurable depth." It refers to the place where Satan and his fiendish cadre are confined until the day of judgment (see 2 Pet. 2:4; Rev. 9:1-2; 11:7; 17:8; 20:1, 3). In the case of the legion inhabiting the demoniac, they repeatedly begged Jesus not to expel them prematurely from the region (Mark 5:10).

E. The Expulsion of the Demons: vss. 11-13

A large herd of pigs was feeding on the nearby hillside. The demons begged Jesus, "Send us among the pigs; allow us to go into them." He gave them permission, and the evil spirits came out and went into the pigs. The herd, about two thousand in number, rushed down the steep bank into the lake and were drowned.

There happened to be a large herd of swine not far off feeding on a "hillside" (Mark 5:11). The Greek noun is more literally rendered "mountain," but this might incorrectly suggest an elevation considerably higher than the biblical text intended to imply. The evil spirits implored that after Jesus expelled them from the man, the Son of God permit them to go into the pigs (vs. 12). He in turn consented to their request. As a result, the legion of demons abandoned their human host, entered the herd (which numbered around 2,000 animals), stampeded down the side of a steep cliff, plunged into the lake, and drowned (vs. 13).

It is not immediately clear from the context why the demons wanted to enter the swine. One common explanation is that this outcome functions as a censure of the owners of the herd, for Jewish law considered these animals to be unclean. Also, eating pigs was strictly prohibited (see Lev. 11:7-8; Deut. 14:8). The latter observations notwithstanding, the theory fails to account for the fact that the region was mainly inhabited by Gentiles. Thus, in all probability, the owners were not members of the Jewish community. A more likely reason for the request is that the evil spirits favored drowning with the herd than being prematurely cast into the "Abyss" (Luke 8:31). Moreover, the episode puts a fine point on the destructive force of these demons—regardless of whether they exploited people or animals. In fact, the spirits were so evil that even the degradation of a human soul was not beneath their diabolical reach.

II. THE GOOD NEWS OF GOD'S MERCY: MARK 5:18-20

A. The Healed Man's Request: vs. 18

As Jesus was getting into the boat, the man who had been demon-possessed begged to go with him.

The Gerasene demoniac, after being freed by Jesus, was found sitting peacefully, clothed properly, and in his right mind (Mark 5:15). He was so grateful for being healed that he pleaded with Jesus to allow him to accompany Him in the boat (vs. 18). One would also expect the people of that region to have honored Jesus because of the changes in the former demoniac. Instead, they responded with fear. Curiosity drew them to the scene, but once they realized all that had happened, they became frightened and began to plead with Jesus to leave their region (vss. 16-17). They saw in Him a power more staggering than the power in demons, yet they didn't understand that Jesus' power is the power of good and not of evil.

This incident verified Jesus' claim to be the owner and master of nature. This included His lordship over the demons and the pigs. Second, the loss of the swine exposed what the people in the area truly valued. They placed greater importance on the animals than on a human being. Also, the swine seemed to be of greater value to them than the Messiah. Third, the pigs' carrying the demons into the depth of the sea is suggestive of the abysmal end awaiting Satan and his evil cohorts at the end of the age.

B. The Savior's Admonition: vss. 19-20

Jesus did not let him, but said, "Go home to your family and tell them how much the Lord has done for you, and how he has had mercy on you." So the man went away and began to tell in the Decapolis how much Jesus had done for him. And all the people were amazed.

Previously, after Jesus had cleansed a man of leprosy, He sternly admonished the recipient of His mercy not to tell anyone what had happened (see Mark 1:43-44). Undoubtedly, Jesus did not want other Jews to obtain a skewed understanding of His claim to be the Messiah. In contrast, while Jesus would not permit the former demoniac to accompany Him in the boat, He did urge the healed man to return to his village and declare to the residents how much the Lord had blessed him. The townspeople were especially to be told about how God showered the man with His "mercy" (5:19). The latter renders the Greek verb *eleeo*, which can also be translated "compassion" or "pity."

One possible reason for the sharp difference in the Savior's admonition is that the former demoniac lived in predominantly Gentile territory. Because there were far fewer Jewish religious leaders and zealots to be found, it was less likely that Jesus' teaching and miracles would be misunderstood to have political overtones or be laced with aspirations of seizing temporal power. In response to Jesus, the grateful man departed and spread the news of Jesus abroad in his homeland.

The latter was the "Decapolis" (vs. 20; literally, "Ten Towns"), a region situated mainly south and east of the Sea of Galilee. The district initially contained 10 independent cities (see Matt. 4:25; Mark 7:31). In later times, additional cities were added to the group. The federation was not primarily distinguished by political aspirations and cooperation. Instead, the inhabitants united around following the Greco-Roman way of life—including its institutions and culture. Moreover, they intentionally refused to embrace the Semitic influences of their neighbors, including those of the Jews to the west, the Nabataeans to the south, and the semi-nomadic tribes in the highland regions to the north.

Discussion Questions

1. Why did the demoniac live in the tombs?
2. What did the crazed man do when he spotted Jesus?
3. Why did the demoniac beg Jesus not to torture him?
4. What was significant about the name the demons gave for themselves?
5. If you were the healed man, would you have wanted to join Jesus as He got in the boat?

Contemporary Application

For many years, Denise would feel sadness when she thought about the condition of her family's spiritual life. She was the only child among her seven siblings who had, so far, trusted in the Messiah for salvation. Neither of her parents showed any interest in the Lord Jesus.

Denise would occasionally hear the testimony of other believers that was the exact opposite of hers. When she would hear them speak of the many generations of godliness that existed in parents and grandparents before them, she would secretly feel ashamed—or even worse, jealous. At times, she would ask herself, Why hasn't Jesus brought spiritual and physical healing to the members of my family?

It was a bright and sunny April morning when Denise was finally set free from the burden of her family's unbelief—or at least the shame of it. As she listened to the visiting speaker in her home church talk about his godly heritage, Denise heard the minister give special thanks to God for all those who were uniquely selected out of ungodly families and homes to begin a new lineage of faith and righteousness.

Moreover, the speaker noted what a wonderful privilege it is to be the first believer or first-generation convert among a clan of unbelievers. As Denise absorbed the reality of the minister's closing thoughts, her heart was filled with praise to the Son, who has the power to redeem the lost.

Begging to Get In

Scripture

Background Scripture: *Mark 7:24-30*
Scripture Lesson: *Mark 7:24-30*
Key Verse: *The woman was a Greek, born in Syrian
Phoenicia. She begged Jesus to drive the demon out of her
daughter.* Mark 7:26.
Scripture Lesson for Children: *Mark 7:24-30*
Key Verse for Children: *A woman . . . came and fell at his
feet.* Mark 7:25.

Lesson Aim

To emphasize how important it is for us to intercede
for each other.

Lesson Setting

Time: *About A.D. 29*
Place: *Tyre*

Lesson Outline

Begging to Get In

  I. Feelings of Desperation: Mark 7:24-26
     A. *The Savior's Desire for Privacy: vs. 24*
     B. *The Arrival of a Distraught Mother: vss. 25-26*
  II. Undeterred Faith: Mark 7:27-30
     A. *The Mother's Tenacity: vss. 27-28*
     B. *The Savior's Approval: vss. 29-30*

Introduction for Adults

Topic: *Pleading for Mercy*

Antonio carried the gun he needed. He would get revenge. The man who had murdered his son would die. Antonio would see to that. But that very night brought an overwhelming hurricane to Honduras. Before he knew it, Antonio found his own life in danger. He climbed a tree to escape a torrent of flood water underneath him.

Antonio lost everything, except his family. He found them in a school that had become a shelter. With other things to worry about, his need for revenge dropped out of sight. Relief workers offered a home and a Savior to Antonio. With many old barriers broken down, Antonio had begun a new life, one in which he began to value and show mercy.

Introduction for Youth

Topic: *Determined to Find True Treasure*

Mothers agonize when their children get sick. They also worry about their children getting into trouble. And Christian mothers pray that their children will trust in Jesus for salvation—the true treasure from an eternal perspective.

A teenage daughter was surprised to find her mother waiting for her when she came home late one night. Suddenly it dawned on the girl that her mother truly cared about her. The daughter asked, "Mom, you really do worry about me, don't you?"

Mothers love and care for their children. That's why they lie awake at night waiting for the car to pull into the garage. Christian mothers pray for the needs of their children. Such moms understand that there is more to provide for their children than food, shelter, and clothing. In addition, these mothers also seek to provide emotional and spiritual nourishment. How satisfying it must be when their children realize their mother's love for them!

Concepts for Children

Topic: *A Woman's Faith*

1. A mother with a sick daughter had the faith and courage to go to Jesus on the young child's behalf.
2. Difficult circumstances sometimes call for unusual faith and courage.
3. Jesus wants us to trust in Him and be saved.
4. Having faith in the Lord can help us deal with difficult situations.
5. The Lord is pleased when we, in faith, pray for the needs of others.

Lesson Commentary

I. FEELINGS OF DESPERATION: MARK 7:24-26

A. The Savior's Desire for Privacy: vs. 24

Jesus left that place and went to the vicinity of Tyre. He entered a house and did not want anyone to know it; yet he could not keep his presence secret.

According to Mark 7:24, Jesus discerned that it was time to leave "that place." This probably would have been the vicinity of Gennesaret (see Matt. 14:34; Mark 6:53). This was a well-watered plain (approximately four miles long and less than two miles wide) located on the northwest bank of the Sea of Galilee. In the valley's fertile soil farmers grew figs, olives, palms, and several other types of trees. According to local belief, the numerous mineral springs in the area could heal the infirm and crippled who flocked to them. The crowds in the region were so desperate and needy that they begged Jesus to allow their sick to simply touch the edge of His cloak in the hope that they might be cured. He granted the people's requests and healed all who touched Him (see Matt. 14:35-36; Mark 6:55-56).

Undoubtedly, all these events took their toll physically on the Savior (see John 4:6). Also, He probably did not want to clash with the religious establishment of Jerusalem at that time. Thus, it made sense for Him to get away from the crowds so that He could focus on training His disciples. He decided to leave Galilee and travel 30 or 40 miles northwestward to the area of Tyre and Sidon, where He found a place to stay (Matt. 15:21; Mark 14:24). In the first century of the common era, these cities were busy ports in Phoenicia on the coast of the Mediterranean Sea. Both were renowned as centers of commerce, especially with respect to the maritime industry. Along with Beirut, Tyre and Sidon are the major cities of modern Lebanon.

According to Mark 7:24, Jesus' desire for privacy included remaining secluded in someone's home (perhaps a Jewish resident) during His stay in the region of Tyre and Sidon. Nonetheless, He could not escape notice for long. Eventually, news of His arrival spread. This enabled people who had heard about the famed worker of miracles to learn about His presence and seek Him out. Jesus, however, was not flattered by such attention. Indeed, because God the Son knew what was in the hearts of people (see 1 Sam. 16:7; 1 Kings 8:39), He refused to entrust Himself to or seek approval from these or any other would-be followers. Moreover, the Savior did not need anyone to tell Him about the true nature of people, for He already knew it perfectly (see John 2:24-25).

B. The Arrival of a Distraught Mother: vss. 25-26

In fact, as soon as she heard about him, a woman whose little daughter was possessed by an evil spirit came and fell at his feet. The woman was a Greek, born in Syrian Phoenicia. She begged Jesus to drive the demon out of her daughter.

Mark 7:25 takes note of a distraught mother whose young daughter was inhabited and controlled by an "evil spirit." The malicious entity tormented the little girl terribly (Matt. 15:22). When the woman heard about Jesus and learned He could heal people of their afflictions, she did not waste any time to discover His whereabouts, come before Him, and fall prostrate at His feet. Mark 7:26 says the uninvited guest was a "Greek." The latter term renders a noun that emphasizes the woman's Gentile (that is, non-Jewish) ethnicity and heritage. She was of "Syrian Phoenician origin," which means she was a female native of Phoenicia in Syria.

Syria (also known as Aram) was a region situated along the northwest corner of the Mediterranean Sea. Syria was also located directly north of Palestine. Throughout biblical times, the political boundaries of Syria remained ill-defined, being inhabited by a loose affiliation of villages and city-states. The region would be roughly equivalent to the modern states of Lebanon and Syria, along with small portions of Iraq and Turkey. In Jesus' day, Syria was a province of the Roman Empire. Like Palestine, ancient Syria had a narrow coastal plain, a ridge of mountains, a rift valley, and a semiarid zone of grassland that transitioned into desert. Syria's two main rivers were the Orontes (which flowed north and west into the sea) and the Leontes (which flowed south and west into the sea).

The name *Phoenicia* is probably derived from the Greek word *phoenos*, which means "blood red." The Bible refers to the Phoenicians as one of the Canaanite peoples. The Phoenicians were a Semitic group who became famous seafarers. They established colonies on shores and islands throughout the Mediterranean Sea area. Their most important settlement was Carthage, which they founded in the ninth century B.C. and which later became the center of an independent empire that for a time rivaled the Roman Empire.

Matthew 15:22 says Jesus' visitor was a "Canaanite woman." During the time of the Judges (beginning around 1375 B.C.), the Canaanites were the principal enemies of the Israelites. These were the people the Israelites chiefly sought to drive out of the land. The Canaanites were descendants of Canaan, the son of Ham (Gen. 10:6, 15-20), and most likely lived in the region some 800 years before the Israelites crossed the Jordan River and began battling the various indigenous tribes. The Canaanites included the Hittites, the Jebusites, the Amorites, and the Hivites (to name a few groups of people; 15:19-20). They lived in well-developed cities, each with its own ruler and army.

Most of the Canaanites were polytheistic, with their idols being Baal, Dagon, and Asherah, to which numerous shrines were erected. God originally called upon the Israelites to conquer and drive out the Canaanites before they could live peacefully in the land. But the Israelites neither completely conquered them nor drove them from the land (Judg. 1:28). In the first century of the common era, Canaan no longer existed as a nation. During Jesus' earthly ministry, "Canaanite" (Matt. 15:22) not only referred to the descendants of the Jews' ancient enemies, but also designated their pagan cultural successors.

Mark 7:26 succinctly notes that the Gentile mother implored the Savior to expel the demon from her tormented daughter. The Greek verb rendered "drive . . . out" is a strong term that can mean to "compel one to depart." Matthew 15:22 is more explicit concerning what the distraught mother said. She cried out, "Lord, Son of David, have mercy on me!" Here we find the Gentile woman speaking with reverence toward Jesus. Perhaps the manner in which she referred to the itinerant rabbi from Nazareth shows that the mother had some recognition that Jesus—King David's most illustrious descendant (see Luke 1:32-33)—was the promised Messiah of the Jews. The text, however, does not indicate that she was a proselyte (that is, a convert to Judaism).

Matthew seems to be intentionally contrasting the faith of a Gentile and the unbelief of the Jewish teachers and rulers who interrogated Him earlier. In this regard, the Greek noun rendered "Lord" (Matt. 15:22) is a title of honor and respect. The verb rendered "mercy" denotes the presence of compassion toward someone who is in an afflicted or wretched condition. For the mother, this would apply to her daughter, who was being tormented by an evil spirit.

II. UNDETERRED FAITH: MARK 7:27-30

A. The Mother's Tenacity: vss. 27-28

"First let the children eat all they want," he told her, "for it is not right to take the children's bread and toss it to their dogs." "Yes, Lord," she replied, "but even the dogs under the table eat the children's crumbs."

Matthew 15:23 indicates that at first Jesus remained silent. Then His disciples, noting that He had not spoken a word, begged Jesus to send away the distraught mother. Evidently, they were annoyed by the woman's persistence, especially the way in which she kept begging Jesus for help. While the comments of the disciples might sound harsh and uncaring to us, possibly these men were afraid that contact with this Gentile woman would make them unclean. As a matter of fact, respected Jewish teachers of that day rarely, if ever, volunteered to speak with a woman in public, especially not a Gentile (see John 4:9).

Apparently, Jesus ignored the disciples' unkind suggestion. While Jesus initially did not respond to the Canaanite woman, He did not heed His followers' urgings at all. When the Savior finally spoke, He addressed the mother so as to clarify His position. His Father sent Him to save the Jews, whom Jesus referred to as the "lost sheep of Israel" (Matt. 15:24). Expressed differently, Jesus' primary mission during His earthly ministry did not (at least on the surface) include helping Gentiles like the Canaanite woman. Tragically, even when the Son conducted His earthly ministry among His own people in their homeland, they failed to receive Him as the Messiah (see John 1:11). Indeed, His own nation, including the religious elite of His day, refused to accept and welcome Him as their Savior and Lord (see John 12:37-41; Acts 7:51-53).

In the midst of this emerging circumstance, we find a Gentile of the opposite gender courageously coming to Jesus for help. Perhaps in His initial response, He sought to test the mother's faith, as well as demonstrate to the disciples the depth of her willingness to depend completely on Him. The encounter clarified how dearly the Father held the Jewish people in His heart. Also, the presence of the Canaanite mother imploring Jesus anticipated the eventual proclamation of the Gospel to Jews and Gentiles alike across the globe (see Matt. 20:19; Acts 1:8).

Matthew 4:12-16 conveys a similar truth. Verse 14, in particular, states that Jesus' relocation to Capernaum fulfilled what was written in Isaiah 9:1-2. This passage alludes to the suffering that northern Israel experienced under Assyrian rule. God had humbled His people, especially the tribes of Zebulun and Naphtali. Under the dominion of foreign rulers, this region became known as Galilee of the nations (or "of the Gentiles"). God had promised to reverse His judgment by allowing northern Israel to receive His blessing. He fulfilled that promise by enlightening the Jews and Gentiles living near the Sea of Galilee (Matt. 4:15). They had once walked in spiritual darkness and death, but as the Savior ministered to them, they were graced with the light of His presence and truth (vs. 16; see also Isa. 42:6; 49:6). Jesus' ministry to Gentiles in Galilee anticipated the worldwide proclamation of the Gospel to come.

The Redeemer's statement in Matthew 15:24 about His mission did not discourage His Gentile visitor. Instead, she knelt before Him and pleaded once more for His help. The Greek verb rendered "knelt before" indicates that the mother's plea was more than an act of supplication. It now took the form of worship toward the Lord. The verb rendered "help" carries the idea of bringing aid or relief at the moment of greatest need. By again calling Jesus "Lord," the Canaanite woman demonstrated the faith that she had in the Savior to heal her daughter—faith that was especially poignant for its desperation and persistence. What is also reflected in the mother's petition is her intense love for her daughter and herself—healing for her daughter and mercy for herself.

Jesus replied, once again letting the woman know that His spiritual works rightfully belonged to the Jews, who were the chosen children of God. It would not be right to take the good things of God from His covenant people and give them to the Gentiles (vs. 26). Jesus illustrated His point by describing a common domestic situation in which a family is eating dinner while small household dogs are begging for food. He stated that it was not right to take food from the children and throw it to the dogs. The Greek noun translated "dogs" (Mark 7:27) referred not to savage, wild animals that scavenge among the garbage in the streets, but to house pets loved by the owners yet not equal to the owners' children.

Jesus' statement has a dual meaning. On one level, it refers to the focus of Jesus' mission. In this case, "children" are Jews, the "dogs" are Gentiles, and the "bread" is the Gospel. It is hardly likely, of course, that the woman understood this meaning of Jesus' words. More likely, she understood them on a practical level. The woman had interrupted Jesus' retreat with His disciples. For Jesus to help her, then, would have required Him to take His time and energy away from the disciples and give them to the woman. On this level of meaning, the "children" are the disciples, the "dogs" represent the woman, and the "bread" is Jesus' ministry.

The woman still was not put off by Jesus' reply to her request. Amazingly, the mother responded with perseverance and wit, letting the Savior know that she would take whatever He would offer. The woman did not contradict or argue with Jesus. The mother remained respectful yet persistent in her petition. After all, she was desperate, and Jesus was her only hope. In this exchange, we find the woman extending Jesus' analogy for her own purposes. The meal did not have to be interrupted and the children's bread be given to the dogs. All the dogs needed were a few crumbs dropped during the meal (vs. 28). Put another way, the woman was saying that Jesus could quickly and easily fulfill her request, and then get back to teaching His disciples.

B. The Savior's Approval: vss. 29-30

Then he told her, "For such a reply, you may go; the demon has left your daughter." She went home and found her child lying on the bed, and the demon gone.

Jesus recognized the depth of the Gentile mother's faith. Despite the Savior's initial discouraging remark, the woman did not tell Him how worthy she was. Neither did she claim that she was as good as a Jew. Instead, throughout her pleas, she reverently showed her devotion to Jesus. The mother embodied the attributes of humility, openness to the power of God, and persistence in her requests of the Lord that characterize godly people in any age.

The Gentile's answer pleased Jesus. He may even have laughed at the way she turned His statement to her own benefit. The Savior, in referring to her as "woman" (Matt. 15:28), gave emotional force to His response to the mother's desperate plea. The Greek noun rendered "woman" was a polite form of address, being similar to such contemporary expressions as "Madam" or "Ma'am." Jesus was impressed with the magnitude and extent of this Gentile's faith.

The Greek noun rendered "faith" includes a range of meanings and nuances, from mere assent to complete dependence. In turn, these form the theological basis for having eternal life, knowing the truth, receiving the Son, obeying His teachings, encountering the Father, and averting judgment. The biblical concept of faith is not static or passive. Instead, it is dynamic and active. Moreover, this vibrant faith reaches out to appropriate the forgiveness that Jesus offers through His atoning sacrifice on the Cross. This is a circumstance in which such faith goes beyond mere belief and mental apprehension to a wholehearted commitment to Jesus, the object of the believer's trust.

In light of the mother's reply, the Savior directed her to return to her daughter, who was now well and whole, for the demon had been expelled from her (Mark

7:29). Matthew 15:28 says that from that moment on, the young girl was healed of her spiritual affliction. When the Gentile woman arrived at her home, she discovered that her child was lying on her bed and in her right mind (Mark 7:30). The evil spirit was no longer present within creating unimaginable havoc and anguish. Ironically, many Jews would lose God's blessing and salvation because they rejected Jesus, and many Gentiles would find salvation because they recognized and accepted Him.

Discussion Questions

1. Why did Jesus decide to leave the vicinity of Gennesaret and head toward the area of Tyre and Sidon?
2. Why was Jesus unable to keep His presence a secret?
3. Why did the Syrophoenician woman believe that Jesus could expel the demon from her daughter?
4. What was Jesus' intent in making use of the analogy recorded in Mark 7:27?
5. If you were the Syrophoenician woman, how do you think you would have made your request to Jesus?

Contemporary Application

God knows our every thought and feeling. No one else can have such an intimate understanding of us. At the same time, Scripture is clear that God seeks communion with us through prayer. By bringing our concerns to God, we strengthen our relationship with Him. Not only is it good for us to present our needs and desires to God directly, but also it is in prayer that we open ourselves up to hear His answers.

Otherwise, God's relationship with us is something like a husband who knows that his wife loves him only because he's heard her telling the neighbors about her feelings for him. It would mean so much more to him, however, if she would tell him face-to-face. When we neglect to take our problems to God, we neglect the one who is totally in control of the universe and our lives.

We show our faith in the Lord by how persistent we are with our prayers. Do we pray halfheartedly, with the feeling that says, "Oh, God wouldn't want that anyway"? Or do we have such conviction and faith that we press on? Even when we think God is silent, and even when circumstances become more and more discouraging, we must faithfully pursue our petitions to God.

When U.S. speed skater Dan Jansen received a gold metal for winning the 1,000-meter race at the Winter Olympics in Lillehammer, Norway, in 1994, people around the globe praised Jansen's perseverance. After failing to medal in seven previous races in four Olympics, Jansen's persistence finally paid off. We need to have the same persistence when we pursue our petitions to God. We must not give up, for the Lord hears our every petition and He does respond.

Opting Out!

Scripture

Background Scripture: *Mark 10:17-31*

Scripture Lesson: *Mark 10:17-31*

Key Verse: *Jesus looked at him and loved him. "One thing you lack," he said. "Go, sell everything you have and give to the poor, and you will have treasure in heaven. Then come, follow me."* Mark 10:21.

Scripture Lesson for Children: *Mark 10:17-31*

Key Verse for Children: *At this the man's face fell. He went away sad, because he had great wealth.* Mark 10:22.

Lesson Aim

To stress the importance of giving Jesus first place in our lives.

Lesson Setting

Time: *About A.D. 30*

Place: *Judea and Perea*

Lesson Outline

Opting Out!

I. Jesus and the Rich Man: Mark 10:17-22
   A. *The Rich Man's Question: vs. 17*
   B. *The Lord's Answer: vss. 18-19*
   C. *The Rich Man's True Need: vss. 20-22*

II. Jesus and His Disciples: Mark 10:23-31
   A. *The Lord's Explanation: vss. 23-25*
   B. *The Lord's Declaration: vss. 26-27*
   C. *The Lord's Promise: vss. 28-31*

Introduction for Adults

Topic: *The Gain in Giving*

Have you ever listened to famous people list their priorities in television interviews? Some will say their careers, families, or friends. Occasionally, someone will mention God, but that is rare. Whatever people may say, we can discover their priorities by what they do.

Even Christians may say that God comes first, but an examination of how they spend their time and money may reveal that some other things outrank God. How easy it is to slip into putting our careers first, or our financial security, or our health. It seems hard to find time to worship God and witness for Him.

The rich young ruler in this week's lesson thought he had his priorities straight, because he kept most of God's commandments. But Jesus knew that law keeping was not enough, for money was the man's idol, and Jesus had taught, "You cannot serve both God and money" (Matt. 6:24).

Introduction for Youth

Topic: *True Treasure Costs*

When one young man at gunpoint robs another youth of his digital media player, we know that materialism has control over the first individual. Adolescents have been attacked for a pair of athletic shoes. And teens from wealthy homes try to validate themselves by wearing expensive designer clothes.

Wherever we look, we see the unmistakable presence of materialism. So we can appreciate why Jesus told the rich young man to sell everything he owned. Jesus was emphatic about this because He knew how susceptible we all can be to the lure of having lots of money, clothes, cars, and so on.

Teens can try to imitate the lifestyle of the rich, but they are destined to be disappointed, for no matter how much they acquire, they will come up empty and lose eternal life. It's much better in the near term and for eternity to give everything to Jesus now. He not only takes care of us, but He also gives us an inner joy that money cannot buy.

Concepts for Children

Topic: *A Rich Man Refuses to Follow*

1. A rich man came to Jesus and asked what he had to do to earn eternal life.
2. Jesus mentioned several Old Testament laws, for the man claimed to be a good person.
3. When Jesus told the rich man to sell all he had, he went away sad, for he valued his wealth more than following Jesus.
4. Jesus told His followers that, while it's hard for the rich to be saved, nothing is impossible with God's special favor (or grace).
5. The Father wants us to trust in the Son for salvation, not in ourselves or others.

Lesson Commentary

I. JESUS AND THE RICH MAN: MARK 10:17-22

A. The Rich Man's Question: vs. 17

As Jesus started on his way, a man ran up to him and fell on his knees before him. "Good teacher," he asked, "what must I do to inherit eternal life?"

The episode recorded in Mark 10:17-31 occurred in the winter of A.D. 30. When we look at the details of the various Gospel accounts, we discover that the man who ran up to Jesus was not only rich, but also a leader and young in age (that is, probably less than 40 years old; see Matt. 19:16, 20, 22; Mark 10:17, 22; Luke 18:18, 23). Add to this his record of law keeping, and we can see that he was quite a noteworthy person. The descriptions found in the Synoptic Gospels could have fit one of the local Jewish council or court representatives.

Such observations notwithstanding, the distinguished person lacked at least one thing, namely, assurance of eternal life. Perhaps based on rumors he had heard about Jesus, the inquirer sought out the itinerant preacher from Nazareth for the answer to his quest. Yet quite unlike another rich man, Nicodemus, who sought Jesus at night (see John 3:1-2), this man ran to Jesus in broad daylight, in full public view, and fell before Him in a position of respect.

Evidently, the young man whom Jesus encountered on His way to Jerusalem expected to be given a task he could accomplish to win favor with God. It is clear that the ruler was thinking in terms of earning salvation rather than receiving eternal life as the Father's gift from the Son. When the Pharisees had asked their question about divorce, they had been mainly interested in getting Jesus to say something that would put Him in a bad light with the people. However, in the case of the rich young leader, the question probably reflected a burning concern. We might paraphrase his query as "What is missing?" He had been raised to follow the law, but he still felt unfulfilled. There was a spiritual void within.

B. The Lord's Answer: vss. 18-19

"Why do you call me good?" Jesus answered. "No one is good—except God alone. You know the commandments: 'Do not murder, do not commit adultery, do not steal, do not give false testimony, do not defraud, honor your father and mother.'"

In his initial greeting, the young man referred to Jesus as "Good teacher" (Mark 10:17). The Greek adjective translated "good" denotes what is distinguished, upright, or honorable. "Teacher" renders a noun that in this context refers to distinguished rabbis who instructed others in truths about God, His commandments, and His expectations for humankind. Undoubtedly, to point the young man's thinking in the proper direction, Jesus asked, "Why do you call me good?" (Mark 10:18). The rich young ruler, in using the adjective rendered "good," implied something about Jesus' essential nature.

Next, the Savior declared that no person is truly good. Indeed, only God is infinitely holy and so He alone could be called "good." Jesus' point was that true goodness is not found in sinful people or the deeds they perform. Rather, there is only one source of supreme goodness, namely, God. It would be incorrect to conclude that Jesus was denying His own goodness. Behind His statement is the awareness of His unity with the Father and the Spirit. Also, Jesus wanted the young man to seriously consider the implications of calling the Savior "good" before using the term.

Jesus next said that if the aspiring leader truly prized the life God gave, he should obey "the commandments" (vs. 19; see Deut. 30:15-20). The latter renders a Greek noun that refers to precepts, injunctions, and edicts of God, particularly those recorded in the Old Testament. It would be incorrect to conclude from Jesus' statement that He thought heeding the Mosaic law could earn eternal life, for this can only be received as a gift through faith. Rather, Jesus' strategy was to help His inquirer recognize his inability to obtain eternal life through good works. Jesus could have done the ruler's thinking for him by telling him that salvation can never be merited by what one does. Instead, Jesus worked with the man on his current level of understanding and led him to confront the truth on his own terms and in his own way.

According to Matthew 19:18, the man asked which commandments he should keep. Jesus' response in Mark 10:19 focused on those Ten Commandments that concerned one's relationship with other people. The Messiah cited prohibitions against murder, adultery, stealing, perjury, defrauding (which is akin to coveting), and dishonoring parents. He also stressed the importance of people loving others as much as themselves (Matt. 19:19). The Ten Commandments are also known as the Decalogue, meaning "ten words." Both Jews and Christians esteem them above other statutes that Moses conveyed to the Israelites. Indeed, they comprise the basic requirements for proper living among God's chosen people.

C. The Rich Man's True Need: vss. 20-22

"Teacher," he declared, *"all these I have kept since I was a boy." Jesus looked at him and loved him. "One thing you lack,"* he said. *"Go, sell everything you have and give to the poor, and you will have treasure in heaven. Then come, follow me." At this the man's face fell. He went away sad, because he had great wealth.*

The young man claimed to have wholeheartedly observed all the commandments Jesus mentioned since he was "a boy" (Mark 10:20). This probably is a reference to the inquirer's *bar mitzvah* at the age of 13 when all Jewish youths assumed personal responsibility for heeding the commandments. The aspiring leader evidently thought Jesus needed to give him a longer list, so that he could set about observing these directives too. Obviously, the official had not yet grasped the fact that keeping the law can never save anyone. It can only disclose our sin and the need we have for a Savior (Rom. 7:7-12; Gal. 3:24). Also, for the ruler obedience to the law was a matter of external compliance. He evidently did not realize that inner conformity was also imperative and that it is impossible for people to fully achieve this by themselves.

According to Mark 10:21, Jesus looked at His inquirer intently and felt love for him. The Greek verb rendered "loved" denotes the unselfish, unconditional compassion of the Messiah. Such love is prompted more by will than by emotion. It seeks to reach out to others in need, even when the object is unworthy of being loved (see John 3:16). The editorial remark in Mark 10:21 shows how Jesus' love for all people was individualized in this situation. Out of compassion, the Savior told the young man something he did not want to hear, namely, to sell all he had and give the money to the poor. Jesus assured the man he would have "treasure in heaven." By doing this, he would show that earthly wealth no longer prevented him from exclusively following the Lord.

The Greek verb rendered "lack" pointed to an area of the inquirer's spiritual life that was deficient. Jesus drew attention to this when, according to Matthew 19:21, He addressed the aspiring leader's desire to be "perfect" (see 5:48). The latter renders an adjective that can also be translated "mature" or "full grown." In this context, it refers to the complete absence of lack in any area of one's spiritual life. Regrettably, this was not the case with the rich young ruler, for he was unduly attached to his material possessions.

Jesus had touched the inquirer's heart, and the man was devastated. The Greek verb rendered "face fell" (Mark 10:22) can metaphorically refer to the sky being covered with dark clouds. The verb translated "sad" denotes the presence of grief, distress, or anguish. In the case of the aspiring leader, he became gloomy and went away dejected, for he did not want to part with his earthly riches for the treasures of heaven. Jesus never specifically stated the one thing the man lacked. Nonetheless, as soon as He instructed the ruler to sell whatever he owned, the one shortcoming took control of his heart and dictated his response. He chose his possessions over eternal life.

II. JESUS AND HIS DISCIPLES: MARK 10:23-31

A. The Lord's Explanation: vss. 23-25

Jesus looked around and said to his disciples, "How hard it is for the rich to enter the kingdom of God!" The disciples were amazed at his words. But Jesus said again, "Children, how hard it is to enter the kingdom of God! It is easier for a camel to go through the eye of a needle than for a rich man to enter the kingdom of God."

After the wealthy official left, Jesus focused His attention on His disciples. He said that it was difficult for the rich to enter the kingdom of God (Mark 10:23). The Savior's remark caused the Twelve to be "amazed" (vs. 24). The latter translates the Greek verb *thambeo*, which also can be rendered "astonished" or "perplexed." Their shocked response shows that they had accepted the common thinking of that day regarding the presence of wealth as an ironclad indication of God's favor (see Prov. 10:22). Jesus, of course, rejected this mistaken notion.

The Savior was even more direct when He declared again that it was very hard to get into the divine kingdom. This was true for all people, not just the rich. In fact, it was impossible. Jesus clarified His assertion by noting that it was easier for a camel to pass through a needle's eye than for a rich person to make the passage into heaven (vs. 25). Camels were the largest and most common beasts of burden in Palestine in New Testament times.

According to an old tradition, Jesus' word picture referred to a low gate in the wall of Jerusalem. This gate, which was for those who arrived after the main gates had been shut for the night, was called "the eye of the needle." People could get through easily, but camels could crawl through only with great difficulty—on their knees—and only if their cargo was unloaded. According to this tradition, Jesus' point was that the rich can enter the Kingdom only if they get down on their knees (in other words, humble themselves) and unload their possessions.

In some ways this tradition is attractive, but there is no reliable evidence that there ever was a gate called "the eye of the needle." It seems more consistent with Jesus' style of teaching and His use of humor and exaggeration to believe He meant a literal camel and a literal needle. He was talking about an impossibility, not a difficulty. Only God can save a human being.

B. The Lord's Declaration: vss. 26-27

The disciples were even more amazed, and said to each other, "Who then can be saved?" Jesus looked at them and said, "With man this is impossible, but not with God; all things are possible with God."

Jesus' provocative statement was designed to elicit a response from His followers, and it did. In fact, the disciples were even more "amazed" (Mark 10:26). The latter translates a Greek verb that can be loosely rendered "struck with astonishment" or "feeling overwhelmed." Jesus' followers were so shocked that they wondered how anyone could be "saved." The latter translates a verb that in this context refers to deliverance from the penalties of divine judgment. Evidently, the Twelve agreed with the religious leaders, who taught that those who had many material possessions were most blessed by God. If, therefore, the rich could not enter heaven, how could the poor ever hope to do so?

Now Jesus gave the answer that His provocative statement had anticipated. Entering heaven is impossible for people, but all things are possible for God (vs. 27). Put another way, while no one (not even the rich) can earn eternal life through godly living, the Father gives it freely to those who believe in the Son. Admittedly, while our sinfulness makes it impossible for any of us to achieve salvation on our own, the wealthy have special temptations to sin. Yet God can achieve the impossible; He can change any human heart.

C. The Lord's Promise: vss. 28-31

Peter said to him, "We have left everything to follow you!" "I tell you the truth," Jesus replied, "no one who has left home or brothers or sisters or mother or father or children or fields for me and the gospel will fail to receive a hundred times as much in this present age (homes, brothers, sisters, mothers, children and fields—and with them, persecutions) and in the age to come, eternal life. But many who are first will be last, and the last first."

Apparently, the Twelve were still thinking in terms of payment and reward. Peter, at least, reflected this mind-set when he reminded the Savior (perhaps with an attitude of smugness) that the entire group had abandoned everything in order to become His disciples (Mark 10:28). Evidently, Peter and the other eleven thought they deserved more recognition than others for the sacrifices they had made to accompany Jesus. Thankfully, the Messiah decided not to debate how genuinely unselfish the Twelve had been up to this point. Instead, Jesus affirmed their commitment, imperfect though it was.

Jesus specifically mentioned His followers giving up all financial claims and inheritance rights in connection with their family (including their parents and siblings) and ancestral estate (including their homes and fields). The Messiah reassured His disciples that in the "present age" (vs. 30), He would shower them with innumerable spiritual blessings. Their generous reward included becoming part of the worldwide body of Christ, along with its numerous members (including, spiritual brothers, sisters, mothers, fathers, children, congregations, and so on) and the possibility of suffering for one's faith. Concerning the latter, Jesus declared in Matthew 5:10 that divine blessing rested on those who were persecuted because of their decision to live for God. Though believers might suffer for their devotion to the Messiah, they were assured that the kingdom of heaven belonged to them.

Jesus' followers should not be shocked when they are slandered, physically harmed, or targeted for malicious rumors (as was the case for believers martyred during the reign of Nero). Though they feel the intense pain of such injustices, they can persevere by holding to the promise of God's richest blessing (vs. 11). The Savior gave two reasons His harassed followers could accept their circumstances with an attitude of joy (vs. 12). First, they ought to realize that their eternal reward will exceed their wildest expectations. Second, they can remember that God's enemies also mistreated His prophets. Beyond the horizon of the present is the "age to come" (Mark 10:30) and with it the promise of "eternal life." Jesus promised that in the end times, when renewal and restoration comes and He reigns on His glorious throne, the Twelve will also sit on 12 thrones and judge the 12 tribes of Israel (Matt. 19:28). Some interpreters take the Savior's pledge literally, while others see in it a figurative expression.

Jesus capped His teaching on this subject with a prediction that, in the messianic kingdom, the status and prestige savored by the elite will be reversed. Many who are now regarded as being the greatest will one day be regarded as the least important. Conversely, those who appear to be least important now will one day be the greatest (Mark 10:31). Unlike the religious teachers, Jesus knew that the rich, far from being shining examples of piety, are often the worst of sinners. In contrast, many of the poor and despised are in fact the most faithful servants of God. When the Lord establishes full and final justice, not appearances but realities will form the basis of judging.

Discussion Questions

1. What was the rich man looking for in his encounter with Jesus?
2. What did the man say to justify his personal sense of righteousness?
3. What were the commandments that the man had tried to keep?
4. Why is it more important to obey the truth than to do things that simply make us feel spiritually good?
5. How can we maintain the right priorities with our material possessions?

Contemporary Application

When I was a child, my pastor would give the invitation to make a commitment to Christ. This was the most challenging part of the worship service for me. After the sermon had been preached, the minister would stand, often coming from behind the pulpit, and invite people to receive Jesus as their Savior. Regardless of whether anyone joined the church, the invitation was given each Sunday with urgency and zeal.

Jesus calls us to be like the good soil in Matthew 13, receiving His seed—the Gospel—joyfully and with total commitment. We are to prayerfully listen to God's Word when it comes to us, not only when we first hear the Gospel, but also every time thereafter. We should have the same attitude as the psalmist who prayed, "Your word is a lamp to my feet and a light for my path" (Ps. 119:105).

It is sometimes difficult to discern God's truth in the midst of a world that often justifies immorality and sin as socially acceptable. In fact, we find the attitude of "everybody's doing it" all around us. Therefore, as Christians we need to continuously commit ourselves to being increasingly responsive to the Bible—from the call of salvation onward. The Lord's bountiful goodness and blessings come to us when we hear and obey His Word.

This week's lesson makes it clear that it is not enough to mentally acknowledge that Jesus died for our sins. We must also have a deepening trust in His sacrifice and a growing awareness that He saves us from eternal separation from God and eternal bondage to sin. All of our so-called good deeds are worth nothing toward our salvation. Jesus paid it all, for only He is qualified to do so. That's why we must trust in Him—and only Him—for eternal life.

A Holy People

Scripture

Background Scripture: *1 Peter 1*
Scripture Lesson: *1 Peter 1:13-25*
Key Verses: *Just as he who called you is holy, so be holy in all you do; for it is written: "Be holy, because I am holy."*
1 Peter 1:15-16.
Scripture Lesson for Children: *Acts 1:6-14; 2:1-4; 1 Peter 1:15*
Key Verse for Children: *Be holy in all you do.*
1 Peter 1:15.

Lesson Aim

To discover ways to cultivate hope, holiness, and love in our lives, especially during trials.

Lesson Setting

Time: *The early 60s of the first century A.D.*
Place: *Rome*

Lesson Outline

A Holy People

   I. Being Holy: 1 Peter 1:13-16
      A. *The Reality of Jesus' Return: vs. 13*
      B. *The Admonition to Obey God: vs. 14*
      C. *The Exhortation to be Holy: vss. 15-16*
  II. Revering God: 1 Peter 1:17-21
      A. *The Impartiality of God: vs. 17*
      B. *The Redemption Provided by the Savior: vss. 18-19*
      C. *The Intent of the Father through His Son: vss. 20-21*
 III. Loving Others: 1 Peter 1:22-25
      A. *The Command to Love: vs. 22*
      B. *The Reason to Love: vss. 23-25*

Introduction for Adults

Topic: *The Beauty of Nonconformity*

A young man had received his Ph.D. degree and then applied for teaching positions around the United States. After an exhausting search, he was offered a position in a university in Canada. He, his wife, and their two children discovered what it meant to be called to a new life. It was a stressful challenge for them, but because they understood this offer to be God's call, they accepted it.

Peter's argument to his scattered Christian readers was something like that. Be assured of the Father's call in the Son. Look at what the Father has guaranteed you in the Son. Look at the price of your redemption. Look at your high calling to be a holy, royal priesthood. Then move out in hope, obedience, and faith.

Our call comes not once but many times in our lives. When we are assailed by doubts, troubles, fears, and depression, we must remember our call and trust the living God.

Introduction for Youth

Topic: *Called to Be Holy*

What's the biggest thing we could be called to? President? Not many of us want that. Football or basketball star? Possibly. Movie, music, or television stardom? Perhaps. A good job and happy family? Yes. A holy, royal priesthood? What's that?

We have to dig deeply to understand Peter's imagery of the Father's high calling in His Son. Fundamentally, God does not call us to a vocation. He calls us to Himself, to be His faithful, trusting, hopeful, and holy children. Because He redeemed us with the Son's blood, He wants us to confess Him as Lord and testify about Him to others. That's a tough calling. It's a divine summons to be part of something really big, something that involves holy living.

Concepts for Children

Topic: *Waiting and Watching*

1. Jesus told His followers to wait for the power of the Holy Spirit.
2. Jesus' followers gathered for prayer while they waited.
3. When the Spirit finally came, Jesus' followers received power to live for Him.
4. Jesus' followers did not delay acting in the Spirit's power.
5. The letter of 1 Peter calls on us to become more holy in the way we live.

Lesson Commentary

I. BEING HOLY: 1 PETER 1:13-16

A. The Reality of Jesus' Return: vs. 13

Therefore, prepare your minds for action; be self-controlled; set your hope fully on the grace to be given you when Jesus Christ is revealed.

In 1 Peter 1:13, the apostle discussed the value of mental preparedness. "Mind" renders a Greek noun that refers to one's ability to think, understand, and feel. The apostle exhorted his readers to get their "minds" ready "for action." A more literal rendering is "binding up the loins of your mind." This idiomatic expression draws attention to the fact that, in Bible times, many people dressed in loose clothing. If they wished to move about quickly or perform tasks requiring significant freedom of movement, they would prepare themselves by tucking the folds of their robe under their belt. The apostle drew upon this imagery to urge his readers to be disciplined in their thinking and prepare themselves for vigorous and sustained spiritual exertion.

Peter urged his readers to "be self-controlled." This renders a Greek verb that refers to those who are sober-minded, calm, and temperate. The emphasis is on believers exercising sound judgment in every area of their lives. One way to do this is to submit to the control of the Spirit (see Eph. 5:18). When the mind of the Christian is free from unwholesome thoughts, it is better able to concentrate on what is pure and pleasing to the Lord. Peter also commented on the believers' "hope." This renders a Greek verb that denotes an eager and confident expectation of good things to come.

Believers were to rest assured that the Father would bestow His grace on them when the Son was revealed at His coming. "Revealed" translates a Greek noun that stresses the unveiling of Jesus' glory and greatness. In this present age, the Father has veiled the presence of the Son. Though the recipients of Peter's letter had never seen Jesus, their love for Him was unquestionable. Also, despite the fact that they could not see the Messiah, they continued to trust in Him for salvation (vs. 8). At His second advent, Jesus' followers will be fully and finally delivered from sin's presence. They will also be glorified and dwell forever with the triune God in heaven.

B. The Admonition to Obey God: vs. 14

As obedient children, do not conform to the evil desires you had when you lived in ignorance.

Peter referred to his readers as "obedient children" (1 Pet. 1:14). "Obedient" renders a Greek noun that refers to those who have a compliant and submissive spirit. As members of God's spiritual family, they refuse to "conform" themselves to the behavior and customs of the world (see Rom. 12:2). This disposition contrasts sharply with the way believers thought and acted before trusting in the Son. While separated from the Father, they knew nothing of His love and law. Also, before their conversion, they "lived in ignorance" (1 Pet. 1:14). The latter translates a noun that denotes those who are morally blinded to divine truth. Tragically, the unsaved wander about in spiritual darkness, and their sinful longings shape and control their lives. The apostle used a noun that is translated "evil desires" to refer to the forbidden cravings and longings of the sinful human heart.

C. The Exhortation to be Holy: vss. 15-16

But just as he who called you is holy, so be holy in all you do; for it is written: "Be holy, because I am holy."

Peter affirmed that the God believers worship and serve is "holy" (1 Pet. 1:15; see Pss. 71:22; 78:41; 89:18; 99:9; Isa. 1:4; 5:19, 24; 6:3; Hos. 11:9). The Greek adjective underlying this translation, when used in reference to God, emphasizes that He is superior to His creatures both physically and morally. Expressed differently, whatever the Lord thinks or does is characterized by purity, goodness, and perfection. In short, there is no trace of evil in God, and He abhors all that is wicked and false.

The holy God, who has called us to salvation, wants us to be holy in every area of life (1 Pet. 1:16; see Lev. 11:44-45; 19:2; 20:7, 26). This means we are to be cleansed from sin to serve the Lord. Our desires, motives, thoughts, words, and acts should be characterized by purity. We should detest sin and love righteousness. The moral perfection of God Himself is the standard we follow. Even after we put our trust in the Son, we continue to struggle with sinful desires. However, we soon learn from experience that it is impossible on our own to adopt the Father's priorities and focus. That is why we must rely on the Spirit to empower us to obey and enable us to overcome sin. When we call on the Lord's power, He frees us from the grip of sin.

II. Revering God: 1 Peter 1:17-21

A. The Impartiality of God: vs. 17

Since you call on a Father who judges each man's work impartially, live your lives as strangers here in reverent fear.

Christians looked to the Lord for salvation. To call Him "Father" (1 Pet. 1:17) was nothing new, for believers in the Old Testament era referred to Him in this way (see Ps. 89:26; Jer. 3:19; Mal. 1:6). The Israelite conception of the fatherhood of God portrayed Yahweh as the creator and architect of the nation. Jesus shed new light on the relationship of believers with the Lord when He addressed God as His Father and when Jesus taught His disciples to pray to the Father (see Luke 11:2; John 17:1). This new relationship revolutionizes our prayer lives. We approach the Father not as slaves, apologetic and fearful, but rather as children of the King.

Peter cautioned, however, against presuming that because of this relationship, God will excuse our sinful behavior. The Lord will one day judge each person's work objectively and fairly (1 Pet. 1:17). Expressed differently, there will be no element of favoritism in God's evaluation of all that we have done. Though the Father will not condemn His spiritual children for their sins (see Isa. 53:4-5; 1 Pet. 2:24), He will evaluate their deeds and reward them accordingly (see Rom. 14:10-12; 1 Cor. 3:12-15). Whatever rewards God bestows for faithful service are not based on merit, for He is the one who prompted these works in the first place.

Peter noted that, in this world, believers are "strangers" (1 Pet. 1:17). The latter renders a Greek noun that conveys the idea of resident aliens dwelling in a foreign land. The apostle was stressing the Christian's pilgrim status on earth. He also emphasized the importance of relating to God in "reverent fear." This does not mean we approach the Lord in cringing terror. Rather, we relate to our heavenly Father and Judge with humility and respect.

The concept of fear falls into two broad categories. First, it can refer to a sense of alarm caused by the anticipation of danger, pain, or disaster. Second, fear can denote a feeling of awe and reverence toward a supreme being. Both aspects of fear are evident in the Old Testament. When the Lord revealed His presence to His people, they were dreadfully aware of His holiness and their sinfulness (Exod. 19:16-19; Isa. 6:5). The Israelites also revered God because of His majesty, power, and holiness (Ps. 34:9). They demonstrated their respect and awe by obeying Him (Prov. 8:13; 16:6).

Both aspects of fear are also evident in the New Testament. A sickening dread will grip those whom God judges in the end times (Rev. 6:15-17). For Christians, however, there is no sense of dread, for "perfect love drives out fear" (Rom. 8:1; 1 John 4:18). Out of reverence for God, not doubt and anxiety, believers strive to grow and mature (Phil. 2:12). This is the least they can do as an expression of their gratitude for God's mercy.

B. The Redemption Provided by the Savior: vss. 18-19

For you know that it was not with perishable things such as silver or gold that you were redeemed from the empty way of life handed down to you from your forefathers, but with the precious blood of Christ, a lamb without blemish or defect.

The lives of those to whom Peter wrote were at one time "empty" (1 Pet. 1:18). The latter renders a Greek adjective that denotes what is futile and useless, at least from an eternal perspective. Some think the apostle was talking about Gentiles who had worshiped pagan deities and lived merely for themselves. Others think Peter was referring to Jews who had followed the unbiblical traditions their ancestors taught (vs. 18). Most likely, Peter was addressing both Jews and Gentiles.

Peter reminded his readers of the tremendous cost of their redemption. The Greek verb that is translated "redeemed" speaks of freedom from the bondage of sin through the payment of a price. In this context, the focus is on the shed blood of the Son (vs. 19; see Matt. 20:28; Mark 10:45). His atoning sacrifice is infinitely more valuable than anything the world has to offer. For instance, fallen humanity values costly metals such as silver and gold. One day, however, God will destroy all of these items, along with the rest of the created order (see 2 Pet. 3:11-13).

From at least the time Abel offered the firstborn from his flock to the Lord (see Gen. 4:4), people have shed the blood of an animal as an act of sacrifice to God. Indeed, this ritual pervades the Old Testament, in which blood sacrifice is an atonement for sin. The ceremony, however, was never completely effective (see Heb. 10:1-4). True atonement could only occur through the shed blood of the Lamb of God, Jesus, who died on our behalf to cleanse us from sin once and for all (see John 1:29, 36; 1 Cor. 5:7; Heb. 7:27; Rev. 5:6).

Of special note is the ritual in which priests would sacrifice lambs on the altar in the temple. In order to be acceptable, these sacrifices had to be free from any defect (see Lev. 22:20-25). Jesus was like a lamb that had no blemish or imperfection (1 Pet. 1:19). His life was sinless, qualifying Him to atone for the sins of the world (see 2 Cor. 5:21; Heb. 7:26; 9:14). We should never cease to be grateful for the shame and suffering the Son endured on the cross for our sake. He did not have to do it, but He did it because He loves us.

C. The Intent of the Father through His Son: vss. 20-21

He was chosen before the creation of the world, but was revealed in these last times for your sake. Through him you believe in God, who raised him from the dead and glorified him, and so your faith and hope are in God.

There are two ways of understanding the Greek verb rendered "chosen" (1 Pet. 1:20). According to some, the term is merely talking about God's foresight. In other words, the Father knew before He created the world that He would have to redeem sinners through the sacrifice of His Son. Others think the term implies purpose. In other words, in eternity past the Father selected the Son as the sole provider of redemption.

"These last times" was a manner of expression used by Old Testament prophets to speak of the end of human history. Now and in New Testament times, the phrase refers to the whole messianic era, which began with Jesus' life on earth. At other times the phrase seems to refer to the period immediately preceding Jesus' second advent. He originally came to earth to redeem the lost, and through Him we put our "faith" (vs. 21) in God and chose to remain faithful to Him. The Father raised His Son from the dead and bestowed glory on Him. For this reason we also rest our hope in God. These truths remind us that the Son is the only mediator between sinful people and the Father (see 1 Tim. 2:5). Jesus' sacrifice provides the only access to the Father (see John 14:6).

III. LOVING OTHERS: 1 PETER 1:22-25

A. The Command to Love: vs. 22

Now that you have purified yourselves by obeying the truth so that you have sincere love for your brothers, love one another deeply, from the heart.

"Purified" (1 Pet. 1:22) renders a Greek verb that denotes being cleansed morally and spiritually. The Holy Spirit uses the believers' obedience to God's truth to bring about this sanctifying process (see John 6:63; 15:3; 17:17). As a result, believers display a "sincere love" (1 Pet. 1:22) for one another. "Sincere" translates an adjective that can also be rendered "unfeigned" or "without hypocrisy." The term rendered "love for your brothers" primarily indicates the fondness, affection, or affinity that exists between family members or close friends.

The second term rendered "love" refers to compassion that is prompted more by will than by emotion. Peter, while commending his readers for the affection they had already demonstrated, urged them to pursue an even deeper compassion for each other (see 1 Thess. 4:9-10). Here we see that once believers experience forgiveness and reconciliation with God, it is only natural for them to reach out to others with sensitivity and kindness. Though at first such affection might seem natural, it takes a concerted effort to deepen that love, especially toward those who do not return the warmth that is being unconditionally offered.

B. The Reason to Love: vss. 23-25

For you have been born again, not of perishable seed, but of imperishable, through the living and enduring word of God. For, "All men are like grass, and all their glory is like the flowers of the field; the grass withers and the flowers fall, but the word of the Lord stands forever." And this is the word that was preached to you.

Peter reminded his readers that they had been "born again" (1 Pet. 1:23). This phenomenon denotes the inner re-creating of the fallen human nature of sinners when they trust in the Son. The new birth is not accomplished by perishable, biological means, but by sovereign working of the Holy Spirit. Moreover, this new life does not come from something that dies. Rather, it originates from a "living and enduring" source, namely, God's Word. In this context, the apostle specifically had in mind the life-giving message of the Gospel (see John 1:12-13; Jas. 1:18; 1 John 3:9).

In 1 Peter 1:24-25, the apostle quoted the Septuagint (or ancient Greek) translation of Isaiah 40:6-8 to highlight the contrast between the perishable nature of human life and the ever-enduring nature of God's Word. The apostle noted that people wither like grass and their glory fades like wildflowers, simply by the natural means of the aging process. Though grass dries up and flowers fall to the ground, the good news of Jesus' death and resurrection will stand forever. Peter noted that this was the same message he and the other apostles had proclaimed to the lost so that they might be saved.

Discussion Questions

1. Why did Peter stress the necessity of his readers preparing their "minds for action" (1 Pet. 1:13)?
2. In what sense is God holy?
3. What difference does Jesus' resurrection and glorification have on the believer's "faith and hope in God" (vs. 21)?
4. What specific ways can believers "love one another deeply" (vs. 22)?
5. How can you use God's "living and enduring" (vs. 23) Word to grow spiritually?

Contemporary Application

We have firsthand, written accounts of the Gospel. Thus, the message of salvation is not as mysterious to us as it was to the prophets (1 Pet. 1:10-12). Nevertheless, it also may not be as special to us as it was to Peter's first readers. A considerable amount of time has passed since that hope was first realized. Thus, we sometimes become dulled to the spiritual reality that eternal life begins here and now. This leaves us without the hope we need to get through life's trials.

Hope helps us because it tells us that the present is not all there is. Being targeted for ridicule by someone at work, being ignored by family members, or losing someone close to us are crises. But they are not crises in which there is no comfort from God. Trials may cause others to look down on us. But with God no disappointment is final.

This is why hope helps us put trials in the appropriate perspective. We expect trials to occur and we expect them to hurt. But with hope, we do not expect to be devastated by them. We can develop a mind-set of determination in which we can endure anything because we know the future that is coming is better than anything we have known before.

How can we can look beyond today and stay open to unknown factors? It is because we have learned that God often uses trials to refine us. We may even be thankful someday for how the trial has transformed us.

A Chosen People

DEVOTIONAL READING

Deuteronomy 10:10-15

DAILY BIBLE READINGS

Monday November 2
*Deuteronomy 10:10-15
Chosen Out of All People*

Tuesday November 3
*Psalm 33:4-12 A Happy
People*

Wednesday November 4
*Psalm 33:13-22 Hope in
God and God's Love*

Thursday November 5
*Acts 10:34-43 Chosen as
God's Witnesses*

Friday November 6
*Acts 4:31-37 A People One
in Heart and Soul*

Saturday November 7
*1 Peter 2:11-17 Free
Servants of God*

Sunday November 8
*1 Peter 2:1-10 God's Own
People*

Scripture

Background Scripture: *1 Peter 2:1-17*
Scripture Lesson: *1 Peter 2:1-10*
Key Verse: *You are a chosen people, a royal priesthood, a holy
nation, a people belonging to God, that you may declare the
praises of him who called you out of darkness into his wonder-
ful light. 1 Peter 2:9.*
Scripture Lesson for Children: *Acts 4:31-37; 1 Peter 2:9*
Key Verse for Children: *No one claimed that any of his pos-
sessions was his own, but they shared everything they had.*
Acts 4:32.

Lesson Aim

To consider the importance of living in unity as God's
chosen people.

Lesson Setting

Time: *The early 60s of the first century* A.D.
Place: *Rome*

Lesson Outline

A Chosen People

   I. The Basis for Holy Living: 1 Peter 2:1-3
       A. *Abandoning Vices: vs. 1*
       B. *Craving God's Word: vss. 2-3*
  II. The Formation of a Holy Community:
       1 Peter 2:4-10
       A. *The Son as a Living Stone: vs. 4*
       B. *The Son's Followers as Living Stones: vss. 5-6*
       C. *The Consequence of Rejecting the Son: vss. 7-8*
       D. *The Distinctives of God's Chosen People: vss. 9-10*

Introduction for Adults

Topic: *Chosen to Proclaim*

"All for one and one for all" is a great rallying cry for French musketeers, political movements, and football teams. It sounds so wonderful. It assumes that each individual will lay aside his or her own preferences for the sake of others.

But when we allow Jesus to break down barriers, we do much more than paper over our differences. We have to confess and acknowledge that hostility does exist. We also have to admit that, unless we allow Jesus to change us from within, we won't be able to achieve oneness in human relationships.

Because Jesus gives us new hearts and new motivations, we can seek His help and power to get along with everyone, regardless of our differences. We accept people as they are, and see them as objects of God's love in the Gospel, which He has chosen us to proclaim. We also show humility and love—demonstrating the Messiah's virtues to people who are very different from us—so that we can all become one family in Christ.

Introduction for Youth

Topic: *From No People to Chosen People*

Human differences are a fact of life, and we spend most of our lives trying to accommodate them. Of course, some people never try. In extreme cases, people fight and die to keep their distinctives alive. Even when our differences do not lead to bloodshed, they cause unhappiness and despair.

Considering how hard it is to resolve problems brought on by racial, religious, national, and economic differences, we are tempted to say it is hopeless. But the Gospel of Christ offers us the only hope we have to bring people together, despite their differences.

Our mission as Christians is to help people really understand who Jesus is and what He can do. Of course, we have to claim our new status as part of God's family. We have to demonstrate in Christ's body how we can overcome our differences. We must never give up on God's plan to bring individuals together as His chosen people, believers who willingly live in peace and harmony under Christ's lordship.

Concepts for Children

Topic: *Sharing Possessions*

1. The Holy Spirit gave Jesus' followers the power to tell others about God.
2. Jesus' followers found joy in being with one another.
3. Jesus' followers shared everything they had so that no one was in need.
4. Jesus' followers knew that God wanted them to live for Him and serve others.
5. The letter of 1 Peter reminds us that God has chosen us to share the Gospel.

Lesson Commentary

I. THE BASIS FOR HOLY LIVING: 1 PETER 2:1-3

A. Abandoning Vices: vs. 1

Therefore, rid yourselves of all malice and all deceit, hypocrisy, envy, and slander of every kind.

The recipients of Peter's letter had obeyed the truth of the Gospel and were born again (see 1 Pet. 1:3). In light of this, the apostle urged them to abandon iniquity in all its forms. The Greek verb translated "rid yourselves" (2:1) conveys the figurative nuance of casting aside vices just as a person would a dirty garment. "Malice" renders a noun that includes ill will that destroys fellowship among believers. "Deceit" translates a noun that refers to all forms of guile and duplicity. The related concept, "hypocrisy," renders the noun *hupokrisis*. The latter denotes acting under a feigned role and connotes the presence of dissimulation. This would include such wrongs as lying, fraud, and two-facedness.

"Envy" translates a Greek noun that refers to a feeling of discontentment or resentment that is aroused by a jealous longing for the possessions, qualities, or good fortune of another person. "Slander" renders a noun that is more literally translated as "evil speaking." The word includes the presence of false charges, misrepresentations, and malicious statements. It is important to remember that Peter was addressing Christians here, people who had obeyed the truth and had been spiritually regenerated. For believers to abandon a litany of vices is a humbling and rigorous process. Nonetheless, by the power of the Spirit, they are able to substitute ungodly thoughts, feelings, and actions for ones that honor the Lord.

B. Craving God's Word: vss. 2-3

Like newborn babies, crave pure spiritual milk, so that by it you may grow up in your salvation, now that you have tasted that the Lord is good.

It's not enough simply to jettison iniquity and immorality. Believers must also embrace a life of virtue and uprightness. This involves a complete transformation of the believer's entire life. Paul taught that this process begins with the "renewing" (Rom. 12:1) of one's "mind." The latter is the control center of one's thoughts, attitudes, and emotions (see Eph. 4:22-23). As believers renounce the ways of the world, their minds are renewed. This spiritual transformation is not a onetime event, but a daily, ongoing experience.

First Peter 2:2 emphasizes the importance of God's Word to believers' spiritual growth and maturity. The apostle used the analogy of "newborn babies" to make his point. Physical birth is a shocking experience for infants. Babies suddenly emerge from the security of their mother's womb into an environment that seems cold and uninviting. For the first time, they must concern themselves with breathing, eating, and crying. They eventually must learn to walk and communicate to others what they "crave."

Newborn infants have a natural craving for their mother's milk. In a figurative sense, God's Word is like "spiritual milk." The Greek adjective that is rendered "pure" conveys the idea of being unadulterated, guileless, and sincere. Peter's emphasis is not so much on the elementary aspects of divine truth. Rather, he is stressing Scripture's wholesome, trustworthy, and nourishing character. As believers regularly partake of God's Word, they are enabled to "grow up" in relation to their "salvation."

Like Peter, Paul knew that Scripture contains resources believers need to become spiritually grounded and stand firm in their faith. For instance, God's inspired Word can keep them from becoming fooled by religious frauds. The Bible also offers practical solutions for living according to God's plan. From Scripture they are taught, rebuked, corrected, and thoroughly trained in righteous living (2 Tim. 3:16). In fact, it is the Bible—with words that have been breathed by God Himself—that equips believers to do good (vs. 17).

In 1 Peter 2:3, the apostle quotes Psalm 34:8, in which David urged God's people to experience His blessings to the fullest. Israel's king used the analogy of a savory meal to emphasize how full and satisfying one's relationship with the Lord can be. Over time, believers deepen their conviction that God is truly "good" (1 Pet. 2:3). The latter translates a Greek adjective that refers to the kindness and graciousness of the Lord. His generosity is evident, for example, in redeeming the lost from sin. The believing sinners' initial satisfying taste of salvation whets their appetite for more spiritual food.

II. THE FORMATION OF A HOLY COMMUNITY: 1 PETER 2:4-10

A. The Son as a Living Stone: vs. 4

As you come to him, the living Stone—rejected by men but chosen by God and precious to him.

First Peter 2:3 compares the spiritual nourishment from God's Word to the milk newborn infants crave. Verse 4 uses another analogy—that of a temple made from stones—to stress the position of honor that believers have in the Messiah. The apostle began by stressing the importance of coming to the Lord Jesus. This, of course, includes initial repentance and faith. Nonetheless, the verb tense of the original also suggests a continual drawing near to the Savior.

In a figurative sense, the Messiah is the "living Stone" or rock, for He imparts new life to all who trust in Him. Likewise, He establishes a deep and abiding relationship with His followers. Other passages of Scripture call the risen Messiah the living bread and the source of life and light for all believers (see John 1:4; 6:51). The salvation purchased by the Son's atoning sacrifice on the cross opens a "new and living way" into God's presence (see Heb. 10:20). Jesus gives His followers living water, that is, eternal life (see John 4:10). The Savior also provides for them streams of living water, which is a reference to the Holy Spirit (see 7:38-39).

Despite all the wonderful things that could be said about the Messiah, most people "rejected" Him. The latter renders a Greek that refers to the disapproval and repudiation of someone. Although Jesus created the world and lived on earth for a time, the world spurned His messianic claims. Even His own people, the Jews, in large part repudiated His assertion to be the Son of God (see John 1:10-11). In fact, both Jews and Gentiles had a hand in sentencing and executing the Savior (see Acts 2:23).

Though people rejected the Son, the Father chose and honored Him. Indeed, the Son is precious to the Father and the object of His approval (see Matt. 3:17; Mark 1:11; Luke 3:22). After the Son died on the cross, the Father raised Him to the highest place and honored His name above all others. Consequently, all people will one day bow the knee to the Son and acknowledge Him as Lord (see Phil. 2:8-11).

B. The Son's Followers as Living Stones: vss. 5-6

You also, like living stones, are being built into a spiritual house to be a holy priesthood, offering spiritual sacrifices acceptable to God through Jesus Christ. For in Scripture it says: "See, I lay a stone in Zion, a chosen and precious cornerstone, and the one who trusts in him will never be put to shame."

If Jesus is the living Stone, His followers are comparable to "living stones" (1 Pet. 2:5). In this analogy, the apostle was stressing the believers' spiritual union with and resemblance to the Messiah. Paul underscored the new life the Savior gives to believers when he called Jesus "a life-giving spirit" (1 Cor. 15:45). The Redeemer takes His people and uses them to build a "spiritual house" (1 Pet. 2:5) or temple. The background for this comparison is the Jerusalem shrine, which was the place where the Lord manifested His presence. The Holy Spirit imparts new life to believers and indwells them so that they become the true edifice of God (see 2 Cor. 6:16; Eph. 2:19-22; Heb. 3:6).

Believers are not only living stones for God's temple, but also a "holy priesthood" (1 Pet. 2:5). In the Old Testament era, priests represented the people before God. Every person who trusts in the Son is part of the priesthood of believers. They have equal and immediate access to the Father and personally serve Him. Moreover, the Spirit enables the entire body of Christ to offer "spiritual sacrifices" to the Father. The Son, as the Advocate for His followers (see 1 John 2:1), makes these offerings acceptable to the Father. These spiritual sacrifices include praise, good works, and charitable giving (see Rom. 12:1; Phil. 4:18; Heb. 13:15-16). The priesthood of believers also represents God before humankind, intercedes for people before God, and reflects the Lord's holiness.

Isaiah 28:16 is quoted in 1 Peter 2:6 to refer to the Messiah as a choice and precious "cornerstone" (see Eph. 2:20). In ancient construction, a cornerstone joined two walls. Like this stone, Jesus is the one in whom the "whole building is joined together" (vs. 21). With Isaiah 28:16 as the scriptural backdrop, Peter affirmed the Messiah is the chief foundation stone God laid in Zion. Those who trust in Jesus for salvation will never be "put to shame" (1 Pet. 2:6). The latter translates a verb that can also mean to dishonor, disgrace, humiliate, or disappoint.

C. The Consequence of Rejecting the Son: vss. 7-8

Now to you who believe, this stone is precious. But to those who do not believe, "The stone the builders rejected has become the capstone," and, "A stone that causes men to stumble and a rock that makes them fall." They stumble because they disobey the message—which is also what they were destined for.

Some people trust in the Messiah, recognizing that He is the "precious" (1 Pet. 2:7) cornerstone. Others, however, reject Him. Peter quoted from Psalm 118:22 to stress the supreme importance of the Son in determining a person's eternal destiny. The stone that the builders did not want turned out to be the "capstone" (1 Pet. 2:7). In ancient times, the latter was used to unite the two sides of an arch and hold it together. The apostle was saying that the Son was the most important stone in the Father's spiritual temple.

In verse 8, Peter quotes from Isaiah 8:14 to note the effect that the Messiah has for some people. To those who refuse to believe the Gospel, Jesus is like a stone that causes them to stumble and a rock over which they trip and fall. The apostle commented that these individuals are so offended by the message of truth that they completely reject it. Furthermore, this lamentable outcome is the destiny God had planned for them.

There are three primary ways to understand the last part of 1 Peter 2:8. One group thinks that God decrees all unbelief to end in eternal destruction. A second group argues that God sovereignly predetermines who will spiritually fall and be lost. A third group maintains that God in His foreknowledge sees the response of unbelief that some have to the Gospel, and based on this awareness of their response determines them to be lost. Regardless of which perspective is taken, it is clear that those who reject the Messiah suffer eternally tragic consequences.

D. The Distinctives of God's Chosen People: vss. 9-10

But you are a chosen people, a royal priesthood, a holy nation, a people belonging to God, that you may declare the praises of him who called you out of darkness into his wonderful light. Once you were not a people, but now you are the people of God; once you had not received mercy, but now you have received mercy.

First Peter 2:9 stresses the wonderful future that awaits God's people. The apostle's intent was to show that there is no shame or disappointment for having believed in the Messiah. Indeed, believers are a "chosen people." This truth is reminiscent of God's having selected Israel from all the nations of the earth to be His special people (see Deut. 10:15). He did this because He loved them and because He wanted the world to know how great He is (see 1 Sam. 12:22). Just as God called the Israelites His chosen people in the Old Testament, so Peter indicated that New Testament believers are the elect of God.

It is a privilege to be a child of God. Likewise, it is one of the spiritual blessings we enjoy as followers of the Savior. He enables us to become a "royal priesthood" (1 Pet. 2:9). The emphasis here is on the entire body of Christ serving in a priestly capacity. Of course, this does not contradict the notion of believers relating to God on an individual basis. This verse can be more loosely rendered "the king's priesthood." The latter emphasizes the fact that the church is a priesthood and that it belongs to the King of kings (see Rev. 19:16).

Peter further declared that the recipients of his letter were a "holy nation" (1 Pet. 2:9). By this he meant that God had established and set apart the church for His distinctive use. The Lord once declared that Israel was a "holy nation" (Exod. 19:6). Based on this, some think the church is the new Israel of God and replaces Israel in His redemptive plan. Others, however, think Israel and the church remain distinct entities with distinct roles in God's program. Regardless of which view is taken, it is clear that New Testament believers belong to God. The Lord wants them to declare to the world the wonderful things He has done. This includes the Father's noble acts of creating the world and providing redemption through the Son. Peter specifically mentioned the Lord's calling his readers out of spiritual darkness into the marvelous light of salvation (1 Pet. 2:9; see Acts 26:18). "Wonderful" (1 Pet. 2:9) renders the Greek adjective *thaumastos*, which denotes something that is amazing, astounding, or extraordinary in character.

The apostle reminded his readers what their relationship to God was like before they were redeemed. At one time they were not the Lord's people, but now they belong to Him as His chosen and precious spiritual children. In the past they had never received mercy, but now they enjoy the Father's mercy through faith in the Son (vs. 10). Throughout Scripture "mercy" refers to God's display of favor to those who have offended Him. In His compassion, the Lord forbears punishing those who have violated His will. Instead, He chooses to withhold judgment. This is a free act on His part, for the recipients of His mercy can make no direct claim to it.

Peter's statements had once applied to the Israelites. During the nation's period of rebellion, the Lord called His people *Lo-Ruhamah* (not loved) and *Lo-Ammi* (not my people; see Hos. 1:6, 9). The Lord promised to one day restore the Israelites so that He could once again call them His people, whom He loved (2:1, 23). Interestingly, Paul applied Hosea 1:10 and 2:23 to the Gentiles (see Rom. 9:25-26). God took a group of individuals who were not His people—the Gentiles—and brought them into an intimate relationship with Himself. Whereas the Gentiles were originally not God's people, now by divine grace and mercy, they were called "children of the living God."

Discussion Questions

1. Why did Peter urge his readers to rid themselves of vice?
2. What role does God's Word serve in promoting the spiritual growth of believers?
3. Why would anyone chose to reject Jesus, the "living Stone" (1 Pet. 2:4)?
4. In what sense are believers a "holy priesthood" (vs. 5) in their service to God?
5. What sorts of "praises" (vs. 9) does God want believers to declare?

Contemporary Application

In 1959, a Caucasian man named John Howard Griffin changed his appearance to make himself look as though he were an African American. Feeling that he never could glimpse the plight of blacks unless he experienced life from a different vantage point, he altered the pigment of his skin with oral medication, sun-lamp treatment, and various kinds of stains. He then set out on travels throughout the South. The results, he found, were unbelievable.

Griffin reported receiving treatment that was almost inhuman. There were vehicles in which he was not allowed to ride. There were restaurants where he could not eat. There were hotels that would not give him a room for the night. And there were rest rooms he was not permitted to use. He was persecuted, slighted, and cheated. Griffin wrote about his treatment in his book entitled *Black Like Me*.

This man's experience helped him to become more aware of the wicked ways in which racial prejudice was being expressed in North America prior to the civil rights movement. And while the latter did not wipe out racial prejudice, it did help to sensitize many people to the need for justice and equality for all people, regardless of gender, race, color, or creed.

Often it is not until we ourselves feel the sting of an injustice or inequity that we take notice of the existence of prejudice. But God's people are chosen and called to be free from prejudices of all kinds, regardless of whether we have experienced them. As we actively ask God to make known and eradicate our own prejudices—especially through the proclamation of the Gospel—then we can see clearly to lead others into prejudice-free living.

A Suffering People

Scripture

Background Scripture: *1 Peter 4*
Scripture Lesson: *1 Peter 4:12-19*
Key Verse: *Those who suffer according to God's will should commit themselves to their faithful Creator and continue to do good.* 1 Peter 4:19.
Scripture Lesson for Children: *Acts 5:12-13, 17-21, 26-29, 40; 1 Peter 4:16*
Key Verse for Children: *"We must obey God rather than men!"* Acts 5:29.

Lesson Aim

To emphasize the importance of turning to God for strength and perspective in times of suffering.

Lesson Setting

Time: *The early 60s of the first century A.D.*
Place: *Rome*

Lesson Outline

A Suffering People

I. Divine Presence in Suffering: 1 Peter 4:12-13
   A. *Suffering Described as a Trial by Fire: vs. 12*
   B. *Participating in the Sufferings of Christ: vs. 13*

II. Divine Perspective on Suffering: 1 Peter 4:14-19
   A. *The Abiding Presence of the Spirit: vs. 14*
   B. *The Proper and Improper Reasons for Suffering: vss. 15-16*
   C. *The Time of Divine Reckoning: vss. 17-18*
   D. *The Faithful Creator of Suffering Believers: vs. 19*

Introduction for Adults

Topic: *Facing Opposition*

On February 7, 2008, the Imperial Sugar refinery in Port Wentworth, Georgia, exploded and burned for seven days. In the aftermath of the blast, nine employees were killed and dozens more were injured.

According to Kathy Lohr of *National Public Radio,* Pastor Michael Kavanaugh made the property of his church available to offer help. The parish is located "just across the street from the plant." For instance, congregants set up the "front of the church" as a "triage area after the explosion." According to Kavanaugh, "We brought tables out. They were hanging the saline bottles from the pear trees in front of the church."

Perhaps the initial recipients of Peter's first letter were just as brave and determined in helping one another during the fiery ordeal that had come to try their faith. Despite the hardships they faced, Peter encouraged them to remain courageous, especially knowing that the "Spirit of glory and of God" (1 Pet. 4:14) rested on them.

Introduction for Youth

Topic: *Feel the Pain!*

When Marilyn felt called by God to be a missionary, she cried, "Please don't send me to Haiti!" She feared the nation's intense poverty, disease, and voodoo culture. Yet she soon found herself there, doing work that was hard and punishing—and extremely fulfilling. "I was terrified at first," Marilyn said. "But God changed me. I spelled out to Him everything I didn't want to do, and He said, 'That's okay. We'll do them together.'"

Marilyn wasn't just experiencing a trial. She was volunteering for one. Yet her statement of what she sensed God said to her encapsulates God's message to us. We are reminded that, if we depend on Him, we'll walk through life together with Him. Marilyn experienced painful trials and suffering. Yet she praised God for the opportunity to endure them for His sake. We can do the same.

Concepts for Children

Topic: *Speak Out!*

1. Peter and John were arrested for being faithful followers of Jesus.
2. Peter and John refused to keep quiet about Jesus.
3. Some angry people beat Peter and John because they told others about Jesus.
4. The Holy Spirit did many wonderful things through Jesus' followers.
5. The letter of 1 Peter encourages us to find our joy and strength in the Lord, especially when life seems difficult.

Lesson Commentary

I. DIVINE PRESENCE IN SUFFERING: 1 PETER 4:12-13

A. Suffering Described as a Trial by Fire: vs. 12

Dear friends, do not be surprised at the painful trial you are suffering, as though something strange were happening to you.

Peter addressed his readers as "dear friends" (vs. 12). The latter renders a Greek adjective that is derived from a verb that means "to love dearly." The reference is to people whom one feels tender affection for and highly esteems. In the case of the apostle and his readers, he wanted them to know how much he cared for them. In all that he said, he had their best interests at heart.

It would have been hard for the believers of northwest Asia Minor to consider the possibility of enduring further mistreatment as followers of the Messiah. Indeed, they were "surprised." The latter translates a Greek verb that refers to the presence of astonishment over encountering something that is extremely difficult. In the case of Peter's readers, they were undergoing a "painful trial." This phrase renders a noun that is more literally translated "burning," especially in contexts that discuss various processes used to refine metals (see 1:7). In 4:12, the emphasis is on the experience of calamities that can undermine a person's character. The fiery ordeal the believers suffered was not a onetime event, but rather an ongoing series of agonizing trials and tribulations.

The original literally says that God, in permitting His spiritual children to be maltreated, was "testing" them. The latter translates a Greek noun that refers to any adversity or affliction that God sends to make clear the nature and extent of a Christian's faith, commitment, and holiness. Apart from knowing this divine intent, it would be easy for the first recipients of Peter's letter to think that they were going through "something strange."

The latter renders a Greek adjective that literally denotes a person or object that is foreign or alien. Figuratively, the term refers to a circumstance or experience that is unheard of or radically different from what someone was used to encountering. In the hours preceding Jesus' death on the cross, He warned His followers that unbelievers would hate them, just as they had despised Him (see John 15:18-19). Indeed, it would not be easy for them to go through times of hardship. Yet God could use agonizing hardships to strengthen the faith of His people.

B. Participating in the Sufferings of Christ: vs. 13

But rejoice that you participate in the sufferings of Christ, so that you may be overjoyed when his glory is revealed.

Instead of viewing suffering negatively, Peter urged his friends to adopt a more constructive attitude and to "rejoice" (1 Pet. 4:13). Initially, it might seem counterintuitive to be cheerful at the prospect of having a part in the "sufferings of Christ." Nonetheless, believers were to count it a privilege to "participate" in them. The latter translates a verb that refers to those who share and partner with others in a common cause or experience.

In would be incorrect to conclude from Peter's statement that believers who suffered made up for any lack in the atoning work of the Messiah. Rather, the apostle was saying that his readers were blessed to endure afflictions for the cause of the Savior. In fact, they were to view suffering for the faith as something to be welcomed, not loathed. Peter stressed that Jesus would eternally reward His disciples for suffering on His behalf. When the Son returned again in glory, His followers would share in it. At that time, persecuted believers, like those living in Asia Minor, would be full of joy. They would see that their faith in Jesus was not in vain, for He would vindicate their commitment to Him.

We find a similar attitude toward suffering in Paul's letters. For instance, the apostle spoke of knowing the Messiah in terms of sharing in His sufferings (Phil. 3:10). By this Paul meant that his own experiences of being persecuted for the faith would help him to better understand the adversity and trauma Jesus endured on the cross. Moreover, the apostle wanted to so identify with Jesus' death that it meant a complete break with Paul's former sinful life (see Rom. 6:4-11). For the apostle, this likewise meant becoming as humble and submissive to the will of the Father as the Son was when He defeated sin and death through His crucifixion.

II. DIVINE PERSPECTIVE ON SUFFERING: 1 PETER 4:14-19

A. The Abiding Presence of the Spirit: vs. 14

If you are insulted because of the name of Christ, you are blessed, for the Spirit of glory and of God rests on you.

In 1 Peter 4:14-18, the apostle made several conditional "if" statements. He realized that some of his readers were not suffering for their faith. Nonetheless, many were, and he wanted them to know that God was aware of their circumstances and would help them make it through. The Greek verb that is rendered "insulted" (vs. 14) is a strong term denoting the presence of reproach, slander, or revilement. The recipients of Peter's letter had identified themselves with the "name of Christ," and enemies of the faith were maligning them for it.

In Bible times, a person's name was thought to give expression to the essence of that individual's character, temperament, and aptitude. The title "Christ" comes from the Greek adjective *Christos*, which means "anointed one." It is equivalent to "Messiah," a word derived from Hebrew. Jews in the first century of the common era believed that a man would appear as God's anointed prophet, priest, and king to bring salvation to His chosen people. The Jews, however, had defined salvation mostly in political terms. Perhaps that is why many of them failed to recognize the true identity of Jesus, who fulfilled the most comprehensive definition of the Messiah.

Peter said that when his readers were persecuted for their faith in the Savior, God blessed them in such situations. In particular, the Father caused the "Spirit of glory" to rest on them in a unique way. Indeed, the third person of the Trinity helps believers to endure mistreatment and remain faithful to the Son. Verse 14 quotes Isaiah 11:2, which is part of a prophecy about the promised Messiah of Israel. God's Anointed One would continue the dynasty of David in fulfillment of the promise recorded in 2 Samuel 7:16. Also, the Spirit of the Lord would rest upon the Messiah, empowering Him to establish at long last true righteousness and justice (Isa. 11:2-5).

B. The Proper and Improper Reasons for Suffering: vss. 15-16

If you suffer, it should not be as a murderer or thief or any other kind of criminal, or even as a meddler. However, if you suffer as a Christian, do not be ashamed, but praise God that you bear that name.

The Greek verb that is translated "suffer" (1 Pet. 4:15) refers to being treated in a deplorable manner. Admittedly, not all the suffering that believers experienced in Bible times was due to their faith. On occasion, they broke the law, and in these instances the authorities were right to punish them. Peter said that Christians should not be guilty of criminal activities such as murdering and stealing. They should not even meddle in other people's affairs. All these offenses were morally wrong and brought shame, not honor, to the cause of Christ.

The more common situation involved a believer suffering as a "Christian" (vs. 16). The Greek noun *Christianos* was probably used by unsaved Gentiles at first to slander believers (see Acts 11:26). The term denoted someone who belonged to or followed Christ. King Herod Agrippa II knew about the word, for he used it when talking to Paul (see 26:28). Even though outsiders used the term in a derogatory manner, the church adopted it as an appropriate title. Christians were not ashamed to be associated with Jesus or to be known as His disciples.

Undoubtedly, in the first century of the common era, there was some social stigma connected with being persecuted for one's faith in the Messiah. Peter drew attention to this circumstance when he used a Greek verb that rendered "ashamed" (1 Pet. 4:16). The latter includes feelings of dishonor or disgrace. Regardless of what the unsaved might think about Christians, God never thinks worse of His spiritual children when they are maltreated for their commitment to the faith. Indeed, the Father is pleased when they offer Him "praise" for their association with the Son. The Greek verb that is translated "praise" can also be rendered "extol," "magnify," or "celebrate." In this verse, we learn that when believers give glory to the Father in the presence of His enemies, they honor the name of the Son.

C. The Time of Divine Reckoning: vss. 17-18

For it is time for judgment to begin with the family of God; and if it begins with us, what will the outcome be for those who do not obey the gospel of God? And, "If it is hard for the righteous to be saved, what will become of the ungodly and the sinner?"

"Judgment" (1 Pet. 4:17) is used to refer to a future time of divine evaluation of humankind. During the early days of the church, when Peter proclaimed the Gospel to Cornelius and his household in Caesarea (Acts 10:1, 23-24), he testified that the Father had appointed the Son as the "judge of living and the dead" (vs. 42). Paul likewise noted that the Father would judge the secrets of human hearts through His Son (Rom. 2:16). Jesus Himself affirmed that the Father had given Him the "authority" (John 5:27) to execute judgment due to the fact that He is the "Son of Man."

The Messiah is fully just in His evaluation and judgment of humankind. He first begins with the "family of God" (1 Pet. 4:17). In this verse, the apostle was explaining that God allowed others to afflict His people—who were collectively His spiritual temple (see 2:5)—so that they might be strengthened in their faith and purified in their conduct. The Lord was not being callous in allowing believers to endure suffering. Through this refining process, they would become more like the Savior.

Peter noted that if God judges those who followed Him first, it is hard to imagine how terrible the judgment will be for those who refused to obey His message of salvation. "Gospel" translates a Greek noun that can also be rendered "good news" or "glad tidings." This concept has Roman and Jewish roots. Among Romans, the noun was used to describe good news about events in the emperor's life, such as his enthronement. These events were thought to affect the entire world. Jewish roots of the term are found in the Old Testament prophecy books, especially Isaiah. There the announcement of the future time of salvation is called "good news" (see 52:7). With the advent of the Messiah, the prophesied time of salvation was inaugurated and marked the beginning of a new era for the world, of both Jew and non-Jew.

In 1 Peter 4:18, the apostle substantiated his point by quoting the Septuagint version of Proverbs 11:31. Here we learn that retribution for sin is certain. Since it is assured that God deals justly with the righteous on earth when they sin, imagine how much more He will punish the wicked. A similar thought appears in 1 Peter 4:18. The righteous are saved from God's wrath, but not on the basis of their good works. Rather, salvation is secured through Jesus' redemptive work on the cross. Now, if the upright barely escape eternal condemnation, then those who reject the Messiah are surely lost. The latter included the "ungodly," those who are destitute of any reverence toward God. Also included is the "sinner," which translates a noun that refers to those who are especially wicked.

D. The Faithful Creator of Suffering Believers: vs. 19

So then, those who suffer according to God's will should commit themselves to their faithful Creator and continue to do good.

Peter addressed those who suffered for obeying God. The apostle referred to this circumstance as being in accordance with "God's will" (1 Pet. 4:19). Christianity is not a religion of escape. Neither is it a way to avoid trouble, hardship, and difficulty. Peter knew that those who commit themselves to following the Savior will, in this world, face opposition. Paul also taught a similar truth in 2 Timothy 3:12, specifically, that those who want to live godly lives "will be persecuted." Likewise, during the apostle's first missionary journey, he declared to believers that "we must go through many hardships to enter the kingdom of God" (Acts 14:22).

Peter urged his readers to entrust their lives and futures to the Lord. "Commit" (1 Pet. 4:19) translates a Greek verb that in some contexts refers to depositing with another something of value that needs to be kept safe at all costs. In 1:5, the apostle noted that the Father watches over those who trust in His Son. The Greek verb that is rendered "shielded" conveys the idea of vigilantly defending a fortress. Believers can count on God's protection regardless of the hardships they might encounter.

The latter is not an empty or baseless hope, either, for God is the believers' "faithful Creator" (4:19). The adjective rendered "faithful" points to the Lord's trustworthy and dependable character. Also, because He is the all-powerful Creator of the universe (see Gen. 1:1; Heb. 11:3; Jas. 1:17-18), He has the ability to fulfill what He has pledged. With respect to His spiritual children, He will not abandon them, but constantly watches over them. In light of these reassuring truths, Peter urged his readers to continue doing what was right (for instance, obeying laws and respecting authority; see 1 Pet. 2:11-17).

Discussion Questions

1. Why would the readers of Peter's letter possibly be surprised by the fiery ordeal they were experiencing?
2. How is it possible to rejoice in the midst of suffering for the cause of Christ?
3. What are some valid and invalid reasons for believers to experience suffering?
4. How can believers resist feeling ashamed when they are persecuted for their faith?
5. How is it possible for believers to continue to do good in the midst of being physically maltreated and verbally abused by unbelievers?

Contemporary Application

The world is filled with people who despise the message of the Gospel and are eager to challenge Christians when they proclaim the Good News. We should not be surprised by this. As the world around us becomes increasingly secular, our loyalty to Christ will come under more frequent attack. Our culture entices us to seek material prosperity, achieve personal pleasure, and fulfill our every desire for a life of ease.

Because these nonreligious values and attitudes bombard us from the media and have nearly universal acceptance, we may be as unconscious of them as we are of the invisible ocean of air in which we live and breathe. This makes living in the culture all the more dangerous.

Sometimes these challenges against our commitment to Jesus are open and obvious. Militant opponents may try to restrict religious expression or caricature believers as old-fashioned and bigoted. In such an environment, we need to be clear about the nature of our relationship to Christ.

For instance, we no longer belong to ourselves, since our precious Savior has purchased us by His death on the cross (1 Pet. 1:18-19). It follows that we are to love Him with all our heart and to follow Him with all our energy. Moreover, we are not to feel at home in this world of sin and selfishness, because our citizenship is in heaven, where the Savior lives to intercede for us. We need to remind ourselves of the truths that were important to us when we first placed our faith in the Messiah.

How did the early church withstand the challenges to their commitment? Their victory flowed from genuine discipleship. Jesus' followers personally believed in Him and committed themselves to His service. Our ability to overcome begins at the same point—with a personal trust in the Son that expresses itself in determination to serve Him. Moreover, our commitment to serve our Lord has to draw upon the strength that only the Holy Spirit provides to those who are united with the Savior.

A Faithful People

Scripture

Background Scripture: *2 Peter 1:3-15*
Scripture Lesson: *2 Peter 1:3-15*
Key Verse: *His divine power has given us everything we need for life and godliness through our knowledge of him who called us by his own glory and goodness.* 2 Peter 1:3.
Scripture Lesson for Children: *Acts 8:26-32; 2 Peter 1:3*
Key Verse for Children: *An angel . . . said to Philip, "Go south to the road. . . ." So he started out.* Acts 8:26-27.

Lesson Aim

To encourage the adoption of a plan for spiritual growth and commit to following it.

Lesson Setting

Time: *Between A.D. 65–68*
Place: *Rome*

Lesson Outline

A Faithful People

I. Being Faithful and Fruitful: 2 Peter 1:3-11
    A. *Living in a Way that Pleases God: vss. 3-4*
    B. *Growing in Christian Virtues: vss. 5-6*
    C. *Cultivating Christlike Love: vs. 7*
    D. *Opting for Spiritual Growth and Productivity: vss. 8-9*
    E. *Validating the Reality of One's Salvation: vss. 10-11*
II. Heeding Scripture: 2 Peter 1:12-15
    A. *Being Reminded of the Truth: vss. 12-13*
    B. *Making the Truth Clear: vss. 14-15*

Introduction for Adults

Topic: *Pursuing Virtue*

The young woman flew off to see her family in South America. She was meticulous about her preparations. She thought she had everything she needed. But when she arrived, she found that she had forgotten to pack one of her prescription medicines. She called home and her husband took care of the matter.

Our pride tells us that we have everything we need to pursue virtue on our own. But Peter would say that such an attitude is counterproductive. An attitude of pride prevents us from grasping all that the Father has done for us in the Son. Because we, as believers, share in His divine nature and His promises, we can claim His power and wisdom and be bold about our faith and godliness.

We have everything we need in the Savior. The Lord, in turn, has commissioned us to use His resources to grow in His grace for His glory.

Introduction for Youth

Topic: *Got What It Takes?*

A church was built more than 100 years ago in an affluent Midwestern suburb. It flourished and grew to some 900 members. Facilities were added to accommodate people and programs. But somewhere along the way the congregation stopped growing. Its numbers dwindled to less than 100.

Such stories are not unusual. They testify to the fact that churches don't always have what it takes to remain vibrant. Indeed, it's possible for entire congregations to stop growing, shrink in numbers, and die. We can point to many reasons for this phenomenon, including the possibility that individual members lost their vision for what God had called them to do.

All Christians—regardless of their age, gender, and social or economic status—must keep growing in faith. That's why Peter's concrete reminders are so important. We can easily become sidetracked. Personality clashes sap our energies. We must keep adding qualities of spiritual power to ourselves and our churches.

Concepts for Children

Topic: *Following Directions*

1. At the direction of God, Philip went out on a mission.
2. When Philip met an Ethiopian reading from the Book of Isaiah, he asked whether the man understood the words he was reading.
3. The Ethiopian invited Philip to explain Isaiah's message.
4. Second Peter reminds us that God has provided us with everything that is essential for a life of faith.
5. In light of what God has done for us, let us obey Him.

Lesson Commentary

I. BEING FAITHFUL AND FRUITFUL: 2 PETER 1:3-11

A. Living in a Way that Pleases God: vss. 3-4

His divine power has given us everything we need for life and godliness through our knowledge of him who called us by his own glory and goodness. Through these he has given us his very great and precious promises, so that through them you may participate in the divine nature and escape the corruption in the world caused by evil desires.

The call to holiness that is so evident in 1 Peter also resonates strongly in 2 Peter. In 1:2, the apostle stressed getting know the Father and Son more and more. Then, in verse 3, Peter noted that, through our increased knowledge of the Lord, we become more responsive to His "divine power." The emphasis here is on living a godly life. The apostle explained that our knowledge of the the Son and His provision of the Father's own power makes it possible for us to pursue "life and godliness." Further incentive can be found in the truth that the Lord has invited us to share in His own "glory and goodness."

There is also an emphasis on having "everything we need" to be godly. A heretical group known as the gnostics were telling Christians that they did not have everything necessary to live a godly life. They supposedly also needed to be enlightened by a secret gnostic knowledge. Many cults today claim to lay hold of a secret saving knowledge that can be obtained only through various levels of teaching. In fact, the revelation that God has provided is sufficient, not only for our salvation, but for an abundant life as well.

Ultimately, our focus is not on acquiring the world's fame and fortune, for these are fleeting. Instead, it is to live in a manner that pleases God. The Lord has made this possible by bestowing on us "very great and precious promises" (vs. 4). The Greek noun that is rendered "promise" had a special meaning in ancient Hellenic culture. It was used in connection with public announcements of events that concerned everyone, as in the notification of public games and sacrifices to gods. The word implied some type of emphatic, state-sponsored proclamation.

The implication in this verse is that here were promises that were made decidedly and openly (not quietly and privately) for the benefit of all believers. It was a pledge given voluntarily, without coercion. Perhaps the most profound promise is that we will "participate in the divine nature." The idea here is not that we will gradually become divine, but that we grow in a host of Christian virtues. The more we pursue holiness, the more we will shun our evil desires and the "corruption" of the world that it spawns.

When Peter said that Christians can "participate in the divine nature" he took a risk by using the language of his opponents to express an eternal truth. The gnostics believed a person could become divine through secret knowledge and enlightened thinking. The truth is that though we will never become little gods, we can participate fully in the spiritual life offered by the one true God (see Rom. 8:9; Gal. 2:20; Col. 1:27; 1 Pet. 2:23; 1 John 5:1), especially as we worship Him in all His glory (while looking forward to our own glorification) and imitate His goodness.

B. Growing in Christian Virtues: vss. 5-6

For this very reason, make every effort to add to your faith goodness; and to goodness, knowledge; and to knowledge, self-control; and to self-control, perseverance; and to perseverance, godliness.

In light of all the provisions we have in the Redeemer, we can be faithful and fruitful in our lives. We start by making a maximum "effort" (2 Pet. 1:5) to appropriate our God-given blessings. The English phrase "add to" doesn't do justice to the full, rich meaning of Peter's original statement. The underlying Greek verb originally described bearing the expense of a chorus to be used in the dramatic presentations of the early Hellenic tragedies. The person selected to do this was responsible for the cost, training, and upkeep of such a chorus of performers. Eventually, the word came to mean providing the cost for any public duty or religious service to make it more than mediocre. Thus the verb meant to supply generously, even lavishly, beyond the bare need.

In the present context, the idea is that believers must dedicate themselves lavishly, strengthening their faith by the development of the characteristics Peter mentioned. Of central concern is their growth in holiness. At the moment of salvation, Christians are made holy in a legal sense; in other words, they are declared righteous in God's eyes. That event is called *justification.* Then, throughout their lives, the Holy Spirit works to bring their moral condition into conformity with their legal status. Expressed differently, He helps to make them actually holy. This process is called *sanctification.*

Sanctification is the work of God (1 Thess. 5:23). Nonetheless, the Bible contains many exhortations for believers to do their part in becoming more holy (Phil. 2:12-13). "Faith" (2 Pet. 1:5) is the starting point, and to it believers are to add "goodness." This is one of several moral excellencies that Peter mentioned. The idea is that, with unwavering trust in the Savior as their foundation, believers press on in a disciplined way to cultivate integrity and rectitude in their lives. Peter next mentioned "knowledge." While an objective understanding of revealed truth is included, the apostle also had in mind a practical application of that truth.

When Jesus' followers heed the teachings of Scripture, it will lead to "self-control" (vs. 6). Peter was referring to a mastering of one's carnal desires. Because believers know God and are empowered by Him, they are able to control their fleshly passions. In turn, they become more patient. They are less likely to be discouraged and succumb to temptation, and more likely to persevere in doing what is right. This ability to endure allows "godliness" to flourish. Christians become more reverent and devoted to the Lord, and less preoccupied with themselves.

C. Cultivating Christlike Love: vs. 7

And to godliness, brotherly kindness; and to brotherly kindness, love.

A heightened loyalty to God results in believers having increased "brotherly kindness" (2 Pet. 1:7). This mutual affection is displayed in serving one another, sharing with one another, and praying for one another. These activities, in turn, foster genuine "love." This form of compassion is not flustered by the personal cost of reaching out to others in need. This sincere love seeks the highest good of others for the glory of the Savior.

D. Opting for Spiritual Growth and Productivity: vss. 8-9

For if you possess these qualities in increasing measure, they will keep you from being ineffective and unproductive in your knowledge of our Lord Jesus Christ. But if anyone does not have them, he is near-sighted and blind, and has forgotten that he has been cleansed from his past sins.

Peter urged believers to continue growing in their life of godliness. Indeed, he wanted to see the various "qualities" (2 Pet. 1:8) he listed earlier to be present and developing in their lives. "Increasing measure" renders a Greek verb that can also be translated "increase in abundance" or "superabound." The tense of the verb indicates that the situation the apostle described is to be an active and ongoing experience for believers.

It would be erroneous to think that the virtues mentioned in verses 5 through 7 can be added in a mathematically precise, sequential fashion. Instead, they are developed together and evidenced gradually over many years of walking with the Lord. The goal, of course, is that these moral excellencies will be present in us without limit (vs. 8). Their abundance indicates spiritual health in Christians. Peter noted that if believers continue to grow in this way, they will become increasingly productive and fruitful, rather than "ineffective" and "unproductive," in their knowledge of the Savior.

Once again we see that knowing God is more than an intellectual exercise. This truth stands regardless of what religious frauds might otherwise assert. Knowing more and more about the Lord Jesus Christ is intended to foster spiritual vitality. The other alternative is to fail to develop the graces Peter mentioned, which results in spiritual loss. The apostle declared that those opting for this are blind and shortsighted, for they have failed to fully appreciate the cleansing and forgiveness from "past sins" (vs. 9) secured by the Messiah. "Cleansed" translates a Greek verb that refers to Christians being purged from the guilt associated with their transgressions through the atoning sacrifice of the Son.

E. Validating the Reality of One's Salvation: vss. 10-11

Therefore, my brothers, be all the more eager to make your calling and election sure. For if you do these things, you will never fall, and you will receive a rich welcome into the eternal kingdom of our Lord and Savior Jesus Christ.

Peter was discussing two different mind-sets. One is transfixed on the concerns of this present life, while the other is sensitive to eternal, spiritual realities. Though we live in the world, the things of God should be our supreme focus. Thus, we are to make every effort to confirm our "calling and election" (2 Pet. 1:10). In his first letter, Peter pointed out that God's election of His people to salvation was because of His foreknowledge (see 1 Pet. 1:2). So, the apostle urged believers to seize the opportunity to increase their assurance of salvation by cultivating the virtues he had described in 2 Peter 1:5-7.

Peter was not saying that Christians can make their salvation more secure by their works. Good deeds are never to be considered spiritual "fire insurance." The tense of the Greek verb, which is rendered "make" (vs. 10), can also be translated "to make for oneself." This means that the increasing assurance of salvation is a benefit of consistent obedience to God. With this kind of assurance, God's people can expect a joyous welcome into His eternal kingdom (vs. 11). Here we see that there is more to heaven than just getting through the proverbial pearly gates. Scripture is full of promises of reward to those who are faithful. The greeting believers will receive when they enter God's presence will be rich because of the blessings the Father has lavished upon those who belong to Him through the redemptive work of His Son.

By remaining loyal to the Father and ministering to our fellow believers, we show that we truly "participate in the divine nature" (vs. 4), that we fully appreciate the atoning sacrifice of the Son, and that we value His "very great and precious promises" to us. Such a consistent life-orientation indicates we will not succumb to doubt or despair concerning our spiritual status. Rather than spiritually stumble and "fall" (vs. 10), we will be assured of our salvation. This assurance also includes our eventual entrance into "the eternal kingdom" (vs. 11) of the Messiah. The Lord, in turn, will honor our life of faithful service with more abundant privileges in heaven.

II. HEEDING SCRIPTURE: 2 PETER 1:12-15

A. Being Reminded of the Truth: vss. 12-13

So I will always remind you of these things, even though you know them and are firmly established in the truth you now have. I think it is right to refresh your memory as long as I live in the tent of this body.

At times even mature believers can wane in their diligence to grow in the Lord. This is especially true in moments of hardship. Peter, perhaps realizing this, was determined to remind his readers about the truths he had previously shared. The apostle's decision did not mean that his readers were ignorant of the truth or had failed to stand firm in it. Peter's intention was to ensure they remained "firmly established" (2 Pet. 1:12) in the faith and diligent in applying it to their lives. The Greek verb that is rendered "firmly established" can also be translated "to make stable" or "to fix securely in place."

In some way, Peter had become increasingly aware of the short time he had left "in the tent of this body" (vs. 13). This is a metaphorical reference to his body being laid aside like a tent. John 21:18-19 records a statement Jesus made concerning the way in which Peter would die. Perhaps the apostle had this in mind as he approached the end of his life. The Greek noun that is translated "tent" can also be rendered "tabernacle." It is clarifying to note that Paul literally referred to the physical body we live in as an "earthly house" (2 Cor. 5:1), which we temporarily inhabit while we wait to put on our new, heavenly bodies (vs. 4).

Contrary to what the gnostics claimed, neither Peter nor Paul believed the physical body was unimportant or inherently evil. In fact, Paul referred to our bodies as "temples of the Holy Spirit" (1 Cor. 6:19). Peter and Paul used various metaphorical expressions for the physical body to carry the idea of a temporary dwelling. While he was on earth, Peter would use the tabernacle of his body in obedience to God's will. Death was simply putting aside the physical dwelling so that the soul could depart to be with God. That structure (so to speak) would be raised again on the day of resurrection.

B. Making the Truth Clear: vss. 14-15

Because I know that I will soon put it aside, as our Lord Jesus Christ has made clear to me. And I will make every effort to see that after my departure you will always be able to remember these things.

Peter said he knew that his upcoming death was near. He figuratively referred to the event as a removal of his earthly tabernacle. The Greek verb that is translated "know" refers to a definite awareness of the facts. In the apostle's case, the Messiah previously revealed to him what would eventually happen to him (see John 21:18-19). This impression is reinforced by the past tense of the verb that is rendered "made clear" (2 Pet. 1:14).

"Departure" (vs. 15) translates a Greek noun that metaphorically refers to Peter's imminent exit from his current earthly existence. In light of what the apostle realized would happen to him, we can certainly appreciate his strong desire to reinforce to his readers the teaching of Scripture. His goal was to make the truth clear so that they could more readily recall and apply it. The destructive teachings of spiritual frauds (see 2:1-4) made the apostle's task all the more imperative.

Discussion Questions

1. What does God's divine power provide for believers?
2. What is the basis for growing in the Christian virtues that Peter listed?
3. Why did Peter want to continue reminding his readers of their hope in Christ?
4. What can believers do to ensure they are spiritually maturing?
5. How can believers fight the tendency to forget the truths of the faith?

Contemporary Application

Trusting in Jesus as Savior is the beginning of a Christian's growth process. The Holy Spirit then works in our lives to produce the virtues listed in this week's Scripture lesson text. The order of the virtues is not a sequence in time, as if stages of the Christian life were being described; rather, the qualities Peter enumerated were to occur simultaneously and lead to a well-rounded and productive Christian life.

While the Spirit makes it possible for us to grow and mature as believers, we must also cooperate with Him in the process. That is why Peter urged us to "make every effort" (2 Pet. 1:5) to cultivate the character qualities he listed in verses 5-7. Faith is the starting point, and the climax of the virtues mentioned by the apostle is love, the preeminent fruit of the Christian life.

From this we see that the church is not a playpen, but rather a construction area where the Spirit desires to work in the lives of Jesus' followers. Why, then, do the lives of many believers exhibit little growth? Why do many remain childish?

One reason is that selfishness saps the energy that God wants us to use for growth. We too often focus on satisfying ourselves rather than on pleasing the Lord. For instance, Paul was concerned that the Corinthians were still spiritual babies because they were fighting among themselves (1 Cor. 3:1-4).

Sadly, temper tantrums in Christian circles are still common. Many of us are also spiritually lazy. Maturing in the Lord looks too much like hard work. We may wonder, "What awful trials will Jesus send if I tell Him that I desire to grow?"

An initial step toward growth is admitting that we need God's help. We must look beyond our fear and selfishness. Since the Father has provided the Spirit to help us grow, we can become partners with Him to transform our lives and help us become more like the Son.

Consequently, the virtues listed in this week's Scripture lesson text are the result of our working together with God. Each time we choose to obey the Lord and not just please ourselves, the fruit becomes more abundant. Also, as we strive to mature, God will do for us what we cannot do for ourselves.

A Hopeful People

DEVOTIONAL READING

Psalm 42

DAILY BIBLE READINGS

Monday November 23
*Psalm 42 I Shall Again
Praise God*

Tuesday November 24
*Psalm 31:21-24 Be Strong,
Take Courage*

Wednesday November 25
*Psalm 71:1-6 God Is My
Hope*

Thursday November 26
*Psalm 119:81-88 Hope in
God's Word*

Friday November 27
*Romans 4:16-24 Hoping
against Hope*

Saturday November 28
*Acts 14:21-28 Strengthen
and Encourage*

Sunday November 29
*2 Peter 3:1-13 Waiting for
the Day of God*

Scripture

Background Scripture: *2 Peter 3*
Scripture Lesson: *2 Peter 3:1-13*
Key Verse: *The Lord is not slow in keeping his promise, as some understand slowness. He is patient with you, not wanting anyone to perish, but everyone to come to repentance.*
2 Peter 3:9.
Scripture Lesson for Children: *Acts 14:21-28;
2 Peter 3:18*
Key Verse for Children: *[Paul and Barnabas were]
strengthening the disciples and encouraging them to remain
true to the faith. Acts 14:22.*

Lesson Aim

To stress that we look forward to a new heaven and earth.

Lesson Setting

Time: *Between A.D. 65–68*
Place: *Rome*

Lesson Outline

A Hopeful People

   I. The Certainty of Jesus' Return: 2 Peter 3:1-7
      A. Reminders of the Truth: vss. 1-2
      B. Mockers of the Truth: vss. 3-4
      C. Past Examples of Divine Judgment: vss. 5-6
      D. A Future Time of Divine Judgment: vs. 7
  II. The Challenge to Be Morally Pure: 2 Peter 3:8-13
      A. The Patience of God: vss. 8-9
      B. The Day of the Lord: vs. 10
      C. The Importance of Godly, Holy Living: vs. 11
      D. The Hope of a New Heaven and Earth: vss. 12-13

Introduction for Adults

Topic: *The Best Is Yet to Come*

Every believer encounters challenges, frustrations, and opposition. These steps to maturity in the Savior are like foothills that sometimes block the view of the lofty snowcapped peaks. But because the peaks are there, Christians, like a mountain hiker, can push onward and upward.

What is the highest peak of biblical hope? It is the return of Jesus and eternal life in His presence. That hope should lighten every step and quicken the heart of all believers. Most importantly, they realize that the best part of God's plan for them is yet to come. Because the Lord is the "God of hope" (Rom. 15:13), He is able to "fill you with all joy and peace as you trust in him, so that you may overflow with hope by the power of the Holy Spirit."

Introduction for Youth

Topic: *Got Hope?*

The story is told of how a village incorrectly thought a vagrant passing through their town was the government inspector. They not only treated him as royalty but also quickly set into motion a plan to cover up years of fraud. Their mistaking the man for someone else cost them dearly.

This fable is a reminder of how important it is to search for hope in the right place—namely, the Messiah of the Bible—not some figment of our imagination. Jesus is no longer a newborn baby in a manger. Nor is He merely a wise and loving person. He is the Lord of life, the King of kings, and the Savior of the world.

Down through the centuries, people of faith recognized these truths about Jesus. The returning Savior was for them light, hope, and salvation. In fact, all who receive Jesus by faith can partake of the forgiveness and grace He now offers.

Concepts for Children

Topic: *Encouraging Others*

1. Paul and Barnabas went to several cities in a place called Asia Minor to tell people about Jesus.
2. Paul and Barnabas were persecuted for their faith, as were those who accepted the Gospel.
3. Even when they were rejected by many people, Paul and Barnabas did not lose courage.
4. When Paul and Barnabas returned to the cities they had visited earlier, they encouraged the believers.
5. Second Peter encourages us to be faithful and grow spiritually as followers of Jesus.

Lesson Commentary

I. THE CERTAINTY OF JESUS' RETURN: 2 PETER 3:1-7

A. Reminders of the Truth: vss. 1-2

Dear friends, this is now my second letter to you. I have written both of them as reminders to stimulate you to wholesome thinking. I want you to recall the words spoken in the past by the holy prophets and the command given by our Lord and Savior through your apostles.

Peter concluded his letter with words of endearment used four times between this point and the end of the epistle. The Greek noun that is rendered "dear friends" (2 Pet. 3:1) can also be translated "beloved" and is derived from a verb that is often rendered "love." Peter wanted his readers to know that he cared for them. The apostle's mention of his "second letter" may refer to 1 Peter, though this is not conclusive. It's also possible there might have been a lost letter. Even some of Paul's letters were apparently never found (see 1 Cor. 5:9; Col. 4:16).

Peter wrote several times to the Christians living in Asia Minor to warn them about the false teaching of spiritual frauds and remind them of key apostolic truths. The goal was to "stimulate [them] to wholesome thinking" (2 Pet. 3:1). The Greek verb that is translated "stimulate" can also be rendered "to awaken" or "to stir up." "Wholesome" translates an adjective that refers to what is pure, sincere, or unsullied. The noun that is translated "thinking" is more literally rendered "mind" and refers to the human faculty of understanding, feeling, and desiring centered in the brain.

In short, the apostle wanted to refresh the memory of his readers and thereby encourage them to do some honest consideration of what they had been taught. The latter included all that God's holy prophets had spoken long ago. Their oracles are recorded in the Old Testament, which initially was the primary collection of sacred writings used by believers in the first century. Peter also wanted the Christians in Asia Minor to recall what he and the other apostles taught. This especially concerned what their Lord and Savior, Jesus Christ, had commanded them to do—namely, to be morally vigilant, especially as they awaited His return in glory.

B. Mockers of the Truth: vss. 3-4

First of all, you must understand that in the last days scoffers will come, scoffing and following their own evil desires. They will say, "Where is this 'coming' he promised? Ever since our fathers died, everything goes on as it has since the beginning of creation."

Peter used a tense of the Greek verb that is rendered "you must understand" (2 Pet. 3:3) to emphasize that the issue he was about to discuss was morally imperative for his readers to grasp. It concerned "the last days." The phrase is sometimes used in the Old Testament to refer generally to events that would take place in the future, both near and distant. When the New Testament speaks of "the last days," it refers to events connected with Jesus' return. The phrase also includes the period from the Savior's first advent to His second advent.

Peter used this same phrase in his first letter to describe the age in which his readers were already living (1 Pet. 1:20). He also used it in his sermon on the day of Pentecost, when he pointed to the giving of the Holy Spirit as fulfillment of events that the prophet Joel had foretold would take place in "the last days" (Acts 2:17). Paul used the phrase in his prediction of the general decline in conditions that were to occur prior to Jesus' return (2 Tim. 3:1). Both Peter and Paul recognized that the "last days" had already arrived.

Peter literally noted that, as the end of the age drew near, "scoffers in their scoffing" (2 Pet. 3:3) would arise. The Greek noun that is translated "scoffers" refers to the fraudulent prophets and teachers mentioned in 2:1. They already had infiltrated the faith community in Asia Minor, and they would continue to plague the body of Christ until His return (see Matt. 24:3-5, 11, 23-26; 2 Tim. 3:1-5; Jude 18). The charlatans were guilty of deriding God's Word and being propelled by their "own evil desires" (2 Pet. 3:3; see 2:13-22). Scoffing in regard to revealed prophetic truth is more than mere jesting. In ignorance some will speak jokingly about spiritual matters, and this grieves the Spirit of God. Scoffing, however, is a calculated effort to discredit an accepted truth. The mockers Peter warned about were especially menacing, for they were familiar with the Scriptures and the apostles' inspired interpretation of the Lord's commands.

Peter focused on the Christian belief attacked by these scoffers with the greatest intensity, namely, the Messiah's promise of His second advent (see Matt. 10:23; 16:28; 24:3, 32-36; Mark 9:1; Acts 1:11). The early church believed that when Jesus returned, He would bring to fruition the work of salvation. Indeed, believers were characterized by an intense anticipation of the Savior's return. Jesus had laid the groundwork with His teaching on end-time events in Matthew 24 (see Mark 13; Luke 21). The Christians in Peter's day lived with the expectation of the Son's advent, just as believers should do today.

Regrettably, the false teachers mocked the believers' hope, reminding them that nothing had changed "since the beginning of creation" (2 Pet. 3:4). "Our fathers" might refer to the patriarchs (Abraham, Isaac, and Jacob; see Acts 3:13; Rom. 9:5; Heb. 1:1), or perhaps even to the first Christian martyrs such as James and Stephen (see Heb. 13:7). In any case, the religious frauds' implicit argument was that if Jesus had not yet returned, He would never do so.

C. Past Examples of Divine Judgment: vss. 5-6

But they deliberately forget that long ago by God's word the heavens existed and the earth was formed out of water and by water. By these waters also the world of that time was deluged and destroyed.

Peter noted that the spiritual frauds intentionally suppressed some key biblical facts. One truth is that, at the dawn of time, God used His powerful utterance to command the heavens and the earth into existence (2 Pet. 3:5; see Pss. 33:6; 148:5). Concerning the planet, Genesis 1:6-10 reveals that God formed it out of water and by means of water. Moreover, He separated the land from the world's oceans, which continue to surround the continents to this day.

The Lord not only had the power to create the earth with the use of water, but He also had the right to destroy the same planet by means of water (2 Pet. 3:6). The apostle was referring to the flood that inundated and wiped out all who inhabited the world in Noah's day (that is, except for Noah and his family, who were all safe in the ark). This obliteration was complete, in that "everything on dry land that had the breath of life in its nostrils died" (Gen. 7:22).

D. A Future Time of Divine Judgment: vs. 7

By the same word the present heavens and earth are reserved for fire, being kept for the day of judgment and destruction of ungodly men.

The conclusion Peter drew was that the same God who in the past destroyed the earth with water will one day destroy both the existing "heavens and earth" (2 Pet. 3:7) with fire. Fire is a symbol of destruction and purification. In both the Old and New Testaments, God is said to be "a consuming fire" (Deut. 4:24; Heb. 12:29). The fire of hell is portrayed as unquenchable (Matt. 3:12; Mark 9:43; Luke 3:17). As well, the work of the Holy Spirit is compared to fire and has the power to renew (Matt. 3:11; Acts 2:3, 19). Jesus stated that He had "come to bring fire on the earth" (Luke 12:49). Even believers, who will escape condemnation, will have the quality of their works tested by fire (1 Cor. 3:13).

Peter noted that just as the wicked were destroyed in the Flood, so will it be at the end of time, when the entire universe is destroyed by fire (2 Pet. 3:7). It will be a time of "judgment and destruction" reserved specifically for the "ungodly." The Greek noun translated "judgment" refers to a future day in which God tries and sentences fallen humanity. The noun translated "destruction" points to the eternal misery in hell that awaits the wicked. The account of the Flood proved the inevitability of divine judgment and testified to God's patience. Even more importantly, the biblical record was evidence of the reliability of Scripture. Thankfully, just as God preserved Noah and his family from the Flood, so He will deliver those who have trusted in the Messiah for salvation.

II. THE CHALLENGE TO BE MORALLY PURE: 2 PETER 3:8-13

A. The Patience of God: vss. 8-9

But do not forget this one thing, dear friends: With the Lord a day is like a thousand years, and a thousand years are like a day. The Lord is not slow in keeping his promise, as some understand slowness.

He is patient with you, not wanting anyone to perish, but everyone to come to repentance.

The religious charlatans had insisted that the delay in the promised coming of the Messiah proved that it was never going to happen. To counter this destructive error, Peter sought to clarify for his readers how God viewed time. Again the apostle used words of endearment as he encouraged these believers not to let an important fact escape their notice (2 Pet. 3:8). Evidently, he summarized the words of Moses recorded in Psalm 90:4.

It would be incorrect to conclude that Peter presumed to suggest a date when the end of history would come. Jesus made it clear that only the Father knew the exact time of the Son's second advent (see Matt. 24:36). The apostle's point was that God does not regard time as humans do. Whereas people are always conscious of days and months and years, God is above time, and its passing does not affect Him in the ways it affects His creatures.

Peter noted that just because the Son had not yet returned did not mean that the Father was "slow in keeping his promise" (2 Pet. 3:9). "Slow" renders a Greek verb that can also mean "to delay" or "to be hesitant." Despite what the false teachers alleged, Peter considered the apparent delay of Jesus' return, not as a doubt-producing dilemma, but as a means of God's grace. The Greek verb that is rendered "patient" literally means "to be long-spirited" and figuratively refers to a forbearing disposition. The Lord was lengthening the period of time in which people could repent and be delivered from eternal destruction.

B. The Day of the Lord: vs. 10

But the day of the Lord will come like a thief. The heavens will disappear with a roar; the elements will be destroyed by fire, and the earth and everything in it will be laid bare.

When God's patience is finally exhausted, "the day of the Lord" (2 Pet. 3:10) will come suddenly, as a thief who strikes in the darkness (see 1 Thess. 5:2; Rev. 3:3; 16:15). Jesus also taught that His second advent would be unexpected, like the intrusion of a burglar (see Matt. 24:42-44; Luke 12:39-40). But unlike the housebreaker, Jesus will have every right to take whatever He wishes, for there is no power, position, or possession that does not already belong to Him.

Peter used strong language typical of end-time passages to describe three events that will happen when the Messiah returns. First, the heavens will vanish with a "roar" (see Isa. 13:10-13; 34:4; Rev. 6:14). The latter renders a Greek adverb that denotes the presence of a horrific noise similar to a whirling, rushing sound. Second, the "elements" (2 Pet. 3:10) will melt away in a fiery blaze. The noun translated "elements" refers to the celestial bodies in the universe (sun, moon, and stars) as well as the chemical compounds out of which they are made (earth, air, fire, and water).

Third, the planet and every deed done on it will be "laid bare." The latter renders a Greek verb that points to the truth that one day every human creation will be exposed and judged by God. Another textual reading uses a verb that means "to burn up" or "be consumed by fire." In this case, the idea is that everything on earth will be obliterated. In turn, humanity will be left to stand exposed and accountable before God.

C. The Importance of Godly, Holy Living: vs. 11

Since everything will be destroyed in this way, what kind of people ought you to be? You ought to live holy and godly lives

Peter had spelled out in vivid terms the terrifying events that will take place when the Messiah returns. The apostle had not done so to produce a trembling fear in the hearts of his readers, for he had assured them of their hope in the Redeemer. Since eventually all earthly things will be completely destroyed, believers should want all the more to live in a manner that is pleasing to God. Specifically, they are to be "holy and godly" (2 Pet. 3:11) in their conduct. Moreover, because death for any of us is but a heartbeat away, and because the Son could come soon, we should feel an urgency to glorify the Father in our daily living.

D. The Hope of a New Heaven and Earth: vss. 12-13

As you look forward to the day of God and speed its coming. That day will bring about the destruction of the heavens by fire, and the elements will melt in the heat. But in keeping with his promise we are looking forward to a new heaven and a new earth, the home of righteousness.

A difference of opinion exists concerning the phrase "speed its coming" (2 Pet. 3:12) in regard to the "day of God" (which is another way of referring to the day of the Lord). Some think the phrase is merely a description of the eagerness with which believers anticipate the Messiah's return. Others, however, relate Peter's statement to the belief that Christians can do things to hasten the Lord's advent. A recorded prayer of the early Christians, "Maranatha! Come, Lord Jesus" (see 1 Cor. 16:22; Rev. 22:20), corresponds with this perspective.

Peter repeated his earlier declaration that the heavens will be burned up and dissolve, and the celestial bodies will melt in a blaze (2 Pet. 3:12). The apostle quickly reassured Christians that, though the fire would destroy creation, God promised to provide "a new heaven and a new earth" (vs. 13). The latter anticipates John's statement in Revelation 21:1. Both of these verses likely have their roots in the words of Isaiah 65:17 and 66:22.

The Greek adjective that is rendered "new" (2 Pet. 3:13) denotes what is fresh and pristine. The idea is that either the new creation will be a total replacement for its old counterparts or will emerge from the same. The old universe had been spoiled by the fall of Adam and Eve and by all their descendants, resulting in the deterioration of nature. The cleansing fire of God's holiness will make everything new at the end of the age, renovating, renewing, and purifying the heavens and the earth. In turn, the new creation will be a place in which one finds "righteousness." The latter translates a noun that points to the presence of such virtues as integrity, purity, and rectitude.

Discussion Questions

1. Why did Peter write his second letter?
2. What lessons did Noah's flood offer for those who were troubled by the apparent delay in Jesus' return?
3. If the Father is faithful to His promise, why has the Son not yet returned?
4. What are two things believers are to do until Jesus' return?
5. What virtues will characterize the new heaven and earth?

Contemporary Application

Peter was deeply concerned about the false teachers who had crept into the infant churches and beguiled many weak-minded Christians into believing doctrines that distorted the Gospel. Peter wrote his second epistle to urge his fellow believers to beware of these frauds, who were headed to certain "destruction" (2 Pet. 3:7).

We must be resolute in denouncing any teaching that falsifies the person and work of the Savior. If we remain silent when Jesus is said to be anything less than what He truly is, we permit dishonor to His name. That is something we can never do. Peter was also concerned that believers were losing their eagerness for Jesus' return. In response, the apostle assured his readers that the Lord will keep His promise to come again. They thus were not to be dismayed that He had not yet returned.

Now, nearly 2,000 years later, many Christians still think that Jesus' return will occur in the long-distant future. Most importantly, some do not anticipate His coming with excitement and longing. They, instead, occasionally pray about it and at times discuss it as a theological issue. But do we truly yearn for Jesus' second coming?

Since so much time has passed, and since many of us live quite comfortably, it is understandable that Jesus' return does not impact us as it should. Yet, as Peter said, "With the Lord a day is like a thousand years" (vs. 8). To the Father, the Son's return is imminent, and so it should be to us as well.

We always need to look forward to Jesus' coming again because that thought will help us live godly lives. If we truly love the Lord, none of us want Jesus to return right when we are sinning. Instead, we want Him to find us living holy lives. Then, at His return, He will say to us, "Well done, good and faithful servant!" (Matt. 25:21). In light of these thoughts, what kind of fruit are we bearing in our witness?

The Lineage of David

Scripture

Background Scripture: *Ruth 4:13-17; Matthew 1:1-17*
Scripture Lesson: *Ruth 4:13-17; Matthew 1:1-6*
Key Verse: *The women living there said, "Naomi has a son."
And they named him Obed. He was the father of Jesse, the
father of David.* Ruth 4:17.
Scripture Lesson for Children: *Ruth 4:13-17;
Matthew 1:1-6*
Key Verse for Children: *"Praise be to the LORD, who this
day has not left you without a kinsman-redeemer." Ruth 4:14.*

Lesson Aim

To learn that God brings diverse people together for
His purposes.

Lesson Setting

Time: *1375–1050 B.C. (Ruth); 6–5 B.C. (Matthew)*
Place: *Judah and Moab (Ruth); Nazareth of Galilee
(Matthew)*

Lesson Outline

The Lineage of David
  I. The Descendants of Boaz: Ruth 4:13-17
     A. *The Birth of Ruth's Son: vs. 13*
     B. *The Well Wishes of the Local Women: vss. 14-15*
     C. *The Extended Family Tree: vss. 16-17*
  II. The Ancestry of the Messiah: Matthew 1:1-6
     A. *The Savior's Genealogy: vs. 1*
     B. *The Savior's Relationship to Abraham and David:
        vss. 2-6*

Introduction for Adults

Topic: *A Son Is Born*

Best-selling author Rick Bragg came from a poor family. He wrote about the Christmas gift he received every year—boxes of underwear. That was it. The perfect gift for him was to be at home with his mother, brothers, aunts, uncles, and cousins. That was enough to make Rick happy.

We don't need a lot of stuff to make this upcoming holiday season a perfect one. Even the perfect gifts wear out, break, turn to rust, get lost, or are stolen. We can't pin our hopes for happiness on any one gift, that is, except the gift of eternal life the Father gives us in birth of His Son, Jesus Christ.

The holiday season gives us an opportunity to identify what's really most important and valuable to us. Thank God for good friends—and even new underwear—but most of all for Jesus.

Introduction for Youth

Topic: *Skeletons in Jesus' Closet?*

The Gospel of Matthew traces Jesus' family history to show His standing as the Messiah of God. We learn that Jesus is a descendant of Abraham, the ancestor of all Jews, and David, Israel's greatest king. Matthew wanted his Jewish readers to know that Jesus was the perfect King who fulfilled the Old Testament prophecies about the Messiah's line.

Note that the roster of ancestors includes some interesting characters, such as Rahab, the Jericho prostitute, and Ruth, the Moabitess. From this we see that Jesus is not only the royal Deliverer, but also the Savior of all humankind. We also discover that God's work in history is not limited by human failures or sins, and that He works through ordinary people like us to accomplish His will.

Concepts for Children

Topic: *The Family Tree*

1. Ruth, Naomi's daughter-in-law, was an important part of Naomi's family.
2. Ruth is an example of someone who became a follower of God.
3. God blessed the family of Boaz and Ruth with a son named Obed
4. Obed became one of Jesus' ancestors.
5. The Father wanted His Son to be born so that He might save us from our sins.

Lesson Commentary

I. THE DESCENDANTS OF BOAZ: RUTH 4:13-17

A. The Birth of Ruth's Son: vs. 13

So Boaz took Ruth and she became his wife. Then he went to her, and the LORD enabled her to conceive, and she gave birth to a son.

Ruth 1:1 places the account of the book in the period when judges ruled Israel, or about 1375–1050 B.C. Furthermore, it appears that Ruth was the great-grandmother of David, who was born about 1040 B.C. Thus, we can calculate roughly that Ruth and the other characters in the narrative lived sometime in the 1100s B.C. The written version of the account—at least in the form we now know it—apparently was not produced until long after the events it describes. Over the years, the narrative of Ruth and her family would have been passed down orally.

Some people consider the book to be a love story because it concludes in a marriage and a birth. Others see it as an account glorifying some ancestors of King David or as an illustration of the way the ancient Hebrews cared for their relatives. Such views notwithstanding, perhaps the best way to look at the narrative is as an example of how a faithful person is rewarded with protection and care. If we are seeking to live for the Father by loving and obeying His Son, then we can see ourselves in Ruth and Naomi, and we can see God in Boaz.

The book is so well written that some have alleged it to be fictional. Most conservative Bible scholars deny that charge. One confirmation of the book's reality can be seen in the linking of David to a Moabite ancestor: Ruth. Israel had its conflicts with Moab at various times, and it is unlikely that anyone would invent a story to place a Moabite in David's family tree. Furthermore, it has been suggested that David's decision to entrust his parents to the care of the king of Moab for a time may have been due to his connection to Moab through Ruth (see 1 Sam. 22:3-4).

In the opening scene of Ruth, we encounter a destitute Moabite widow. Then, as the narrative unfolds, we journey with her as she chooses to live among God's people and glean in the grain fields. In one episode, when Ruth returned home to Naomi, Naomi learned at last just whose field her daughter-in-law had been gleaning. Naomi arranged for the two to have a second meeting. This time Boaz was so taken with Ruth that he arranged to buy Elimelech's remaining property from Naomi and thus, according to the laws of that time, "inherit" the responsibility of marrying the widow Ruth.

This is a circumstance in which Boaz acted as a "kinsman-redeemer." The latter (literally, *ga'al*) is a term that indicates the recovery of persons or property sold into bondage (see Lev. 25:26; Ruth 4:4-12). It also signifies any payment given in exchange for a vow (see Lev. 27:13, 15, 19, 20) or tithe (see 27:31).

The kinsman-redeemer was a near relative who intervened on behalf of the individual in trouble or danger. There was a close bond or relationship between the two. Within ancient Israel, it was a privilege and a duty for the near relative to extend help.

Once the promised land was apportioned to the tribes of Israel, each family took pains to make sure that its portion remained in the family; but sometimes land could be lost through poverty. The law provided for this problem by giving family members the right and responsibility to repurchase family lands. Thus the nearest relative to the one who had sold the land was known as the "redeeming relative" or "kinsman-redeemer" (see Lev. 25:25).

In ancient times, such a person was a kind of family vindicator. If a relative's life had been taken, the related redeemer could bring about vindication for the victim (Num. 5:8). Also, if the family had been forced to forfeit property, the kinsman-redeemer had the right to redeem it before the Year of Jubilee (Lev. 25:10-17). Moreover, according to marriage customs, a brother-in-law (or another close male relative) should marry his brother's widow in order to provide family heirs. This was the cultural custom behind the Book of Ruth.

With respect to Boaz, he removed the one obstacle to marriage by negotiating with the nearer relative. The entire transaction between the unnamed redeeming relative and Boaz took place in the presence of the elders of Bethlehem at the city gate (Ruth 4:1). Then Boaz went ahead and wed Ruth and began to be physically intimate with her. In the providence of God, Ruth became pregnant and "gave birth to a son" (vs. 13). The Bible often speaks of God's determining birth or barrenness.

Archaeological excavations indicate that numerous ancient Israelite cities had an open space or plaza just inside the main gate. As the center of public life, the town plaza was used for a wide variety of purposes. Formal and informal gatherings were held there. Judicial proceedings and military exhibitions would be conducted. At the plaza, people could buy and sell merchandise, find employment, hold celebrations, make speeches, socialize, and sometimes even sleep (see Deut. 25:7; Judg. 5:8, 11; 1 Sam. 19:8).

B. The Well Wishes of the Local Women: vss. 14-15

The women said to Naomi: "Praise be to the LORD, who this day has not left you without a kinsman-redeemer. May he become famous throughout Israel! He will renew your life and sustain you in your old age. For your daughter-in-law, who loves you and who is better to you than seven sons, has given him birth."

Although Boaz and Ruth were the newborn child's biological parents, the honor for the birth belonged to Naomi, who had at last been given the heir she had been denied through the deaths of her two sons. Accordingly, the women of the town celebrated her good fortune. She had not been left barren.

Instead, they hoped that this newborn would become famous in Israel—a hope that would come true in the lineage that produced the great King David and, later, the Lord Jesus (Ruth 4:14).

The local women prayed that the newborn would restore Naomi's youth and care for her in her old age. The women then offered a tribute to Ruth, stating that she was better to Naomi than "seven sons" (vs. 15). In ancient times, a successful family was one with many sons. As a matter of fact, in some Hebrew settings a family with seven sons was considered ideal. For one woman in that culture to be regarded as better than seven sons was a monumental compliment.

C. The Extended Family Tree: vss. 16-17

Then Naomi took the child, laid him in her lap and cared for him. The women living there said, "Naomi has a son." And they named him Obed. He was the father of Jesse, the father of David.

Naomi took the newborn in her arms, placed him on "her lap" (Ruth 4:16), and became his caregiver. In this way, Naomi symbolically adopted the child as her own. While this may strike modern readers as odd, it was the fulfillment of dreams that Naomi had believed were dead forever. The local women seem to have been involved in naming the child, though that was not a common practice. They gave the boy the name "Obed" (vs. 17), which means "servant." They hoped he would be a faithful follower of the Lord. It was a fitting name for a child who would become the grandfather of King David.

The book ends with a genealogy stretching from Perez to David. Who could have imagined that the Lord would bring together a loyal young Moabite woman and a faithful older Israelite man to become ancestors of the great King David—and of the greater King Jesus? If God can do that, He can also bring about resolutions to our difficult problems and add new blessings to our lives.

II. THE ANCESTRY OF THE MESSIAH: MATTHEW 1:1-6

A. The Savior's Genealogy: vs. 1

A record of the genealogy of Jesus Christ the son of David, the son of Abraham.

Matthew introduces us to the King of all the earth, showing us His humble beginnings, proclaiming to us His teachings, and convincing us with His miracles. It was during the reign of Herod the Great that God fulfilled His Word by sending His Son, Jesus Christ, to be born on earth as a human being. Like the other Gospel writers, Matthew was an author who carefully selected the material he included in his account of Jesus' life and ministry. The vignettes Matthew provided were intended to demonstrate that Jesus was the Jewish nation's long-awaited Redeemer. Matthew also wrote to show that Jesus was the fulfillment of all for which Israel had hoped.

The Jewishness of Jesus is emphasized in Matthew's Gospel perhaps more than in any other. The Greek of 1:1 literally says "the book of the genealogy of Jesus Christ." The idea is that the writer began his account by presenting the birth record of the Messiah. This is in keeping with ancient Jewish custom, in which God's people exercised great care to preserve records of family trees. Matthew's opening presentation involved going back to Abraham, the progenitor of the faith. The writer then traced the line through David, the great king, to show that Jesus was the lawful heir to the throne. Expressed differently, He had the proper credentials to be Israel's Savior. This was important to demonstrate, for the Old Testament prophets said that the Messiah would be a descendant of David.

"Jesus" is the Greek transliteration of the Hebrew name *Joshua*, which means "Yahweh saves." As well, "Christ" (from the Greek) and "Messiah" (from the Hebrew) both mean "the Anointed One." When taken together, they indicate that the Father chose, appointed, and empowered His Son to redeem the lost (see Luke 1:30-33). Starting with Matthew 1:22-23, numerous Old Testament prophecies are said to be fulfilled in connection with Jesus' life and ministry. The idea of fulfillment is mentioned again in the following verses: 2:6, 15, 17, 23; 4:14; 8:17; 12:17; 13:14, 35; 21:4; 26:56; and 27:9.

Since Matthew seems to have written for a predominantly Jewish audience, his Old Testament citations and his emphasis on Jesus being a "son of David" (1:1) and a "son of Abraham" all point to Jesus being the promised Messiah. (The Greek noun *huios*, which is rendered "son," could also refer to a grandson or even a distant descendant.) Furthermore, Matthew emphasizes that the events in Jesus' life filled the prophecies about the Messiah in the smallest details, from where and how He was born to how much money would be involved in His betrayal (27:9). Indeed, Jesus said that the entire Old Testament—namely, "the Law [and] the Prophets" (5:17)—in a sense was fulfilled in His coming.

B. The Savior's Relationship to Abraham and David: vss. 2-6

Abraham was the father of Isaac, Isaac the father of Jacob, Jacob the father of Judah and his brothers, Judah the father of Perez and Zerah, whose mother was Tamar, Perez the father of Hezron, Hezron the father of Ram, Ram the father of Amminadab, Amminadab the father of Nahshon, Nahshon the father of Salmon, Salmon the father of Boaz, whose mother was Rahab, Boaz the father of Obed, whose mother was Ruth, Obed the father of Jesse, and Jesse the father of King David.

Many scholars who have compared the genealogies recorded in Matthew 1:1-17 and Luke 3:23-37 think that Matthew traced Jesus' lineage through Joseph, while Luke delineated it through Mary. Matthew presented his account of the ancestral origin of the Messiah by dividing His genealogy into three groups of 14 "generations" (Matt. 1:17). One way the generations could be divided is that the first group begins with Abraham and ends with King David (vss. 2-6), the second begins with Solomon and ends with Jeconiah and his brothers before exile (vss. 7-11), and the third group begins with Jeconiah's family after the exile and ends with the Messiah (vss. 12-16). When taken together, this list of names shows that the progress of biblical history had reached its fulfillment with the coming of the Redeemer (see Heb. 1:1-2).

The Greek adjective rendered "all" (Matt. 1:17) does not mean the writer's lists of names in Jesus' birth record includes every ancestor. For instance, in the second grouping of the genealogy, Matthew omitted the names of four Davidic kings. It would be incorrect to conclude from this that the writer somehow made a mistake, for there are other examples in the biblical record in which names were intentionally omitted from the genealogical listing (see 1 Chron. 6:3-15; Ezra 7:1-5). One plausible explanation for the exclusion of four Davidic kings is that they were all under a divine curse.

Some of the names in Matthew's genealogy are familiar, such as people like Abraham, Isaac, and Jacob. Scholars have long been fascinated by the names of the women included in Matthew: Tamar (1:3), Rahab and Ruth (vs. 5), and Uriah's wife, Bathsheba (vs. 6). Perhaps the main point is that God's love and purposes have not been limited to decent people of a particular race. In His wisdom, the Father chose to have His Son identified with both women and men, and with people who had their failures as well as their successes.

The nationality and character of the four women Matthew included in Jesus' genealogy made it all the more peculiar that their names should be represented on such a list. Rahab was a Canaanite from Jericho, Ruth was a Moabitess, and Tamar and Bathsheba were famous mainly for their participation in public scandals. While Rahab and Ruth displayed great faith, they were not of Jewish descent. While the other two probably trusted God, they were known for their sin, not their faith.

Perhaps Matthew wanted to show the overly proud Jews that Gentiles and women played a significant role in the Messiah's birth. Or perhaps Matthew wanted to stress that God's grace extended to everyone and that He could bring good out of all circumstances. The women are evidence of God's unusual workings in the past to prepare for the Messiah's coming. Their life histories showed that Jesus was not just the descendant of kings but the one who would save His people from their sins (see vs. 21).

As noted earlier, the Gospel of Luke also contains an extensive genealogy that traces Jesus' ancestry back from Joseph to Adam (3:23-37) and ends with the phrase "son of God." The list of names indicates that the person whom John baptized in the waters of the Jordan River (vss. 21-22) was none other than a descendant of Adam, the patriarchs, and David; the representative of all humanity; and the divine Messiah. In the incarnate Son of God, all the aspirations of the Old Testament are completely and eternally bound. Likewise, the destiny of all humanity is held together.

Discussion Questions

1. What led Boaz to decide to marry Ruth?
2. Why was the birth of Ruth's son of historical significance to God's people?
3. What is noteworthy about Obed being the grandfather of David?
4. Why did Matthew present the birth record of Jesus?
5. Why did Matthew possibly include the names of women in the genealogy of Jesus?

Contemporary Application

Homeless, hungry refugees often fill our television screens. We watch them clamor and fight for food and clothing being thrown from trucks. Ruth, a refugee of sorts from Moab, found shelter in Bethlehem. What kept Ruth going? It was her faith in God and courage to remain devoted to His people. Ruth had no earthly prospects and was reduced to foraging for food. Yet she did not quit, for she knew that trusting and obeying the Lord was her highest goal.

Many adults can relate to the struggles Ruth experienced—losing a loved one, moving to a strange place, struggling to make ends meet, and so on. Believers also know that peers who do not share their faith in Christ sometimes treat them like outcasts. They should be encouraged to remain loyal to their Christian faith and heritage. They can do so knowing that the Lord will be with them every step of the way.

Foreshadowing Jesus' Birth

DEVOTIONAL READING

Micah 5:1-5

DAILY BIBLE READINGS

Monday December 7
Micah 5:1-5 A Ruler from Bethlehem

Tuesday December 8
Matthew 23:29-39 I Sent You Prophets

Wednesday December 9
Mark 1:1-8 Preparing the Way

Thursday December 10
Luke 1:26-29 The Lord Is with You

Friday December 11
Luke 10:21-24 What Prophets Desired to See

Saturday December 12
Luke 1:68-75 Prophets from of Old

Sunday December 13
Isaiah 7:13-17; Luke 1:30-38 The Promise Fulfilled

Scripture

Background Scripture: *Isaiah 7:13-17; Luke 1:26-38*
Scripture Lesson: *Isaiah 7:13-17; Luke 1:30-38*
Key Verse: *"Therefore the Lord himself will give you a sign: The virgin will be with child and will give birth to a son, and will call him Immanuel."* Isaiah 7:14.
Scripture Lesson for Children: *Luke 1:26-38*
Key Verse for Children: *"The Holy Spirit will come upon you, and . . . the holy one to be born will be called the Son of God."* Luke 1:35.

Lesson Aim

To note that God's plan overcomes all obstacles.

Lesson Setting

Time: *735 B.C. (Isaiah); 6–5 B.C. (Luke)*
Place: *Judah (Ruth); Nazareth and the hill country of Judea (Luke)*

Lesson Outline

Foreshadowing Jesus' Birth

I. The Sign of Immanuel: Isaiah 7:13-17
  A. *The Lord's Indignation: vs. 13*
  B. *The Virgin-born Son: vs. 14*
  C. *The Promised Disaster: vss. 15-17*

II. The Astonishing Message: Luke 1:30-38
  A. *Mary's Pregnancy Foretold: vss. 30-31*
  B. *Jesus' Greatness Foretold: vss. 32-33*
  C. *Mary's Miraculous Conception Explained: vss. 34-35*
  D. *Elizabeth's Pregnancy Declared: vss. 36-37*
  E. *Mary's Humble Response: vs. 38*

Introduction for Adults

Topic: *An Unexpected Sign*

The Bible's accounts regarding angelic-human encounters are designed not just to excite our interest, but also to inspire our faith and obedience. The Bible tells us about God's calls to many individuals under a variety of circumstances, yet somehow we find it hard to believe that He can and will summon any of us to serve Him.

When God calls, He always gives sufficient evidence for us to respond obediently and not turn away. Sometimes, we demand signs to confirm God's call, but Jesus rebuked those of His day who demanded signs.

The life of Jesus is sufficient to inspire our commitment, loyalty, and service. God has called us in His Son. Therefore, it is reasonable for Him to expect faithful obedience from us. God calls us first to trust in Jesus for salvation, and then to faithful service in our homes, churches, schools, and communities.

Introduction for Youth

Topic: *Guess Who Is Coming to Dinner*

A man who had lost his job found that he also had to face the protracted illness of his adolescent son and the death of his mother-in-law. The man thought about going back to a local university for an advanced degree, but in the meantime he took a temporary position.

One day, the man answered the phone and the person on the other end offered him an attractive position. He had received an unexpected calling. In this way, God was faithful and provided for him and his family.

One day God spoke to Mary through the appearance of the angel Gabriel, and Mary was unprepared for what God had to say. Nevertheless, because Mary knew God, she trusted Him to take care of her, despite the fact that she was going to become pregnant through the miraculous work of the Holy Spirit.

Would we stagger and stumble at something like that? Probably. When God surprises us, we will want to say *yes*, especially if we are serious about obeying Him.

Concepts for Children

Topic: *Receiving Good News*

1. Isaiah foretold the birth of Jesus.
2. The angel Gabriel brought good news to Mary.
3. Gabriel told Mary that she would give birth to a special child, who would be called the Son of God.
4. The angel told Mary that her relative Elizabeth was pregnant in her old age.
5. This account is an example of how God performs miracles in people's lives.

Lesson Commentary

I. THE SIGN OF IMMANUEL: ISAIAH 7:13-17

A. The Lord's Indignation: vs. 13

Then Isaiah said, "Hear now, you house of David! Is it not enough to try the patience of men? Will you try the patience of my God also?"

In 734 B.C., Israel and Syria joined forces to attack Jerusalem (Isa. 7:1-2). Ahaz evidently was about to depart from Jerusalem to see how his defenses would hold up against a protracted siege. It was at this moment that the Lord directed Isaiah to go out to meet Ahaz. The place of meeting between Isaiah and Ahaz was the aqueduct of Jerusalem's upper pool (vs. 3). The aqueduct was located beside a road near a place where people went to launder their clothes. Ahaz was possibly at this source to inspect the city's water system in anticipation of a siege by his enemies—the Israelites and the Arameans.

Isaiah was to take his first son, Shear-Jashub, with him. The lad's name means "a remnant will return." It underscored the fact that while God would use Assyria to bring destruction on Israel and Judah, a righteous remnant would survive and live in the land of promise as God's faithful servants. The prophet, knowing this, urged Ahaz to keep his wits about him and not be alarmed by the threat posed by Syria and Ephraim. Isaiah declared that the kings of Syria and Ephraim were comparable to the two ends of smoldering sticks that were about to be extinguished (vs. 4). In other words, Judah's powerful invaders would be reduced to nothing in a short while.

The kings of Syria and Ephraim had intended to march their armies against Judah and lay siege to the capital city. They wanted to so terrorize Judah that the fighting spirit of Ahaz and his people would be broken. Because Rezin and Pekah wanted to overthrow Jerusalem, the Lord would allow Assyria to crush Damascus and Samaria (vs. 5). The invaders wanted to create a gap in Jerusalem's wall so that the city could be completely overrun. Once the capital was under their control, Rezin and Pekah would make Judah their puppet state. They planned to depose Ahaz, a descendant of David, and place a non-Israelite on the throne. One view is that "the son of Tabeel" (vs. 6) was from a prominent Syrian family.

Isaiah assured Ahaz and his people that the threat posed by Syria and Ephraim was temporary. Their diabolical plan would neither stand nor come to pass, for God would use Assyria to wipe out Damascus and make Samaria her vassal (vss. 7-9). Such truths notwithstanding, the threat posed by Damascus and Samaria deeply distressed Ahaz. Realizing this, the Lord spoke again to him through Isaiah (vs. 10). The Hebrew noun rendered "sign" (vs. 11) can also be translated "confirming token." The Lord invited Ahaz to ask for some tangible assurance that what God had pledged would come to pass. Nothing

Ahaz might ask would be too difficult for God to perform.

Knowing how threatened Ahaz felt and how weak his faith was at this point, the Lord sought to strengthen the monarch's confidence in Him. That is why the Judean king could make his request as deep as the place where the dead were buried or as high as the heavens were above the earth. Ahaz sounded very spiritual when he declared, "I will not ask; I will not put the LORD to the test" (vs. 12). In reality, Ahaz did not want a sign from the Lord because he had made up his mind to solicit help from Assyria (see 2 Kings 16:7-9). Ahaz tried to rationalize his disobedience by piously referring to Deuteronomy 6:16, a passage that prohibited Israel from putting God to the test. Isaiah summoned Ahaz to listen to what the Lord had to say. The king not only was arrogant enough to try the patience of people but also egotistical enough to try the patience of God with his rebellious decision (Isa. 7:13). Though the king refused to ask for a sign, the Lord would still supply one.

B. The Virgin-born Son: vs. 14

"Therefore the Lord himself will give you a sign: The virgin will be with child and will give birth to a son, and will call him Immanuel."

The Lord's prophet declared that a "virgin" (Isa. 7:14) would conceive, give birth to a son, and name him "Immanuel." The latter means "God with us" (Matt. 1:23). "Virgin" (Isa. 7:14) translates the Hebrew noun *'alma*. This denotes a young woman of marriageable age who had never had intimate relations with a man. There is some debate over the identity of the virgin mentioned in this verse. Those who see the passage as having only real fulfillment in the Messiah interpret the virgin to be Mary, the mother of Jesus. Others think she was an unmarried woman known to Ahaz. More probable is the view that the virgin was to be the second wife of Isaiah. Those who hold to this view think that Isaiah's first wife, the mother of Shear-jashub (vs. 3), had previously died. The prophet then married the woman who would become pregnant, bear a son, and name the newborn Immanuel. It is maintained that at the time of the prophecy, the woman was unwed and a virgin.

There are also differences of opinion concerning the interpretation of the prophecy recorded in verse 14. One group thinks the virgin and her son were people who lived only in the time of Ahaz. The problem with this view is that it ignores what is said in Matthew 1:23. A second group interprets Isaiah 7:14 as being only a prophecy of Jesus' miraculous conception and birth. It is maintained that what Isaiah said finds no real fulfillment in Ahaz's time. The problem with this view is that it neither does full justice to Isaiah 7:14 nor to the context in which it appears. If this view were true, how could Isaiah's prophecy have been a word of assurance to Ahaz? A third group thinks the virgin and her son were people who actually lived in the time of Ahaz. Thus, what Isaiah foretold had real significance to the king. It is also maintained that Isaiah's prophecy finds ultimate fulfillment in the miraculous conception and birth of the Messiah. The strength of this view is that it seeks to take both Isaiah 7:14 and Matthew 1:23 equally seriously.

C. The Promised Disaster: vss. 15-17

"He will eat curds and honey when he knows enough to reject the wrong and choose the right. But before the boy knows enough to reject the wrong and choose the right, the land of the two kings you dread will be laid waste. The LORD will bring on you and on your people and on the house of your father a time unlike any since Ephraim broke away from Judah—he will bring the king of Assyria."

Isaiah gave his prophecy to Ahaz around 734 B.C. Within two years (that is, 732 B.C.) the two kings invading Judah would no longer be threats to Ahaz. The Hebrew noun rendered "curds" (Isa. 7:15) refers to a fermented milk product similar to yogurt. Some think curds along with honey denote the abundance of food. It seems better, however, to understand that Isaiah had in view the plain diet of an agrarian community. The picture is one in which the farmland has been devastated (vss. 22-25). With the pursuit of farming rendered impossible, only a simple diet based on what livestock produced would be possible.

The devastation referred to in verse 15 took place in 732 B.C. The child referred to in verse 14 thus would be about two years old. Clearly, he would not know enough yet to refuse evil options and choose good ones. Because Samaria's countryside would be ravaged by Assyria, many agricultural products would not be available for the child's consumption. Only simple, basic foods such as curds and honey would be attainable to eat.

Despite the devastation, God promised to deliver Judah from Damascus and Ephraim (vs. 16). Ahaz had dreaded northern Palestine because of the threat that Rezin and Pekah had posed to him. Yet in due time both these assailants would die, forcing them to abandon the territories they once ruled. Sadly, Ahaz decided to solicit the help of Tiglath-Pileser III. Judah became Assyria's vassal rather than her ally. Ahaz also had to pay Assyria a heavy tribute of silver and gold from the treasuries of both the temple and the royal palace in Jerusalem (2 Chron. 28:16-21).

Ephraim originally departed from Judah in 931 B.C., when the once united kingdom was divided in two. That was a time of significant distress, turmoil, and humiliation for the people of God (1 Kings 12:16-24). Isaiah prophesied that God would use the Assyrians to distress and humble Judah even more (Isa. 7:17). The enemy would invade the nation, conquer its cities, overthrow its fortresses, and devastate its vineyards and farmlands (vss. 18-25). Such would be the high price God's people would pay for not trusting in Him. This calamity occurred in 701 B.C. when Sennacherib's armies swarmed over Judah (2 Kings 18:13-16). Even though God graciously spared Hezekiah and his subjects

(19:35-37), it was not until the Assyrians had brought the Hebrew people very low in the process.

II. THE ASTONISHING MESSAGE: LUKE 1:30-38

A. Mary's Pregnancy Foretold: vss. 30-31

But the angel said to her, "Do not be afraid, Mary, you have found favor with God. You will be with child and give birth to a son, and you are to give him the name Jesus."

In the divinely appointed time, God sent the angel Gabriel to a young woman living in a village of Galilee called Nazareth (Luke 1:26). Mary was betrothed to a man who was descended from King David, the family from which the prophets had said the Messiah would come (vs. 27). For Jewish women at this time, betrothal could occur as early as 12 years old, and the betrothal period lasted for about a year. The angel had good news for Mary. The phrase "highly favored" (vs. 28) means that the Lord had singled her out for a special blessing. Through her, God would bestow His grace upon many. Gabriel's salutation, however, was troubling to Mary. Indeed, the presence of the angel was strange and perplexing. Naturally, Mary was thrown into turmoil (vs. 29).

It was vital for God to send Gabriel to speak with Mary before she became pregnant because she was a virgin and her pregnancy would cause her distress and shame. In addition, she would have no idea who this child was. Gabriel came to prevent any fears and anxieties that Mary might otherwise have felt. The angel also came so that the young woman could prepare for this great event. But before Gabriel continued his message, he calmed Mary's fears. He had come to bring her good news, not to alarm her (vs. 30). The angel then told Mary how God was to bless her. He would enable her to give birth to a Son, whom she would name "Jesus" (vs. 31).

B. Jesus' Greatness Foretold: vss. 32-33

"He will be great and will be called the Son of the Most High. The Lord God will give him the throne of his father David, and he will reign over the house of Jacob forever; his kingdom will never end."

As was noted earlier in the lesson, Isaiah had prophesied that a virgin would conceive and bear a son (Isa. 7:14). Mary's infant was that child, this miracle being possible because He would also be the "Son of the Most High" (Luke 1:32). Furthermore, He would fulfill what Isaiah had foretold about the one who would rule on David's throne (Isa. 9:6-7). God had promised David that his kingdom would be established forever (2 Sam. 7:16). In fact, David's descendants reigned over Judah until the Exile (586 B.C.). The angel's reference to the "throne of his father David" (Luke 1:32) meant that God would now restore the broken line of David's succession. Indeed, Gabriel revealed to Mary that her Son would fulfill that promise by reigning forever (vs. 33).

C. Mary's Miraculous Conception Explained: vss. 34-35

"How will this be," Mary asked the angel, "since I am a virgin?" The angel answered, "The Holy Spirit will come upon you, and the power of the Most High will overshadow you. So the holy one to be born will be called the Son of God."

Mary asked the obvious question. How could she, who had not been physically intimate with any man, become pregnant (Luke 1:34)? While Mary's question provides Scripture's best verification for the virginal conception of Jesus, her words also show a strong and thinking mind. She was confident enough in her relationship with God to ask appropriate questions. Incidentally, both Mary and Zechariah asked Gabriel how God could do the seemingly impossible. The difference in their queries is that Mary asked how it was possible, while Zechariah (evidently in doubt) asked, "How can I be sure of this?" (vs. 18). Zechariah asked for a sign, which Gabriel granted in the form of Zechariah's muteness.

Gabriel probably anticipated Mary's confusion, for he was prepared to explain God's message to her. He said Jesus would need no man to father Him, for the Spirit of God would come upon Mary (vs. 35). When the Holy Spirit later came upon Mary, she became the instrument of Jesus' incarnation. Being the "Son of God," Jesus is holy, not because He was dedicated to God, but because He is God.

D. Elizabeth's Pregnancy Declared: vss. 36-37

"Even Elizabeth your relative is going to have a child in her old age, and she who was said to be barren is in her sixth month. For nothing is impossible with God."

Although Mary had not asked Gabriel for a sign, he pointed toward evidence that God's power was already at work. He mentioned Mary's relative Elizabeth, who had long been barren but was now pregnant (Luke 1:36). The angel assured Mary that what he said to her would come to pass, for with God nothing is impossible (vs. 37). Human promises sometimes fail, especially when people lack the resources or inclination to keep them. God, however, always fulfills His word.

E. Mary's Humble Response: vs. 38

"I am the Lord's servant," Mary answered. "May it be to me as you have said." Then the angel left her.

Mary's response to Gabriel perhaps helps explain why God had chosen her. Many disturbing questions may have been running through her mind: *Will Joseph believe the unimaginable? What will my friends and neighbors think when they learn I am pregnant? Will I be branded the worst of sinners, rather than God's chosen instrument?* Nevertheless, Mary did not argue with the angel. Instead, she humbly submitted to God when He gave her a responsibility (Luke 1:38). Scripture describes faith as "being sure of what we hope for and certain of what we do not see" (Heb. 11:1). Mary had such faith. Though she did not fully understand Gabriel's message, she accepted God's promise. Faith says, "I will believe the 'impossible' as fact because the Lord says so." We put our faith into action when we obey God in this way.

Discussion Questions

1. Why did the Lord declare through Isaiah that Ahaz would be given a sign?
2. What is significant about the name of the child to be born to the virgin?
3. Why was Mary initially afraid when Gabriel appeared to her?
4. How would it be possible for Mary, a virgin, to become pregnant with the Christ child?
5. What was the nature of Mary's response to Gabriel before he departed?

Contemporary Application

The man experienced blurred vision and went for an eye examination. He was sure it was a cataract. After extensive tests, the physician gave him the grim news. He had suffered a mini-stroke in his optic nerve. Then came this crushing admission: "There's nothing we can do to correct the problem."

We so blindly think that modern medicine can do something about every malady that we are not prepared when physicians tell us there is nothing they or we can do. Experiences like this drive us to God in prayer. We know that ultimately only the Lord can heal us and take care of us. We also know that only the love of Jesus can take us through difficult experiences like the one mentioned above.

The account of Ahaz and Isaiah reminds us of God's mercy and comfort. It also underscores the futility of refusing to turn to the Lord in faith and devotion. Some people, of course, feel differently. They ask, "Why trust God when you can do it yourself?" That philosophy permeates society. Christians also find themselves tempted to work their way out of jams by themselves. Plain old simple trust is hard to come by. Why is this so?

For one thing, we appear foolish not to take advantage of everything we can do for ourselves. We have so much money, training, education, skills, and power. We also have modern science and modern medicine, so who needs God? Such worldly thinking, of course, is shallow and shortsighted.

Because we believe in God, we have many opportunities to encourage others who face insurmountable problems. Our calling is to bring hope and comfort to the fearful, as Isaiah tried to do for Ahaz.

We offer Jesus—the Christ child whom Gabriel announced to Mary—to people who do not know the Savior. We offer prayer and the strength that comes from claiming the Lord's promises in the Bible. And we offer testimonies of what the Redeemer has done for us.

Emmanuel Is Born

Scripture

Background Scripture: *Matthew 1:18-25*
Scripture Lesson: *Matthew 1:18-25*
Key Verse: *"[Mary] will give birth to a son, and you are to give him the name Jesus, because he will save his people from their sins."* Matthew 1:21.
Scripture Lesson for Children: *Matthew 1:18-25*
Key Verse for Children: *"[Mary] will give birth to a son, and you are to give him the name Jesus, because he will save his people from their sins."* Matthew 1:21.

Lesson Aim

To recognize that God guides people one step at a time.

Lesson Setting

Time: *6–5 B.C.*
Place: *Nazareth of Galilee*

Lesson Outline

Emmanuel Is Born

   I. The Skepticism of Joseph: Matthew 1:18-19
      A. The Pregnancy of Mary: vs. 18
      B. The Decision of Joseph: vs. 19
  II. The Intervention of God: Matthew 1:20-25
      A. The Unusual Dream: vss. 20-21
      B. The Fulfillment of Prophecy: vss. 22-23
      C. The Obedience of Joseph: vss. 24-25

Introduction for Adults

Topic: *A Unique Birth*

How long can we hold on to a promise before we give up? From 1993 to 2001, three missionary wives clung to the hope that their missing husbands would be found alive. They weren't.

Eight years seems like a long time until we consider how long the God-fearing Jews held on to the Lord's promise of a Messiah. We can hardly appreciate the overwhelming joy they must have found at the news that God the Son came to earth by being miraculously conceived and born as a human being.

How long can we cling to the hope of the Messiah's return? Do we find a renewed sense of hope concerning His return when we celebrate His first advent? We must keep His return in mind even while we thank the Father for the Son's birth.

Introduction for Youth

Topic: *Look Who Just Dropped In*

When our orthodox Jewish friends celebrate Passover, they set a place at the table for Elijah, for they expect him to return to earth at any time to announce that the Messiah is coming. Thus, with the greatest care, they make preparation for the Savior's advent.

What kind of preparation are we making to celebrate the marvelous fact that the Messiah has, indeed, already come? Has our preparation consisted only of festive decorations and the placing of gifts under a tree? What about our spiritual preparation? Do we understand something of the fantastic preparations God made from eternity past for the coming of His Son? Have we prepared our hearts and minds to properly celebrate His advent?

Concepts for Children

Topic: *What a Special Day!*

1. An angel of the Lord told Joseph about Mary's special baby.
2. Old Testament prophets foretold the virgin birth of Immanuel, which means "God is with us."
3. Joseph obeyed what the angel told him to do.
4. The Holy Spirit enabled Mary to give birth to Jesus.
5. Jesus' birth fulfilled God's promise to be with us and save people from their sins.

Lesson Commentary

I. THE SKEPTICISM OF JOSEPH: MATTHEW 1:18-19

A. The Pregnancy of Mary: vs. 18

This is how the birth of Jesus Christ came about: His mother Mary was pledged to be married to Joseph, but before they came together, she was found to be with child through the Holy Spirit.

In Matthew 1:18, we find the start of Matthew's explanation concerning the birth of Jesus the Messiah. Mary most likely belonged to the tribe of Judah, and possibly was herself a descendant of David (Matt. 1:1-16; Luke 1:32). We see much of the events of Jesus' early life through Mary's eyes, especially as she treasured all sorts of episodes and pondered in her heart what they might mean (Luke 2:19, 51). This information, unique to Luke, has led some to conclude that Mary was one of the eyewitnesses Luke interviewed when he gathered material for his Gospel (1:2).

Mary was also an eyewitness to Jesus' first miracle—the turning of water into wine at the wedding feast in Cana of Galilee (John 2:1-11). On another occasion, Mary and Jesus' brothers wished to see Him while He was teaching the multitudes (Luke 8:19). When Jesus was crucified, Mary stood near the cross. It was then that Jesus gave her over to the care of John (John 19:25-27). After Jesus' resurrection, Mary was in the upper room along with the rest of the disciples as they awaited the coming of the Holy Spirit (Acts 1:14).

There is little information about Joseph in the Gospels. He was a descendant of David, the husband of Mary, and the legal guardian of Jesus. By trade, Joseph was a carpenter (Matt 13:55). It can be deduced from Scripture that Joseph possessed great integrity and firm moral conviction (1:19). Regardless of what God desired of him, Joseph was willing to obey (1:24; 2:14, 21). Because he was a devout Jew, Joseph no doubt made sure Jesus received good spiritual training during His adolescent years in Nazareth (Luke 2:39-40, 51-52). Joseph is last mentioned when Jesus was 12 years old (vss. 42-48). Many think Joseph had died by the time Jesus entered His public ministry (4:14-15).

Matthew 1:18 explains that Mary was espoused, or betrothed, to Joseph. If Mary and Joseph were of the ages typical for marriage in their time and place, she was perhaps in her early teens and he may have been somewhat older. The parents usually arranged marriages in Jesus' day, though a young man or woman could sometimes decline a particular person the parents had chosen.

Many times, the marriage depended on a person's ancestry, property, and the size of a bride's dowry. Sometimes the marriage was arranged to distant relatives in order to keep wealth in the family. The betrothal period involved a much more formal commitment than an engagement does today. During that time, the couple were considered husband and wife but abstained from sexual relations. They spent their time preparing for their wedding day—the man by preparing the place where they would live together, and the wife by preparing herself for the day.

Mary and Joseph must have dreamed about what their life together would be like. Yet neither of them could have imagined the extraordinary privilege and responsibility that would be theirs—the raising of God's Son. The Bible describes several incidents in which God blessed the wombs of women. Sarah, Hannah, and Elizabeth were recipients of God's gracious intervention; but the miracle of Jesus' conception was different. The Holy Spirit came upon Mary, and thus she became pregnant. No human male fathered Jesus. Unlike crude pagan tales of miraculous appearances of gods and goddesses (such as in the Greek myths), Matthew avoided lurid details and sensational embellishments of Jesus' birth; instead, Matthew wrote about these matters with quiet restraint.

B. The Decision of Joseph: vs. 19

Because Joseph her husband was a righteous man and did not want to expose her to public disgrace, he had in mind to divorce her quietly.

In those days betrothal was a legally binding pledge between a man and a woman. In fact, Matthew called Joseph the "husband" (Matt. 1:19) of Mary while they were still betrothed. This contract required that each partner remain faithful to the other. The betrothed couple began living together when the bridegroom took the bride to his house and consummated the marriage. A betrothal could be dissolved only by a bill of divorce. This was easier to obtain in the betrothal period than it was if the marriage vows had been completed and the marriage sexually consummated. Once the marriage vows were complete, a divorce was generally harder to get. It was supposed to be allowed only in cases of adultery. However, the Pharisees corrupted the law and allowed divorce to occur for many reasons, even things as mundane as a wife burning a husband's meal.

Interestingly, when children put on nativity plays each Christmas, Joseph and Mary are coveted roles. Yet Joseph himself did not initially want any part of the situation he found himself in with Mary. We can only imagine the anxiety that Joseph must have felt when he learned that Mary was pregnant. Thoughts of unfaithfulness no doubt surfaced in his mind. Joseph could have brought Mary before a court and exposed her alleged sin. However, since Joseph would not allow Mary to be disgraced, he decided to divorce her privately, which the Jewish law permitted.

Matthew called Joseph a "righteous man." In context, that was an affirmation of Joseph's character. It was as solid as the wood he used in his carpentry trade (see 13:55). Of course, Joseph was righteous not just because of what he did, but because of who he believed (see Rom. 4:3). Scripture teaches that righteousness comes through faith (see 1:17), and Joseph acted from a firm faith in

God. Because of Joseph's piety, he could not wed Mary, believing she had been unfaithful. If Joseph had taken any other course of action, he would have tacitly acknowledged that he was the father of the child. This would have been a circumstance of guilt by association. For a man of integrity like Joseph, that prospect was an unthinkable threat to his reputation.

II. THE INTERVENTION OF GOD: MATTHEW 1:20-25

A. The Unusual Dream: vss. 20-21

But after he had considered this, an angel of the Lord appeared to him in a dream and said, "Joseph son of David, do not be afraid to take Mary home as your wife, because what is conceived in her is from the Holy Spirit. She will give birth to a son, and you are to give him the name Jesus, because he will save his people from their sins."

It was normal for Joseph to be confused and upset over Mary's apparent promiscuous behavior. After all, what man would marry a woman who had become pregnant by someone else during their engagement? The Lord, however, caused an angel to appear to Joseph in a dream to assure him that Mary had not been unfaithful to him. In the ancient world, people believed that dreams were a window into knowing the future. This sentiment proved to be true in the case of Joseph. The angel addressed him as the "son of David" (Matt. 1:20). This reflects the fact that Joseph was a descendant of Israel's greatest king. Additionally, this is another indication that Jesus, as the legal son of Joseph, would have the right to sit on the throne of David.

God's heavenly messenger revealed that the child in Mary's womb had been conceived by the Holy Spirit. Just as God's Spirit was instrumental as the agent of the natural Creation (Gen. 1:2), even so the Spirit of God was the divine agent in the conception of Jesus' human nature (Luke 1:35). Creation before the Fall was pronounced "very good" (Gen. 1:31), and likewise Jesus' human nature was preserved from any taint of inherited sin.

The angel's words indicate that the issue involving Mary had weighed heavily on Joseph's mind. Nevertheless, the appearance of the angel convinced Joseph that, despite how the situation appeared, it was God's will that he wed Mary. The angel's message must have also comforted Joseph. Being reassured of Mary's faithfulness and being told what to do probably motivated him to want to be her protector, as well as the protector of her child. Next, the angel announced that Joseph was to give the name "Jesus" to the male child in Mary's womb (Matt. 1:21). As Joshua—Moses' successor—had led the Israelites into the promised land, so Jesus—God's Son—would lead many into God's salvation.

When faced with a decision, we often seek God's guidance to know what to do. But how should we expect to receive His guidance? For instance, Joseph received direct guidance in four separate dreams from an angel of the Lord

(1:20; 2:13, 19, 22). While it is possible that God could still directly guide us in like manner, we find His guidance more often in the counsel of His Word and Spirit (see John 14:16; 16:7-15; 1 Cor. 2:10-12). When faced with a decision for which we need divine guidance, James 1:5 is instructive. We learn that if we need wisdom, we can ask our generous Lord, reassured that He will grant our request. God gives that wisdom through Scripture (2 Tim. 3:16-17), the counsel of others (Prov. 15:22), trust in Him (3:5-6), and our willingness to consider a matter patiently rather than rushing into something (19:2). As with Joseph, God's guidance usually comes incrementally rather than all at once, for He wants us to look to Him and trust Him. Just as Joseph did, we can also obey the direction God gives us.

B. The Fulfillment of Prophecy: vss. 22-23

All this took place to fulfill what the Lord had said through the prophet: "The virgin will be with child and will give birth to a son, and they will call him Immanuel"—which means, "God with us."

Matthew wrote his Gospel to address the needs of the early Christian church members, especially those from a Jewish background. He wanted to establish that Jesus truly was the promised Messiah of the Hebrew Scriptures (for examples, see 16:15, 16; 27:37). Since Matthew wanted to prove that Jesus fulfilled all the Old Testament predictions about the Messiah, he referred at least 12 times to the ancient prophecies (key examples: 1:22-23; 21:4-5; 26:55-56). In addition, Matthew quoted or alluded to the Old Testament Scriptures more than 90 times.

In 1:22, the Lord's angel revealed to Joseph that Mary's pregnancy was the fulfillment of what previously had been foretold. Specifically, Isaiah had described the unusual birth of Jesus about eight centuries before it happened (Isa. 7:14). As was noted in lesson 2, a coalition of the kings of Israel and Syria threatened to destroy the kingdom of Judah and the Davidic dynasty. Isaiah admonished Ahaz, the king of Judah, to trust God and ask for a sign of His protection; but instead Ahaz foolishly placed his trust in the Assyrians.

In response, Isaiah angrily told Ahaz that God's sign would be a virgin birth (Matt. 1:23). Whether or not a prophecy came to pass determined the truth of a prophet's message. Isaiah's prophecy was true because a virgin did conceive and give birth to a child. Why did Isaiah refer to Jesus as Immanuel? In the Hebrew, the name *Immanuel* highlights the character of the promised Messiah of God. Isaiah's prophecy was about a person who would come as the embodiment of God's character and nature. In every way Jesus truly is "God with us," namely, the sovereign, eternal Lord dwelling among people as a human being.

There is some debate over the exact identification of "Immanuel" in Isaiah 7:14. One group thinks he was the son of a woman known to Ahaz. This view raises a host of chronological and theological problems that are difficult to resolve. These problems make this view less favorable. A second group thinks Immanuel was a son of Isaiah. Because Isaiah 7:10-17 and 8:1-10 are similar in form, some conclude that Immanuel and Maher-Shalal-Hash-Bez (which means "quick to the plunder, swift to the spoil") were two names for the same child. Others, however, regard Immanuel and Maher-Shalal-Hash-Bez as Isaiah's second and third sons, respectively. Immanuel would be a promise of divine deliverance, while Maher-Shalal-Hash-Bez would be a promise of divine judgment. Ultimately, of course, the promise of the virgin-born child is fulfilled in Jesus, since Mary was unmarried at the time of Jesus' conception.

The preceding information reminds us that Bible prophecy is a complex subject. When Old Testament passages seem to refer to the Messiah, we have to remember that those verses were first addressed to a particular contemporary audience that found meaning in them. Also, when Old Testament verses are quoted in the New Testament in relationship to Jesus as the Messiah, the New Testament writers saw in the verses another meaning that may or may not have been recognized by the prophet when he spoke them (see 1 Pet. 1:10-12). With respect to Isaiah 7—9, these chapters could be seen as a single connected prophecy announcing the eventual destruction of both Israel and Judah. The child Immanuel then becomes the one who will later bring light to Galilee, the land of the Gentiles (9:1-2), and be called the "Wonderful Counselor, Mighty God, Everlasting Father, [and] Prince of Peace" (vs. 6)—Jesus Christ.

C. The Obedience of Joseph: vss. 24-25

When Joseph woke up, he did what the angel of the Lord had commanded him and took Mary home as his wife. But he had no union with her until she gave birth to a son. And he gave him the name Jesus.

After Joseph awoke, he obeyed the angel of the Lord by subsequently marrying Jesus' mother (Matt. 1:24). Since the idea of a virgin birth cannot be found clearly anywhere in ancient Jewish literature outside of Isaiah's prophecy, this angelic revelation must have startled Joseph. Nevertheless, he did not regard his dream as a fantasy, but as an actual visitation from God's messenger. More importantly, Joseph believed what the angel had told him, and this is why he named Mary's child "Jesus" (vs. 25).

When the angel told Joseph to take Mary home and he did, Joseph showed that his trust in the Lord was great. His reputation was still at stake, yet he submitted that to the Lord. Joseph knew that Mary and he were not guilty of immorality. Though others in their acquaintance might have presumed otherwise, Joseph would not allow that to deter his obedience. There is no explanation as to why Joseph abstained from physical intimacy with his wife until Jesus was born in Bethlehem of Judea. (Some think Joseph had been instructed by an angel to do so.) Joseph's decision to wait, however, suggests that he had great respect and reverence for the presence of the Lord upon Mary.

Discussion Questions

1. What brought about Mary's pregnancy?
2. Why did Joseph initially decide to divorce Mary?
3. Why did an angel of the Lord encourage Joseph to remain betrothed to Mary?
4. What are some Old Testament messianic prophecies that the birth of the Christ child fulfills?
5. What does Joseph's obedience to the angel of the Lord's command suggest about Joseph's character?

Contemporary Application

"I believe," said the great African theologian Augustine, "that Christ was born of a Virgin because I read it in the Gospel." How many people today can say the same thing with sincere conviction? Probably only a small percentage can do so.

The idea that a woman can conceive a baby without any involvement of a man is absurd to the modern mind, which limits beliefs to within scientific boundaries; but as the ancient Apostles' Creed illustrates, the Virgin Birth is a core belief of orthodox Christianity. If this doctrine is taken away, the rest of our faith begins to crumble. If Jesus had been the offspring of Joseph and Mary by ordinary means, Jesus could not have died for the sins of the entire world.

It is certainly a miracle that Jesus was born of a virgin, but it is also a miracle that a person can trust in the Word of God enough to believe that His birth truly occurred in this way. People cannot believe in this event on their own. God must perform a miracle and grant this kind of faith to them.

During Christmastime, of course, we see the baby Jesus and sing about Him; and few people openly question that He was born in Bethlehem many centuries ago. Many people, nevertheless, are skeptical of the Virgin Birth and assume that it is a myth that His early followers added to embellish His life story.

In the midst of the prevailing doubt in our society, do you know whether your students have experienced the miracle of God and believed the Gospel account of Jesus' birth? If so, then they believe the miracle of miracles—that the Creator returned to His creation as the sinless human being, Jesus. He was conceived in a virgin and was born that we no more may die, but instead receive our own second birth.

Knowing who Jesus is means knowing who He is not. He is not merely a religious teacher or a great philosopher. He is the Messiah, the Son of God. We hear about people whose lives have been transformed when they come to know who Jesus is. Some of the accounts are so moving that they stir us deeply, making us want to shout or cry for joy. We need to praise Jesus for not only what He has done in our lives but for who He is—God Himself, the Creator, Redeemer, and Lord.

Confirming Jesus' Birth

DEVOTIONAL READING

Proverbs 9:7-12

DAILY BIBLE READINGS

Monday December 21
*Proverbs 9:7-12 The
Beginning of Wisdom*

Tuesday December 22
*2 Chronicles 1:7-12 Give Me
Wisdom*

Wednesday December 23
*Psalm 90:11-17 Gaining a
Wise Heart*

Thursday December 24
*Proverbs 3:13-23 Those Who
Find Wisdom*

Friday December 25
*Matthew 2:1-6 Where Is the
Child?*

Saturday December 26
*Matthew 2:10-15
Overwhelmed with Joy*

Sunday December 27
*Matthew 2:7-9, 16-23
Finding and Protecting Jesus*

Scripture

Background Scripture: *Matthew 2*
Scripture Lesson: *Matthew 2:7-9, 16-23*
Key Verse: *When [the magi] saw the star, they were overjoyed.*
Matthew 2:10.
Scripture Lesson for Children: *Matthew 2:1-12*
Key Verse for Children: *[The magi] saw the child with his
mother Mary, and they bowed down and . . . presented him
gifts of gold and of incense and of myrrh.* Matthew 2:11.

Lesson Aim

To understand that people all over the world worship
Jesus.

Lesson Setting

Time: *About 3 B.C.*
Place: *Jerusalem and Bethlehem*

Lesson Outline

Confirming Jesus' Birth

  I. The Visit of the Magi: Matthew 2:7-9
     A. *The King's Instruction to the Magi: vss. 7-8*
     B. *The Magis' Worship of Jesus: vs. 9*
  II. The Messiah's Protection: Matthew 2:16-23
     A. *The Murder of the Innocent: vss. 16-18*
     B. *The Return to Nazareth: vss. 19-21*
     C. *The Fulfillment of Prophecy: vss. 22-23*

Introduction for Adults

Topic: *Searching for a Child*

The editors of a newspaper decided to find out what their readers remembered most about Christmas. The editors asked them to write letters describing their most memorable Christmas experiences. The more than 300 respondents wrote about joy and thanksgiving, as well as about unhappiness and even disappointments. The editors picked what they thought was the best letter.

As an underprivileged girl of eight, the letter writer noted that she had been given a doll by the volunteer firefighters of her town. But she didn't keep it. Her five-year-old neighbor girl also wanted a doll, so she decided to give away the cherished doll she had just received.

As this week's lesson shows, that's the heart of Christmas—giving, not getting. The magi persisted and overcame great difficulty, at considerable risk, not to get something for themselves, but to search for the Christ child and give something away. Why? Because they recognized that it was their privilege to respond to God's great gift to them, namely, to worship the promised Messiah of Israel.

Introduction for Youth

Topic: *Kings at the Front Door*

My father had a practice that was somewhat exasperating to me as a teenager. I would ask him whether I could do something, or go somewhere, or participate in some activity. Instead of making my decision for me, he would often answer, "Let your conscience be your guide." Though I was looking for an easy way out, my dad forced me to take personal responsibility for my actions.

My dad's response presupposed that I have a conscious. His answer also assumed that I had the training and background to know the difference between right and wrong. Moreover, his response presumed that I had the ability to apply different rules to specific situations. My dad was right, for he knew that my conscience was the voice of God in my soul (see Rom. 2:14-15).

God wants us to do what is right. When faced with a difficult or morally perplexing situation (such as the magi experienced), we can turn to Scripture for guidance and let the Lord use it to speak to our soul about what we should do.

Concepts for Children

Topic: *Worship the King!*

1. The magi asked King Herod where Jesus, the King of the Jews, had been born.
2. The magi searched for and found Jesus by following the star.
3. The magi discovered that Jesus was worth seeking.
4. When the magi found Jesus, they worshiped Him and gave Him gifts.
5. Jesus is pleased when we choose to worship and serve Him.

Lesson Commentary

I. THE VISIT OF THE MAGI: MATTHEW 2:7-9

A. The King's Instruction to the Magi: vss. 7-8

Then Herod called the Magi secretly and found out from them the exact time the star had appeared. He sent them to Bethlehem and said, "Go and make a careful search for the child. As soon as you find him, report to me, so that I too may go and worship him."

While Joseph, Mary, and the Christ child were in Bethlehem, "Magi from the east" (Matt. 2:1) visited them. The magi functioned as advisors to monarchs, and they practiced astrology and dream interpretation. Since they studied the movement of the stars, the magi who searched for Jesus were no doubt especially intrigued by the star that led them to Bethlehem. Some think they originated from Media or Persia, since the Greek term *magoi* comes from the Persian word *magav*. Other experts accept the ancient view that they came from Babylon. Still others think the magi came from South Arabia, partly because of trading links between the two areas dating back to the time of King Solomon.

The number of magi has been the subject of much speculation. The Eastern Christian Church believes 12 wise men worshiped Jesus. Western tradition says there were three, and their names were Caspar, Melchior, and Balthasar. In any case, the magi did not visit Jesus when He was a newborn, unlike the shepherds who found Him in a manger crib. Instead, they visited Jesus in a house, possibly several weeks to two years after His birth.

According to verse 2, the magi living east of Judea witnessed an unusual light in the sky. Verse 9 suggests this "star" may have hung so low that the magi could see it and follow it to their desired destination in the city. Some have suggested the star was an optical illusion or a figurative star in the hearts of the magi that moved them to the right location. Others think the star was a natural phenomenon (such as a supernova or the conjunction of two planets), while others maintain it was a supernatural phenomenon (namely, a unique light that appeared at God's command). Unlikely is the claim made by some that Matthew was mistaken because stars do not typically behave in the manner he described.

Regardless of the exact nature of the star, the magi recognized its importance. In the world of that time, there was an expectation of the coming of a great ruler, and this idea was linked with Jewish prophecy. Somehow the magi associated the star with the Jewish expectation of a king, especially the Messiah's birth. Accordingly, the magi traveled to Jerusalem to begin a search for this person. While in the Jewish capital, the magi began asking for directions to the person who had recently been born King of the Jews. They explained that they had seen this monarch's star and had journeyed to Palestine in order to pay homage to Him.

Some Bible interpreters think the phrase "we saw his star in the east" (vs. 2) means the magi were east of Palestine when they first caught a glimpse of the light. Others translate the phrase as "we saw his star in its rising." This rendering suggests that the magi had taken note of the star as it had appeared in the nighttime sky, and had become intrigued by it. Also, since Herod was known as the king of the Jews, it makes sense that the magi would inquire of him concerning the birth of the promised Messiah of Israel. The magi were perhaps familiar with Balaam's prophecy about a star that would come out of Jacob (Num. 24:17), though the magi needed Herod's religious experts (the scribes) to tell them about Micah's prophecy concerning the location of Israel's future leader (Mic. 5:2; Matt. 2:6).

We don't know who the magi initially asked for information, but their appearance in town set a chain of events in motion. It wasn't long before news reached the imperial court. When King Herod heard what the foreign visitors were saying, he became "disturbed" (Matt. 2:3). This renders a Greek term that denotes the presence of extreme agitation and alarm. Herod recognized that the Magi were talking about the Messiah. Though not a Jew himself, Herod well knew that prophets had foretold the appearance of a Jewish king and deliverer.

The last thing Herod wanted was a rival king among the Jews, who intensely hated him. As well, the rumors of a messianic figure might embolden the people to rise up against Herod. But in order for Herod to eliminate his rival, he needed more information. So when he heard what the magi were saying, he was scared that he might have a new rival—no less a rival than the Messiah. The people of Jerusalem were disturbed as well, probably not because of what the magi were saying but because Herod was perturbed. They knew the kind of violence of which he was capable.

In order to find out where the Messiah was to be born, Herod assembled a team of religious experts—chief priests and teachers of the law (vs. 4). It's possible Herod knew the location of the birthplace himself, but wanted the religious experts to confirm it. The chief priests were most likely members of the high priest's family as well as other prominent priestly leaders. The teachers of the law were biblical scholars who maintained the oral traditions of the Jews and promoted the study and practice of the Mosaic law.

After meeting together, the Jewish scholars named Bethlehem in Judea as the birthplace of the Messiah (vs. 5). This response is consistent with the common Jewish view of the day that the Messiah would be born in Bethlehem (John 7:42). The theological experts based their reply on the prophecy of Micah 5:2, proclaimed hundreds of years earlier. Micah had said that despite this village's apparent insignificance, out of it would come a shepherd for the people of Israel. Matthew evidently modified the verse a bit to emphasize the village's theological significance (Matt. 2:6).

Herod now knew the whereabouts of the Messiah. But the king also needed to know when the child had been born. No doubt Herod was already intending to slaughter every boy of the appropriate age in Bethlehem, so he needed to find out about how old his rival was. Therefore, crafty Herod's next move was to summon the magi for a private discussion to learn when the star had appeared (Matt. 2:7). They evidently named a date within the past two years (see vs. 16).

Having gotten the information he wanted about the child's time of birth, Herod then sent the magi on to Bethlehem with his encouragement to search diligently for the Christ child. The ruler told them that when they had found this newborn King of the Jews, they were to report their findings to Herod because he wanted to visit the child and pay homage to Him (vs. 8). This was utter hypocrisy, of course. The king's desire was to murder Jesus, not worship Him.

B. The Magis' Worship of Jesus: vs. 9

After they had heard the king, they went on their way, and the star they had seen in the east went ahead of them until it stopped over the place where the child was.

When the magi left Herod, the "star" (Matt. 2:9) they had previously seen went ahead of them on the short journey to Bethlehem until it stopped above Jesus' location. (This description of the light's movement would seem to count against the theory that the "star" was a supernova or some other natural phenomenon.) The magi were "overjoyed" (vs. 10) at what they saw. After all, their search was over, for they had found the King. Their excitement paralleled the great joy brought to the Christmas shepherds by the heavenly heralds (Luke 2:10).

Since a period of time had elapsed since Jesus' birth, the family had moved into a house in Bethlehem. The magi entered that house and saw Jesus with His mother, Mary. As they had planned, the magi prostrated themselves in worship before the King of the Jews (Matt. 2:11). Next, the magi opened containers they had brought with them and gave Jesus gifts of gold, frankincense, and myrrh. Many people have tied symbolic significance to each of these three gifts, but that is only speculation. Frankincense was a perfume and medicine gathered by making incisions in certain trees and collecting their aromatic white gum. Myrrh, the resin extracted from a small shrub, was used in perfume, incense, and embalming (John 19:39). All the items were expensive, worthy of a king. Joseph and Mary may have used these gifts in years to come to help them take care of Jesus.

Herod had told the magi to report their findings to him, and at that time the magi had probably not suspected Herod of any evil motives. Remarkably, Herod also trusted the magi to be his detectives, for he did not send anyone with them. Due to Herod's sinister plans, God warned the magi in a dream not to go back to Herod. So they returned to their home country by a different way, that is, by avoiding any travel through Jerusalem (Matt. 2:12).

II. THE MESSIAH'S PROTECTION: MATTHEW 2:16-23

A. The Murder of the Innocent: vss. 16-18

When Herod realized that he had been outwitted by the Magi, he was furious, and he gave orders to kill all the boys in Bethlehem and its vicinity who were two years old and under, in accordance with the time he had learned from the Magi. Then what was said through the prophet Jeremiah was fulfilled: "A voice is heard in Ramah, weeping and great mourning, Rachel weeping for her children and refusing to be comforted, because they are no more."

Perhaps not long after the magi had departed, Joseph had a dream in which an angel of the Lord appeared to him. The heavenly emissary warned Joseph to take his wife and her child and flee to Egypt, for Herod was about to conduct a thorough search to locate and murder Jesus. The angel directed Joseph to remain in Egypt until he was told to return to Palestine (Matt. 2:13). As a true servant of God, Joseph obeyed the divine instructions. He hurriedly took Jesus and Mary and departed for Egypt, secretly leaving during the night to avoid detection (vs. 14). Some think Joseph left within 24 hours after the magi had departed.

During the time of the Messiah, there were Jewish colonies in several prominent Egyptian cities. Some think Joseph and his family may have lived in one of these communities. The family remained in Egypt until the death of Herod in the spring of 4 B.C. Jesus' flight to—and, later, His return from—Egypt fulfilled Hosea 11:1: "Out of Egypt I called my son" (Matt. 2:15). Hosea 11:1 originally referred to God's bringing Israel out of foreign domination. But Matthew applied this verse to Jesus, the ideal Israelite in whom all the hopes of the nation were fully realized. In the Messiah all the promises of God come to fulfillment.

When Herod found out that the magi had tricked him, he became furious. He ordered his men to murder all the boys who lived in or near Bethlehem and who were two years old and younger. Herod's order was based on what he had learned from the magi. Given Herod's temperament and previous crimes, it is not surprising to read about his atrocities in and around Bethlehem. The king who had murdered members of his own family evidently had no qualms about commanding assassins to search every house in the city, snatch young boys from their parents, and put them to death (Matt. 2:16).

Verse 17 says the horrible massacre fulfilled Jeremiah 31:15. The prophecy, which is repeated in Matthew 2:18, originally referred to the bitter sorrow felt by the Israelites as their youths were carried away into exile by foreign conquerors. Under divine inspiration, Matthew viewed the life of the Messiah as the ultimate expression of what the nation had experienced in its history.

B. The Return to Nazareth: vss. 19-21

After Herod died, an angel of the Lord appeared in a dream to Joseph in Egypt and said, "Get up, take the child and his mother and go to the land of Israel, for those who were trying to take the child's life are dead." So he got up, took the child and his mother and went to the land of Israel.

After King Herod's death in 4 B.C., an angel of the Lord again appeared to Joseph in a dream (Matt. 2:19). Joseph was told to take his family out of Egypt and return to Palestine, for the threat on Jesus' life no longer existed (vs. 20). Joseph did not hesitate to obey the command of the Lord. He took his wife and her son and returned to the land of Israel (vs. 21).

C. The Fulfillment of Prophecy: vss. 22-23

But when he heard that Archelaus was reigning in Judea in place of his father Herod, he was afraid to go there. Having been warned in a dream, he withdrew to the district of Galilee, and he went and lived in a town called Nazareth. So was fulfilled what was said through the prophets: "He will be called a Nazarene."

Joseph may have planned to return to Bethlehem, intending to settle there permanently. But if so, Joseph's plans changed when he learned that Archelaus had succeeded his father, Herod, as king in Judea. (Archelaus reigned from 4 B.C.–A.D. 6.) Joseph rightly feared Archelaus, for the latter was notoriously malicious and oppressive in his political tactics. Moreover, Joseph was warned in another dream not to resettle in Judea. Thus, he decided to relocate his family to the region of Galilee (Matt. 2:22).

Joseph and his family eventually settled in Nazareth (vs. 23). This was a logical choice, for Nazareth had been the hometown of both Joseph and Mary (Luke 1:26-27; 2:4, 39). The origin of the name "Nazareth" is uncertain. One view is that it is related to the Hebrew verb *natsar*, which means "to guard" or "to watch." Accordingly, the term has been applied to watchtowers (see 2 Kings 17:9; 18:8). If this etymology is followed, "Nazareth" could imply that the original city was perched on or near a hill (see Luke 4:16-30).

Another view is that "Nazareth" is related to the Hebrew noun *netser*, which means "sprout," "branch," or "shoot" (see Isa. 11:1). According to Matthew 2:23, when Joseph's family relocated to Nazareth (Greek, *Nazaret*), it fulfilled prophecy. However, the prophetic declaration "He will be called a Nazarene" cannot be found in the Old Testament. One possibility is that Matthew was making a play on the Hebrew noun *netser*. Expressed differently, the *netser* (which is translated "Branch") would be called a Nazarene (Greek, *Nazoraios;* in other words, the saying is a pun; see Zech. 6:12).

In Jesus' day, Nazareth was a relatively insignificant village of Lower Galilee. The town resides in a basin north of the Valley of Jezreel (or Plain of Esdraelon) about 1,300 feet above sea level. Nazareth is also about 20 miles from the Mediterranean Sea and 15 miles from the Sea of Galilee, which places it near several of Palestine's key trade routes. The moderate climate and ample yearly rainfall makes the area suitable for agriculture. From the third century B.C. until the present, people have lived in Nazareth.

Discussion Questions

1. Who were the magi, and why were they interested in the birth of the Christ child?
2. How were the magi able to find the Christ child?
3. Why did Herod order the murder of all the boys living in Bethlehem who were two years old and younger?
4. Why did an angel of the Lord direct Joseph to relocate his family to Israel?
5. In what way did Joseph's decision to settle in Nazareth fulfill prophecy?

Contemporary Application

The birth of Jesus produced a wide spectrum of responses—some threatened, some uncaring, and some joyful and eager—that we still see today. Like Herod, some people are openly hostile to Jesus. They regard Him as a threat to the way they want to run their lives. Was there a time in your life when you responded with hostility to Jesus and His claims? If so, what changed your attitude?

There are others like the chief priests and teachers of the law who know the religious routine, but are unmoved by it. They even have some Bible knowledge, but they couldn't care less. Jesus simply isn't for them in any life-changing way. They are content to be religious, but not converted. Have you had someone recently respond with indifference to your Gospel witness? How did it make you feel?

In contrast to antagonistic and ambivalent responses, the magi worshiped Jesus. When they got information about Him, they acted on it. They were not the same. It took their time and persistence, but they found the Messiah. They gave Him the noblest gifts they could bring. Can we afford to do anything less? When we realize the love the Father has for us in His Son, shouldn't we respond with praise?

Our worship of the Savior can come in a variety of forms. One person might think of the overwhelming sensation of adoration experienced by repeating "O for a Thousand Tongues to Sing" amid thousands of people at an evangelistic event. Another Christian might think of being moved to tears amid the Rocky Mountains by the praise chorus "The Greatest Thing." Another individual might recall a worshipful insight triggered during a quiet Communion service. What outstanding experiences of homage can you remember that God might want you to share with others?

Proclaimed in Baptism

DEVOTIONAL READING

Acts 8:26-38

DAILY BIBLE READINGS

Monday December 28
*Matthew 21:23-27 The
Origin of John's Baptism*

Tuesday December 29
*Luke 7:24-30 John, More
than a Prophet*

Wednesday December 30
*John 1:24-34 John's
Testimony of Jesus*

Thursday December 31
*Romans 10:8-17 Calling on
the Name of Jesus*

Friday January 1
*Matthew 3:7-10 The
Necessity of Repentance*

Saturday January 2
*Romans 6:1-11 Buried and
Raised with Christ*

Sunday January 3
*Matthew 3:1-6, 11-17 Jesus
Baptized by John*

Scripture

Background Scripture: *Matthew 3*
Scripture Lesson: *Matthew 3:1-6, 11-17*
Key Verse: *A voice from heaven said, "This is my Son, whom
I love; with him I am well pleased."* Matthew 3:17.
Scripture Lesson for Children: *Matthew 3:1-6, 13-17*
Key Verse for Children: *A voice from heaven said, "This is
my Son, whom I love; with him I am well pleased."*
Matthew 3:17.

Lesson Aim

To stress that the Messiah's advent calls for change.

Lesson Setting

Time: A.D. *26*
Place: *Wilderness of Judea*

Lesson Outline

Proclaimed in Baptism

I. John Prepares the Way: Matthew 3:1-6
   A. *The Arrival of John: vss. 1-2*
   B. *The Fulfillment of Prophecy: vs. 3*
   C. *The Lifestyle of John: vs. 4*
   D. *The Response of the Crowd: vss. 5-6*

II. John Baptizes Jesus: Matthew 3:11-17
   A. *The Messiah as Judge: vss. 11-12*
   B. *The Arrival of Jesus: vs. 13*
   C. *The Consent of John: vss. 14-15*
   D. *The Affirmation of Jesus: vss. 16-17*

Introduction for Adults

Topic: *Declaring Identity*

Martin Koukal, a cross-country skier for the Czech Republic, was excited. Martin had the opportunity to represent his tiny country at the Winter Olympic Games in Nagano, Japan, in February 1998. As exciting as that was, it was nothing compared with the fact that he would get to meet one of the greatest hockey players in the world.

A hockey player himself since age 11, Martin had heard that the NHL players would be staying in the Olympic Village. That meant that he would get to meet one of his heroes and fellow countrymen, Jaromir Jagr, the Pittsburgh Penguins forward, and possibly get his autograph for himself and his little brother.

Martin Koukal is no different than your students. They tend to be attracted to unique persons, particularly celebrities. People were attracted to John the Baptizer, but he used his unique identity to point to a far more important individual—God's own Son! The Lord wants us to abandon our sin and turn to Him in faith.

Introduction for Youth

Topic: *Splitting the Heavens*

Often young people are attracted by strange figures whose dress and lifestyles drive their parents crazy. Probably, in A.D. 26, if your kids had gone to hear John the Baptizer, you would have been equally skeptical, for this man did not look or behave like the "respectable" establishment.

During the late 1960s, the Jesus people and the Jesus people movement swept across the United States. Thousands of long-haired youths, wearing dirty, torn jeans, responded to the simple Gospel of Jesus Christ, again confounding adults and church leaders. Today many of these converts serve the Lord in strategic Christian leadership positions, as well as in their professions.

What counts is not what people wear or eat, but whether their lives back up what they profess to believe. Young people need authentic leaders who refuse to go blindly along with the contemporary pagan culture, and who instead stand for truth and righteousness. John—who saw the heavens open and the Spirit descend on Jesus (Matt. 3:16)—was that kind of person.

Concepts for Children

Topic: *Taking on the Task*

1. Baptism was important to Jesus.
2. Jesus showed humility and obedience to God when He came to John for baptism.
3. John realized that Jesus was superior to him in every way.
4. The Father's voice from heaven said that Jesus was His Son.
5. God is pleased with us when we choose to live for Jesus.

Lesson Commentary

I. John Prepares the Way: Matthew 3:1-6

A. The Arrival of John: vss. 1-2

In those days John the Baptist came, preaching in the Desert of Judea and saying, "Repent, for the kingdom of heaven is near."

The name "John" (Matt. 3:1) means "the Lord is gracious." This name was given to John before he was born. It was linked to the message he would preach as an adult. He prophesied that the Father was sending the long-awaited Messiah, who would bring salvation to the lost. John began his preaching ministry in the desert of Judea. This is a hot and arid tract of land extending from the plateau of Jerusalem and Bethlehem east to the Jordan River and south to the Dead Sea.

John's message was forthright: "Repent, for the kingdom of heaven is near" (vs. 2). The Baptizer told people to do so because "the kingdom of heaven" was near. The Messiah's reign was about to begin, demanding a radical change in the behavior of those who hoped to be citizens of this new Kingdom. The Bible describes God's kingdom as being heavenly (2 Tim. 4:18), unshakable (Heb. 12:28), and eternal (2 Pet. 1:11).

The heavenly kingdom embraces all who walk in fellowship with the Lord and do His will. It is governed by God's laws, which are summed up in our duty to love the Lord supremely and love others as ourselves. Also, this kingdom, which was announced by the prophets and introduced by Jesus, will one day displace all the kingdoms of this world, following the return of the Messiah.

B. The Fulfillment of Prophecy: vs. 3

This is he who was spoken of through the prophet Isaiah: "A voice of one calling in the desert, 'Prepare the way for the Lord, make straight paths for him.'"

The Father chose John the Baptizer for an important task. He was to prepare the way for the advent of the Son, as foretold in Malachi 3:1 and Isaiah 40:3. Interestingly, Mark 1:2 states that both of these verses were penned by the prophet Isaiah. This is a circumstance in which the entire Old Testament is regarded as God's unified revelation. Also, because Isaiah serves as a gateway (of sorts) to the remainder of the prophetic writings, it was acceptable for an ancient writer such as Mark to begin his Old Testament quotes as he did.

As with Mark 3:2, Matthew 3:3 regarded John's appearance as a fulfillment of Isaiah 40:3-5. In Bible times, there were no superhighways. When an important dignitary was expected to travel through the country, a messenger would go out in advance to tell the people to prepare the way for the dignitary's arrival. This meant they had to improve roads by cutting down trees, leveling steep hills, and generally clearing away obstacles. Figuratively speaking, this represented the ministry of John the Baptizer. He was the Lord's messenger who prepared the hearts of people for the coming of the Messiah.

C. The Lifestyle of John: vs. 4

John's clothes were made of camel's hair, and he had a leather belt around his waist. His food was locusts and wild honey.

No person could miss John, for his clothing and his eating habits made him a standout. He wore a garment made of camel's hair, with a leather belt around his waist. He ate locusts and wild honey (Matt. 3:4). Insects were one of the few foods available in the desert, and they were considered clean to eat by Jewish law (see Lev. 11:21-22).

All of this was appropriate for a man of the desert. But John's lifestyle might also have served to denounce greed, self-indulgence, and pride. Moreover, it has been noted that John's lifestyle resembled that of Elijah, the desert prophet of Old Testament times who was to return in some way to Israel before the Messiah's arrival (see 2 Kings 1:8; Mal. 4:5). Like Elijah, the Baptizer demanded sincerity and repentance rather than hypocrisy and empty religious rituals. To be sure, John had a unique ministry. He was not the Messiah, as he freely told anyone who asked him (John 1:19-23). His job was to awaken people to their need for repentance, a message Jesus Himself would bring to them later (Matt. 4:17).

D. The Response of the Crowd: vss. 5-6

People went out to him from Jerusalem and all Judea and the whole region of the Jordan. Confessing their sins, they were baptized by him in the Jordan River.

John was not the kind of person one might expect to get the job of being the forerunner for the Messiah. As far as we know, John never served as a priest, even though he was born into a priestly family. Neither did he serve as a scribe, Pharisee, or Sadducee. Despite John's peculiarities, many people from Jerusalem and the surrounding districts flocked to hear him preach (Matt. 3:5), and John "baptized" (vs. 6) them in the Jordan River. The Greek verb *baptizo* means "to dip repeatedly," "to immerse," or "to submerge." The converts confessed, or acknowledged, their sins—an appropriate response to John's powerful message. Even today, when we put our trust in the Messiah, He enables us to come to terms with our sin.

John the Baptizer received his title from the ministry he practiced in the Jordan River. Baptism is a rite related to religious cleansing, and forms of the ritual are performed in many religions. It is not possible to determine with certainty when the practice of baptism began. Baptizing Gentile converts to Judaism (called "proselytes") occurred even before John's time. Also, many

Old Testament passages refer to ceremonial washings (Exod. 29:4; Lev. 14:8). Several prophets used the washing image to speak of inner cleansings (Isa. 1:16; Jer. 4:14; Ezek. 36:25; Zech. 13:1).

Some think that John learned the baptism ritual he performed from the Essenes of Qumran, an ascetic Jewish sect in Palestine that flourished during the time of Christ. The Essenes were separatists who emphasized ceremonial purity and devotion to the Mosaic law. The baptism of the Essenes was a daily practice, most likely performed to remove ritual uncleanness. The Essene rite also had strong end-time implications, for they devoted themselves to personal purity in preparation for the final cosmic war between God's chosen and the wicked.

John's baptism was not intended to be practiced every day. In addition, John baptized others in public, while the Essenes at Qumran self-administered their washings in private. What makes John's baptism unique was that he called candidates who desired to undergo the procedure to repent and be cleansed spiritually. Thus, his baptism was not just for the ceremonially unclean or for Gentiles. Instead, his rite was for everyone—whether Jew or Gentile—who repented. John's baptism was intended to prepare people for the coming of God's Anointed One. While John's baptism did not actually bestow forgiveness of sins, it signified that God had forgiven those who had repented.

II. JOHN BAPTIZES JESUS: MATTHEW 3:11-17

A. The Messiah as Judge: vss. 11-12

"I baptize you with water for repentance. But after me will come one who is more powerful than I, whose sandals I am not fit to carry. He will baptize you with the Holy Spirit and with fire. His winnowing fork is in his hand, and he will clear his threshing floor, gathering his wheat into the barn and burning up the chaff with unquenchable fire."

A large number of Jewish religious leaders, Pharisees and Sadducees, were among those who came to hear John. These men belonged to the two leading religious and political parties in Palestine. The Sadducees tended to be aristocrats with relatively liberal views on religion, while the Pharisees were mostly commoners who were strict about the law. The Sadducees did not believe in an afterlife or in divine intervention on the earth. Because of that, the Sadducees sought to enjoy their limited time on earth with fabulous homes and wealth. They had the most to lose from any threat to the nation that might come from the appearance of someone claiming to be the Messiah.

In the time of Jesus, there were about 6,000 Pharisees. They would be classed as a conservative, ritualistic party and were more popular with the people because of their anti-foreign attitude and high regard for the Scriptures. In the Sanhedrin (the supreme religious court of justice in that day), the Pharisees held a majority. They believed the oral law with its many interpretations and traditions to be just as binding as the Old Testament. They went to great lengths to perform all the prescribed religious duties and to keep themselves separated from everything that they considered unclean. Hypocrisy was their most notorious and persistent sin. The Pharisees believed in a future state and the resurrection of the dead. They also kept the messianic hope alive, though their concept of the Messiah tended to be erroneous.

When John spotted the members of the two groups, he called them all a "brood of vipers" (Matt. 3:7), that is, the offspring of poisonous snakes. What a way to talk to some of the most powerful people in the nation! But John knew they were hypocrites who led others astray. He also asked, "Who warned you to flee from the coming wrath?" The way these men left Jerusalem to find him evidently reminded John of the way vipers slither out of underbrush when they sense danger. While these men had heard about John's message of judgment and wanted to hear him for themselves, John knew they still felt smug about their standing with God. So he summoned them to prove the genuineness of their commitment to God by bringing forth the fruit of repentance (vs. 8).

The Baptizer declared that if the religious leaders wanted God's favor, being repentant and fruitful was the way to act, rather than to rely on their descent from Abraham (vs. 9). John undoubtedly shocked these men when he made it clear that a person's Jewish ancestry had no saving value. Probably pointing at stones lying by the riverbank, the Baptizer declared that if the Lord so desired, He could make children for Abraham from those stones. Returning briefly to his earlier imagery of fruit bearing, John said that trees that failed to bear good fruit were in imminent danger of being cut down and burned (vs. 10). Of course, what he meant was that any person—even religious experts—who did not repent and start behaving more righteously would be judged. What John said next made it clear who would do the judging.

John had been baptizing people with water as a sign that pointed to and confirmed their repentance. But another person was coming who was far mightier than John. This man was so great that John felt he was not worthy to remove this person's sandals, which was considered one of the most menial tasks in Jewish society at the time (vs. 11). The Messiah would baptize people, not with water, but with the "Holy Spirit" and "fire." Baptism with the Holy Spirit occurred at Pentecost and (according to many) continues to occur as people come to faith in the Lord. As for baptism with fire, John may have just been referring to judgment for the wicked, though he may also have been referring to a purifying effect on the righteous.

In any case, it was the judgment aspect of fire that John emphasized. He said that, in a figurative sense, the coming one (namely, Jesus; see Ps. 118:26; Dan. 7:13; 9:25-27; Mal. 3:1) held a winnowing fork in His hand. This was a tool similar to a pitchfork that was used to pick up grain. Thus, John compared the Messiah to a farmer at harvesttime who, after the grain has been threshed, stores the valuable wheat in his barn and burns up the useless chaff (Matt. 3:12). The chaff represents the unrepentant, while the wheat represents the righteous. The fire for the chaff was "unquenchable." John was saying that all who failed to repent would suffer eternal judgment.

B. The Arrival of Jesus: vs. 13

Then Jesus came from Galilee to the Jordan to be baptized by John.

John played a key role in the inauguration of the Redeemer's public ministry. Although John had foretold that the Messiah was coming, he was shocked when one day Jesus approached him at the Jordan and asked to be baptized (Matt. 3:13). John later said of that time, "I myself did not know [Jesus]" (John 1:31). Perhaps this indicates the two had not seen each other for years, or John may not have known Jesus was the Messiah until John saw the Spirit rest on Jesus like a dove. After Jesus' baptism, John humbly recognized that his ministry would decline even as Jesus' ministry increased (3:27-30). However, their ministries still paralleled each other, as they both suffered at the hands of the authorities and faced prison and death.

C. The Consent of John: vss. 14-15

But John tried to deter him, saying, "I need to be baptized by you, and do you come to me?" Jesus replied, "Let it be so now; it is proper for us to do this to fulfill all righteousness." Then John consented.

The Greek verb rendered "tried to deter" (Matt. 3:14) implies that John did all he could to prevent the baptism of Jesus from happening. John reasoned that it would be far more appropriate for him to be baptized by the Messiah, not the other way around. Jesus listened, but could not agree. He explained that by being baptized, He would "fulfill all righteousness" (vs. 15). This means that Jesus, though sinless, voluntarily conformed with all that God required of sinful people. With this visible display of solidarity, Jesus also showed that He is our genuine representative and intercessor with God. Moreover, Jesus, as the Suffering Servant, died on the cross as an atoning sacrifice for sin, in obedience to the divine will (see Isa. 42:1-4; 53:11). When John heard Jesus' explanation, he consented to baptize his Lord.

D. The Affirmation of Jesus: vss. 16-17

As soon as Jesus was baptized, he went up out of the water. At that moment heaven was opened, and he saw the Spirit of God descending like a dove and lighting on him. And a voice from heaven said, "This is my Son, whom I love; with him I am well pleased."

As Jesus emerged from the waters of the Jordan, He apparently spent a few moments in prayer (see Luke 3:21). Suddenly the heavens opened, and the Spirit descended in the form of a dove that settled on the Son (Matt. 3:16). This was an anointing experience, an equipping of Jesus for His ministry to come ahead. Then a voice from heaven said, "This is my Son, whom I love; with him I am well pleased" (vs. 17; see Ps. 2:7; Isa. 42:1). In this way the Father verbally gave His approval of Jesus so that all around could hear it. He declared that He took delight in His Son. Here we learn that both the Holy Spirit and the Father were together empowering and authenticating the Redeemer for His ministry and work.

Discussion Questions

1. Why did John the Baptizer proclaim a message of repentance?
2. Why did John dress in such an unusual manner?
3. Why did people confess their sins as they were being baptized by John?
4. Why did John sense the need to emphasize Jesus' superiority?
5. Why did John initially try to deter Jesus from being baptized?

Contemporary Application

The implication of John's ministry is that repentance calls for radical changes in one's life. Most believers know about the marvelous change in the apostle Paul's life when he became a follower of Jesus Christ, especially how Paul encountered the Lord on the road to Damascus, repented of his hatred and persecution of believers, and then preached love and forgiveness. Yet few know the story of Tetsuya (Tet) Tanaka.

Tet was a young Japanese soldier during World War II. He was a devout servant of the emperor and the Japanese military. He obeyed orders without question, even when he was commanded to nail boards to a Korean church so the worshipers could not flee through the doors and windows of the church. Nevertheless, when others set the church on fire, he could never forget the screams of people from within.

Shortly after the war, Tet heard an American missionary preach the Gospel. Tet wanted to put his faith in the Son, but he felt that because of what he had done, he was too sinful to receive God's forgiveness. Only after Tet fell on his knees before the missionary, who had become his friend, and repented openly before God, did Tet become a true believer.

Nevertheless, Tet still felt terribly remorseful for the crimes he had committed in Korea. Despite his inbred prejudices against the Korean people, Tet had to return to the site of the ravaged Korean church and ask for forgiveness from the relatives of the murdered people. It was then that he became a missionary among the Korean people and a devoted servant to their spiritual and physical needs.

Like Tet, we need the conviction of the Spirit to lead us to repent of the things we do that displease God. But more than that, we need to follow up on our convictions with changes in our lifestyles. Steps will differ according to what changes are needed, and God in His grace will be with us throughout the process.

Strengthened in Temptation

DEVOTIONAL READING
Hebrews 2:10-18

Scripture

Background Scripture: *Matthew 4:1-11*
Scripture Lesson: *Matthew 4:1-11*
Key Verse: *Jesus said to him, "Away from me, Satan! For it is written: 'Worship the Lord your God, and serve him only.'"* Matthew 4:10.
Scripture Lesson for Children: *Matthew 4:1-11*
Key Verse for Children: *"Worship the Lord your God, and serve him only."* Matthew 4:10.

Lesson Aim

To emphasize that temptations target our vulnerable areas.

Lesson Setting

Time: A.D. 26
Place: *Wilderness of Judea*

Lesson Outline

Strengthened in Temptation
I. The Son Trusts His Father's Provision: Matthew 4:1-4
    A. *The Setting: vss. 1-2*
    B. *The First Temptation: vss. 3-4*
II. The Son Trusts His Father's Protection and Plan: Matthew 4:5-11
    A. *The Second Temptation: vss. 5-7*
    B. *The Third Temptation: vss. 8-10*
    C. *The Attendance of Angels: vs. 11*

Introduction for Adults

Topic: *Facing Temptation*

Medical tests scare us and we worry and pray at the same time, hoping for negative results. Would it not do much to revive our souls and the life of our churches if we took spiritual tests with the same degree of seriousness?

Perhaps we are not as concerned about the health of our souls as we are about the health of our bodies. Jesus was terribly weakened in body during 40 days in the wilderness. Yet His primary concern was for the well-being of His soul and His obedience to His Father.

God brings us to places of moral and spiritual testing so we can grow stronger in faith and obedience. The key, of course, is to know how to pass the test.

Introduction for Youth

Topic: *Who Am I Anyway?*

When we think we won't have trouble with something, we often do. The resulting unpleasant experience can lead us to question our identity as Christians. We are able to regroup when we turn to the Lord for discernment concerning our areas of weakness and vulnerability. The goal is for us to experience victory when the devil attacks.

Being tempted is not wrong, but giving in is. The devil keeps after us, poking and probing our weak points. That's why we need God's wisdom and help. He knows our hearts and failings. His Word teaches us that through Jesus' indwelling presence and power, we can win.

We need close friends to talk with about our temptations and weaknesses. After all, everyone one of us needs support and encouragement. We can also learn from each other, for our temptation is usually similar to the enticements being experienced by other believers. Most of all, we need to walk closely with Jesus every day. Abiding in Him can keep us from falling into sin.

Concepts for Children

Topic: *Resisting Wrong*

1. Jesus' time of temptation followed the special moment of His baptism.
2. The devil tried to test Jesus' power and authority as God's Son.
3. Jesus was not fooled by the devil's use of Scripture.
4. Jesus turned to Scripture in His response to the devil's temptation.
5. Jesus wants us to use Scripture to resist temptations from the devil.

Lesson Commentary

I. THE SON TRUSTS HIS FATHER'S PROVISION: MATTHEW 4:1-4

A. The Setting: vss. 1-2

Then Jesus was led by the Spirit into the desert to be tempted by the devil. After fasting forty days and forty nights, he was hungry.

The temptation of Jesus draws attention to His unique status as the divine Messiah. He was now anointed with God's Spirit (Matt. 3:16), which signified the Son's inauguration into His public ministry (Acts 10:37-38). Matthew 4:1 and Luke 4:1 both say that the Holy Spirit led Jesus into the wilderness in order that the devil could tempt Him. Mark 1:12 literally says that the Spirit "thrust [Jesus] into the wilderness." One is left with the impression that this event occurred by divine necessity and in private (see Deut. 8:2). The Greek adjective rendered "desert" (Matt. 4:1) denotes an uninhabited region, though not necessarily a parched or arid locale (such as a desert). The identity of the specific area near the Jordan River to which this verse refers remains unknown.

At various times in Jesus' earthly life, He experienced events that paralleled important episodes in Israel's history. For instance, the nation, as God's "son" (Exod. 4:23), was led by Moses into the desert (15:22). Then, for the next four decades (see Deut. 1:3), the Lord tested His people as they wandered in the wilderness (Exod. 15:25; 16:4; 20:20; Deut. 8:2-5). Tragically, as Scripture reveals, that generation of Israelites failed the divine test, even though they enjoyed the provision of the Father (see Deut. 2:7; Neh. 9:21; Ps. 78:17-22) and the presence of the Spirit (see Neh. 9:20; Isa. 63:7-10). Their unbelief led them to transgress the Lord repeatedly (see Num. 14:33; 32:13; Ps. 95:10-11; Heb. 3:7-19). In contrast, Jesus, as the ideal Israelite and representative of the human race, not only endured real testing, but also triumphed over it in the power of the Spirit.

The "devil" (Matt. 4:1; see Luke 4:2) was the entity who harassed Jesus. "Devil" (Matt. 4:1) renders the Greek adjective *diabolos*, which means "slanderer" or "false accuser." Mark 1:13 refers to Jesus' nemesis as "Satan." The latter renders a noun that literally means "adversary." Both the names "devil" (Matt. 4:1; Luke 4:2) and "Satan" (Mark 1:13) refer to a preeminent and powerful rogue angel. Sometime before God created human beings, the devil rebelled against the Creator and became the archenemy of God and humanity. Scripture reveals that Satan is a murderer, liar, and the "father of lies" (John 8:44); the one who "leads the whole world astray" (Rev 12:9); and "the ruler of the kingdom of the air" (Eph. 2:2) at work in the hearts of those who refuse to obey God.

The prince of demons wanted to draw away the Son from obeying the Father's will. In particular, the devil "tempted" (Matt. 4:1) Jesus throughout and (especially) toward the end of His sojourn in the wilderness. Depending on the context, the Greek verb behind the NIV translation can mean either "to test" or "to entice to sin." As the representative for sinful humanity, Jesus had to endure real temptation and triumph over it. Verse 2 states that during Jesus' time in the wilderness, He fasted "forty days and forty nights," which in turn left Him famished. Therefore, when the devil launched his final attacks, the Savior was at a disadvantage. As we know from our own experience, temptation, anxiety, and worry tend to threaten most powerfully during our moments of physical exhaustion. Despite the devil's repeated efforts, he failed to lure the Son to transgress against the Father. As a result of this encounter, the Messiah proved that He is the Father's loyal and beloved Son (see 3:17).

"Forty" (4:2) is a number to which some scholars assign sacred significance. Various Old Testament luminaries also had life-shaping experiences that lasted 40 days, including Moses (Exod. 34:28; Deut. 9:9, 18), David (1 Sam. 17:16), and Elijah (1 Kings 19:8). The temptation episode is a reminder that the Son, as the "author and perfecter of our faith" (Heb 12:2), inaugurated a new exodus to provide redemption for the people of God (see 1 Cor. 10:1-5). Jesus, of course, is not simply a new Moses. More importantly, the Son, as the divine Messiah, utterly transcends Israel's lawgiver as well as all other prominent individuals in the Old Testament (see Heb. 3:1-7). Indeed, the Son alone is the Father's ultimate revelation to humankind (see John 1:18; 14:9; Heb. 1:1-3).

B. The First Temptation: vss. 3-4

The tempter came to him and said, "If you are the Son of God, tell these stones to become bread." Jesus answered, "It is written: 'Man does not live on bread alone, but on every word that comes from the mouth of God.'"

Some claim that evils spirits, such as the "tempter" (Matt. 4:3), are helpful beings from other planes of existence who have come to aid people on their evolutionary journey to enlightenment. Others have said that demons are the personification of an innate intelligence within humankind. Still others call Satan and his devilish cohort hallucinations of our unconscious minds that are maintained in thought and action. In contrast to these incorrect notions is the clear teaching of Scripture. From it we learn that demons are any of the angels of God's creation who chose to side with Satan in his rebellion against the Lord.

These spirits are real, supernatural beings who strive to deceive people, thwart the will of God, and undermine the work of the church (1 Cor. 10:20-21; 1 Tim. 4:1; Jas. 2:19; Rev. 9:20; 16:14). Because of Jesus' atoning sacrifice, Satan and his demonic cadre are defeated foes (Luke 10:17-18; John 12:31; 16:11; Col. 2:15; Heb. 2:14) awaiting certain doom (Matt. 25:41; 2 Pet. 2:4; Jude 6; Rev. 20:10). At the end of the age, demons will be forced to bow to the lordship of

Christ (Matt. 22:44; Phil. 2:10).

This fate is well deserved, especially when we learn about the diabolical way in which the evil one operates. Consider Satan's first attempt to entice Jesus to sin. The "tempter" (Matt. 4:3) said that since Jesus is the "Son of God," He should turn some of the stones that were lying about into bread. "Son of God" is a messianic title that the New Testament writers applied to the Lord Jesus (see Rom. 1:4; Rev. 2:18). The phrase emphasizes the special and intimate relationship that exists between the first and second persons of the Trinity (see Matt 16:16; Luke 1:35).

Jesus, as the divine Son, reveals the Father to humankind by perfectly fulfilling His plan of redemption. Hebrews 1:5 and 5:5 quote Psalm 2:7 in connection with the Messiah being the Son of God. Most likely, the Israelites applied this verse to the descendants of David, whom they crowned king. However, Psalm 2:7 ultimately refers to the Savior. This is made clear in Acts 13:33. When the Father raised the Son from the dead, the Father conferred great dignity on Him by declaring Him to be His Son (something that had been true of Jesus for all eternity). Jesus' divinity is another emphasis implicit in the phrase "Son of God" (Matt. 4:3). It indicates that Jesus is to be identified with the Father and considered fully and absolutely equal to Him (see John 5:18; 10:30, 36).

Jesus, while in the wilderness, could have used some bread after a 40-day fast, just as the Israelites needed manna to sustain them in the wilderness (Exod. 16:13-36). But it would have been wrong for the divine Messiah to utilize His power for a purely selfish purpose. His power was meant for His redemptive ministry. The devil was probably attempting to get the Son to show distrust in His Father's provision. The Father had designed the fast for His Son and would provide for Him at the proper time. Satan, however, wanted the Son to rebel by taking matters into His own hands. Rather than yield to the tempter's suggestion, Jesus quoted Deuteronomy 8:3. This verse teaches that people live not only by consuming food. They also need to take in God's Word for spiritual nourishment (Matt 4:4). Jesus could do without bread, but He could not do without obedience to God (see Luke 4:3-4).

The relationship between temptations and testing is very close. The section of Deuteronomy 8 that Jesus quoted to Satan deals with the Israelites and the test that the Lord put them through in the wilderness. Moses told the Hebrew people that "God led you all the way in the desert these forty years, to humble you and to test you in order to know what was in your heart, whether or not you would keep his commands" (vs. 2). By feeding the people manna, God saved them from starvation and made them dependent on Him for food, so that they would learn that His followers must depend on Him to meet all their needs (vs. 3). Like the Hebrews, Jesus faced the temptations in the wilderness, but unlike those who refused to enter the promised land (see Num. 13—14), the Son passed His test and remained faithful to the Father.

157

II. THE SON TRUSTS HIS FATHER'S PROTECTION AND PLAN: MATTHEW 4:5-11

A. The Second Temptation: vss. 5-7

Then the devil took him to the holy city and had him stand on the highest point of the temple. "If you are the Son of God," he said, "throw yourself down. For it is written: "'He will command his angels concerning you, and they will lift you up in their hands, so that you will not strike your foot against a stone.'" Jesus answered him, "It is also written: 'Do not put the Lord your God to the test.'"

The devil next escorted Jesus to Jerusalem and positioned Him on the "highest point of the temple" (Matt. 4:5). In all likelihood, this was the southeastern portion of the shrine complex, where there was a steep drop-off to the Kidron Valley over 100 feet below. The tempter invited Jesus to prove in a spectacular way that He was God the Son. Supposedly, He could throw Himself down from the apex of the shrine and trust the Father to protect Him (vs. 6). A common interpretation of Malachi 3:1 held that the Messiah would appear in the sky, descend to the temple, and proclaim deliverance. Apparently, Satan wanted Jesus to combine such an appearance with a sensational descent, complete with angels, to win popular approval for His kingdom.

The tempter cleverly misquoted Psalm 91:11-12 by leaving out the phrase "to guard you in all your ways." This passage teaches that God provides His angels to watch over His people when they live in accordance with His will (see Exod. 19:4-5; Deut. 32:10-11). Satan claimed that the Father would protect the Son as He plummeted to the ground. But since such a stunt would not be within the will of God, the promise of divine protection would not apply.

Rather than yield to the devil's suggestion, Jesus quoted from Deuteronomy 6:16, saying, "Do not put the Lord your God to the test" (Matt 4:7; see Luke 4:9-12). We humans cannot dictate the terms of divine intervention by arranging situations of need. This would be foolish presumption, an attempt to deny the mutual accountability and responsibility woven into our personal relationship with God. Yet, He freely grants what we need in order to grow in Him.

B. The Third Temptation: vss. 8-10

Again, the devil took him to a very high mountain and showed him all the kingdoms of the world and their splendor. "All this I will give you," he said, "if you will bow down and worship me." Jesus said to him, "Away from me, Satan! For it is written: 'Worship the Lord your God, and serve him only.'"

In the third and final temptation, Satan transported Jesus to a "very high mountain" (Matt. 4:8). In a moment of time, the devil paraded before the Son all the nations of the world and their glory, promising them to Him if He would fall before the tempter in "worship" (vs. 9). Through the Messiah's death and resurrection, the Father intended to free the world from the oppressive control of Satan (see Heb 2:14-15) and give the Son the nations throughout the earth as His rightful inheritance (Ps. 2:8). Therefore, rather than oblige His tempter, Jesus commanded, "Away from me, Satan!" (Matt 4:10). There was good reason for this command. It stands written in Deuteronomy 6:13 and 10:20 that worship and service are to be given only to God. In the midst of temptation, Jesus showed an unwavering commitment to do the will of the Father (see Luke 4:5-8).

Many who have studied the temptations have wondered whether Satan actually took Jesus to the pinnacle of the Jerusalem temple and to a high mountaintop, or if the devil presented those situations to Jesus in a vision. After all, no mountain is high enough to literally view "all the kingdoms of the world" (Matt. 4:8) at once. Could the evil one actually force the Messiah to go to the shrine or the mountain, or did Satan cause Jesus to visualize the situations supernaturally?

Some object that the temptations could not have been real if Jesus was not actually taken to the temple and the mountain. Others argue, however, that the prophet Ezekiel and the apostle John were taken places through visions and that what happened was quite real to them. Another noteworthy example was the apostle Paul, who was not sure at times whether his visions were "in the body or out of the body" (2 Cor. 12:2). If Jesus' temptations did take place through a supernatural vision, we can be sure that they were real to Him, as if He were actually there.

C. The Attendance of Angels: vs. 11

Then the devil left him, and angels came and attended him.

When the devil had completed every temptation, he departed from the Lord (Matt 4:11). Even so, when the next opportunity came, Satan would tempt Jesus again (Luke 4:13). Matthew 4:11 notes that angels came and attended to Jesus' needs (possibly throughout His 40-day sojourn; see Mark 1:13). We are not told how they ministered to the Savior, but it is safe to assume that they brought nourishment as well as encouragement. Previously, angels offered care and support to the Israelites during their wanderings in the wilderness (see Exod. 14:19; 23:20, 23; 32:34; 33:2) and food to Elijah when he fled to Horeb for safety from Ahab (see 1 Kings 19:3-8).

Mark 1:13 says that during the Messiah's sojourn in the wilderness, He was out among the wild animals. In the Savior's day, far more wild animals roamed the countryside than today, including lions that prowled the wooded areas along the Jordan River (Jer. 5:6; 49:19). The mention of wild beasts adds drama to Jesus' confronting evil. Another reason for mentioning these creatures is that Mark possibly wanted to emphasize the divine protection Jesus received in the midst of the danger He faced.

A third reason for mentioning wild animals may be that untamed beasts were associated with evil powers. The historical episode, in a sense, became a symbol of the cosmic struggle of good and evil in which the Son was engaged. Likewise, the wild beasts might be connected to the hope of the messianic era, when animal enemies such as the wolf and the lamb will live in peace (see Isa. 11:6-9; 32:14-20; 65:25; Hos. 2:18).

A fourth reason might come from Mark's audience. If Mark was writing his Gospel for Gentile Christians about A.D. 64–67, particularly those in Rome (see 1 Pet. 5:13), they would be facing persecutions from Nero that often included being thrown to the lions for refusing to worship the emperor. The early Christians could take comfort in the fact that Jesus, too, had confronted wild animals.

Discussion Questions

1. Why did the Spirit lead Jesus out into the wilderness?
2. Why do you think Satan targeted Jesus when He was very hungry?
3. What is significant about the three temptations Jesus experienced?
4. Why did Jesus refuse to give in to these temptations?
5. What did Jesus prove about Himself by resisting the attacks of the devil?

Contemporary Application

Hardly a day passes that we are not tempted to violate God's will and sin. Yet, for the most part, the world makes fun of those who take temptation seriously and try to resist it. The powerful lie of popular culture is that yielding (in other words, not resisting) is the best way to have fun. In contrast, if the church takes Jesus seriously, we must also take temptation seriously. We cannot pretend to be His followers and take no thought about protecting ourselves from the devil.

Often, the evil one outsmarts us because we can't see the traps he lays for us. Some of us get so accustomed to following the world's values that we don't realize we have sold out to Satan. We follow whatever seems to be the popular thing to do, regardless of whether it is God's will.

To successfully combat the devil's strategy, we need to abide in Jesus and heed His teachings. After all, He relied on Scripture to withstand the assaults of Satan, and so do we. Indeed, every moment invested in Bible study and prayer will return huge dividends for us as we experience spiritual victory in our lives.

We also need to remember that temptations in themselves are powerless. The devil cannot make us do anything. As with the case with Job, Satan can come against us in many ways, yet God sets the limits in which the evil one can operate. We never lose the power to choose between right and wrong. Even though these trials can ensnare us, the Father offers victory through the power of the risen Son.

Acts of Healing

Scripture

Background Scripture: *Matthew 9:27-34; 11:2-6*
Scripture Lesson: *Matthew 9:27-34; 11:2-6*
Key Verse: *"The blind receive sight, the lame walk, those who have leprosy are cured, the deaf hear, the dead are raised, and the good news is preached to the poor."* Matthew 11:5.
Scripture Lesson for Children: *Matthew 9:27-34*
Key Verse for Children: *The crowd was amazed and said, "Nothing like this has ever been seen in Israel."* Matthew 9:33.

Lesson Aim

To note that Jesus' compassion reaches out to human hurts.

Lesson Setting

Time: A.D. *28*
Place: *Capernaum and other towns of Galilee*

Lesson Outline

Acts of Healing
  I. Healing the Blind and Mute: Matthew 9:27-34
    A. *The Blind Men's Request: vss. 27-28*
    B. *The Messiah's Healing Touch: vss. 29-31*
    C. *The Expulsion of a Demon: vss. 32-34*
  II. Responding to John the Baptizer: Matthew 11:2-6
    A. *The Baptizer's Question: vss. 2-3*
    B. *The Messiah's Reply: vss. 4-6*

Introduction for Adults

Topic: *Works of Healing*

Sickness and death confront us on every hand. Even though we try to hide the realities, we cannot escape them. The battle against aging, disease, and death occupies our greatest minds and consumes vast resources. In fact, experts project that U.S. health care spending will reach 4.2 trillion dollars in 2016, or 20 percent of the nation's Gross Domestic Product (GDP).

Jesus constantly encountered people who were sick, blind, crippled, and dying. He did not dodge them but went out of His way to help them. Since then, His followers have done likewise. Filled with compassion as He was, they have been at the forefront in ministries of healing and caring.

Jesus invites us not only to be made whole by Him, but also to reach out to others in need with tangible acts of kindness. Jesus heals today. Indeed, He touches people through believers who demonstrate His compassion, love, and power.

Introduction for Youth

Topic: *Yes, Lord*

Jesus loves to say "yes" to our prayer requests. This includes petitions to heal. That's the good news we must spread among teenagers. Many of them have painful hurts—not always because of their own misdeeds, but also due to the misdeeds of others, including their own parents.

Adolescents need to know that Jesus can heal one's body, soul, and spirit. He brings wholeness to those who seek Him. He responds to rugged faith, no matter how desperate our needs. No one's case is beyond the love and help of Jesus.

Our greatest task is to keep Jesus at the center of our appeal to youth—not rules, dogma, or religious organizations. We have to jettison all the arguments and tangents, so that young people will be brought face-to-face with the Savior.

Concepts for Children

Topic: *Healing People*

1. The two blind men did not give up in asking Jesus for help.
2. Jesus asked the two whether they believed He could heal them.
3. The opening of the men's eyes to sight proved they were correct in trusting Jesus.
4. The crowds were amazed that Jesus could heal the man who was unable to speak.
5. Jesus wants us to bring all our needs to Him in prayer.

Lesson Commentary

I. HEALING THE BLIND AND MUTE: MATTHEW 9:27-34

A. The Blind Men's Request: vss. 27-28

As Jesus went on from there, two blind men followed him, calling out, "Have mercy on us, Son of David!" When he had gone indoors, the blind men came to him, and he asked them, "Do you believe that I am able to do this?" "Yes, Lord," they replied.

Matthew 9 opens with Jesus returning to Capernaum and healing a paralyzed man (vss. 1-8). Capernaum was the home of some of Jesus' disciples and served as the Lord's headquarters during a large portion of His public ministry. It was a fishing village built on the northwest shore of the Sea of Galilee. Capernaum hosted a Roman garrison that maintained peace in the region. Major highways crisscrossed at Capernaum, making it militarily strategic. Because of its fishing and trading industries, the city was something of a melting pot of Greek, Roman, and Jewish cultures. Visitors to the site today can see the remains of an early Christian church believed to have been constructed on the site of Peter's home.

After healing the paralytic, Jesus continued to establish His core group of disciples by calling Matthew, a tax collector (vss. 9-13). Then some of John the Baptizer's followers questioned Jesus about the failure of His disciples to fast. Jesus revealed that, as the Messiah, He was not going to fit into the unyielding legalistic traditions of the religious elite of His day (vss. 14-17). Next, a synagogue ruler named Jairus approached Jesus and asked Him to raise the religious leader's daughter from the dead. Along the way, Jesus healed a woman who had trouble with hemorrhaging for 12 years. When Jesus arrived at the home of Jairus, the Savior brought the deceased girl back to life (vss. 18-26).

The previous mentioned episodes remind us that during Jesus' earthly ministry, He was surrounded by people who clamored for His attention almost constantly, except perhaps when He withdrew for times of prayer before daybreak. The Messiah was subjected to pressures, experienced fatigue and stress, and was the target of critics. The latter accused Jesus of speaking and acting in a sacrilegious manner toward God (vs. 3), of associating with morally questionable people (vs. 11), and of disregarding humanly-devised rites and rituals (vs. 14). Despite these challenges, Jesus never became irritable when people crowded around Him and pleaded for some kind of help.

No person in history was ever confronted with the number or size of human demands as was Jesus. Other public figures were known to lose their cool and snap at those around them, but not the Son. His patience and compassion toward the hurting and helpless knew no limits. Matthew and the other Gospel writers gave examples of the patience and compassion that Jesus demonstrated through His healings. These miracles were never stunts. In fact, Jesus seemed to go out of His way to avoid being sensational or making a great spectacle out of the people whom

He healed. The miracles were acts of kindness and revealed that the power of God was manifesting itself in the world through Jesus, the Messiah.

A case in point would be the incident recorded in verses 27 through 31. As Jesus continued on His journey, two blind men followed Him (presumably trailing behind the entourage of disciples), shouting loudly. "Son of David" (Matt. 9:27) was a common expression among the Jews of that era that referred to the promised Messiah of Israel (see 12:23; 21:9; 22:42). "Have mercy" (vs. 27) renders a Greek verb that refers to showing compassion or pity on someone. With respect to the two blind men, they were entreating Jesus to give them their sight. The pair seemed to realize that they did not deserve to be healed and that the granting of their request would be a display of God's grace.

After Jesus had entered a house (providing some privacy away from the crowds), the blind men approached Him, possibly with the assistance of others. Following Jesus indoors was a noteworthy display of faith. Perhaps to encourage their faith, Jesus asked them, "Do you believe that I am able to do this?" (vs. 28). Both men affirmed their confidence in His ability to give them their sight. This exchange brings to mind Hebrews 11:1, which reveals that faith is a present and continuing reality. Specifically, it is the confident assurance that gives substance to what we "hope for." Faith is also the evidence for our conviction of the certainty of "what we do not see." More generally, faith refers to a person's trust in God. In another sense, it is used in the New Testament to refer to the body of truths held by Jesus' followers.

During Jesus' public ministry, it was not official Judaism that accepted His messianic claims, but the outcasts of society. Consider the episode in the Fourth Gospel regarding how Jesus healed a man on the Sabbath who had been born blind (John 9:1-7, 13-16). The controversial healing gave Jesus the opportunity to talk about spiritual blindness (vss. 39-41). Theologically speaking, we are all born blind on a spiritual level and only Jesus can give us sight. We will not be able to see the truth until we come to Jesus in faith and allow Him to regenerate us. In the same way that the blind men came to Jesus, we must believe that He is the divine Messiah and that He is able to heal our spiritual blindness.

B. The Messiah's Healing Touch: vss. 29-31

Then he touched their eyes and said, "According to your faith will it be done to you"; and their sight was restored. Jesus warned them sternly, "See that no one knows about this." But they went out and spread the news about him all over that region.

"Faith" (Matt. 9:29) can be understood as having four recognizable elements. First is cognition, an awareness of the facts; second is comprehension, an understanding of the facts; third is conviction, an acceptance of the facts; and fourth is commitment, trust in a trustworthy object. Popular opinion sees faith as irrational. It is supposedly believing in something even when your mind tells you not to. In contrast, the biblical concept of faith includes both reason and experience. Such faith, however, is not limited to what we can see. It makes unseen spiritual realities perceivable, not by willing them into existence, but by a settled conviction that what God has said about them is true.

Jesus touched the eyes of the two blind men and said they would be helped because they had chosen to believe in Him (Matt. 9:29). They had trusted in the Redeemer to give them sight, and that is exactly what happened: "Their sight was restored" (vs. 30). Jesus' messianic claims and authority were further confirmed by this miracle. This in-breaking of the Father through the Son was done out of compassion for suffering persons and without fanfare, though eyewitnesses undoubtedly were astounded.

Why did Jesus command the men not to tell anyone what had happened? The Savior insisted on this with good reason. Instead of being regarded as just a miracle worker, Jesus wanted people to listen to His claims and accept His spiritual healing. He also wanted to avoid precipitating a crisis with the religious leaders before His earthly ministry was fulfilled. But despite Jesus' instructions, the two formerly blind men traveled throughout the region of Galilee spreading the news of what He had done (vs. 31).

C. The Expulsion of a Demon: vss. 32-34

While they were going out, a man who was demon-possessed and could not talk was brought to Jesus. And when the demon was driven out, the man who had been mute spoke. The crowd was amazed and said, "Nothing like this has ever been seen in Israel." But the Pharisees said, "It is by the prince of demons that he drives out demons."

As Jesus and His followers began to leave the house, a demon-possessed man who could not speak was brought to Him (Matt. 9:32). After Jesus drove out the demon, the man was able to talk. This miracle so astonished the crowd that they exclaimed, "Nothing like this has ever been seen in Israel" (vs. 33). The people could see that Jesus had amazing power and authority. However, some Pharisees in the crowd did not attribute the Messiah's power to God. Instead, they cynically asserted that Jesus drove out demons "by the prince of demons" (vs. 34; see also 12:22-29). The religious leaders believed Jesus used Satan's power to perform His miracles. This clearly was a slanderous comment to make against the Son of God.

In a later episode involving the religious leaders of Jerusalem, they alleged that Jesus was a "Samaritan" (John 8:48) and demon-possessed. The Savior's antagonists might have used the first contemptuous statement to insinuate either that He was a foreigner to the covenant promises (see Eph. 2:12) or of illegitimate parentage (see John 6:41). Another possibility is that the dual remarks alleged Jesus to be not only a heretic but also insane. In any case, the Messiah only responded to the second charge.

After denying that He was demon-possessed, the Son declared that He honored His Father and that His opponents dishonored Him (8:49). Jesus could make the first claim because what He said and did represented God's will. In terms of the second claim, Jesus' critics, by slandering Him through their erroneous accusations, were guilty of blasphemy, for He is God the Son. Despite the sarcastic remarks of His antagonists, Jesus' agenda did not include self-promotion. He did not need to get praise for Himself, for His heavenly Father would glorify Him through His resurrection from the dead (see 17:5). The Father in turn would judge those who spoke derisively about His Son (8:50).

II. Responding to John the Baptizer: Matthew 11:2-6

A. The Baptizer's Question: vss. 2-3

When John heard in prison what Christ was doing, he sent his disciples to ask him, "Are you the one who was to come, or should we expect someone else?"

After Jesus expelled the demon from the mute (Matt. 9:32-34), the Savior traveled widely, preaching and healing as He went. He had compassion for the people, for they needed spiritual leadership. He instructed His disciples to pray for more spiritual harvesters (vss. 35-38). An examination of chapter 10 indicates that Jesus did not operate alone. He chose and empowered 12 disciples, or followers, to proclaim the Gospel. As they ministered to people, these disciples were to remain dependent on Jesus and be prepared for a variety of responses to their message. Jesus warned His followers about the possibility of severe persecution, encouraging them not to feel fearful when it happened. In the time of testing, the disciples were to acknowledge their total allegiance to the Son and remain unwavering in their devotion to Him. They could do so, knowing that the Father would eternally reward them.

After Jesus had finished instructing the Twelve, He went off to teach and preach in the towns of Galilee (11:1). Verse 2 makes reference to John the Baptizer being imprisoned (see 4:12). The reason for this is given in 14:3-5. The wilderness prophet had run afoul of Herod Antipas because his bold moral pronouncements got a little too personal for Herod's taste. When Herod the Great died, his kingdom was divided among four of his seven sons, including Antipas. Herod Antipas was given control of Galilee and Perea, and he ruled these regions from 4 B.C. to A.D. 39. His career thus coincided with the lives and ministries of John the Baptizer and Jesus, and the realm of Antipas's authority included the areas these two men most often frequented.

John condemned Antipas for marrying Herodias, whom the tetrarch took from his brother Philip. (The word "tetrarch" designated the ruler of a fourth part of a region.) Herodias happened to be Herod's niece as well as his sister-in-law. John correctly identified this action as immoral, for the law of Moses barred a man from marrying the wife of his living brother (see Lev. 18:16; 20:21). Nonetheless, as a result of this condemnation, Herod had John arrested, bound, and thrown into jail (Matt. 14:3-4). The Jewish historian Josephus said John was imprisoned in the fortress at Machaerus, which was located in Perea not far from the Dead Sea.

Herod did not want to stop at imprisoning John. Antipas also wanted to kill the prophet. Herodias, too, held a grudge against John and wanted to see him executed (see Mark 6:19). But Antipas stopped short of ordering the execution because he feared the hostility of the crowds, who considered John a prophet (Matt. 14:5). Antipas's decision was apparently a bone of contention between him and his wife.

While John was languishing in prison (11:2), he might have expected Jesus to declare Himself the Messiah, claim David's throne, and deliver the Jews out of Roman oppression. Perhaps when John heard about Jesus' deeds, the reports surprised the Baptizer because those deeds were miraculous healings and not demonstrations of God's judgment against Israel's enemies. Perhaps this is why John sent two of his disciples to ask Jesus whether He was the Messiah (vs. 3). Since John's doubts probably arose from incorrect expectations and not because of a lack of faith, he possibly was going through a time of depression as the prophet Elijah had done when he fled to Beersheba (see 1 Kings 19:3-4). Thus, John needed reassurance. One school of thought suggests that John asked his question (recorded in Matthew 11:3) for the sake of his disciples. But the context of his query indicates that his concern was personal. John clearly wanted to know whether Jesus was the Messiah.

B. The Messiah's Reply: vss. 4-6

Jesus replied, "Go back and report to John what you hear and see: The blind receive sight, the lame walk, those who have leprosy are cured, the deaf hear, the dead are raised, and the good news is preached to the poor. Blessed is the man who does not fall away on account of me."

Jesus responded to John's doubts by summarizing His ministry in the language of Isaiah (Matt. 11:4). Bystanders saw the Messiah give sight to the blind, enable the cripple to walk, cure lepers of their skin disease, give the deaf the ability to hear, and restore the dead to life. These miracles were accompanied by the proclamation of the "good news" (vs. 5) to the impoverished. Jesus' response is a paraphrase of numerous Old Testament passages that described the promised time of salvation (for example, Isa. 26:19; 29:18-19; 35:5-6; 42:7, 18; 61:1). In short, Jesus was telling John that what He did and said harmonized with what was prophesied in the Old Testament about the Messiah.

The Greek verb translated "fall away" (Matt. 11:6) can also be rendered "stumble" or "take offense." In this verse, Jesus was saying that those who accepted, rather than rejected, His messianic claims were "blessed" by God. The underlying Greek adjective conveys the idea of being the privileged recipient of the Lord's favor (see 5:3-11). The implication is that John's personal struggle with doubts was not sin. After several months in prison, the Baptizer understandably had questions about the nature of Jesus' ministry. John did not wallow in doubts, but made an effort to resolve them. By doing so, John received an answer (and affirmation) from Jesus that must have encouraged the Baptizer. Jesus, by describing His ministry in terms of Isaiah's prophecy, said in effect to John, "Yes, My cousin, I am the one for whom you have been preparing others so faithfully." John and his disciples were not to expect another. The Anointed One of God had come, even though He was not living up to their expectations. Thus, they were not to be ensnared by doubt concerning Jesus, but rather accept Him as the Messiah.

Discussion Questions

1. What were the two blind men affirming about Jesus when they referred to Him as the "Son of David" (Matt. 9:27)?
2. Why do you think Jesus asked the blind men whether they believed He could heal them?
3. Why would the Pharisees accuse Jesus of operating in the power of Satan to expel demons?
4. What sorts of Old Testament messianic prophecies did Jesus' actions and words fulfill?
5. Why do you think Jesus chose not to publicly rebuke John for his doubts?

Contemporary Application

Jaded, technologically-equipped people respond to accounts about Jesus' healings with a yawn, and go about their business as usual. They rarely stop to examine the implications of what Jesus did. However, when God interrupts their plans, they start looking for answers.

Jesus raised the dead, healed the sick, cured the blind, and cast out demons. He also taught people what it means to become a child of God and enter His kingdom. Those are the truths recorded in the Gospels accepted by Christians.

Nonetheless, in contemporary culture, believers often must first establish their credentials as trustworthy, loving friends. Many people aren't ready to hear about Jesus until they first see some compassion. They seek acceptance from His followers, who confess they also are vulnerable to sickness and death.

No one escapes what is common to all people. But when we cast our lot with Jesus, we find hope, strength, peace, and healing. Even when believers go through the proverbial valleys of affliction, they do not journey alone. Jesus is always with them to give comfort and strength. That is the same experience they can share with those who do not know the Savior.

Declared in Prayer

DEVOTIONAL READING

John 11:38-44

DAILY BIBLE READINGS

Monday January 18
John 11:38-44 A Listening Father

Tuesday January 19
Matthew 6:5-8 Whenever You Pray

Wednesday January 20
Matthew 14:22-33 Praying Alone

Thursday January 21
Matthew 19:13-15 Prayer and Blessing on Children

Friday January 22
Matthew 5:43-48 Pray for Your Persecutors

Saturday January 23
Matthew 21:18-22 Prayer and Faith

Sunday January 24
Matthew 11:25-30 The Father's Gracious Will

Scripture

Background Scripture: *Matthew 11:25-30*
Scripture Lesson: *Matthew 11:25-30*
Key Verse: *"Come to me, all you who are weary and burdened, and I will give you rest."* Matthew 11:28.
Scripture Lesson for Children: *Matthew 11:25-30*
Key Verse for Children: *"Jesus said, "I praise you, Father, Lord of heaven and earth."* Matthew 11:25.

Lesson Aim

To learn that Jesus cares enough about believers to offer them eternal peace and rest.

Lesson Setting

Time: A.D. *28*
Place: *Galilee*

Lesson Outline

Declared in Prayer

I. The Father Revealed in the Son: Matthew 11:25-27
   A. *The Son Praises the Father: vss. 25-26*
   B. *The Son's Relationship with the Father: vs. 27*

II. The Invitation of the Son to Humanity: Matthew 11:28-30
   A. *The Son's Offer of Rest: vs. 28*
   B. *The Son's Assurance of Rest: vss. 29-30*

Introduction for Adults

Topic: *Inviting the Weary*

To approach God boldly is not to approach Him flippantly. Some people are so casual with God that they take His name in vain. In contrast, some people are so unfamiliar with God that they find it hard to pray to Him. They might not even try, despite the fact that their soul is weary from all their spiritual burdens.

Christians enjoy confidence before the Father because they know the Son has opened the door to fellowship with Him. God is holy; yet He gave His Son to save us from judgment and death. The only way we can approach the Father without fear is through His Son. In fact, no one comes to the Father except through His Son (John 14:6).

We can pray and worship with boldness because Jesus sits at the Father's right hand. The Son, who is the source of our eternal rest, intercedes for us as our merciful and faithful High Priest. Because He is our heavenly representative, we are freed to worship God with joy and invite others to do the same.

Introduction for Youth

Topic: *I Don't Get It!*

Brian's case was fairly typical. His parents divorced and he lived with his dad, who had a hard time building a good relationship with him. Brian got into trouble at school. He developed emotional problems and was hospitalized. To put it simply, Brian could not fill the vacuum in his life caused by a broken family.

Many adolescents rightly claim, "I can't figure out who *really* cares for me." They lack strong family ties. They don't have any good friends. They wander fruitlessly from one activity to another and often get into deep trouble.

Without sounding sanctimonious, we should try to introduce teens like Brian to Jesus. In order to do so, we must enjoy a valid faith ourselves. We must be able to explain how Jesus makes a difference, even when no one else seems to care.

Concepts for Children

Topic: *Giving Thanks*

1. Jesus' prayer was one of thanksgiving to God.
2. Jesus was joyful that great truths were being shown to His followers.
3. Jesus expressed His desire to tell God's truths to those who wanted to receive them.
4. Learning from Jesus brings us rest from weariness and heaviness.
5. When we share the good news about Jesus with others, they, too, can find rest in Him.

Lesson Commentary

I. THE FATHER REVEALED IN THE SON: MATTHEW 11:25-27

A. The Son Praises the Father: vss. 25-26

At that time Jesus said, "I praise you, Father, Lord of heaven and earth, because you have hidden these things from the wise and learned, and revealed them to little children. Yes, Father, for this was your good pleasure."

Last week we learned that while John the Baptizer was in prison, he sent some of his followers to ask Jesus whether He was the Messiah. In turn, Jesus affirmed His identity to them (Matt. 11:1-6). After they left, Jesus declared to a crowd that John was a great servant of God who had prepared the way for the Redeemer's advent (vss. 7-19). During the Baptizer's time of prophetic service, he exhorted people to repent, for with the arrival of the Messiah, the divine kingdom was at hand (3:2). Likewise, Jesus' own preaching included an emphasis on repentance (see 4:17).

The Greek verb translated "repent" conveys the idea of changing one's mind. In a religious sense, it signifies a turnabout in attitude toward God and life's priorities. Repentance is part of the conversion process. Through the working of the Holy Spirit, sinners come to the point at which they are ready to turn away from sin and place their trust in the Messiah for salvation. Such an outcome pleases God, who does not want "anyone to perish" (2 Pet. 3:9), but for "everyone to come to repentance." Expressed differently, the Lord wants all people "to be saved and to come to a knowledge of the truth" (1 Tim. 2:4).

The divine attitude explains why Jesus invested much time, energy, and effort ministering in the towns of Galilee. This included performing many miracles (Matt. 11:20), which served several purposes. First, they confirmed His claim to be the Messiah. Second, they validated the Son's assertion that He was sent by the Father and represented Him. Third, they substantiated the credibility of the truths Jesus declared to the people of Israel. Fourth, they encouraged the doubtful to put their trust in Him. Fifth, they demonstrated that the one who is love was willing to reach out to people with compassion and grace.

Tragically, despite all the miracles Jesus performed in Galilee, many of the people living in the region did not turn from their sins. Consequently, Jesus began to denounce openly the cities where He had ministered. "Woe" (vs. 21) was an exclamation of grief. It is equivalent to saying, "How terrible it will be," or, "What sorrow awaits." In other words, such towns as Korazin and Bethsaida faced divine judgment for rejecting the Messiah. Their residents were primarily Jews. The Redeemer said that even the Gentile towns of Tyre and Sidon would have repented if they had seen His miraculous deeds. In truth, the latter cities would be treated better on the "day of judgment" (vs. 22).

Verse 23 indicates that the residents of Capernaum thought highly of themselves. As a matter of fact, they were so self-assured that they envisioned being exalted to heaven. Jesus, however, declared that no such honor would be theirs. Instead, they would be thrown down to Hades—the place where the unrighteous dead resided until judgment day (see Luke 10:15; 16:23; Rev. 20:13-14). Moreover, Jesus declared that if the miracles He performed in Capernaum had occurred in Sodom, the city would still exist (Matt. 11:23).

Genesis 19:1-29 records how the Lord destroyed Sodom, along with Gomorrah, because its inhabitants were exceedingly degenerate and wicked. Amazingly, on judgment day, God would show more mercy to the former residents of Sodom than to those of Capernaum (Matt. 11:24). Before we criticize the people of Korazin, Bethsaida, and Capernaum too quickly, we should remember it is still easy to overlook the ways God works in our lives. We should be careful not to take the Lord or His miracles for granted. We are accountable for how we respond to Jesus' blessings in our lives.

Next, the Son directed His attention to His heavenly Father. The Greek verb rendered "praise" (vs. 25) denotes the giving of thanks and honor. Such was appropriate for the Father to receive, especially since He is the "Lord of heaven and earth." *Kurios* is the noun translated "Lord" and can also be rendered "master" or "owner." When used in reference to God, *kurios* is a title of honor that expresses respect and reverence. This is appropriate, for He exists independently of the material universe and is not subject to its limitations. Moreover, because God is all-powerful and all-knowing, He is able to bring about whatever He wills. This remains true, even though His judgments are unsearchable and His ways are unfathomable to humankind (Rom. 11:33).

The Father's ownership encompasses all of heaven and earth, which He created (see Gen. 1:1). This includes the "highest heavens, and all their starry host" (Neh. 9:6), the "earth and all that is on it," and the "seas and all that is in them." Psalm 33:6 reveals that the Lord commanded everything into existence by means of His "word," even the "breath of his mouth." According to Psalm 102:25, the vast stretches of the universe are the "work of [His] hands." He is so powerful that, metaphorically speaking, He dresses Himself in a robe made out of light and stretches out the heavens like a tent curtain (104:2). He uses the clouds as His chariot and He rides upon the wings of the wind (vs. 3). Moreover, the Lord of all creation placed the earth firmly on its foundations, ensuring that it will never be upended (vs. 5).

In Jesus' prayer to the Father, the Son acknowledged that it was the divine will for the simple truths of the Gospel to remain "hidden" (Matt. 11:25) from those who claimed to be "wise and learned." "Hidden" renders a Greek verb that denotes what has been concealed or kept secret. In contrast, the Father revealed the good news of salvation to "little children." "Revealed" translates a verb that refers to what has been disclosed or made known. It was the Father's "good pleasure" (vs. 26), or gracious will, to enable ordinary, unpretentious people such as the Twelve to grasp the overall significance of Jesus' redemptive mission (including the miracles He performed and the truths He taught). In contrast, the arrogant elitists of the day remained disinterested in and dismissive of the Gospel.

In 1 Corinthians 1, Paul noted that while the message of the Cross has the power to save lives eternally, to unbelievers its message is sheer folly. Also, as long as unbelievers reject the message of the Cross as foolish, they are doomed to perish (vs. 18). In contrast, to those who are saved through their faith in God, the message of the Cross is a demonstration of divine power. Quoting Isaiah 29:14, Paul said the Lord used the message of the Cross to destroy the wisdom of the worldly wise and to annihilate the understanding of those who imagined themselves clever (1 Cor. 1:19).

In their quest to understand the meaning of life, the unsaved solely relied on humanly devised means. But the Father did not intend for worldly wisdom to be the basis for knowing Him. Rather, He intended for people to come to know Him through His Son, Jesus Christ (vs. 21). The Gospel proclaims a truth that human wisdom alone cannot comprehend. What seemed like a stumbling block to the Jews and like foolishness to the Greeks—Christ crucified—was the only way for people to come to a true knowledge of God (vss. 22-23). The Father chose a means of salvation that could disturb even the world's greatest philosophers—individuals who saw in it only foolishness. By operating in this way, God opened wide the door of salvation (vss. 24-25).

B. The Son's Relationship with the Father: vs. 27

"All things have been committed to me by my Father. No one knows the Son except the Father, and no one knows the Father except the Son and those to whom the Son chooses to reveal him."

The Son declared that "all things" (Matt. 11:27)—especially matters of eternal importance—had been handed over to Him by His Father (see Dan. 7:14; Matt. 28:18; 1 Pet. 3:22). This circumstance was in keeping with the intimate relationship that existed between them (and the Holy Spirit) from all eternity within the Godhead. Specifically, the Father was the only one who truly knew the Son. Likewise, the Son was the only one who truly knew the Father. The Messiah did not seek to horde the knowledge He had of the Father. Rather, the Son came to earth to "reveal" (Matt. 11:27) the Father to the lost.

Similar truths are found in the Fourth Gospel. In John 10:15, the Son noted that He and the Father had a mutual, intimate knowledge of one another. We learn in 17:2 that the Father had given the Son authority over all humanity. His gift of eternal life to believers exemplified that authority. The Son defined eternal life as enjoying a personal relationship with the Father based on knowing Him as the one true God. Furthermore, it is only possible to truly know the Father through faith in the Son, whom the Father had sent to reveal Himself (vs. 3). In short, eternal life was a growing relationship with the triune God that begins, not just when the believer dies, but at the moment of conversion.

II. THE INVITATION OF THE SON TO HUMANITY: MATTHEW 11:28-30

A. The Son's Offer of Rest: vs. 28

"Come to me, all you who are weary and burdened, and I will give you rest."

One striking difference between Jesus and the religious leaders of His day was their tendency to make many laws out of a few and His gift of making few laws out of many. They had identified a law for every Hebrew letter (613 of them) in the Ten Commandments. Generally, they emphasized the laws about external behavior, such as maintaining ritual cleanness and observing the Sabbath. The attempt of common people to keep these multitude of extraneous rules and regulations was like an oppressive burden that sapped them of their spiritual vitality.

The Greek verb that is translated "weary" (Matt. 11:28) refers to the fatigue and exhaustion that results from seemingly endless toil, burdens, or grief. "Burdened" renders a verb that denotes the presence of a gigantic load. In this case, a metaphorical pile of contrived rites and unwarranted precepts were leaving sincere worshipers of God feeling defeated and demoralized. Jesus invited them to come to Him in faith and find eternal "rest." The latter translates a verb that refers to the quiet, calm, and repose associated with believing in the Son for salvation.

In Hebrews 3:16-19, the author concluded that the wilderness generation of Israelites failed to enter God's rest. The writer began chapter 4 by saying that Christians can possess the promise to enter God's rest. The "rest" he was referring to is both spiritual and eternal. This rest that had been offered to the Israelites hundreds of years earlier was symbolic of the spiritual rest that culminated in the salvation offered by the Messiah. The author warned his readers against failing to accept the rest made available through faith in Christ. The writer told them not to be like the generation of Israelites who had failed to accept God's rest in the promised land. Believers were to make every effort not to fall short of God's promise (vs. 1). Here we learn that faith is the key to the door of God's rest. Indeed, the only proper response to what God has done and what He has made known is trusting in and obeying Him.

The author of Hebrews referred to several different kinds of rest. (1) Creation rest (vss. 3-4): God rested after Creation. Therefore, God has prepared a rest that His people may enter. (2) Canaan rest (vs. 8): Joshua led the Israelites into the promised land, where they entered into God's rest. Deuteronomy 12:9 refers to the land of Canaan as the Israelites' "resting place." (3) Continuing rest (Heb. 4:9-11): the fact that David wrote about God's rest (Ps. 95) around 400 years after the Israelites had entered the promised land meant for the author of Hebrews that God's rest is continuously offered to those who have faith in the Lord. How did the writer intend for his readers to apply these concepts of rest to their own lives? The following are a few possibilities: (1) Christian rest: when people become Christians, they enter into God's rest. (2) Consecration rest: people enter into God's rest at some point after conversion when they fully surrender their lives to the Lord and allow Him to work through them. (3) Celestial rest: people cannot enter God's rest completely until they go to heaven.

B. The Son's Assurance of Rest: vss. 29-30

"Take my yoke upon you and learn from me, for I am gentle and humble in heart, and you will find rest for your souls. For my yoke is easy and my burden is light."

"Yoke" (Matt. 11:29) translates a Greek noun that refers to the wooden bar or frame people in ancient times placed on the necks of animals so that they could pull a load (such as a wagon or plow). In a non-literal sense, the yoke represented subordination and servitude. Thus, when Jesus invited His disciples to take His yoke and put it on their shoulders, He was implying a high level of commitment to Him and His teachings. Unlike the excessive and unreasonable burdens the legalists of the day foisted on others (see Acts 15:10), the "yoke" (Matt. 11:30) Jesus offered was comparably "easy" and the "burden" that came with following Him was relatively "light" (see 1 John 5:3).

These verses shatter the mistaken notion that being a follower of Jesus was free of any expectations or obligations. In fact, remaining a disciple of the Messiah was demanding. Jesus' followers agreed not only to obey Him in all He has said, but also to order their priorities for His sake. They sought to serve Him as a slave would serve a master. The disciples of Jesus wanted to be like Him in their thoughts and actions. Furthermore, their desire was to abide in His words and heed His commands. The followers of the Messiah did not merely perpetuate His teachings, transmit His sayings, or imitate His life. They bore witness in their own words and actions that their Lord dwells within them. Thus, Jesus was much more than a mere teacher or guru to His disciples. For them He was the indwelling presence of God.

Such a high level of commitment need not frighten would-be converts to the Messiah. After all, they would find Him to be "gentle" (Matt. 11:29). The latter translates a Greek adjective that refers to someone whose temperament is meek and mild. "Humble" renders an adjective that denotes someone who is modest and unpretentious in nature. All these descriptions aptly applied to Jesus of Nazareth, who promised to give to His followers "rest" for their weary "souls" (see Exod. 33:14; Jer. 6:16). Jesus' remarks indicate that He was not soliciting the approval and praise of any human being, least of all the religious leaders (see John 5:41). His decision was especially prudent, given how deeply He knew their hearts.

In particular, the Messiah discerned that His opponents were devoid of love from God and for God (vs. 42). After all, they rejected the Son, who came in the authority of the Father. In contrast, Jesus' antagonists welcomed those who came in their own lesser authority (vs. 43). With such rampant hypocrisy, it is no wonder the legalists refused to believe in the Redeemer. Tragically, they more highly valued obtaining respect and praise from their peers than caring about the honor that came from the true and living God (vs. 44). In a sense, then, they idolized one another, rather than loving the triune God with all their heart, soul, and strength (see Deut. 6:4-5). Failing to do the latter was a fundamental breach of the foremost commandment of the law they highly venerated (see Exod. 20:3-6; Deut. 5:7-10; Matt. 22:36-38; Mark 12:28-30).

Discussion Questions

1. Why was it appropriate for Jesus to give praise to the Father?
2. Why would the Father hide from the unsaved the kingdom truths taught by the Son?
3. In what sense do the Father and Son know each other?
4. To whom has the Son made the Father known and why specifically them?
5. What is the nature of the "rest" (Matt. 11:28) Jesus offers believers?

Contemporary Application

Does Jesus really care? This is a question that frequently crosses our minds when we face tough times. The devil immediately sows seeds of doubt, suggesting that, if Jesus really loved us, we would not be going through a difficult experience.

Intellectually, we know Jesus cares, but it is difficult to allow that fact to override our emotional pain, doubts, and fears. That's one reason why the teaching about Jesus as our gentle and humble Savior is so important and valuable.

When we're down, we can tell Jesus how we feel and that we know He experienced what we are called to endure. Because He suffered as one of us in His humanity, we know we are not alone. He has gone before us and He wants us to come to His Father's heavenly throne for help.

We find great encouragement for ourselves and others when we ask Jesus to show us what it means to obey in the midst of suffering. And we have a significant message of hope to those who have never known Jesus as their High Priest.

Revealed in Rejection

DEVOTIONAL READING

Isaiah 53:1-9

DAILY BIBLE READINGS

Monday January 25
  Isaiah 53:1-9 A Man of Suffering

Tuesday January 26
  Hosea 4:1-6 No Knowledge of God

Wednesday January 27
  Mark 7:5-13 Rejecting God's Command

Thursday January 28
  Proverbs 3:5-12 The Lord Disciplines Those He Loves

Friday January 29
  Luke 4:16-22 Is Not This Joseph's Son?

Saturday January 30
  Luke 4:23-30 Rejected at Home

Sunday January 31
  Matthew 13:54-58 Thwarting God's Power by Unbelief

Scripture

Background Scripture: *Matthew 13:54-58; Luke 4:16-30*
Scripture Lesson: *Matthew 13:54-58*
Key Verses: *[Jesus] did not do many miracles there because of their lack of faith.* Matthew 13:58.
Scripture Lesson for Children: *Matthew 13:54-58*
Key Verse for Children: *"Jesus said to them, "Only in his hometown and in his own house is a prophet without honor."* Matthew 13:57.

Lesson Aim

To remain strong in the faith and endure whatever hardships we are going through.

Lesson Setting

Time: A.D. *28*
Place: *Nazareth*

Lesson Outline

Revealed in Rejection

I. The Initial Shock of the Populace to Jesus: Matthew 13:54-56
    A. *Teaching in the Synagogue of Nazareth: vs. 54a*
    B. *The Astonishment of the People: vss. 54b-56*
II. The Outright Rejection of the Populace of Jesus: Matthew 13:57-58
    A. *The Outrage of the People: vs. 57*
    B. *The Disbelief of the People: vs. 58*

Introduction for Adults

Topic: *Overcoming Rejection*

Ever since Jesus was rejected by the people in Nazareth, Christians have had a tough time with unbelieving spouses, children, and relatives. In some parts of the world, the church's obedience to Christ's call is exercised in the face of serious political and religious opposition. Even when Christians do deeds of mercy for victims of disasters, their religious foes do all they can to keep the people from hearing about Jesus. For many Christians, rejection takes the form of subtle discrimination in their offices, factories, and schools.

Jesus accomplished His mission despite opposition and unbelieving peers. And so can we. He lives in us. He empowers our mission. When we do His will, regardless of the opposition, He will honor and bless our faithfulness. As 1 Corinthians 15:58 reminds us, our "labor in the Lord is not in vain."

Introduction for Youth

Topic: *Coming Home . . .*

Hang in there! This saying is a relative newcomer to our English lexicon. You won't find it in the Bible, but the idea is there. And Jesus is our model for how to do it. He did not quit when He visited the people living in His hometown of Nazareth and they refused to believe in Him.

Joni Eareckson Tada tells how she refused to abandon her faith even when she was paralyzed after an accident. Her life was transformed by God's love and the love of her friends and family. She has since encouraged countless numbers of believers to hang in there.

When Jesus is firmly embedded in our hearts, He gives us strength to overcome ridicule and rejection. Opposition reinforces our determination to do God's will and fulfill His plans for our lives. We can do so, for we know that Jesus will never leave or forsake us (Heb. 13:5).

Concepts for Children

Topic: *Dealing with Rejection*

1. People in Jesus' hometown of Nazareth thought they knew Him.
2. The people's limited knowledge of Jesus as the Messiah led them to doubt His teachings.
3. The people also began to question Jesus' deeds of power.
4. The people's rejection of Jesus left Him feeling disappointed.
5. Jesus is sad when people we know do not want to believe in Him.

Lesson Commentary

I. THE INITIAL SHOCK OF THE POPULACE TO JESUS: MATTHEW 13:54-56

A. Teaching in the Synagogue of Nazareth: vs. 54a

Coming to his hometown, he began teaching the people in their synagogue.

In A.D. 28, after Jesus condemned the unrepentance of some towns and announced that severe judgment awaited all who rejected Him, He urged the people to turn to Him in faith, for only He could satisfy their eternal needs (Matt. 11:20-28). Then, when questioned by Israel's religious leaders, Jesus declared that He was Lord of the sabbath. Jesus backed up His claims by healing a man with a shriveled hand on the sabbath. All that Jesus said and did proved that He was the Father's chosen, humble, and victorious servant (12:1-21). When the Pharisees accused Jesus of operating in Satan's power, Jesus countered by claiming that He operated in the power of the Spirit. The Messiah stated that attributing His miracles to Satan was an unpardonable offense, that the real character of people is evident by the fruit of their lives, that all who rejected Him would be condemned on judgment day, and that the Father's true children obeyed the Son (vss. 22-50).

Matthew 13 presents various parables Jesus taught concerning the kingdom of heaven. By using parables, He ensured that only His followers grasped His teaching. The parable of the sower concerns a farmer scattering seed on different types of soil and illustrates that there are a variety of responses to the proclamation of the Gospel (vss. 1-23). In Jesus' parable of the weeds, a farmer's wheat field was sabotaged by an enemy who planted weeds in it. The farmer decided to let the wheat and the weeds grow together until the harvest (vss. 24-30). Next, Jesus used parables about a planted mustard seed and yeast in dough to explain the growth potential of the kingdom of heaven. The little seed produces a large plant and yeast causes a lot of bread to rise. By teaching parables like these, Jesus fulfilled Scripture (vss. 31-35).

At the disciples' request, Jesus interpreted the parable of the weeds. It was about the future judgment, when the wicked (weeds) are punished and the righteous (wheat) are blessed (vss. 36-43). Jesus told the parables of the treasure and of the pearl to illustrate the worth of God's kingdom. The parable of the net is another story of divine separation of the righteous and the wicked. Since the disciples claimed to understand these parables, Jesus told them one more, about a homeowner, to encourage them to share their spiritual insights with others (vss. 44-52).

After Jesus had finished teaching a variety of parables to His followers, He left for a new location (vs. 53). The Savior may have been at Capernaum while teaching the parables. If so, He would have traveled about 20 miles in a southwest direction to get to Nazareth, the town where He spent His childhood years (vs. 54; see 2:23). Mark 6:1 indicates that Jesus was accompanied by His disciples. As in other towns of Galilee, in Nazareth Jesus preached in the local synagogue and performed a few miracles (Matt. 13:54). Perhaps Jesus used the occasion to talk about His redemptive mission, especially in the context of fulfilling messianic prophecies recorded in the Old Testament.

During the period of the Exile, after the temple in Jerusalem was destroyed, the Jews started meeting in places called synagogues. The term comes from a Greek noun that means "an assembly of people." It referred to both the place where attendees met to pray, read Scripture, and hear teaching, and the people who gathered at the place. The synagogue served as a substitute for the temple, where the Jews always worshiped before the Exile in 586 B.C. Wherever 10 Jewish families lived, they formed a synagogue. We do not know exactly how many synagogues there were in Israel in the first century of the common era, but we know nearly 400 of them existed in Jerusalem when the Romans burned the holy city in A.D. 70. Although later synagogues were more ornate, most people in first-century Galilean synagogues probably sat on mats on the floor.

Not long after Jesus' encounter with Satan in the wilderness (see Luke 4:1-13), Jesus had visited Nazareth (about A.D. 27). By then, His reputation had mushroomed, due in part to His ministry throughout Galilee (vss. 14-15). On the sabbath, He attended the local synagogue. Since there was no professional clergy (rabbis held secular trades to earn their living), the synagogue leader could invite anyone to teach. As a visiting rabbi and hometown celebrity, Jesus was invited to be the guest speaker. At the appropriate time in the service, He was handed the scroll of Isaiah, which He unrolled and from which He read in Hebrew (vss. 16-17). Presumably, He then translated the passages into Aramaic, which was the common language of the people. Jesus read Isaiah 61:1-2, which was a messianic prophecy. The passage foretold that the era of the Messiah would be a time of liberation and change. Then Jesus gave the scroll back to the attendant and sat down to teach (Luke 4:18-20).

Most Jews hoped for a powerful leader to arise and deliver them from the Romans, who dominated them. So when Jesus announced that this messianic prophecy was now being fulfilled (vs. 21), He had the worshipers' full attention. Some were impressed, but others were not so sure. Amazed by Jesus' message, the audience began to talk among themselves (vs. 22). Jesus knew He had a skeptical group on His hands, but He met their doubts head-on. He acknowledged that they would want Him to prove Himself, especially to see dramatic evidence of His power. But because they could not imagine God raising up one of their own to be a prophet, He would not show them God's power (vss. 23-24; see Matt. 13:58). Jesus drove His point home, reminding the skeptical worshipers that because God's chosen people doubted, they had missed blessings that the Gentiles then received. Jesus cited an instance in the time of Elijah and another in the time of Elisha (Luke 4:25-27; see 1 Kings 17:8-16; 2 Kings 5:1-14).

Hearing about the widow of Zarephath and the leper from Syria infuriated Jesus' hearers. It was bad enough for Jesus to say He was the fulfillment of messianic prophecy. Now He was saying that His audience was unworthy of God's blessings. The people surged toward Jesus. They pushed and shoved, moving Him toward a bluff at the edge of town, intending to toss Him over the side. But He slipped away from the mob and escaped (Luke 4:28-30). Luke does not say this escape was a miracle, but it probably was. By rejecting Jesus, the Nazarenes allowed the blessings of God to slip away from them. They showed they were unworthy by refusing to listen. In obstinate pride, they thought they knew better than Jesus.

B. The Astonishment of the People: vss. 54b-56

And they were amazed. "Where did this man get this wisdom and these miraculous powers?" they asked. "Isn't this the carpenter's son? Isn't his mother's name Mary, and aren't his brothers James, Joseph, Simon and Judas? Aren't all his sisters with us? Where then did this man get all these things?"

In A.D. 28, many who heard Jesus speak in the synagogue at Nazareth were astonished at His teaching, wisdom, and miracles, all of which pointed to the inauguration of the divine kingdom (Mark 6:2). "Amazed" (Matt. 13:54) renders a Greek verb that denotes the presence of emotions ranging from surprise to shock. "Wisdom" translates a noun that refers to the skillful handling of life problems. Biblical wisdom also involves the exercise of sound judgment and the application of scriptural truths to one's conduct. Divine prudence guides the believer to live in an upright, virtuous, and well-pleasing manner. In the case of Jesus, this was seen in His commitment to the Father, the Son's devotion to the Father's will, and the Son's obedience to Scripture.

In short, the inhabitants of Jesus' hometown were flabbergasted at what they heard. Some possibly resented the idea that a former, seemingly ordinary local resident had surpassed them in importance. Tragically, though, their bewilderment led to doubt, not belief. The Nazarenes had long been familiar with Jesus and His family. They knew His mother (Mary), His four half brothers (James, Joseph, Simon, and Judas), and His half sisters (vss. 55-56). (In Bible times, large families were common.) The lack of any mention of Joseph suggests he had died by this time (Mark 6:3). Some Bible interpreters have considered Jesus' brothers and sisters to be children of Joseph's from a previous marriage. However, there's no evidence of that, so they most likely were the younger children of Joseph and Mary, born after Jesus. Incidentally, two of Jesus' brothers—James and Judas—are believed to have later authored the New Testament books that bear their names. (Jude is the abbreviated form of Judas.)

The Nazarenes recalled how Jesus had worked among them as a carpenter. Some of the residents may still have been using wooden items Jesus had made or repaired. The Nazarenes also knew He was without formal rabbinic training (see John 7:15). Because of this general knowledge, the people rejected Jesus' claims to be the Messiah. They thought they knew Him too well as a common man to accept Him as their Lord and Savior. It should come as no surprise that Jesus, like His legal father, Joseph, worked as a carpenter. It is possible that Jesus continued to practice His trade while traveling about to teach and heal.

Some think the latter is so because Jesus derived no income from His ministry. Only officials of the temple and religious courts drew salaries. The rest of the religious teachers and leaders were either independently wealthy or supported themselves through a trade or profession. Jesus did receive support from several wealthy women (Luke 8:1-3). Also, Jesus was welcomed as a guest in many homes. Interestingly, of all the complaints His opponents lodged against Him (such as failing to keep the sabbath, eating and drinking with sinners, and claiming to be God), they never accused Him of being lazy. In fact, Jesus' own townsfolk were amazed at His teaching, for they thought of Him just as a carpenter (Matt. 13:55).

The content of verses 54-56 offers several windows into first-century culture. A quick look at these reminds us that Jesus lived in a world quite different from ours. To begin, religious teachers (rabbis) commonly moved around the countryside offering their knowledge to whomever would listen. Also, as noted earlier, leaders of local synagogues often invited these traveling ministers to speak in their worship services. Individuals who wished to receive more intensive training followed a rabbi as his disciples. In this sense, the ministry of Jesus fit right into a pattern familiar to Jews of His day.

English translations of Mark 6:3 call Jesus a "carpenter." That particular occupation would have included woodworking, but also much more. Most people in small villages such as Nazareth lived as poor peasants. Nearly all residents made their living off the land. They raised crops, tended animals, or both. Also, each village would have had at least one handyman. He would build and repair houses, pieces of furniture, tools, kitchen utensils, and almost any of the simple implements of first-century life.

The people of Nazareth referred to Jesus as "Mary's son." Had Joseph still been alive, they might have mentioned that Jesus was his son. Mary was undoubtedly a widow. In ancient times, adult men often married girls who were still teenagers or even younger. That, combined with low life expectancy, contributed to the high percentage of women who lived as widows. When a father died, the eldest son took responsibility of caring for his mother and younger siblings. That likely offers one explanation why Jesus began His public ministry when He was 30 years old. By that time, His younger brothers were old enough to take responsibility for managing the home.

II. THE OUTRIGHT REJECTION OF THE POPULACE OF JESUS: MATTHEW 13:57-58

A. The Outrage of the People: vs. 57

And they took offense at him. But Jesus said to them, "Only in his hometown and in his own house is a prophet without honor."

"Took offense" (Matt. 13:57) renders the same Greek verb that is translated "fall away" in 11:6. The mental image is of someone tripping or stumbling over an object. In short, the inhabitants of Nazareth felt outrage toward Jesus. Much of the Gospel record includes the conflict between belief and unbelief. To those Jews who were able to get past their religious traditions and understand what Jesus was telling them, He became their Messiah. In contrast, to those who were unwilling to do so, He became offensive.

Jesus responded to the townspeople's animosity and refusal to believe with His own version of a common proverb from the period. The Savior declared that a prophet typically is honored everywhere except in his own hometown. This lack of acceptance and respect also came from the person's relatives and even his own family (Mark 6:4). We have a similar saying—familiarity breeds contempt. The Lord implied that His former neighbors had refused to consider His words and works objectively. Perhaps they thought He was no better than they were.

B. The Disbelief of the People: vs. 58

And he did not do many miracles there because of their lack of faith.

Because the residents of Nazareth were filled with unbelief, Jesus drastically limited the number of "miracles" (Matt. 13:58) He performed among them. The most He opted to do was heal a few sick people by laying His hands on them (Mark 6:5). In the Gospels, the normal order is faith first, healing second. While Jesus marveled at the unbelief He encountered in Nazareth, He did not interpret His rejection there as failure on His part. After all, He had been faithful in preaching the Word and ministering to people. The Nazarenes, however, had been faithless.

It would be incorrect to suppose that Jesus lacked power. Rather, He chose not to do many miracles in His hometown because of the people's unbelief (vs. 6). As long as they refused to believe, no teaching or miracle would convince them to follow Him. Also, if Jesus had performed more miracles in a climate of antagonism and cynicism, the people's guilt would have increased. Thus, the Nazarenes missed out on the benefits of Jesus' power due to their agnosticism. By rejecting Jesus, the people of Nazareth forfeited eternal joy with the Father. They also allowed the blessings of God to slip away from them. They showed they were unworthy by refusing to listen. The same outcome is true for all who reject the Messiah. As Hebrews 11:6 makes clear, anyone who wants to come to God must believe that He exists and that "he rewards those who earnestly seek him" (Heb. 11:6).

The unpleasant episode at Nazareth taught Jesus' disciples to expect opposition. They could see that a negative response to the Gospel message was not necessarily due to a flaw in the messenger. Even the greatest Messenger was not received by all. He was rejected by those who thought they knew Him best. We, too, can take comfort from this episode. While we should be grieved over unbelief wherever we find it, we do not need to punish ourselves over that lack of faith in others. If we have been faithfully presenting the Gospel, then the failure is not our own.

Discussion Questions

1. What possibly motivated Jesus to minister in His hometown of Nazareth?
2. What was it about Jesus' itinerant ministry that caused such a stir among the inhabitants of Nazareth?
3. Why did the local residents in Jesus' hometown take offense at Him?
4. Why would Jesus say that prophets tended to be without honor in their towns of origin?
5. In what way did the Nazarenes display a lack of faith in Jesus?

Contemporary Application

Being committed to Jesus during times of hardship isn't easy. Our faith is tested when we encounter unanticipated expenses, a job loss, family problems, or a severe illness. The way we choose to deal with these crises can make a difference in our relationship with God and the testimony we present to the unsaved.

There are numerous ways we can remain strong in Christ despite hardships. We should avail ourselves of the Lord's grace. God's grace saves us, and it also keeps us spiritually healthy. As we grow in grace, we draw closer to the Lord and become stronger in our faith. We can spend time with the Lord in prayer, sharing with Him our concerns and struggles. We can seek the counsel of mature, godly believers about how to handle a difficult situation. We can remain strong in Christ by regularly fellowshipping with other believers. God can use their encouragement and support to get us through a crisis.

Being strong in Christ does not mean that God will shield us from all difficulties. In fact, hardships seem to come at the most inconvenient times, and we seldom feel prepared to deal with them. In those moments, we should never lose hope or give in to our despair. Jesus is always present and ready to help us endure our trials. God can use our unwavering commitment to Him to encourage other believers to look to Christ for help.

The faces of hopelessness are evident in every walk of life. The businessman who has a substance abuse problem, the teenager who discovers that she is pregnant, the housewife who is the victim of spousal abuse, and the family members who feel trapped in unending poverty are examples of those who struggle with despair. Sadly, many are convinced there is no relief from their hardships. Yet the good news is that regardless of our struggles, there's hope in Christ. This truth has sustained and enabled believers throughout the years to rise above their difficulties.

A Canaanite Woman

DEVOTIONAL READING

Isaiah 42:1-9

DAILY BIBLE READINGS

Monday February 1
Luke 2:25-35 Revelation to the Gentiles

Tuesday February 2
Romans 2:1-11 God Shows No Partiality

Wednesday February 3
Acts 13:44-49 A Light for the Gentiles

Thursday February 4
Isaiah 60:1-5 Nations Come to Your Light

Friday February 5
Revelation 21:22-27 Nations Walk by God's Light

Saturday February 6
Romans 15:7-13 In Him the Gentiles Hope

Sunday February 7
Matthew 15:21-28 Great Is Your Faith!

Scripture

Background Scripture: *Matthew 15:21-28*
Scripture Lesson: *Matthew 15:21-28*
Key Verses: *"Woman, you have great faith! Your request is granted."* Matthew 15:28.
Scripture Lesson for Children: *Matthew 15:21-28*
Key Verse for Children: *Jesus answered, "Woman, you have great faith! Your request is granted."* Matthew 15:28.

Lesson Aim

To share the love of Jesus with others around us.

Lesson Setting

Time: *About A.D. 29*
Place: *The Region of Tyre and Sidon*

Lesson Outline

A Canaanite Woman

I. A Plea for Mercy: Matthew 15:21-22
   A. *The Savior's Departure to Tyre and Sidon: vs. 21*
   B. *The Desperation of a Gentile Mother: vs. 22*

II. An Amazing Display of Trust: Matthew 15:23-28
   A. *The Consternation of the Disciples: vss. 23-24*
   B. *The Determination of the Mother: vss. 25-27*
   C. *The Granting of the Mother's Request: vs. 28*

Introduction for Adults

Topic: *Hope for Healing*

Brad Ketterling was born prematurely with only 15 percent of normal hearing. He grew up in a non-Christian home and learned little about Christ. His grandmother encouraged him to attend church, but Brad saw little purpose in that. He could not adequately hear the program. Someone gave him a couple of Christian comic books and their message brought Brad to salvation.

While attending Bible college, Brad received a call to ministry among the deaf, but rejected that possibility. God continued to work on Brad, and today he gives full time to working with others like him who cannot hear. He easily empathizes with the struggles of the deaf. They bond well with him because of his own impairment. Now working in Los Angeles, Brad ministers fruitfully by bringing the hope of healing found through the Gospel to those in spiritual need.

Introduction for Youth

Topic: *Hope for Healing*

The members of the church that saved teens encounter tend to be ordinary people. However, when empowered by the Holy Spirit and full of faith in Jesus' promises, the Lord can enable them to step out of their ordinariness into the amazing lives to which the Lord has called them.

Jesus is also calling saved teens to be willing and ready to serve Him. The Savior wants them to minister to every aspect of other people's needs. And Jesus is able to do through adolescents all that He has planned. Saved teens are qualified to be a part of His plan, not because of who or what they are, but because of who Jesus is and what He has made them by His spiritually healing and transforming power.

Concepts for Children

Topic: *Believe and Receive*

1. Jesus' power was so well known that even foreigners sought Him.
2. Jesus explained that the Father sent Him to the Jewish people.
3. The bold faith of the Gentile mother resulted in Jesus healing her daughter.
4. Jesus hears you even when you think He does not.
5. Jesus will give you what you need.

Lesson Commentary

I. A PLEA FOR MERCY: MATTHEW 15:21-22

A. The Savior's Departure to Tyre and Sidon: vs. 21

Leaving that place, Jesus withdrew to the region of Tyre and Sidon.

Last week we learned that while Jesus was in His hometown of Nazareth, the residents responded to Him with disbelief and disrespect (Matt. 13:54-58). The Messiah had been ministering for a while in Galilee. At roughly the same time He was rejected in Nazareth, word about Him finally reached "Herod the tetrarch" (14:1), that is, Herod Antipas. The ruler mistakenly thought Jesus was John the Baptizer resurrected. After Herod had John beheaded, the Baptizer's disciples buried his body and reported the sad news to Jesus (vss. 2-12).

Having heard how Antipas responded to the news of His preaching and miracles, Jesus decided to leave the area by boat. He felt a need to get away and spend some time by Himself in prayer (see vs. 23). Jesus traveled alone to an isolated location. The solitary place was in the area of Bethsaida, a town probably located on the northeast shore of the Sea of Galilee. Jesus was unable to remain alone for long, however, for large crowds of people had heard of His whereabouts and followed Him on foot from the towns of Galilee (vs. 13).

As Jesus arrived at the shore and began to disembark, He saw a large crowd already there waiting for Him (vs. 14). This incident reveals that Jesus was tremendously popular among the people and that they looked to Him to fill a spiritual vacuum in their lives. Although what Jesus wanted most to do was to be alone and pray, when He saw the needy people, He "had compassion on them." This means He was filled with pity and concern for them. With genuine love, He willingly healed the sick of their afflictions. Thus He deferred the fulfillment of His own desire for prayer. At the end of the day, Jesus miraculously fed the thousands of people present (vss. 15-21).

As the day drew to a close, Jesus directed the Twelve to get into a boat without Him and cross over to the other side of the lake, that is, the west side. Meanwhile, the Savior "dismissed the crowd" (vs. 22) and then ventured up the side of a mountain to spend the night in prayer. As the sun set, Jesus was finally alone with the Father (vs. 23). The text does not say what Jesus prayed about. He may have talked to the Father about the needs of the people, the direction of His earthly ministry, and His coming crucifixion. Certainly the Son recognized the importance of spending private time with His Father in prayer.

While Jesus was beginning to pray, the disciples had already gone far out on the lake. But their boat began to be slowed by a head wind and beat by the waves (vs. 24). The disciples evidently spent most of the night trying to get across the lake against the storm. During the fourth watch—that is, in the hours immediately preceding the dawn—Jesus came to rescue His friends. However, He did not take a boat, for He did not need one. He came to His disciples by walking on the water (vs. 25). This means He overcame the wind, waves, and gravity. Peter went out to meet the Lord on the water, but began to sink when he looked at the storm around him (vss. 26-30).

Jesus, still in full control of the situation, quickly extended His hand and took hold of Peter. The Savior wasted no time in focusing on Peter's real problem—he had allowed doubt to squash his faith (vs. 31). If he had remained unwavering in his trust, he would have experienced no difficulties. From this incident Peter learned that any task done for the Messiah must be accompanied by faith from start to finish. The moment Jesus and Peter returned to the fishing boat, the turbulent wind died down (vs. 32). The Twelve, completely dumbfounded over what had taken place, fell prostrate in worship before the Redeemer and exclaimed, "Truly you are the Son of God" (vs. 33).

After the crisis had passed, the boat landed and moored at Gennesaret (vs. 34). This was a fertile plain located on the northwest bank of the Sea of Galilee. The numerous mineral springs in the area, according to local belief, could heal the infirm and crippled who flocked to them. When the people of the region realized who Jesus was, the news of His presence spread quickly throughout "all the surrounding country" (vs. 35). As a result, a large crowd hurriedly carried their sick to Him. The throng was so desperate and needy that they begged Jesus to allow their sick simply to touch the edge of His cloak in the hope that they might be cured. He granted the people's requests and healed all who touched Him (vs. 36).

Meanwhile, a delegation of Pharisees and teachers of the law traveled north from Jerusalem to interrogate Jesus. They asked why His followers did not wash their hands before eating. The leaders believed that refusing to do so made the disciples ceremonially unclean. In Jesus' response, He stated that the religious leaders had elevated humanly devised rules above God's commands in the Hebrew sacred writings concerning the issue of maintaining ritual purity (see Lev. 11—15; Num. 5:1-4; 19). Jesus then declared to a crowd that it is what springs from the hearts of people that defiles them, not what they eat (Matt. 15:1-20; Mark 7:1-23).

The latter exchange serves as a reminder that, over the course of Jesus' earthly ministry, the Pharisees and scribes grew increasingly opposed to Him. They envied His popularity, resented His challenges to their traditions, and hated His exposure of their hypocrisy. Undoubtedly, the Jewish leaders wondered whether Jesus had political aspirations and worried about how His increasing influence would affect their control over the people. The Pharisees and scribes allowed their petty concerns to blind them to the truth that Jesus was their Messiah.

In light of the acrimony surrounding Jesus' encounter with the religious leaders from Jerusalem, the Savior decided to leave the vicinity of Gennesaret (see Matt. 14:34; Mark 6:53). In fact, He left the entire region of Galilee, where He had been ministering, and traveled 30 or 40 miles northwestward to the area of "Tyre and Sidon" (Matt. 15:21). These were Phoenician cities located on the coastal plain between the mountains of Lebanon and the Mediterranean Sea. Both cities were known for their maritime exploits and as centers of trade. The Jews living in Judea would have regarded Phoenicia and its cities as pagan territory.

B. The Desperation of a Gentile Mother: vs. 22

A Canaanite woman from that vicinity came to him, crying out, "Lord, Son of David, have mercy on me! My daughter is suffering terribly from demon-possession."

Evidently, Jesus lodged in the home of a local Jewish resident. Though the time away was supposed to be a retreat, it didn't turn out that way. Jesus' reputation had preceded Him, and even in this Gentile region people came to hear His teachings and benefit from His miracles (see Mark 7:24). Matthew 15:22 focuses attention on a "Canaanite woman" who lived in that region. This manner of expression was the Jewish way of referring to non-Jews residing in Phoenicia in Jesus' day (see Mark 7:26). The emphasis in Matthew 15:22 is on the woman's Gentile heritage. To be specific, she was a descendant of the pagan population of Palestine. During the time of the Judges (beginning around 1375 B.C.), the Canaanites were the principal enemies of the Israelites. Also, the Canaanites were the people the Israelites chiefly sought to drive out of the promised land.

This woman was also a distraught mother, for her daughter was demon-possessed. Evidently, the mother heard or saw something in Jesus to make her believe He would help her. That faith was strengthened by the woman's compassion for her child. Because of the mother's faith in Jesus, she did what the residents of Jesus' hometown would not do: she presented her plea to Him for His help. The Canaanite referred to Jesus as "Lord, Son of David" (Matt. 15:22), which suggests that she had some awareness of His messianic identity. Moreover, the woman explained that her daughter was possessed by an evil spirit, and that the demon was severely tormenting her. Mark 7:26 says the woman kept begging Jesus to expel the malicious entity from her daughter. This underscores how desperate and helpless the woman felt.

II. AN AMAZING DISPLAY OF TRUST: MATTHEW 15:23-28

A. The Consternation of the Disciples: vss. 23-24

Jesus did not answer a word. So his disciples came to him and urged him, "Send her away, for she keeps crying out after us." He answered, "I was sent only to the lost sheep of Israel."

Despite the woman's persistent pleas for help, Jesus did not give her a reply (Matt. 15:23). Though Jesus meant all along to help the woman, He decided before doing so to test her faith. The disciples, however, were bothered by the woman's persistent begging and urged Jesus to send her away, perhaps after granting her request. Sadly, they showed no compassion for her or sensitivity to her needs. Jesus noted that the Father had sent Him to help the people of Israel—His lost sheep—not the Gentiles (vs. 24). Jesus did not say this to imply that Jews were the only ones to be saved. Rather, they were to become the first agents through whom Jesus would extend His Gospel throughout the world (see John 4:22; Rom. 1:16).

B. The Determination of the Mother: vss. 25-27

The woman came and knelt before him. "Lord, help me!" she said. He replied, "It is not right to take the children's bread and toss it to their dogs." "Yes, Lord," she said, "but even the dogs eat the crumbs that fall from their masters' table."

The Gentile mother was undeterred. She approached Jesus, knelt before Him in worship, and cried out, "Lord, help me" (Matt. 15:25). Jesus' statement in verse 26 describes a common domestic situation in which a family is eating dinner while small household dogs are begging for food. Jesus said the order in which the appetites should be satisfied is children first, dogs second.

This statement has a dual meaning. On one level it refers to the focus of Jesus' mission. In this case, "children" are Jews, the "dogs" are Gentiles, and the "bread" is the Gospel. It's hardly likely, of course, that the mother understood this meaning of Jesus' words. More likely, she understood them on a personal level. To be specific, she had interrupted Jesus' retreat with His disciples. For Jesus to help her, then, would have required Him to take His time and energy away from the disciples and give them to the woman. On this level of meaning, the "children" are the disciples, the "dogs" represent the woman, and the "bread" is Jesus' ministry.

The Messiah's reference to the mother's kinfolk as the "dogs" was not necessarily a derogatory term. Dog was a common Jewish reference for the Gentiles and was based on their making no distinction between clean and unclean foods. In essence, when it came to eating, the Gentiles used about as much discretion as a pack of hungry dogs. Many Bible scholars also point out that the Greek *kynarion*—the term Jesus used—referred to house dogs or little puppies, not to wild, scavenging beasts.

Although the Canaanite woman was from a different ethnic background than the Jews, she apparently knew enough about the Jewish faith—and had enough insight into the Jews' longing for their Redeemer—to recognize Jesus as the fulfillment of the messianic prophecies. This realization explains why the mother still was not put off by Jesus' reply to her request. The woman extended the Savior's analogy for her own purposes. The meal did not have to be interrupted and the children's bread be given to the dogs. All the dogs needed were a few crumbs dropped during the meal (vs. 27). In other words, the mother was saying that Jesus could quickly and easily fulfill her request, and then get back to teaching His disciples.

C. The Granting of the Mother's Request: vs. 28

Then Jesus answered, "Woman, you have great faith! Your request is granted." And her daughter was healed from that very hour.

The Gentile woman's answer pleased Jesus. He may even have laughed at the way she turned His statement to her own benefit. Then He rescued her daughter from the evil spirit (Matt. 15:28). Ironically, many Jews would lose God's blessing and salvation because they rejected Jesus, and many Gentiles would find salvation because they recognized and accepted Him. The basic principle here is that people persist in faith because they know who Jesus is and that He will honor their commitment to Him. The Messiah's love and power are always available, but our desires are not always granted immediately. To test us, Jesus sometimes does not answer. His silence may seem unbearable. But then we should recall the Canaanite mother and keep coming back to Jesus in faith.

Like the woman from the vicinity of Tyre and Sidon, we should demonstrate boldness in seeking God's help. Often we are too easily discouraged from our spiritual pursuits. We need the humility to know we deserve nothing, but the determination to draw upon the riches of God's grace. Commenting on the mother's faith, Martin Luther wrote: "This was a most beautiful and shining faith, and is a notable example, showing the method . . . of wrestling with God. For we ought not at the first blow immediately to cast away courage and all hope, but we must be urgent, we must be prayerful, we must seek and knock."

In this account, the mother was not perfect. Thankfully, Jesus does not demand perfection before we can place our faith in Him. The woman came to Jesus just as she was. She accepted her identity, and did not recoil at Jesus' words. We, too, should be willing to come to Jesus just as we are without any pretense. This incident also reminds us of the need for faith throughout our spiritual lives. Faith is not only for conversion. Living day by day with Jesus requires us to trust Him to take care of us. This is hard when we see the risks that are involved, but we can make it if we keep focused on our strong Savior.

All through Scripture, God seems to wait in answering requests, even though He fully intends to meet the need. With respect to the Canaanite mother, at first Jesus did not pay attention to her, even though He knew that He would eventually heal her daughter. Why would the Lord make the woman wait? Why did He initially remain silent to her desperate appeals? By delaying His response, Jesus seemed to be assessing the woman's faith and giving her the opportunity to express her belief in a way that brought praise from the Savior. In addition to that, His initial responses made the woman recognize all the more how great of a blessing she received. Her faith was strengthened, and she learned that the Lord rewards those who earnestly seek Him.

After leaving Tyre, Jesus traveled about 25 miles north to Sidon. He then headed southeast through the territory of Herod Philip. Jesus cut a wide path around the eastern shore of the Sea of Galilee and eventually ended up in the region of Decapolis (Mark 7:31). After the journey, Jesus climbed a hill and sat down, most likely to rest and teach His disciples (Matt. 15:29). These were critical days for them. As they traveled together, Jesus taught them who He was and what His plans were. They needed to absorb as much as they could, for serious trouble loomed ahead. However, Jesus' presence could not remain a secret for long. A vast crowd brought Him a wide assortment of people with severe physical difficulties (such as lameness, blindness, crippledness, and muteness). When the infirmed were laid before Jesus, He healed all of them (vs. 30). What a powerful testimony to His compassion and mercy!

Discussion Questions

1. Why did Jesus decide to leave Galilee and travel to the region of Tyre and Sidon?
2. How do you think the Canaanite woman felt as her daughter experienced demon-possession?
3. If you were among the disciples, do you think you would have responded similarly or differently to the mother's persistent plea for help?
4. How did the mother remain respectful in her response to Jesus, even when she voiced a dissenting view to His statement in Matthew 15:26?
5. Why did Jesus finally decide to grant the mother's request?

Contemporary Application

To love the way the Savior does involves making a conscious decision. The Lord Himself is the best example of this. As Romans 5:8-10 teaches, God chose to reach out to us in love even when we were His enemies. Despite our sin, God decided to bring peace and wholeness to our relationship with Him.

There will be times when we do not feel like loving other people. It is in those moments that we need to look to God for supernatural help. He is ready and willing to give us the strength to love in a Christlike fashion; but first we must submit ourselves to God's will.

In addition, when God enables us to love despite our desire not to, nonbelievers will see the power of Christ's love working through and in us. In a morally corrupt society in which people yearn for a power greater than what they have, so as to give them meaning and value, the love of Christ in us will draw them to Him. Here, then, is another reason to choose love—to surrender our will to Jesus' will and thus be a beacon to others.

If we are to be more loving, we must also examine our attitudes and actions. We need to consider how we love others in our ministries and relationships. Furthermore, we should look for ways in which we can be more loving.

Declared by Peter

Scripture

Background Scripture: *Matthew 16:13-27*
Scripture Lesson: *Matthew 16:13-27*
Key Verse: *"You are the Christ, the Son of the living God."*
Matthew 16:16.
Scripture Lesson for Children: *Matthew 16:13-20*
Key Verse for Children: *Simon Peter answered, "You are the
Christ, the Son of the living God."* Matthew 16:16.

Lesson Aim

To discover that acknowledging Jesus as the Messiah
demands unwavering commitment.

Lesson Setting

Time: A.D. *29*
Place: *Caesarea Philippi*

Lesson Outline

Declared by Peter
   I. The Confession of Peter: Matthew 16:13-20
      A. *Jesus' Question: vs. 13*
      B. *Various Responses: vss. 14-16*
      C. *Jesus' Pronouncement of Blessing on Peter:
         vss. 17-20*
  II. The Prediction of Jesus: Matthew 16:21-27
      A. *Jesus' Foretelling of His Death and Resurrection:
         vs. 21*
      B. *Jesus' Response to Peter's Rebuke: vss. 22-23*
      C. *Jesus' Explanation of Discipleship's Cost: vss. 24-27*

Introduction for Adults

Topic: *Declaring Allegiance*

Helen Keller grew up without being able to see or hear. Despite her visual and auditory handicaps, she became one of America's most famous women. She graduated from college and had an illustrious career as a writer and speaker. As a young girl, she was told the good news about Jesus for the first time. It was reported that, upon hearing the Gospel, Helen Keller exclaimed, "I already knew that such a God existed. I simply did not know His name!"

In the life, death, and resurrection of the Lord Jesus, we learn the name and personality of the eternal, living God. It's not a mistake, then, for us to declare our allegiance to the Messiah, for we know that through faith in Him our home in heaven is guaranteed.

Introduction for Youth

Topic: *I Know Who You Are!*

Have you ever noticed how Jesus is portrayed in literature, onstage, or onscreen? In *Jesus Christ Superstar,* He is an idealistic, but deluded, would-be Messiah. In *Godspell,* Jesus is a lovable innocent who becomes a crucified clown. Jesus is a well-intentioned charlatan in *The Passover Plot,* while He is a fierce champion in the film titled *The Gospel According to Saint Matthew.* And in *The Last Temptation of Christ,* Nikos Kazantzakis portrays Jesus as a man who did not want to be the Messiah.

So, who is Jesus to the teens in your class: a superstar, a sap, or a Savior? Peter had no difficulty whatsoever in affirming Jesus as the Messiah. Hopefully, your students can say the same.

Concepts for Children

Topic: *Who Am I?*

1. Jesus asked His followers what others thought about Him.
2. The twelve followers mentioned different names that people gave for Jesus.
3. Jesus wanted to know who His followers said He was.
4. Peter said that Jesus is the Messiah.
5. Jesus said that He would safeguard all His followers throughout the world.

Lesson Commentary

I. THE CONFESSION OF PETER: MATTHEW 16:13-20

A. Jesus' Question: vs. 13

When Jesus came to the region of Caesarea Philippi, he asked his disciples, "Who do people say the Son of Man is?"

Jesus decided to leave Galilee and travel north to the region around the city of Caesarea Philippi (Matt. 16:13). Caesarea Philippi was a city located in the upper Jordan Valley and along the southwestern slope of Mount Hermon. Behind the town, which was about 1,150 feet above sea level, rose bluffs and rugged mountain peaks. The area was one of the most lush in Palestine, with an abundance of grassy fields and groves of trees. The city was also strategically located, standing as a sentinel over the plains in the area. For many years, a cave and spring there had been associated with the worship of Canaanite gods. Later, a shrine was built on the site and dedicated to the Greek nature gods. Herod the Great built a temple to Rome and Augustus in the town, and later Herod's son, Philip the tetrarch, refurbished the city and named it Caesarea Philippi.

Jesus may have chosen this spot to ask His followers who He was so He could draw a stark contrast between Himself and the pagan worship for which this area was famous. In questioning the disciples about His identity, Jesus referred to Himself as the "Son of Man." This phrase was His most common self-description. He wanted to teach that, as the Messiah, He combined two Old Testament roles: Son of Man (Dan. 7:13-14) and Servant of the Lord (Isa. 52:13—53:12). Daniel described a Son of Man to whom God gives an everlasting kingdom, while Isaiah described a Servant of the Lord who suffers on behalf of others. Jesus knew that He must perform the role of the suffering Servant. But He also knew that eventually He would receive glory as the Son of Man.

B. Various Responses: vss. 14-16

They replied, "Some say John the Baptist; others say Elijah; and still others, Jeremiah or one of the prophets." "But what about you?" he asked. "Who do you say I am?" Simon Peter answered, "You are the Christ, the Son of the living God."

Jesus undoubtedly knew what the people were saying about Him, but He asked the question as a prelude to help the Twelve obtain a clearer understanding of His identity. The disciples reported a variety of opinions concerning who Jesus was. It seems that popular opinion stated that Jesus was one of the great figures of the past reincarnated, though there was no agreement on which great figure. Some thought He was John the Baptizer, while others thought He was an earlier prophet, such as Elijah or Jeremiah (Matt. 16:14).

While mistaken about Jesus being a reincarnation, the people recognized correctly that Jesus was a prophet and that He stood in line with God's faithful servants of the past. If they had understood Him more fully, though, they would have known that He was someone totally new. People today, of course, are still uncertain about Jesus' true identity. Those who think of Him as a great reformer (like John the Baptist), a great miracle worker (like Elijah), or a great teacher (like some other Old Testament prophets) usually imagine they are holding Jesus in high esteem, when in reality they have misunderstood Him altogether. In short, Jesus did not receive a pleasing report. But He expected better from the Twelve. Thus, He put the question directly to them: "Who do you say I am?" (vs. 15).

Peter responded, perhaps speaking for the rest of the Twelve as first among equals. Peter's affirmation of Jesus' identity revealed greater insight than that of the people at large. Peter noted correctly, "You are the Christ" (vs. 16). The title *Christ* comes from the Greek term *christos*, which means "anointed" (with ointment or oil). It is equivalent to *Messiah*, a word derived from the Hebrew term *mashiach*. The latter initially referred to persons installed in a special office, such as a king or priest. The anointing with oil implied that the king approved the person to under-take his or her divinely appointed role.

Eventually, *mashiach* (and *christos*) came to designate God's royal agent, whom He would send to free Israel and restore the nation in righteousness. The Jewish hope for a messiah to deliver and purify the nation was defined mainly in political terms. Consequently, most of Jesus' contemporaries failed to recognize His true identity as the promised Messiah of Israel. In accordance with Old Testament prophecy, the Savior's mission included dying on the cross and rising from the dead (Luke 24:7, 44-47).

Matthew 16:16 relates that Peter also called Jesus the "Son of the living God." This phrase draws attention to the divine, exalted status of Jesus as the Messiah (Matt. 1:20-23; Luke 1:31-33; Acts 13:33; Rom. 1:3-4). When the Gospels refer to Him as the Son of God, the emphasis is on His unparalleled knowledge and saving work. In Peter's role as the spokesperson for the Twelve, he recognized Jesus as the true Messiah of Israel, even though He wasn't fulfilling popular expectations of the Savior as a political figure. Peter also understood that Jesus is more than just human; He is divine.

C. Jesus' Pronouncement of Blessing on Peter: vss. 17-20

Jesus replied, "Blessed are you, Simon son of Jonah, for this was not revealed to you by man, but by my Father in heaven. And I tell you that you are Peter, and on this rock I will build my church, and the gates of Hades will not overcome it. I will give you the keys of the kingdom of heaven; whatever you bind on earth will be bound in heaven, and whatever you loose on earth will be loosed in heaven." Then he warned his disciples not to tell anyone that he was the Christ.

"Simon" (Matt. 16:17) refers to Peter, a fisherman from Galilee. He was the son of Jonah (see John 1:42; 21:15-17) and one of the Twelve whom Jesus called to be His disciples (Matt. 4:18-20; Mark 1:16-17; Luke 5:1-11; John 1:40-42). Jesus said that

Peter was "blessed" (Matt. 16:17). In other words, he was highly favored by God because his spiritual awareness did not come to him through any human agency or power, but from the heavenly Father. In light of Peter's blessing, Jesus commented on his name. The Savior made a play on words when He declared, "You are Peter, and on this rock I will build my church" (vs. 18). "Peter" renders the Greek noun *petros*, which means "stone." "Rock" translates the noun *petra*, which refers to a massive formation of bedrock. "Church" renders the noun *ekklesia*, which literally refers to those who are "called out." In verse 18, the term denotes the global community of Christians, while in 18:17 it refers to a local congregation of believers.

There are differing views concerning what Jesus meant by His statement in 16:18. One option is that Peter's confession is the "rock" upon which the church is built. A second option is that Jesus Himself is the "rock" (see Acts 4:11-12; 1 Cor. 3:11; Eph. 5:23; 1 Pet. 2:5-8). A third option is that Peter, as a representative and leader of the Twelve, is foundational to the church (see Eph. 2:20-21). Regardless of which view is preferred, there is no ambiguity to Jesus' declaration that the "gates of Hades" (Matt. 16:18) will not "overcome" His church. "Hades" (like "sheol," its Hebrew counterpart) is used to denote the place of the dead. The Greek verb translated "overcome" refers to one entity winning the victory over another entity. Through this figure of speech, Jesus was promising that not even the forces of evil and death will vanquish the community of the redeemed. More broadly speaking, while the apostles played a foundational role in the spiritual construction of the church, Jesus is the most important stone of the edifice. Also, those who affirm Jesus as the Messiah and trust in Him for salvation (as Peter did in his confession) represent the type of spiritually regenerate people on which the church is built. In turn, the Savior enables them to prevail against the forces of darkness.

In verse 19, the Lord promised to give the "keys of the kingdom of heaven" to Peter. In Jesus' day, keys were a symbol for authority and power. In this verse, "keys" probably refers to the exercise of spiritual authority in God's kingdom. The nature of this spiritual authority is elaborated upon in terms of binding and loosing. There would be a correspondence between binding and loosing on earth and binding and loosing in heaven. But what, exactly, is the binding and loosing? One possibility is that as Peter heralded the Gospel, he would play a part in determining who would not believe in Jesus (binding) and who would believe (loosing). Another possibility is that Peter would have authority in church discipline cases to determine whether a sinner had not repented (binding) or had repented (loosing). A third possibility is that Peter would have the authority to tell Christians what they could not do (binding) and what they could do (loosing).

The question of the meaning in verse 19 is complicated by uncertainty over the proper way to translate the verse. Some render it as the NIV does ("will be bound . . . will be loosed"), which might imply that God will ratify decisions made on earth. Others translate the verse as the NASB does: "Whatever you shall bind on earth shall have been bound in heaven, and whatever you shall loose on earth shall have been loosed in heaven." This rendering implies that decisions made on earth would be in keeping with decisions already made by God. The ideas of binding and loosing are referred to again in 18:15-18. That connection implies that Peter and the other disciples had the authority to confront sin among the members of the church. Put another way, God sanctioned the leaders of a congregation to discern (based on the teaching of Scripture) and declare who had repented of a sin that had been committed (and was therefore loosed) and who had not repented (and was still bound; see John 20:23). This observation suggests that the "keys" (Matt. 16:19) Jesus gave to Peter were also given to all other believers.

Jesus strictly warned Peter and the rest of the Twelve not to tell anyone that He was the Messiah (vs. 20). The reason is that Jesus knew His followers needed additional time to learn more about Him before they could accurately declare the truth of His messiahship. Also, Jesus may have wanted to avoid drawing excessive attention to Himself at this time, the kind of attention that might make people think He would free them from the control of Rome. Furthermore, Jesus probably wanted to avoid intensifying the opposition of the religious leaders against Him, for doing so might lead to His arrest before the divinely appointed time. Should that happen, Jesus' enemies probably would have openly denounced Him as a heretic and tried to kill Him before He had intended.

II. THE PREDICTION OF JESUS: MATTHEW 16:21-27

A. Jesus' Foretelling of His Death and Resurrection: vs. 21

From that time on Jesus began to explain to his disciples that he must go to Jerusalem and suffer many things at the hands of the elders, chief priests and teachers of the law, and that he must be killed and on the third day be raised to life.

It's true that Jesus was the fulfillment of Old Testament prophecies concerning Israel's Savior. In addition, He was the suffering Servant—something His disciples did not yet understand. Jesus thus moved swiftly to tell them why He had come to this world. He came to die. This was Jesus' first specific teaching about His death. It was not a brief speech; rather, it gave particular details surrounding His crucifixion. In this regard, Jesus made five points about His future: (1) He would go to Jerusalem; (2) He would suffer; (3) He would be rejected by the religious leaders; (4) He would be executed by the authorities; and (5) He would rise from the dead (Matt. 16:21).

B. Jesus' Response to Peter's Rebuke: vss. 22-23

Peter took him aside and began to rebuke him. "Never, Lord!" he said. "This shall never happen to you!" Jesus turned and said to Peter, "Get behind me, Satan! You are a stumbling block to me; you do not have in mind the things of God, but the things of men."

Peter was so shocked by Jesus' prediction of His suffering, rejection, and death, that the statement concerning His resurrection apparently meant nothing to the disciple. In Peter's mind, Jesus had violated all he understood about the mission of the Savior. Along with the majority of the Jews, Peter evidently was looking for a Messiah who would defeat Rome and establish Israel as the dominant power in the region (if not the entire world). As a result, Peter took upon himself the role of counselor. As Jesus talked openly about the future with His disciples, Peter took Him aside and "began to rebuke him" (Matt. 16:22). The Greek verb translated "rebuke" means "to express strong disapproval of someone." In Peter's case, he was sternly censuring Jesus not to talk in the way He had.

The Greek phrase rendered "Never, Lord!" is more literally translated "[God be] merciful to you." It's as if Peter was wishing that the Father, in His mercy, would spare His Son from having to endure the Crucifixion. In contemporary English, we might say, "Heaven forbid, Lord!" Peter also declared that God would never let anything as horrible as this happen to the Messiah, especially since the disciple imagined that a glorious, earthly reign awaited his Master. It's amazing that, despite Peter's recent confession, he now utterly failed to understand that it was necessary for Jesus to suffer and die.

As Peter was in the process of chastising Jesus, the Savior did an amazing thing. He turned and declared that Peter's words were satanic. In fact, Peter was behaving as Jesus' adversary. Thus, Jesus referred to him harshly as "Satan" (vs. 23). Expressed differently, Satan was using Peter to tempt Jesus to abandon the Father's will. Peter's ideas about the career of the Messiah were worldly, not godly. Indeed, Peter's words echoed the same kind of temptation Satan used in the wilderness to try to get Jesus to stumble (4:1-11). Peter had not become Satan; but by Peter's words, he had become an unknowing agent of the devil. Later, Peter warned his readers of Satan's tactics in attempting to devour his prey (1 Pet. 5:4).

C. Jesus' Explanation of Discipleship's Cost: vss. 24-27

Then Jesus said to his disciples, "If anyone would come after me, he must deny himself and take up his cross and follow me. For whoever wants to save his life will lose it, but whoever loses his life for me will find it. What good will it be for a man if he gains the whole world, yet forfeits his soul? Or what can a man give in exchange for his soul? For the Son of Man is going to come in his Father's glory with his angels, and then he will reward each person according to what he has done.

Peter had modeled the wrong reaction to Jesus' messiahship. It was left to Jesus to explain the proper response. Because this was something everyone should know, Jesus addressed all the disciples. Jesus said that He was not the only one who would need to take up a cross. Anyone who followed Him would have to take up a cross too (Matt. 16:24). Bible students have long considered what it might mean to deny oneself. It might mean giving up control of our lives to the Lord. It might mean rooting out aspects of our sinful nature that are slowing down our spiritual growth. It might mean being willing to give up our own comfort to serve others. It might mean all of this.

Jesus explained in Matthew 16:25 that if we try to keep, or preserve, our physical lives for ourselves, we will ultimately lose them. However, if we surrender our lives for the sake of Jesus and the Gospel, we will find true life. The questions appearing in verse 26 drive home the point that there is no benefit in losing what is of eternal value to gain what is of temporal value. Eternal life is of much more value than success, prosperity, or even a long earthly life. The one who wins without Jesus still loses.

The shame of the cross may cause some people to avoid Jesus and not want to be identified with Him. But those who are ashamed of Jesus now will have to face being rejected by Him when He returns. At that time, the "Son of Man" (vs. 27) will appear, accompanied by a multitude of angels, in the glory of His Father. Then, Jesus will judge and reward everyone according to their deeds (see Matt. 25:31-46; John 5:25-30).

Discussion Questions

1. Why did Jesus ask His disciples about the opinions of others concerning His identity?
2. How was it possible for Peter to declare Jesus to be the Messiah?
3. What do you think Jesus meant in Matthew 16:18 when He stated, "On this rock I will build my church"?
4. In what way had Peter become a stumbling block to Jesus (vs. 23)?
5. What does it mean for believers to take up their cross and follow Jesus?

Contemporary Application

Many people see Jesus as a wise philosopher, a social revolutionary, or a kind healer, but their knowledge makes no difference in the way they live. They neither love the Lord nor serve Him. In fact, they don't really see Jesus clearly. We will have difficulty understanding Jesus' teachings—especially about His suffering messiahship and heavenly glory—if we are not committed to obeying Him.

Have we strengthened our commitment to Jesus so we can see Him more clearly and love Him more dearly? We may have known about Jesus since we were young children, but do we recognize Him as the divine Messiah so we can follow Him more nearly? Being committed to Jesus does not mean being devoted to Him occasionally. It does not come and go like the wind. No, full commitment affects every phase of our lives. Such commitment to Jesus illumines His teachings more and more day by day.

As we become more committed to Jesus, we desire to spend more time studying God's Word, are more attentive when God's Word is taught, and discuss God's Word with family and friends. The more interaction we have with God's Word, the more we understand Jesus' teachings. In addition, our commitment to Jesus deepens, and our experiences make Jesus' teachings clearer. We gain new God-given insights into the same teachings.

Witnessed by Disciples

DEVOTIONAL READING

2 Peter 1:16-21

DAILY BIBLE READINGS

Monday February 15
2 Peter 1:16-21 Eyewitnesses of Jesus' Majesty

Tuesday February 16
John 1:6-13 Witness of the True Light

Wednesday February 17
Matthew 12:22-28 The Kingdom Has Come

Thursday February 18
Matthew 20:29-34 Beseeched the Lord, David's Son

Friday February 19
Matthew 21:1-11 Hailed as the Son of David

Saturday February 20
Acts 3:11-16 To This We Are Witnesses

Sunday February 21
Matthew 17:1-12 Listen to Him

Scripture

Background Scripture: *Matthew 17:1-12*
Scripture Lesson: *Matthew 17:1-12*
Key Verse: *[Jesus'] was transfigured before them. His face shone like the sun, and his clothes became as white as the light.* Matthew 17:2.
Scripture Lesson for Children: *Matthew 17:1-8*
Key Verse for Children: *A voice from the cloud said, "This is my Son, whom I love; with him I am well pleased. Listen to him!"* Matthew 17:5.

Lesson Aim

To assess how our commitment to the Messiah can strengthen our understanding of His teachings.

Lesson Setting

Time: *A.D. 29*
Place: *Near Caesarea Philippi*

Lesson Outline

Witnessed by Disciples

I. The Mountaintop Experience: Matthew 17:1-3
   A. *The Journey to the Mountain: vs. 1*
   B. *The Son's Transfiguration: vs. 2*
   C. *The Appearance of Moses and Elijah: vs. 3*
II. The Father's Voice: Matthew 17:4-8
   A. *The Suggestion Made by Peter: vs. 4*
   B. *The Declaration Made by the Father: vs. 5*
   C. *The Reassuring Presence of Jesus: vss. 6-8*
III. The Son's Instructions: Matthew 17:9-12
   A. *The Messiah's Prohibition: vs. 9*
   B. *The Messiah's Explanation: vss. 10-12*

Introduction for Adults

Topic: *Mountaintop Experiences*

The Noxubee County Library in Macon, Mississippi, is an excellent repository of information. Books fill the shelves in the well-stocked facility. Computers and other up-to-date equipment make the building a center for everyone in the area wanting knowledge.

The Noxubee County Library has an interesting past. In 1907, the three-storied brick structure started out as a jail and was used as a place of incarceration for 70 years. In 1982, a group of citizens determined to renovate the building and use it to house the county's collection of learning resources.

Today, library users walk through cell doors to reach bookshelves. The rope hook and the trapdoor for the gallows are still in place. The people of Macon had the vision to convert the structure from a dingy place of incarceration to a delightful space for information.

Even in the bleakest of times, Christians are able to see a future because of the Savior. He promised one day to transport us to the celestial "Mount Zion, to the heavenly Jerusalem, the city of the living God" (Heb. 12:22).

Introduction for Youth

Topic: *I See You!*

James Truslow Adams, in his book *The Epic of America* (published in 1931), first referred to the American dream. He envisioned the country as a "land in which life should be better and richer and fuller for everyone, with opportunity for each according to ability or achievement." Many once thought the dream of financial success and power was achievable. Supposedly, hard work would pay off and be rewarded with wealth and prestige.

Sadly, today's youth do not follow that formula to the American dream. Instead, many believe that the American dream is now achieved, not by hard work, but by inheriting wealth from a family member or by winning a lottery! Because of the odds against either of these events occurring, most young people feel as if they have no hope in the future.

The ultimate dream or hope of a believer, whether young or old, is one day to "see [Jesus] as he is" (1 John 3:2). Our confident expectation resides in His eternal kingdom, not in material wealth or earthly power.

Concepts for Children

Topic: *A Special Appearance*

1. Peter, James, and John went with Jesus up on a very high mountain.
2. Peter, James, and John were with Jesus when Moses and Elijah appeared.
3. Jesus talked to Moses and Elijah in the presence of the Savior's followers.
4. Everyone who was there heard the Father say that He loved His Son.
5. The Father is pleased with us when we obey His Son, the Lord Jesus.

Lesson Commentary

I. THE MOUNTAINTOP EXPERIENCE: MATTHEW 17:1-3

A. The Journey to the Mountain: vs. 1

After six days Jesus took with him Peter, James and John the brother of James, and led them up a high mountain by themselves.

Matthew 16:28 records Jesus' statement that some of His hearers would not "taste death" before they saw the "Son of Man coming in his kingdom." There are differing ways of understanding the latter. Some think the coming of Jesus and His kingdom "with power" (Mark 9:1) refer to His resurrection from the dead. Others say the reference is to the birth of the Christian church at Pentecost. Still others think the reference is to the Transfiguration. In any case, not long after making the preceding pronouncements, Jesus split up His group, taking three of the disciples with Him up the side of a high mountain (Matt. 17:1). Some see a parallel with the episode in which Aaron, Nadab, and Abihu accompanied Moses up Mount Sinai (see Exod. 24:1). This suggestion harmonizes with the truth that Jesus is the end-time prophet as Moses foretold in Deuteronomy 18:15.

Why Jesus specifically chose Peter, James, and John is subject to debate. The Bible does describe Peter's special role because of his confession concerning Jesus (16:16-19), John as the disciple whom Jesus loved (John 13:23), and James as the first of the Twelve to be martyred for the Lord (Acts 12:2). In general, Peter, James, and John enjoyed an especially close relationship with the Savior, and now they would be privileged to witness a special revelation of the Messiah's glory. In addition to this occasion, Jesus allowed only Peter, James, and John to accompany Him when He raised the daughter of Jairus from the dead (Mark 5:37; Luke 8:51) and while Jesus prayed in the Garden of Gethsemane (Matt. 26:37; Mark 14:33).

The context of Matthew 17 seems to indicate that the Transfiguration occurred on a "high mountain" (vs. 1) that was in the vicinity of Caesarea Philippi. Because Mount Tabor, the traditional site of the event, is some distance from the city and only 1,800 feet in height, it is unlikely that it took place there. Mount Hermon fits better in that it is close. Also, three different mountains to the southeast of Caesarea Philippi are each over 4,000 feet. Any of these could fit the context and provide the solitude Jesus desired for the Transfiguration.

B. The Son's Transfiguration: vs. 2

There he was transfigured before them. His face shone like the sun, and his clothes became as white as the light.

While Jesus was praying on the mountain, He was "transfigured" (Matt. 17:2). The Greek word used is a variant of *metamorphoo*, which means an essential change in form. This term is the origin of our English word *metamorphosis*. The glow on Jesus' face was translucent, coming from within, like a lampshade's luminance when the bulb inside is turned on. Matthew noted that Jesus' countenance shone with the brightness of the sun and His clothes turned as white as light. In the Bible, God's glory is often associated with light. Thus in the Transfiguration, Jesus' heavenly glory was being unveiled. It must have been a marvelous sight.

Moses' face had also shone with the glory of God when the lawmaker had come down from Mount Sinai. His brightness, however, had been external and fading (see Exod. 34:29-35). In contrast, Jesus' glory was internal and always present, though it was veiled by His human form, that is, except during His transfiguration. The most profound way in which Jesus' followers witnessed His glory was through His death on the cross, followed by His resurrection and ascension (see John 7:39; 12:23, 28; 13:31-32; 17:1, 4-5). At His second coming, Jesus' glory again will be totally revealed to the entire world (see Matt. 25:31).

C. The Appearance of Moses and Elijah: vs. 3

Just then there appeared before them Moses and Elijah, talking with Jesus.

As if the Lord's transfiguration in glory was not enough, two former heroes of the faith—Moses and Elijah—appeared and began talking with Jesus (Matt. 13:3). We know from another Gospel that the subject of their conversation was Jesus' approaching death (see Luke 9:31). It's been suggested that these two men, in particular, appeared because Moses (the nation's number-one lawgiver) represented the Law and Elijah (a premier prophet) represented the Prophets. Their appearance was a visual reminder that Jesus fulfilled the Law and the Prophets, that is, the whole Old Testament revelation.

Concerning Elijah, his name means "Yahweh is my God," and it summarized well the message of his life. Elijah began prophesying about 875 B.C. during the 22-year reign of King Ahab. Nothing is known about Elijah's family and little is known about his life before the initial confrontation with Ahab. First Kings 17:1 identifies Elijah as being from Tishbe in Gilead, a region that extended to the upper reaches of the part of Israel east of the Jordan River.

The Bible regards Elijah as a rugged and tough wilderness dweller, much like John the Baptizer (2 Kings 1:8). Elijah's unquestioning devotion to God made the prophet a bold and persuasive spokesperson for the Lord. Elijah spent most of his time announcing the dire consequences for the Israelites of breaking their covenant with God. But Elijah's presence and the power of his ministry testified to the concern of the living God, who called His people to return to Him. James 5:17 describes Elijah as being a man with the same human frailties that all people have; yet he also "prayed earnestly" that there would be no rain. Consequently, none fell "on the land for three and a half years" (see 1 Kings 17:1; 18:41-46). In the end, God took Elijah directly to heaven in a chariot of fire (2 Kings 2:11-12).

II. THE FATHER'S VOICE: MATTHEW 17:4-8

A. The Suggestion Made by Peter: vs. 4

Peter said to Jesus, "Lord, it is good for us to be here. If you wish, I will put up three shelters—one for you, one for Moses and one for Elijah."

The Old Testament prophets had foretold the Messiah's suffering and glory to follow (1 Pet. 1:10-11). Peter, however, having just witnessed Jesus' glory during His transfiguration, evidently assumed that His glorification was immediately coming. Peter clearly didn't grasp the significance of Jesus' transfiguration, at least not while it was occurring. On behalf of the other two disciples, Peter spoke to Jesus and offered to build "three shelters—one for you, one for Moses and one for Elijah" (Matt. 17:4). It seems that Peter's intent in building huts was to prolong the experience. His wording shows that he was thinking of Jesus as being on a par with the other two. Peter failed to recognize that Moses and Elijah were secondary figures compared to Jesus. Furthermore, though Peter's motive seemed laudable (at least on the surface), his timing was out of sync with that of God and the Old Testament messianic prophecies. In short, Peter was eager to experience Jesus' promised glory without the suffering that Jesus had foretold.

The Jewish feast of Tabernacles forms the backdrop of Peter's remarks. This feast (also known as Sukkoth, Ingathering, Shelters, Booths, and Tents) was celebrated in autumn after the harvest. The observance lasted seven days, making it the most extended festival of the Jewish year. During this time, participants lived in tents or shelters made from branches and leaves. It was a sacred season when God's people commemorated the way the Lord graciously provided for the Israelites during their years of wilderness wandering. The feast was also a time to thank God for allowing the year's harvest to be completed (see Lev. 23:33-43; Num. 29:12-39; Deut. 16:13-17).

B. The Declaration Made by the Father: vs. 5

While he was still speaking, a bright cloud enveloped them, and a voice from the cloud said, "This is my Son, whom I love; with him I am well pleased. Listen to him!"

Peter's mistake was pointed out to him by none other than the Father. While Peter was still speaking, a bright cloud (representing God's presence) enveloped the people on the mountaintop. In the Bible, God is often associated with clouds, such as when He led the Israelites in the Sinai wilderness. The Father, while speaking from the cloud that enveloped the mountain, gave the Son His stamp of approval (Matt. 17:5). Incidentally, the Father made the same declaration at Jesus' baptism, which signified the start of His earthly ministry (see 3:17). Now that Jesus was about to experience the Cross, the Father's voice saying, "This is my Son" (Matt. 17:5), affirmed Jesus' earthly ministry before His disciples.

It is worth noting that the Father, in making this pronouncement, rebuked Peter by pointing out that Jesus was not just another hero of the faith, but rather His very Son. Furthermore, the Father expressed His love and approval of Jesus. The Son had come to earth with a difficult mission, yet He was being completely obedient to God. In light of this, the three disciples—and all people—should have listened to and obeyed Jesus' words. Admittedly, the Twelve had often listened to Jesus' teachings, but frequently they did so without understanding or obeying His words. So now, the Father commanded that the Son's teachings were to be taken to heart and heeded. Doing so was appropriate in light of the difficult days that lay ahead.

C. The Reassuring Presence of Jesus: vss. 6-8

When the disciples heard this, they fell facedown to the ground, terrified. But Jesus came and touched them. "Get up," he said. "Don't be afraid." When they looked up, they saw no one except Jesus.

The three disciples, terrified by hearing the voice of God, fell prostrate (Matt. 17:6). The ancient Israelites had felt the same kind of fear when they had heard the voice of God from the cloud on Mount Sinai. With genuine sensitivity and compassion, Jesus came, gave the disciples a reassuring touch, and said, "Get up. . . . Don't be afraid" (vs. 7). Jesus' actions reflected His deep affection for these three men. When the disciples looked up, Jesus alone was with them; Moses, Elijah, and the cloud were gone (vs. 8). The extraordinary experience was over.

Some six decades after Jesus' resurrection and ascension, the apostle John found himself in the presence of the divine Messiah. But now John's closest friend was exalted, honored, and glorified. As he stood before the risen Lord, the apostle dropped to his knees as though he were dead (see Rev. 1:17). Isaiah, Ezekiel, and Daniel had similar responses when suddenly exposed to the glorified presence of God (see Isa. 6:5; Ezek. 1:28; Dan. 8:17). This was not the same experience John had when he leaned toward the Messiah at the Last Supper. The Savior touched John, perhaps both to strengthen him physically and comfort him emotionally. The Son encouraged the apostle not to be afraid, for He is the first and the last (see Rev. 1:17). This is a divine title that appears elsewhere in Scripture in reference to the Lord (see Isa. 41:4; 44:6; 48:12). It means essentially the same thing as the title "the Alpha and Omega" (Rev. 1:8).

III. THE SON'S INSTRUCTIONS: MATTHEW 17:9-12

A. The Messiah's Prohibition: vs. 9

As they were coming down the mountain, Jesus instructed them, "Don't tell anyone what you have seen, until the Son of Man has been raised from the dead."

As the Lord and His three followers descended from the mountain, the disciples were probably bursting to tell the others what they had witnessed. But Jesus directed them not to tell anyone about it—not until after He was raised from the dead (Matt. 17:9). It would only be after His resurrection that the disciples could correctly grasp the significance of the Transfiguration. And Jesus certainly didn't want to give the impression that He was about to establish a glorified earthly kingdom.

On other occasions, Jesus had made a similar statement about not publicizing His messiahship (for example, when Peter said that Jesus is the Messiah; see Matt. 16:16-20; Mark 8:29-30). Even though the disciples had accepted Jesus as the Messiah, they were still in some ways spiritual infants. Perhaps they were not quite ready to explain a vision they did not yet fully comprehend—at least not until after Jesus' resurrection. In any case, the time was not right for the people at large to know Jesus' identity as the Messiah.

The Transfiguration was important for several reasons. First, it unveiled the splendor of the Redeemer, the Son of God, authenticating His messiahship. Second, the vision of Jesus confirmed and expanded what He had been teaching His followers about Himself. Third, the Transfiguration revealed the great depth to which the Savior had humbled Himself in becoming a human being. Fourth, the mountaintop experience encouraged the Twelve to remain faithful to one who would be executed on a cross because, despite the immediate prospect of suffering and shame, they could look forward to a future of unending glory with their almighty Lord.

B. The Messiah's Explanation: vss. 10-12

The disciples asked him, "Why then do the teachers of the law say that Elijah must come first?" Jesus replied, "To be sure, Elijah comes and will restore all things. But I tell you, Elijah has already come, and they did not recognize him, but have done to him everything they wished. In the same way the Son of Man is going to suffer at their hands."

Having been reminded that Jesus was going to die, the disciples asked why the scribes taught that Elijah would appear first, that is, before the advent of the Messiah (Matt. 17:10). It didn't make sense to the disciples that Jesus, who they now knew to be the Messiah, would have to die, especially if Elijah came first and initiated widespread repentance (see Mal. 3:1; 4:5-6). Of course, the disciples had just seen Elijah, but they assumed that this was not the return of the prophet that Malachi had foretold. Understandably, then, the Twelve wondered why Elijah had not come to prepare the way for Jesus.

Jesus did not contradict the scribes' teaching about Elijah's coming, which was certainly part of God's eternal plan (see Rev. 11:3-6). Instead, Jesus affirmed that the scribes were correct in teaching that Elijah would precede the Messiah (Matt. 17:11). But Jesus pointed out that the scribes had failed to recognize that Elijah had already come (vs. 12). Of course, Jesus was talking about John. The Baptizer was not a reincarnation of Elijah, but rather one who fulfilled the role of Elijah by preaching repentance and preparing the way for Jesus. The scribes had not only failed to recognize John for who he was, but they had even gone further and contributed to his persecution and eventual murder. This anticipated Jesus' own suffering at the hands of the nation's leaders.

When the Savior had said these things, it became clear to His three disciples that the Elijah who had already come was John (vs. 13). The Baptizer was the person whom the prophet Isaiah had promised would prepare the way of the Lord (Isa. 40:3). John's ministry also found fulfillment in what the prophet Malachi had described when he spoke of Elijah preparing the hearts of the people for the advent of the Lord (Mal. 4:5-6). Jesus, in confirming John's role, both affirmed the Baptizer's ministry and Jesus' own work as the Messiah.

Discussion Questions

1. Why did Jesus possibly take only Peter, James, and John with Him up a high mountain?
2. What is significant about Moses and Elijah appearing and talking with Jesus?
3. Why did the Father deem it necessary to affirm His love of and approval for His Son?
4. Why did Jesus direct Peter, James, and John not to tell anyone about the Transfiguration until after Jesus' resurrection?
5. In what way did Jesus' response to His disciples' question about Elijah actually refer to John the Baptizer?

Contemporary Application

Jesus selected Peter, James, and John to witness the Transfiguration probably because they had proved themselves to be the more committed followers. Then through this amazing mountaintop episode, they gained a greater understanding of Jesus and His teachings.

Peter, recalling his encounter with Jesus during His transfiguration, later wrote, "We were eyewitnesses of his majesty" (2 Pet. 1:16; see also vss. 17-18). The apostle's memory of this incident no doubt increasingly encouraged him, James, and John, especially as their commitment to the Lord deepened. Moreover, as Peter's devotion to the Messiah became stronger, he probably looked forward to greater understanding of Jesus' teaching. Each step in the apostle's walk with the Lord helped him to comprehend more of what the Savior wanted him to tell others concerning the Gospel.

We can follow Peter's footsteps, and if we do, we can also look forward to a deeper understanding of our Lord's teachings. This is especially true as we become more committed to Him. It's exciting to know that God's Word will become clearer to us as we deepen our relationship with the Redeemer. In fact, the more experiences we have with the Son, the more we can anticipate the new truths He has in store for us.

Our world often tells us what is wrong with our faith in the Savior and how dull Christianity seems. The spiritual journey, however, can be a thrilling adventure of discovery to which we are always looking forward with excitement. After all, what awaits us is always a clearer awareness of our good Shepherd.

Anointed by a Woman

Scripture

Background Scripture: *Matthew 26:6-13*

Scripture Lesson: *Matthew 26:6-13*

Key Verse: *"I tell you the truth, wherever this gospel is preached throughout the world, what she has done will also be told, in memory of her."* Matthew 26:13.

Scripture Lesson for Children: *Matthew 26:6-13*

Key Verse for Children: *"Wherever this gospel is preached throughout the world, what she has done will also be told, in memory of her."* Matthew 26:13.

Lesson Aim

To consider the importance of showing devotion to Jesus.

Lesson Setting

Time: A.D. *30*

Place: *Bethany*

Lesson Outline

Anointed by a Woman

   I. The Woman's Act of Kindness: Matthew 26:6-7

      A. *The Location: vs. 6*

      B. *The Anointing: vs. 7*

  II. The Savior's Endorsement of the Act: Matthew 26:8-13

      A. *The Disciples' Indignation: vss. 8-9*

      B. *The Savior's Rebuttal: vss. 10-13*

Introduction for Adults

Topic: *Extravagant Love*

We've all seen classic movies where the young female lead decides she doesn't want to marry her handsome young betrothed. She rips off her diamond engagement ring and hurls it into the dust. He throws himself at her and begs her to change her mind, but it's too late.

Scriptwriters did not invent this story line. The basics have been acted out since the dawn of time, but perhaps nowhere more dramatically than in Judas Iscariot's broken commitment to Jesus. Judas was the pinnacle of betrayal because he turned his back on the Son of God. Judas threw Jesus' extravagant love into the dirt. Judas traded the Lord of glory for money.

How refreshing it is to see the brilliance of the woman who poured out her life savings on Jesus. She didn't trade Jesus for money; instead, she gave all she had to Him. That's an act of devotion we rarely see, even though opportunities abound for us to show how much we love Jesus.

Introduction for Youth

Topic: *I Kneel before You*

Governments hang traitors for selling military secrets. Sometimes we feel like doing that to friends who betray us. We trust our friends with our personal secrets, but sometimes they cannot keep a confidence and word leaks out that some of our secrets are public knowledge. While we condemn this in others, we have to be careful we are not guilty of doing it ourselves.

Consider how close Judas Iscariot was to Jesus; yet Judas could not control his desire to turn Jesus in for money. The Judas account powerfully reminds us how vulnerable we are to sin. When it comes to keeping true to our Christian promises, we must be careful lest we betray Jesus for a brief joke.

Judas' treachery looks especially dark when we compare it to the woman who came up to Jesus and anointed Him. The woman risked everything to worship and honor Him. So must we.

Concepts for Children

Topic: *A Special Act of Love*

1. Mary poured expensive perfume on Jesus' head.
2. Jesus said that Mary's act of kindness prepared Him for His burial.
3. Jesus reminded His followers that He would not always be with them in the flesh.
4. Jesus said that Mary would always be remembered for her act of love.
5. Jesus is pleased when we do things that show our devotion to Him.

Lesson Commentary

I. THE WOMAN'S ACT OF KINDNESS: MATTHEW 26:6-7

A. The Location: vs. 6

While Jesus was in Bethany in the home of a man known as Simon the Leper.

The last week of Jesus' earthly ministry occurred in the spring of A.D. 30. His triumphal entry into Jerusalem took place on Sunday (Matt. 21:1-11). Then, on Monday, Jesus cleared the temple (vss. 12-13) and cursed a fig tree (vss. 18-19). Next, on Tuesday, Jesus was interrogated by the religious leaders (vss. 23-27) and taught in the temple (21:28—23:39). After leaving the shrine, Jesus continued to give teachings and respond to His disciples' questions (24:1—25:46).

When Jesus had finished teaching (26:1), He noted to His followers that the Jewish Passover would begin in two days. He explained that it was the will of the Father for Him, the Son of Man, to be handed over to His enemies and nailed to a cross (vs. 2). This statement points to a sobering reality, namely, that humankind did not recognize the Messiah when He came to earth (John 1:10). Perhaps even more distressing is that many of the Jewish people failed to accept Him as their Savior (vs. 11).

The plot to kill Jesus was set in motion when the leading religious authorities gathered at the residence of Caiaphas, "the high priest" (Matt. 26:3). He was the son-in-law of Annas, the previous high priest. The Roman procurator Valerius Gratius appointed Caiaphas around A.D. 18, and he was subsequently removed from office around A.D. 37. At this nefarious meeting, the attendees discussed how they might arrest Jesus by means of stealth (vs. 4). Then, after capturing the Messiah, they wanted to "kill him." The ringleaders were afraid, however, to carry out this gruesome act during the Passover because they sensed that Jesus was too popular to arrest openly. Thus they decided to wait and thereby avoid inciting a riot among the people (vs. 5).

It's appropriate that the setting of Matthew 26 is the Jewish Passover. This was the yearly festival of national redemption. The Passover lamb was killed in the afternoon of the fourteenth of Nisan (a month corresponding to March/April). The Passover meal was eaten after sunset (the start of a new day, the fifteenth) but before midnight. The Feast of Unleavened Bread began on the fifteenth and continued through the twenty-first day of the same month. By Jesus' time, the two feasts were treated as one, so that essentially Passover was a weeklong festival. Just as at the original Passover, lambs were slain as substitutes for firstborn children, so now Jesus would die as the fulfillment of that symbol. He was our Passover Lamb, dying in our place (see 1 Cor. 5:7).

The anointing described in Matthew 26:6-13 was probably the same one mentioned in John 12:1-8. Jesus had been going through towns and villages, telling the good news about God's kingdom. Along with the Twelve, a number of women accompanied Him from time to time (Luke 8:1-3), perhaps including Mary and Martha, the sisters of Lazarus (John 11:1-3). These three were among Jesus' most devoted followers and perhaps part of an inner circle of Jesus' associates. As the Savior and His disciples were traveling along, they came to Bethany (Matt. 26:6). This was a village located about two miles southeast of Jerusalem on the eastern slope of the Mount of Olives, the hill outside the holy city where Jesus prayed and was arrested. While Jesus was at Bethany, He was welcomed into the home of "Simon the leper." The religious elitists of the day would claim that Jesus' decision to lodge there made Him ritually unclean (see 8:1-4). Some have speculated that Jesus had previously cleansed Simon from leprosy and that he was either a member of the family of Lazarus, Mary, and Martha, or a close friend.

B. The Anointing: vs. 7

A woman came to him with an alabaster jar of very expensive perfume, which she poured on his head as he was reclining at the table.

John 12:3 reveals that Mary was the woman of Matthew 26:7 who came to anoint Jesus. Mary was the sister of Martha and Lazarus. An examination of Luke 10:38-42 indicates that Mary and Martha could not have been more different. Martha was task-oriented. She enjoyed opening up her house to visitors, but she wanted to make sure things were just right. In contrast, Mary was relationship-oriented. She likely enjoyed having visitors, too. Yet, she wasn't averse to setting aside the tasks associated with being hospitable so that she could spend time with her guests.

John 11:1-44 recounts the episode in which Jesus restored Lazarus to life. According to 12:2, Martha prepared a meal for Him and the rest of the guests. Possibly the dinner was given in honor of the Messiah to thank Him for what He had done for Lazarus. Indeed, Lazarus reclined at the table with the Savior, no doubt giving Him his undivided attention. In those days, guests in wealthy homes normally did not eat a meal while sitting at a table; instead, they leaned on cushions with their left arm and ate food with their right hand. Their head would be near the table and their feet extended away from it.

Showing hospitality was an important custom in the biblical world. Jews in the Old Testament and Christians in the New Testament were encouraged to be kind to strangers and to take care of the needs of passersby (see Rom. 12:13). Hospitality was shown in many ways. The most common was to wash the feet of visitors. This offered much-needed relief to those who traveled long distances over the dusty roads in Israel. It was also common to prepare meals for visitors. This often consumed a great deal of time, especially as hostesses baked bread, cooked meat, and did whatever else was necessary to provide substantial meals for guests. Animals accompanying visitors were also looked after and were given food, water, and shelter.

When guests left, they were often given supplies to help them in their travels. This could include the provision of food, water, and articles of clothing. The host might even accompany departing visitors for a short distance as they continued their journey. Showing hospitality in a practical way met the physical needs of visitors. It was also crucial for maintaining social relationships. Asking someone to set this aside would not have been taken lightly.

It is understandable why Mary wanted to show her love and respect for Jesus. Perhaps after some forethought, Mary decided to bring Jesus one of her most valuable possessions. This was an "alabaster jar" (Matt. 26:7) containing a rose-colored ointment made from the roots and stems of the Indian nard plant. Mary broke the neck of the jar, which contained only one application. She then poured the ointment on Jesus' head and feet. As Mary did this, the sweet smell of the perfume diffused throughout the house (John 12:3). In Jesus' day, slaves usually took care of the guests' feet. Thus, Mary's actions were a sign of humility. In Jewish culture, most women would not unbind their hair in public. But Mary did not allow this social convention to stop her from showing devotion to the Messiah. The sacrificial aspect of Mary's action is underscored by the expense of the perfume she used to anoint Jesus.

Nard is an herb with rose-purple flowers and fibrous roots that give off a pleasant aroma. In Bible times, people dried the roots of this plant and used them to make perfume or ointment. The Romans anointed their heads with the product. Nard can be found throughout western Asia and is also native to the high elevations of the Himalayan Mountains. The perfume made from the nard that is mentioned in the Bible most likely originated in the Himalayas (Song of Sol. 1:12; 4:13-14; Mark 14:3; John 12:3). Merchants transported the product in carefully sealed alabaster jars. The seal ensured both the preservation and the conservation of the perfume. The customer would break the seal only when he or she intended to use the ointment. Because merchants shipped nard over great distances, the product was very expensive. In New Testament times, a pint of pure nard cost about a year's wages (see Mark 14:3-5). Because of its great expense, the product was used only by the wealthy, and then only for the anointing of special guests.

II. THE SAVIOR'S ENDORSEMENT OF THE ACT: MATTHEW 26:8-13

A. The Disciples' Indignation: vss. 8-9

When the disciples saw this, they were indignant. "Why this waste?" they asked. "This perfume could have been sold at a high price and the money given to the poor."

The disciples, perhaps at the instigation of Judas (John 12:4), objected to this apparent "waste" (Matt. 26:8). Supposedly, Mary could have sold the "perfume" (vs. 9) for a sizable sum of money, which then could have been donated to the poor. But, as John 12:6 reveals, the real concern of Judas was not to help the poor but rather to pilfer as much of the money as possible from the disciples' funds for his own use.

Perhaps to a casual observer, the idea advanced by Judas sounded pious. But the author of the Fourth Gospel explained that Judas did not really care about the poor. He was irritated because Mary's action prevented Judas from having more money to filch, since he was the group's treasurer and sometimes stole the money. Interestingly, the cost Mary bore to show devotion to the Messiah was several times the amount Judas later accepted to betray Jesus (see Matt. 26:5). It is also worth noting that the remarks Judas made were inconsiderate of the Redeemer and unnecessarily harsh toward Mary.

B. The Savior's Rebuttal: vss. 10-13

Aware of this, Jesus said to them, "Why are you bothering this woman? She has done a beautiful thing to me. The poor you will always have with you, but you will not always have me. When she poured this perfume on my body, she did it to prepare me for burial. I tell you the truth, wherever this gospel is preached throughout the world, what she has done will also be told, in memory of her."

Thankfully, Jesus defended Mary's action. The Savior questioned why the disciples, undoubtedly spearheaded by Judas, were "bothering this woman" (Matt. 26:10). After all, she had done a "beautiful thing." By this Jesus indicated that Mary had performed a loving act of service, which was especially appropriate in light of His approaching death and "burial" (vs. 12). In those days, it was a Jewish custom to anoint the body of a deceased loved one with sweet-smelling oil and spices prior to burying the corpse. The Messiah was alluding to the fact that, in less than a week, the authorities would arrest, condemn, and crucify Him.

Mary's action underscored the supreme value of Jesus' atoning sacrifice and the great depth of Mary's devotion to Him. Mary's unselfish deed shone all the more brighter because of its contrast with the way the disciples were competing for power (Mark 10:37, 41). Even more strikingly, Mary's generous act contrasted with the way Judas was about to trade Jesus to the religious leaders for money. It is no wonder that, as believers proclaimed the Gospel worldwide (that is, the Christian message of salvation), they would talk about Mary's noble deed "in memory of her" (Matt. 26:13).

Jesus' remark that there will always be poor people (most likely an allusion to Deut. 15:11) should not be taken as an indication that He lacked concern for the poor (Matt. 26:11). In fact, He was always the champion of the oppressed and the afflicted. For instance, Jesus previously had stressed the ongoing need to help the poor (see 25:34–36). In the anointing at Bethany, the Redeemer affirmed another important truth, namely, that it is never a waste to give one's best to honor the Lord. Jesus' comment in 27:11 meant that His followers would have many opportunities to help the needy. But only a short time remained for His disciples to show Him their love before He died.

When residents from the rural areas around Jerusalem learned that the Savior was in Bethany, many flocked to see Him. They also wanted to see Lazarus, whom they learned Jesus had restored to life (John 12:9). The miracle involving Lazarus prompted many to reject the religious leaders and put their faith in Jesus. Because this turn of events stoked the fears of the chief priests, they made plans to have both Lazarus and Jesus murdered (vss. 10-11). Judas Iscariot would play a pivotal role in helping the authorities eliminate the itinerant preacher from Galilee. However, the exact reason for the decision of Judas to betray Jesus remains open to debate.

We have only sketchy background details about Judas from the Gospel accounts. His surname, "Iscariot," may refer to his hometown, either Kerioth of Moab or Kerioth-hezron in southern Judah. If the latter is true, he would be the only Judean among the disciples, and Judeans looked down upon Galileans. Another suggestion is that Judas's name is a Semitic version of the Latin word *sicarius*, the name for a radical Zealot who carried a dagger, but there is no evidence in the Gospels that he was a Zealot. His name always appears last in the lists of the apostles (Matt. 10:4; Mark 3:19; Luke 6:16), no doubt reflecting the writers' hatred of what he did. John, in fact, does not hesitate to state that Judas was a thief.

One motive, then, for Judas's betrayal could have been greed. After all, he took 30 pieces of silver from the religious leaders to betray Jesus (Matt. 26:14-16). Only when he saw Jesus being tried for execution did Judas fully realize what he had done (27:3-10). Another theory is that Judas was very patriotic. More specifically, he betrayed Jesus when he realized that the Lord was not going to establish an earthly kingdom, or Judas hoped that the betrayal would cause Jesus to establish His kingdom immediately. While Satan deceived Judas into betraying Jesus, Judas still remained fully responsible for his actions (see John 13:2, 27).

Whatever the reason Judas had for betraying Jesus, Matthew 27:3 says Judas regretted what he had done. In turn, his feelings of remorse led to a lame attempt to atone for his own sin. When he tried to give back the betrayal money, the religious leaders ridiculed him. In despair, Judas hanged himself, an act described in vivid detail by Peter in the Book of Acts (1:16-20). The chief priests then used this "blood money" (so to speak) to buy a field to bury the indigent poor, fulfilling Old Testament prophecy (Matt. 27:6-10).

After Judas agreed to betray Jesus, the Redeemer had His followers make preparations to eat the Passover. Next, during the meal, Jesus revealed that Judas would break faith with Him. Then, after the Messiah instituted the Lord's Supper, He and the Twelve sang a hymn and went out to the Mount of Olives. While there, Jesus foretold that Peter would deny Him, and then He prayed. In the events that followed, Judas betrayed Jesus with a kiss, the authorities arrested Him, and His disciples abandoned Him. Caiaphas then interrogated Jesus, and the Sanhedrin condemned Him to death and treated Him abusively. Meanwhile, out in the courtyard, Peter denied his allegiance to the Messiah three times (26:17-75).

Though Judas was associated with the Messiah, heard His teaching, and witnessed His works, Judas did not have an abiding spiritual union with the Son. Rather than bearing fruit, the life of Judas ended in destruction. The Savior also chose Peter to be one of His disciples. Jesus taught him the same truths and gave him the same sorts of opportunities to witness that He had given Judas. Peter did not begin his life as a disciple with great success, but after some pruning (such as his denial of the Son and later reinstatement), Peter bore much fruit. He found the key to a productive life in a living relationship with the Savior.

Discussion Questions

1. What would have possibly motivated Jesus to lodge in Bethany at the home of Simon the leper?
2. Why were the disciples indignant at the sight of Mary anointing Jesus?
3. Why did Jesus come to Mary's defense regarding her act of kindness to Him?
4. How should Jesus' statement regarding the poor be understood?
5. Why did Jesus want the memory of Mary's action honored by future believers?

Contemporary Application

Most of your students would say they are devoted to Christ. But are they doing enough to show their devotion to Him? It is clear they are committed enough to go to church and attend Sunday school. But how much further does their commitment extend?

Having the class think about the following questions will help them evaluate whether their devotion to Christ is sufficient: How often do I pray? How much time do I spend studying God's Word? Am I involved in the church or in other Christian ministries as extensively as I should be? How frequently do I share the Gospel with non-Christians?

The intent in asking these questions is not to make your students feel guilty. Rather, it is to encourage them to candidly assess their relationship to and service for the Redeemer. Some of the class members might conclude that they are not doing enough to show their devotion to Jesus, while others might determine they should be doing more. A few students might decide they are doing as much as the Lord wants.

Your students should also examine their attitude toward serving the Lord. Are they motivated by greed or by gratitude? As they minister to others, is their goal to advance their own cause or glorify the Savior? Do the class members serve the Lord begrudgingly or are they eager to do so? Do they take the initiative to show their devotion to Him or do others have to spur them into action?

Commitment to Jesus is not a one-way street where He expects us to do everything. In reality, the Lord works in and through us as we show our devotion to Him. Without His strength and provisions, we could not possibly do what He wants. It is the presence and power of the Son in our lives that enables us to set aside our desires and give ourselves wholeheartedly in service to Him.

Mission to the Community

Scripture

Background Scripture: *Jonah 1:1-3; 3:1-9*
Scripture Lesson: *Jonah 1:1-3; 3:1-9*
Key Verse: *The Ninevites believed God. They declared a fast, and all of them, from the greatest to the least, put on sackcloth.* Jonah 3:5.
Scripture Lesson for Children: *Jonah 1:1-3; 3:1-9*
Key Verse for Children: *Jonah obeyed the word of the* LORD *and went to Nineveh.* Jonah 3:3.

Lesson Aim

To repent of rebellious attitudes or actions in our relationship with God.

Lesson Setting

Time: *About 793–753 B.C.*
Place: *Israel; the Mediterranean Sea; Nineveh*

Lesson Outline

Mission to the Community

   I. God's Call: Jonah 1:1-4
       A. *The Assignment: vss. 1-2*
       B. *The Refusal: vs. 3*
  II. Jonah's Compliance: Jonah 3:1-4
       A. *God's Command: vss. 1-2*
       B. *Jonah's Preaching: vss. 3-4*
 III. Nineveh's Repentance: Jonah 3:5-9
       A. *Displaying Sorrow: vss. 5-6*
       B. *Issuing a Decree: vss. 7-9*

Introduction for Adults
Topic: *Influencing Community Change*

William Wilberforce was born on August 24, 1759, to wealthy merchant parents. He studied at Cambridge University, where he became a long-lasting friend of William Pitt, the future prime minister of Great Britain. In 1780, Wilberforce became a member of the British parliament, where he earned a reputation for wild living.

Wilberforce's lifestyle dramatically changed when he put his faith in the Lord Jesus. Not long after, the English member of parliament became interested in social reform, especially improving the working conditions of factory laborers in Britain. Then, an abolitionist named Thomas Clarkson persuaded Wilberforce to press for an end to the trafficking of black slaves from Africa to the West Indies. It took almost two decades of persistence and hard work before the slave trade was finally abolished in 1807.

Wilberforce, like Jonah, stands as an example of someone who heeded the call of God to make a difference in the society of his day. Like other saints of old, we too have a divine commission to be agents of change in our world. And it all begins with the proclamation of the Gospel.

Introduction for Youth
Topic: *Mission Unwanted!*

Perhaps you are familiar with the scene. A parent walks into an adolescent's bedroom and asks him or her to turn down the music being played. But the teen can't hear the request because the music is being played too loudly.

Even more frustrating than this is the situation in which young people do not heed God. They have allowed their minds to be pumped so full of the world's messages that God's truth is never given the slightest bit of attention. Sadly, God's will for them is pushed aside for the allurement of temporal distractions.

The remedy to this problem is for youth to redirect their attention back to God. This isn't necessarily difficult, though at first it might be challenging. But once it is done, a wonderful opportunity exists for real change and lasting spiritual growth. The transformation that can occur is quite profound!

Concepts for Children
Topic: *Jonah Obeyed*

1. Jonah disobeyed God's command.
2. The men aboard the ship begged God to end the violent storm.
3. Even though Jonah was disobedient, God provided a safe place for him inside the belly of a huge fish.
4. After the fish spit Jonah onto dry land, the prophet took God's message to the Ninevites.
5. The Ninevites accepted God's message and prayed they would not perish.

Lesson Commentary

I. GOD'S CALL: JONAH 1:1-4

A. The Assignment: vss. 1-2

The word of the LORD came to Jonah son of Amittai: "Go to the great city of Nineveh and preach against it, because its wickedness has come up before me."

Unlike the other Minor Prophets, the Book of Jonah is not a collection of oracles. Instead, it is an account of a period in the life of a prophet, namely, "Jonah son of Amittai" (1:1). Virtually nothing is known about Amittai. According to 2 Kings 14:25, Jonah lived in the northern kingdom of Israel. Jonah was originally from Gath Hepher, a town in the territory of the tribe of Zebulun located about three miles northeast of Nazareth (Josh. 19:13). According to 2 Kings 14:25, Jonah had foretold Jeroboam II's restoration of the territory of Israel from the entrance of Hamath (a city in central Syria) to the Dead Sea. Since Jeroboam II reigned from 793–753 B.C., Jonah's life and ministry most likely occurred in the early eighth century B.C. This made him a contemporary of two other Old Testament prophets, Hosea and Amos.

We don't know whether Jonah was the author of the book that bears his name or whether someone else wrote the book about him. Jonah's prophecy falls into two distinct parts. The first portion shows us Jonah's attempt to escape God's call to preach in the Assyrian city of Nineveh. The second part depicts Jonah's reluctant obedience to that command. Although Assyria's power was temporarily on the wane in Jonah's day, Assyria had cruelly oppressed Israel and other neighboring states. This helps us understand Jonah's opposition to go to Nineveh. Jonah's nationalism and his righteous indignation made it difficult for him to accept God's willingness to show mercy to Assyrians.

God's command to Jonah is more literally rendered, "Arise! Go!" (vs. 2). In other words, the prophet was to immediately depart, for his mission was urgent. The Lord had commissioned Jonah to journey about 550 miles northeast to the "great city of Nineveh." In all likelihood, this means Nineveh, as the last capital of the mighty Assyrian Empire, was a sprawling urban center. God wanted Jonah to announce judgment against Assyria's large capital city for its many crimes. In a sense, Nineveh stood for all the evil deeds committed by its inhabitants, including the rulers of the entire empire.

The Hebrew term rendered "wickedness" is typically used in contexts that deal with abuse, exploitation, and immorality. Probably, therefore, those atrocities were occurring in Nineveh (see Isa. 10:13; Nah. 3:1, 10, 19). Jonah 1:2 graphically portrayed these misdeeds as rising heavenward into the holy presence of God. Expressed differently, the Lord of all creation was fully aware of the abominations taking place in Nineveh and He was prepared to punish the people for their transgressions.

B. The Refusal: vs. 3

But Jonah ran away from the **LORD** *and headed for Tarshish. He went down to Joppa, where he found a ship bound for that port. After paying the fare, he went aboard and sailed for Tarshish to flee from the* **LORD***.*

From the latter part of the account, we gather that God conditioned His judgment on the response of the Ninevites. If they reacted favorably to Jonah's message, the Lord would withhold His judgment. But if they reacted unfavorably, He would visit them with calamity. The possibility of the Ninevites' repenting and forestalling God's judgment did not appeal to His prophet (see Jonah 4:2), for the Assyrians were enemies of Israel. Although Assyria was currently in a period of decline, it was still a threat. Indeed, Jonah was aware of all the harm that Assyria had done to Israel and Israel's neighbors in the past.

Jonah would have preferred to see the enemy destroyed rather than delivered. That is why the prophet tried to run away from God's presence by going to Tarshish. A literal rendering of verses 2 and 3 brings out the wordplay in the Hebrew text. In response to the divine command to "Arise! Go!," Jonah "rose to flee." Three times the book tells us that God's prophet tried to run away from the Lord (twice in verse 3 and once in verse 10). Despite this emphasis, Jonah probably did not really think he could get away from God. After all, Scriptures existing in his time taught that God is present everywhere (see Ps. 139:7-12). Indeed, Jonah showed himself familiar with this concept (Jonah 1:9).

Most likely, then, the prophet was trying to escape from fulfilling God's command. We can imagine Jonah thinking, *Let somebody else have the dirty job of preaching to the Assyrians!* Since Nineveh lay to the east, Jonah fled to the west. His plan was to go to Tarshish, a Mediterranean seaport that some have identified with ancient Tartessus, a Phoenician colony located in southwest Spain. Others have identified Tarshish with Tarsus in Cilicia, Carthage in North Africa, and Sardinia (an Italian island south of Corsica). Regardless of which of these locations is correct, it is clear that Jonah meant to get far away from Israel by crossing the Mediterranean Sea.

For this purpose, Jonah first went to Joppa (today's Jaffa, Israel), a small port city on the Mediterranean coast about 35 miles northwest of Jerusalem. When the prophet found a vessel that was sailing to Tarshish, he paid the passenger fare and boarded the ship. The Bible does not tell us what kind of vessel Jonah boarded. It may, however, have been one of the "ships of Tarshish" that are frequently mentioned in the Old Testament (see 1 Kings 22:48; Ps. 48:7). The name of these ships does not mean that they were all built in Tarshish, any more than all "China clippers" were built in China. Some scholars have suggested that the word *Tarshish* comes from a term used in the ancient mining industry. If so, the phrase "ships of Tarshish" may originally have meant "ore ships."

Reports indicate that the ships of Tarshish were large merchant vessels capable of transporting heavy cargoes. They were powered by double banks of oars. From

20 to 30 sailors usually manned the oars of these ancient vessels. During violent storms, the mariners would tie ropes around the hull to prevent the ship from falling apart (a practice called frapping). In Jonah's day there were also warships. These vessels had long streamlined hulls with a ram in front. The ships were highly maneuverable and capable of high nautical speeds. The Greeks were quite skilled in using this type of ship. Because of their speed, warships were often used to carry urgent messages during times of war and peace.

Jonah thought that by being on a cargo vessel, he could evade God's call. However, the error of the prophet's thinking is brought out by the repetition of the Hebrew verb rendered "went down" (vs. 3). If the prophet was in the Jerusalem temple when he first received his commission (see 2:4, 7), he had to physically travel downhill to get to Joppa (1:3). Next, he went down into the cargo hold of the ship (vs. 5). Eventually, he went down to the bottom of the sea inside the belly of a large sea creature (2:6). It was only after he repented that God brought him back up from the threshold of death (vs. 7).

Ultimately, one must acknowledge the presence of the miraculous in the life of Jonah. The provision of the huge fish was not just a coincidence. Rather, the Lord sovereignly ordained that Jonah would be preserved alive in the internal organs of the creature for approximately three days and three nights. From inside the fish, Jonah prayed to the Lord. In this petition, the prophet recalled what had gone on in his mind while he was sinking into the depths of the sea. In Jonah's most dangerous predicament, he had cried out to God for help, and He favorably responded to the request by graciously sparing the prophet's life. This had renewed Jonah's faith and determination to serve the Lord (2:1-9).

In his prayer from inside the fish, Jonah said, "From the depths of the grave I called for help" (vs. 2). Here "grave" translates the Hebrew noun *Sheol.* This word referred to the place of the dead. The Israelites (as well as other ancient peoples) evidently believed that the dead occupy a gloomy underworld place: Sheol. They also believed that in Sheol the dead are mere shadows of themselves, living in darkness and silence and inactivity. To Jonah, sinking into the sea felt like descending to Sheol. And indeed, if it were not for God's mercy in sending a fish to save Jonah, he would have gone to the place of the dead.

II. JONAH'S COMPLIANCE: JONAH 3:1-4

A. God's Command: vss. 1-2

Then the word of the **LORD** *came to Jonah a second time: "Go to the great city of Nineveh and proclaim to it the message I give you."*

Jonah had repented of his rebellious attitudes and actions. He also determined in his heart to do what God had commanded. The prophet was now ready to be sent on his way to Nineveh to proclaim a message of judgment. Thus, the Lord commanded the fish to release Jonah. In turn, the sea creature cast the prophet onto dry land (2:10). Next, God revealed His will to the prophet a second time (3:1). The Lord directed Jonah to immediately travel to Nineveh, the sprawling metropolis of the great empire of Assyria, and declare to its inhabitants a somber message of judgment (vs. 2).

B. Jonah's Preaching: vss. 3-4

Jonah obeyed the word of the LORD and went to Nineveh. Now Nineveh was a very important city—a visit required three days. On the first day, Jonah started into the city. He proclaimed: "Forty more days and Nineveh will be overturned."

Unlike before, this time Jonah did not hesitate to heed the command of God. Instead of running away, the prophet went at once to Nineveh (Jonah 3:3). The biblical text says nothing about Jonah's journey to Nineveh, which probably occupied two months or more. Jonah would have taken ancient trade routes along the Fertile Crescent that arched northward from Israel and then eastward and southward into Mesopotamia, following rivers much of the way. The book focuses not on the journey but on what happened once Jonah got to Nineveh.

Verse 3 comments on Jonah's destination this way: "Nineveh was a very important city." The Hebrew original can also be translated "Nineveh was a city important to God." The phrase could indicate the Lord's concern for its inhabitants, or it may simply point to Nineveh's prominence in the ancient world. The verse comments that "a visit [to Nineveh] required three days." This probably does not mean that the city was so big it would take Jonah three days to walk through it. Archaeological surveys reveal that in the eighth century B.C., Nineveh was only three miles across at its widest point.

One explanation for the biblical comment suggests that the surrounding territory was included as a part of Nineveh. In that case, three days might have been required to walk from the frontier of Nineveh's territory to the center of the city itself. A second possibility is that Jonah might have pronounced his somber warning throughout the first day's journey (vs. 4). A third option is that protocol, not size, is in view. According to this explanation, a foreigner with a message for the city was regulated by city officials. Such a person could speak publicly, but had to leave the city by the end of the third day.

In any case, it's not hard to imagine Jonah venturing through various small streets and markets as he announced God's judgment. What a stir he must have caused! The inhabitants learned that in 40 days their great city would be destroyed. Jonah's message to the Ninevites may seem ambiguous. Was the overturning inevitable, or did the 40 days comprise a waiting period in which the Ninevites might avert the overturning? The Hebrew verb translated "overturned" had a number of meanings. It could refer to an overthrow, a judgment, a turning upside down, a reversal, a change, a deposing of royalty, or a change of heart. No matter what Jonah's warning specifically meant, his hearers took it quite seriously.

III. Nineveh's Repentance: Jonah 3:5-9

A. Displaying Sorrow: vss. 5-6

The Ninevites believed God. They declared a fast, and all of them, from the greatest to the least, put on sackcloth. When the news reached the king of Nineveh, he rose from his throne, took off his royal robes, covered himself with sackcloth and sat down in the dust.

The inhabitants of Nineveh not only believed Jonah's message of judgment (which he received from God), but also the people proclaimed a city-wide fast. They put on sackcloth to display their grief and anguish over what the prophet of the Lord had announced against them. Sackcloth was a coarse fabric woven from the hair of goats or camels. All the people of the city wore the rough material, from the most important to the least important residents (Jonah 3:5).

The immediate response of the inhabitants to Jonah's preaching seemed genuine. Even the king got caught up in the wave of repentance sweeping through his city (or at least he found it politically expedient to lead a bandwagon that had already started to roll.) We don't know if this king was ruler of the city only or ruler of the whole Assyrian Empire. The monarch traded his robes of state for an uncomfortable garment of sackcloth and left his impressive throne for a humble seat in the dust. In this way, he set an example for his people (vs. 6).

B. Issuing a Decree: vss. 7-9

Then he issued a proclamation in Nineveh: "By the decree of the king and his nobles: Do not let any man or beast, herd or flock, taste anything; do not let them eat or drink. But let man and beast be covered with sackcloth. Let everyone call urgently on God. Let them give up their evil ways and their violence. Who knows? God may yet relent and with compassion turn from his fierce anger so that we will not perish."

Along with his nobles, the king issued a decree for the people of Nineveh (Jonah 3:7). Presumably, this edict was read aloud in public places or was posted where the literate could read it. The dictum proclaimed a total fast (no food, no water) for people and for domestic animals. Since no person can go more than a few days without water, the king evidently wanted a short but severe fast. Furthermore, the decree required the people and the animals to wear sackcloth. Perhaps the king wanted the rich ornamentation on harnesses and bridles exchanged for sackcloth coverings (vs. 8). To us, the inclusion of animals in the monarch's edict might seem bizarre. But such measures, though rare, were not unheard of in the ancient world. The historians Herodotus and Plutarch recorded that at a later date Persian mourning rites included animals.

The Ninevite king's decree called for more than the trappings of repentance. In addition to fasting and wearing sackcloth, the people of Nineveh were to "call urgently on God." Their prayer was to be both public and earnest. Also, they were to turn from their despicable and vicious conduct. The Hebrew term rendered "evil ways" refers generally to immoral behavior. The word translated "violence" speaks of social injustice. Earlier, God had said that the city's wickedness had come up before Him (1:2), and now something was being done about that wickedness. The reason the monarch gave for his edict was the possibility that God might yet be willing to change His mind and hold back His intense anger (literally, "the burning of His nostrils"; 3:9). In turn, this would forestall the death of Nineveh's many inhabitants (compare 1:6). Clearly, the king hoped that the overturning Jonah had proclaimed was conditional, not inevitable (3:4). The idea is that maybe with repentance and reformation on the part of the Ninevites, God's mercy might yet save the metropolis.

Discussion Questions

1. Why do you think God chose Jonah to proclaim a message of judgment against Nineveh?
2. At first, why did Jonah balk at the Lord's command to go to Nineveh?
3. Why was Jonah so compliant the second time around to obey the Lord's command?
4. What explanation is there for the amazing response of the Ninevites to Jonah's proclamation?
5. If you were Jonah, how do you think you would have felt as you witnessed the impact of your prophetic ministry in Nineveh?

Contemporary Application

There is no middle ground with respect to God's commands. He wants us to be fully committed to doing His will. He cannot bless any rebellious attitudes or actions in our relationship with Him.

That is why we should repent of thoughts and deeds that are in opposition to the will of the Lord (1 John 1:9). Repentance involves being sorry for doing something wrong and choosing not to do it again. The truly repentant believer rejects attitudes and actions that are insubordinate and adopts those that are in harmony with God's commands (2 Cor. 7:8-12).

Repenting is never easy or enjoyable. This is because we are saying *no* to our sinful desires and tendencies and saying *yes* to God and the teachings of His Word. We are choosing to die to our unwholesome urges and submitting as the will of the Lord replaces them. We are putting to death our old sinful ways and allowing the life of the Spirit to be present in all we do (Rom. 6:1-14).

We will never regret repenting of our rebellious attitudes and actions. Our joy in serving the Lord will be renewed and our ability to witness effectively for Him will be enhanced. We will be better able to relate to others in a godly manner and we will be more sensitive to the leading of the Spirit. Repentance can also be a major factor in our becoming more Christlike and mature.

A Community to Redeem

Scripture

Background Scripture: *Jonah 3:10—4:11*

Scripture Lesson: *Jonah 3:10—4:5*

Key Verse: *"O* LORD, *is this not what I said when I was still at home? That is why I was so quick to flee to Tarshish. I knew that you are a gracious and compassionate God, slow to anger and abounding in love, a God who relents from sending calamity."* Jonah 4:2.

Scripture Lesson for Children: *Jonah 3:10—4:5*

Key Verse for Children: *"I knew that you are a gracious and compassionate God, slow to anger and abounding in love."* Jonah 4:2.

Lesson Aim

To become more compassionate and forgiving.

Lesson Setting

Time: *About 793–753* B.C.

Place: *Nineveh*

Lesson Outline

A Community to Redeem

  I. The Compassionate Lord: Jonah 3:10

     A. Repentance throughout Ninevah: vs. 10a

     B. Mercy from God: vs. 10b

  II. The Pouting Prophet: Jonah 4:1-5

     A. Jonah's Displeasure: vs. 1

     B. Jonah's Request: vss. 2-3

     C. God's Question: vs. 4

     D. Jonah's Brooding: vs. 5

Introduction for Adults

Topic: *Jealousy of Others*

This week's lesson emphasizes two of God's characteristics that saved adults are to exhibit in their lives—compassion and forgiveness. Sadly, these were absent from Jonah's life. He censured God for choosing not to destroy the Ninevites. And Jonah resented the fact that God would forgive a people who were terribly evil. God chose to show compassion, and Jonah held a grudge because of it.

Many people are like Jonah. It's far easier to harbor bitterness and seek revenge than to forgive. It's human nature for people to want misfortune to fall on their enemies rather than show compassion. In fact, adults sometimes work at staying angry with others or even become upset when God doesn't punish the wicked.

The key is for class members to stop focusing on the harm or injustice that's been done to them. If they can set that aside for a moment, they will be better able to see that the one who has hurt them is a hurting person too. With the Spirit's help, adults can do what they could never do on their own, namely, to show compassion and forgiveness to the unlovable.

Introduction for Youth

Topic: *Redeem Them?*

The Book of Jonah leaves us hanging. We don't know if Jonah ever got to the point of being glad that God was merciful to the people of Nineveh. But there is one fact we do know. God expects saved teens to make a top priority the redemption of the lost through the proclamation of the Gospel.

Because of their sinful nature, believing adolescents, like Jonah, find it hard to be merciful to those who have hurt them. But unlike Jonah, saved teens know the Messiah and have the Holy Spirit dwelling within them. Therefore, they can be compassionate and forgiving.

Even if people have been hard on the members of your class, that does not mean it is right for them to hate or unlovingly condemn bullies. Believing adolescents should not set preconditions on showing God's compassion to troublemakers. If the students are truly Christlike, they will display the love of God to other people in an unconditional and unselfish manner, regardless of how they have treated their peers.

Concepts for Children

Topic: *All People Are Valued*

1. Jonah's message had an amazing effect on the Ninevites.
2. Jonah became so angry that he wished to die.
3. God showed Jonah His power by using a vine, a worm, a hot wind, and a blazing sun.
4. God taught Jonah that all humans have value regardless of their past.
5. God wants us to be loving and forgiving to others.

Lesson Commentary

I. THE COMPASSIONATE LORD: JONAH 3:10

A. Repentance throughout Ninevah: vs. 10a

When God saw what they did and how they turned from their evil ways.

Last week's lesson focused on Jonah's initial disobedience of God's command for him to deliver a warning of judgment against the people of Nineveh. We learned that the Lord, in His superabundant love, gave the prophet another opportunity to serve Him. God revealed His will a second time by telling Jonah to travel to Nineveh and proclaim to its inhabitants a somber message of judgment. In response, the inhabitants took to heart what the prophet declared and repented. Even the king of Nineveh joined his subjects in expressing sorrow (Jonah 3:1-9).

The Hebrew word for "repentance" used in the Book of Jonah literally means "to turn." Repentance implies that we have been moving in the wrong direction. When we turn back to God, we do so with mind, heart, and body. A similar emphasis is found in the Gospels, where the notion of repentance signifies a turnabout in attitude toward God and life's priorities. Indeed, repentance is portrayed as part of the conversion process. Through the working of the Holy Spirit, sinners come to the point at which they are ready to turn away from sin and place their trust in Christ for salvation.

There is some uncertainty about the nature of the Ninevites' repentance. Some think the people were genuinely converted to faith in the Lord, while others think their remorse was superficial and temporary. Regardless of which view is preferred, the repentance of the Ninevites is remarkable by any standard. Yet it is easier to understand if we take into account factors that may have affected the Ninevites' frame of mind in the mid-eighth century B.C.—the probable time when Jonah appeared in their midst.

Political threats to Assyria's stability may have made the Ninevites uneasy about their future. Riots and rebellions cropped up around the Assyrian Empire between 772 B.C. and 758 B.C. The kingdom of Urartu took land and major cities away from the Assyrians between 760 B.C. and 750 B.C. There also occurred natural events that would certainly have been viewed as signs of God's displeasure. A violent earthquake shook the region sometime between 772 B.C. and 755 B.C. Famine left many hungry in the years 765 B.C. to 759 B.C. A total eclipse of the sun occurred on June 15, 763 B.C. Prepared by this combination of disasters and evil omens, the people of Nineveh could easily have been quick to believe a foreign prophet warning that God would overturn their city in forty days.

Of course, the grace of God working in the lives of the Ninevites was the ultimate cause of their heartfelt response. From a human perspective, they should have reacted stubbornly to Jonah's message of judgment. The Lord, however, enabled the inhabitants of Assyria's sprawling metropolis to recognize the error of their ways and to embrace the truth proclaimed by Jonah. When we are swamped with troubles of our own making, we do well to remember the Ninevites' spiritual turn-about. If there is rebellion within us, it is not too late to turn to the Lord. In turn, He will be merciful to us.

B. Mercy from God: vs. 10b

He had compassion and did not bring upon them the destruction he had threatened.

Because the Ninevites had turned from their moral evil, God, in response, relent-ed from the calamity He had threatened to bring upon them (Jonah 3:10). This cir-cumstance mirrors what Nineveh's king had hoped, namely, that the overturning proclaimed by Jonah was conditional, rather than inevitable (vs. 9). As verse 10 reveals, the monarch's hope was well placed, for God did indeed have compassion on the Ninevites. In a manner of speaking, He shelved His plan to bring destruc-tion on the city in the near future. At the end of 40 days, no calamity would take place.

The Lord, in canceling His threatened punishment, was not being arbitrary or inconsistent, but revealing His earnest desire for as many people as possible to "come to repentance" (2 Pet. 3:9). All along, His warning of judgment on the peo-ple of Nineveh had been conditional and tentative. Expressed differently, God had planned from the beginning to anchor His response to the reaction of the Ninevites. Since they responded favorably to the oracle proclaimed by His spokesperson (Jonah), God treated the inhabitants favorably. Ultimately, it was not the Lord who changed His mind, but the people of Nineveh who changed.

II. THE POUTING PROPHET: JONAH 4:1-5

A. Jonah's Displeasure: vs. 1

But Jonah was greatly displeased and became angry.

The Ninevites' repentance impacted Jonah much differently than it affected God. The prophet was quite upset (Jonah 4:1), or as the Hebrew text literally says, "It was evil to Jonah, a great evil." The enormity of his displeasure is further emphasized by the statement that he "became angry." The biblical text literally says "it burned to him." The contrast between the Lord and His prophet could not have been greater. While the Lord hand relented from judging the Ninevites, the anger of His emissary burst into flames.

Jonah not only hated the people of Assyria, but also did not want them to receive divine mercy. So strong was his nationalistic pride that he would have preferred to see the enemies of Israel destroyed even after they had turned from their sins. Previously, Jonah had welcomed and enjoyed the love and mercy that the Lord had showered on him. Nevertheless, the prophet did not want others to be treated the same way. If Jonah truly represented the Lord, he should have sought to be as com-passionate and forgiving to others as God had been to him. In chapter 4, we read about the interaction between the Lord and His spokesperson after the completion of Jonah's preaching tour in Nineveh.

B. Jonah's Request: vss. 2-3

He prayed to the LORD, *"O* LORD, *is this not what I said when I was still at home? That is why I was so quick to flee to Tarshish. I knew that you are a gracious and compassionate God, slow to anger and abounding in love, a God who relents from sending calamity. Now, O* LORD, *take away my life, for it is better for me to die than to live."*

Jonah complained to the Lord that his worst fears had been realized. The prophet noted that when he previously was in Israel, he anticipated that the Ninevites might repent and that God would spare them from being judged. To forestall such an outcome, the distraught prophet had tried to flee to Tarshish and avoid the divine command. In short, Jonah wanted nothing to do with the possibility of the Lord showing mercy to Israel's enemy.

The prophet was well aware of how "gracious and compassionate" (Jonah 4:2) God could be. The Hebrew adjective rendered "gracious" draws attention to the forbearance of the Lord toward those who deserve His wrath. Similarly, the adjective translated "compassionate" underscores God's kindness and mercifulness to sinners. His patience is so great that He is slow to get angry. The biblical text literally says, "long of nostrils." This idiomatic expression is based on the human tendency for the nose to flare its nostrils when a person becomes angry. Moreover, Jonah affirmed that the Lord is filled with "love." The latter translates a noun that refers to the unfailing mercy of the Lord. This is seen in His willingness to relent concerning threatened judgment.

In Jonah's description, he echoed earlier scriptural portrayals of God's forgiving nature (see Exod. 34:6-7; Num. 14:18; Neh. 9:17; Ps. 86:15; 103:8; 145:8-9; Joel 2:13; Nah. 1:3). Yet the prophet's ability to eloquently convey biblical truth was undercut by his spiteful disposition. He should have realized how wrong it was for him to gloat over the prospect of Nineveh's destruction. Also, he should have turned away from his irresponsible attitude. This would have included acknowledging to God that He was right for showing mercy to the people of Nineveh.

In a rebellious pout, Jonah asked the Lord to take his life. He evidently thought that it would be better for him to die than to live and see God spare Israel's oppressors (Jonah 4:3). In contrast, months earlier, when the prophet had been sinking beneath the surface of the Mediterranean Sea, he had called out to the Lord to spare his life (2:2). Hebrews 12:15 warns that bitterness defiles. Jonah is an example of that principle in action. His hatred of the Assyrians was so great that it eventually displaced his appreciation for God. By rejecting the Lord's attributes of grace and forgiveness, the prophet was rejecting God Himself.

C. God's Question: vs. 4

But the LORD *replied, "Have you any right to be angry?"*

The Lord could have severely chastised His stubborn, narrow-minded prophet, yet He did not do so. Instead, God displayed as much compassion and forgiveness to Jonah as He had to the Ninevites. Accordingly, rather than grant Jonah's request, the Lord asked him a question. This was God's approach to get His despondent spokesperson to think about the implications of his attitude and actions. There are two possible ways of understanding Jonah 4:4. According to the NIV rendering, the Lord asked whether His emissary had any justification for being so upset. In an alternate translation, the Lord asked whether Jonah was so deeply grieved that he would rather be dead than alive.

Clearly, Jonah had no right to be angry and wish he were dead. Anger is not always bad, and more than one biblical character expressed anger at God. But in this case, Jonah's anger was wrong because he had no legitimate reason for it. Here we see the prophet operating according to a double standard. He had been glad when God delivered him from his predicament, but he became incensed over God's mercy toward the Ninevites. Jonah should have accepted the fact that whatever the Lord does is right. Furthermore, the prophet should have had the same forgiving attitude toward the Ninevites that God displayed.

D. Jonah's Brooding: vs. 5

Jonah went out and sat down at a place east of the city. There he made himself a shelter, sat in its shade and waited to see what would happen to the city.

Jonah's anger was not the kind that evaporated rapidly. Even the Lord's question did not dissolve the prophet's bitterness over the repentance in Nineveh. After Jonah's visit to the huge urban center, he did not immediately return to Israel. Instead, he first took up temporary residence in the plain "east of the city" (Jonah 4:5). With Nineveh in view, he constructed a booth of some kind using whatever materials were available. His plan was to wait and see what fate awaited the city. Evidently, he still harbored some hope that God might destroy Nineveh.

The shelter Jonah constructed provided shade for him from the heat of the day and relief from the chill of the night. Possibly he had stone or clay to make the walls of his hut. But since timber was scarce in that area, he may not have had the materials to make much of a roof. At any rate, the shelter offered marginal protection from the elements, but not enough to make him really comfortable (vs. 6). To this day, shade is an important consideration for people living in the hot climate of the Middle East.

Noting the situation, God "provided a vine" (vs. 6), which grew up "overnight" (vs. 10), to "ease [Jonah's] discomfort" (vs. 6). The precise identification of the Hebrew noun rendered "vine" is uncertain. Other renderings include "gourd" and "little plant." In any case, whereas before Jonah had been very angry with God concerning the Ninevites (see vs. 1), now the prophet was overtaken with delight at God's provision (vs. 6). The leafy plant was a source of pleasure in an otherwise disagreeable circumstance for Jonah. He may even have interpreted the vine as a sign of God's renewed favor toward him.

The prophet's happiness was short-lived. He apparently got only one day's enjoyment out of the plant, for the next morning God arranged for a worm to attack and eat through the stem of the plant. In turn, it dried up (vs. 7). Then, when the sun began to shine, the Lord sent a hot "east wind" (vs. 8). As the sun beat down on the prophet's head, he "grew faint" and despaired of life. In his misery, Jonah concluded that death would be far better than withering away in the blazing heat of the day. Undoubtedly, God permitted the dire turn of events to teach His emissary a lesson.

As before (see vs. 3), the reason for Jonah's death wish was his anger. However, this time he was peeved at the destruction of the leafy plant, not at the repentance of the Ninevites he so intensely despised. Again, God tried to get the prophet to consider the unreasonableness of his agitation. The Lord asked whether Jonah had any right to be upset over the demise of the vine (vs. 9). As before (see vs. 4), the implied answer to the Lord's query was no. Amazingly, Jonah declared that he was fully justified in being perturbed. He retorted that his anger was so intense that he wanted to die.

Aren't we often the same way? We don't like it when someone shows us that we are in the wrong. Even if we see their point, we often stick to our wrongdoing out of pride or willfulness. But if it's God who is showing us where we are wrong, we'd better let our stubbornness crumple up and go away. Besides, we'll feel good about making a change once we've gone ahead and made it.

Jonah still hadn't gotten the point. So God showed how the vine was not the real issue. The vine was an object to teach a lesson. By arguing from the lesser to the greater, the Lord compared the vine to Nineveh. The vine was just a plant. It was short-lived and moreover Jonah had no responsibility for it (vs. 10). But Nineveh, on the other hand, had a large population of people and animals (vs. 11). They needed to hear the truth about God, especially concerning His displeasure with their wicked ways.

In the Lord's extended dialogue with Jonah, He was trying to get His emissary to recognize his skewed perspective. If it was legitimate for Jonah to pity a single plant, why should he be angry with God for showing compassion and forgiveness to the repentant Ninevites? From a moral standpoint, the inhabitants could not discern their right hand from their left (4:11). In the Lord's unfailing love, He mercifully reached out to the Ninevites with a message of warning and hope. Through Jonah's proclamation, they were spared from otherwise certain destruction. The prophet should have been thankful, not vexed, over the fact that God had used him to deliver the city's inhabitants from wickedness and devastation.

Jonah showed that he was unwilling to forgive people who had been harsh toward his fellow Israelites. Furthermore, the prophet demonstrated that he thought he knew better than God what He should do. While Jonah did not run away to Tarshish the second time the Lord summoned him to preach in Nineveh, a spirit of rebellion still dwelt in the emissary's heart. The tension raised by God's final question to Jonah is never resolved. We are not told whether the prophet learned the lesson God had taken such pains to teach. Clearly, he stands as a warning to succeeding generations of the dangers created by despising the Lord's blessings.

Discussion Questions

1. Why would God want one of His people to proclaim His judgment against a pagan people? What does this say about God?
2. What did Jonah disclose about himself when he became angry with the Lord?
3. If you had been in Jonah's situation, how would you have felt about God's response to the Ninevites?
4. Why was Jonah wrong for pouting?
5. If you were Jonah, what would you have wanted to see happen to the Ninevites?

Contemporary Application

Imagine the most terrible crime someone could possibly commit against you. How would you feel after being so cruelly treated? How readily would you be willing to extend forgiveness if that person eventually came and asked to be pardoned for the hurt he or she had inflicted?

It would be extremely difficult for most of us to be compassionate and forgiving to someone who has severely mistreated us. The sinful response would be to lash out in anger, hold a grudge, or seek to get even. The godly response would be to forgive the person who has been abusive or destructive in his or her behavior. Although this is rarely easy to do, it is the only response that meets with God's approval and will be blessed by Him.

First John 4:7 urges believers to love one another because love comes from God. By striving to show the Lord's compassion to others, we reveal that we are His children and truly know Him. Conversely, when we do not love as the Lord does, we show that we do not know God, who is characterized by pure and unbounded compassion for others, as we should (vs. 8). According to verse 11, believers should seek to be as loving to others as God has been to them.

By imitating our compassionate and forgiving God, we can bring comfort to the needy. We can help them see the love of God as it works through us. We can even inspire others to begin showing compassion and forgiveness. In a cold world, a little love can produce some unexpected and much-needed warmth.

Family as Community

Scripture

Background Scripture: *Ruth 1:1-16*

Scripture Lesson: *Ruth 1:1-9, 14, 16*

Key Verse: *Ruth replied, "Don't urge me to leave you or to turn back from you. Where you go I will go, and where you stay I will stay. Your people will be my people and your God my God."* Ruth 1:16.

Scripture Lesson for Children: *Ruth 1:1-9, 14, 16*

Key Verse for Children: *"Don't urge me to leave you or to turn back from you. Where you go I will go, and where you stay I will stay. Your people will be my people and your God my God."* Ruth 1:16.

Lesson Aim

To note that God honors steadfastness in family relationships.

Lesson Setting

Time: *1375–1050 B.C.*

Place: *Judah and Moab*

Lesson Outline

Family as Community

I. The Predicament: Ruth 1:1-9
    A. *Famine: vss. 1-2*
    B. *Death: vss. 3-5*
    C. *A Plan: vss. 6-9*

II. The Pledge: Ruth 1:14, 16
    A. *Ruth's Commitment: vs. 14*
    B. *Ruth's Faith: vs. 16*

Introduction for Adults

Topic: *Commitment to a New Community*

What causes waning commitment among adults to the members of their faith community? Each of us struggles with a different set of weaknesses. Some adults struggle with sexual immorality, and it is difficult for them to be faithful to their spouses. Other adults harbor deep anger toward a family member or friend who has hurt them in some way. Still other adults can't seem to help but break the trust of a loved one by relating confidences to others.

Honesty, forgiveness, unselfishness, and loyalty are God-honoring character traits for the new community of God's people. As we study Ruth's loyalty to Naomi, we will be encouraged to examine our own relationships, reshape our loyalties, and overcome grief in our lives.

Introduction for Youth

Topic: *Who's in the Family?*

Adolescents soon learn that short-term loyalties, like fireworks, blaze intently for a brief time and then vanish. They also come to discover that constant loyalty glows like a light bulb pointing the way through a dark tunnel.

This week's lesson makes it clear that, as Orpah's loyalty faded, she returned home; but Ruth's commitment was permanent. Even when her initial plans for marriage tragically ended, she devoted herself to her mother-in-law, Naomi, and to the God of Israel. Ruth even submitted to His plan for her life.

Jesus' last earthly promise to His disciples in Matthew 28:20 was "And surely I am with you always." Christian love is not commitment by convenience, which disappears when life becomes difficult. Real love says, "I'll be there for you when times are tough for you." Saved teens need Christian fellowship, especially in hard places. The Lord did not intend that any of them should go it alone, but journey with others who belong to the family of God.

Concepts for Children

Topic: *Bonding with Relatives*

1. Naomi, Orpah, and Ruth experienced great loss when their husbands died.
2. Naomi decided to return to Judah from Moab.
3. Orpah decided to remain in Moab, but Ruth said she wanted to go with Naomi to Judah.
4. Ruth refused to separate from Naomi.
5. God wants us to be as loyal to Him and His people as Ruth was to Naomi.

Lesson Commentary

I. THE PREDICAMENT: RUTH 1:1-9

A. Famine: vss. 1-2

In the days when the judges ruled, there was a famine in the land, and a man from Bethlehem in Judah, together with his wife and two sons, went to live for a while in the country of Moab. The man's name was Elimelech, his wife's name Naomi, and the names of his two sons were Mahlon and Kilion. They were Ephrathites from Bethlehem, Judah. And they went to Moab and lived there.

As was noted in the first lesson of the previous quarter, Ruth 1:1 places the account of the book in the period when judges ruled Israel, or about 1375–1050 B.C. These individuals, though involved in some judicial matters, were primarily God's instruments of deliverance from Israel's oppressors. During this era of biblical history, Israel's true form of government was a theocracy. This means that no matter who led the people, the Lord alone was their King. As the nation's leader, God raised up a number of judges between Joshua's death and the coronation of Saul. Some of these were major judges, military leaders whose deeds and accomplishments are recounted at length. Others were minor judges, individuals about whom little is known apart from their names.

Most of the judges did not rule over all of Israel. Deborah and Barak, for example, were unable to gain the cooperation of the tribes of Reuben, Gilead, Dan, and Asher in their war against the Canaanites. Gideon did not include Ephraim in his battles, and almost caused a civil war because of it. Furthermore, the era of the judges was a depressing period in Israel's history. Each time God's people went through the cycle of sin, oppression, repentance, and deliverance, they seemed to sink deeper into alienation from the Lord. Spiritual compromise was the norm. They kept giving in to the pagan ways of their neighbors, and each time God sent powerful oppressors until they cried out for deliverance. When the Israelites were ready to listen, God raised up a judge to lead them.

This was a time of tremendous political upheaval in the ancient Near East. The Hittite Empire, which had once controlled a region extending from southeastern Asia Minor to northern Lebanon, was overthrown by an influx of Sea Peoples, who included the Philistines. Though their southward advance was checked by the Egyptians, these Sea Peoples remained in Canaan and dominated the area for many years. During this time, Egypt's power and influence began to wane. The Assyrians were so preoccupied with other matters that they exercised only a marginal influence in the regions south of Lebanon. These circumstances gave the Israelites considerable freedom to strengthen their control of Palestine. Despite their military victories under the leadership of Joshua, the Israelites continued to wage war with various tribal groups in Canaan. They also were repeatedly attacked by nomadic groups from Moab, Ammon, and the eastern desert.

If we did not have the Book of Ruth, we might think that the period of the judges was about nothing but warfare and that the only people who really mattered then were the great tribal heroes. But thankfully we do have the Book of Ruth, and it shows us the other side of that time period. Instead of having a large scope and telling about battles, it is a relatively brief account about domestic relations. Instead of being peopled with heroes and villains, its characters are ordinary, godly individuals, mainly women. Thus, it shows us that while the fate of tribes and nations was being decided, everyday life was still going on. Better yet, it shows us that while Israelite society as a whole was caught in a downward spiral of apostasy, there were some individuals who remained loyal and faithful to God.

Throughout history, it was common for families to up and move to a new community because of job or economic circumstances. In Ruth 1:1-2, we learn that a family from Bethlehem in Judah did the same. Elimelech, the husband, and his wife, Naomi, had two sons, Mahlon and Kilion. Although the name of the family's hometown, Bethlehem, means "House of Bread," there was a famine in the area that made survival tough. Just as hunger had forced Jacob's sons to seek food in Egypt (Gen. 42:1-2), starvation drove Elimelech and Naomi from Bethlehem to Moab. Moab was an area across the Salt Sea (Dead Sea) from Bethlehem. Moab's territory stretched from the south of the sea to its middle, and the edge of the Syrian desert formed the kingdom's eastern boundary.

The entire territory measured only 60 miles north to south and 20 miles east to west, while several ravines divided it. Through the middle of Moab from north to south ran "The King's Highway," a route of strategic military and commercial importance. Moab was a well-organized kingdom. The Moabites' buildings were well constructed and their cities well fortified. Meanwhile, their lands could be used for farming and ranching. Wheat and barley grew especially well in this region. Also, part of the area in the hills above the Salt Sea was fertile, and it was obviously untouched by the famine that forced Naomi's family out of the territory of Judah.

The decision of Elimelech and Naomi to move their family to this alien land must have been difficult. The couple knew that their reception might not be a friendly one because of ancient hatred between the Moabites and the Israelites (Judg. 3:12-14). This animosity stretched back to the time of Balaam, a prophet who was hired by the frightened king of Moab to curse the Israelite people who were approaching his country from Egypt (Num. 22:1-8). Overruled by God, however, Balaam's curses became blessings for God's people (23:19-20).

B. Death: vss. 3-5

Now Elimelech, Naomi's husband, died, and she was left with her two sons. They married Moabite women, one named Orpah and the other Ruth. After they had lived there about ten years, both Mahlon and Kilion also died, and Naomi was left without her two sons and her husband.

Sometime after Elimelech and Naomi's arrival in Moab, tragedy struck. Elimelech's death left Naomi dependent on her sons (Ruth 1:3). Apparently Mahlon and

Kilion liked Moab well enough to marry and settle down (vs. 4). These marriages would have been frowned upon by orthodox Israelites, for whom Moab long represented temptation to immorality. For instance, during the Israelites' wandering in the wilderness, their men had been easily seduced by Moabite women (Num. 25:1-5). During the third and second millennia B.C., the religion of the Moabites was similar to that of their neighbors, the Canaanites. Over time, the two peoples' religious practices became distinct. Chemosh was the Moabites' national god, and they became known as "the people of Chemosh." This idol was believed to be a god of war who led his people to victory.

Ten years after Naomi's family had moved to Moab, tragedy struck again. The names of Naomi's sons indicate they were physically weak (perhaps from birth). Mahlon means "weak" or "sick," and Kilion means "failing" or "annihilation." Ruth and Orpah were probably widowed soon after their weddings (Ruth 1:5). After Mahlon and Kilion died, all three women were left without support. In ancient patriarchal societies, women depended on male relatives for protection and care. Sadly, widows were usually ignored and destitute.

As the head of his household, Elimelech would have maintained rights to ancestral property in Bethlehem, even after having moved to Moab. But when both he and his two sons died, the only ways Naomi could regain the property were through two legal customs: the "levirate" law and the "redemption of the land" law. The levirate law—sometimes called the "levirate marriage"—was the custom of a widow marrying her dead husband's closest male relative, usually his brother (Deut. 25:5-10). Any offspring born from this union would carry both the name and the inheritance of the former husband. (In Naomi's case—since she was beyond childbearing years—her daughter-in-law, Ruth, became her substitute in marriage and bore a son to perpetuate the family name.)

C. A Plan: vss. 6-9

When she heard in Moab that the Lord had come to the aid of his people by providing food for them, Naomi and her daughters-in-law prepared to return home from there. With her two daughters-in-law she left the place where she had been living and set out on the road that would take them back to the land of Judah. Then Naomi said to her two daughters-in-law, "Go back, each of you, to your mother's home. May the Lord show kindness to you, as you have shown to your dead and to me. May the LORD grant that each of you will find rest in the home of another husband."

Eventually, word came from Bethlehem that the famine had ended (Ruth 1:6). Naomi made the courageous decision to return home. She and her daughters-in-law faced the prospect of crossing about 50 miles of barren desert. The risks of this journey were great: heat exhaustion, starvation, and attacks by beasts or bandits. However, for Naomi, death on the road would be no worse than destitution and loneliness in a foreign land. Naomi's daughters-in-law were determined to go with her, a decision that underscored how much they appreciated her (vs. 7). Soon, however, Naomi told the women to go back to their families, find husbands, and start life over. Despite her need for their support, the older woman unselfishly set her daughters-in-law free.

Naomi could not provide husbands for these two women, and she cared too much for them to let them live as widows, especially since they had been good to her sons and herself. Perhaps Naomi also wanted to protect Ruth and Orpah from abusive discrimination, which they might face in Bethlehem (vs. 8). Naomi softened the blow of her directive by giving Orpah and Ruth a double blessing. In the first part of the blessing, Naomi wished the Lord's kindness on them. And in the process of doing so, she expressed her appreciation for the kindness the young women had shown to her sons and to herself. In the second part of the blessing, Naomi wished her daughters-in-law rest in a new husband's home (vs. 9). In this case "rest" meant ceasing from toil and trouble and experiencing lifelong protection and blessing from the Lord.

We can see from Naomi's double blessing that she did not hesitate to speak about Yahweh, the Israelites' God, in the presence of her Moabite daughters-in-law. Indeed, Naomi's words show that she believed He was the one who had the power to bless them. Naomi kissed Orpah and Ruth to show her love for them. At this the young women wept. Through the tears, however, both declared their intention to continue with Naomi (vs. 10). Clearly, Naomi's love for them had evidently made a powerful impact on them.

In the Old Testament, "love" typically renders a Hebrew term that literally means "goodness" or "kindness." For centuries English versions traditionally rendered this word as "mercy." But more recent scholarship suggests that such renderings as "loyal love" or "steadfast love" may more accurately capture the essence of the term. (This is also the word rendered "love" in Jonah 4:2, which we studied in last week's lesson.) Loyal love is evident throughout the Book of Ruth.

Behind the love of God is His fidelity to the covenant relationship He has with His people. Such love is not an inconsistent and volatile emotion, as it might be among humans. Instead, His love is unselfish and unconditional, being prompted more by will than by feeling. God's love reaches out to His needy people, even though they are unworthy of His affection (Deut. 7:8-9). It is because of His love that the Lord redeemed His people from slavery in Egypt (4:37). And in the future day of redemption, the God of love will also gently lead His people and provide for their every need (Hos. 11:4).

II. THE PLEDGE: RUTH 1:14, 16

A. Ruth's Commitment: vs. 14

At this they wept again. Then Orpah kissed her mother-in-law good-by, but Ruth clung to her.

Despite the initial pledges made by Ruth and Orpah, Naomi repeated her command for them to return home (Ruth 1:11). Israelite tradition formed the backdrop of her reasoning. As noted earlier, in ancient times it was usually considered a man's duty to marry his brother's widow so as to see that she was taken care of. Naomi, however, had no more sons to marry Ruth and Orpah. Also, Naomi did not expect to marry and have more sons, and even if she did bear sons, it would take too long for them to reach marriageable age (vss. 12-13). Thus, if the young women traveled to Judah with her, Naomi wouldn't be able to give them more of her sons to marry.

This second attempt to turn the young women back somewhat worked. After a few more tears and more kissing, Orpah headed home (vs. 14). This decision to return to Moab is not a reproach on her character; rather, she was showing a practical concern for herself. Also, her tearful parting from Naomi indicates a fondness for the older woman. Here we see that occasionally loyalty means allowing loved ones to do what is best for them, even if such an action means loss for us. In Naomi's case, her prospect for surviving and thriving in Judah were reduced with the departure of Orpah. Yet, despite this, Naomi remained sensitive to the needs of her daughter-in-law.

B. Ruth's Faith: vs. 16

But Ruth replied, "Don't urge me to leave you or to turn back from you. Where you go I will go, and where you stay I will stay. Your people will be my people and your God my God."

While Orpah made a commonsense decision, Ruth opted to place Naomi's needs first. This decision is all the more remarkable in light of Naomi's statement about Orpah. Since she was returning to "her people and her gods" (Ruth 1:15), it appeared reasonable for her sister-in-law to follow her back home. Ruth, however, refused to do so and even asked that Naomi stop trying to dissuade her. Ruth was convinced that if she returned to her people, it would mean abandoning Naomi and leaving her more vulnerable than before.

Ruth's clinging to Naomi indicated a love stronger than formal regard. Self-centered choosing wants to know, "What's in it for me?" Loyalty like Ruth's asks, "What can I do for you?" In her pledge of loyalty, Ruth made four choices (vs. 16). First, she decided to forsake the comforts of home to travel across the desert. Second, she would live where Naomi lived, even in poverty. Third, Ruth would identify herself with Naomi's people, even though she knew they might reject her. Ruth's most significant commitment—the fourth one—was to Yahweh, the God of Israel: "your God [will be] my God."

Loyalty like Ruth's doesn't mushroom in moments of crisis; rather, it develops through long association. Ruth had already been a source of strength to Naomi after Elimelech died. By sharing their grief, the two women had learned to trust each other. Ruth had probably never read the Scripture or heard a biblical sermon. Her knowledge of Israel's God had come from observing Naomi. The older woman's witness, even in times of great suffering, had shaped the younger woman's faith. Living up close and personal, family members know whether our actions match our testimony. Would our example convince someone to follow the Lord?

Discussion Questions

1. How do you think Elimelech and Naomi felt as famine overtook their land?
2. Given their options, why do you think this couple decided to settle in Moab?
3. After the death of Naomi's husband, what must it have been like for Naomi to find wives for her two sons?
4. What sorts of struggles might have Naomi and her two daughters-in-law faced as they decided to leave Moab?
5. What does Ruth's response suggest about her character? How do you see yourself in comparison to her?

Contemporary Application

According to the English dictionary, loyalty must always have an object. You cannot simply be loyal; you have to be loyal to someone or something. This week's lesson challenges us to remain loyal in our relationships. Certainly Ruth is a wonderful example of loyalty in her relationship with Naomi.

The world's brand of loyalty often says, "I will scratch your back if you will scratch mine." Christian loyalty, however, means giving without expecting anything in return. Consider Ruth. When she left Moab, she had no assurance of a happy future. Jesus similarly set aside His heavenly glory to do His Father's will. Jesus likewise taught His disciples that sacrificial service was the route to contentment.

The unity believers have in Christ goes deeper than any other bond. As Paul said to the Ephesians, Christians share "one Lord, one faith, one baptism" (Eph. 4:5). The unity believers have in their faith is shown by their mutual loyalty in Christ; and such loyalty is demonstrated in compassion toward others. As 1 John 3:11 says, we should love one another. Loyalty is also shown in obedience to God, for as Jesus declared in John 14:15, if we love Him, we will keep His commandments.

Consider the fact that, after Naomi arrived in Bethlehem, she told her neighbors that her life had become bitter (Ruth 1:20). Ruth chose to share this suffering. We, too, as believers seek to rejoice with our fellow Christians and share in their sorrows (Rom. 12:15). Together we celebrate a wedding, deliver groceries to a family going through a financial crisis, stand by a hospital bed, or weep beside an open casket.

Loyalty to Christ furthermore means choosing to act for the good of another. Ruth's trip with Naomi was arduous. Such loyalty like this always costs time and energy; and helping someone else often destroys our well-planned schedules. God's most effective servants are those who are willing to stop what they are doing to help someone in need.

Acceptance in Community

DEVOTIONAL READING

Romans 12:9-18

DAILY BIBLE READINGS

Monday March 22
Romans 12:9-18 Live
Peaceably with All

Tuesday March 23
Romans 1:8-15 A Debtor to
Others

Wednesday March 24
James 2:8-13 Mercy
Triumphs

Thursday March 25
James 3:13-18 Wisdom from
Above

Friday March 26
Isaiah 56:3-8 For All Peoples

Saturday March 27
Ephesians 2:11-20 Members
of God's Household

Sunday March 28
Ruth 2:5-12; 3:9-11 Blessed
with Acceptance

Scripture

Background Scripture: *Ruth 2—3*
Scripture Lesson: *Ruth 2:5-12; 3:9-11*
Key Verse: *"And now, my daughter, don't be afraid. I will do*
for you all you ask. All my fellow townsmen know that you are
a woman of noble character." Ruth 3:11.
Scripture Lesson for Children: *Ruth 2:1-12*
Key Verse for Children: *"May the LORD repay you for what*
you have done. May you be richly rewarded by the LORD, the
God of Israel, under whose wings you have come to take
refuge." Ruth 2:12.

Lesson Aim

To treat others kindly and respectfully, regardless of
their gender, race, or economic status.

Lesson Setting

Time: *1375–1050 B.C.*
Place: *Judah*

Lesson Outline

Acceptance in Community
  I. The Kindness of Boaz to Ruth: Ruth 2:5-12
      A. *The Decision to Glean in the Field of Boaz: vs. 5*
      B. *The Explanation Provided by the Overseer: vss. 6-7*
      C. *The Instructions Given by Boaz: vss. 8-9*
      D. *The Commitment of Ruth to Naomi: vss. 10-12*
  II. The Affirmation Made by Boaz to Ruth:
      Ruth 3:9-11
      A. *The Request Made by Ruth: vs. 9*
      B. *The Willingness of Boaz: vss. 10-11*

Introduction for Adults

Topic: *Gaining Acceptance*

Why do many adults refuse to accept people of another gender, race, or economic status? Fear is one of the greatest barriers for adults to overcome. John Perkins, who has made great strides in bridging ethnic gaps, writes about this fear in his book *With Justice for All.*

What Perkins says about racial relationships can also be extended to relationships between people of different genders and economic statuses. Adults who stretch across the gap of race, economics, or gender reach into the unknown, and naturally most of us have misgivings about the unknown. Thus, as Perkins suggests, bearing the burdens of others not only erases the unknown factor but also helps us exhibit God's concern for others.

Empathy is difficult for adults, especially since it presupposes looking at a situation through the emotions and perspective of another. Yet without empathy we will never achieve reconciliation and begin to treat others kindly and with respect.

Introduction for Youth

Topic: *We Welcome You*

Kindness is easily pushed aside in a culture that persists in looking out for number one. With our focus on satisfying our own needs comes an appalling lack of interest in and concern for others. Many social tragedies could be averted if we spent more time developing the habit of welcoming others and less time on seeking self-fulfillment.

"I'm too busy" is one of the most frequent excuses for not taking the time to help people in need. This is sad, for in many cases people are starving for companionship and encouragement. Elderly people are easily forgotten, and young people complain that their parents do not care about them.

The Book of Ruth shows teens that one person can make a difference. Boaz did not allow his concern for profits to overshadow the needs of a foreign widow. He not only gave her food to eat, but also tried to meet her deeper needs—all at considerable expense to himself. He sets the example for showing kindness to others.

Concepts for Children

Topic: *Welcome to the Community*

1. To provide food for Naomi and herself, Ruth picked leftover grain in the field of Boaz.
2. Ruth found favor with Boaz, who invited her into his community.
3. Boaz told Ruth why he was so kind to her.
4. Boaz and Ruth found their future in each other.
5. God is pleased when we are kind to others.

Lesson Commentary

I. THE KINDNESS OF BOAZ TO RUTH: RUTH 2:5-12

A. The Decision to Glean in the Field of Boaz: vs. 5

Boaz asked the foreman of his harvesters, "Whose young woman is that?"

In last week's lesson we learned that Naomi urged her daughters-in-law to return home, for she was too old to have sons who could become their husbands. Orpah returned to her family, but Ruth went with Naomi. The two women continued their journey, finally arriving in Bethlehem just as the barley harvest was beginning (Ruth 1:11-22). Yet, as poor, defenseless widows, they depended on the kindness of friends, relatives, and even strangers for their daily bread. Soon help came in the form of harvesttime.

At this point in the narrative we are introduced to another major character: Boaz. He was a relative of Elimelech and one of the important men in town (2:1). The Hebrew text literally says "a man mighty in substance." Elsewhere in the Old Testament, this phrase is frequently translated as "mighty man of valor." While Boaz might not have been a warrior, he still was a wealthy and influential person in Bethlehem. Though Naomi had sought to send her daughters-in-law back to their homes, Boaz would prove to be a relative who would protect Ruth and Naomi.

As widows and immigrants, the two women had to find a source of income. Since it was the time of the barley harvest, Ruth offered to go into the fields and glean, that is, pick up grain missed or dropped by the harvesters. Ruth might have learned from Naomi that the Hebrew law made provision for the poor to do this (see Lev. 19:9; 23:22). But of course, it was not in the financial interest of farmers to allow gleaning, so Ruth hoped to find some who would look favorably upon her and allow her to glean (Ruth 2:2). Here we find the Moabitess taking the role of a subordinate servant as she sought permission from landowners. In turn, they could decide to show kindness by permitting her glean in their fields behind their harvest workers.

Naomi gave Ruth permission. And so it was that Ruth found herself gleaning in a field belonging to Boaz, though at this time the Moabitess did not know his identity. The Hebrew text of verse 3, when rendered more literally, says "she chanced, chanced" or "she happened to happen upon." The narrative is written from the limited perspective Ruth had at the time. From her viewpoint, she just randomly chose a spot in someone's field to pick grain. People of faith, however, realize from reading the entire account that God was providentially involved in leading the Moabitess to the land owned by Boaz, one of Elimelech's near relatives.

As Ruth was gleaning that morning, Boaz himself arrived on the scene. The Hebrew text of verse 4 literally says "and look." By using this literary device, the narrator draws readers into the account. It's as if the audience was right there in the fields outside of Bethlehem and witnessing the appearance of Boaz. He greeted the harvesters with the blessing, "The Lord be with you!" From this we know Boaz was a godly man. The response of the workers—"The Lord bless you!"—indicates that they admired and liked their employer.

Boaz noticed an unfamiliar woman in his fields. He asked the servant in charge of the harvesters to identify the stranger. The Hebrew phrase rendered "Whose young woman is that?" (vs. 5) expected a response about Ruth being someone's daughter, wife, or servant. In Bible times, the culture was patriarchal. Typically, an unmarried woman would have belonged to her father, while a married woman would have belonged to her husband. In the case of Ruth, since she had neither a father nor a husband, her next of kin was Naomi (due to the fact that Ruth was Naomi's daughter-in-law).

B. The Explanation Provided by the Overseer: vss. 6-7

The foreman replied, "She is the Moabitess who came back from Moab with Naomi. She said, 'Please let me glean and gather among the sheaves behind the harvesters.' She went into the field and has worked steadily from morning till now, except for a short rest in the shelter."

The overseer reported to Boaz that Ruth was a young woman who recently returned with Naomi from the region of Moab (Ruth 2:6). The foreman repeated her request for permission to follow the harvesters and gather grain among the bundles they made from the sheaves. The servant in charge of the laborers noted that Ruth arrived early in the morning and had been working steadily until now. The latter did not preclude the fact that the Moabitess had taken a short break in the "shelter" (vs. 7). This probably was a hut made out of branches such as was sometimes constructed in a field. The gist is that Ruth not only worked hard, but also rested for a brief period of time.

C. The Instructions Given by Boaz: vss. 8-9

So Boaz said to Ruth, "My daughter, listen to me. Don't go and glean in another field and don't go away from here. Stay here with my servant girls. Watch the field where the men are harvesting, and fol-low along after the girls. I have told the men not to touch you. And whenever you are thirsty, go and get a drink from the water jars the men have filled."

Boaz approached Ruth and greeted her as "My daughter" (Ruth 2:8). This form of address was friendly and welcoming. It possibly indicates that Boaz was older than Ruth, but by how many years remains unclear. In that era, gleaners might wander from one field to the next in search of food wherever they might find it. Boaz encouraged Ruth to stay in his field and follow the women in his crew closely. By remaining relatively close to the women who worked for Boaz, Ruth would get the first chance at what they left behind and be able to collect considerably more grain than would otherwise be possible. Also, Boaz could better guarantee Ruth's safety.

On that score, Boaz reassured Ruth by informing her that he had instructed the men in his work crew to leave her alone. In short, she did not have to fear being sexually molested by them. Moreover, Boaz arranged for Ruth to quench her thirst after hot hours in the fields. By being able to drink from what the men had drawn (most likely carried from a well some distance away), she would save herself the laborious, time-consuming process of having to stop and fetch water for herself (vs. 9).

D. The Commitment of Ruth to Naomi: vss. 10-12

At this, she bowed down with her face to the ground. She exclaimed, "Why have I found such favor in your eyes that you notice me—a foreigner?" Boaz replied, "I've been told all about what you have done for your mother-in-law since the death of your husband—how you left your father and mother and your homeland and came to live with a people you did not know before. May the LORD repay you for what you have done. May you be richly rewarded by the LORD, the God of Israel, under whose wings you have come to take refuge."

In response to the unusual kindness shown by Boaz, Ruth knelt down in his presence with her forehead to the ground. This was a sign of extreme humility and gratitude. Boaz had done more for Ruth than the social laws of conduct had required, and Ruth responded accordingly by thanking him in a profound way. Yet, even as Ruth demonstrated her gratitude, she wondered what she had done to merit his actions. "Favor" renders a Hebrew noun that emphasizes undeserved kindness. The attentiveness of Boaz seemed even more pronounced to Ruth given the fact that she was a "foreigner" (Ruth 2:10), not an Israelite.

The reason for Boaz's thoughtfulness and generosity were straightforward. He was impressed with the kindness and devotion Ruth had displayed toward her mother-in-law (and a relative of Boaz). This included the sacrifice Ruth made to leave her native land and people to remain with Naomi. Boaz recognized that no law or custom obliged Ruth to do so. Even though she had already fulfilled her duties as a daughter-in-law, she still had chosen to be loyal and devoted to her mother-in-law (vs. 11).

In response, Boaz offered a prayer on behalf of Ruth. Boaz asked the Lord to recompense Ruth for her kindness to Naomi. Behind the statement made by Boaz is the belief that God would fully repay Ruth's efforts. At the same, Boaz acknowledged that Ruth had come to believe in Israel's God for herself. By saying that Ruth had come under the metaphorical wing's of the Lord, Boaz was picturing a little bird snuggling under its mother's pinions. Some think Boaz was referring to the fact that Ruth was now living in the territory of God's people. Another possibility is that Boaz believed Ruth had a personal faith in the Lord (vs. 12). In humility, Ruth responded with her own wish that Boaz would continue to look on her favorably. Also, Ruth expressed her thanks to him again (vs. 13).

It must have been uncommon for a landowner to invite an impoverished widow to join his harvest crew for lunch, but that's what Boaz did for Ruth a little later. He gave her the opportunity to eat bread with sauce. Then Boaz gave Ruth roasted grain, which would have been a treat at harvesttime. Freshly reaped grain was left attached to the stalks and held in the fire, which would burn away the chaff and roast the kernels of grain. Ruth's portion was large, as she had some left over (vs. 14).

After Ruth left the dining place, Boaz instructed his male crew members to make sure Ruth had a lot of grain to pick up. If she gathered among the sheaves—where the poor were not normally allowed—she was not to be harassed. Furthermore, they were to deliberately leave some grain for her, again without harassing her (vss. 15-16). The provisions made by Boaz were designed to benefit Ruth without robbing her of self-respect. Under the favorable conditions fostered by Boaz, Ruth gleaned until dusk, when the crew would have finished its work. Then she threshed her barley, which means she separated the valuable kernels from the unwanted chaff, in this case probably by beating it with a stick. The grain that resulted amounted to about an ephah, or about three-fifths of a bushel. This was a good day's yield for a gleaner (vs. 17).

After Ruth returned home, she showed Naomi the ephah of grain and the leftovers from her lunch. This was a greater bounty than Naomi had expected to see. Plainly gleeful, Naomi quizzed Ruth about her work and blessed the person who had helped her (vss. 18-19). Ruth gave the information Naomi requested. If anything, this increased Naomi's excitement. She again blessed Boaz, noting that he had show kindness to "the living and the dead" (vs. 20). This possibly means he had been generous to the family of Elimelech when they previously had lived in Bethlehem. And now Boaz was doing the same out of respect for the deceased husband of Naomi.

Until this point Ruth had been ignorant about her family relationship with Boaz. So now Naomi explained that he was not only a "close relative" but also a family guardian. In Israelite custom, the later was a person who took on the responsibility of caring for a relative. Naomi saw Boaz in that role, and indeed he might have, too. That would explain his going out of his way to help Ruth at the field that day. Ruth noted that Boaz had invited her to continue gleaning in his fields until the end of the grain harvest (vs. 21). Naomi encouraged Ruth to take Boaz up on his offer, for she would be safer with his crew than with others (vs. 22).

II. THE AFFIRMATION MADE BY BOAZ TO RUTH: RUTH 3:9-11

A. The Request Made by Ruth: vs. 9

"Who are you?" he asked. "I am your servant Ruth," she said. "Spread the corner of your garment over me, since you are a kinsman-redeemer."

Naomi had a rather unique idea for encouraging Boaz to marry Ruth. When Naomi had heard that Boaz would be winnowing barley at the threshing floor that evening, Naomi knew the time to act had come. Evening was the usual time for winnowing, for that was when breezes picked up strongly enough to blow away the chaff after the grain was tossed into the air. Naomi told Ruth to make herself attractive by washing and perfuming herself and dressing well (Ruth 3:3). Boaz had seen Ruth wearing field clothes and covered with perspiration, dirt, and bits of barley stalks. Now he would see her at her best.

Next, Ruth was to go to the threshing floor and wait until Boaz was in a good mood as a result of eating and drinking his fill. There may have been a party going on at the threshing floor to celebrate the harvest. Ruth was also to note when he lay down to sleep so that in the dark later she would not mistake some other man for Boaz. As he slept, Ruth was to pick up the edge of his cloak (used as a blanket) and lie next to his feet (vs. 4).

Obediently, Ruth agreed to follow Naomi's instructions and proceeded to do so (vss. 5-6). Though the daughter-in-law might not have been consulted in the choice of her second husband, she showed no hesitation to cooperate in getting him. At the threshing floor that night, Boaz ate and drank and then went to sleep at the end of the grain pile. A little later, Ruth stealthily went to him and lay down at his feet (vs. 7). Then, around midnight, Boaz awoke and noticed that a woman was laying at his feet. Naturally, Boaz asked her who she was. Ruth gave her name and then asked him to cover her with the corner of his garment (vss. 8-9). Ruth wanted Boaz to perform the symbolic act to indicate his intention to marry her.

In those days when a man covered an unmarried woman with his garment, that was a symbol of wanting to take her into his care by marrying her. (This ritual is practiced even today in some Arab cultures.) Thus Ruth would be indicating her desire for him to marry her. Interestingly, the Hebrew noun rendered "garment" (vs. 9) can also mean "wings." It is used in 2:12 when referring to Ruth's refuge under God's wings. Here she was to seek further safety under the symbolic "wings" of Boaz. This imagery unveils the essence of Ruth's petition. This was not just a request for marriage, but for Boaz to function in the fullest sense as a guardian of the family interests. This included raising a child in the name of Ruth's former husband, purchasing the land of Elimelech, and caring for Ruth and Naomi— essentially adopting a new family.

B. The Willingness of Boaz: vss. 10-11

"The LORD bless you, my daughter," he replied. "This kindness is greater than that which you showed earlier: You have not run after the younger men, whether rich or poor. And now, my daughter, don't be afraid. I will do for you all you ask. All my fellow townsmen know that you are a woman of noble character.

Boaz could have reacted angrily, but instead he blessed Ruth and praised her for what she had done (Ruth 3:10). Boaz considered Ruth seeking him as her husband to be a greater act of kindness toward Naomi than had been even Ruth's earlier decision to accompany her mother-in-law (compare 2:11-12). Boaz knew Ruth could have found a man younger than him, perhaps even having more wealth. But Ruth had sought to attach herself to Boaz, for Ruth knew that as a family guardian he might take care of Naomi. Expressed differently, Ruth had taken the interests of her mother-in-law into consideration when she had pursued a husband.

Boaz assured Ruth that he would try to fulfill his duty as the guardian of the family interests. Boaz added that Ruth's "noble character" (3:11) was known throughout the town. Thus the marriage of Boaz to Ruth would be acceptable to the community even though she was a foreigner. Nonetheless, Boaz did bring up one possible impediment to the plan. There was a man in Bethlehem who was a closer relative to Naomi and Ruth than was Boaz (vs. 12). Accordingly, this person had the greater right to act as a family guardian. Boaz promised to find out the other man's intensions in the morning. If this person did not want to marry Ruth, Boaz would do it. With these encouraging words, Boaz urged Ruth to finish her night's sleep where she was (vs. 13).

Discussion Questions

1. What sort of character qualities did Ruth demonstrate to the overseer of Boaz's harvesters?
2. Why did Ruth show such extreme humility and gratitude to Boaz?
3. Why do you think Ruth chose early on to be so devoted to her mother-in-law?
4. In what sense had Ruth sought refuge in the God of Israel?
5. If you were Ruth, would you have chosen to be married to someone such as Boaz, as opposed to a man who was richer and younger?

Contemporary Application

Of the various themes that can be traced in the Book of Ruth, the idea that God is close at hand seems to be one of the most significant. Though He is hidden in terms of His being, the movements of events and characters flowed under His constant supervision. He controlled famine and harvest, chose the destiny of individuals, took the lead in bringing people together, and even guided in conception.

The active involvement of people in remaining faithful and doing what is right is also important in the book. Each of the characters had a role to play in discovering and working out the plan of God. Along the way they learned that the paths of God are not always smooth, but may involve poverty, hard work, complications, and grief.

Yet in this account, loyalty is rewarded. Making a personal sacrifice to maintain the values and laws of God resulted in the activity of God on the faithful's behalf. And faith in the face of tragedy, minimal as that faith might have been in its wrestling match with human emotions, resulted in the tender redemption of God. Last, the strength and experience of a godly man led a path through the harassment of rough laborers and the red tape of legal counsel to redeem the lives of two struggling people. His loving act sustained a lineage that includes not only King David but also Jesus Christ.

Facing Pain and Joy

Scripture

Background Scripture: *John 13:21-30; 16:16-24;
20:11-16*
Scripture Lesson: *John 16:16-24; 20:11-16*
Key Verse: *"In a little while you will see me no more, and
then after a little while you will see me."* John 16:16.
Scripture Lesson for Children: *John 13:21-30; 20:11-16*
Key Verse for Children: *Mary Magdalene went to the disci-
ples with news: "I have seen the Lord!"* John 20:18.

Lesson Aim

To explore the significance of Jesus' resurrection.

Lesson Setting

Time: A.D. *30*
Place: *Jerusalem*

Lesson Outline

Facing Pain and Joy
  I. Joy to Replace Grief: John 16:16-24
      A. *The Disciples' Confusion: vss. 16-18*
      B. *The Savior's Explanation: vss. 19-20*
      C. *The Analogy of Childbirth: vss. 21-22*
      D. *The Provision of the Father: vss. 23-24*
  II. An Encounter with the Risen Lord: John 20:11-16
      A. *Seeing the Angels: vss. 11-12*
      B. *Seeing the Lord Jesus: vss. 13-14*
      C. *Recognizing the Lord Jesus: vss. 15-16*

Introduction for Adults

Topic: *Loss and Life*

One of the common testimonies of people whose heart ailments have been treated with bypass surgery is that they have found new life. Instead of feeling weak, tired, and short of breath, they now have energy to do things they could not do before.

Christ's resurrection does the same sort of thing for us in the spiritual realm. At one time we were "dead in . . . transgressions and sins" (Eph. 2:1). But when we trusted in Jesus for salvation, we passed from death to life (vs. 5). This is possible because we have been identified with Christ's death, burial, and resurrection (Rom. 6:1-4).

If we think of our old, sinful life as dead and buried, we have a powerful motive to resist sin. We now have the option of consciously choosing to treat the temptations and desires of the old nature as if they were dead. Such is possible because of the wonderful new life we have in Jesus.

Introduction for Youth

Topic: *Double Whammy: Pain and Joy!*

Every teen knows about pain and joy in their lives. And while some youth have little hope for the future, apparently many more are optimistic. When polled by *TIME/CNN* and asked what happens after death, 61 percent of Americans felt that they would go to heaven. Joni Eareckson Tada, a quadriplegic since she was 17, trusts in full-body resurrection and the glorification of the body in heaven.

Believers around you highlight the biblical account and announcement. Jesus rose from the dead! Death has been conquered!

Concepts for Children

Topic: *From Sorrow to Joy*

1. Jesus announced that Judas Iscariot would betray Him.
2. Jesus identified Judas by offering him a piece of bread.
3. The disciples did not understand what Jesus was telling them.
4. After Jesus rose from the dead, He first appeared to Mary Magdalene.
5. Just as Mary told Jesus' followers about resurrection, we can tell others about our risen Lord.

Lesson Commentary

I. JOY TO REPLACE GRIEF: JOHN 16:16-24

A. The Disciples' Confusion: vss. 16-18

"In a little while you will see me no more, and then after a little while you will see me." Some of his disciples said to one another, "What does he mean by saying, 'In a little while you will see me no more, and then after a little while you will see me,' and 'Because I am going to the Father'?" They kept asking, "What does he mean by 'a little while'? We don't understand what he is saying."

John 16 is one the Bible's chief passages describing the Holy Spirit and His work. Jesus revealed that the Spirit of God, like a legal counselor, would act as a prosecutor to bring about the world's conviction. He does not merely accuse the world of wrongdoing, but also presents indisputable evidence to prove the world's sinfulness. The Spirit would establish the case of the Father and Son against nonbelievers by presenting evidence in three different areas: sin, righteousness, and judgment (vs. 8). In terms of the first area, the Spirit convicts the world of sin because people do not believe in the Son of God (vs. 9). Jesus might have meant that the classic sin was unbelief, or that sin remains because of unbelief, or both. In any case, the Holy Spirit convicts people of sin because they reject and repudiate the Redeemer's message.

With respect to the second area, the righteousness of God was manifested in the life and character of His Son. The Messiah's return to the Father vindicated His character and established Him as the standard of all righteousness. But when the Son returned to the Father, He was no longer visible to His disciples and the world (vs. 10). It was now the Holy Spirit's responsibility to convict the world according to the standard of righteousness set by the eternal Word. In connection with the third area, the Son told His disciples that the Father has already condemned Satan, the prince of this world. In fact, the Messiah's crucifixion and resurrection sealed the defeat of the evil one. Since the world has followed the prince of darkness, the world stands condemned with him (vs. 11).

The purpose for the Spirit's advent was not only to convict the world of its guilt, but also to guide the disciples into all truth. The divine-human Word wanted to share these truths with His friends, but He knew that what the Holy Spirit would later convey to them would be too much for them to presently bear (vs. 12). Jesus might have meant that this knowledge was too difficult for them to understand, or too difficult to emotionally absorb, or perhaps both. In any case, the Spirit would help them understand these truths in the future and give them the ability to incorporate them into their lives.

The Spirit never worked independently from the Father and the Son. The Spirit would pass along to Jesus' followers whatever was given to Him (vs. 13). Just as the Son glorified His heavenly Father during His earthly ministry, the primary function of the Holy Spirit's ministry was to glorify the Son. The Spirit did this by taking the teachings of the eternal Word and making them known to believers (vs. 14). Anything the Messiah conveyed to the Spirit was given to the Son by His Father (vs. 15). This verse describes the intimate communion, concert, and cooperation among the three persons of the Godhead.

Finally, Jesus told His disciples that soon He would be leaving them, but a little later they would see Him again (vs. 16). Jesus was alluding to His imminent arrest, trial, execution, and burial. During that time, they would abandon Him and not see Him. After His resurrection, however, they would again see Him. Some think the phrase "after a little while" refers either to the coming of the Spirit following the ascension of the Son or to the Messiah's second advent. But, as 14:19 and 16:22 suggest (see also 7:33; 12:35; 13:33), it is more likely that 16:16 is referring to Jesus' post-resurrection appearances to His disciples. Indeed, Scripture reveals that He manifested Himself to them several times before His ascension into heaven (see Matt. 28; Mark 16; Luke 24; John 20—21; Acts 1:3-8; 9:1-19; 1 Cor. 9:1; 15:5-7).

Jesus' statement about departing, returning, and going to the Father perplexed His disciples (John 16:17). They especially struggled to make sense of His words recorded in verses 10 and 16, which refer to His ascension and crucifixion, respectively. While Jesus had not connected these two events, His followers nonetheless considered them to be linked. Their desire to understand the Savior prompted them to keep on repeating fragmentary portions of His statements (vs. 18). Jesus, of course, was receptive to their desire to grasp the significance of His words.

B. The Savior's Explanation: vss. 19-20

Jesus saw that they wanted to ask him about this, so he said to them, "Are you asking one another what I meant when I said, 'In a little while you will see me no more, and then after a little while you will see me'? I tell you the truth, you will weep and mourn while the world rejoices. You will grieve, but your grief will turn to joy."

Jesus could see that His disciples wanted to query Him about His statements. While Jesus had supernatural knowledge of all people (see John 1:47-48; 2:24-25; 4:17-18; 6:61, 64), the writer of the fourth Gospel was not necessarily referring to it in 16:19. Most likely, the open back-and-forth dialogue between His disciples made it obvious that they wanted Him to clarify what He meant when He declared that they would not see Him for a "little while," but then after an unspecified period of time, they again would see Him.

"I tell you the truth" (vs. 20) is more literally rendered "Truly, truly, I say to you." It's as if Jesus was in a courtroom and bearing solemn witness to the facts. In this case, He acknowledged that His crucifixion and burial would cause His followers to wail and lament over what they presumed was His demise. Meanwhile, unsaved humanity—whom Jesus referred to as the "world"—would celebrate their apparent triumph over the "Lord of glory" (1 Cor. 2:8). Though the disciples would be sad for a while, it would not last forever. Indeed, their grief would be turned into joy over the news of the Savior's resurrection from the dead (see John 20:20).

The Greek noun rendered "world" (16:20) is *kosmos* (from which we get our English term "cosmos"). In its most basic usage, *kosmos* referred to an ornament, such as in 1 Peter 3:3, where it is used to mean the "adornment," namely, the ornamentation of jewelry and clothing. The noun can also be used of the universe with its orderly ornamentation of stars and planets. Eventually *kosmos* came to refer to the earth, since (from the human perspective) that is the most important part of the universe, and also people, since they are the most significant inhabitants of the planet.

In the Fourth Gospel, "world" most often refers to the majority of people and their temporal pursuits (including their goals, aspirations, values, and priorities). Since most rejected the Messiah, "the world" in this Gospel sometimes denotes humanity in opposition to Him. John's "world" is hostile to the Savior and to His followers because of their association with Him (7:7; 15:18–19). Yet despite the world's hatred of God, He still loves it and gave His Son so that its people might receive eternal life (3:16). How ironic it is that even though the world came into being through the Messiah, it remained ignorant of His identity (1:10). Even many of the Jews, God's chosen people, rejected Jesus as the Messiah during His earthly ministry (vs. 11).

C. The Analogy of Childbirth: vss. 21-22

A woman giving birth to a child has pain because her time has come; but when her baby is born she forgets the anguish because of her joy that a child is born into the world. So with you: Now is your time of grief, but I will see you again and you will rejoice, and no one will take away your joy.

Jesus used the common analogy of childbirth to clarify for the disciples what He meant. When a mother's period of gestation is completed, the ensuing birth of her child is filled with "pain" (John 16:21; see Isa. 26:17-19; 66:7-15; Hos. 13:13-14). The underlying Greek term rendered "pain" (John 16:21) can also be translated "distress," "sadness," or "grief," which strengthens the conceptual link with Jesus' statement recorded in verse 20. The joy of bringing a newborn into the world displaces the "anguish" (vs. 21) and suffering that was previously felt.

In a similar way, Jesus' disciples presently experienced "grief" (vs. 22) and distress over His impending suffering. At that time, of course, they did not realize that His atoning sacrifice at Calvary was necessary to redeem the lost. Once Jesus had conquered death through His resurrection and appeared to His followers, they would rejoice (see Isa. 66:14, where God speaks similar words of hope concerning Jerusalem). The disciples' response was appropriate, for the presence of the risen Lord signaled the dawning of the messianic age (which would be consummated at the Redeemer's second advent). Furthermore, no one (whether human or demonic in origin) would be able to rob the disciples of their deep-seated gladness (see John 10:28; 15:11; Phil. 1:6).

D. The Provision of the Father: vss. 23-24

In that day you will no longer ask me anything. I tell you the truth, my Father will give you whatever you ask in my name. Until now you have not asked for anything in my name. Ask and you will receive, and your joy will be complete.

Jesus further explained that once He had risen from the dead and physically appeared to His disciples, they would "no longer ask [Him] anything" (John 16:23). The Greek verb translated "ask" refers to a search for information, which is seen in people putting forth questions in an effort to satisfy their curiosity. After Jesus' ascension, the Holy Spirit would come to the disciples to reveal to them truth from the Father and the Son (see 14:26; 16:12-14). In point of fact, the Spirit would enable the disciples to fully know and understand the truth.

Next, Jesus solemnly assured His followers about the importance of them praying to His heavenly Father. A different Greek verb is rendered "ask" in the latter part of 16:23. The term relates to the offering of petitions, which Jesus directed His disciples to do in His name. The idea is not that Jesus' name is like a magical formula that believers tack on to the end of their prayers to increase the likelihood of them being answered. Rather, Jesus was saying that His followers were operating as His representatives and making requests to the Father with the Son's delegated authority (see 14:13-14; 15:16).

Prior to Jesus' crucifixion, the disciples offered prayers to the Father and made petitions to the Son. Expressed differently, they had not made their requests to the Father in the name of the Son. After Jesus' resurrection and ascension into heaven, this would change. The disciples would directly address the Father with newfound confidence. They had the assurance that when they asked in the delegated authority of the Son, the Father would respond to their requests. In turn, their "joy" (16:24) would be made "complete."

Here we see that prayer is essential to effectively doing God's work. When we make our requests known to the Father through the name of the Son, He Himself will do them. Of course, Jesus did not mean that He will always fulfill the request in the way we desire. Moreover, Jesus is referring to requests whose primary purpose is to glorify God, and thus are in line with God's will. These conditions do not limit the power of prayer. Instead, they require us to make our requests consistent with the character of the Son and in accordance with the Father's will. Once we focus our requests on fulfilling the will of God, we will desire nothing less and reap the fruit of abundant joy.

II. An Encounter with the Risen Lord: John 20:11-16

A. Seeing the Angels: vss. 11-12

But Mary stood outside the tomb crying. As she wept, she bent over to look into the tomb and saw two angels in white, seated where Jesus' body had been, one at the head and the other at the foot.

The promise of Jesus' resurrection alluded to in John 16:16-24 finds its fulfillment in John 20. Verse 1 recounts how Mary Magdalene discovered the empty tomb. In turn, her reporting of the same prompted Peter and the "other disciple" (vs. 2), who most likely was John, to confirm what Mary saw. When John went inside the tomb, he saw the evidence and believed that Messiah had risen from the dead (vs. 8). John's awareness, however, was incomplete, for neither he nor the rest of the disciples understood the Scripture concerning the Resurrection (vs. 9). Once Peter and John were done examining the scene, they went back to their homes (vs. 10).

Evidently, Mary had returned to the tomb with Peter and John. At this point, Mary did not understand that Jesus had risen from the dead. Mary thought bandits had stolen the Lord's body (vs. 2), and this possibility so traumatized Mary that she "stood outside the tomb crying" (vs. 11). At some point, Mary decided to look into the tomb, and when she did, she saw two white-robed angels sitting at the head and foot of the place where the body of Jesus had been lying (vs. 12).

B. Seeing the Lord Jesus: vss. 13-14

They asked her, "Woman, why are you crying?" "They have taken my Lord away," she said, "and I don't know where they have put him." At this, she turned around and saw Jesus standing there, but she did not realize that it was Jesus.

Even while Mary was reexamining the tomb, she continued to weep. This prompted the angels to ask her, "Woman, why are you crying?" (John 2:13). Mary explained that she was grieved over the fact that the body of the Lord had somehow been stolen. Mary still did not realize that the all-powerful Word had risen from the dead. When Mary glanced over her shoulder, she saw someone standing behind her. Though she did not recognize Him, the person was Jesus (vs. 14).

C. Recognizing the Lord Jesus: vss. 15-16

"Woman," he said, "why are you crying? Who is it you are looking for?" Thinking he was the gardener, she said, "Sir, if you have carried him away, tell me where you have put him, and I will get him." Jesus said to her, "Mary." She turned toward him and cried out in Aramaic, "Rabboni!" (which means Teacher).

The Savior, with undeniable compassion, asked Mary why she was weeping and whom she was trying to find (John 20:15). Mary, while still in a state of shock, mistakenly thought that Jesus was the local gardener. The reason for Mary's inability to recognize Jesus is uncertain. Perhaps it is because Mary's tears blurred her eyes, or possibly the memories of Jesus' bruised and battered body were still etched in Mary's mind. Another option is that the Lord supernaturally prevented Mary from recognizing Him until He chose for her to do so.

In any case, it took a direct statement from Jesus to Mary to get her to see that she was talking to the Savior (vs. 16). On that first Easter morning, tears, defeat, and despair clouded Mary's heart and mind. She was loving and brave, but she needed a special word from the good Shepherd to grasp the reality of His resurrection. Suddenly, Mary's sorrow turned to joy, and she exclaimed, "Rabboni!" Mary had spoken in Aramaic, which was the language the people of Palestine commonly used in Jesus' day. The author of the fourth Gospel explained to his readers that this term meant "Teacher."

Excitedly, Mary tried to hold the Savior, but He stopped her (vs. 17). It was not that Jesus forbade Mary to touch Him at all. Rather, the phrase "Do not hold on to me" conveys the idea of "stop clinging to me." Mary wanted to cling to the Lord she thought she had lost, but He had an ascension for Himself and an assignment for her. Mary was to return to the disciples with the great news of the Redeemer's victory over death. Mary could not run fast enough to tell them (vs. 18).

Discussion Questions

1. Why do you think Jesus' disciples struggled to understand the statement He made in John 16:16?
2. Why would Jesus permit His followers to be filled with sadness, while at the same time the world would be filled with joy?
3. What does it mean to make petitions in the name of Jesus? What does it not mean?
4. Why did Mary, after seeing the empty tomb, stand outside of it and cry?
5. What is significant to you about the risen Lord first revealing Himself to Mary?

Contemporary Application

We may tend to minimize the despair and darkness of those who saw the death of Jesus because we know that He rose from the dead. But the first-century disciples did not know the rest of the account when Jesus was crucified. At times our position is similar to theirs. This side of heaven we see only death and despair, when in reality God has rescued us from both and is preparing a place for us with Him (John 14:1-2).

Jesus' victory over death is the foundation for our faith and the source of our hope. Paul stressed that we can stand on these unshakable facts: Jesus died for our sins and was resurrected on the third day (1 Cor. 15:3-4). Also, if that victory over death had not happened, our faith would be in vain and those who die would be truly lost (vss. 17-18). Thankfully, Jesus rose from the dead, and His resurrection is just the first, for all believers will follow in His path (vs. 20).

Through the Son's resurrection, the Father has rewritten the presumed ending of our life accounts. Death is just the beginning of a new chapter in our walk with Him. The resurrection hope should shine in our moments of darkness, reminding us that the tomb was empty. Moreover, we can join all believers in giving thanks to the Father for the victory we have through the Son (vs. 57).

Love in the Community

Scripture

Background Scripture: *1 John 2:7-17*
Scripture Lesson: *1 John 2:9-11, 15-17*
Key Verses: *Whoever loves his brother lives in the light, and
there is nothing in him to make him stumble.* 1 John 2:10.
Scripture Lesson for Children: *1 John 2:9-11, 15-17*
Key Verse for Children: *And now these three remain: faith,
hope, and love. But the greatest of these is love.*
1 Corinthians 13:13.

Lesson Aim

To stress the value of living in God's light, not in the
darkness of the world.

Lesson Setting

Time: *Around A.D. 96*
Place: *Possibly Ephesus*

Lesson Outline

Love within the Community
  I. Compassion for Others: 1 John 2:9-11
    A. *Light versus Darkness: vs. 9*
    B. *Love versus Hatred: vss. 10-11*
  II. Abhorrence of All That Is Sinful: 1 John 2:15-17
    A. *Love for God versus Love for the World: vs. 15*
    B. *What the World Offers: vs. 16*
    C. *Abiding Forever: vs. 17*

Introduction for Adults

Topic: *Living in the Light of Love*

Depending on where we live, we are required to take our automobiles for periodic inspections, either for mechanical worthiness or for emission controls. When our vehicles pass the inspection, we are free to enjoy all the privileges of driving these marvels of technology.

John's letter is something like that. He writes so that his readers can pass the test and enjoy the blessings of eternal life in Christ. That's why his epistle is so practical. He gives clear pass-fail grades. "If you do this, you pass. If not, you fail."

All of us need John's reminders about letting the light of God's love shine in every aspect of our lives. After all, professing faith in Christ is supposed to make a difference. The changes include loving God rather than the pagan ways of the world and displaying compassion instead of hatred toward our fellow human beings.

Introduction for Youth

Topic: *Love Rules!*

What is it like to live in the light of God's love, as 1 John 2:10 emphasizes? Have you ever entered a dark room or an abandoned apartment, turned on the light, and watched the cockroaches scurry away? Living in the light means we do not have to run away when God shines the truth of His Word on our lives. It means we welcome His inspections. According to the apostle John, it means letting the love of Jesus guide our conduct.

That's a tough assignment and sometimes we fail to make the grade. But Jesus forgives us when we confess our sins. He pardons our transgressions. That's why it's so important to stay close to Him, whatever our circumstances. Jesus not only tells us how to be compassionate, but also helps us to display it when we rely on Him.

Concepts for Children

Topic: *Love Binds Us Together*

1. The apostle John encouraged us to obey Jesus' teachings.
2. Our behavior shows whether we are Christians.
3. As we live for Jesus, we grow stronger in our faith.
4. The presence of Christlike love in us helps others to see that we belong to Jesus.
5. Love is the key to living in a way that pleases the Lord.

Lesson Commentary

I. COMPASSION FOR OTHERS: 1 JOHN 2:9-11

A. Light versus Darkness: vs. 9

Anyone who claims to be in the light but hates his brother is still in the darkness.

First John was authored primarily to combat the emerging heresy of Gnosticism, which was influencing the churches in John's day. Key foundational elements of Gnostic teaching included these beliefs: (1) virtue is inferior to knowledge; (2) only a few chosen people can understand the true meaning of Scripture; (3) to explain the existence of evil, God must have had a cocreator; (4) the Incarnation must be rejected because a spiritual deity would not unite with a material body; and (5) there can be no bodily resurrection since the body is evil and the spirit is good.

John's pre-Gnostic opponents might have been led by a man named Cerinthus. They denied that Jesus was the Son of God who had come in the flesh. To an extent, they denied their own sinfulness and that righteous conduct was necessary to remain in good standing within the church. Apparently the proponents of these views had once been a part of the established church in Asia Minor, but at some time made a distinct break from this fellowship. It seems members of this subversive group were attempting to lure the faithful away from the apostles' authoritative teachings. For this reason John wanted to make it clear that these people were false teachers—in fact, he considered them antichrists.

This week's lesson teaches us to recognize the incompatibility of the darkness of the world and God's light. We discover that fellowship with the world leads to judgment, while fellowship with the Father and His Son leads to eternal life. For believers who want to know if they have genuine, intimate fellowship with God, John suggested a simple test. Christians should ask themselves whether they are obeying God (1 John 2:3). In contrast to Gnosticism, which emphasized accumulating secret knowledge about God, John stressed action-oriented faith. Genuine faith requires conduct that conforms to God's will and commands. Obedience to the divine commands is a fundamental test of a Christian's faith. The importance of obedience is a recurring theme in 1 John (see 3:22-24; 5:2-3).

If obedience is a test of knowing God, then anyone who claims to know the Lord but does not follow His commands cannot be telling the truth. In John's view, if the claim to know God is not accompanied by upright actions, then the claim is worthless and the one who makes it is a liar (2:4). If the person who claims to know God but does not obey His commands is a liar, then the one who does obey God's commands shows that he or she knows Him. The fullness of God's love will be demonstrated in that person's life. God's love is perfected in him or her in the sense that the obedient believer experiences a fuller, richer expression of God's love (vs. 5). All believers enjoy God's saving love, but obedience carries the divine love to a deeper level. We know we are in fellowship with God if we obey His commands.

Expressed differently, we know that our fellowship is genuine if our lives imitate that of Christ (vs. 6). The Son set the standard for living in complete obedience to the Father's will.

After encountering John's extensive discussion about the subject of obedience to God's commands, some of the apostle's readers may have wondered, "Are there any commands we might be unaware of?" The Gnostics were claiming to have the inside scoop on a secret saving knowledge, so John's readers may have been struggling with doubts. Warmly, John made it clear to his friends that he was not presenting some new requirement or obligation, but an old command that they had heard since the Gospel was first proclaimed (vs. 7). The command that John had in mind was apparently to "walk as Jesus did" (vs. 6) and its natural corollary, to love one another (vs. 10).

Whatever the false teachers were telling John's readers, he wanted one truth to be understood. Their obligation was not to some new idea or teaching, but to the message they had heard from the beginning of their Christian experience. The Greeks had two different words for "new." One referred to something that was new in regard to time or recently had come into existence. The other word, the term used in verse 7, referred to something that was new in regard to quality or attribute. Accordingly, because of Jesus' example, the command to love was something new in character and virtue.

When Jesus first gave the command to love one another, He called it new (1 John 2:8; see John 13:34). The apostle presented it again as if it were still new. The commandment to love was first truly realized in the Son and then in His followers. John made reference to this truth in terms of the true light of the Messiah already shining brightly. Because the apostle saw the victory of light over darkness as something previously begun, he urged his readers to hold fast to what they had already heard and not be influenced by the teaching of the opponents. The commandment to love others did not belong to the old era that was passing away. It belonged to the new era of righteousness that was introduced by Jesus' incarnation and made possible by His atoning work on the cross. It follows that any professing Christian who claims to follow Jesus but harbors hatred toward others is still living in the old era of darkness (1 John 2:9).

B. Love versus Hatred: vss. 10-11

Whoever loves his brother lives in the light, and there is nothing in him to make him stumble. But whoever hates his brother is in the darkness and walks around in the darkness; he does not know where he is going, because the darkness has blinded him.

Believers who demonstrate genuine love for others are living in the light of the new era in the Messiah; and because of this, there is nothing in them that would cause others to stumble (1 John 2:10). Professing believers, however, who nurse grudges and cultivate bitterness, remain spiritually darkened. These people lose their bearings as they stumble around in the dark (vs. 11).

As in other portions of John's writings, he minced no words about the vileness of abiding in the darkness of sin and the virtue of dwelling in the light of the Savior. Darkness is the haunt of all that is unrighteous and corrupt, while light is the haven of whatever is pure and wholesome. Both the Old and New Testaments equate light with the truth of the Word (Ps. 119:105; 2 Cor. 4:4). We also learn from Scripture that the Lord detests every aspect of iniquity. Moreover, He enjoins believers to have nothing to do with the fruitless deeds of darkness. Instead, they are to rebuke all forms of wickedness and expose the evil character of the same (Eph. 5:11).

II. ABHORRENCE OF ALL THAT IS SINFUL: 1 JOHN 2:15-17

A. Love for God versus Love for the World: vs. 15

Do not love the world or anything in the world. If anyone loves the world, the love of the Father is not in him.

In the prologue of his letter, the apostle gave his readers two reasons for writing to them (see 1 John 1:1-4). The first was to foster fellowship between his Christian readers and the apostles, then ultimately with God Himself. The second objective was to make the apostle's joy complete. In the remainder of chapter 2, John expanded upon these objectives by detailing how he wanted to see them fulfilled. The warnings and admonitions John gave in 1:5—2:11 might lead one to believe that the apostle was dissatisfied in some way with the spiritual state of his readers. First John 2:12-14 suggests just the opposite. The apostle commended his readers for their relational knowledge of God and their reliance upon the Lord for victory in spiritual warfare.

In these verses, the apostle prefaced the broader objectives of his letter with the words "I am writing to you . . ." (see also verse 7). Writing letters, for personal and business reasons, was a common practice in Bible times. Since there were no telephones or faxes in those days, the most accurate way to convey a message to someone was to put it in written form. In the Old Testament, for example, there are many references to letter writing. Among these are David's letter of instruction to Joab regarding the fate of Uriah the Hittite (2 Sam. 11:14-15), Jezebel's letters plotting Naboth's death (1 Kings 21:8-10), and King Sennacherib's official letter to his subject Hezekiah (2 Kings 19:14). Of course, most of the epistles in the New Testament were originally written as letters to be read publicly.

In 1 John 2:12-14, the apostle referred to his readers in three ways: as "dear children," "fathers," and "young men." Several suggestions have been made to explain John's reasons for using these titles. Some say they are actual age groupings. Others believe that the classifications refer to spiritual maturity rather than chronological age. Many scholars think John was making reference to all the readers in each category. Certain characteristics and experiences suggested by each life stage apply to every Christian.

As "children" John's readers (and all believers) were forgiven because they belonged to their heavenly Father (vs. 12). Their status as adopted children assumed a reconciled relationship with God based on the atoning work of Christ. In the second reference to his readers as children (vs. 13c), John took note of their knowledge of the Father. John used two different Greek words in his characterization of his readers as "children." In verse 12, the word means "little born ones," which is a reference to newborn infants. In verse 13, however, the term John used suggests young children who are no longer infants. As newborn Christians his readers began their spiritual lives barely able to recognize their Father's face. But now, because of their fellowship with God, they had come to know their heavenly parent in a closer and more intimate way.

As "fathers," said John, his readers had "known him who is from the beginning" (vss. 13a, 14a; both comments to the fathers are identical). Whether "him" refers to God the Father or God the Son is unclear, but for John's purposes either would fit equally well. John's point was that his readers in their maturity had experienced true fellowship with God—both the Father and the Son (along with the Spirit). In the designation of his readers as "young men" (vs. 13b), John highlighted their victory over the evil one, or Satan. As warriors who had engaged the evil enemy in spiritual battle, they had been triumphant. In his second reference to the "young men" stage (vs. 14b), John suggested that in their spiritual struggle his readers had not only overcome the enemy but had been strengthened in the process.

While the spiritual state of John's readers was healthy, the apostle still felt compelled to warn them about the dangers of getting too intimate with the world. In the preceding verses, the apostle reminded his readers about the benefits they enjoyed as children of God. Their sins were forgiven, they knew the true God, and they had been victorious in the spiritual battle over Satan. In verses 15-17, the apostle encouraged believers to take the high road mandated by their divine calling. He commanded his readers not to love the world or anything in it (vs. 15a).

In 1 John 2:15, the Greek noun for "world" is *kosmos*. As noted in lesson 5, it refers to the secular, ungodly, humanistic system under Satan's control. At every turn this system opposes God and actively seeks to subvert His plan of salvation for humankind. For this reason, John wanted it understood that one cannot love that world and all that it has to offer and love God at the same time (vs. 15b; compare Jas. 4:4). A clear choice had to be made—love God and hate the world or love the world and hate God. The two options are mutually exclusive. The truth of John's words is evident in the lives of countless believers today. Many Christians desperately try to follow God while embracing the very system that despises Him and everything for which He stands. While believers are permitted to use the things in the world (see 1 Cor. 7:31), none of these things must ever take God's place in their affections or interfere with God's will and plan for their lives.

B. What the World Offers: vs. 16

For everything in the world—the cravings of sinful man, the lust of his eyes and the boasting of what he has and does—comes not from the Father but from the world.

John explained that everything in the world has its origin in this pagan, godless system, not from the Father. In describing what the world has to offer, John specifically named three vices. First is "the cravings of sinful man" (1 John 2:16). The Greek word translated "cravings" here is sometimes rendered "lust," as in the phrase "lust of the eyes." Regardless of which translation is preferred, the word most often signifies the sinful desires that come from within the human heart.

There are times in the New Testament when the Greek word is used in a positive sense to express an attraction for something worthy or good (as in Luke 22:15). Most often, however, it is connected with inappropriate sexual passion. This is especially true of the word's use in New Testament letters. Paul warned, for example, that God may give the unrighteous "over in the sinful desires of their hearts to sexual impurity" (Rom. 1:24). He exhorted Timothy to "flee the evil desires of youth" (2 Tim. 2:22). And Peter urged believers to "abstain from sinful desires" (1 Pet. 2:11) because they wage war against the soul and produce corruption in the world (2 Pet. 1:4).

The second vice the apostle John identified as having its origin in the world is "the lust of [the] eyes" (1 John 2:16). This speaks of the temptations that assault believers from the outside. Jesus called the eye "the lamp of the body" (Matt. 6:22). If the eyes were good, in the moral sense, then the body and the spirit would remain clean. If the eyes were bad, in the same moral sense, then body and spirit would be tainted by sin. Allowing the eyes to dwell upon an object of desire, whether it be a person or thing, will eventually lead to sinful attitudes and actions.

The third vice in John's list of worldly offerings involved boasting about what one has and does (1 John 2:16). The meaning here, while difficult to be precise, seems to refer to the arrogance that can come with success. Ultimately, all of our talents and abilities come from God, so there is never anything to boast about when it comes to what we've accomplished with our skills. The only appropriate response to the blessings in our lives is gratitude, not gratuitous boasting.

C. Abiding Forever: vs. 17

The world and its desires pass away, but the man who does the will of God lives forever.

In John's view a believer should have nothing to do with any of the worldly values he described. In fact, according to the apostle, it is only logical to reject the world and cling to God. The empty values and hollow promises of the world are even now in the process of passing away. Obedience to God and His will, on the other hand, leads to life everlasting (1 John 2:17). Jesus defined eternal life as enjoying a personal relationship with the Father based on knowing Him as the one true God. Furthermore, it is only possible to truly know the Father through faith in the Son, whom the Father had sent to reveal Himself (John 17:3). In short, eternal life is a growing relationship with the triune God that begins, not just when the believer dies, but at the moment of conversion. How foolish it is to remain on a sinking ship when God has tossed a lifeline within the grasp of every human being.

Discussion Questions

1. How is it possible for individuals to claim to be living in the light of God's truth and yet hate a fellow believer?
2. What can believers do to help others recognize they are walking around in spiritual darkness?
3. What does it mean to love the world, especially since God created the universe and everything in it?
4. What are some things people lust for that can ultimately bring about their downfall?
5. What connection do you see between doing the will of God and living forever?

Contemporary Application

John's letter identifies three marks of a genuine relationship with Christ. One is walking in righteousness. Broadly speaking, this means upright living. If we want to be followers of Christ, we must be willing to live His lifestyle. That means changing any attitude or action that is not in keeping with the example Christ set for us.

A second mark of believers should be their obedience to God. Imagine that someone had been pretending to be your friend because that person felt obligated to or was trying to look good in front of others. If you became aware of this, the "friendship" would be meaningless.

We must not have that kind of relationship with God, namely, one characterized by legalistically obeying His commands. Our obedience, like Christ's, should come from our love for God, not from just doing what He says we should do. Then others will notice the joy we have in our relationship with the Lord.

A third mark of a genuine relationship with Christ is loving other believers. Jesus said, "By this all men will know that you are my disciples, if you love one another" (John 13:35). When Christians demonstrate sacrificial, not self-seeking, love toward each other, they stand out in our "me-first" world.

In 1965, Jackie DeShannon wrote and performed the top ten single "What the World Needs Now Is Love." The chorus for this popular song stated that love is "the only thing that there's just too little of" and that "sweet love" is "not just for some but for everyone."

Few people would claim that DeShannon's sentiments don't apply today. In an era in which people tend to live for themselves and take advantage of others to satisfy their own desires, the world needs a special kind of love. It's not the sort, though, that remains confined to our hearts. We need the love of Christ, a practical love that seeks the benefit of others, a caring love that is active and sincere.

Connecting in Community

DEVOTIONAL READING

Romans 5:1-11

DAILY BIBLE READINGS

Monday April 12
Romans 5:1-11 Reconciled with God

Tuesday April 13
John 5:39-47 Refusing Christ

Wednesday April 14
Matthew 5:17-20 Fulfilling the Law

Thursday April 15
Luke 11:42-44 Neglecting the Love of God

Friday April 16
John 8:39-47 Hearing and Accepting the Word

Saturday April 17
Ephesians 3:14-19 Rooted and Grounded in Love

Sunday April 18
Matthew 22:34-40 The Great Commandment

Scripture

Background Scripture: *Matthew 5:17-20; 22:34-40*
Scripture Lesson: *Matthew 22:34-40*
Key Verses: *"Love the Lord your God with all your heart and with all your soul and with all your mind."* Matthew 22:37.
Scripture Lesson for Children: *Matthew 22:34-40*
Key Verses for Children: *"Love the Lord your God with all your heart and with all your soul and with all your mind . . . Love your neighbor as yourself."* Matthew 22:37, 39.

Lesson Aim

To make love for God and others the highest priority in our lives.

Lesson Setting

Time: A.D. *30*
Place: *Jerusalem*

Lesson Outline

Connecting in Community

I. The Issue of the Law's Most Important Commandment: Matthew 22:34-36
   A. *Silencing the Sadducees: vs. 34*
   B. *Being Challenged by the Pharisees: vss. 35-36*

II. The Centrality of Love: Matthew 22:37-40
   A. *The Importance of Loving God: vss. 37-38*
   B. *The Importance of Loving Others: vss. 39-40*

Introduction for Adults

Topic: *The Necessity of Love*

   Booker T. Washington, the noted African-American educator, was taking a walk with a Caucasian friend when a pedestrian roughly elbowed Washington into the gutter. His friend was furious and asked him, "How can you tolerate such an insult?" Washington replied, "I defy any man to make me hate him."

   This is what true Christian love does—it defies all the bitterness and hatred in the world. It also sweeps aside all the barriers that separate people. Because Jesus makes a difference in our social relationships, Christians can extend the love of God to others.

   Jesus' emphasis on the importance of loving our neighbor forces us to look deep inside ourselves. How easy it is for us to say we love God, but then do nothing for others. Also, how hard it is for us to cast aside our own desires for the sake of showing compassion to our fellow human beings.

Introduction for Youth

Topic: *Let's Be Connected*

   The expert in the Mosaic law who questioned Jesus was experienced in creating diversion, and, sadly, many people today follow his tactics. They find it relatively easy to talk about spirituality. But they find it difficult to stick to the main point, namely, their need for Jesus to save them from their hypocrisy and self-righteousness.

   It's a huge step for us to confess that we aren't good enough to merit eternal life. Perhaps that's why some people talk about the sins of others without ever facing the reality of their own transgressions. They have no desire to repent of their sins and be saved. They also have no interest in being merciful even to their enemies.

   From Jesus' emphasis on the importance of loving our neighbor we can glean three principles. First, lack of love is often easy to justify, even though it is never right. Second, our neighbor is anyone of any race, creed, or social background who is in need. Third, love means acting to meet the person's need. When we reach out to others in this way, we establish a true and lasting relational bond with them. In short, it helps us to be connected with them.

Concepts for Children

Topic: *Love One Another!*

1. God desires us to love Him with all our being.
2. We learn to love God by keeping His commands.
3. Part of keeping God's commands includes loving others around us.
4. Loving others the way Jesus has loved us is what life is all about.
5. Sometimes we don't do what God desires. We can ask Him to forgive us and give us the strength to do what is right.

Lesson Commentary

I. THE ISSUE OF THE LAW'S MOST IMPORTANT COMMANDMENT: MATTHEW 22:34-36

A. Silencing the Sadducees: vs. 34

Hearing that Jesus had silenced the Sadducees, the Pharisees got together.

In the spring of A.D. 30, Jesus traveled with His disciples to Jerusalem. It was Sunday, and as they drew near the city, He sent a couple of His followers ahead to a village to procure a donkey. In fulfillment of Scripture, Jesus chose to enter the capital riding on the donkey. Meanwhile, the crowds treated Him like a king entering the city. They sang praises and carpeted His path with their coats and with branches (Matt. 21:1-11). It wasn't long, however, until He made some people angry.

On Monday, Jesus went into the temple and drove out those who were selling sacrificial animals and exchanging money. His motivation was to keep the temple a pure place of worship. While there, He healed the sick and the children sang praises to Him. The Pharisees were critical of this, but Jesus would not compel the children to quiet down (vss. 12-17). Next, while Jesus walked with His disciples, He spotted a fig tree in full leaf, which was usually an indication that it had fruit. But upon finding no fruit on the tree, Jesus cursed it and pronounced that it would never bear fruit again. When the tree withered, the disciples asked why it happened. The Savior used the opportunity to teach them about the power of faith in prayer (vss. 18-22).

On Tuesday, Jesus returned to the temple and began to teach. Some of the chief priests and elders of the Jews approached Him and asked by whose authority He was speaking. Jesus rebuffed them by asking a question in return concerning the authority of John the Baptizer. Since the priests were unwilling to risk an answer, Jesus refused to answer them as well. Instead, He rebuked them for rejecting John's message. Then the Savior told the parable of the two sons—one who said he would not work, but did anyway, and the other who agreed to work, but did not (vss. 23-32).

The first son in this parable of the two sons represented the social outcasts of Jewish society, such as the tax collectors and prostitutes. At first, they were disobedient to God. Yet when these people recognized the truth that had been proclaimed by John, they believed. The second son in Jesus' parable represented Israel's religious leaders. Although they pretended to obey God, they had actually rebelled against Him. Despite their pious activities and sophisticated rituals, they were far from genuinely serving the Lord, having rejected John's message. The religious leaders were looked upon as shining examples of righteousness in their day, while the common people were considered to be further from pleasing God. The Savior did not hesitate to reveal that the situation was actually more like the opposite of that stereotype.

As Jesus' last week progressed, He continued to give teachings and respond to questions. In the parable of the tenants, the Messiah indicated that all who rejected Him would be eternally condemned, while all who received Him would be eternally blessed. In the parable of the wedding banquet, Jesus taught that though many people are invited to put their faith in Him, a much smaller number actually do so. In His encounter with the Pharisees and Herodians, He stressed that obligations to God and people should be honored. When Jesus was interrogated by the Sadducees, He revealed that marriage will not exist in the resurrection (21:33—22:32).

Beneath the surface of the Sadducees question regarding marriage was their desire to know with whom He sided. Did He agree with them that there is no resurrection, or did He agree with the Pharisees, who believed in life after death? Jesus responded by turning to the Sadducees' favorite authority: Moses. From a passage on the burning bush (Exod. 3:6), Jesus demonstrated that resurrection is a reality. In speaking to Moses, God had indicated that He is currently related to people who had long been dead. That meant they had not ceased to exist. If the Sadducees knew the Scriptures, they would see that this is true. Also, if they knew the power of God, they would realize that He can provide a new existence for believers that is radically different from this one.

Matthew 22:33 reveals that as the crowds listened to Jesus, they were astounded by what they heard Him teach. A similar response is recorded in 7:28-29, appearing at the end of a lengthy teaching segment called the Sermon on the Mount. In both instances, the authorities and common people alike had encountered someone who had not received the formal religious training the elites of His day had obtained. Yet, despite Jesus' lack of the proper credentials, He taught with distinctive power and persuasiveness. The legal experts of the day typically cited other scholars to support their statements. But when Jesus taught, He spoke as the Son of God. This meant His authority, which was divine, not only exceeded that of the legalists of the day, but also that of Moses, the great lawgiver.

Of course, the Sadducees did not share this view of Jesus. They not only regarded Him as a threat to their power, but also someone who had to be challenged and whose growing influence and popularity had to be squashed. To their chagrin, however, their most recent attempt to do so failed (see 22:23-33). Indeed, Jesus had "silenced" (vs. 34) His opponents, in which the underlying Greek term refers to muzzling an animal. In a manner of speaking, the allegedly untrained itinerant rabbi from Nazareth had made the Sadducees look foolish. It probably did not take long for the Pharisees to learn about this development, and it spurred them into action. They assembled to figure out how they might put Jesus to the test and in the process discredit Him before the onlooking crowds in the temple.

B. Being Challenged by the Pharisees: vss. 35-36

One of them, an expert in the law, tested him with this question: "Teacher, which is the greatest commandment in the Law?"

One of those who listened to Jesus debate with the Sadducees was an "expert in the law" (Matt. 22:35). The reference here is to the law of Moses. Perhaps the unnamed professional theologian was among the best and brightest of his peers at interpreting the commandments. Evidently, if anyone could upstage Jesus of Nazareth, it would be the lawyer. His strategy was to trick Jesus into offering an opinion about a hotly debated issue concerning the law. Then His opponents could use what He said against Him. In addressing Jesus as "Teacher" (vs. 36), the religious expert was being polite, even though he probably did not regard Jesus as an equal. In contrast, the four Gospels present the Son as the premier teacher and interpreter of the law (see 5:17-21).

The Pentateuch (the first five books of the Old Testament) discloses that the Mosaic law was a unique body of commandments that God revealed to His people to direct them in their worship, guide them in their relationship with Him, and regulate the nature of their social interactions with one another. The law was more than a mere record of ordinances and decrees. It represented the will of God for His people. Accordingly, those who violated the law transgressed God Himself, for He authored the law. Moreover, the law was the precise expression of God's pure and perfect moral standard. In a manner of speaking, it was the measuring stick by which the Lord evaluated all human actions (see Rom. 3:20).

In Jesus' day, the Pharisees and other sectarian groups were devoted in their study of the law and meticulous in their observance of the same. This is reflected in the question the legal expert put before Jesus: "which is the greatest commandment in the Law" (Matt. 22:36). The specialist was not asking the Nazarene to select the one commandment that people could least afford to disobey. Rather, the lawyer was asking whether there was a class of codes, even one specific decree, that was preeminent in representing the entire body of commandments.

As was noted in lesson 8 last quarter,, one striking distinction between Jesus and the religious leaders of His day was their tendency to make many laws out of a few and His gift of making few laws out of many. They had identified a regulation for every Hebrew letter in the Ten Commandments (613 edicts, 365 being negative and 248 being positive). Generally, they emphasized laws about external behavior, such as maintaining cleanness and keeping the sabbath. Allegedly, these humanly-devised interpretations (called the oral law) had as much force and authority as the written law. In contrast, Jesus called them—perhaps with some disdain—"traditions" (Mark 7:9).

II. THE CENTRALITY OF LOVE: MATTHEW 22:37-40

A. The Importance of Loving God: vss. 37-38

Jesus replied: "'Love the Lord your God with all your heart and with all your soul and with all your mind.' This is the first and greatest commandment."

In contrast to the religious contemporaries of His day, Jesus summarized the entire

Mosaic law very briefly. The Greek word rendered "love" (Matt. 22:37) refers to showing compassion and kindness in a social and moral sense. When the New Testament writers use the verb in reference to God's love for humanity, the emphasis is on Him showing mercy to those who do not deserve to receive it. In response, the recipients of His grace are to love Him above everything else. This emphasis is reflected in Jesus' declaration that the devotion people have to God needs to involve their "heart," "soul," and "mind." Together, these words are a way of saying "entire being." Expressed differently, every part of us (our emotions, volition, and reasoning) should be involved in our worship of and service to God.

Jesus was quoting Deuteronomy 6:5 and noted that it was the "first and greatest commandment" (Matt. 22:38). In Deuteronomy 6:4, Moses told the Israelites to "hear," which translates the Hebrew word *shema*. For centuries in Jewish tradition, verses 4-9 have been known as the Shema. It contains the fundamental truth of Israel's religion and are the creed of Judaism. Pious Jews today recite the Shema several times a day. In fact, early rabbis called for Jews to recite these verses once in the morning and once in the evening. In Moses' exhortation to the Israelites, the lawgiver wanted them to listen carefully to a divinely revealed insight: "The LORD our God, the LORD is one" (vs. 4).

Actually, as the NIV margin note shows, the Hebrew can be translated in several different ways. Other possibilities include "The LORD our God is one LORD" and "The LORD is our God, the LORD is one." One meaning of the phrase certainly is that Yahweh was the only real God. Taken in the context of the time in which it was written, this statement is especially remarkable in that the Israelites had not even encountered other monotheists. From Egypt to Canaan, every people the Israelites dealt with worshiped a pantheon of gods and goddesses. The statement "the LORD is one" expresses not only the uniqueness of God, but also the unity of God. There is no essential division or multiplicity in God. The Christian doctrine of the Trinity is consistent with this by teaching that God exists as three Persons who are of one essence.

Moses, however, was not just making a statement about God; the lawgiver was also giving a command to the people. They were always to worship only the Lord their God and never divide their devotion between the one true God and other false gods. Furthermore, they were to teach their children to do the same. Moses then exhorted the Israelites to love their God with all their heart, soul, and strength (vs. 5). The Hebrew word that is translated "heart" in this verse is meant to include the mind and will as well as the emotions. Put another way, God wanted all His people's feelings, thoughts, and decisions to be an expression of their love for Him. In every way, their day-to-day existence was to reflect a kind of love that would not spare even one's life for the love of God. Indeed, they were to love Him with all that was in their power. Together these three terms—"heart," "soul," and "strength"—demanded total devotion to the one true God, an attitude that was required if a person was to be obedient to the commandments of the Lord.

B. The Importance of Loving Others: vss. 39-40

"And the second is like it: 'Love your neighbor as yourself.' All the Law and the Prophets hang on these two commandments."

In Matthew 22:39, Jesus followed up His previous statement by noting that Leviticus 19:18 was of equal importance. It says we are to love our neighbors as ourselves. The idea is that we need to work out our love for God in daily life. A supreme love for God will always find expression in unselfish love for others. The importance of doing the latter is seen in Jesus' statement recorded in Matthew 22:40, namely, that the entire Old Testament depends on loving God and others. Expressed differently, the Mosaic legal code is illumined and deepened by the presence of Christlike love (see Matt. 5:17; 7:12; Rom. 8:4; 13:8-10). Furthermore, just as the Savior loved us and gave His life for our eternal benefit, we also should reach out to others in a caring manner (see 1 John 4:7-11).

In A.D. 29, Jesus had an encounter with an expert in religious law regarding Deuteronomy 6:5 and Leviticus 19:18. Jesus approved of the scribe's response and urged him to put his insight into action (Luke 10:25-28). For whatever reason, though, the lawyer felt uncomfortable with his own answer. Perhaps he knew that his behavior didn't measure up to the standard he had quoted. Thus, the scribe raised a technicality, hoping to justify his failure. He would be glad to love his neighbor, he implied, if only Jesus would tell him who his neighbor was (vs. 29).

In Jesus' day, the widespread opinion among scribes and Pharisees was that one's neighbors only included the upright. Supposedly, the wicked were to be hated because they were enemies of God. The religious leaders defined the wicked as sinners (such as tax collectors and prostitutes), Gentiles, and especially Samaritans. Psalm 139:21-22 was used to legitimatize this view. It's true that a love for righteousness will lead to a hatred of evil. However, this does not make it right to be hostile and malicious toward sinners.

The upright should abhor the corrupt lifestyle of the lost but never harbor a vindictive loathing of them as human beings. Instead, the godly should display a brokenhearted grieving over the sinful condition of the lost. Such is undergirded by a genuine concern for the eternal condition of the lost (Matt. 5:44-48; Luke 6:27-36). Tragically, the scribes and Pharisees had made a virtue out of being antagonistic toward the sinful. The result was a renunciation of Leviticus 19:18, the command to love one's neighbor.

By telling the parable of the Good Samaritan (Luke 10:30-35), Jesus shattered the legalistic notion of hating one's enemies. Though Jesus' parable takes place in a rural setting, it speaks to a number of urban issues: racial and ethnic divisions, violent crime, and even the struggle of small businesses to collect their debts. The Samaritan—the good neighbor—does not eliminate these problems, but he does act as an agent of mercy to overcome them in small but effective ways. The Samaritan's example challenges us to consider how we can be good neighbors to others, regardless of their racial or ethnic background. Ultimately, God is interested in mercy, not maintaining prejudice.

Mark 12:28-31 also records the episode found in Matthew 22:34-40. Mark 12:32-34 adds that when Jesus quoted the two most important commandments, it stirred up something in the religious expert and prompted him to respond to Jesus' words. The scribe repeated Jesus' comments and added that love was superior to the sacrificial system. This assertion was an improvement over the common teaching of the time that love and sacrifices were equal. The teacher was not yet a believer in Jesus, but he did have some understanding of the nature of the Kingdom.

Discussion Questions

1. How do you think the religious leaders felt after Jesus had silenced the Pharisees?
2. Why do you think the Pharisees decided to question Jesus about which commandment in the Mosaic law was the greatest?
3. Why is it important to love God with all one's heart, soul, and mind?
4. What does it mean to love one's neighbor in the way Jesus stated?
5. What are some ways we can be a neighbor to those around us?

Contemporary Application

There is a lawyer's instinct in all of us that seeks careful definitions of our Christian duties. This suggests we suffer from a cold creedalism that can strangle tangible expressions of love. However, God's command to love all people transcends legal niceties (1 John 4:21). We cannot separate our duties to others from our duties to God. Saying the right words, praying the right prayers, and singing the right hymns cannot make up for a lack of love (1 Cor. 13:1-3).

We have to confess our coldness and our preoccupation with ourselves. And we have to admit how hard it is to find the time and the resources to show Christlike love to hurting people. Together, we must encourage one another to make our churches places where love springs into action. Otherwise, we may look outwardly holy, but be inwardly full of hypocrisy.

This week's lesson reminds us of the importance to give love for God and others the highest priority in our lives. We are more likely to help others if we remember the last time someone helped us. If we maintain a safe distance from those in need, we can avoid feelings for them, but Jesus tells us we don't have an excuse good enough to stay at arms length from them (so to speak). We should stop and extend mercy to anyone we have the opportunity and resources to help.

Inclusion in Community

DEVOTIONAL READING

Psalm 65:1-8

DAILY BIBLE READINGS

Monday April 19
Psalm 65:1-8 God Is the Hope for All

Tuesday April 20
Psalm 86:8-13 All Nations Shall Come

Wednesday April 21
Isaiah 2:1-4 Come and Learn God's Ways

Thursday April 22
Revelation 15:3-4 King of the Nations

Friday April 23
Matthew 25:31-40 Ministry to All

Saturday April 24
Luke 14:7-14 Humility and Hospitality

Sunday April 25
Luke 14:15-24 Invite All to Come

Scripture

Background Scripture: *Luke 14:7-24*
Scripture Lesson: *Luke 14:15-24*
Key Verse: *"Go out quickly into the streets and alleys of the town and bring in the poor, the crippled, the blind and the lame."* Luke 14:21.
Scripture Lesson for Children: *Luke 14:7-14*
Key Verses for Children: *"For everyone who exalt himself will be humbled, and he who humbles himself will be exalted. . . . and you will be blessed."* Luke 14:11, 14.

Lesson Aim

To examine our own responses to God's invitation.

Lesson Setting

Time: *A.D. 30*
Place: *On the way to Jerusalem*

Lesson Outline

Inclusion in Community

  I. An Attendee's Exclamation: Luke 14:15
  II. The Parable about the Great Banquet: Luke 14:16-24
     A. *A Spurned Invitation: vss. 16-20*
     B. *An Expanded Invitation to Others: vss. 21-24*

Introduction for Adults

Topic: *All Are Invited*

Greed causes people to do strange things. For instance, most of us have seen a community of family members split over the handling of estates. We have seen landlords cheat tenants. We have seen harsh quarreling over insignificant accounts.

On the other hand, most of us have been greatly blessed by generous people within our respective faith communities. Prosperous farmers have given away property and wealth. Wealthy businesspeople have given huge amounts to Christian causes.

What makes the difference? The difference is that greedy people cannot release themselves to God's care, while generous people trust God to take care of them. How liberating it is to accept God's invitation to become a member of His spiritual family. The Gospel invites everyone to respond and be saved.

Introduction for Youth

Topic: *A Beggar's Banquet*

The values of young people are strongly shaped by role models in sports and entertainment. They see the stars revel in unparalleled wealth. They watch as athletes refuse to show up for practice because they are being paid only three million dollars a year.

Against this popular culture comes the teaching of Jesus, who said we are fools if all we work for is money and possessions. Young people are driven, not for millions, but for cars, stereos, clothes, and sports equipment. Jesus said it's all a lot of stuff that in the end does not mean a thing.

Real life is found not in things but in saying yes to God's invitation to be saved. Money and possessions cannot buy happiness, and they deceive us into thinking all is well with our souls, when we really are in grave danger. That's why Jesus urges us to feast at the table of spiritual blessings He freely offers. We can do so by putting our faith in Him for eternal life. All are invited to the celestial banquet.

Concepts for Children

Topic: *Everyone Is Included*

1. Jesus was at a dinner taking place in the home of an important person.
2. Jesus saw that those who came wanted to sit in the most desired places around the dinner table.
3. Jesus encouraged everyone there to stop being proud and seek to be humble and kind to others.
4. Jesus does not want us to think we are more important than others.
5. Jesus is pleased when we reach out to others with His love.

Lesson Commentary

I. AN ATTENDEE'S EXCLAMATION: LUKE 14:15

When one of those at the table with him heard this, he said to Jesus, "Blessed is the man who will eat at the feast in the kingdom of God."

We learn from Luke 14:1 that Jesus accepted an invitation one sabbath to dine at the house of a prominent Pharisee. Religious leaders dining at his home (possibly a synagogue official) were watching the Lord Jesus closely to detect any sabbath-breaking conduct. The Jewish sabbath began at sunset on Friday and ended at sunset on Saturday. Sabbath restrictions kept people from carrying any loads or traveling great distances until sunset.

The sabbath regulations began in the time between the Old and New Testaments as a way to protect and preserve the spirit of the day. The scribes who first wrote the rules wanted to guarantee a proper observance of the sabbath and ensure that people did not break the fourth commandment. But the sabbath regulations became a burden rather than a blessing. They deprived people of many opportunities to enjoy the day and serve the Lord. Several times during His earthly ministry, Jesus confronted the legalistic views of the Pharisees concerning the sabbath.

Verse 2 says that a man (either another guest or a bystander) suffering from dropsy was right in front of Jesus. This ailment (also known as edema) involved the abnormal swelling of limbs, which resulted from excessive amounts of fluid accumulating in the cavities and tissues of the body, especially the legs. In Jesus' day, the religious leaders believed restoring someone to health on the sabbath was work and thus violated their longstanding traditions (see 13:14). Jesus, being aware of this, asked the Pharisees and experts in the interpretation of religious law whether they thought it was legal to heal someone on the sabbath (14:3). Would they end up defending tradition or advocate doing good? Their silence indicated they chose the first option, while Jesus approved the second one.

Accordingly, the Redeemer took hold of the man, healed him, and sent him away (vs. 4). Then Jesus turned to the religious leaders and asked which of them did not work on the sabbath (vs. 5). After all, if they had a child (some manuscripts read "donkey") or an ox that had fallen into a well on a sabbath day, they would immediately pull out the person or animal. In short, deeds of mercy were permissible on the sabbath. Again, Jesus' critics chose to remain silent (vs. 6), rather than be humiliated by His words of censure (see 13:17).

In Jesus' day, the Jewish social spectrum was broad and layered. The upper class consisted of the priestly and lay aristocracies and the scribes. The priestly nobility included the high priest, any retired high priests, and the chief priests who administered temple affairs. The middle class consisted of Jews of pure descent, among whom were found the ordinary priests (who served in the temple), the Levites (who served as temple musicians and servants), merchants, artisans, and farmers.

The lower classes embraced all Jews who were not of pure descent as well as Jewish slaves, Jews with slight blemish (proselytes), Jews with a grave racial blemish (eunuchs), and Jews who worked in despised trades. Gentile slaves and Samaritans held the lowest rank in this social order.

Jesus, who was familiar with these social conventions, observed how the guests in His presence chose places of honor at the table of the prominent Pharisee hosting the meal (vs. 7). In New Testament times, the seating arrangement at gatherings indicated much about the honor and respect extended to those present. At dinner feasts, the closer one sat to the host, the higher the honor. In fact, many Jewish homes had two levels, with honored guests seated on the higher floor. The seat to the right of the host was a place of special honor, with the seat to the left next in rank (see Matt. 20:20-21). Other seats were ranked in descending honor, with the seat on the lower floor and next to the door being the lowest. To be left standing, or seated on the floor, was the humblest position of all (see Jas. 2:3-4).

To emphasize the importance of humility, Jesus told a parable involving those present receiving an invitation to a wedding feast. He urged them to resist the temptation to recline in the place of honor (Luke 14:8). In that day, meals were not eaten while sitting in upright chairs at a table. Instead, people would recline on their left elbows on the cushioned floor, with their head being closest to the low table and their feet being farthest away. Jesus raised the possibility that the host might ask a guest who had taken one of the best spots to vacate it for someone else who was more distinguished or highly respected. Social convention would then require that the person who had been publicly disgraced to move to a place of least importance (for example, whatever spot was left at the foot of the table; vs. 9).

In that culture, avoiding public embarrassment and shame was important. For that reason, Jesus emphasized the wisdom of taking the place of least importance at a banquet. Then, when the host approached, the humble individual would be asked in the presence of all the other guests to move to a more important spot— at the head of the table. As a result, the deferential guest would be honored in front of all those sharing the meal with him or her (vs. 10). The moral of Jesus' parable appears in verse 11. God will humble the proud, who strive to exalt themselves before others. In contrast, God will exalt or honor the humble. This principle, which is repeated elsewhere in Scripture (see Prov. 3:34; 25:6-7; Matt. 18:4; 23:12; Luke 11:43; 18:14; 20:46; Jas. 4:10; 1 Pet. 5:6), was not worldly advice on how to manipulate a situation to make oneself look good. Rather, Jesus was advocating the cultivation of genuine humility among His followers.

Perhaps Jesus was one of those seated in a place of honor near the head of the table. If so, we can imagine Him turning to His host to emphasize the importance of showing unconditional generosity. For instance, when the leader of the Pharisees hosted a dinner or a banquet, Jesus urged him to break with social convention. The goal should not be to invite friends, close family members, other relatives, or rich neighbors (in other words, the powerful and well-to-do), who would feel obliged to extend an invitation in return as a repayment for the display of hospitality (Luke 14:12).

Instead, when planning an elaborate meal, the host was urged to invite people who did not have the ability to reciprocate—"the poor, the crippled, the lame, the blind" (vs. 13). God would take note of and approve this display of graciousness. He would also eternally bless His followers for acting in this way. In verse 14, the Greek term rendered "blessed" conveys the idea of endowing someone with productivity or fruitfulness in service to the Lord. Although the kind and caring host would receive no recompense from his or her guests, God would reward him or her at the resurrection of the righteous (see Dan. 12:2; John 5:28-29; Acts 24:15). The latter event will occur at the return of the Messiah, who will sit on His glorious throne and honor those who served others in His name (see Matt. 25:31-46).

God's kingdom is defined by His righteousness. The latter means that God acts justly and fairly in all His decisions and actions (Dan. 9:14). God declares as righteous those who acknowledge their sin and put their faith in Him for forgiveness and eternal life (Mark 2:17; Luke 18:14). In contrast, the unsaved have a false sense of righteousness, for they trust in their moral accomplishments to make others think they are living in accordance with God's holy standards (Matt. 23:38; Luke 18:9). Thus, it is clear that people cannot attain a right relationship with God based on their merits. Instead, God must impute, or transfer, to them an upright standing. This takes place through faith in the Son. Expressed differently, the Father sees us as righteous because of our identification with His Son (Rom. 3:21-26; Gal. 3:6; Phil. 3:9). Those who lack God's righteousness, but hunger and thirst for it, will receive it in full (Matt. 5:6). Also, those who are burdened with the load of self-righteousness are invited to find their rest in the Savior (11:28-30).

The righteousness Jesus commanded included showing hospitality to others. Jews in the Old Testament and Christians in the New Testament were encouraged to be kind to strangers and to take care of the needs of passersby. Hospitality was shown in many ways. The most common was to wash the feet of visitors. This offered much-needed relief to those who traveled long distances over the dusty roads in Israel. It was also common to prepare meals for visitors. This often consumed a great deal of time as hostesses baked bread, cooked meat, and did whatever else was necessary to provide substantial meals for guests. Animals accompanying visitors were also looked after and were given food, water, and shelter. When guests left, they were often given supplies to help them in their travels. This could include food, water, and articles of clothing. The host might even accompany departing visitors for a short distance as they continued their journey. Showing hospitality in a practical way met the physical needs of visitors. It was also crucial for maintaining social relationships.

As far back as the law of Moses, God told His people to give alms (or gifts) to the poor and needy (Exod. 23:11; Deut. 15:7, 11). The prophets of the Old Testament saw alms as a right of the poor. Several prophets warned that when the poor were not taken care of, there was no justice in the land (Isa. 10:1-4; Jer. 5:26-29; Amos 5:12-15). This type of thought led to the idea that righteousness could be obtained through giving alms, and it could also help in obtaining forgiveness of sins. The Pharisees of Jesus' day also believed that almsgiving entitled them to divine favor in moments of trouble. By the time of Jesus' earthly ministry, righteousness and almsgiving were seen as the same thing by many Jews. Jesus encouraged giving to the poor, for He said in Matthew 6:2, "when you give," not "if you give." But Jesus also stressed the need for the right motive. The giver should not take a pious act, such as giving to the poor, and make it a sign of spirituality for others to see.

In response to Jesus' exhortation recorded in Luke 14:12-14, another guest declared to the Savior that those who get to eat in the kingdom of God are blessed (vs. 15). The man who said this was reflecting a Jewish tradition that there would be a great feast when the Messiah came (Isa. 25:6). This tradition was correct (Rev. 19:9), and Jesus Himself taught that it was (Matt. 8:11; Luke 13:29). However, the man who made the statement evidently thought that the future messianic banquet was reserved for him and other religious people like him. So Jesus decided to tell a story illustrating how the guests who eventually will attend the messianic banquet are not necessarily the ones who were expected.

II. The Parable about the Great Banquet: Luke 14:16-24

A. A Spurned Invitation: vss. 16-20

Jesus replied: "A certain man was preparing a great banquet and invited many guests. At the time of the banquet he sent his servant to tell those who had been invited, 'Come, for everything is now ready.' But they all alike began to make excuses. They first said, 'I have just bought a field, and I must go and see it. Please excuse me.' Another said, 'I have just bought five yoke of oxen, and I'm on my way to try them out. Please excuse me.' Still another said, 'I just got married, so I can't come.'"

On the surface Jesus' parable is simple. A man plans a special dinner and makes certain that his friends are notified beforehand (Luke 14:16). When the time comes for the actual dinner, he sends his servant to alert the guests (vs. 17). In the ancient world, meals were often major social events. It was important who was invited and who was not, who accepted and who declined. Even where the guests sat at the table when the meal was finally served was important. The words used in verse 16 for "great banquet" indicate that this event was no ordinary meal. It was a special occasion, and it would have been an honor to receive an invitation.

It was customary at that time (and still is, in some parts of the Middle East) for a second invitation to be given once the meal was ready. And so a servant would be dispatched to remind the guests of their earlier commitment. Although the intended guests had already received one invitation and evidently had accepted it, they now offered excuses (vss. 18-20). In essence, these three were saying, "Sorry, I'd rather not come." They may have had plans in mind when they received the original invitation. If so, it would have been more appropriate to have declined at the outset. The curious thing is why they refused the second time. Either they felt that they had obligations that were more important than maintaining the goodwill of their host or they feared that they would not enjoy the occasion. If the latter, they thought they would have more fun following the call of their own hearts than being stuck for several hours at the host's dinner party.

In any case, one invited guest declined because he wanted to check out a new field. Another preferred to test his new oxen. And the third chose to stay with his bride. None of these excuses was adequate to justify breaking a commitment to attend the feast. With this story Jesus was suggesting to the Pharisees around the table that they had much in common with the three guests. Although they expressed their devotion at every opportunity and heartily endorsed the prospect of an eternity with God, Jesus knew that they were, at the same time, finding reasons why they would not be able to attend His own banquet—the feast of salvation.

B. An Expanded Invitation to Others: vss. 21-24

"The servant came back and reported this to his master. Then the owner of the house became angry and ordered his servant, 'Go out quickly into the streets and alleys of the town and bring in the poor, the crippled, the blind and the lame.' 'Sir,' the servant said, 'what you ordered has been done, but there is still room.' Then the master told his servant, 'Go out to the roads and country lanes and make them come in, so that my house will be full. I tell you, not one of those men who were invited will get a taste of my banquet.'"

When the host learned from his servant that his guests would not be coming, he was quite angry (Luke 14:21). If they had no desire to be with him, he would open his doors to those who would welcome his invitation. After all, the food was prepared and the table set. It should not go to waste. Thus, instead of leading a dinner party for well-to-do people, the host called in the poor, the disabled, the outcasts, and the needy of society. Yet even after his new guests were gathered, still there was enough room at the banquet (vs. 22). And so the host gave a second call, inviting whoever he might gather from the roads and lanes. Persuasion rather than brute force is implied in the phrase "make them come in" (vs. 23).

Food, drink, and fellowship would be powerful tools of persuasion for needy people. In a spiritual sense, the Lord offers us blessings greater than anything the world has to offer. With respect to Jesus' parable, He was speaking quite clearly to His host and the other guests. They were the ones who should have embraced Him—the ones who were best equipped to understand exactly who He was and what His coming meant for Israel and the world. But they would not have Him. Thus Jesus would invite those who were willing to come when He called (vs. 24).

Discussion Questions

1. Why do you think one of the invited guests felt compelled to exclaim that those attending a banquet in the divine kingdom would be truly blessed?
2. How do you think the host felt when he heard the excuses his peers made to

Lesson 8

Quarter 3

explain why they could not attend his banquet?
3. Why did the host decide to invite the outcasts of society to his banquet?
4. What do you think was the point of the parable Jesus told regarding the great banquet?
5. What things should we as Christians say to make sure people truly understand God's invitation to them?

Contemporary Application

The people in Jesus' parable who gave various excuses did so to get out of attending a great banquet. But these excuses are not very different from those we hear in our day when neighbors or co-workers respond to our invitation to come to church with us.

"We just bought a house and have so much work to do on it!" "We're taking the family out for a test drive in the new van." "My husband isn't really into church-going, but we're planning to take the kids when they're old enough." While missing a church service will not result in catastrophe, it is an occasion on which many people have said no to God. And saying no has become a habit for them.

Jesus' parable is about constantly listening for God's call and constantly striving to respond. As His parable makes plain, refusing the host's invitation to a banquet is a sign of a deeper concern, a symptom of a relationship that is not all it could or should be.

As a child I was a little embarrassed when my father, a minister, would challenge someone who had made some halfhearted comment like "Well, I can't say religion's ever done much for me." "Christianity," my father would counter, "is not a religion; it's a way of life." Now I see he was right.

In the early part of the last century, Cambridge professor Sir Arthur Quiller-Couch wrote that "to the Greeks, their religion, such as it was, mattered enormously. They built their Theatre upon it . . . which means that it had sunk into their daily life and permeated their enjoyment of it."

Our Christian faith should influence all we do, especially since it is based on the truth and not on myth. The extent to which it does so is a good measure of how well we have done at saying yes to God's invitations on a daily basis. If we are not always alert to what God wants us to do, then we will follow after things that will take us away from God, who knows what is best for us and how best for us to serve others.

Our favorable response to God's invitation is based on the truth that the final form of His kingdom will be glorious and joy-filled. It is a place where our weaknesses and imperfections will be no more, where we will rejoice in the presence of a loving and merciful heavenly God. Why not keep these images in mind throughout the coming week, especially as you weigh your response to God and His call on your life?

A Faithful Community

Scripture

Background Scripture: *Colossians 1*
Scripture Lesson: *Colossians 1:1-14*
Key Verses: *We have not stopped praying for you and asking
God to fill you with the knowledge of his will through all spiri-
tual wisdom and understanding.* Colossians 1:9.
Scripture Lesson for Children: *Colossians 1:1-14*
Key Verse for Children: *We have heard of your faith in
Christ Jesus and of the love you have for all the saints.*
Colossians 1:4.

Lesson Aim

To live by the great facts of the Father's blessings to us
in His Son.

Lesson Setting

Time: *About A.D. 60*
Place: *Rome*

Lesson Outline

A Faithful Community

  I. Giving Thanks for God's Transforming Work:
Colossians 1:1-8
     A. *Introductory Greeting: vss. 1-2*
     B. *Faith, Love, and Hope: vss. 3-6a*
     C. *Evangelistic Fruit: vss. 6b-8*
  II. Giving Thanks for God's Provisions:
Colossians 1:9-14
     A. *Divine Wisdom Bearing Spiritual Fruit: vss. 9-10*
     B. *Divine Power Resulting in Patience: vss. 11a*
     C. *Divine Inheritance, Redemption, and Forgiveness:
vss. 11b-14*

Introduction for Adults

Topic: *Understanding and Living Truth*

Tony faithfully shared the truth about Jesus with a friend who wanted to discuss religion in general. Tony gently refused and left his friend with one question: "Do you have eternal life?" Tony explained that the real issue is life, not religion. One day several months later the friend came to Tony and said, "I've got eternal life!" He had trusted in Jesus for salvation.

The truth about Jesus becomes a reality in our lives when we put our faith in Him. He said that He came to give us life in all its fullness (John 10:10). No one else can do this. We need life because we are spiritually dead in sin. Indeed, there is no true life available to us, other than through faith in the Son.

So we have to make choices. Even Peter, a disciple of the Lord, had to decide. When Jesus confronted Peter, the latter answered, "Lord, to whom shall we go? You have the words of eternal life" (John 6:68). Later, Jesus declared, "I am the way and the truth and the life" (John 14:6). When we receive Jesus by faith, then we truly start to live!

Introduction for Youth

Topic: *Living Faithfully—Together*

One day a disciple of Jesus named Philip demanded of the Savior, "Lord, show us the Father and that will be enough for us" (John 14:8). Many young people are asking for the same sort of thing. They want to see the authenticity of Christianity displayed among believers who live faithfully together. Youth rightly expect to see the Father at work in the lives of those who profess to be followers of His Son.

Jesus is the only one who perfectly bears the "image of the invisible God" (Col. 1:15). Even so, because believers are spiritually united to the Son by faith, they too can demonstrate the reality of God's presence in their lives by being virtuous in their actions. As the community of faith loves and serves others, the lost will catch a glimpse of the presence and power of God.

Jesus said that He would manifest God to others by living in believers. Jesus also promised to confirm the truth of the Gospel when believers work together in loving and obeying Him. For these reasons, Christians stand in the gap between God and the unbelieving world.

Concepts for Children

Topic: *Learn Together*

1. Paul wrote letters to encourage and teach Jesus followers.
2. Paul sent a believer named Epaphras to help the believers living in a city named Colosse to learn more about Jesus.
3. Paul prayed for the spiritual growth of the believers in the church at Colosse.
4. Paul thanked God for the love the Colossian believers had for Jesus.
5. The Lord is pleased when we join other believers to learn more about Jesus.

Lesson Commentary

I. GIVING THANKS FOR GOD'S TRANSFORMING WORK: COLOSSIANS 1:1-8

A. Introductory Greeting: vss. 1-2

Paul, an apostle of Christ Jesus by the will of God, and Timothy our brother, to the holy and faithful brothers in Christ at Colosse. Grace and peace to you from God our Father.

Since the Christians in Colosse evidently did not personally know Paul, he introduced himself as "an apostle of Christ Jesus" (Col. 1:1). Most likely, Paul did this to immediately establish his authority among his readers. Moreover, he added that God Himself had commissioned him to this high office in the Church. Therefore, the Colossians were not to read, and perhaps even dismiss, the apostle's letter as merely a list of suggestions from an outside observer. They were to follow his instructions as though they had come from the Messiah Himself.

Paul could be confident that the Colossians would respond appropriately for two reasons. First, one of Paul's most devoted friends was Epaphras, who was from Colosse and apparently was responsible for the founding of a church there. Epaphras had probably communicated his respect for Paul to the believers in Colosse prior to the writing of this letter. Second, the Colossian church was probably an extension of Paul's evangelistic ministry while he resided in Ephesus for three years during his third missionary journey (around A.D. 53–57). Unlike the Corinthians and Galatians, the Colossians did not force Paul to write a defense of his apostolic authority.

In Paul's introductory greeting to the Colossians, he included Timothy's name, as he had done in 2 Corinthians, Philippians, 1 and 2 Thessalonians, and Philemon. Though Paul was the sole writer, the inclusion of Timothy's name was probably intended to strengthen Paul's right to teach the Colossian believers. Timothy was well respected in the Christian communities in Asia Minor. Furthermore, Paul continued to follow the ancient custom of letter writing by identifying the recipients of this epistle in his salutation. Interestingly, he did not address his letter to the "church" in Colosse, as he had done, for example, with 1 Corinthians (see 1:2). Instead, the apostle referred to the recipients as "the holy and faithful brothers in Christ at Colosse" (Col. 1:2). Paul was being more specific than in his other letters by describing here what kind of people ought to make up the Church.

First, Christians ought to be "holy." They should regard themselves as being distinct from the rest of the world. This is not to say that they must be isolated from the rest of society, but rather that they should always keep themselves free from the evils of this world. God has called us to a life of moral purity dedicated to serving the Lord Jesus. In one sense, what the Savior has done for us on the cross has already made us a holy people, belonging to God. We need only be faithful to our covenant with Him. Second, Christians ought to be "faithful." Because the Colossians were exposed to dangerous heresies that were creeping into the church in Colosse, Paul felt compelled to refute these destructive teachings. Quite wisely, Paul noted the faithfulness of his readers before he addressed their pastoral needs. He praised the steadfastness of the Colossians to the Gospel despite the variety of false teachings they faced.

Paul transformed the ancient style of the greeting portion of his letter by amplifying Greek terms with Christian meaning. In the ancient Greek world, people commonly used the word rendered "grace" to greet one another. In Paul's letter, however, its related term means more than just "best wishes." In a Christian context, "grace" denotes God's favor and concern for those people with whom He has renewed His relationship. Furthermore, Paul's mention of "peace" refers to the restored fellowship we have with the Father through the blood of the Son. Thus, Paul was not merely addressing his original readers with a conventional greeting but also focusing on the unique blessing of salvation they had in Jesus.

B. Faith, Love, and Hope: vss. 3-6a

We always thank God, the Father of our Lord Jesus Christ, when we pray for you, because we have heard of your faith in Christ Jesus and of the love you have for all the saints—the faith and love that spring from the hope that is stored up for you in heaven and that you have already heard about in the word of truth, the gospel that has come to you.

Paul used a prayer of thanksgiving to praise the Colossians for their celebrated faith in the "Lord Jesus Christ" (Col. 1:3). With this prayer the apostle probably wanted not only to commend these believers but also to encourage them to remain faithful to the Son. Even in his salutation, Paul was already preparing the ground on which to argue his case against the heresies that were troubling the believers in Colosse.

Paul's tact here was similar to that in his letter to Philemon, who was a member of the Colossian church and possibly even a leader. Paul undoubtedly wrote both letters at the same time in Rome and sent them by way of the same messenger, Tychicus. Prior to urging Philemon to receive his runaway slave, Onesimus, back as a useful brother in the Lord, Paul extolled Philemon's strongest virtues. In a sense, Paul was building up his readers—both Philemon and the Colossians—before instructing them to do what was right according to the Gospel.

One doctrinal truth of the Christian faith that Paul hammered away at throughout his letter is the deity of Christ. At the very outset of Colossians, Paul identified Jesus as the Son of God the Father (1:3). Of course, God is the Father of all His chosen children, but Paul was making it unmistakably clear that Jesus has a special and exalted relationship with the first person of the Godhead. Epaphras had probably reported to Paul about the vibrant spiritual condition of the Colossians. Others had likely affirmed Epaphras's good news. Paul was exceedingly pleased with their living faith and their active love for one another. It was always important to Paul that faith in Christ continually be demonstrated outwardly in behavior toward others. The Colossians evidently showed true love and concern for other Christians not only in their own church but also in other churches (vs. 4).

The Greek meaning of Epaphras's name is "lovely," and he must have been just that to Paul. He was not only a fruit of Paul's ministry in Asia Minor but also fruitful in extending that ministry beyond Paul's personal reach. As Paul's delegate from Ephesus and as a Christian teacher, Epaphras in all likelihood was mainly responsible for the Lord's work in Colosse, Laodicea, and Hierapolis (see 4:12-13), as well as other towns in Phrygia. Furthermore, Epaphras shared many of Paul's hardships, such as being at one point a prisoner with the apostle in Rome (see Philem. 23).

In another letter Paul wrote, "Now these three remain: faith, hope and love" (1 Cor. 13:13). These three Christian virtues were important to the apostle, and he echoed them again at this point in his letter to the Colossian believers. Paul did not want the false teachers to rob the Colossians of the hope that the Gospel gives to believers. This would also negatively affect their faith and love in the Son. Quite possibly the false teachers had argued against a heavenly blessing being a part of one's salvation in the Lord Jesus. Therefore, Paul contrasted the truth of God's Word—the message the Colossians had heard from the apostle's fellow workers—against the lies circulated by these heretics (Col. 1:5-6a).

C. Evangelistic Fruit: vss. 6b-8

All over the world this gospel is bearing fruit and growing, just as it has been doing among you since the day you heard it and understood God's grace in all its truth. You learned it from Epaphras, our dear fellow servant, who is a faithful minister of Christ on our behalf, and who also told us of your love in the Spirit.

One of the key elements of the false doctrine Paul and other New Testament writers condemned was that only a few elite people can acquire the deep knowledge of the mysteries of the cosmos. A pseudo-Christian version of this doctrine, which emerged in Colosse, was that only a few Christian initiates could discern the deeper spiritual truths of Jesus' teachings. Paul's statement that the Gospel was bursting forth into the world and multitudes were receiving it was in vivid contrast to this deviant teaching (Col. 1:6b).

The Colossians did not have to just take Paul's word for the tremendous success in the spread of the Gospel. They could recall their own experience and how the message of the Savior had converted many of them. Moreover, it seems they were growing not only in numbers but also in spiritual maturity, especially as they comprehended the full truth of God's grace. This feature of the Gospel did not restrict who could come to faith in the Son. Instead, it opened the door so that many could be welcomed into God's kingdom.

Next, Paul mentioned a person who was dear to the believers in Colosse—Epaphras (vs. 7). Apparently the result of Epaphras's labors in Phrygia was the birth and initial growth of the Colossian church. He may have become a Christian as a result of Paul's preaching in Ephesus. Under Paul's tutelage Epaphras became a dynamic evangelist and was sent to Colosse, his hometown. There he was Paul's valued and trusted delegate to spread the good news about the Savior. Epaphras became a beloved teacher and minister to the Colossian church.

While Epaphras served as a pastoral leader within the Colossian church, he probably yearned to visit his spiritual mentor during Paul's house arrest. Epaphras might have even been concerned about the troubling heresies current in Colosse and wanted Paul to address this issue in a letter to his flock. By enlisting the apostolic authority of Paul to refute these false teachings, Epaphras might become able to rescue some who were close to being persuaded. In any case, he had joined Paul in Rome with the blessings of the Colossian believers and told the apostle about the great love these people possessed in the Holy Spirit (vs. 8).

II. GIVING THANKS FOR GOD'S PROVISIONS: COLOSSIANS 1:9-14

A. Divine Wisdom Bearing Spiritual Fruit: vss. 9-10

For this reason, since the day we heard about you, we have not stopped praying for you and asking God to fill you with the knowledge of his will through all spiritual wisdom and understanding. And we pray this in order that you may live a life worthy of the Lord and may please him in every way: bearing fruit in every good work, growing in the knowledge of God.

Paul continued to pray openly for the Christians in Colosse. In his prayers, he disclosed their critical need for spiritual discernment. He wanted their faith in the Son to be grounded in divine truth and not be perverted by the beguiling, false teachings that were becoming increasingly bold in attacking the good news about the Messiah. Paul again noted how Epaphras had brought him the marvelous news about their growing faith in and fruitful service for the Redeemer. For this reason the apostle and his associates had fervently prayed for their readers without ceasing (Col. 1:9). Such praise of their walk with the Lord naturally touched Paul's heart and inspired him to care even more deeply for their spiritual welfare. He demonstrated his parental concern in the way he prayed for them.

After Paul acknowledged how ardently he had prayed for the Colossians, he used three terms to stress his deepest concern for them—"knowledge," "wisdom," and "understanding." The Colossians probably understood clearly what Paul was referring to. In fact, the apostle may have been repeating the same Greek words—*epignosis, sophia,* and *sunesis*—that the false teachers were regularly using to promote their seductive doctrines. However, Paul's petition to God was that He bestow, not esoteric knowledge to a selected elite, but "all spiritual wisdom and understanding" concerning how He wanted the Colossian believers to live. Furthermore, the apostle declared that such knowledge can come to us only through the Holy Spirit and not through human speculation.

Having the right kind of knowledge, however, was not enough to Paul. Believers must also demonstrate that God-given knowledge in their behavior toward the Lord and others. Indeed, the absence of Christlike virtues is proof that one lacks the kind of knowledge the apostle urged the Colossians—and us—to have. Foremost in Paul's prayer was that the lives of believers be commendable in God's eyes so that we might delight Him in everything we do, say, and think.

And how do we please God? One way is by "bearing fruit in every good work" (vs. 10). The insights we gain as believers are meaningless if we don't touch the lives of others. Moreover, a Spirit-led, Christlike life invariably causes believers to grow in their "knowledge of God." There are two possible ways of understanding this statement. Paul might have been referring to the spiritual maturing of the minds of Christians, or he might have been talking about the spread of the Gospel and the enlarging of the church in Colosse. It is quite possible that the apostle had both meanings in mind since both are naturally connected to each other.

B. Divine Power Resulting in Patience: vss. 11a

Being strengthened with all power according to his glorious might so that you may have great endurance and patience.

Paul reminded the Colossians that none of the fruit they bore was possible apart from God empowering them. The Lord was working in their lives and bringing about the fruits of "endurance" (Col. 1:11) and "patience" in their Christian character. Both of these virtues are needed to combat dangerous heresies. Endurance enables believers to prevail in the midst of hostility, and patience helps them remain under self-control despite the unsettling nature of such confrontations.

C. Divine Inheritance, Redemption, and Forgiveness: vss. 11b-14

And joyfully giving thanks to the Father, who has qualified you to share in the inheritance of the saints in the kingdom of light. For he has rescued us from the dominion of darkness and brought us into the kingdom of the Son he loves, in whom we have redemption, the forgiveness of sins.

Paul would not leave us thinking we should view difficult circumstances with a heavy heart. He did not want believers to focus strictly on the ordeals they must endure when they affirm God's truths. Like the apostle, we can "joyfully" (Col. 1:11) thank God that He has accepted us into His kingdom, sharing the eternal benefits that all God's spiritual children enjoy. Indeed, it is the Lord Himself who has made us worthy to share in this marvelous heritage.

Just as Paul had contrasted the heretical doctrines of the false teachers with the Gospel of Christ, so the apostle made a distinction between "the kingdom of light" (vs. 12) and "the dominion of darkness" (vs. 13). Paul's use of "light" and "darkness" is packed with multiple contrasting meanings, such as truth and falsehood, good and evil, redemption and damnation. Yet what also cannot be missed is the apostle's unmistakable point that the false teachers were emissaries of darkness, while he would continue to preach the message that gives light to the truth about the Messiah.

The Father reserves the kingdom of light for His saints—that is, those whom He has redeemed and set apart as His own (vs. 14). Moreover, Paul said this kingdom belongs to the one the Father loves—His Son, the Lord Jesus, who died for our sins. The dominion of darkness is that place that is separated from God. Because the Redeemer has secured divine forgiveness for us through the blood He shed on the cross, He has liberated us from the dominion of darkness and delivered us into His eternal kingdom.

Discussion Questions

1. What do you think it means for believers to be called God's "holy and faithful" (Col. 1:2) people?
2. What connection do you see between faith in the Lord Jesus and being compassionate to His followers?
3. Why do you think Paul placed such a strong emphasis on bearing spiritual fruit as a result of believing the Gospel?
4. How does the power of God enable us to demonstrate endurance and patience in tough situations?
5. Why was it necessary for the Father to qualify us to share in the eternal inheritance offered by the Son?

Contemporary Application

How quickly our culture saturates our minds with so-called "truths" that affect our wills and emotions. Every day we are bombarded with messages about how to stay well, how to get rich, how to succeed, how to be popular, and so forth. When things don't work out the way these messages suggest, we wonder what's wrong with us.

As followers of the Savior, we can't escape these messages about the world's values. So we have to fortify our minds with the facts the Father has revealed to us in His Son. Divine truths are not broadcast the same way the worlds advertisements are publicized. Consequently, we have to work hard to set aside time to think matters through from a scriptural perspective.

Every day we can pick up our Bibles and build our faith. We can read texts like Colossians 1 and rejoice in the goodness of the Lord. We can realize that the really important things in life are the Father's choice of us as His spiritual children, His incomparable blessings made available through faith in His Son, His redemption and forgiveness, and His guarantee of an eternal inheritance.

When we think about these divine provisions, somehow what the world tells us fades into insignificance. Our lives achieve purpose, order, and composure. We find grace and peace that no one can take away from us.

An Established Community

Scripture

Background Scripture: *Colossians 2:1-19*

Scripture Lesson: *Colossians 2:1-10*

Key Verse: *See to it that no one takes you captive through hollow and deceptive philosophy, which depends on human tradition and the basic principles of this world rather than on Christ.* Colossians 2:8.

Scripture Lesson for Children: *Colossians 2:1-10*

Key Verses for Children: *Just as you received Christ Jesus as Lord, continue to live in him, rooted and built up in him.* Colossians 2:6-7.

Lesson Aim

To recognize that the truth about the Son exposes false religious ideas.

Lesson Setting

Time: *About A.D. 60*

Place: *Rome*

Lesson Outline

An Established Community

I. Spiritual Understanding in the Son: Colossians 2:1-5
 A. *Ministering Among Believers: vs. 1*
 B. *Recognizing the Centrality of Christ: vss. 2-3*
 C. *Maintaining a Strong Faith in Christ: vss. 4-5*

II. Spiritual Fullness in the Son: Colossians 2:6-10
 A. *Becoming Rooted and Grounded in Christ: vss. 6-7*
 B. *Rejecting False Teachings: vs. 8*
 C. *Affirming Christ's Deity: vss. 9-10*

Introduction for Adults

Topic: *Distinguishing Truth from Deceit*

With a broad grin, Bob met me at the appointed time, well dressed, Bible in hand. On the exterior, he could have fit in at any of the Bible-believing churches in our college town.

As we sat together over a cup of tea in the student union, his mood was upbeat. Although we had only met the day before, Bob jumped into a comfortable conversation with me, pointing out Scripture and sharing his life story. I listened, genuinely interested.

Then Bob came to his conversion experience. He had come to believe a "faith plus works Gospel"—with a strong emphasis on works. Although highly-educated and well-versed in Scripture, he didn't understand that people cannot enter the kingdom of God on their own merits.

When we add to the good news about Jesus, we distort the truth, deceive ourselves, and mislead others. In this case, more is less.

Introduction for Youth

Topic: *Stand Firm*

Both inside and outside the church the presence of commitment is seriously lacking. People shun commitment because they think it will prevent them from doing what they want. This attitude is extremely harmful among Christians who profess to believe in the vital doctrines of the faith.

For instance, a hesitancy to stand firmly on the truth of the Gospel can lead to spiritual confusion. It is only when we, as believers, preserve the integrity of the Good News, that the doctrinal foundation of the church will withstand the attacks of spiritual frauds.

Concepts for Children

Topic: *Grow Strong Together*

1. Paul encouraged the believers living in Colosse to grow in their understanding of Jesus.
2. Paul also encouraged his readers to drive deep roots of faith in Jesus.
3. Paul reminded his readers that the Father forgave them because of their faith in Jesus.
4. Paul warned his readers not to be tricked by false teaching about Jesus.
5. We should study the Bible to learn more about Jesus.

Lesson Commentary

I. SPIRITUAL UNDERSTANDING IN THE SON: COLOSSIANS 2:1-5

A. Ministering among Believers: vs. 1

I want you to know how much I am struggling for you and for those at Laodicea, and for all who have not met me personally.

Paul was primarily concerned with a heresy that had crept into the Colossian church. Some false teachers were evidently promoting an extreme form of Judaism, which demanded strict adherence to rituals and regulations. Other false teachers were introducing elements of early Gnosticism, a belief system that diminished the supremacy of the Messiah. Paul argued brilliantly in this letter that the Son is indeed truly divine, uniquely sovereign, and entirely capable as the reconciler of sinful humanity to the Father.

After the apostle declared that God had chosen him to bring the Gospel to the Gentiles and to serve those who received it, he narrowed his scope to the recipients of this letter. First, he told them that he labored rigorously for them. He wanted them to know that his concern and calling extended to them, though he had not personally founded or visited their church. Quite possibly he had not even met most of them. Nevertheless, he felt a special bond with them (Col. 2:1).

In addition, Paul's concern included the believers in Laodicea and the nearby region. Like the Colossians, these Christians also had not seen Paul in the flesh. Paul intended to rectify this, however, by visiting them once he was released from his house arrest in Rome. His intention appears in his Letter to Philemon, in which he said, "Prepare a guest room for me, because I hope to be restored to you in answer to your prayers" (vs. 22). Philemon was a member of the Colossian church, and he received Paul's letter from Tychicus at the same time Tychicus delivered this letter.

B. Recognizing the Centrality of Christ: vss. 2-3

My purpose is that they may be encouraged in heart and united in love, so that they may have the full riches of complete understanding, in order that they may know the mystery of God, namely, Christ, in whom are hidden all the treasures of wisdom and knowledge.

Paul continued to discuss the purpose of his apostolic ministry by expressing the hopes he had for his readers. First, he desired that they would take heart from his message. Though the apostle criticized at great length the false teachings present within their fellowships, his letter was not intended to discourage them. Instead, he believed that a faith anchored on a right understanding of the Messiah could be only an encouragement to them as persevering Christians in a hostile world (Col. 2:2).

Second, Paul strived for unity among believers. When believers have a proper view of the Son and what He has done for us, His love flows through us, binding us together in a spirit of love. Whereas false teachers create confusion and disorder, the apostolic message called for believers to love one another and be one in their faith and service in the Redeemer. Third, Paul did not want his readers to be spiritually ignorant. In fact, he desired that they fully comprehend God's truths and thus be blessed in every way. To be a Christian possessing such godly wisdom is to be spiritually wealthy indeed.

And what is this invaluable knowledge, which Paul called "the mystery of God"? It is Jesus Christ—knowing who He truly is and what He has really accomplished. Here we see that Paul's objective in ministry was to reveal the Father's eternal plan of redemption in the Son. The Greek noun rendered "mystery" generally denotes that which is hidden or secret. For the apostle, a "mystery" is a truth that was once undisclosed but has now been revealed through Christ. With the advent of Son, the divine secret is meant to be understood by all believers (see Rom. 16:25-27; Col. 1:25-27).

In Paul's day, so-called "mystery" cults were widespread throughout the Western world. The apostle often used the Greek noun rendered "mystery" to provide a counterpoint to the false doctrine that only a small circle of initiates possessed ultimate truth. Instead, he taught that the Son's earthly ministry, death, burial, and resurrection have fully unveiled the Father's once mysterious plan. According to the apostle, this mystery included various aspects of the truth that is found in the Messiah: 1) the incarnation of the Son (1 Tim. 3:16); 2) the eternal ramifications of Jesus' death and resurrection (1 Cor. 15:51); and 3) the comprehensiveness of Jesus' atoning work (Eph. 3:2-6).

Colossians 2:3 states that the Son is the reservoir of all of the Father's wisdom and knowledge. A similar set of truths can be found in 1 Corinthians 1. Paul declared that the Messiah is "the power of God and the wisdom of God" (vs. 24). Indeed, the Father has made the Son to be "wisdom" (vs. 30) for us, along with our source of "righteousness, holiness and redemption." It is only through the resources of the Son that we can know the Father. God had hidden this personal understanding of Himself until the advent of the Messiah. The wisdom and knowledge we have in the Savior is to be treasured and not used to exalt ourselves above others.

C. Maintaining a Strong Faith in Christ: vss. 4-5

I tell you this so that no one may deceive you by fine-sounding arguments. For though I am absent from you in body, I am present with you in spirit and delight to see how orderly you are and how firm your faith in Christ is.

At this point Paul rebuked the heretics. These people prided themselves on being spiritually wiser, aggressively promoted their false doctrines about the Messiah, and verbally assaulted Paul's reputation and teachings among the Colossian believers. However convincing these determined troublemakers were with their seemingly credible assertions, the apostle warned the Colossians not to be tricked into believing their claims (Col. 2:4). It would be incorrect to conclude that the apostle was arguing against the study of philosophy as a discipline. Instead, the apostle was warning against adopting any point of view or teaching that was contrary to the Gospel (see Gal. 1:6-9).

Undoubtedly, Paul would have preferred to be with the believers living in Colosse so that he could deal directly with their problems. But, of course, his Roman imprisonment prohibited him from performing this pastoral duty. Presumably, the apostle was confident that his spiritual presence would arouse their respect for his authority. Hopefully, this respect would spur them on to follow his written instructions eagerly and carefully. Therefore, he reminded them that he was among them, though not physically, certainly in spirit (Col. 2:5).

For the time being, Paul expressed his pleasure with the "orderly" conduct of his readers. The apostle was drawing from a military image to describe how they unified their ranks against the Messiah's foes. As a matter of fact, the religious frauds were not able to break the morale of the Colossians. In addition, Paul commended them on how they stood steadfastly in their faith in the Son. It is evident from the apostle's remarks that the heresies he condemned in this letter had not engulfed the Colossian congregation. However, Paul was intent on equipping them with doctrinal arguments that would demolish the theological claims of the false teachers among them. A unified front, empowered by the Holy Spirit, is by far the strongest weapon against falsehood that Christians have at their disposal.

II. SPIRITUAL FULLNESS IN THE SON: COLOSSIANS 2:6-10

A. Becoming Rooted and Grounded in Christ: vss. 6-7

So then, just as you received Christ Jesus as Lord, continue to live in him, rooted and built up in him, strengthened in the faith as you were taught, and overflowing with thankfulness.

Despite Paul's praise for the believers in Colosse, he still felt compelled to admonish them to keep away from the forces that wanted to lead them astray. When the apostle's readers first heard the good news about the Savior, they embraced it with joy and zeal. But perhaps their initial enthusiasm had started to fade. For this reason Paul admonished them to draw upon deeper spiritual resources as they continued to anchor their lives in the Son (Col. 2:6). It is all too common for many believers to go through a so-called "honeymoon period" just after conversion. During this time, the new believer might begin to feel invulnerable to emotional or spiritual pain and expect these feelings to last a lifetime. After awhile, however, as the pressures of following the Savior begin to mount, the pain inevitably comes. A mark of spiritual maturity is to let go of false expectations and to keep growing despite temporary discomforts.

What does it mean to live our spiritual lives in Christ? Paul provided three answers to this question. First, we are to be "rooted and built up" (vs. 7) in the Redeemer. This phrase brings two pictures to mind. One is of a plant rooted in the ground; the other is of a structure being built above ground. This mixed metaphor actually combines two important features of the growth of one's Christian faith. At the same time we are growing upward in Christ, our roots in the faith should also be deepening. Second, we are to be "strengthened in the faith." Specifically, Paul was exhorting the Colossian believers to rely on the teachings Epaphras had given them. These instructions were consistent with what Paul had taught and were certainly in harmony with other apostolic teachings. Expressed differently, they were to stay committed to the truth of the Gospel, which empowered them to live in harmony with the Father's will.

Third, we are to be "overflowing" with gratitude. This includes being thankful that Jesus died for our sins and now lives in us. For these and other reasons, we should show our appreciation to the Father and the Son (along with the Spirit) in all that we do. Paul prayed that this attitude would mark the lives of the Christians in Colosse. This attitude should most certainly mark the lives of believers today as well. As before, Paul's objective in giving this much emphasis to the Messiah was so that people would come to know Him and devote their lives to Him. With respect to the Colossian believers, the apostle wanted them to understand who Jesus truly is and what He had done for them. This knowledge would protect them from doctrinal error and invigorate their faith. This type of knowledge can do the same for us who are rooted and grounded in Christ.

B. Rejecting False Teachings: vs. 8

See to it that no one takes you captive through hollow and deceptive philosophy, which depends on human tradition and the basic principles of this world rather than on Christ.

Paul warned the believers in Colosse not to be fooled into believing the deceitful doctrines of the false teachers who had slipped in among them. Quite possibly these heretics were present when the apostle's letter was read to the church members and were livid at hearing his censure of them. Nevertheless, Paul was not one who made any effort to spare the feelings of those who tried to lead believers into doctrinal or moral error. The apostle's language in Colossians 2:8 vividly portrays the consequence of being misled by a philosophy that is empty of any value and deceptive in its intent. Those who were captivated by it are like people who are kidnapped or captured during a war. In short, the false teachers were spiritual enemies who treacherously preyed upon Jesus' followers.

Paul went on to characterize this evil philosophy as being man-made. God had not revealed this doctrine; rather, it was the product of corrupted human minds. Moreover, this philosophy was based on the strictly human ideas found in the world. They consisted of instructions on acquiring secret knowledge and codes, angel worship, eating and drinking practices, and religious rituals. Yet very little of it reflected the well-known public teachings of the Savior. The precise meaning of the Greek term rendered "basic principles" is debated among scholars. One option is that it refers to the rudimentary teachings of fallen humanity. A second option is that the focus is on how elemental spiritual forces operated in and controlled the world (under the permission and authority of God).

Paul and the other apostles attacked the foundations of Gnosticism during the first century A.D. Despite their efforts, this heretical doctrine flourished in the second and third centuries A.D. Famous second-century Gnostics such as Marcion and Valentinus taught that the Messiah was one of many angels who got past forces of darkness to bring the secrets of the spiritual realm to an unenlightened world. Following the apostles' example, the church fathers Irenaeus (A.D. 130–200), Tertullian (A.D. 160–225), and Hippolytus (A.D. 170–236) devoted much of their writing to exposing this philosophy, which seemed so compelling to many believers of the day. Irenaeus likened a Gnostic commentator to one who tore up the picture of a king and put it back together to resemble a fox. Many modern occultic and cultic groups claim to be influenced by second-century Gnosticism.

C. Affirming Christ's Deity: vss. 9-10

For in Christ all the fullness of the Deity lives in bodily form, and you have been given fullness in Christ, who is the head over every power and authority.

At this point in his letter, Paul sensed the importance of affirming the deity of the Son. In Colossians 1:19, the apostle declared that the Father was "pleased" to have His full divine nature reside in the Son. This is a permanent dwelling, not a temporary one. Again, in 2:9, the apostle stated that the essence of God in its entirety resided in the Messiah—even in His human body. This statement unequivocally rejects the view that the Son did not have a bodily form and that the human body is evil. More importantly, this verse affirmed both the divine and human natures of the Savior. He is God who has lived as a human being.

Paul declared in verse 10 that believers have been brought to "fullness in Christ." By this the apostle meant they were complete through their spiritual union with Him. Paul dismissed the claim of the false teachers who said believers are deficient because they need further spiritual enlightenment. The apostle also rejected the idea that believers must practice additional religious rituals in order to reach spiritual perfection. The Son, who is Lord over all the powers and forces in the supernatural and the natural realms, has already provided everything we need for salvation and spiritual growth. Jesus is not one of many aeons or angels, but the supreme commander over every power and authority.

Before the advent of the Messiah, the Israelites were members of a special covenant with God (Rom. 9:4-5). This covenant was affirmed by their males being physically circumcised. Now, following the advent of the Messiah, there is a new sign that indicates who are God's people. It is no longer a physical sign but a spiritual one that Savior has performed, and not just for men, but for men and women. That sign is a circumcision of the heart in which sin is cut away. Indeed, Paul said, it is "circumcision done by Christ" (Col. 2:11), and it is by this that we enter into a covenant of grace with God—both Jew or Gentile (see Eph. 2:11-19; 1 Pet. 2:10).

Paul associated baptism with circumcision (Col. 2:12). The apostle vividly paralleled the act of baptism with the dramatic events at the end of Jesus' earthly ministry. After the Son died on the cross, His friends buried His body. But then God raised Him from the dead never to physically die again. In baptism, we are symbolically buried and raised from the dead never to experience spiritual death. In truth, Jesus has washed away our sins with the blood He shed on the cross. As a result of our identification with Him by faith, our old sinful selves, along with their passions and desires, were nailed to the cross (Rom. 6:6; Gal. 5:24). We can now be in a right relationship with the Father because the Son's redemptive work at Calvary atoned for our sins completely.

Discussion Questions

1. What do you think motivated Paul to labor so hard on behalf of the believers in Colosse?
2. Why did Paul choose to refer to the Father's redemptive plan in the Son as the "mystery of God" (Col. 2:2)?
3. On a day-to-day basis, what difference does it really make to be rooted and grounded in Christ?
4. What can believers do to avoid being captivated by the teachings of "hollow and deceptive philosophy" (vs. 8)?
5. How can we help one another when we feel we lack something to be more devoted to Jesus?

Contemporary Application

The Father has made every provision for our spiritual vitality through faith in the Son. Yet many believers often appear to be defeated. And if not defeated, they do not seem to reflect much enthusiasm about their Christian commitment.

It's one thing to lose a battle if we lack adequate resources, but quite another if we have the resources but refuse to use them. Perhaps one reason for the church's lack of power is that too many believers are not aware of all they possess in the Son. They lack the passion for discovering the wealth of their spiritual riches in union with Him.

When we confess Jesus as Lord, we acknowledge that He alone can win our spiritual battles. Yet we seem to go on as if everything depended on our own cleverness and ingenuity. We find it hard to trust Jesus alone. We also find it difficult to abandon pagan human philosophies and traditions for the truth of the Gospel.

Jesus made a public spectacle of our spiritual enemies. The cross is our sign of triumph. In Jesus our sins are forgiven, our old nature has been crucified, and we are raised to new life. Thus, there is no excuse for settling for anything less than a victorious life in Christ.

A Chosen Community

Scripture

Background Scripture: *Colossians 3*

Scripture Lesson: *Colossians 3:12-17*

Key Verses: *As God's chosen people, holy and dearly loved, clothe yourselves with compassion, kindness, humility, gentleness and patience.* Colossians 3:12.

Scripture Lesson for Children: *Colossians 3:12-17*

Key Verse for Children: *As God's chosen people, . . . clothe yourselves with compassion, kindness, humility, gentleness and patience.* Colossians 3:12.

Lesson Aim

To live as God's chosen and grateful people.

Lesson Setting

Time: *About A.D. 60*

Place: *Rome*

Lesson Outline

A Chosen Community

I. Living as God's Chosen People: Colossians 3:12-14
   A. *Being Clothed with Christian Virtues: vs. 12*
   B. *Binding Christian Virtues with Love: vss. 13-14*

II. Living as God's Grateful People: Colossians 3:15-17
   A. *Ruled by Christ's Peace: vs. 15*
   B. *Indwelt by Christ's Message: vs. 16*
   C. *Undergirded by Heartfelt Thanks: vs. 17*

Introduction for Adults

Topic: *A Sense of True Belonging*

Human differences are a fact of life, and we spend most of our lives trying to accommodate them. Of course, some people never do. In extreme cases, people fight and die to keep their distinctives alive. Even when our differences do not lead to bloodshed, they cause unhappiness and despair.

As we look at how hard it is to resolve problems brought on by racial, religious, national, and economic differences, we are tempted to conclude there is no hope. But the Gospel is a message of inclusion in which people from all walks of life are given an opportunity to belong to the community of the redeemed. Indeed, the Good News offers people the only true hope of spiritual unity among those with seemingly insurmountable differences.

Our mission as Christians is to help people really understand who Jesus is and what He can do. Of course, we have to claim our new status as part of God's family. We also have to demonstrate in Christ's spiritual body how we can overcome our differences. And we must never give up God's plan to bring people together in peace and harmony under the Savior's lordship.

Introduction for Youth

Topic: *Hey, I've Been Chosen!*

Sociologists tell us we have yet to see the fruit of family breakdown in the U.S. But anyone in touch with teenagers knows very well how bitter that fruit is in their lives. Many of them long to become members of a close, loving family.

Sadly, what we used to consider the traditional family barely survives. Many teenagers live with single parents, or as part of so-called "blended" families. They are trying to make some sense out of separation and divorce.

The good news for young people is that God has chosen them to be a part of His spiritual family. All it involves is for them to put their faith in Jesus for salvation. When they do, the local church should be there to welcome them into a fellowship known for its unconditional love and forgiveness.

Concepts for Children

Topic: *Act in Love Together*

1. When we become Jesus' followers, we learn how important it is to say no to sin.
2. The Bible helps us to spot sinful practices in our lives.
3. By reading the Bible, we also learn how to make good choices.
4. Even after studying the Bible, there will be times when we get angry or say mean things to others.
5. Jesus is pleased when we say we were wrong and ask Him to forgive us.

Lesson Commentary

I. LIVING AS GOD'S CHOSEN PEOPLE: COLOSSIANS 3:12-14

A. Being Clothed with Christian Virtues: vs. 12

Therefore, as God's chosen people, holy and dearly loved, clothe yourselves with compassion, kindness, humility, gentleness and patience.

Earlier in Paul's letter, he decried the ascetic (self-denying) practices of the false teachers in the Colossian church (see Col. 2:20-23). This is because they were trying to use human willpower to restrain their sensual indulgences. Apart from faith in the Son and the power of the indwelling Spirit, all such efforts to control the sin nature are bound to fail. This does not mean it is wrong to advocate and practice self-control. Indeed, Paul exhorted his readers to do so. The key to their success was their faith in Christ for salvation and identification with His death, burial, and resurrection (3:3). They had the assurance that at His second advent, they (along with all believers) would be revealed with Him in glory (vs. 4).

In short, Paul wanted the believers at Colosse to live as God's chosen people. This included no longer sinning and being enslaved to evil. Figuratively speaking, they were to "put to death" (vs. 5) whatever earthly desires were lurking within them. The apostle listed five vices that are indicative of the old fallen nature. These included "sexual immorality," or illicit sexual relations; "impurity," or moral uncleanness; "lust," or carnal cravings; "evil desires," or depraved covetousness; and "greed" or the insatiable hunger for material possessions—which is idolatry. Paul followed his admonition with a stern warning. The Father will not ignore unrepented sins. Instead, He will show His displeasure with these vices on the day of judgment when the Son returns. Divine retribution will fall on all who have sold themselves out to such wickedness (vs. 6).

Evidently, most of Paul's readers were Gentiles from pagan backgrounds. They had probably indulged in the sins he just described. Now, however, Jesus had forgiven and renewed them and given them a new way in which to live. Therefore, they were not to be characterized by their former heathen existence (vs. 7). After all, this old way of life was buried in the past for the true follower of Christ. To reinforce the apostle's point, he listed a second catalog of vices that have more to do with verbal offenses (vs. 8). Paul commanded his readers to get rid of "anger," or outbursts of temper; "rage," or the violent expression of hatred; "malice," or vindictive spite; "slander," or destructive gossip; and "filthy language," or vulgar speech. Moreover, they were not to lie to one another (vs. 9). The apostle may have been noting actual spiritual maladies within the congregation at Colosse. The problem could have been a source of mistrust and conflict that was beginning to flare up in the church.

Paul presented a vivid picture of what it means to turn away from a life of sin and walk in newness of life in Christ. It is like taking off old, dirty clothes and putting

299

on new, clean garments. Expressed differently, we are to strip off all the disgusting habits we had when we were nonbelievers and clothe ourselves with godly behavior that reflects the character of the Son. This is only possible as the Spirit empowers us to do so. As a result of putting on a new self in Christ, believers are "renewed in knowledge" (vs. 10). In turn, they come to understand their Creator better and conduct themselves in a manner that is pleasing to Him. For the remainder of the believers' sojourn on earth, Jesus renews their minds and transforms their thinking, with the result that they choose to do God's perfect will (see Rom. 12:2).

In this new way of living, there are no distinctions between any of us who belong to Christ. To reinforce this truth, Paul gave examples from his day of social barriers that separated groups of people (Col. 3:11). Between Gentiles and Jews, race was an issue. Differing religious practices divided the circumcised from the uncircumcised. The elites of society regarded barbarians and Scythians as being uncivilized brutes. Class distinctions separated slaves from those who were free. Against this backdrop, it must have seemed quite radical for Paul to declare that "Christ is all, and is in all." By this the apostle meant that Jesus unites all of us, despite our vast differences, because He dwells in all believers.

Parallel truths are found in Galatians 3:28. Paul wrote that the Son's advent made it possible for believers to become the Father's spiritual children. Also, through faith, they are baptized into and clothed with the Messiah. Jesus' incarnation also broke down worldly divisions, such as those based on distinctions of race, social status, and gender. This means that such distinctions have no bearing on who can become a follower of Christ. It also means that all people in society should be seen as persons of worth. The three social distinctions Paul mentioned were significant ones in his day. Prejudice existed between Jews and non-Jews over religious, political, and cultural issues. Hundreds of thousands of people in the Roman Empire were enslaved by others. Women had limited legal rights and were often looked down upon by men. Thankfully, through the valid influence of Christian principles, many of these social divisions have been abolished.

Paul, in his letter to the Colossians, did not just tell his readers to abandon all forms of sin. He also exhorted them to demonstrate and cultivate Christlike virtues. The motivation for doing so was their status as "God's chosen people" (3:12). Put another way, they were the elect of God. As such, the Lord considered them to be His "holy and dearly loved" spiritual children. By putting to death the vices of the old self and putting on Christian love, they demonstrated the reality of the new life they had in the Son. They also promoted harmony within their fellowship. It was not enough for them as individual Christians to be like the Savior. In fact, it was more important for them to be like the Son as a unified Church. In this way, they collectively represented themselves as the Messiah's bride to the world, "without stain or wrinkle or any other blemish, but holy and blameless" (Eph. 5:27).

To further encourage a holy way of life, Paul listed five virtues that should spiritually clothe believers (Col. 3:12). The apostle's purpose was to remind his readers (and all Christians) that they were to practice what the Son had taught His followers and measure up to what the Father created them to be. Paul first urged the Colossians to array themselves with a heart of "compassion" or mercy. This refers to an affectionate sympathy for others, especially for those in need. Second, the apostle affirmed the value of kindness. His readers were to have a generous and helpful regard in their dealings with others. Humility was third on Paul's list. He certainly was not advocating self-mortification as the false teachers had done, but was speaking of a meekness in behavior and attitude that is respectful and not haughty or pretentious.

Fourth, the apostle wanted the believers in Colosse to exhibit gentleness. By this he meant showing congenial consideration toward others. Although people regard meekness as a sign of weakness, Paul did not view this trait as a flaw, especially since Jesus Himself had the characteristic. The Redeemer said, "Take my yoke upon you and learn from me, for I am gentle and humble in heart" (Matt. 11:29). Finally, the apostle stressed the importance of "patience" (Col. 3:12). He wanted his readers to have a tolerant and forgiving spirit toward those who wronged them. All of these characteristics have relational aspects to them. As we exercise and cultivate these virtues in our relationships with other believers, we will individually and collectively become more Christlike.

B. Binding Christian Virtues with Love: vss. 13-14

Bear with each other and forgive whatever grievances you may have against one another. Forgive as the Lord forgave you. And over all these virtues put on love, which binds them all together in perfect unity.

Paul's next admonition pertained to forgiveness. Even within the Church believers often rub each other the wrong way, and it's easy to harbor a grudge against a Christian brother or sister. The apostle, however, instructed the Colossians to resist such a temptation and instead be forbearing and forgiving when they felt they had been mistreated (Col. 3:13). Furthermore, making allowance for the faults of others and being willing to overlook an offense were the means by which believers clothed themselves with the Christian virtues listed in verse 12.

Paul then recalled how the Lord forgave us. The implication is that if Jesus could pardon us, who have wronged Him infinitely more than we have been mistreated, how much easier it should be for us to forgive those who have frustrated us. Of course, Paul knew that forgiving is not an easy thing to do. Yet the apostle also believed that the Son empowers us to be like Him, especially as the Holy Spirit conforms us to the Savior's image. This gives us the ability to be patient with one another no matter how great a loss someone has caused in our lives. Most of all, Paul asked the Colossians to clothe themselves with "love" (vs. 14). Metaphorically speaking, Christlike compassion is like an overcoat that rests on top of all the other virtues. When Jesus' followers are dressed in this manner, they will enjoy perfect unity. The Messiah will have knit us all together in a single, multicolored, multipatterned tapestry by His transforming love.

II. LIVING AS GOD'S GRATEFUL PEOPLE: COLOSSIANS 3:15-17

A. Ruled by Christ's Peace: vs. 15

Let the peace of Christ rule in your hearts, since as members of one body you were called to peace. And be thankful.

After Paul described the kind of conduct the Colossian believers should maintain, he explained how it was possible for them to obey his instructions. In essence, he said they must live day-by-day totally under the lordship of Christ. This involved letting the peace that He supplied control their thoughts, emotions, and actions. The Greek term rendered "peace" (Col. 3:15) denoted the presence of harmony and tranquility. Unlike worldly forms of concord, this peace was a special, personal gift from the Savior (John 14:27). Moreover, this peace is the embodiment of the Messiah, "for he himself is our peace" (Eph. 2:14).

Since the biblical writers thought of the heart as the center of a person's being, Paul, in effect, was calling upon believers to submit their entire being to the control of the Redeemer's peace. The reason for doing so is that God has "called [us] to peace" (Col. 3:15). Moreover, God wants Christians to live in harmony, not as separate individuals, but as a unified community of believers. Since we are all members of one spiritual body, of which Jesus is the appointed head (see 1:18; 2:19), we must not let our selfishness disrupt the health of His body. Paul also directed us to be thankful. He didn't ask us to just express gratitude to the Father, but to have a constant attitude of thankfulness for being a redeemed member of the Son's spiritual body. The apostle wanted believers to be a thankful people who appreciated what the Savior was doing within them.

We find similar exhortations in Philippians 4:6-7. Paul told his friends not to worry about any self-centered concerns. Such anxiety can become all-consuming. It takes our minds off what is important to God and focuses attention on ourselves. We can become self-absorbed, unable to rejoice during hard times and to be gentle with friends and foes alike. So what is the best remedy for anxiousness? Paul's prescription is prayer. When we turn to God and surrender our anxieties to Him, God's peace can reach our innermost parts. The apostle did not imply that our burdens will vanish, nor was he talking about a state of mind. In fact, it is an inner peace that can come only from God and is beyond our comprehension.

In addition, the Father's peace will guard our hearts and minds in the Son. The Greek word rendered "guard" (vs. 7) is a military term that depicts a sentry maintaining his watch. Since Philippi was a garrison town, the believers living there would have immediately comprehended the meaning of Paul's metaphor. Every day they would have seen Roman sentries standing guard at the gates. In the same way a trained soldier guards a base, God's peace stands guard over our hearts and minds. The peace of God can come only through our Lord Jesus Christ, who made peace between God and us through the blood He shed on the cross. Thus we are in the Savior's protective custody only when we are yielded to His lordship. And for those who are, He will leave His peace with us, giving us an inner tranquility the world may claim but can never truly know.

B. Indwelt by Christ's Message: vs. 16

Let the word of Christ dwell in you richly as you teach and admonish one another with all wisdom, and as you sing psalms, hymns and spiritual songs with gratitude in your hearts to God.

Living as God's grateful people includes letting the message about Christ, in all its richness, to completely fill our lives (Col. 3:16). This admonition means more than just a simple reading and rote memorization of the Bible. It is allowing the Word of God to affect every aspect of our existence. For instance, we allow Scripture to shape our decisions and determine our thinking patterns. We also seek to live by it on a daily basis. As Christ's message dwells in us richly, we are better able to instruct and exhort one another in a prudent and discerning manner.

Moreover, the Spirit enables us to draw upon all the wisdom provided by the Savior as we go about our daily lives. Indeed, the "word of Christ" is the basis for us singing "psalms, hymns and spiritual songs . . . to God" with our "hearts" filled with "gratitude." The "psalms" were probably the canticles found in the Old Testament Psalter. The "hymns" most likely were lyrics composed by Christians to honor God. The "songs" may have been called "spiritual" either to distinguish them from similar compositions by non-Christians or because they referred to spontaneous singing in the Spirit.

The idea is that the words in our worship songs are meant to express the compassion and truth of the Savior. These hymns can either be taken from the Old Testament psalms or be newly written lyrics of praise. Whatever the type of music, it is clear that the Spirit should guide the words, the music, and the singer. Furthermore, we are to praise the Father and the Son in song with not just with our lips but more importantly with all our heart—that is, our whole being. In Ephesians 5:19-20, Paul wrote that those who are filled with the Spirit desire to worship the Father. Here, too, the apostle associated worship with music. The Ephesians were to communicate among themselves with a wide variety of music. In addition to communicating with one another by means of music, the Ephesians were to "sing and make music" in their hearts to the Lord. This is a way of giving thanks to the Father for all He has given us in the Son.

Music has always been a vital feature of all cultures. It has also had a prominent role in the worship ceremonies of God's people. The first description of music among the Israelites was when Moses and Miriam in song celebrated their crossing of the Red Sea (Exod. 15:1-21). At that time, Miriam used tambourines and danced. Besides the tambourine or timbrel, the lyre, harp, lute, flute, cymbals, and trumpets were common in ancient Israel. In fact, King David was a master at playing the harp (1 Sam. 16:23). These observations notwithstanding, it is uncertain to what extent musical instruments were used in Christian worship during the first century of the common era. In any case, music was inseparable from Christian worship. Indeed, the first believers, and Christians since, have proclaimed their faith and theology in psalms, hymns, and songs from the Spirit.

C. Undergirded by Heartfelt Thanks: vs. 17

And whatever you do, whether in word or deed, do it all in the name of the Lord Jesus, giving thanks to God the Father through him.

Paul urged the believers in Colosse to do everything in Jesus' name (Col. 3:17). Put differently, they were to think, behave, and minister in light of the Messiah's supreme authority and character. Since the Lord has claimed us with His atoning blood, we belong to Him. Accordingly, His name should be stamped on all that we do and say as His representatives to the unsaved. This includes us expressing gratitude through the Son to the Father.

Discussion Questions

1. What difference has being part of "God's chosen people" (Col. 3:12) made in your life?
2. Why is it important for our lives to be clothed, in a manner of speaking, with Christian virtues?
3. How challenging is it for you to bear with others who have wronged you?
4. How likely is it for the peace of Christ to rule in your heart when you are feeling stressed out?
5. How might you use the singing of Christian hymns to encourage and exhort other believers?

Contemporary Application

Every day we seem to be confronted by a new crisis of some kind. What would the evening news be if there were no crises to report? But perhaps the most significant crisis of all never makes the news. Our churches must realize that a crisis exists when believers fail to follow God's principles for holy living. It's a crisis when believers adopt a ho-hum attitude toward the standards of godly living revealed in the Bible.

God has provided all we need to throw off the old life and put on the new one. There can be no doubts about His governing principles. But until we realize the danger of neglecting God's spiritual resources, we will not swing into action.

Action begins by evaluating how much time we spend feeding our hearts and minds on the truths of the Gospel. Confession and repentance are demanded. We also have to regularly use Paul's checklist of virtues and vices. Where we fall short, we must acknowledge the err of our ways. We should also seek the help of others to keep us on the road to godly living. As we rejoice and praise the Lord together, we allow the words of the Savior to penetrate our hearts and minds.

At Home in the Community

Scripture

Background Scripture: *Philemon*

Scripture Lesson: *Philemon 8-18*

Key Verse: *Confident of your obedience, I write to you, knowing that you will do even more than I ask.* Philemon 21.

Scripture Lesson for Children: *Philemon 8-18*

Key Verse for Children: *If you consider me a partner, welcome him as you would welcome me.* Philemon 17.

Lesson Aim

To see how Christian love has a way of equalizing people.

Lesson Setting

Time: *About A.D. 60*

Place: *Rome*

Lesson Outline

At Home in the Community

I. Paul's Plea: Philemon 8-11
   A. *Appealing on the Basis of Love: vss. 8-9a*
   B. *Appealing on the Basis of Spiritual Kinship: vss. 9b-11*

II. Paul's Plan: Philemon 12-18
   A. *Returning Onesimus: vss. 12-13*
   B. *Obtaining Philemon's Consent: vss. 14-16*
   C. *Establishing a Partnership with Philemon: vss. 17-18*

Introduction for Adults

Topic: *Doing the Right Thing*

By God's grace, we no longer have slavery in this country. Admittedly, the working conditions of migrant farm workers and so-called "sweat shops" take their human toll. Thankfully, some employers make a special effort to treat even unskilled laborers in a "brotherly" way.

One man recalls, "I'd never worked so hard when I was a youth as the summer I was hired out to a neighboring farmer. But he was a good man and treated me well. He was also a wise Christian and saw that I was not cut out for farm work. One day he relieved me of my summer's commitment and told me I would be happier doing something else, which was true. He was one of many people who made a great investment in my spiritual well-being."

God gives us many opportunities to grace the lives of others. We have to see their potential as Christian brothers and sisters. Paul saw great potential in a runaway slave. The apostle wanted the man's owner to see his slave in a new light—as a fellow-believer in Christ. When we see people that way, we can do the right thing by investing our lives in them.

Introduction for Youth

Topic: *Homeward Bound*

All of us want to be accepted, regardless of our past mistakes. Tragically, the lives of many young people are scarred by sin before they come to faith in Christ. Sometimes it's hard for older believers to accept them. Imagine how difficult it was for Philemon to welcome his homeward bound slave—who previously had wronged him and fled—and treat him as a fellow believer.

As Christians, we are called to do the unthinkable and the impossible in human relationships. We don't keep bringing up past mistakes. We welcome people into our church because Jesus accepts them. Former enemies can become fast friends in Christ. Such is the power of the Gospel.

When we cross boundaries to show Christian love, we gain new opportunities to point people to Jesus. Unbelievers find it hard to accept the Savior if we do not first unconditionally accept them.

Concepts for Children

Topic: *Act as Friends*

1. Paul wrote personal letter from prison to Philemon, a dearly-loved friend.
2. Paul wrote on behalf of Onesimus, Philemon's runaway slave, who had become a new believer.
3. Paul offered to pay Philemon for anything that Onesimus owed Philemon.
4. Paul asked Philemon to accept Onesimus back as a fellow believer rather than as a slave.
5. In God's family, we show Jesus' love to others who have done wrong to us.

Lesson Commentary

I. PAUL'S PLEA: PHILEMON 8-11

A. Appealing on the Basis of Love: vss. 8-9a

Therefore, although in Christ I could be bold and order you to do what you ought to do, yet I appeal to you on the basis of love.

Philemon is one of the letters Paul wrote during his first imprisonment in Rome (about A.D. 60). The apostle's epistle to Philemon focuses on slavery, particularly on the fate of a slave named Onesimus. Philemon was a slave owner who lived in the Lycus Valley in Asia Minor and was an influential member of the church at Colosse. Slavery was prevalent in the Roman Empire. In fact, during the early Christian period, one out of every two people in the empire was a slave. Onesimus may have stolen from his master, Philemon, and then run away. Onesimus made his way to Rome, where he met Paul, who led him to faith in the Messiah. Shortly thereafter, Onesimus faced his Christian duty of returning to his master.

Philemon wasn't the sole slaveholder in the Colossian church (see Col. 4:1), and this letter gives a few general guidelines other Christian masters could follow in their relationships to their slave brothers and sisters. Paul didn't deny the rights of Philemon over his slave, but the apostle asked this believing master to practice Christian brotherhood with his wayward slave. At the same time, Paul offered to pay personally whatever Onesimus owed. The letter the apostle wrote is not a polemic against slavery as such, but a suggestion as to how Christian masters and slaves could live their faith within a very evil system. It is conceivable that Philemon did free Onesimus and send him back to Paul (Philem. 14). It has also been suggested that Onesimus became a minister of the church at Ephesus.

Paul said that whenever he prayed about Philemon, he thanked God for the good reports he had heard about him (vs. 4). Specifically, the apostle had learned about Philemon's faith in Jesus and his "love for all the saints" (vs. 5), that is, God's holy people. In Christian circles, it was getting around that Philemon was a true believer whose faith made a difference in how he treated people. Paul prayed for Philemon as well as about him. This prayer, recorded in verse 6, has been taken two ways. On the one hand, Paul may have prayed that Philemon would share his faith, which would lead to his gaining a full understanding of Christian blessings. On the other hand, the apostle may have prayed the opposite: that Philemon would gain an understanding of blessings that would lead to his sharing his faith. Both interpretations are plausible.

Paul noted that Philemon's love for God's people had given the apostle considerable "joy and encouragement" (vs. 7). Philemon showed his kindness for his fellow Christians by "refresh[ing] the hearts of the saints." This perhaps means Philemon was able to cheer up his fellow believers, especially as they experienced difficult trials. He may also have helped them to be spiritually rejuvenated in their service for the Lord. Since Philemon was known for showing love to other Christians, Paul was bold enough to ask him to show that sort of love again. To be specific, the apostle wanted Philemon to forgive Onesimus for running away and receive him back as a brother in Christ. This would be a real test of Philemon's love for the saints.

Paul was an apostle of the Lord Jesus and a prominent leader in the church. Paul also was Philemon's spiritual parent, having led Philemon to the Lord. Paul thus had the authority to order Philemon to do the proper thing (vs. 8). However, the apostle did not want to resort to such stern tactics to persuade his dear Christian friend to fulfill a duty. Paul chose to appeal to Philemon on the basis of love rather than authority (vs. 9). The apostle did not want his child in the faith to feel forced into showing mercy to Onesimus. Paul wanted the decision to come voluntarily from Philemon.

In Paul's day, the majority of slaves were laborers performing such duties as cooking, cleaning, and farming. A minority served as tutors, physicians, artisans, and managers of households. More skilled and better educated slaves generally enjoyed better food, clothing, and shelter than their unskilled and uneducated counterparts. Under Roman law slaves were not considered legal persons. They could be bought and sold like animals. Additionally, slaves were not allowed to represent themselves in court, inherit property, or select a mate. Nevertheless, the law protected them against mistreatment by their masters. There were two basic situations in which slaves could obtain freedom: they could either be emancipated by their masters or they could purchase their freedom with funds they accumulated over time. Sometimes an owner might grant freedom to all the slave members of a household. On other occasions a freed slave might be forced to leave family members behind.

B. Appealing on the Basis of Spiritual Kinship: vss. 9b-11

I then, as Paul—an old man and now also a prisoner of Christ Jesus—I appeal to you for my son Onesimus, who became my son while I was in chains. Formerly he was useless to you, but now he has become useful both to you and to me.

As plain "Paul" (Philem. 9), rather than as the "great apostle," the spiritual parent of Philemon appealed to him on behalf of Onesimus. Yet as plain Paul, the veteran church leader still deserved respect on two counts. First, he was an elderly man. Most likely, he was about 60 years old—an advanced age at that time. In that society, elderly people were generally looked upon as wise and worthy of respect. Second, Paul was "a prisoner of Christ Jesus." The apostle was under house arrest in Rome while he awaited appeal of his case before Caesar. Paul had been arrested on a false charge at the instigation of Jews who didn't like his preaching of the Gospel to Gentiles (see Acts 21:27-31). Thus, the apostle was a "prisoner" (Philem. 1) as a result of obeying the Savior. Paul deserved respect because he was suffering for the Lord.

As a man worthy of respect, the apostle was appealing to one of his spiritual sons

(Philemon) on behalf of another spiritual son (Onesimus). God had graciously enabled Paul to lead Philemon's slave to faith in Christ. Ironically, this took place while the apostle was under house arrest in Rome. Though in chains himself, Paul was able to lead Onesimus to spiritual freedom (vs. 10). The apostle's efforts were not wasted either. Onesimus—whose name means "useful"—proved to be useful, Paul punned. Perhaps at one time Onesimus was uncooperative and unruly toward Philemon. However, now that Onesimus was a believer, he was profitable both to Philemon, his master, and to Paul, his mentor (vs. 11).

II. PAUL'S PLAN: PHILEMON 12-18

A. Returning Onesimus: vss. 12-13

I am sending him—who is my very heart—back to you. I would have liked to keep him with me so that he could take your place in helping me while I am in chains for the gospel.

Undoubtedly, it was difficult for Paul to send Onesimus back to Philemon. Since meeting the runaway slave and leading him to Christ, Paul had grown quite close to Onesimus. It was as if the apostle's heart—his very self—accompanied Onesimus back to Colosse (Philem. 12). The apostle's desire had been for Onesimus to remain with him and continue to help him. Since as a prisoner Paul's mobility was limited (due to the chains he had to wear), he needed help from others to bring him food and run other errands for him. Also, if Onesimus had remained with the apostle and continued providing help for him, the recent convert would in a sense have been taking his master's place in assisting Paul. As the apostle's spiritual son, Philemon owed Paul support, which Onesimus could have provided if the apostle had decided to keep him around (vs. 13).

B. Obtaining Philemon's Consent: vss. 14-16

But I did not want to do anything without your consent, so that any favor you do will be spontaneous and not forced. Perhaps the reason he was separated from you for a little while was that you might have him back for good—no longer as a slave, but better than a slave, as a dear brother. He is very dear to me but even dearer to you, both as a man and as a brother in the Lord.

Out of respect for Philemon, Paul did not want to make a decision concerning Onesimus unless Philemon agreed to it. If Philemon was to do a good deed for Paul, it should have been from his own willingness, not out of compulsion (Philem. 14). The apostle, having decided to send Onesimus back, wanted to help Philemon adopt the right attitude toward Onesimus. While Philemon would at first naturally be upset with Onesimus for running away, the apostle tried to get Philemon to see the experience in light of the larger purposes of God. For instance, perhaps the Lord had allowed the temporary separation of slave from master to occur so that the two could be together (spiritually) on a permanent basis (vs. 15).

Moreover, Onesimus was now more than a slave to Philemon. He was a beloved fellow believer in Christ. Paul admitted that he had grown fond of Onesimus and valued his help. But the apostle thought Philemon should hold Onesimus even more dear. Whereas Paul had known Onesimus only a short while, Philemon had longstanding ties with him. Philemon, thus, should have valued Onesimus as a human being and as a fellow believer (vs. 16). Paul clearly taught that, because of what Jesus had done in the heart of Onesimus, the relationship between master and slave had to change.

Some readers of the book think the apostle was going further and hinting that Philemon should give Onesimus his freedom. If Onesimus was better than a slave spiritually, it made sense for him to be better than a slave legally as well. While in all the centuries that have passed since Paul's day slavery has thankfully disappeared, our social customs still tend to dictate the way people deal with one another. That's natural, but we should never let such customs interfere with the love we owe our fellow believers in the Lord.

C. Establishing a Partnership with Philemon: vss. 17-18

So if you consider me a partner, welcome him as you would welcome me. If he has done you any wrong or owes you anything, charge it to me.

Paul knew that Philemon considered him to be a partner in the work of the Gospel. In particular, they shared common interests, desires, and goals. The apostle asked his coworker in the faith to regard Onesimus in the same way. Philemon was to welcome his converted slave just as he would welcome Paul (Philem. 17). The apostle was gracious in offering to pay any sum Onesimus may have owed Philemon (vs. 18). Possibly Onesimus had stolen some money or property when he had run away. Or perhaps the apostle was thinking about the loss of economic value from Onesimus that Philemon had suffered while Onesimus was away. The apostle did not want such financial losses to prevent Philemon from welcoming Onesimus back.

Paul wanted to assure Philemon of his sincere intent to do what he said. Evidently, most of the apostle's letter was dictated to a secretary, who then wrote down what was said. At this point, however, Paul took hold of the pen and began writing with his own hand. He may have written only verse 19, or he may have continued writing to the end of the letter. In either case, his handwriting would help to make the letter serve as a legal promissory note obligating the apostle to fulfill what he pledged. While Paul was willing to pay Philemon the sum Onesimus owed, he pointed out that he should not have to do so. After all, Philemon owed his very soul to Paul, for the Lord had used the apostle to bring Philemon to a saving knowledge of the truth. The spiritual debt Philemon owed Paul far exceeded the monetary debt that Onesimus owed Philemon. The apostle brought up this fact to keep matters in proper perspective.

Due to the fact that Philemon owed so much to Paul, the apostle asked for "some benefit" (vs. 20) from him. The Greek word translated "benefit" (*oninemi*) is similar in sound to the name Onesimus. In short, Paul was using another pun to get his point across. Earlier in his letter, the apostle had commended Philemon for refreshing the hearts of God's people (see vs. 7). Now Paul asked his partner in the faith to do the same for him with respect to Onesimus (vs. 20). Probably the benefit, or refreshment, Paul was seeking was that Philemon would send Onesimus back to the apostle to help him. Paul had not felt comfortable keeping Onesimus without first asking Philemon's permission. But if Philemon voluntarily lent the slave to Paul, that would be a different matter.

Paul realized that his request to Philemon was substantial. Nevertheless, the apostle was confident that Philemon would do all that was asked of him. In fact, Paul was convinced Philemon would do even more than this (vs. 21). Probably the apostle meant that Philemon should free Onesimus as well as send him to Paul. The apostle had one additional request to ask of his friend. He wanted Philemon to prepare a place for Paul to stay when he next visited Colosse (vs. 22). If Philemon was wealthy enough to own slaves and had a home large enough to accommodate a church, he must have had a guest room that a traveling apostle could use for a while.

Among many of the social classes of the Roman Empire, showing hospitality to strangers was considered an inviolable obligation. For example, Greeks considered displays of friendliness and generosity to foreigners a mark of a civilized culture. In contrast, the lack of hospitality was viewed as a sign of barbarity. When a guest or stranger was received by the host, the host was duty bound to provide shelter and sustenance. In addition, the host did as much as possible to ensure that the traveler's needs were met for the next segment of the journey. This included the provision of water, food, clothing, and even money. The hospitality was given freely and graciously, for there was always the possibility that one day the host might be a stranger or weary traveler in need of help.

Although Paul was imprisoned in Rome, he anticipated that he would soon be released by the authorities. Undoubtedly, the possibility of the apostle's visiting Colosse would spur Philemon to comply with Paul's request regarding Onesimus. Paul realized that his release from prison would be due to the powerful working of God in response to the prayers of many believers, such as Philemon. Tradition says that Paul was set free sometime after writing this letter. However, it is not known whether he ever made it to Colosse.

Many scholars think Paul took one more missionary journey before being arrested again. Most likely, it was during this time that he wrote 2 Timothy. Earlier in Rome, he had been kept under house arrest. This time, however, he sensed that the outcome would be different. Paul spoke about how he had finished his work and completed the race. However, he did not intend that this epistle to Timothy would be his last contact with the minister. Instead, the apostle hoped Timothy would be able to come visit him in Rome. Church tradition states that Paul was executed by the emperor Nero near the end of his reign of terror. Nero committed suicide in A.D. 68, so Paul probably wrote this last letter around A.D. 67 or 68.

Discussion Questions

1. If you were Philemon, how would you have felt after receiving Paul's letter?
2. How do you think Onesimus felt about the prospect of going back to Philemon?
3. What obstacles did Philemon have to overcome to receive Onesimus back as a fellow believer?
4. Why didn't Paul order Philemon to take back his runaway slave?
5. Why is our willingness to welcome others such a strong witness to the power of the Gospel?

Contemporary Application

What principles can we draw from Paul's letter to Philemon to help us to welcome others in Christ? First, Paul asks all of us to lay aside prejudices and grudges. We have to allow the love of the Savior to wipe the slate clean (in a manner of speaking). As believers, we confess our sins to one another. We thank God that all of us can make fresh starts.

Another encouragement is that it is possible in Christ to develop very strong bonds of partnership, love, trust, and respect across barriers that normally keep people apart. We have to admire Paul's bravery in making such an audacious request of Philemon in that culture. But when we know our fellow believers in Christ, we can take such risks. We can trust our friendships to see us through tough times.

The world watches how we treat one another in the church. It's an amazing testimony of Jesus' power when unbelievers see believers overcome distrust and prejudice. When the unwelcome are made welcome, people truly see Jesus in us.

At Risk in the Community

Scripture

Background Scripture: *Jude*
Scripture Lesson: *Jude 3-7, 19-21, 24-25*
Key Verses: *Have mercy on some who are wavering; save others by snatching them out of the fire; and have mercy on still others with fear.* Jude 22-23.
Scripture Lesson for Children: *Jude 3-7, 19-21, 24-25*
Key Verse for Children: *Contend for the faith that was once for all entrusted to the saints.* Jude 3.

Lesson Aim

To refuse to let false teachers take advantage of us.

Lesson Setting

Time: *About A.D. 65*
Place: *Unknown*

Lesson Outline

At Risk in the Community

I. A Warning about Apostates: Jude 3-7
  A. *The Importance of Defending the Faith: vss. 3-4*
  B. *The Demise of Apostates: vss. 5-7*
II. A Call to Faithfulness: Jude 19-21, 24-25
  A. *The Divisiveness Caused by the Apostates: vs. 19*
  B. *The Importance of Devotion to God: vss. 20-21*
  C. *The Expression of Praise to God: vss. 24-25*

Introduction for Adults

Topic: *Tempering Judgment with Mercy*

John's wife suffered from a brain tumor and the physicians gave her two months to live. The months dragged by and she grew less and less responsive. John lapsed into bitterness and despair. His wife lingered and gradually John began to recover. His outlook brightened. He knew that he had to keep his faith, no matter what. Eight months later his wife passed away.

For many Christians like John, keeping faith is a battle against overwhelming despair. For others, it's a battle against various religious and intellectual arguments. That's what it was like for John's son, who was convinced that the Christian faith held nothing for him. At first, he was tempted to pass judgment on Christianity. But then the mercy of God prevailed in his heart. Thankfully, John's son gave Jesus a more serious look during his mother's illness.

Whatever our battlegrounds, faith in the truth of the Gospel is the issue. If we yield on this point, we have no hope for ourselves or for others.

Introduction for Youth

Topic: *Are You for Real?*

When Roger graduated from college, one of his professors expressed disappointment that he had not been able to shake what he called Roger's "Sunday school" faith. The academic had assumed that when Roger got a college education, he would outgrow his beliefs.

Roger, however, learned how to grow in and defend his faith, because in college he joined a Christian group and studied the Bible, prayed, and told other students about Jesus. There were times when Roger's faith was attacked in class, especially by those who pretended to be sympathetic to Christianity. In response to these frauds, Roger consulted the library shelf where the Christians had placed a number of scholarly books that held the Bible to be true and trustworthy.

Keeping the faith required hard work, perseverance, knowledge, and Christian fellowship. Roger knew he could not go through college in neutral as far as his faith was concerned. If he did not spiritually grow, he would lapse into indifference and unbelief. So, he took the offensive and won the battle.

Concepts for Children

Topic: *Hold On to Truth*

1. Jude was a follower of the Lord Jesus.
2. Jude wrote a letter to other believers about the importance of obeying the Savior.
3. Jude also encouraged his friends in the faith to beware of false teachers.
4. Jude wanted the readers of his letter not to be tricked by these evil people.
5. Jude reminded his readers that the Father would watch over them. He also watches over us in our walk with Him.

Lesson Commentary

I. A WARNING ABOUT APOSTATES: JUDE 3-7

A. The Importance of Defending the Faith: vss. 3-4

Dear friends, although I was very eager to write to you about the salvation we share, I felt I had to write and urge you to contend for the faith that was once for all entrusted to the saints. For certain men whose condemnation was written about long ago have secretly slipped in among you. They are godless men, who change the grace of our God into a license for immorality and deny Jesus Christ our only Sovereign and Lord.

An examination of Jude 4-18 and 2 Peter 2:1-22 indicates that one relied directly on the other or both used a third source that no longer exists. Most New Testament scholars think Peter relied on Jude. If that is so, Jude had to be written long enough before Peter's death in the late A.D. 60s to have been recognized as authoritative. Assuming Jude precedes 2 Peter, it may have been written about A.D. 65.

Jude made extensive use of Old Testament allusions. This may indicate he wrote to an audience in Palestine. The false teachers Jude warned against seem to have interpreted the doctrine of salvation by grace to imply that sins were acceptable or even desirable as stimulants for more grace (Jude 4). The bogus teachers John's epistles combated held false views about the full humanity and full deity of Christ. Jude's (and 2 Peter's) false teachers seem primarily to have tried to join the gracious Gospel of Christ to immorality.

Jude's original intent was to write to his dear friends in the faith about "the salvation we share" (Jude 3), and he was "very eager" to offer pastoral counsel. The presence of false teachers, however, prompted Jude to redirect his attention. Spiritual frauds were threatening believers with a counterfeit gospel. The danger was so great that Jude exhorted his readers to "contend for the faith." This refers to the body of apostolic truth "that was once for all entrusted to the saints." God, in His grace, gave His inspired and infallible Word to His holy people, and they were to uphold and defend it against heretics.

Jude referred to the charlatans as "godless men" (vs. 4) who had crept in undetected among the fellowship of believers. The frauds purported that the "grace of our God" permitted people to live in a manner characterized by lewdness and immorality. The charlatans also denied the necessity of obeying Jesus Christ. Long ago Scripture revealed that the impious were eternally marked out for "condemnation." Their decision to be unrestrained in their wickedness was the reason they faced this gloomy end. Thus, they bore full responsibility for their judgment.

B. The Demise of Apostates: vss. 5-7

Though you already know all this, I want to remind you that the Lord delivered his people out of Egypt, but later destroyed those who did not believe. And the angels who did not keep their positions of authority but abandoned their own home—these he has kept in darkness, bound with everlasting chains for judgment on the great Day. In a similar way, Sodom and Gomorrah and the surrounding towns gave themselves up to sexual immorality and perversion. They serve as an example of those who suffer the punishment of eternal fire.

Jude had much more to say about the false teachers in his readers' midst. In this portion of the letter, Jude compared the religious frauds to three groups of sinful persons from the past: (1) the unbelieving Israelites of the Exodus generation, (2) wicked angels, and (3) the sinful inhabitants of the Plain of the Jordan. Each of these groups was judged by God, as the false teachers would be. Before bringing up the examples of judgment, Jude said, "You already know all this" (vs. 5) and "I want to remind you." Jude's readers were familiar with the Old Testament and other Jewish writings. But he wanted to refresh their memories and make pointed comparisons. In later parts of the letter, Jude followed the same strategy.

For his first example of judgment, Jude noted that the Lord first rescued the Israelites from Egypt (see Exod. 12). Then, later, He caused an entire generation of His chosen people to perish in the wilderness as a consequence of their refusal to believe (see Num. 12—14). In this verse, some Greek manuscripts read "Jesus," instead of "the Lord." This would imply that Jesus directly acted in the early history of Israel as a nation. In any case, long before Jude's time, God delivered the Israelites from their Egyptian taskmasters. Next, the chosen people crossed the Sinai peninsula to a point near the promised land. Then Moses sent out 12 men to explore Canaan.

Afterward, the spies reported that the region was a rich land well worth having. But the majority of the spies advised against an attempt at conquest because the people who lived there were strong. Hearing this, the Israelites became afraid and would not believe that God would deliver the Canaanites into their hands. For their doubt and disobedience, God sentenced the entire nation to 40 years of wandering in the wilderness. During that time, virtually the whole of a generation died. Like the Exodus generation of Israelites, the false teachers in Jude's time did not have faith. Also, like the disbelieving Israelites, the teachers would be judged.

Jude's second example of judgment concerned fallen angels, who refused to operate within the limits of their prescribed authority. Instead, they went outside the bounds of their proper places. For this act of rebellion, the Lord keeps them securely chained in prisons of utter darkness. They remain locked up until the great day of final judgment, when they will be eternally condemned (vs. 6). The false teachers, like the angels, would be judged. One important, unanswered question is the following: In what sense are evil angels kept in darkness and bound with chains? The Bible clearly describes demons as active in human affairs. Therefore, they must have some freedom. Perhaps the binding refers to divine limitations upon their authority and their freedom, or maybe the binding involves only some demons.

For Jude's third example of judgment, he noted that Sodom, Gomorrah, and the neighboring towns indulged in "sexual immorality" (vs. 7) and every kind of heinous "perversion." The account of this episode is told in Genesis 18:16—19:29. In Abraham's time, the five cities in the Plain of the Jordan were filled with wicked, debased people. The men of Sodom, for example, were violent homosexuals. Not even ten righteous people could be found in Sodom, so God destroyed the cities of the plain (with one exception). Like the people from the cities of the plain, the false teachers were immoral and perverse. The people from the cities of the plain—as a result of being destroyed by burning sulfur from the sky—became a example of the eternal fire of God's judgment that awaits all who rebel against Him. Jude regarded the spiritual charlatans of his day as being in line for the same kind of everlasting condemnation.

II. A CALL TO FAITHFULNESS: JUDE 19-21, 24-25

A. The Divisiveness Caused by the Apostates: vs. 19

These are the men who divide you, who follow mere natural instincts and do not have the Spirit.

Jude called the false teachers wretched "dreamers" (Jude 8) because they claimed to have inspired dreams and visions. This became the basis for them flaunting all forms of authority, whether civil or spiritual, and living immorally. They feared neither God nor people and even reviled "celestial beings." To illustrate the danger of doing the latter, Jude referred to a case involving Satan, the leader of the demons. While disputing with the devil over the body of Moses, the archangel Michael refrained from rebuking Satan, leaving that up to God. Verse 9 is thought to refer to a story in *The Assumption of Moses,* a Jewish writing that no longer exists. The Old Testament does not record Michael's dispute with Satan over the body of Moses.

The religious frauds not only were self-deluded and pretentious but also boorish, especially as they spoke "abusively against whatever they [did] not understand" (Jude 10). Put another way, their unregenerate state prevented them from comprehending eternal truths, especially those related to the things of the Spirit. Jude compared the false teachers to "unreasoning animals" who operated by impulse and instinct. Despite their confidence about the things they asserted, the frauds had been corrupted in their own thinking. Consequently, their baseless and senseless actions would bring about their demise.

Verse 11 says concerning the spiritual charlatans, "Woe to them!" This cry was a typical prophetic warning of divine judgment on sinners. Sooner or later, the false teachers would get their just desserts. This truth is illustrated by the brief comparisons Jude made between the religious frauds and three Old Testament villains—Cain, Balaam, and Korah. Verse 12 reveals that the false teachers were shameless, selfish, and filthy minded. Jude described the barren deeds of the apostates as "clouds without rain" that were blown along by the wind but never brought any water to the arid land.

The charlatans were also like trees at harvest time with either withered "fruit" or no fruit at all. Though the apostates promised much, their lives were spiritually empty and only fit for uprooting, thus being "twice dead." The "shame" (vs. 13) of the false teachers churned up like foam produced from the "wild waves of the sea." Expressed differently, the promises of the frauds brought chaos and disgrace. Their aimless and untrustworthy lives were comparable to "wandering stars" that brightly appeared for a moment but proved unreliable for charting a course. The everlasting "blackest darkness" associated with hell was their eternal end.

The frauds were noted for their constant murmuring and complaining and for doing whatever their "evil desires" (vs. 16) dictated. Such arrogance also manifested itself in speech characterized by boasting. Moreover, they were brash enough to flatter people to gain an "advantage." The godly, in contrast, seek to praise God and encourage His people. The righteous also shun evil desires and reach out to others in need. Thus, rather than exploiting and manipulating people, believers make great sacrifices to proclaim the truth so that the lost might be saved.

Numerous apostolic warnings appear in Scripture that, in coming generations, the church will be attacked by spiritual frauds. For instance, Paul referred to them as "savage wolves" (Acts 20:29); and Peter called them "false prophets" (2 Pet. 2:1) who taught "destructive heresies." Jude urged his readers to "remember" (Jude 17) these and other declarations made by "the apostles of our Lord Jesus Christ." They specifically revealed that, in the era spanning the first and second comings of the Messiah, "scoffers" (vs. 18) will arise who will follow after "their own ungodly desires."

The impious will belittle inspired revelation, flaunt divine authority, and indulge themselves in unrestrained immorality. Jude wanted his readers to know that the false teachers had infiltrated their ranks and were dividing their congregations. The apostates had a worldly-minded disposition, which prompted them to "follow mere natural instincts." In brief, they took their cues from Satan, not God. Additionally, the frauds were unregenerate, for they did not have "the Spirit" (vs. 19) indwelling them.

B. The Importance of Devotion to God: vss. 20-21

But you, dear friends, build yourselves up in your most holy faith and pray in the Holy Spirit. Keep yourselves in God's love as you wait for the mercy of our Lord Jesus Christ to bring you to eternal life.

In response to the threat posed by the spiritual frauds, Christians were to continually build their lives on the bedrock of their "most holy faith" (Jude 20). They were also to keep praying "in the Holy Spirit." The idea is that believers can only combat the false teachers in the power of the Spirit and the true teaching of God's Word. Furthermore, Jude urged his readers to keep themselves grounded "in God's love" (vs. 21). With the love of the Father as the anchor of their souls, believers could remain united in their faith and committed to one another. They were also to wait eagerly for "the mercy of our Lord Jesus Christ." This is a reference to the Savior's return, at which time believers will be resurrected, resulting in their full and final reception of "eternal life."

C. The Expression of Praise to God: vss. 24-25

To him who is able to keep you from falling and to present you before his glorious presence without fault and with great joy—to the only God our Savior be glory, majesty, power and authority, through Jesus Christ our Lord, before all ages, now and forevermore! Amen.

Among Jude's readers were those "who doubt" (Jude 22). This possibly refers to people who were genuinely wavering in their faith. These sincere doubters deserved mercy from Jesus' followers. A second group appears to be those who were further entrenched in unbelief. Jude urged his readers to make every effort to "show mercy" (vs. 23) to them "with fear." God was able to make the witness of believers so persuasive that unbelievers could be snatched out of "the fire" of judgment. A third group were the apostates, whose lives, like "clothing," were "stained," or defiled, by moral filth. Believers, while abhorring the depravity of the false teachers, were to show mercy on them. The adage of "hating the sin but loving the sinner" seems applicable here.

Jude capped his letter with one of the Bible's most glorious doxologies (passages of praise). While Jude recognized that the danger posed by the religious frauds was severe, he was not pessimistic. If it were up to his readers alone to combat the charlatans, they would have been in real trouble. But they were not alone. God would help them, specifically by preventing them from spiritually stumbling. The Lord would also bring the readers of Jude's epistle (along with all believers) into His "glorious presence" (vs. 24). Indeed, they would stand before Him rejoicing and without blemish.

The false teachers wanted to see Jude's readers soiled with sin, as they themselves were. But the recipients of Jude's epistle had already been washed clean of sin by trusting in Christ. They could keep from sinning if they remained faithful and dependent on the Lord. Like those first-century believers, we too are presented with situations in which sinning seems the easiest thing to do. But we don't have to give in to that temptation. We can turn to God in prayer and say, "No, I just won't do it; I won't disobey the Lord, whom I love." The God who safeguards us and welcomes us into His presence is worthy of every honor we can give—or even think of. To the Father, our Savior, through the Son, our Lord, belongs all "glory, majesty, power and authority" (vs. 25).

This was true in the past (before all time), it is just as true now (in the present), and it will remain true for all eternity (beyond all time). In Jewish thought, history could be divided into two ages, often called "the present age" and "the age to come." Jews believed that the Messiah would usher in the age to come. Christians, who know Jesus as the Messiah, recognize that the age to come has already broken in on the present age. But the final age hasn't entirely come. That awaits the second coming of Christ. Jude believed that, in a sense, he was living in the last times, when scoffers would arise (see vs. 18).

Discussion Questions

1. What were some of the characteristics of the false teaching Jude warned about?
2. How did Jude graphically describe the false teachers?
3. What vices did Jude associate with the false teachers?
4. What actions did Jude recommend for believers to guard against false teaching?
5. How might we someday have to contend for the faith?

Contemporary Application

Jude urged his fellow believers in Christ to grow in their spiritual maturity; but, at the same time, he knew they would have to contend with the evil that had crept into the churches. Despite the attempts of ungodly people to lead believers into immorality, apostasy, and division, Jude reminded the faithful that God will keep them from falling, especially as they continuously build up their faith in Christ.

The same types of temptations and problems that emerged in the churches in the first century still persist. That is why it is imperative that we obey Jude's exhortations, which include praying in the Holy Spirit, remaining in God's love, and showing mercy to others.

Here we see that a strong faith is an active faith. Yet only Christ can give us the power to truly pray, love, and be compassionate and wise in our dealings with others. When we feel tempted to submit to fleshly desires, when we hear heretical teachings about Christ, or when we encounter conflict within the church, then we must immediately turn to Jesus for strength, wisdom, and encouragement.

It is also important that we build up one another in the Lord. No one should live in complete isolation from others. Since God intended for us to live in community, we need each other. And we need to help each other, especially as we strive together to be the people Christ wants us to be.

Visible to God

Scripture

Background Scripture: *1 Thessalonians 1*
Scripture Lesson: *1 Thessalonians 1*
Key Verse: *You welcomed the message with the joy given by the Holy Spirit.* 1 Thessalonians 1:6.
Scripture Lesson for Children: *Acts 17:1-9; 1 Thessalonians 1:8-10*
Key Verse for Children: *You became a model to all the believers.* 1 Thessalonians 1:7.

Lesson Aim

To learn to be a model of faith for others to imitate.

Lesson Setting

Time: *About A.D. 51*
Place: *Written from Corinth to the church in Thessalonica*

Lesson Outline

Visible to God

  I. Paul's Greeting: 1 Thessalonians 1:1
  II. Paul's Thanksgiving: 1 Thessalonians 1:2-6
      A. *Faith, Love, and Hope: vss. 2-3*
      B. *Gospel Power: vss. 4-6*
  III. Paul's Commendation: 1 Thessalonians 1:7-10
      A. *Spreading Faith: vss. 7-9*
      B. *Anticipation: vs. 10*

Introduction for Adults

Topic: *Witness in Daily Life*

Evangelist D. L. Moody said that there are three kinds of faith in Christ: 1) struggling faith, like a person in deep water desperately swimming; 2) clinging faith, like a person hanging to the side of a boat; and, 3) resting faith, like a person safely within the boat (and able to reach out with a hand to help someone else get in).

The Thessalonians had the third kind of faith. They were not only able to survive despite persecution, but the witness of their daily lives was also a shining example to other Christians throughout the region. They were even an encouragement to Paul during his own distress and persecution. By resting in God's hands and placing their faith in Him, the Thessalonians were able to "reach out their hands" (so to speak) to others, giving them hope, encouragement, and faith.

Introduction for Youth

Topic: *Seeing Is Believing*

What messages do we send to others about the Christian faith? If all their knowledge and understanding depended on what they observed in our lives, what would they know, believe, and do?

From Paul's first letter to the Thessalonians we learn that the message concerns repentance and faith. We turn from our sins and give ourselves in faith to Jesus. But we also learn that we need one another. Being a Christian links us intimately with our fellow believers.

The message is all about faith, but it is also about love, joy, and endurance through the power of the Spirit. Even the great pioneering apostle of our faith needed to know that the Thessalonians loved him. He wanted to be sure of their love as well as their faith. Similarly, when we make a faith commitment to the Lord Jesus, we make a love commitment to one another. When the lost see the latter at work in our lives, it provides a powerful incentive for them to believe in Christ for salvation.

Concepts for Children

Topic: *Be an Example to Others*

1. What Paul said about Jesus encouraged people to put their faith in Him.
2. There were some, however, who did not like what Paul was saying about Jesus.
3. Sometime later, Paul wrote a letter to believers living in a city called Thessalonica.
4. The Thessalonians not only put their faith in Jesus, but also helped others do so, too.
5. The Lord Jesus is pleased when He finds us encouraging others to believe in Him for eternal life.

Lesson Commentary

I. PAUL'S GREETING: 1 THESSALONIANS 1:1

Paul, Silas and Timothy, to the church of the Thessalonians in God the Father and the Lord Jesus Christ: Grace and peace to you.

First and Second Thessalonians speak to the faith, love, and hope of believers in the context of anticipating the Savior's return. But these epistles are not primarily speculative. Rather, they reveal strong bonds of concern and love in God's family. The Thessalonian letters show not only the hope of living eternally with the Messiah but also the need for godly living in the meantime. We see the pain, hard work, and rejoicing that come with being a follower of the Lord Jesus.

Paul's second missionary journey (Acts 15:39—18:22; between A.D. 49–52) forms the initial historical backdrop for his epistles to the Thessalonians. While the apostle is the primary author for both letters, he may, however, have had some help from Silas and Timothy, two of his missionary associates. Paul had chosen Silas to be his partner after a dispute with his previous coworker, Barnabas (Acts 15:36-40). Paul had recruited the youthful Timothy early on in the journey, at Lystra (16:1-3).

In both letters all three men are listed in the opening salutation (1 Thess. 1:1; 2 Thess. 1:1). Generally, throughout these epistles Paul used the plural "we," including Silas and Timothy with him. But sometimes he used "I," and twice he interjected his name without theirs. The evidence for the apostle's authorship lies not only in the letters themselves but also in the writings of early church leaders. Several Christian writers in the years following Paul's death cited him as the author of the Thessalonian letters. By the second century A.D., the epistles were universally accepted as the apostle's own.

During Paul's second missionary journey, he and his associates gradually worked their way down the eastern coast of what is now Greece. First, they did evangelistic work in Philippi. Then the party moved on to Thessalonica (17:1-9). The city was located on the Thermaikos Gulf below the Hortiates mountains on the northwest corner of the Aegean Sea. Thessalonica was founded in 315 B.C. by Cassander, the king of Macedonia. Cassander named the city in honor of his wife, Thessalonike, the daughter of King Philip II of Macedon and step-sister of Alexander the Great. In 146 B.C., the Romans made Thessalonica the capital of the province of Macedonia and the seat of Roman administration.

As a free city of the empire, Thessalonica enjoyed a number of commercial and civic privileges. This included the right to mint its own coinage and the absence of a Roman garrison within its walls. The city was near the Egnatian Way, the major trade route joining Rome and the eastern portions of the empire. This increased Thessalonica's stature as a major hub of communication and mercantile exchange. This vibrant seaport was also the most populous and cosmopolitan town in Macedonia.

Thessalonica not only was a prosperous commercial center, but also the capital of one of the four divisions of Macedonia. Also, Thessalonica had an active Jewish community, giving Paul his first occasions for ministry in the city. He preached for three sabbaths in the local synagogue. He told the local Jews that the crucified Jesus of Nazareth was the promised Messiah. Some Jews believed, but a larger number of "God-fearing Greeks" (vs. 4)—Gentiles who worshiped in the synagogue—became Christians. Also, some prominent women of the city joined the church.

Some of the unbelieving Jews raised a ruckus, forcing Paul to leave Thessalonica. After visits to Berea and Athens, he went on to Corinth, where he stayed for about a year and a half. Meanwhile, the new believers in Thessalonica continued to be harassed by unbelieving Jews. These Jewish troublemakers created doubt about Paul's authority and integrity, pointing to his sudden departure and long absence. His message was a delusion, they claimed, and they insinuated that he was only in the ministry for the money. These conditions were aggravated by questions that arose among the believers about events of the end times. Also, some Thessalonians were not living on a consistently high moral plane. All in all, it was a persecuted, somewhat shaky church in Thessalonica to which Paul wrote these letters.

By matching up known historical facts and clues within the epistles, many Bible scholars have concluded that Paul wrote the Thessalonian letters a few months apart in A.D. 50 or 51. When the apostle wrote 1 Thessalonians, several months had passed since he had seen the new believers in Thessalonica. At the time, he was living and ministering in Corinth. As was just noted, the recipients of the letter were not a perfect church; nor did the congregation hold any property. The church also did not have a highly trained professional staff. However, the Thessalonian believers possessed sterling spiritual resources. As Paul said, they were "in God the Father and the Lord Jesus Christ" (1:1).

How had the Thessalonians reached that amazing position? It was by trusting in Redeemer for salvation. Paul had persuaded the Thessalonians that Jesus is the Messiah (Acts 17:3-4). They had "welcomed the message" (1 Thess. 1:6) the apostle proclaimed and had "turned to God" (vs. 9) from their sinful ways. To these richly endowed people, Paul extended a wish of grace and peace (vs. 1). This was Paul's typical salutation. Some scholars think that by using those words he combined the Greek (grace) and Hebrew (peace) greetings commonly used in his day.

II. PAUL'S THANKSGIVING: 1 THESSALONIANS 1:2-6

A. Faith, Love, and Hope: vss. 2-3

We always thank God for all of you, mentioning you in our prayers. We continually remember before our God and Father your work produced by faith, your labor prompted by love, and your endurance inspired by hope in our Lord Jesus Christ.

The missionary team led by Paul gave continual thanks to God for the new converts in Thessalonica. The apostle and his colleagues also prayed for their fellow believers on a regular basis (1 Thess. 1:2). Unlike prayer sessions in many churches today, Paul did not waste time spouting vague generalities to the Lord. As the three evangelists prayed to God the Father, they recalled the work resulting from the faith of the Thessalonians, the deeds motivated by their love, and the perseverance stemming from their hope in the return of the Lord Jesus Christ (vs. 3). This triad of virtues was hammered out on the anvil of persecution and sustained by the believers' unshakable confidence that the Savior would vindicate their faith at His second coming (see 2 Thess. 1:3-10).

B. Gospel Power: vss. 4-6

For we know, brothers loved by God, that he has chosen you, because our gospel came to you not simply with words, but also with power, with the Holy Spirit and with deep conviction. You know how we lived among you for your sake. You became imitators of us and of the Lord; in spite of severe suffering, you welcomed the message with the joy given by the Holy Spirit.

The missionary team affectionately referred to their readers as their dear Christian friends. The Thessalonians learned that God loved them and chose them to be His own people (1 Thess. 1:4). Before God made the world, He decided that they would be holy and without fault in His eyes (Eph. 1:4). The Father also decided in advance to adopt them into His own family (vs. 5).

God used the proclamation of the Gospel to bring about the conversion of Paul's readers (1 Thess. 1:5), who were predominately Gentile. The Greeks were accustomed to traveling teachers who presented clever philosophies that they could take or leave. But the evangelists had not brought another academic theory, nor had they given a classroom lecture. Instead, the team had preached in Thessalonica with divine power, as seen in the Thessalonians' redemption from spiritual bondage. The Holy Spirit worked through the proclamation of the Good News to convict them about their sin, about God's righteousness, and about the coming judgment (John 16:8). The Spirit also gave them full assurance that the message they heard was true.

Moreover, the believers in Thessalonica could tell by the virtuous way in which Paul, Silas, and Timothy lived that they were true representatives of God (1 Thess. 1:5). The example set by Paul as an apostle was especially pivotal. Our English word *apostle* comes from the Greek noun *apostolos*, which means "messenger," "envoy," or "ambassador." The latter comes from a verb meaning "to send." Thus, the noun refers to a person who is sent on behalf of another.

In the New Testament, "apostle" is used mainly to refer to the group of leaders within the early church who had seen the risen Messiah and were specially commissioned by Him to proclaim His saving truth to others (Acts 1:21-22). Jesus originally gave the title to His closest followers, the Twelve (Luke 6:13). Then, after His resurrection, the term was applied to a wider circle of authoritative preachers and witnesses of the resurrected Lord (Acts 14:4, 14). Paul's claim to be an apostle was questioned by others. However, he based his apostleship on the direct call of the exalted Lord, for Jesus had appeared to Paul while the latter was traveling on the road to Damascus (9:1-9).

Given the testimony of Paul and his associates to the Thessalonians concerning the Gospel, it's no surprise that they welcomed the truth. This remained the case even in the midst of severe suffering. In this way, they followed the example of the Lord Jesus and His messengers (1 Thess. 1:6). Acts 17:5-9 tells us one way in which the Thessalonian believers endured hardship. Some local Jewish leaders stirred up a mob, which dragged some of the converts before the city officials. The Christians were soon released, but undoubtedly the attacks did not end at that point.

Opposition did not quench the Thessalonians' faith. Despite the heavy price they paid, they welcomed the Gospel with joy. That is not how things happen naturally. How could they do that? Their joy was "given by the Holy Spirit" (1 Thess. 1:6). Joy is part of the fruit of the Spirit (Gal. 5:22). One distinctive work of the Spirit is that He enables believers to rejoice in spite of—or even because of—their hardships. This is a significant New Testament theme (John 16:22; Rom. 5:3-5; 1 Pet. 4:13).

III. PAUL'S COMMENDATION: 1 THESSALONIANS 1:7-10

A. Spreading Faith: vss. 7-9

And so you became a model to all the believers in Macedonia and Achaia. The Lord's message rang out from you not only in Macedonia and Achaia—your faith in God has become known everywhere. Therefore we do not need to say anything about it, for they themselves report what kind of reception you gave us. They tell how you turned to God from idols to serve the living and true God.

We can imagine the evangelists, while at Corinth (in the Roman province of Achaia), telling their fellow believers about the new converts at Thessalonica (in the Roman province of Macedonia). As a result of the second group's enduring faith, despite the presence of persecution, they became an example for all the Lord's followers throughout Greece (1 Thess. 1:7). Indeed, because of the Thessalonian believers, the good news about the Messiah had echoed forth, like the carillon of a mighty cathedral, to people in many outlying regions. Their testimony was no doubt aided by the fact that their city stood in a strategic geographic position.

Wherever the missionaries ventured, they met people who had heard about the Thessalonians' faith in God (vs. 8). In turn, this made it unnecessary for the evangelists to elaborate any further about the commitment of their dear friends to the Savior and His followers. It seemed as if people everywhere kept talking about the warm manner in which the Thessalonians had welcomed Paul, Silas, and Timothy. Others were also impressed with the new converts' firm decision to abandon their idols and serve the living and true God (vs. 9).

In Paul's day, people throughout the Roman Empire worshiped various deities. Each city had its own favorite god or goddess and set aside festival times, which resembled a Mardi Gras. Astrologers were popular, as they are today, claiming to predict the future according to the stars. Deification of the Roman emperor was being pushed. Mystery cults (so-called because of their secret rites) flourished. For example, the worship of Mithras, popular with Roman soldiers, took place in a cave around a statue of Mithras killing a bull. New members studied the rites, were baptized, and ate a sacred meal to commemorate a meal Mithras ate with the sun god before ascending to heaven. Also popular in Paul's time was the worship of Isis, an Egyptian goddess said to reign over heaven, and Osiris, her husband and brother, whom she had raised from the dead. Archaeological digs reveal the likely remains of many sites of pagan worship.

In responding to the Good News, the Thessalonians had indicated more than an outward allegiance. They had enlisted to serve the one true God. Such an act is called repentance. Faith and repentance go hand in hand; one cannot claim valid faith if there is not a corresponding change in lifestyle. True repentance means turning away from one thing to follow another. Intellectually, it means we change our mind and decide to go in the opposite direction. It is a complete reversal in life.

B. Anticipation: vs. 10

And to wait for his Son from heaven, whom he raised from the dead—Jesus, who rescues us from the coming wrath.

The missionaries described both the beginning of Christian faith—turning from idols to God—and its outworking: waiting for the return of the Savior (1 Thess. 1:10). Waiting is not to be confused with idleness, but rather speaks to the essence of the Christian's life direction. As believers serve (activity), they also wait. This is not a contradiction, as it may seem. The certainty of Jesus' coming provides stability and purpose. It also keeps people from wandering into misguided ventures and aspirations.

The evangelists taught that the true God is not an image carved of stone; He made himself visible in the person of the Messiah, who came from heaven to earth to rescue us from the coming wrath. To certify His deity—that He truly came from heaven—Jesus conquered death and rose again. Those who trust in Him can be assured that He is coming back and that they will be spared God's judgment in the future. "The coming wrath," of course, is going to be exercised by God because of the sin and rebellion against His truth and against His Son that have characterized human history. Jesus Himself spoke of God's wrath resting on those who do not believe Him (John 3:36).

Discussion Questions

1. Why is it encouraging to learn that believers belong to "God the Father and the Lord Jesus Christ" (1 Thess. 1:1)?

2. What are some ways that we, as believers, can give thanks to God for one another?

3. Why are the Christian virtues of love and hope pivotal to our labor done in the name of Christ?

4. How might the presence of suffering affect our proclamation of the Gospel to others?

5. In what tangible ways do others see our service to the "living and true God" (vs. 9)?

Contemporary Application

Just as the Thessalonians trusted and obeyed God, so should your students. Their obedience to Him should impact every area of their lives—from home to school to work. They do the will of God when they give their best effort in their daily routines and face difficult circumstances with an attitude of hope. They are also obedient to His will when they exercise caution about the things they read, watch, and hear.

The Lord wants saved adults to share their faith with others. Some might do it in a large-group setting, while others might witness one-on-one. It's also God's will that your students spend time with Him in prayer. While some prefer to do it in the morning, others might opt to pray at night. Regardless of how they carry out God's will for their lives, their actions should be undergirded by faith. In fact, without faith, they cannot truly please the Lord (Heb. 1:6).

The readiness of the class members to do God's will can lead them down unexpected paths. For instance, the Lord might want them to tell others about Jesus, even when the students are uncertain what the response will be; or the class members could be asked to serve God in a way that is new to them, perhaps singing in the choir or leading a church group.

Adults who wholeheartedly trust God are convinced that He knows what's best for them. They are willing to wait for His timing when it comes to enjoying the blessings of faith. They realize that some of these come in this life, but most are received in eternity.

Your students might continue to struggle with doubts even after they're seasoned in their faith. Instead of allowing uncertainty to control them, they should examine it in the light of what Scripture teaches. The truth of God's Word can calm them when they're feeling anxious about something. The faith of adults in the Lord can also be strengthened by reflecting on their past experiences and those of other believers. God's faithfulness to the class members and others in the past can encourage them when they're going through difficult times, whether in the present or the future.

Pleasing to God

Scripture

Background Scripture: *1 Thessalonians 2*
Scripture Lesson: *1 Thessalonians 2:1-12*
Key Verse: *We speak as men approved by God to be entrusted with the gospel. We are not trying to please men but God, who tests our hearts.* 1 Thessalonians 2:4.
Scripture Lesson for Children: *Acts 17:10-14; 1 Thessalonians 2:1-4*
Key Verse for Children: *We speak . . . not trying to please men but God, who tests our hearts.* 1 Thessalonians 2:4.

Lesson Aim

To emphasize the importance of being a full-time follower of Jesus, no matter how hard it may be.

Lesson Setting

Time: *About A.D. 51*
Place: *Written from Corinth to the church in Thessalonica*

Lesson Outline

Pleasing to God

I. The Motives of the Missionaries: 1 Thessalonians 2:1-4
   A. *Proclaiming the Gospel Despite Opposition: vss. 1-2*
   B. *Seeking to Please God: vss. 3-4*

II. The Conduct of the Missionaries: 1 Thessalonians 2:5-12
   A. *Honesty and Integrity: vss. 5-6*
   B. *Compassion and Care: vss. 7-8*
   C. *Dedication and Devotion: vss. 9-10*
   D. *God-Honoring Priorities: vss. 11-12*

Introduction for Adults

Topic: *Motives for Commitment*

Philip Yancey tells about a monk who once bragged about his dietary discipline. His spiritual director replied, "Don't tell me, my child, that you've spent 30 years without eating meat. But tell me the truth: How many days have you spent without speaking ill of your brother? Without judging your neighbor? Without letting useless words pass your lips?"

The way saved adults conduct their lives before others demonstrates the underlying motives for their walk with Christ. While a half-committed follower might bear little discomfort, a full-time follower knows the sacrifices of a disciplined Christian life. This week's lesson can be used to encourage class members in the latter direction.

Introduction for Youth

Topic: *Setting Good Goals*

Many high school students take a course in Study Skills and acquire the tools for active learning. One of those tools is time management. As part of the course, students learn to prioritize their time and establish good goals for themselves.

For instance, they must decide between wise and unwise activities. Wise use of time aids in production, while unwise use of time is wasted. Students learn to figure out which tasks have to be accomplished and which don't really matter. Time is budgeted so that they learn to see whether an assignment is due tomorrow, next week, or next month.

Jesus called His followers to get their priorities straight. Certain decisions, such as accepting His call to discipleship, were the best and wisest choices. Everything else was less important from an eternal perspective.

Concepts for Children

Topic: *Living a Pleasing Life*

1. When Paul and his friends preached the Gospel in Berea, many believed their message about Jesus.
2. Some people living in Thessalonica were mean to Paul and his friends in Berea and forced them to leave the city.
3. Even though Paul and his friends were mistreated, they did not stop telling people about Jesus.
4. Paul wanted people to know that he and his friends were honest and truthful in what they said about Jesus.
5. We honor God when we try to live for Him, no matter how hard it might feel at times.

Lesson Commentary

I. THE MOTIVES OF THE MISSIONARIES: 1 THESSALONIANS 2:1-4

A. Proclaiming the Gospel Despite Opposition: vss. 1-2

You know, brothers, that our visit to you was not a failure. We had previously suffered and been insulted in Philippi, as you know, but with the help of our God we dared to tell you his gospel in spite of strong opposition.

After commending the Thessalonian believers for their faith, love, and hope as well as for their warm response to the Gospel, Paul recalled how he and his associates had ministered to them. Evidently, his detractors claimed that his team did not really care about the Thessalonians and that their ministry had been lackluster. Allegedly, it was self-centeredness and greed that originally brought the apostle and his peers to Thessalonica. Paul disputed such charges by appealing to the true motives he and his coworkers had for serving among the Thessalonians. Also, he described the positive, long-lasting results of the missionary endeavor. In short, he was a legitimate apostle—one whom God had called. Moreover, it was the Lord who empowered him and his colleagues to proclaim the truth of the Gospel.

Paul summed up the work of his associates in Thessalonica as "not a failure" (1 Thess. 2:1). The Greek text is more literally translated "has not become empty." The idea is that the Lord enabled the declaration of the truth to be purposeful and beneficial. Why did Paul need to remind the Thessalonians about the success of his ministry? Perhaps they were growing insecure or shaky in their faith. As a minority in a pagan city, they worried about their future and about the extent of the suffering they were being called to endure.

The evangelistic outreach had inspired a harsh response—first in Philippi and then in Thessalonica. Paul had left both cities because of it. "Suffered" (vs. 2) renders a term that means to undergo hardship, while "insulted" translates a word that denotes the presence of outrageous, degrading treatment. The Thessalonians were aware of these hardships and the way in which the Lord helped His emissaries. Indeed, despite the presence of intense hostility and resistance from the unsaved, the missionaries had the courage to declare the Good News to the Thessalonians.

Outwardly, it appeared as if the enemies of the Gospel had won a victory. But looking back, the apostle declared victory instead. He had made a daring move in bringing the Gospel to Thessalonica in the first place, and he was not about to surrender now. Declaring victory was a tremendous morale booster. Too often, it seems, believers today take a superficial look around and wonder whether Jesus really is Lord. They see so much suffering and hardship. Is the Gospel really God's power, or is the enemy of the Gospel winning? We need to be reminded that in spite of opposition and human weakness, the church is not a failure and the Gospel has not been stripped of its life-changing power.

B. Seeking to Please God: vss. 3-4

For the appeal we make does not spring from error or impure motives, nor are we trying to trick you. On the contrary, we speak as men approved by God to be entrusted with the gospel. We are not trying to please men but God, who tests our hearts.

The missionaries not only preached in spite of opposition, but also they preached the truth openly with no hidden agendas (1 Thess. 2:3). Why did Paul raise this issue? No doubt because of what was being said about he and his associates by various detractors. The apostle answered these critics and distanced himself from the typical wandering philosophers who fed on people's offerings and exploited them with delusions and trickery. It's as if he boldly declared, "We're not one of them!"

By reading between the lines, we can discover what the charges were against the missionaries, especially Paul: erroneous teaching, sexual impurity, and deceit (vs. 3); a love of public acclaim (vss. 4, 6a); and flattery, hypocrisy, and greed (vs. 5). These were serious allegations that deeply troubled the apostle; and understandably, he emphatically denied them. With respect to the charge of "error" (vs. 3), Paul defended the accuracy of his preaching. What he and his coworkers taught centered on Jesus' death and resurrection, and this assertion could be verified. Paul stoutly defended his own encounter with the risen Lord on the Damascus road. The apostle's preaching was not just another religious theory but was anchored in historical events.

"Impure motives" refers to an accusation that Paul had engaged in sexual immorality. Of course, he had not. In fact, the apostle's letters are filled with commands to be sexually pure. One of the major distinctions between Christianity and the pagan religions of the day was that Christianity promoted sexual morality. Furthermore, Paul, as Jesus' ambassador, shunned all forms of subterfuge or trickery. In fact, God had been pleased to entrust the apostle with the Good News.

Paul, having first been redeemed by an appearance of Jesus Himself, was then appointed to take the Gospel to the world. The idea behind "approved" (vs. 4) and "entrusted" is that of passing a series of tests. The apostle had measured up, so to speak, to the highest standards imaginable. Therefore, the nature of his calling and the essence of the Gospel precluded the messenger's use of false, ungodly methods. Because God continued to test Paul, his motivation was to please the Lord, not his hearers. God's test pierced the apostle to the inner being, his heart. Paul was not tested by how many converts he made or by how much money he raised. The integrity of his heart was on the line. These claims also held true for his coworkers.

II. THE CONDUCT OF THE MISSIONARIES: 1 THESSALONIANS 2:5-12

A. Honesty and Integrity: vss. 5-6

You know we never used flattery, nor did we put on a mask to cover up greed—God is our witness. We were not looking for praise from men, not from you or anyone else. As apostles of Christ we could have been a burden to you.

Paul could call up the missionary record of deeds done. He reminded his readers that Jesus' true ambassadors had never puffed them up with "flattery" (1 Thess. 2:5). Likewise, the Lord's emissaries were not phonies. For instance, the evangelists had not used subterfuge to appear to be pious and holy for the sake of bilking others out of their money. The apostle was so sure of this that he called God to be his "witness."

Despite the charge made by detractors, the missionaries did not proclaim the Gospel in order to obtain "praise" (vs. 6) from any person. Indeed, if they had wanted to garner the applause of others, the evangelists would not have preached a message that stoked the fires of persecution. Gaining the public's esteem was the furthest thing from the minds of the missionaries. In a word, both their message and their methods passed the test. Those in public ministries today, as well as believers generally, need to appreciate how much the world looks for purity and integrity. Unfortunately, religious phonies—many of them inspired by greed—plague the church. That's why the church must insist on a ministry that is above reproach.

Paul's thoughts of his time in Thessalonica brought back the most intimate memories, not just of preaching and of opposition, but also of tenderness and of caring. He could have used his apostleship as a means of sponging off the believers, but he had refused to be a "burden" to them. Expressed differently, he and his associates never asserted the prerogatives of their appointment as missionaries to impose themselves upon new converts. Instead of operating as doctrinaire teachers, the evangelists presented themselves as tender care-givers.

B. Compassion and Care: vss. 7-8

But we were gentle among you, like a mother caring for her little children. We loved you so much that we were delighted to share with you not only the gospel of God but our lives as well, because you had become so dear to us.

Paul never backed off from his divine commission; he strongly defended his apostleship when it was necessary (1 Thess. 2:4). Even so, he viewed himself to be operating in an entirely different role toward believers. They needed not only a divine authentication of the message and the messenger but also a loving reminder of where they stood with him. This is evident in Paul's remarks found in verse 7. The gentleness of a mother with her little children evokes the truest image of spiritual leadership and influence. Some scholars go even further and say that the apostle really had in mind a nursing mother. Regardless of whether this is so, the main point is clear: Paul and his colleagues were not dictators but gentle encouragers among the Thessalonians.

The affection of the missionaries for these new converts was heightened when Paul recalled how he and his associates had given the Thessalonians not only words ("the gospel of God," vs. 8), but also their very lives. The ambassadors for Christ had proved their love by their deeds. Even in a relatively short span of time, the hearts of the evangelists and the new converts had been melded together as one. The Thessalonians were dear to their spiritual parents because the latter had become vulnerable and transparent before them.

C. Dedication and Devotion: vss. 9-10

Surely you remember, brothers, our toil and hardship; we worked night and day in order not to be a burden to anyone while we preached the gospel of God to you. You are witnesses, and so is God, of how holy, righteous and blameless we were among you who believed.

When someone shares his or her life with another person, this sharing includes not merely outward signs of caring, but in addition the kind of care that is costly and often painful. For Paul and his associates, this meant "toil and hardship" (1 Thess. 2:9). Their jobs wore them down; it wasn't a lark. Why did the missionaries work so hard "night and day"? Why didn't they relax in comfort and live off the gifts of church members instead of supporting themselves with a trade? It's because the evangelists refused to be a burden on anyone while they preached.

In some 10 or 11 years, Paul established churches in four provinces of the Roman Empire: Galatia, Asia, Macedonia, and Achaia. Part of the time he was working at a secular job, making tents. He was what we call a "bivocational missionary" (or "tentmaker"—in honor of Paul). In the Jewish tradition, all boys learned a trade. Not even the rabbis could earn a living by teaching the Mosaic law. Paul's tentmaking trade enabled him to authenticate the Gospel. He could not be accused of preaching for money.

The apostle labored for extended periods of time at Corinth and Ephesus, and he also worked during shorter visits, such as the one at Thessalonica. Paul worked to pay for his room and board, to help pay expenses for his traveling companions, and to give a positive example to his converts (2 Thess. 3:7-9). His work backed up his preaching, so that he might offer the Gospel "free of charge" (1 Cor. 9:18). He deliberately refused his right as an apostle to receive payment (1 Cor. 9:7-12), so that no one might suspect he was preaching only for money.

The church's witness today is strengthened by believers who find ways to meet other people's needs after putting in a full day or week on the job. This builds wholesome respect in the community and opens doors to people who suspect that ministry is carried out only by those who get paid for it. A church will be effective in its community to the extent that people who do not make their living by the Gospel present it to others free of charge.

In 1 Thessalonians 2:10, Paul reflected again on the attacks critics were making on the methods and character of himself and his colleagues. The apostle emphasized how godly they had lived while in Thessalonica. It is amazing that he could write so boldly about their behavior, calling it "holy, righteous and blameless." He reminded his readers that they had observed the conduct of the evangelists, and then he appealed to God as the ultimate witness. The Lord saw not only the missionaries' outward conduct but also the depths of their motives.

Paul's reference to holiness probably means the devoutness of the emissaries' faith and worship. They were dedicated servants of God, being sold out 100 percent to the Messiah. By "righteous," conceivably Paul meant the evangelists' behavior toward other people in the general sense of justice and fair play. They did not curry favors or expect any in return. The Lord's servants were impartial and gave the Gospel freely to all. To be "blameless" meant to give no cause for reproach. People could not call any of the missionaries a phony or hypocrite. They lived what they taught. In this bold affirmation of integrity, Paul set a high standard for the church. The evangelists did not claim to be on a spiritual pedestal, but they could look back on their visit in Thessalonica without regrets for any misconduct. Any Christian can aspire to the same standard, knowing that the validity of the Gospel can be attested by such sterling character.

D. God-Honoring Priorities: vss. 11-12

For you know that we dealt with each of you as a father deals with his own children, encouraging, comforting and urging you to live lives worthy of God, who calls you into his kingdom and glory.

Paul described how he and his colleagues had worked with the Thessalonians, comparing the evangelists to the way a father treats "his own children" (1 Thess. 2:11). Earlier, the apostle had said the missionaries had been gentle, like a mother, among the new converts (vs. 7). Verse 11 reveals that the Lord's emissaries also had assumed a father's role to persuade the Thessalonians to live in a manner that God would consider "worthy" (vs. 12). The evangelists used a variety of means, including exhortation, encouragement, and admonishment.

What was Paul's purpose as a persistent spiritual parent? It was to see his children in the faith measure up to God's expectations. It's true that they could not earn the Lord's favor by their own efforts. Moreover, the apostle did not tell his readers to clean up their lives so they would be good enough to deserve salvation. That would have been impossible. But having committed themselves to Christ, they had a new purpose for living.

Paul urged the Thessalonians to strive to please God because He had called them "into his kingdom and glory." The apostle gave his readers another slant on what it meant to turn from idols. They had lived in the kingdom of darkness, the kingdom of evil powers. Now they had a new destiny: God's kingdom. The Thessalonian believers anticipated entering the divine kingdom and glory in the future, which is part of the Christian hope. But God's kingdom is in place now, and believers are called to live as citizens of it (Rev. 1:9).

The present aspect of the divine kingdom (Col. 1:13) is God's ever-present rule, the working out of His loving and wise plan for the world. As such, it is not always apparent and unbelievers do not acknowledge it. However, one day God's kingdom will come (Matt. 6:10) in all its fullness and be evident to all (25:31-34). At that time, God's glorious power will conquer the forces of evil and unbelief.

Discussion Questions

1. What sorts of positive results could Paul and his associates point to concerning their ministry among the Thessalonians?
2. Upon what basis did the missionaries urge the residents of Thessalonica to put their faith in Christ?
3. How can we, as Jesus' followers, avoid using impure motives and methods to minister to others?
4. What would spur us on to remain faithful in our Christian service, despite the hardships we might encounter?
5. Why is it important for the unsaved to see our lives as being "holy, righteous and blameless" (1 Thess. 2:10)?

Contemporary Application

Some people think that discipleship is for super-zealous Christians, not ordinary ones. This incorrect way of thinking has led to a wishy-washy form of Christianity in the lives of countless believers. Rather than serve Him wholeheartedly, they are superficial in their devotion. They fail to realize that following Jesus is an all or nothing proposition.

Jesus never distinguished between disciples and ordinary Christians. To Him, true believers are also His disciples. They cast everything on Jesus and trust in Him for their salvation. They willingly forsake their old life of sin to experience new life in Him. They have counted the cost and determined that serving Jesus is eternally more valuable than striving for fame, wealth, and power.

Paul, Silas, and Timothy fit this description; and they wanted the same to be true for believers in Thessalonica. More generally, being a faithful follower of Jesus should be a high priority for everyone who affirms Christ as Lord. Those who do so are not disappointed with their decision, for they have found new life, hope, and purpose in the Son. They are liberated from sin and its consequences. They have the hope of eternal salvation. And their purpose in life is to worship and glorify God.

Those who choose to follow the Savior aren't sidetracked by earthly comforts, confused priorities, or divided loyalties. Instead, they are totally submitted, steadfast in their commitment, and absolute in their devotion to the Redeemer.

Sustained through Encouragement

Scripture

Background Scripture: *1 Thessalonians 3*
Scripture Lesson: *1 Thessalonians 3*
Key Verse: *Therefore, brothers, in all our distress and persecution we were encouraged about you because of your faith.*
1 Thessalonians 3:7.
Scripture Lesson for Children: *Acts 18:1-4, 18-23;
1 Thessalonians 3:6-9*
Key Verse for Children: *We were encouraged about you
because of your faith.* 1 Thessalonians 3:7.

Lesson Aim

To consider how to be encouragers to others.

Lesson Setting

Time: *About A.D. 51*
Place: *Written from Corinth to the church in Thessalonica*

Lesson Outline

Sustained through Encouragement

   I. Paul's Desire to See the Thessalonians:
      1 Thessalonians 3:1-5
      A. *Remaining in Athens: vs. 1*
      B. *Sending Timothy: vs. 2*
      C. *Suffering Affliction: vss. 3-4*
      D. *Genuine Pastoral Concern: vs. 5*
  II. Timothy's Encouraging Report:
      1 Thessalonians 3:6-13
      A. *Conveying Good News: vs. 6*
      B. *Standing Firm: vss. 7-8*
      C. *Praying Earnestly: vss. 9-10*
      D. *Seeking Mutual Affection: vss. 11-12*
      E. *Striving for Morally Pure Hearts: vs. 13*

Introduction for Adults

Topic: *Encourage One Another*

Henry Ford, the auto inventor and manufacturer, knew the power of encouragement. He learned it as a young man, at the beginning of his career.

At a dinner one evening at which Thomas Edison was present, young Ford began explaining his engine to men nearest him at the table. He noticed that Edison, seated several chairs away, was listening. Finally, the renowned inventor moved closer and asked Ford to make a drawing.

When Ford finished his crude sketch, Edison studied it intently. Then suddenly he banged his fist on the table. "Young man," he said, "that's the thing! You have it!" Years later, Ford recalled, "The thump of that fist upon the table was worth worlds to me."

Mature Christians find ways to express love and appreciation among themselves and with their peers. From this we recognize that the church is not a business, nor is the ministry merely a profession. What is involved is a relationship characterized by mutual encouragement.

Introduction for Youth

Topic: *Hang in There!*

The television cameras focused on a dejected player who had just missed a crucial shot in a basketball game. At the same time, however, his coach threw a consoling arm around the player's shoulders and said, "Hang in there!" The game may have been lost, but there was more at stake than one game.

All of us can be picker-uppers when those around us stumble. For many, simple words of appreciation can do the trick. So much of our talk is pointless. We need good words, encouraging words, and supportive words to bring Christ's love to people.

Concepts for Children

Topic: *Encourage One Another*

1. In the city of Corinth, Paul was encouraged by his friendship with Aquila and Priscilla.
2. Many in Corinth who heard Paul talk about Jesus put their faith in Him.
3. As Paul traveled with his friends to the city of Ephesus and beyond, he continued to tell people about Jesus and to encourage His followers.
4. Paul told the Thessalonians that their faith and love were a real encouragement to him.
5. We can thank God for the joy other believers bring to us because they have trusted in the Savior.

Lesson Commentary

I. PAUL'S DESIRE TO SEE THE THESSALONIANS: *1 THESSALONIANS 3:1-5*

A. Remaining in Athens: vs. 1

So when we could stand it no longer, we thought it best to be left by ourselves in Athens.

Paul considered himself and his converts to be so closely related to one another that his honor was their honor (2 Cor. 1:14). Thus, by calling the Thessalonian believers his "glory and joy" (2 Thess. 2:18), the apostle primarily meant to get across the idea that he put a high value on them. Because of his absence, some of the Thessalonians may have begun to wonder whether Paul really cared about them. He wanted to erase all doubts about his love for them.

The central issue for the apostle was the faith of the young church at Thessalonica. These new Christians had been battered, and he wasn't there to help. He agonized over their fate while he was in Athens and finally decided to send Timothy to them. How human Paul was to suffer through this separation! Twice he wrote that he could "stand it no longer" (3:1, 5). Frustrated as the apostle was, there wasn't much he could do. Today we would pick up the telephone or send an e-mail, but Paul had no such communications.

B. Sending Timothy: vs. 2

We sent Timothy, who is our brother and God's fellow worker in spreading the gospel of Christ, to strengthen and encourage you in your faith.

Paul was not able to go to Thessalonica himself, so he sent Timothy, even though that meant the apostle was left alone in Athens (1 Thess. 3:2). Timothy was the son of a Gentile father and a Jewish mother. Timothy grew up in Lystra, a city in central Asia Minor. Early on in his life he received religious instruction from his mother and grandmother, both of whom had come to faith in Christ. Paul may have met Timothy on his first missionary journey. During the apostle's second missionary journey, he took Timothy along with him. Paul also had Timothy circumcised, so as to avoid giving offense to Jews they would meet in their travels (Acts 16:1-3; 2 Tim. 1:5).

The Book of Acts does not say whether Timothy was with Paul and Silas at the founding of the Thessalonian church. Timothy may have been there, or he may have still been at Philippi. Paul later sent Timothy to Thessalonica from Athens to find out how the new church was doing. In later years, Paul and Timothy maintained a close relationship. Many of Paul's New Testament letters were written with Timothy or to him. Indications suggest that Timothy was a younger man who could at times be timid. Yet Timothy's years of service proved that Paul's faith in him was well placed.

In 1 Thessalonians 3:2, Paul gave Timothy his highest commendation. The younger man was Paul's brother in the faith and a fellow worker in spreading the Gospel. Paul had called Timothy to be his companion in ministry; and early on, Timothy learned what it meant to have a ministry of encouraging and strengthening new churches. By now, Paul felt entirely confident about sending his younger protegé to Thessalonica with the specific assignment of strengthening and encouraging them in their faith.

C. Suffering Affliction: vss. 3-4

So that no one would be unsettled by these trials. You know quite well that we were destined for them. In fact, when we were with you, we kept telling you that we would be persecuted. And it turned out that way, as you well know.

The Thessalonians needed strength and courage because of their trials, or persecutions. Paul feared that their faith would be "unsettled" (1 Thess. 3:3). The translated word may also mean "disturbed" or "beguiled," which suggests the Thessalonians might not have known what to make of their sufferings. Nonetheless, they had been forewarned, for during his ministry there, Paul had made it clear that persecution was coming.

The apostle wrote that believers were "destined" for all sorts of troubles. Put another way, experiencing hardship was part of God's will for Jesus' followers. Indeed, while Paul and his colleagues were still with the Thessalonians, the missionaries warned them that the disciples of the Lord would suffer affliction; and that is exactly what happened to the evangelists (vs. 4). Such truths notwithstanding, Paul was restless about the Thessalonians' reaction to their trials. The apostle's comments show how he was both a mother and father to them (2:7, 11). Parents keenly understand what it's like to be separated from their children, not knowing how they are handling life's hard knocks.

D. Genuine Pastoral Concern: vs. 5

For this reason, when I could stand it no longer, I sent to find out about your faith. I was afraid that in some way the tempter might have tempted you and our efforts might have been useless.

Paul sensed that the Thessalonians' faith was at stake. He also knew that Timothy could stand by them in the apostle's absence and teach them not to succumb to "the tempter" (1 Thess. 3:5). Paul traced to Satan not only his own isolation but also the danger to the faith of the new converts. The apostle's implication is clear: The believers' trials could cause their faith in Christ to weaken. Such an outcome would have devastated Paul. He could see the possibility of his work going for nothing. This was spiritual warfare at a high level. The forces of light and darkness were battling over the church at Thessalonica. Paul prayed for the church's victory every day and finally decided to send Timothy to call them to perseverance.

II. TIMOTHY'S ENCOURAGING REPORT: 1 THESSALONIANS 3:6-13

A. Conveying Good News: vs. 6

But Timothy has just now come to us from you and has brought good news about your faith and love. He has told us that you always have pleasant memories of us and that you long to see us, just as we also long to see you.

Paul's fears evaporated when Timothy returned to him. Why? It's because Timothy brought good news about the new converts' "faith and love" (1 Thess. 3:6). They had not caved in to Satan's craftiness, and they had not succumbed to trials and persecution. They were remaining steadfast in their faith. Their faith, of course, was in the Lord Jesus, while their expressed love was for His emissary, Paul.

Faith and love were some of the qualities Paul most admired in this church (1:3). Exactly how these qualities had been developed, Paul's letter does not state. Timothy had given Paul all the details about his mission, but the apostle did not rehearse them in his letter. From some of his experiences in other churches, we can safely assume that the group met faithfully—perhaps every night—in someone's home to pray, to read the Scriptures, and to encourage one another.

Paul did recall with appreciation the church's expression of love for him. They remembered him fondly and shared in his desire that they might see one another again. The Greek word translated "pleasant memories" (3:6) speaks of intense feelings. Admittedly, Paul had been in Thessalonica for only a few weeks; yet, deep, lasting friendships formed in this brief time. In today's churches, many people don't try to put down deep roots because they know their jobs will soon require them to move. However, even when Christians are together for only a short period, they can build strong friendships. Those ties can survive despite distance.

B. Standing Firm: vss. 7-8

Therefore, brothers, in all our distress and persecution we were encouraged about you because of your faith. For now we really live, since you are standing firm in the Lord.

Paul had wanted to encourage the Thessalonians in their trials. Now he found himself encouraged by their faith. The apostle referred to his own distress, which was both emotional and physical. The Greek word translated "distress" (1 Thess. 3:7) refers to pressing care, while the term rendered "persecution" denotes crushing trouble. The record in Acts 17:16-34 does not reveal any outright persecution in Athens. Perhaps Paul wrote generally about how he had been treated throughout his second missionary journey. Another possibility is that he may have been thinking about his separation from his readers.

Whatever the cause of his trials, the apostle felt better when Timothy returned with the word that the Thessalonians were persevering despite difficulties and remaining strong in their faith. A great consolation for any Christian worker is to find people standing true to the Lord. The Thessalonians had a right relationship with Him and were not standing in their own strength. Timothy's report encouraged Paul because it pointed him back to God and to His faithfulness and power. That's the true value of mutual encouragement: reminding people that God is still in control and that He hasn't forgotten us.

Paul, prior to learning about the situation involving the believers in Thessalonica, had felt a sense of dread. Now the apostle felt spiritually reinvigorated. It's as if the encouraging report gave him new life (vs. 8). This was a case in which the younger worker, Timothy, was God's instrument of blessing to the older worker, Paul. Timothy's good news of the Thessalonians' "standing firm" in their commitment to Christ strengthened the apostle to continue his evangelistic journey. The Greek verb rendered "standing firm" means to persevere or persist and points to a character quality that demands endurance. Inspired by hope, Christians find an inner strength that enables us to hold up under persecution and hardship. Endurance is one of the virtues by which Christian character can be measured.

C. Praying Earnestly: vss. 9-10

How can we thank God enough for you in return for all the joy we have in the presence of our God because of you? Night and day we pray most earnestly that we may see you again and supply what is lacking in your faith.

As Paul contemplated his strong bond of love with the church at Thessalonica, he realized it was beyond his capacity to express in words. The apostle stressed that he could not thank God enough for the faithfulness of believers in Thessalonica. It was also because of their steadfast faith in the Lord that Paul and his colleagues could enter God's presence in prayer with great joy (1 Thess. 3:9). It was in those moments of heavenly fellowship that the apostle pleaded with God around the clock to be able to see his spiritual children again.

In addition to praying about his desire to revisit the Thessalonians, Paul petitioned God for strength to minister effectively among the new converts. According to verse 10, the apostle wanted to supply what was lacking in their faith. The Greek word translated "supply" is used elsewhere for mending fishing nets, but in the New Testament it usually means to make complete, restore, or equip. After such effusive praise of his friends, what could Paul think they were lacking? All Christians need to grow and develop. No believer can say he or she has fully arrived at optimum growth or potential. We all need continual feeding and strengthening of our spiritual fibers.

So Paul was not bashful about his readers' need for further teaching. Later on in this letter and in 2 Thessalonians, the apostle instructed them about specific matters of conduct—areas in which they were lacking. They had sufficient faith to turn to the Savior from idolatry and they knew the basics of the Gospel, but they needed to become more Christlike in their conduct. Even today, the church needs to be sure that it goes beyond just winning people to the Lord and teaches converts to become mature, godly believers.

D. Seeking Mutual Affection: vss. 11-12

Now may our God and Father himself and our Lord Jesus clear the way for us to come to you. May the Lord make your love increase and overflow for each other and for everyone else, just as ours does for you.

First Thessalonians 2:11-13 bring to a close the intensely personal part of this letter. In a way, these verses form a succinct summary of all Paul wrote to this point. Stylistically, these verses resemble a mini-benediction, one that contains three prayers. Foremost on Paul's mind, of course, was the desire he still had to return to Thessalonica. He realized that Satan was blocking his return. Prayer, therefore, was the apostle's sole recourse. Only the triune God could "clear the way" (vs. 11) for him and his associates to see the Thessalonians again.

Sometimes Christians shy away from such a specific prayer request as Paul's. They think their petition is too trivial a matter to be of any concern to God. But since the Lord knows the number of the hairs on our heads and knows when a single sparrow falls, He certainly cares about our journeys and our desires to be with our loved ones. Separation rightfully inspires intense prayer. Of course, prayer is not simply going to God with a shopping list (in a manner of speaking). It involves opening our hearts to the Lord, even about intimate details of our lives, and seeking His blessing and wisdom.

Paul's second prayer focused on the need for increasing, overflowing love within the Thessalonian fellowship (vs. 12). The apostle did not complain about a lack of love; in fact, he commended their love (1:3; 4:9, 10). But he made it clear that all Christians can grow in love. He wanted to see in his spiritual children abounding love, that is, above and beyond what might be expected. What is distinctively Christian about this love is that it is "for each other and for everyone else" (3:12). It begins with the fellowship of believers, but then extends beyond. Such love springs from those who have truly been transformed by the Gospel; it doesn't just come naturally. In the Christian community, our love should explode into the surrounding territory. When that happens, people are drawn to faith in the Savior, for in the world at large selfishness reigns, not love.

E. Striving for Morally Pure Hearts: vs. 13

May he strengthen your hearts so that you will be blameless and holy in the presence of our God and Father when our Lord Jesus comes with all his holy ones.

Paul's third prayer request looked to the future. He petitioned the Lord to strengthen the "hearts" (1 Thess. 3:13) of his spiritual children. In turn, this would enable them walk in holiness and live above reproach, especially as they awaited the second advent of Christ. The Greek word translated "blameless" (1 Thess. 3:13) points to those who are free from ethical fault or defect, while the term rendered "holy" denotes those who are morally pure.

The apostle eagerly longed for the Lord Jesus' second coming "with all his holy ones." Bible scholars see this as a reference either to angels or to Christians who have died and gone to heaven—or to both. Angels often are in view in other passages related to the Savior's advent (for example, Matt. 13:41; 25:31; Mark 8:38; Luke 9:26; 2 Thess. 1:7). But the Greek term rendered "holy ones" almost always refers to people, and believers will be associated with the Son at His coming (1 Cor. 6:2; 1 Thess. 4:14).

Discussion Questions

1. What specifically about the situation in Thessalonica did Paul find especially hard to bear?
2. For what purpose did Paul send Timothy to Thessalonica?
3. Why did Paul fear that Satan might have somehow undermined the faith of the new converts in Thessalonica?
4. What was it that Timothy reported to Paul that brought him encouragement?
5. What are some areas of your life in which the Lord Jesus can enable your love Him and His followers to "increase and overflow" (1 Thess. 3:12)?

Contemporary Application

Organizations in the West can be very competitive. This is evident from the sports teams that dominate athletics and the fierce rivalry that exists among businesses. Even the entertainment industry is marked by ruthless self-interest.

Individuals are also competitive. Students try to outdo their peers in terms of grades. Employees do whatever they can to climb to the top of their professions. Many people want to drive a better car and own a nicer home than their neighbors.

Worldly competition is ultimately based on a win-lose model. If one person is victorious, the rest are vanquished, for that's the way the game of life is played. Admittedly, most people do not relate well to others in a ruthlessly competitive environment. For instance, if a runner stumbles in a race, the other participants won't stop to help up him or her. They just keep running, thankful there is one less competitor.

Against the preceding backdrop, being an encourager appears to be a revolutionary concept. This is especially the case for adults who are highly competitive. When we encourage others, we're not thinking about eliminating them to get to the top. Instead, we're cultivating relationships and showing love. In this regard, being the greatest among our peers doesn't matter anymore.

From our study of 1 Thessalonians 3 we discover that every Christian and every church at times needs someone to come alongside and offer words of encouragement, strength, and hope. It does no good to pretend that we don't need another believer's help. God places us in the church so that we can be surrounded with spiritual coaches, who can give us wise counsel and tell us that God is faithful.

Demonstrated in Action

Scripture

Background Scripture: *1 Thessalonians 4:1-12*

Scripture Lesson: *1 Thessalonians 4:1-12*

Key Verse: *Finally, brothers, we instructed you how to live in order to please God, as in fact you are living. Now we ask you and urge you in the Lord Jesus to do this more and more.* 1 Thessalonians 4:1.

Scripture Lesson for Children: *Acts 18:24-28; 1 Thessalonians 4:1-2, 9-12*

Key Verse for Children: *When Priscilla and Aquila heard [Apollos], they invited him to their home and explained to him the way of God more adequately.* Acts 18:26.

Lesson Aim

To recognize the godly lifestyle Jesus wants His followers to adopt.

Lesson Setting

Time: *About A.D. 51*

Place: *Written from Corinth to the church in Thessalonica*

Lesson Outline

Demonstrated in Action

    I. Remaining Sexually Pure: 1 Thessalonians 4:1-8
- A. *Living to Please God: vss. 1-2*
- B. *Seeking to Be Holy: vss. 3-4*
- C. *Shunning Lustful Passions: vss. 5-6*
- D. *Heeding God's Injunctions: vss. 7-8*

    II. Putting Others First: 1 Thessalonians 4:9-13
- A. *Cultivating Christlike Love: vss. 9-10*
- B. *Living a Quiet Life: vss. 11-12*

Introduction for Adults

Topic: *Motivation for Action*

On one of the New Hebrides islands in the South Pacific is the lonely grave of a Presbyterian missionary, John Geddie. A marble slab bears the following inscription: "When he came here, there were no Christians; when he went away, there were no heathen."

What made the difference? The basis for Geddie's success was his decision to be godly in his conduct and caring in his service to others. The Lord used Geddie's life witness to win the hearts of the lost, lead them to faith in Christ, and motivate them to actively serve the Lord.

Someone once said, "My life shall touch a dozen lives before this day is done, and leave countless marks of good or ill, before sets the evening sun. This is the wish I always wish and the prayer I always pray: Lord, may my life help other lives it touches on the way."

Introduction for Youth

Topic: *More Love*

We sometimes get the impression that ours is a uniquely mobile society. But our country's history shows that people were always on the move. To keep up with them, churches employed itinerant preachers called circuit riders because they traveled on horseback. Their circuits might include half a dozen churches. These were far-flung congregations needing the love of Christ.

That same mobility is required of us today. Many teenagers have moved three or four times in their brief lives. Some have gone to seven different schools. In the midst of being dislocated, they might feel forgotten, alone, and unloved.

Regardless of wherever we go to meet them, we can take with us the love of Jesus, especially as conveyed in Gospel. Even though the world of adolescents is constantly changing, Jesus' care for them remains the same. Moreover, the good news about Him does not change. We can encourage youth to put down deep roots in the soil of Jesus' love. This will give them the stability they need, even if they have to move to a new school and make new friends.

Concepts for Children

Topic: *Help One Another*

1. In Ephesus, Priscilla and Aquila helped a believer named Apollos become a better teacher of God's Word.
2. Apollos did a better job in helping the believers in Achaia learn more about Jesus.
3. Paul told the believers in Thessalonica to live in a way that pleased God.
4. Paul also encouraged the Thessalonians to love one another and their neighbors.
5. God is pleased when we are sensitive and kind to others.

Lesson Commentary

I. REMAINING SEXUALLY PURE: 1 THESSALONIANS 4:1-8

A. Living to Please God: vss. 1-2

Finally, brothers, we instructed you how to live in order to please God, as in fact you are living. Now we ask you and urge you in the Lord Jesus to do this more and more. For you know what instructions we gave you by the authority of the Lord Jesus.

In 1 Thessalonians 4:1, Paul started giving specific instructions concerning how to live in a way that pleased God. A person's efforts to live uprightly can never be enough to earn salvation. Even so, once we have been saved, our love for God should compel us to do whatever it takes to operate according to His will.

On the strength of his authority as an apostle, Paul had given the Thessalonians practical instructions when he was with them. And they were, in fact, already behaving in a manner that pleased God. But by making more of an effort, they could do better still. That's why Paul repeated the mandates. He not only asked, but also urged them to heed his directives. The apostle did not just dispense good advice; he commanded a specific lifestyle. The Greek word rendered "instructed" signifies a military chain of command, in which orders are handed down. Also, "how to live" is better understood as "how you must live." Verse 2 builds on this idea with Paul's reference to what he and his colleagues, as representatives of the Savior, had taught the new converts in Thessalonica. Here we see that the Christian faith is not only believing certain doctrines but also following clear moral imperatives.

B. Seeking to Be Holy: vss. 3-4

It is God's will that you should be sanctified: that you should avoid sexual immorality; that each of you should learn to control his own body in a way that is holy and honorable.

Of all Paul's instructions to the Thessalonians, perhaps none is more appropriate for our age than the first one, which concerns sexual purity (1 Thess. 4:3). The decline in sexual morality has afflicted not only our culture in general but also the church. We do well, then, to pay attention to the apostle's counsel about sexual behavior. For the Gentile believers in Thessalonica, the idea of restricting physical intimacy to marriage might have initially seemed foreign to them. After all, non-Jews living throughout the Roman Empire had lax ideas about sex. Sexual sins were commonplace; people rarely stopped to think that they might be wrong. Thus it could be hard for Gentile converts to get used to biblically-based standards of sexual morality.

However hard maintaining sexual purity might have been for the Thessalonians (or might be for us), Paul emphasized its importance by telling them it was God's will for them to "be sanctified." The Greek word translated "sanctified" refers to holiness. Christians are to be holy—dedicated distinctively to the Lord, and that has implications for our sexual conduct. For instance, we are to keep away from all forms of immorality, including sexual sin.

At the moment of salvation, Christians are made holy in a legal sense; we are declared righteous in God's eyes. That event is called justification. Then throughout our lives, the Holy Spirit works to bring our moral condition into conformity with our legal status; He helps to make us actually holy. This process is called sanctification. Sanctification is a work of God (5:23). But the Bible contains many exhortations for believers to do their part in becoming more holy (Phil. 2:12-13).

The latter includes our sanctification with respect to sexuality. It not only involves shunning immorality (4:3), but also learning to "control" (1 Thess. 4:4) our physical bodies. The verse is more literally rendered "to gain [or possess] one's own vessel." Here "vessel" is used as a figurative reference for one's body. Paul was admonishing believers to use their bodies in a way that is characterized by holiness and honor. We know from other passages in the Bible that any sexual involvement outside a lawful marriage between a man and a woman is immoral. Secular society may say that living together before marriage is "wise" or that extramarital affairs can be "healthy," but God says we are to avoid engaging in all such sinful sexual behavior. Those activities displease Him.

C. Shunning Lustful Passions: vss. 5-6

Not in passionate lust like the heathen, who do not know God; and that in this matter no one should wrong his brother or take advantage of him. The Lord will punish men for all such sins, as we have already told you and warned you.

Paul set up a contrast between two kinds of self-control: that which the Thessalonian believers were to practice and that which they knew their unbelieving neighbors were practicing. The believers' self-control was to be virtuous and upright. The "heathen" (vs. 5), not knowing God and His ways, controlled their bodies by indulging their "passionate lust." Our sexuality was given to us by God and is therefore normal. But the evil one is always trying to misdirect our physical drives into unacceptable outlets. Despite that, God can help us to maintain vigilance over our thoughts and actions, resulting in a lifestyle that is upright and acceptable to Him. This includes reserving sexual activity for marriage.

Indulging lustful passions not only affects us detrimentally, but also harms others. Verse 6 literally warns believers not to "transgress against or defraud his brother in the matter." Here Paul probably had in mind actual cases of premarital sex and adultery. Concerning the issue of premarital sex, a future spouse is defrauded of the right to receive his or her marriage partner as a virgin. And with respect to adultery, the spouse is cheated out of exclusive sexual rights to his or her marriage partner. Regardless of the exact nature of the offense, Paul declared that the Lord is the avenger in all these cases. The apostle's statement corresponds with what he and his colleagues previously taught the new converts in Thessalonica. In brief, they were solemnly warned that God punishes those who commit "all such sins."

D. Heeding God's Injunctions: vss. 7-8

For God did not call us to be impure, but to live a holy life. Therefore, he who rejects this instruction does not reject man but God, who gives you his Holy Spirit.

Paul explained that God summoned His spiritual children to salvation in Christ so that they would be ethically pure, not filthy. Expressed differently, the divine call was to live in holiness, not wallow in immorality (1 Thess. 4:7). The apostle may have been concerned that his instructions on sexual matters would not be received positively in Thessalonica. Perhaps some would even categorically dismiss his injunctions as being too strict. That concern would explain why he attached warnings to his edicts. Christians need to keep in mind that no sin is impossible for God to forgive. This includes sexual immorality. Violating God's ethical standards for sexuality brings serious consequences, but anyone can come to Christ in repentance and receive His pardon. For this reason the church must consistently hold out the hope of both forgiveness and acceptance, as well as the possibility of living a regenerate and holy life.

The believers in Thessalonica might have safely disregarded Paul's words if he were speaking on his own behalf. But the apostle was giving his spiritual children instructions from God. Consequently, a rejection of Paul's words about proper sexual conduct amounted to a rejection of the Lord. This was a solemn matter. The new converts were admonished to think long and hard before they went their own way in matters involving physical intimacy. What would make it all the more wrong for the Thessalonians to reject the Father was that He had given them the Holy Spirit (as a result of them trusting in the Son; vs. 8). When those in whom the Holy Spirit lives behave in an immoral way, they go against His nature and grieve Him. In brief, the Spirit seeks to dwell in sanctified people.

II. PUTTING OTHERS FIRST: 1 THESSALONIANS 4:9-13

A. Cultivating Christlike Love: vss. 9-10

Now about brotherly love we do not need to write to you, for you yourselves have been taught by God to love each other. And in fact, you do love all the brothers throughout Macedonia. Yet we urge you, brothers, to do so more and more.

In addition to remaining sexually pure, believers are to put others first. Foremost in this regard is cultivating Christlike love. With respect to Jesus' followers in Thessalonica, Paul could commend them for already treating their fellow believers as their spiritual next-of-kin. But he encouraged them to display "brotherly love" (1 Thess. 4:9) all the more.

The church in Thessalonica (like the other congregations the apostle had started in Macedonia) was probably less than a year old at this time. Some of the believers were Jews; others were Gentiles (Acts 17:1-4). Some of the Christians may not have been acquainted with the others for long. There were social and cultural differences to overcome. A mortar was needed to unite the individual believers, and that mortar was Christlike compassion.

Paul declared that on this occasion he did not have to go into detail about "brotherly love" (1 Thess. 4:9). The reason is that God had already taught the new converts to be kind and caring; and in fact, they were loving their fellow believers throughout Macedonia (vs. 10). In short, the Thessalonians had already understood and heeded Paul's message. It may be that the apostle had taught his spiritual children about Christlike compassion while he was with them. But in this letter, Paul did not claim to have done so. Their real teacher of brotherly love, he said, was God.

People don't begin to show Christlike compassion because of something they have heard or read. They don't have brotherly love because they observe others who have it. Rather, those who begin to exhibit genuine kindness do so because the Spirit of God is living within them, teaching and motivating them to show such love. Having been taught Christlike compassion by God, the Thessalonians were showing that affection to one another. Moreover, they did not restrict their displays of caring to those in their particular fellowship. They also had brotherly love for believers in surrounding areas.

At the time Paul wrote 1 Thessalonians, the only churches in Macedonia may have been the ones he and his companions had just started. Apart from the church in Thessalonica, the apostle had begun churches in Philippi and Berea. However, the Gospel may have been swiftly penetrating other parts of the province, which was less than 300 miles wide and long. Christlike compassion, in fact, should extend to wherever believers are found. It may be easier for us to show kindness toward fellow Christians with whom we worship each week. But our love must take in believers who live far away from us and may seem different from us. After all, Jesus' worldwide church is a vast network of local congregations whose links must be maintained through displays of caring.

Despite the fact that the Thessalonians were already loving believers throughout Macedonia, Paul boldly urged them to "do so more and more." The Thessalonians were still young as Christians. Their infant steps of love were promising, but they needed to learn to run. The apostle may have had in mind, partly, material expressions of kindness. Perhaps he wanted the Thessalonians to share with poorer believers some of the good things with which God had blessed them. Since financial and material needs in the church are always more than any one person can meet, we always have an incentive to express our love tangibly in increasing amounts, whenever possible.

B. Living a Quiet Life: vss. 11-12

Make it your ambition to lead a quiet life, to mind your own business and to work with your hands, just as we told you, so that your daily life may win the respect of outsiders and so that you will not be dependent on anybody.

Having urged the Thessalonians on to greater displays of love, Paul next gave three more directives about godly behavior. He urged the new converts were to strive earnestly to lead quiet lives, mind their own affairs, and earn their own living. Probably these were three areas in which some Thessalonians were deficient.

In Paul's first directive, the Greek verb translated "make" (1 Thess. 4:11) indicates a wholehearted pursuit of an objective. The result is a paradox, something like "work energetically to be still." The first directive ("lead a quiet life"), when taken with the second ("mind your own business"), suggests that some of the apostle's readers were minding other people's business. Put another way, they were meddling in the affairs of others, stirring up trouble, or gossiping around town. Such behavior—unfortunately, still known among believers—is wrong and reflects badly on the Savior and His church. If the Thessalonians had kept themselves busy at useful labor, they would not have had time to get in trouble with meddling, troublemaking, or gossiping (compare 2 Thess. 3:11).

Based on that reasoning, Paul told his spiritual children, "Work with your hands" (1 Thess. 4:11). In other words, they were to be diligent about pursuing their jobs and household chores. Greeks despised manual labor, thinking it fit only for slaves. For Jews, however, manual labor had dignity. In the mind of Paul, a Jew, respect for hard work had a place in the church's tradition. Paul had argued for the value of manual labor while he was with the Thessalonians in person. He had given them the rule that anyone who was unwilling to work would not eat (2 Thess. 3:10). The apostle, as a tentmaker by trade, had also modeled a productive lifestyle while he was with the new converts (vss. 3:7-9).

In 1 Thessalonians 4:12, Paul offered two reasons why his readers were to work with their hands. First, they would live in a decent manner in the presence of "outsiders." In turn, this godly lifestyle might earn the respect of the unsaved. Second, the apostle's spiritual children would not have to depend on others to satisfy their ongoing, daily needs. As a result, the believers in Thessalonica could offer the Gospel without charge and remain free from the possibility of being manipulated by unscrupulous donors. We may not always realize it, but unbelievers are watching us to see how we behave. If we have joy and love, and if we live on a high plane of morality, then the unsaved are more likely to be favorably impressed with the Christian faith. However, if we fail to live consistent with what we teach, then unbelievers will conclude that Christianity is full of hypocrisy.

With respect to the unsaved living in Thessalonica, they saw that some of the believers were busybodies and idlers. Thus, the resident pagans could hardly be blamed for concluding that the new religion in town, Christianity, had nothing special to offer. *If that's what it means to be a follower of Jesus, I don't want to be one!* they might have thought. On the other hand, if the believers began to work diligently, then others would start to respect them and might even become interested in learning more about the Savior.

Verse 12 also emphasizes the importance of being self-supporting. As long as the believers in Thessalonica earned their own living, they would "not be dependent on anybody." Evidently, some of them were living off the charity of others. The idle Christians had become a burden to others and could not know the self-respect that comes from taking care of oneself. We should do whatever we can to take care of our own needs before going to others for help. Men and women who are diligent in doing all they can to take care of their family's needs deserve our respect. As far as they are able, they are "not . . . dependent on anybody" but God for their material well-being.

Discussion Questions

1. Why did Paul urge the believers in Thessalonica to live in a way that pleased God?
2. What sort of instructions had Paul and his colleagues previously given to the new converts about godly living?
3. Why is it important for us, as believers, to shun sexual immorality?
4. What are some ways we can fulfill our divine calling to live in moral purity?
5. How might we go about leading a quiet life in our community?

Contemporary Application

"Cocooning" is common these days. We can secure just about anything we want through television shopping networks, delivery food service, and so on. We are told not to leave the comfort of our homes. We can be withdrawn, and yet (in some ways) be part of society.

Jesus, who came to be the servant of all, left us with a different—and far more challenging—model of how we should live and interact with others. Following His example, we must spend less time on ourselves and more on opportunities to spread the Kingdom, live in peace and fellowship with others, accept and honor others, and share His love instead of hatred and vengeance.

When it comes to demonstrating Christlike compassion, there is always room for improvement. Perhaps someone we know has lost his job; we can just tell him we are sorry or we can try to give him some financial help, as we are able. Perhaps someone we know is feeling depressed; we can merely pray for her or we can pray and try to encourage her. These are just some of the ways in which we all can strive to love more and more.

Our society teaches us to be independent and self-sufficient. At some point, however, everyone who needs help should get it. That's especially true in the Christian church, where each member is connected with every other member. After all, we're all part of one spiritual body. Consequently, when we really need something, we should ask for it without shame. And if someone else asks us for help with a legitimate problem, we should give whatever help we can. This is part of what it means to display the love of Christ to others.

God's Cosmic Plan

Scripture

Background Scripture: *1 Thessalonians 4:13—5:28*
Scripture Lesson: *1 Thessalonians 5:1-11*
Key Verse: *For God did not appoint us to suffer wrath but to receive salvation through our Lord Jesus Christ.*
1 Thessalonians 5:9.
Scripture Lesson for Children: *Acts 19:1-10; 1 Thessalonians 5:8-11*
Key Verse for Children: *Let us be self-controlled, putting on faith and love as a breastplate, and the hope of salvation as a helmet.* 1 Thessalonians 5:8.

Lesson Aim

To recognize the godly lifestyle Jesus wants His followers to adopt.

Lesson Setting

Time: *About A.D. 51*
Place: *Written from Corinth to the church in Thessalonica*

Lesson Outline

God's Cosmic Plan
 I. The Day of the Lord: 1 Thessalonians 5:1-3
    A. *The Suddenness of the Lord's Return: vss. 1-2*
    B. *The Certainty of Disaster: vs. 3*
 II. Alertness and Self-Control: 1 Thessalonians 5:4-11
    A. *Children of the Light: vss. 4-5*
    B. *Living in the Light: vss. 6-8*
    C. *Eternally Abiding with Jesus: vss. 9-10*
    D. *Edifying One Another: vss. 11*

Introduction for Adults

Topic: *Finding Hope*

Psychologists tell us that many adults have no sense of their own mortality. They take crazy risks because they think they are immortal. They make career choices based on the best offers, looking for satisfaction in the future based on positions and money.

However, when accidents take the lives of their friends, adults are forced to think about life and their future. Christians step up at times like these and offer a totally different perspective on life and its meaning.

Because Jesus died, rose from the grave, and is coming again, we can anchor our hope firmly in Him. We do not have to be nervous about our future because we know it is with Jesus. Thus, knowing Jesus makes life worthwhile.

Introduction for Youth

Topic: *Committed Forever*

The young fellow had his heart set on going with a group to see a major league baseball game. But on the day of the event, it rained and the trip had to be canceled. The lad's hopes were shattered.

Most of us can relate to how this teen felt. Yes, life is filled with disappointments, but we somehow get over most of them and move on to other things. For instance, the young fellow I mentioned above got to see many baseball games later in his life.

It's helpful to admit, though, that when life gets tougher, and the issues loom larger, we're tempted to weaken in our commitment to the Lord. We might begin thinking of Him as a cosmic Scrooge who wants to cheat us out of fun. However, we know from Scripture that this is a flawed way to view God. We learn that remaining committed to the Lord never brings disappointment. He is our unending source of hope and strength, even in life's darkest moments.

Concepts for Children

Topic: *Hey, I'm a Believer*

1. While Paul was in Ephesus, he baptized new believers.
2. The Holy Spirit gave these new believers the ability to do wonderful things.
3. For two years, Paul and his friends taught at a place in town where people met.
4. The Spirit gives us the ability to remain faithful to Jesus.
5. The Spirit also gives us the ability to love to others around us.

Lesson Commentary

I. THE DAY OF THE LORD: 1 THESSALONIANS 5:1-3

A. The Suddenness of the Lord's Return: vss. 1-2

Now, brothers, about times and dates we do not need to write to you, for you know very well that the day of the Lord will come like a thief in the night.

During his short stay in Thessalonica, Paul declared that Jesus would come again. The apostle also taught about the resurrection of the dead. But Paul evidently had not described how the dead will participate in the events surrounding the Lord's second coming. The apostle knew that if he cleared up the Thessalonians' confusion about death, he would in the process reassure them. Believers, Paul said, need not grieve "like the rest of men, who have no hope" (1 Thess. 4:13). The "rest of men" are, of course, unbelievers.

The apostle argued in verse 14 that since Jesus rose from the dead, believers can be certain they, too, will be resurrected. Moreover, Jesus will bring with Him all the believing dead, in their resurrected form, when He returns as He promised. Because the Messiah survived death, the survival of believers beyond death was as equally certain.

The Thessalonian believers were evidently concerned that their dead loved ones would be at a disadvantage when Christ returned; but that would not be the case. In fact, Paul stated on the authority of the exalted Messiah that the righteous dead will be the first to join the Savior in a resurrection existence (vs. 15). The apostle did not try to say when the Lord's coming will happen. But Paul did say that when it occurs, three signs will accompany it: (1) "a loud command" (vs. 16), (2) "the voice of the archangel," and (3) "the trumpet call of God." The three signs mean the same thing: an announcement of Jesus' coming.

At that time, deceased believers will be the first to be resurrected from the dead in an immortal and glorified form. Then they, along with Christians alive at the time, "will be caught up . . . in the clouds" (vs. 17). The order of events suggests that at Jesus' return, deceased believers will "rise first" (vs. 16) before the events of verse 17 take place. The Greek word translated "caught up" can also be rendered "snatched away." This verb carries the ideas of irresistible strength and total surprise.

In this case, the event the verb describes is often called the "rapture," after a word used in the Latin translation of verse 17. Expressed differently, a time is coming when a whole generation of believers in Christ will be privileged to miss out on death. At Jesus' return, all believers living on the earth will be caught up in the air to meet the Lord. Also, the bodies of raptured believers will be instantaneously glorified, so that they will be like the resurrected believers. The believers who are "caught up" will have a double reunion. They will be reunited with the Savior as well as with their deceased loved ones in the faith. The joy of this gathering is probably beyond our imagination.

This meeting will take place "in the clouds." In the Old Testament, clouds were often associated with God's special activity (see Dan. 7:13). Also, when Jesus ascended to heaven, a cloud hid Him from the apostles' sight; and He will return "in the same way" (Acts 1:11). The clouds will not be a vehicle of the Lord's return; but in some sense they will be recognized as a sign of God's glory and majesty. The main purpose of the rapture is to meet the Lord. When a dignitary paid a visit to a Greek city in ancient times, leading citizens went out to meet him and to escort him on the final stage of the journey. Paul similarly pictured Jesus as being escorted by His own people, those newly raised from the dead and those who will have remained alive. Having met the Lord in a glorified existence, they will never have to leave Him again.

As the Thessalonians thought about the death of their loved ones or the possibility of their own death before Jesus' return, they might have become discouraged. To counteract discouragement, they needed to recall that one day Christ will come in glory and gather all His followers to His side forever. In light of that promise, Paul's readers were to comfort and encourage one another (1 Thess. 4:18).

The Thessalonians had two questions related to Jesus' return. First, they wondered whether believers who die before the Messiah's second advent will miss out on the blessings of that time. Verses 13-18 contains Paul's assurance that not only will the dead in Christ participate in those blessings, but also they will join the Lord in a resurrected existence prior to Christians who are alive at the Second Coming. The apostle's readers also wanted to know how and when all the events connected with Jesus' return will happen (5:1).

Paul reminded his spiritual children of what he had told them before, namely, that the timing of that future day is unknown. The apostle went on to tell his readers that they ought to keep looking forward to the day of the Lord with confidence. Evidently, the Thessalonians were engaging in speculation about the "times and dates" of Jesus' return. Paul gently chided his readers for their useless endeavor. He really should not have had to write to them on this subject, for they knew that the day of the Lord's return will come suddenly and unexpectedly, like a "thief in the night" (vs. 2).

Numerous Old Testament prophets spoke of the day of the Lord. Uniformly, they pictured this future day as a time when God will enter history decisively, executing wrath upon the ungodly (see Amos 5:18-20). New Testament writers frequently mentioned the day of the Lord, relating it specifically to the return of Christ. For these writers, the day of the Lord retained its wrathful character for the wicked (see 1 Thess. 5:2-3). But they indicated that the day of the Lord is also a time of blessing for the righteous (see Eph. 4:30).

Theologians today understand the day of the Lord in differing ways. According to some experts, the Second Coming, the resurrection of the dead, the rapture, and the final judgment all will take place in a brief space of time and together comprise the day of the Lord. According to other specialists, however, the day of the

Lord is a long period that will begin just after the rapture and will end following a thousand-year reign of Christ on earth.

B. The Certainty of Disaster: vs. 3

While people are saying, "Peace and safety," destruction will come on them suddenly, as labor pains on a pregnant woman, and they will not escape.

People will be lulled into false security right up to the time of the day of the Lord. They will be talking about "peace and safety" (1 Thess. 5:3) when destruction suddenly strikes. Paul made reference to a pregnant woman's going into labor. The apostle's main focus was not on the intense pain of labor, but rather on the rapid and unexpected way in which the experience starts. The unsaved, being surprised by the commencement of the day of the Lord, will not escape this future time of unprecedented travail.

The history of human life on the earth is filled with more scenes of destruction than any of us care to contemplate. But in verse 3, commentators believe Paul was referring to a future time of unprecedented difficulties, usually called the Great Tribulation period. This passage does not necessarily mean that all people will die during the future time of harrowing distress, only that the destruction will be terrible and there will be no avoiding it.

The apostle referred to the immediate arrival of a pregnant woman's labor pains to emphasize how quickly God's wrath will strike the wicked. The use of childbirth to illustrate spiritual truth is seen both in the prophets and in the teachings of Jesus (Isa. 13:6-8; Jer. 4:31; Mark 13:8). In rabbinic writings, the sufferings preceding the establishment of the messianic age are often called labor pains. Sometimes, the point is the intense pain of labor, but in 1 Thessalonians 5:3 Paul's point is the sudden onset of labor pains.

II. ALERTNESS AND SELF-CONTROL: 1 THESSALONIANS 5:4-11

A. Children of the Light: vss. 4-5

But you, brothers, are not in darkness so that this day should surprise you like a thief. You are all sons of the light and sons of the day. We do not belong to the night or to the darkness.

Paul returned to his comparison of the thief in the night to make the point that his readers should not be taken by surprise by the day of the Lord. Furthermore, as believers, they should keep alert and be self-controlled. The destruction associated with the day of the Lord will come to many as a complete surprise, revealing their sense of security to be hollow. But Paul's readers had no need to be surprised. The difference was one of expectation.

The apostle's spiritual children were not in the dark about the Messiah's second advent. Admittedly, they could not predict its timing, but they knew that it was coming and they could expect it. Others did not know about that day and, like a homeowner sleeping while being robbed, would not be expecting it (1 Thess. 5:4). This contrast between light and darkness is developed into a running metaphor (comparison) in verse 5. Believers were "sons of the light" and "sons of the day." Moral purity and truth characterized them. In contrast, unbelievers belonged "to the night" and "to the darkness." Impurity and falsehood characterized them. In Jewish speech, to be a "son" of something meant to be characterized by that thing. Moral and spiritual "light" is a distinguishing characteristic of the followers of Jesus Christ, the Light of the World.

Some Bible commentators have suggested that early on in his career, Paul expected to be among those who are still alive at the time of the Lord Jesus' coming. They base this view, first of all, on passages in early letters written by the apostle where he used the word "we," seeming to include himself with those who will be alive (for example, 1 Thess. 4:15, 17). Furthermore, passages in letters written later in Paul's career seem to indicate that the apostle expected to be among those who would die and be resurrected (for instance, 2 Cor. 4:14). Some commentators who favor this view suggest that the primary incident that changed Paul's mind was his close brush with death in the Roman province of Asia (1:8-10). Other commentators believe we cannot know whether the apostle expected to survive until the Savior's return. They point out that Paul regularly identified himself with his readers by saying "we." Therefore, nothing can be proved by his use of that pronoun.

B. Living in the Light: vss. 6-8

So then, let us not be like others, who are asleep, but let us be alert and self-controlled. For those who sleep, sleep at night, and those who get drunk, get drunk at night. But since we belong to the day, let us be self-controlled, putting on faith and love as a breastplate, and the hope of salvation as a helmet.

In 1 Thessalonians 5:6-8, Paul further compared the saved and unsaved. Like people who sleep, unbelievers are spiritually insensitive and unaware of the coming of the day of the Lord (vs. 6). That they get drunk is a representation of their lack of proper self-control (vs. 7). In contrast, believers live in the brightness of spiritual awareness and keep themselves alert and sober. We often think about sobriety in terms of avoiding some form of sin. But in verse 8, Paul had in mind self-control's positive virtues. It means to put on the breastplate of faith and love and to done "as a helmet" the "hope of salvation." Here the apostle was using parts of a Roman legionnaire's armor to symbolize qualities that make up the believer's spiritual armor and perhaps to stress that the Christian life involves spiritual conflict.

Paul more than once used parts of a Roman legionnaire's armor to symbolize qualities that make up the Christian's spiritual armor, as he did in verse 8. The apostle's most complete description of armor is found in Ephesians 6:10-17, where he mentioned a belt, breastplate, footgear, shield, helmet, and sword. He also used armor symbolism in Romans 13:12 and 2 Corinthians 6:7 and 10:4. Paul may have been influenced by the prophet Isaiah, who spoke about the Lord's breastplate of righteousness and helmet of salvation (Isa. 59:17). The recurring symbolism of armor in Paul's writing is vivid evidence that the Christian life involves spiritual conflict.

Along with 1 Thessalonians 5:8, Paul also mentioned the trio of faith, hope, and love in 1:3. Faith is the means by which we enter the Christian life, and day by day we trust in the Lord for our care. The love that exists between God and us prompts us to be compassionate and kind to one another. The hope of salvation means that, while divine wrath awaits unbelievers, we who are Christians will abide forever with the Lord.

C. Eternally Abiding with Jesus: vss. 9-10

For God did not appoint us to suffer wrath but to receive salvation through our Lord Jesus Christ. He died for us so that, whether we are awake or asleep, we may live together with him.

Paul's view of the future was rooted in his assurance of salvation through faith in Christ, who died and rose again for sinners. The apostle did not add any new truth to what he had previously preached, but he pointed to the Cross to clear up his readers' uncertainty and confusion about the death of their loved ones and the day of the Lord. The latter event will indeed bring destruction (1 Thess. 5:3), but this wrath is not meant for Jesus' followers (vs. 9). Christians, of course, along with everybody else, deserve God's wrath because of our sin. But instead of receiving judgment for our deeds, we will "receive salvation" because of what Jesus has done for us at Calvary.

In the end, it does not really matter whether we pass away before Jesus comes, for He died (and rose again from the dead) so that we can abide with Him forever. Whether we are living or deceased, our eternal future will be the same: "we may live together with him" (1 Thess. 5:10). The sleep mentioned in this verse refers, not to spiritual insensitivity, as in verses 6 and 7, but to death, as in 4:13 and 15. Whether living or dead, our destiny will be the same: We will live together with Christ. Everlasting pleasure, not wrath, awaits the followers of Jesus. Our existence has an eternal dimension that will outlast time as we know it. Paul wrote to the Corinthians, "For our light and momentary troubles are achieving for us an eternal glory that far outweighs them all" (2 Cor. 4:17).

D. Edifying One Another: vss. 11

Therefore encourage one another and build each other up, just as in fact you are doing.

Until the Lord Jesus comes, Christians are to encourage and build each other up in their faith (1 Thess. 5:11; compare 4:18). Paul knew this was happening in the church of Thessalonica, but since his readers were perplexed about the day of the Lord, they needed to be reminded to keep on affirming each other. Because of their discouragement, Paul told them to keep on doing their good works for one another. This was no time to let up.

Discussion Questions

1. In what sense will the "day of the Lord" (1 Thess. 5:2) come like a "thief in the night"?
2. How can believers avoid being of the "night" (vs. 5), that is, of "darkness"?
3. Why did Paul admonish his readers to "watch and be sober" (vs. 6)?
4. How should Christians act as they wait for Jesus' return?
5. If you are preparing yourself for Jesus' return, what are you specifically doing?

Contemporary Application

In the midst of the Thessalonians' hardships, Paul reminded them of the Lord's return and urged them to draw comfort from this truth. Even believers face moments of distress and uncertainty, and the reality of Jesus' coming can be a source of consolation for them.

The years of life are filled with change and discovery as well as with emerging talents, aptitudes, and dreams. Nevertheless, some students still struggle with loneliness and depression. There undoubtedly are times when the students, out of the depths of their hearts, cry for something or someone to give them peace and comfort. But before they can experience God's help and consolation, they must first recognize their own human frailty.

Only Christ can fill the void that exists in the lives of every person. When they invite the living Lord to come into their hearts, He supplies the freeing power from the bondage of evil and sin's oppression. He also helps them deal with the loneliness, depression, and insecurity they might feel at times.

Jesus comforts believers through His presence and the promises of His Word. He also consoles them through the indwelling Spirit and the loving support of Christian friends. Such evidences of compassion and care undergird the students in their times of need.

The Lord's unfailing love is the ultimate basis for comfort in difficult times. The mystery of His compassion is that it accepts and meets believers at the point of their deepest need. When they trust God's promises, they experience His solace and blessings in their lives.

It would be wrong for the class members to think that, when God comforts them, all their troubles go away. Being consoled means they receive strength to endure trials and hope to face a potentially troubled future. In fact, the greater difficulty they face, the more God reaches out in love to comfort them.

God has never failed in His promise to console believers. They should not only acknowledge this truth but also thank the Lord for the ways He has consoled them during difficult times in the past. Unlike flowers, which are a temporary delight in their eyes, God's love and care for His spiritual children are everlasting. They thus should express their gratitude to God for being like a shepherd in His care for them, especially when life is rough.

Glory to Christ

Scripture

Background Scripture: *2 Thessalonians 1*
Scripture Lesson: *2 Thessalonians 1:3-12*
Key Verse: *We constantly pray for you, that our God may count you worthy of his calling, and that by his power he may fulfill every good purpose of yours and every act prompted by your faith.* 2 Thessalonians 1:11.
Scripture Lesson for Children: *Acts 20:3-12;*
2 Thessalonians 1:3-4
Key Verse for Children: *Your faith is growing more and more, and the love every one of you has for each other is increasing.* 2 Thessalonians 1:3.

Lesson Aim

To find courage and strength in the Lord during hard times.

Lesson Setting

Time: *About A.D. 51 or 52*
Place: *Written from Corinth to the church in Thessalonica*

Lesson Outline

Glory to Christ

   I. A Future Time of Reckoning:
       2 Thessalonians 1:3-10
       A. *Vibrant Faith and Love: vs. 3*
       B. *Perseverance Despite Persecution: vs. 4*
       C. *Suffering for the Kingdom: vs. 5*
       D. *Divine Justice: vss. 6-7*
       E. *Eternal Destruction: vss. 8-9*
       F. *Jesus' Return: vs. 10*
  II. Prayer for Endurance: 2 Thessalonians 1:11-12
       A. *Living in an Exemplary Manner: vs. 11*
       B. *Bringing Glory to the Savior: vs. 12*

Introduction for Adults

Topic: *Finding Purpose in Life*

Every four years, a small group athletes achieve their dream of competing in the Olympic games. And medal winners reflect the glory of their country's' flags. They proudly stand for the entire world to see because they want to bring glory to their homeland.

In a much larger sense, Christians find purpose in life by reflecting the glory of the Lord Jesus. He is honored in us and we in Him. Therefore, we can see purpose and hope for living. We are encouraged to stand firm in our faith because we know the glory of Jesus is at stake.

In our race of life, we pursue victory for the sake of Jesus. He has called us to eternal glory. In the meantime, though, we may take some hard knocks, we want to stand firm for the sake of His glory. His name is worth all the effort we can make to grow in our faith, hope, and love.

Introduction for Youth

Topic: *Committed*

A skyrocket is exciting to watch, but its beauty doesn't last long. There are people who have Christian experiences as brilliant as skyrockets or like giant Roman candles. They certainly can dazzle our eyes for a while. But then they sputter and go out. Their lives become sad, sick, and disappointing. People who are committed to maintaining a spiritual glow over the years, through good times and bad, help us believe in the faithfulness of God. Their devotion to Christ is deep and constant because it is real.

I think about my aunt who for years has prayed for her brothers and sisters and their families, read and studied her Sunday school lesson each week, and generally thought of others more than herself. When I decided to go to seminary, she was one of the first persons I told, because I knew she would understand my desire to serve the Lord—and she did. Every young person should have someone like my aunt to look up to as a shining example of how one's faith commitment is lived out in everyday life.

Concepts for Children

Topic: *Keep the Faith*

1. Paul and his friends returned to a place called Macedonia.
2. The group next went to a place called Troas, where Paul spoke to Jesus' followers until midnight.
3. A believer named Eutychus went to sleep while listening to Paul and fell out of a window to the ground.
4. God used Paul to restore Eutychus to life.
5. Paul thanked God that the believers in Thessalonica remained faithful to Him, even though they were suffering for being Christians.

Lesson Commentary

I. A FUTURE TIME OF RECKONING: 2 THESSALONIANS 1:3-10

A. Vibrant Faith and Love: vs. 3

We ought always to thank God for you, brothers, and rightly so, because your faith is growing more and more, and the love every one of you has for each other is increasing.

Paul began his second letter to the church at Thessalonica with a traditional greeting from his missionary team, which included Silas and Timothy (2 Thess. 1:1). They were well known to the Thessalonian believers and so needed no introduction. Paul then reminded his spiritual children of their heritage and position: They were members of the church and were rooted in the Father and in His Son, the Lord Jesus Christ (vs. 2).

Perhaps some of the Thessalonians felt somewhat unworthy of the way in which Paul commended them in his first letter (see 1 Thess. 1:2-3). If so, that would help explain why he repeated his affirmation of them in the opening lines of his second letter. The apostle and his associates always had good reason to "thank God" (2 Thess. 1:3) for His work of grace in the lives of Paul's spiritual children. The apostle praised the Lord for the flourishing faith and growing love the Thessalonians had for one another. This remained the case, even though they faced the stress of continuing persecution.

B. Perseverance Despite Persecution: vs. 4

Therefore, among God's churches we boast about your perseverance and faith in all the persecutions and trials you are enduring.

Paul's initial concern was to assure his readers of his steadfast prayers for them. In doing so, he did not offer them an escape plan or a promise of political relief. Instead, the apostle claimed spiritual victory for the Thessalonians. Doing so would have been a morale booster for them. As noted in previous lessons, the Thessalonian believers were enduring "persecutions and trials" (2 Thess. 1:4). No doubt some of the afflictions were physical, but more likely Paul had in mind social stigma, ridicule, the loss of status, and even the loss of their livelihood.

The believers were paying a heavy price for putting their trust in the Savior. Nonetheless, they persevered in their faith. The underlying Greek term indicates the presence of steadfastness, patience, and endurance. So stalwart was the faith of Paul's readers that he and his colleagues proudly told believers in other churches about their fellow Christians suffering in Thessalonica for being disciples of the Lord Jesus.

C. Suffering for the Kingdom: vs. 5

All this is evidence that God's judgment is right, and as a result you will be counted worthy of the kingdom of God, for which you are suffering.

No persecution is easy to take. But if we view our troubles from an eternal perspective, that helps us to endure in faith. Believers have the assurance of Scripture that their devotion to the Lord will be vindicated when He judges the ungodly. The fact that the latter harass and afflict Jesus' followers—such as those living in Thessalonica—vindicates God's eternal condemnation of the wicked (2 Thess. 1:5). The suffering endured by Paul's readers proved that God was preparing them to be "counted worthy" for His kingdom. Their steadfastness, which was a result of God's grace working in their lives, showed they were truly God's people.

Suffering on behalf of the Kingdom was something the Thessalonians shared with Paul and his companions. Through it all, the apostle kept an eternal perspective on life. In the midst of his many adversities, that perspective is what enabled him to remain on an even keel. From any other vantage point, the apostle's suffering must have appeared extremely grievous and long lasting. But as he thought about the glory of the eternal life ahead of him, he regarded his afflictions as merely "light and momentary" (2 Cor. 4:17). When compared to the overwhelming weight of the glory that lay ahead for him, his sufferings were almost weightless.

D. Divine Justice: vss. 6-7

God is just: He will pay back trouble to those who trouble you and give relief to you who are troubled, and to us as well. This will happen when the Lord Jesus is revealed from heaven in blazing fire with his powerful angels.

Old Testament writers wondered why the wicked prosper while the righteous suffer. This theme echoes through the Prophets, the Psalms, and the Book of Job. But in the New Testament, the suffering of believers is seen in an entirely different light. If people in Old Testament times were surprised, New Testament Christians were not, for they had been told by Jesus and the apostles to expect suffering. It was part of their birthright as followers of the Savior. The sorts of afflictions He had to endure would also be experienced by His followers (John 15:18-21; Phil. 1:29).

In light of the biblical perspective conveyed by Paul and his colleagues, the believers in Thessalonica could entrust themselves to God's wise and loving care. The apostle reassured them that God would do what is right. Specifically, the Lord would repay with affliction those who made Paul's spiritual children suffer (2 Thess. 1:6). It would be incorrect to assume that God delights in such an outcome. After all, the Father would prefer that all people repent of their sin and trust in the Son for salvation (see 1 Tim. 2:3-4; 2 Pet. 3:9). The latter truth notwithstanding, in an ethical universe, sin cannot go unpunished. Oppressors seem to think they are immune to God's moral laws because He does not execute judgment immediately. But God will have the last word, for eternal condemnation is the ultimate outcome of sin.

Just as important is the truth that God would eventually send relief to the Thessalonian Christians and the missionaries alike. The believers in the city were enduring hardship and affliction because of the actions of evil individuals. Paul could not say that the situation of his spiritual children would suddenly improve. On the one hand, justice was coming in the form of punishment for the persecutors and relief for the persecuted. On the other hand, that outcome would not necessarily happen until the second advent of the Savior (2 Thess. 1:7).

Paul noted that when Jesus comes again, He will be "revealed from heaven." Right now the Son is veiled from human eyes. But one day He will return in "blazing fire" and be accompanied by an entourage of "powerful angels." At that time, His mighty presence will be disclosed to the entire world. He will come with the clouds of heaven, and everyone will see Him. Indeed, all peoples of the earth will weep at the sight of His holy countenance (Rev. 1:7).

E.   Eternal Destruction: vss. 8-9

He will punish those who do not know God and do not obey the gospel of our Lord Jesus. They will be punished with everlasting destruction and shut out from the presence of the Lord and from the majesty of his power.

Paul looked down the long corridor of history and revealed the ultimate destiny of those who reject the knowledge of the Father and refuse to heed the good news about the Son (2 Thess. 1:8; see Ps. 79:6; Isa. 66:15; Jer. 10:25). Concerning the latter, it means to admit and confess one's sin, repent, and welcome Jesus as Lord and Savior. Here we see that the significance of Paul's writing extended far beyond the immediate hardships being experienced by the believers in Thessalonica. The focus is a consideration of what is in store for all humankind. According to Jesus, unbelievers now live under the threat of God's condemnation and wrath (see John 3:18, 36). Outwardly, they may appear to be secure and comfortable, but they are skating on thin ice (so to speak).

Knowing God and obeying the Gospel are not two different qualifications for escaping divine judgment. One can "know God" (2 Thess. 1:8) in the theological sense only by heeding the Good News. And saving knowledge of the Father comes from trusting in and following the Son. We often use the expression "believe the Gospel." That's a common biblical theme as well. But a person cannot genuinely accept the truth of the Gospel without also abiding by its injunctions. In Romans 1:5, Paul told his readers that his apostolic commission was to call people "to the obedience that comes from faith." To believe, trust, and obey—all are components of a valid, life-changing knowledge of God. Without such an intimate relationship with the Creator and Judge, there is no escaping His punishment.

In 2 Thessalonians 1:9, Paul went on to describe the fate of unbelievers. They will undergo the penalty of eternal "destruction." The latter term does not mean annihilation, but unceasing ruin. It will include banishment from God's holy presence and glorious power (see Isa. 2:10, 19, 21). These are truths people of the world choose to ignore—facts that even some Christians find distasteful and are unwilling to profess publicly. But denial does not change the certainty of eternal punishment awaiting the wicked. The Bible describes the condemnation of the

unrighteous in terms that sound like physical torment. However, there is disagree-
ment among Bible interpreters concerning how literally to understand all these
descriptions.

Undoubtedly, the primary torment of hell will be the awareness of one's eternal
separation from God. The horror of being unendingly cut off from the Lord is
impossible for us to comprehend. Yet we realize it is a just outcome. After all, the
Bible depicts unregenerate humanity as sheep who are lost and have gone their
own way (Isa. 53:6). Tragically, many people choose to live independently of God.
Even so, they still live under the Father's provision of their basic needs. Also, the
Son continues to sustain all life. In light of these truths, to exist for all eternity separated from God's grace would be a living hell.

Based on the preceding information, we can see that when Paul said unbelievers
"will be punished with everlasting destruction" (2 Thess. 1:9), he was referring to
torment in hell. The New Testament provides a number of clues to the nature of
hell. It is a place of raging fire (Heb. 10:27) and a locale of deepest darkness (2 Pet.
2:17). There people weep and gnash their teeth in misery (Matt. 8:12). The inhabitants of hell can expect no relief (Rev. 14:11). Dwelling in hell means a separation
from the Savior (Matt. 7:23) but not from Satan and his demons (25:41). Hell causes the destruction of both body and soul (10:28). It is worse than death (Heb.
10:28-29).

F. Jesus' Return: vs. 10

*On the day he comes to be glorified in his holy people and to be marveled at among all those who have
believed. This includes you, because you believed our testimony to you.*

When Jesus is "revealed from heaven" (2 Thess. 1:7), He will execute just punishment on unbelievers. He will also receive glory from His saints, that is, His "holy
people" (vs. 10). Indeed, everyone who has trusted in Him for eternal life will offer
Him praise and honor. Paul contrasted the fate of humanity's two groups—those
who believe the Gospel and those who reject it. For those who put their faith in the
Savior, His revelation will result in them marveling at His awesome presence.

The Lord Jesus will not be ashamed to associate with His followers. These are the
same ones who are persecuted, oppressed, and treated as worthless by the wicked
in the present age. But these outcasts from society will be the shining trophies of
God's grace. The believers in Thessalonica were included in this group. Thus,
rather than being depressed, they were to be encouraged by the truth of God's justice and His love for them. They would be part of those praising the Son at His
return, for they believed Paul's testimony to them about the Savior. The apostle's
witness focused on the good news of Jesus' death and resurrection for their sins.
This reminds us that the Christian faith rests on verifiable evidence. Assuredly,
that's what Paul proclaimed and the church believed.

II. PRAYER FOR ENDURANCE: 2 THESSALONIANS 1:11-12

A. Living in an Exemplary Manner: vs. 11

With this in mind, we constantly pray for you, that our God may count you worthy of his calling, and that by his power he may fulfill every good purpose of yours and every act prompted by your faith.

Paul, after telling his readers about God's future judgment of unbelievers, redirected the attention of the Thessalonians back to the present. How should they live now? What could they do at this time to make their lives increasingly fruitful and productive? With these sorts of concerns in mind, the apostle once more reminded his spiritual children of his persistent prayers for them. He would neither forget nor abandon them. Rather, he would continue to bring their needs before the throne of God's grace.

Foremost among Paul's concerns was that the believers in Thessalonica would live up to their high and holy calling. Earlier, the apostle assured his readers that they would be "counted worthy of the kingdom of God" (2 Thess. 1:5). By mentioning the nature of his prayers on their behalf, Paul reminded the Thessalonians that they were really living for God and not for themselves. Their lives were to match their calling. Similarly, our highest aspiration should be to live in an exemplary manner. This doesn't mean we can ever earn or merit God's favor, for His mercy and grace are freely given and totally undeserved. But we can be "worthy" (vs. 11) in the sense that we demonstrate that God has chosen us to be His holy people.

Paul also prayed that God, by His great "power," would enable the Thessalonians to accomplish "every good purpose" their faith in the Lord Jesus prompted them to do. This included "every act" inspired by their faith and intended to glorify God. Perhaps at this time Paul's readers were struggling with discouragement and despair, especially as they faced harassment and affliction from unbelievers. The apostle's spiritual children would be heartened to know that he was holding them up in prayer and that God was on their side to complete their work of faith.

B. Bringing Glory to the Savior: vs. 12

We pray this so that the name of our Lord Jesus may be glorified in you, and you in him, according to the grace of our God and the Lord Jesus Christ.

Paul wanted to see the name of Lord Jesus glorified through the Thessalonians' success and fruitfulness in their service for Him (2 Thess. 1:12). When the church prospers in boldness, faith, worship, service, and witnessing, the Messiah is exalted in the wider community. People begin to take notice. They start to wonder what motivates Jesus' followers. The unsaved ask what enables Christians to be so kind and helpful to one another. The all-important calling of the church is to draw attention to the Savior, not to plan programs or to erect buildings. As we exalt and glorify the Lord Jesus, we are also glorified in Him. This takes place because of God's grace working in our lives. In short, He empowers us for Christian service.

Discussion Questions

1. What motivated Paul and his colleagues to give thanks to God for the believers in Thessalonica?
2. How would Paul's readers demonstrate that they had been counted worthy of God's kingdom?
3. How can God be just in punishing the unsaved?
4. What is the nature of the testimony we demonstrate by our lives to the unsaved?
5. What aspects of our service for God do we see bringing Him the most glory?

Contemporary Application

Paul put the Thessalonians' persecution in the right perspective. He told them to endure it with perseverance and faith, to trust in God's judgment, to be confident in His purposes, and to hope in His power. These admonitions are just as relevant today in the lives of believers as they were in the early church.

Consider, for example, the fact that the students live in a time when life's challenges can seem overwhelming, especially when they carry a high risk factor. There are occasions when they try to figure out the best course of action to take and are not sure what to do. This situation, in turn, can leave them feeling discouraged and defeated.

At such times, it helps for believers to reflect on how God has been with them in past situations. Rehearsing previous events and circumstances will reinforce their confidence in God's loving care. They will discover that He can use even unpleasant happenings to shape their lives and strengthen their faith.

Both the students' personal experiences and the testimony of Scripture reinforce the truth that God keeps His promises to His people. His faithfulness takes a variety of forms, and all of them are designed to strengthen believers in their daily walk with Him.

The promises of God are dependable, and they are meant for all believers. For instance, the Lord promises to walk with them through the darkest valleys of life (Ps. 23:4). He pledges to give them His incomprehensible peace (Phil. 4:6-7). He even vows to never forsake them in their time of need (Heb. 13:5).

Often when the students need to trust God's promises, they instead focus on their fears. Doing this, though, restrains their spiritual growth. It can also steer them away from potentially interesting challenges that are high-risk. There are times when God wants believers to set aside their fears and rely on His promises.

In those moments when fear rears its ugly head, the students can find encouragement in the many promises of God's Word. They can examine the ones that relate to their fears and problems, and trust in them. When believers focus their attention on God's promises (rather than their fears), they will be filled with hope, peace, strength, and understanding to get them through their difficulties.

Chosen and Called

Scripture

Background Scripture: *2 Thessalonians 2*
Scripture Lesson: *2 Thessalonians 2:13-17*
Key Verse: *So then, brothers, stand firm and hold to the teachings we passed on to you, whether by word of mouth or by letter.* 2 Thessalonians 2:15.
Scripture Lesson for Children: *Acts 20:16-19, 22-25, 32, 36-38; 2 Thessalonians 2:13-14*
Key Verse for Children: *So then, brothers, stand firm and hold to the teachings we passed on to you.* 2 Thessalonians 2:15.

Lesson Aim

To rely on the Lord for help to stand firm in the faith.

Lesson Setting

Time: *About A.D. 51 or 52*
Place: *Written from Corinth to the church in Thessalonica*

Lesson Outline

Chosen and Called
  I. Being Loved and Sanctified by God:
      2 Thessalonians 2:13-14
      A. *Chosen for Salvation: vs. 13*
      B. *Called to Salvation: vs. 14*
  II. Standing Firm in the Faith:
      2 Thessalonians 2:15-17
      A. *Holding Fast to Biblical Truth: vs. 15*
      B. *Finding Encouragement and Strength in the Lord:
          vss. 16-17*

Introduction for Adults

Topic: *Standing Firm*

We run the risk of skepticism when we read about the physical obstacles the believers in Thessalonica faced and overcame with the help of the Lord. We wonder how we would have responded to the same challenges they endured. Regardless of whether God calls us to go through similar circumstances, the importance of standing firm in the faith remains unchanged.

Jesus' earliest followers succeeded because of their complete commitment to the Savior. They loved Him so much, and they wanted to obey Him so completely, that they persevered and grew in spiritual wisdom and understanding. Through the sanctifying work of the Spirit and belief in the truth of the Gospel, they were able to finish the race of life successfully.

There is no other way for believers today. Despite many popular but false "secrets" on the market, we are challenged to find answers in our unwavering commitment to the Lord Jesus. When we love and serve Him above everything else, He enables us to rise above our difficulties and setbacks.

Introduction for Youth

Topic: *Committed to Stand Firm*

Power from weakness is an oxymoron in today's culture. Smart people tell us to use power to get ahead and make something of ourselves. The importance of power is the unwritten message that undergirds the media's assault of our minds. We are sold power cars, power computers, and power cosmetics.

However, we learn from the Gospel that "In our own power, we are dead." So teenagers are forced to choose between society's power and Jesus' power. He was dismissed by the crowds because He refused to use His power to overthrow the Romans, who had conquered, subjugated, and persecuted the Jews.

Instead, Jesus showed that real, eternal power comes only through His cross. To remain firmly committed to Him requires enormous courage and faith in today's culture. But Paul convincingly showed that by Jesus' power, believers could not only endure hardships, but also live with hope and purpose. The Gospel's power really is better, and it lasts forever.

Concepts for Children

Topic: *Finish the Job*

1. As Paul made his way back home, he sent a message asking the Christian leaders in the city of Ephesus to meet with him.
2. Paul said that others would be mean to him because he followed Jesus.
3. Paul reminded his friends of the love and encouragement they had in Jesus.
4. Paul thanked the Father that people living in the city of Thessalonica had put their faith in the Son for salvation.
5. When we tell others about Jesus, we show how much we love Him.

Lesson Commentary

I. BEING LOVED AND SANCTIFIED BY GOD: 2 THESSALONIANS 2:13-14

A. Chosen for Salvation: vs. 13

But we ought always to thank God for you, brothers loved by the Lord, because from the beginning God chose you to be saved through the sanctifying work of the Spirit and through belief in the truth.

At this point in his second letter to the Thessalonian believers, Paul returned to one of the subjects he had discussed in his first letter (1 Thess. 4:13-18): the second coming of the Savior. At the same time, the apostle amplified on the subject of the coming judgment of God (2 Thess. 1:7-9). Paul was seriously alarmed by a report—supposedly from him—that was upsetting the church at Thessalonica. He told the people there to recognize that what others told them was false (2:1-2), to know what must happen before Jesus' return (vss. 3-4), to know about the restrainer of evil (vss. 5-7), to be aware of spiritual counterfeits (vss. 8-10), and to believe in God's judgment (vss. 11-12).

Why were Paul's readers in such turmoil? He blamed it on a message purported to have come from him. Allegedly, the second coming of the Messiah had already occurred, and the Thessalonians had missed it. Paul categorically denounced the interpretation in a disturbing "prophecy, report or letter" (vs. 2) that certain false prophets had made. The apostle firmly declared that nothing he had ever said or written could be correctly interpreted to mean that the Second Coming had already occurred. The Thessalonians, rather than being shaken, troubled, and excited, could hold on to what the apostle had taught them. He had clearly said that they would not miss the return of Christ (see 1 Thess. 4:17).

To help his readers stand firm, Paul declared something of what will happen in the end times. First, there will be a rebellion against God. Of course, people have always rebelled against God, but this will be worse than anything that has happened before. The apostle underscored the climactic nature of this apostasy by calling it "the rebellion" (2 Thess. 2:3)—one that will far exceed anything else like it in human history (see also Matt. 24:10-12; 1 Tim. 3:1-9; 2 Tim. 4:1). Second, "the man of lawlessness" (2 Thess. 2:3) will be revealed. This title is appropriate, for he will break God's injunctions. Presumably, this person will be the leader of the rebellion. He will defy everything considered to be holy or sacred and even claim that he himself is God (vs. 4; see Isa. 14:13-14; Ezek. 28:2-9; Dan. 11:36). Despite his bombastic assertions, this person is destined for "destruction" (2 Thess. 2:3).

Paul's spiritual children were distraught because they had forgotten or failed to apply what he had told them in person (vs. 5). He reminded them that the ultimate revelation of the powers of darkness is being held back by someone or something. This implies that the current age is not as bad as it could possibly be. Indeed, the full-fledged manifestation of Satan that will be exhibited through his evil

371

henchman has not yet occurred. Currently, his appearance is being delayed according to God's sovereign will (vs. 6). There is no agreement concerning the identity of the restrainer of lawlessness. Options include the following: the Roman Empire and its emperor; the principle of law and government; the preaching of the Gospel; the Jewish state; and the Holy Spirit.

In any case, verse 7 says that during the present age, the hidden "power of lawlessness is already at work" in the world. Perhaps this is akin to the "spirit of antichrist" (1 John 4:3). Expressed differently, even though the Antichrist has not yet appeared, many people presently are opposed to God. Be that as it may, the full force of the diabolical one's mysterious power is being held back until the restrainer is removed. This information implies that a specific series of events must occur prior to return of the Messiah: (1) a sudden acceleration of apostasy (2 Thess. 2:3); (2) the removal of a restraining influence (vss. 6-7); and (3) the complete unveiling of the lawless one, who will be animated by Satan, oppose God, and attempt to exalt himself above God (vss. 4, 9).

As the present era unfolds, Satan and his operatives continue to clash with Jesus' and His followers. Moreover, as the end of the age draws to a close, the battle will reach a point of no return. Regardless of how deplorable the situation becomes, the triumph of the Savior, the vindication of the saints, and the demise of the wicked are assured (vs. 8). In the meantime, the devil's agent of lawlessness will use whatever tactics and schemes are at his disposal to persecute believers and undermine the will of God. Paul provided a graphic description of the wicked one's powers. This self-glorifying individual will be under Satan's control. Indeed, the devil will give his henchman unusual abilities to perform miracles, signs, and wonders. Satan's work will be seen in the most audacious deceptions (vs. 9).

The tragic outcome will be destruction for people who allow themselves to be duped by this Satan-inspired miracle worker. People usually flock after unusual phenomenon, but a miracle in and of itself proves nothing. Works of power will be used to deceive people into worshiping the lawless one. People fall into this snare because they found no place in their hearts for the truth of the Gospel, the acceptance of which leads to salvation (vs. 10). The Good News must not only be acknowledged; it must also be loved. The latter is demonstrated when converts allow God's Word to rule their lives. In contrast, to reject the Gospel is to reject the divine offer of salvation.

Because the unsaved spurn the Good News, the Lord eventually sends on them a deluding influence so that they embrace what is false (vs. 11). In other words, God will use their sin as a punishment against them. He will let them continue in their sinful ways so that they are fooled into believing an assortment of lies. The world is filled with liars and lies, all of them inspired by Satan, the father of lies (John 8:44). But the specific lie Paul was talking about in 2 Thessalonians 2:11 is the bogus claim made by the devil's operation.

The lawless one dupes unregenerate humanity to believe that he is divine and deserves to be worshipped (vs. 4). Those taken in by this deception not only reject the Gospel, but also delight in evil. It's no wonder that God condemns them (vs. 12). This presumably refers to punishment in hell. Here we see that more than intellect is involved in accepting the Gospel. In Scripture, belief always includes the will and the emotions. Paul emphasized the connection between the two. Moreover, refusing to believe the truth and delighting in wickedness are related.

On the one hand, Paul foresaw a time when the Messiah will judge the lawless-ness one, along with all who will follow this satanic deceiver (vss. 8-12). But the apostle hastened to assure his readers that they would not be among those judged. They were destined for blessing by God (vss. 13-14). This is why Paul thanked God for the Thessalonian believers—not so much because of who they were in them-selves as because of who they had become through God's grace to them.

The apostle called his spiritual children those who were "loved by the Lord" (vs. 13). God had demonstrated His love for them by choosing them for salvation. This shows that God's love is not a vague, emotion-charged slogan. Put another way, His love is not the basis of some blind hope for a silver lining in the clouds. The Father's love has been verified in history by what He has done for the church. To be specific, He sent His beloved Son to be the atoning sacrifice for the sins of the entire world (1 John 2:2).

After describing the future, when the Messiah will judge lawless people, Paul turned his attention to the distant past. He noted that from the very "beginning" (2 Thess. 2:13) God chose the believers in Thessalonica to "be saved." The apostle made similar claims in other letters (for example, see Eph. 1:4). These passages are understood in different ways by Christians. Some think that God long ago predes-tined some individuals (but not others) for receiving His salvation. Others say that God formed His plan of salvation long ago but that the matter of who receives sal-vation is determined by the exercise of free human will.

In either case, the salvation of the Thessalonians (and that of all believers) came through the work of the Spirit. He enables the lost to believe the Good News and grow increasingly holy in their lives. Paul emphasized both the Spirit's "sanctifying work" and the individual's "belief in the truth. With respect to the apostle's read-ers, God the Spirit had made unholy people holy, and the people themselves had put their faith in the truth about the Messiah. At this point we should note the con-trast between the Thessalonian believers and the future followers of the lawless one. Those whom God will judge "have not believed the truth" (vs. 12), while the Thessalonians were saved "through belief in the truth" (vs. 13).

B. Called to Salvation: vs. 14

He called you to this through our gospel, that you might share in the glory of our Lord Jesus Christ.

On a practical, historical level, Paul's proclamation of the Gospel had been the means by which God had called the Thessalonians to salvation. No doubt, the apos-tle was pleased and proud to have been used by the Lord in this important way.

One reason God called the Thessalonians to salvation was so that they "might share in the glory" (2 Thess. 2:14) of Jesus. This was a far different destiny than that awaiting the followers of Satan's evil henchman. He would be eternally condemned.

Other Bible passages likewise describe believers as sharing the Messiah's glory—now, and even more so in the life to come. For instance, while the Son prayed to the Father, He said of His disciples, "I have given them the glory that you gave me" (John 17:22). Also, consider some of what Paul wrote: (1) "We, who with unveiled faces all reflect the Lord's glory, are being transformed into his likeness with ever-increasing glory, which comes from the Lord, who is the Spirit" (2 Cor. 3:18); (2) "When Christ, who is your life, appears, then you also will appear with him in glory" (Col. 3:4); and (3) "God . . . calls you into his kingdom and glory" (1 Thess. 2:12). Moreover, Peter said the following: (1) "When the Chief Shepherd appears, you will receive the crown of glory that will never fade away" (1 Pet. 5:4); and (2) "The God of all grace . . . called you to his eternal glory in Christ" (1 Pet. 5:10).

It's hard to comprehend the fact that one day believers will share in Jesus' glory. After all, the Messiah is the sinless Son of God. So who are we to participate in His glory? But out of love, Jesus became like we are so that we might become like He is—and He is glorious. Knowing that God has prepared glory for believers should not make us complacent. On the contrary, it should motivate us to serve the Lord better. Because Christians are destined for glory, we should be concerned about obeying the instructions God has given us in the Scriptures. Also, since believers are destined for glory, we should live as God's hands and mouth in the world—ministering to people's needs and proclaiming the Gospel boldly.

II. STANDING FIRM IN THE FAITH: 2 THESSALONIANS 2:15-17

A. Holding Fast to Biblical Truth: vs. 15

So then, brothers, stand firm and hold to the teachings we passed on to you, whether by word of mouth or by letter.

In light of the Thessalonians' decision to trust in Christ for salvation, Paul urged them to remain steadfast in their faith. This included standing firm on the solid ground of the apostolic teaching they had received from the missionaries. Also, rather than be misled by spiritual frauds, they were to maintain a strong grip on the biblical truths Paul and his colleagues had imparted to them. It did not matter whether it took place directly in person or indirectly by means of letters (2 Thess. 2:15). Either way, the proclamation of the Gospel had been effective as a means to the Thessalonians receiving salvation. Therefore, it was only logical for them to continue to heed what the missionaries had taught them.

B. Finding Encouragement and Strength in the Lord: vss. 16-17

May our Lord Jesus Christ himself and God our Father, who loved us and by his grace gave us eternal encouragement and good hope, encourage your hearts and strengthen you in every good deed and word.

Given the challenges the believers in Thessalonica faced, it would not be easy for them to hold fast to biblical truth. Indeed, they would need help—divine help. So at this point in his letter, Paul prayed that God would encourage and strengthen them. In the apostle's prayer, he invoked both the Lord Jesus Christ—God the Son—and God the Father (2 Thess. 2:16). Perhaps Jesus was mentioned first because the Savior was much in Paul's thoughts. Usually he mentioned the Father first (for example, see 1 Thess. 1:1), but sometimes the apostle reversed the order (for example, see Gal. 1:1). This indicates that he regarded the Father and the Son (along with the Spirit) as equal members of the Godhead.

Paul reminded his readers of what God had done for them. Specifically, He "loved" (2 Thess. 2:16) them and by means of His "grace" bestowed on them everlasting consolation and a firm hope. When speaking of the love of the Father for believers, the apostle may have had in mind the sacrifice of the Son for sinners. Surely no greater evidence of the Father's love could be imagined. Most likely, then, "eternal encouragement" refers to the effects of salvation. Because the Thessalonians had been redeemed, they had received a permanent change of attitude. For similar reasons, the "good hope" was their confident assurance of receiving future kingdom blessings. Put another way, they had every reason to expect kindnesses from the Lord Jesus at His second coming.

The Greek term rendered "encouragement" literally means "a calling to one's side." Expressed differently, one person is called to the side of another to admonish or console. A form of this word is used as a title for the Holy Spirit (see John 14:26). The Greek term also refers to encouragement that prepares for action. So when Paul said that God "gave us eternal encouragement" (2 Thess. 2:16), he was talking about a continuing process of divine strengthening, exhortation, and aid. It would be natural to see the Holy Spirit's involvement in this process.

The love, encouragement, and hope believers receive from the Father through faith in the Son is the basis for Paul's specific prayer request for the Thessalonians. He wanted God to encourage their hearts and strengthen them in every good thing they did and said (vs. 17). Given their situation, these are the areas the apostle thought they needed God's assistance the most. Because of persecution and false teaching in Thessalonica, and perhaps for other reasons as well, Paul's readers needed encouragement. God could give them the spiritual uplift they required. He could also refresh their hearts and give them the grit they needed to go on believing and obeying the truth.

The apostle's spiritual children were already involved in serving others in what they said and did. But as Christians soon find out, ministry can be wearying. So Paul prayed for an injection of new spiritual energy into the Thessalonians as they carried on in their lives of service. When we find ourselves feeling discouraged and weak, we should not forget that God is able to supply us with what we need to get moving again. His resources are more than abundant enough to meet our needs, and He is eager for us to go to Him in prayer for help.

Discussion Questions

1. In what ways did God show His love to the believers in Thessalonica?
2. How does the Holy Spirit use the proclamation of the Gospel to bring about the salvation of the lost?
3. Why is it important for us, as Jesus' followers, to stand firm in the faith?
4. In what ways has the truth of salvation in Christ provided you with "good hope" (2 Thess. 2:16)?
5. What are some specific ways you can serve the Lord in "every good deed and word" (vs. 17)?

Contemporary Application

Have you ever encountered someone who confesses to have trusted in Christ in the past, but after suffering or disappointment, admits to little faith? All believers experience times when their ability to stand firm in the faith is tested. Undoubtedly, some in your class are now facing situations in which their faith needs strengthening.

Second Thessalonians was directed to believers whose commitment to the Lord Jesus was being undermined by persecution and false teaching. If these challenges were left unaddressed, Paul's spiritual children faced the possibility of drifting away from their loyalty to the Savior. Just as an anchor is needed to keep a boat from drifting into danger, so the Redeemer is the anchor of our faith. He is also the bedrock that secures our faith so that it can remain firm in the soil of our lives.

The main point of this imagery is that we are to find encouragement and strength in the Lord. When we do so, we are better able to hold fast to biblical truth. The implication is that Christianity must not be for us an off-again, on-again, "when-it's-convenient" religion. Paul, in his second letter to the Thessalonians, calls us to live consistently close to the Savior. We can do so knowing that when He returns, we will share in His glory.

God's Own Faithfulness

DEVOTIONAL READING

Psalm 89:1-8

DAILY BIBLE READINGS

Monday July 19
  *Psalm 89:1-8 God's
  Steadfast Love*

Tuesday July 20
  *Acts 21:1-14 Ready to Die
  for the Lord*

Wednesday July 21
  *1 Corinthians 1:4-9 God Is
  Faithful*

Thursday July 22
  *Hebrews 6:13-20 A Sure and
  Steadfast Anchor*

Friday July 23
  *Hebrews 10:19-25 Faithful
  Promises*

Saturday July 24
  *1 John 1:5-10 Faithful to
  Forgive*

Sunday July 25
  *2 Thessalonians 3:1-15 God
  Will Strengthen and Guard*

Scripture

Background Scripture: *2 Thessalonians 3*
Scripture Lesson: *2 Thessalonians 3:1-15*
Key Verse: *The Lord is faithful, and he will strengthen and
protect you from the evil one.* 2 Thessalonians 3:3.
Scripture Lesson for Children: *Acts 21:1-14;
2 Thessalonians 3:1-3*
Key Verses for Children: *The Lord is faithful, and he will
strengthen and protect you.* 2 Thessalonians 3:3.

Lesson Aim

To recognize the value of serving the Lord in productive and useful ways.

Lesson Setting

Time: *About A.D. 51 or 52*
Place: *Written from Corinth to the church in Thessalonica*

Lesson Outline

God's Own Faithfulness

  I. Items for Intercession: 2 Thessalonians 3:1-5
      A. *Prayer Requests: vss. 1-2*
      B. *Protection from God: vs. 3*
      C. *Perseverance in the Faith: vss. 4-5*
  II. Idleness as Irresponsibility: 2 Thessalonians 3:6-15
      A. *Avoiding the Slothful: vs. 6*
      B. *Working Hard for the Lord: vss. 7-8*
      C. *Setting a Godly Example: vss. 9-10*
      D. *Leading Orderly Lives: vss. 11-12*
      E. *Seeking to Do Good: vs. 13*
      F. *Disciplining the Slothful: vss. 14-15*

Introduction for Adults

Topic: *Finding Strength*

If we're content to let things go on in a routine sort of way, nobody bothers us. But when we dare to throw down the challenge of a great opportunity for God's glory, opposition suddenly appears. For example, if a church wants to buy property for a new sanctuary, suddenly people start to protest about the traffic, noise, pollution, and so forth.

Paul and his colleagues knew what John Newton wrote about in "Amazing Grace." In this week's Scripture passage, we learn that "wicked and evil people" (2 Thess. 3:2) tried to undermine the efforts of the missionaries. By finding strength in the Lord, the evangelists were able to persevere in their God-given work. In the same way, we can too.

Introduction for Youth

Topic: *Committed to Work*

A young man named Mike was recovering from drug addiction when he went door-to-door looking for odd jobs. One family asked him to spade a garden plot. Mike tore into his task, but soon wearied of it because he had no idea how to use a spade. His enthusiasm did not make up for his inexperience.

The spot Mike worked on looked like a battlefield. Huge holes appeared everywhere. The owner came back aghast. He took Mike aside and showed him how to spade in a more orderly way. Once more Mike tackled the plot. This time he finished the work acceptably.

Most of us need practical help and wise counsel so that we can do God's work in His way. Growing things in God's spiritual garden is not easy. In Paul's time, enemies of the faith tried to undermine the spread of the Gospel. The apostle and his colleagues drew on their experiences with God. They prayed, worked hard, and refused to give up. They joined raw courage to strong faith and finished their God-given responsibilities. Likewise, so can we.

Concepts for Children

Topic: *Live like a Believer*

1. Jesus' followers did not want Paul to go to the city of Jerusalem, where mean people wanted to harm him.
2. Paul was not afraid to put up with hardship so that people might trust in Jesus for salvation.
3. Paul and his friends prayed with believers in the city of Tyre before they went to Jerusalem.
4. Paul asked that the believers in the city of Thessalonica pray for him and his friends so that as many people as possible would hear the Gospel.
5. Paul taught that God can give us the strength to serve Him faithfully.

Lesson Commentary

I. ITEMS FOR INTERCESSION: 2 THESSALONIANS 3:1-5

A. Prayer Requests: vss. 1-2

Finally, brothers, pray for us that the message of the Lord may spread rapidly and be honored, just as it was with you. And pray that we may be delivered from wicked and evil men, for not everyone has faith.

The missionaries, having prayed for the Thessalonians, were not too proud or too vain to ask prayer for themselves. The ministry team requested prayer for the success of their mission and for personal protection. The evangelists specifically wanted to see the Gospel continue to "spread rapidly" (2 Thess. 3:1) and be received with honor. At the time Paul wrote this letter, he and his colleagues were probably in Corinth. So he was thinking especially about the future of Christianity in that major city and in the surrounding territory of Achaia.

The evangelists' second prayer request was for God to rescue them from those who were perverse and cruel. The existence of people who are "wicked and evil" (vs. 2) reminds us that far too many have rejected the saving message of the Gospel. Paul and his colleagues were doing spiritual battle in Corinth with individuals who opposed what was being preached (Acts 18:6, 12-17). Therefore, the prayer support of fellow believers was essential. The Christians in Thessalonica knew how their missionary friends had been abused in their own city by bigoted, depraved people (17:5-9). The ministry team's desire for deliverance from enemies of the Gospel in other places, then, was something their spiritual children could understand.

B. Protection from God: vs. 3

But the Lord is faithful, and he will strengthen and protect you from the evil one.

Persecution was something that the missionaries and the Thessalonians had in common. Paul and his colleagues were suffering from the actions of immoral and reprehensible people (2 Thess. 3:2), and so were the evangelists' spiritual children. So the ministry team assured them again of God's ability to take care of them. That "the Lord is faithful" (vs. 3) means He can be depended upon completely by all who trust in Him. In the case of the believers in Thessalonica, they could rely on Him to give them strength and protection against Satan.

The Greek term rendered "strengthen" emphasizes being made stable, placed firmly, or established. The word translated "protect" means to guard or keep watch over something so that it remains safe. Concerning believers, God preserves them from "the evil one." This phrase is a common New Testament reference for Satan. The devil's eventual doom is certain, but in the present, he is active. Be that as it may, Christians can be sure that God will strengthen us in our continuing battle with this powerful and malevolent opponent. Indeed, God does not establish His people and then leave us on our own. Instead, He guards us continually.

C. Perseverance in the Faith: vss. 4-5

We have confidence in the Lord that you are doing and will continue to do the things we command. May the Lord direct your hearts into God's love and Christ's perseverance.

Paul and his colleagues were certain that God was watching over the believers in Thessalonica. In turn, this truth gave the missionaries "confidence in the Lord" (2 Thess. 3:4) that their new converts were obeying and would continue to obey what they had been taught. Evidently, then, the evangelists associated their commands with effective opposition to the evil one. By believing and living as the ministry team had taught, the Thessalonians could frustrate the plans of Satan.

Undoubtedly, the assurance of Paul and his associates gave much-needed encouragement to the believers in Thessalonica. As they read about this confidence, they would be motivated to trust God afresh to enable them to do His will as it was communicated through the missionaries. At the same time, the evangelists knew how easy it is for believers to go astray and to cave in to fear of the enemy. So the missionaries prayed that their spiritual children would allow the Father to "direct" (vs. 5) their "hearts" into His "love" and "Christ's perseverance."

The Greek phrase rendered "God's love" (vs. 5) can refer to both the love that God gives and the love believers have for Him and others. Similarly, the phrase translated "Christ's perseverance" can denote both the patient endurance Jesus displayed while here on earth and the steadfastness He gives to His followers. The basis for believers remaining faithful to Him is the Lord directing them, in which the Greek word used for "direct" can also mean to "guide" and "lead." The term was sometimes used of guiding a storm-tossed ship into a peaceful harbor. As Christians, we too need to be directed into an ever deeper understanding of the Father's love, especially to rest and rejoice in it. We also need to reflect more and more on the patient suffering of the Son. He endured the cross, despite the shame associated with it (Heb. 12:2), and He is our example in times of testing and persecution.

II. IDLENESS AS IRRESPONSIBILITY: 2 THESSALONIANS 3:6-15

A. Avoiding the Slothful: vs. 6

In the name of the Lord Jesus Christ, we command you, brothers, to keep away from every brother who is idle and does not live according to the teaching you received from us.

As Paul came to the end of his second letter to the believers in Thessalonica, he and his colleagues addressed a serious problem that had developed. Some of the new converts had decided not to work anymore. We can't be sure why. According to one suggestion, the idlers had decided that since Christ was returning soon, there was no point in working. Another possibility is that the loafers thought their fellow church members should support them while they devoted themselves to prayer and study.

Whatever the reason for the idleness in the Thessalonian church, the evangelists did not approve of it. And apparently they thought the disease of idleness might be contagious. So the ministry team commanded the working members of the congregation to stay away from those who lived in an undisciplined, unruly, or disruptive manner (2 Thess. 3:6). The indolent should have known better than to refrain from working. In fact, they had deliberately chosen to disobey what the missionaries had taught about work when they were with the new converts in person (see vs. 10) and when the apostle had written his first letter (see 1 Thess. 4:11-12; 5:14). Thus, the slothful deserved to be shunned by the more obedient church members.

The missionaries commanded the hardworking believers to avoid the idlers. Issuing the directive "in the name of the Lord Jesus Christ" (2 Thess. 3:6) made it especially authoritative. The Greek word translated "command" was used to describe generals giving orders to their troops. The term rendered "idle" denoted soldiers who were lax in discipline. Despite the insistence of the evangelists, they did not bully their readers. The ministry team addressed the troubled Thessalonians as "brothers." This included those who had fallen into slothfulness as well as those who had not.

B. Working Hard for the Lord: vss. 7-8

For you yourselves know how you ought to follow our example. We were not idle when we were with you, nor did we eat anyone's food without paying for it. On the contrary, we worked night and day, laboring and toiling so that we would not be a burden to any of you.

To reinforce their command, the missionaries reminded their spiritual children how the ministry team had lived while in Thessalonica. The evangelists had set an example of a disciplined life that the new converts were urged to imitate (2 Thess. 3:7). Instead of being idle and self-indulgent, Paul and his colleagues had worked hard and even refused to accept a meal without paying for it with the money they had earned. In making this statement, the evangelists did not mean that the Thessalonians had failed to display hospitality. Presumably, they had offered to feed the ministers of the Gospel and take care of their other material needs.

Nonetheless, the evangelists refused to be a financial burden on the new converts. God's servants wanted to become a positive role model for others. Surely Paul recognized the importance of his apostolic ministry. If he and his colleagues had not worked for a living, they would have had more time to spread the Gospel and teach new believers. The latter truths notwithstanding, the missionaries chose to work in toil and drudgery "night and day" (vs. 8) so as not to be an expense to any of the Thessalonians. The testimony of the evangelists underscored the great importance they put on offering an example of hard work. In short, they decided to conduct their spiritual ministry after long hours of physical labor.

C. Setting a Godly Example: vss. 9-10

We did this, not because we do not have the right to such help, but in order to make ourselves a model for you to follow. For even when we were with you, we gave you this rule: "If a man will not work, he shall not eat."

The ministry team sensed the importance of explaining further the rationale for their decision to earn their own living. The evangelists affirmed that they had a right to receive material help from the new converts while ministering among them (2 Thess. 3:9). Despite this, the missionaries deliberately gave up their right for the good of their spiritual children. The evangelists wanted to set a godly example for the other believers to imitate. This was evidently Paul's practice in more than one city (see 1 Cor. 9:1-23).

Previously, when Paul and his associates were in Thessalonica, they noticed that idlers and gossips were infecting the congregation. So the missionaries directed that anyone who refused to work would not get to eat (2 Thess. 3:10). This "rule" or order was a consistent theme of the apostle's teaching, not a cavalier remark. Paul meant that slothful, unruly members of the church should not be permitted to live off the generosity of hardworking Christians. The apostle was not referring to believers who lost their jobs for economic or political reasons, or were unable to work. It goes without saying that the Christians living in Thessalonica needed to care for the poor and unemployed among them. But those who refused to work had no right to such consideration.

D. Leading Orderly Lives: vss. 11-12

We hear that some among you are idle. They are not busy; they are busybodies. Such people we command and urge in the Lord Jesus Christ to settle down and earn the bread they eat.

When it came to the slothful in the church at Thessalonica, the missionaries had some specific individuals in mind. They weren't just being lazy. In some cases, the "idle" (2 Thess. 3:11) had grown undisciplined and unruly in their conduct. Perhaps someone in the congregation had written to Paul about the serious epidemic of indolence. Another possibility is that the reports came from visitors. In any case, the evangelists learned that some believers, instead of doing their own work, were meddling in the work of others. Since these "busybodies" refused to earn a living, they had plenty of time to swap tales about other people and pry into matters that did not concern them. It's still the case that mischief-makers can become a disruptive influence in the church. That's one more reason for making a habit of working hard.

In verse 12, the missionaries spoke directly to the slothful persons. They were commanded in the name of the Lord Jesus Christ to lead orderly lives and work quietly. In this way they were to provide for their own food to eat. While the evangelists addressed the loafers tactfully, the ministers of the Gospel did not mince words. In admonishing the slothful, the missionaries invoked the authority of the

Savior. If the busybodies recognized Jesus as their Lord, then they ought to have obeyed the directives issued by His servants. There was no middle ground here. Instead of freeloading off of others, the idlers were to earn a living just like anybody else.

E. Seeking to Do Good: vs. 13

And as for you, brothers, never tire of doing what is right.

Next, the missionaries shifted their attention back to the hardworking members of the church in Thessalonia. The ministry team affectionately addressed the new converts as "brothers" (2 Thess. 3:13) and encouraged them to never grow weary of doing good (compare Gal. 6:9). The evangelists probably meant, in particular, "doing what is right" by continuing to work. But the exhortation is broad enough to take in other kinds of virtuous activity. Perhaps the offenders would pay no attention to the missionaries. Despite this, the responsible members of the congregation were not to follow the slothful example of their idle peers.

It can be hard to keep on the straight and narrow road when other travelers are veering off and taking one exit ramp after another. Nevertheless, the missionaries urged their spiritual children to seek to do good. For many believers today, idleness is not one of their failings. On the contrary, they work too hard. Indeed, they are workaholics. That is, they devote themselves to their jobs so extensively that their family, their church, and even their own health may suffer for it. Be that as it may, others still need to heed the apostolic warning against idleness. They work too little, depend on the goodness of others too much, and waste time in harmful behaviors. By acting in this way, they are doing what is wrong in God's sight. Let us do whatever we can to strike a healthy balance between overwork and idleness.

F. Disciplining the Slothful: vss. 14-15

If anyone does not obey our instruction in this letter, take special note of him. Do not associate with him, in order that he may feel ashamed. Yet do not regard him as an enemy, but warn him as a brother.

Given the amount of time and attention the missionaries devoted to commenting on the situation in the church at Thessalonica, we can see how seriously they took the matter. In fact, 2 Thessalonians 3:14-15 are quite pointed in their emphasis. The Greek word rendered "obey" (vs. 14) means not only to hear but also to heed what is commanded. The new converts were to be on their guard against those who ignored what the evangelists had instructed in their letter. The responsible members of the congregation were to put the loafers to shame by refusing to "associate" closely with them. The latter is more literally rendered, "Do not mix yourselves up with him."

The goal of disciplining the slothful was to bring about a radical change in their behavior. Here we see the beneficial application of peer pressure to get the unruly to conform their behavior to God's will. The missionaries hoped that the pain of being avoided would effectively prompt the idlers to see the error of their ways. The entire effort was to be carried out in a spirit of Christian love. Those who refused to obey the apostolic mandate were still members of Christ's spiritual body, not enemies (vs. 15). This means that the evangelists were not ordering outright excommunication of the indolent. The goal was the restoration of the idlers to usefulness in the community of faith, not their punishment.

Discussion Questions

1. Why were the missionaries eager for the Gospel to spread rapidly?
2. What are some ways you have seen the Lord protect His spiritual children from the evil one?
3. Why did the evangelists decide not to rely on others to provide for their daily needs?
4. How might the spread of the Gospel be negatively affected by the presence of busybodies in a congregation?
5. Why were the believers in Thessalonica directed not to associate with the slothful in their midst?

Contemporary Application

The Lord's work in any era advances against opposition. Jesus made this clear when He said hell itself would attack, but not prevail against His church (Matt. 16:18). Each generation needs wisdom to discern the enemy's strategy and to develop plans to resist.

Christian adults are often surprised by the opposition they encounter in striving to serve the Lord in ways that are productive and useful. They wrongly assume the path will be easy. But even though the sources of opposition may not be obvious when they begin their work, the opposition will appear. They may be as subtle as discouragement or as blatant as outward attempts to interfere with a believer's service for the Savior.

Sometimes the attacks are overt, such as Paul and his colleagues faced. Other times the attacks are psychological and emotional. We have to be prepared for both. If the enemy cannot sidetrack us with suffering or persecution, for example, we may find ourselves being subverted by sinful attachments. The usual avenues of such attacks are immorality, money, and power.

Therefore, to be strong for God we need wisdom, courage, and faith. We need the kind of wise instructions Paul and his associates gave. We need leaders who will summon us to be diligent in our service. They will call us to prayer, obedience, and disciplined way of life. Our greatest need in the face of hostility is to know how to put on and use the complete armor of God (Eph. 6:10-18).

Sharing God's Grace

Scripture

Background Scripture: *Philippians 1*

Scripture Lesson: *Philippians 1:18b-29*

Key Verse: *Whatever happens, conduct yourselves in a manner worthy of the gospel of Christ. Then, whether I come and see you or only hear about you in my absence, I will know that you stand firm in one spirit, contending as one man for the faith of the gospel.* Philippians 1:27.

Scripture Lesson for Children: *Acts 21:27-28, 31-33; 22:30—23:1, 9-11; Philippians 1:27*

Key Verse for Children: *Conduct yourselves in a manner worthy of the gospel of Christ.* Philippians 1:27.

Lesson Aim

To learn that only Jesus brings true meaning to life.

Lesson Setting

Time: *About A.D. 61*

Place: *Written from Rome to the church in Philippi*

Lesson Outline

Sharing God's Grace

  I. Exalting the Messiah: Philippians 1:18b-26
     A. *Anticipating Deliverance: vss. 18b-19*
     B. *Living and Dying for Christ: vss. 20-21*
     C. *Continuing to Live: vss. 22-24*
     D. *Rejoicing in Christ: vss. 25-26*
 II. Living as Citizens of Heaven: Philippians 1:27-29
     A. *Standing Firm: vs. 27*
     B. *Remaining Fearless: vs. 28*
     C. *Suffering for the Savior: vs. 29*

Introduction for Adults

Topic: *Overcoming Obstacles*

A woman asked a pastor to visit her father in the hospital. He had suffered a heart attack after a flood had wiped out his business.

The woman thought her father would be open to spiritual counsel and turn to Jesus in faith. Perhaps the former business owner would take the flood as God's warning for him to repent. Sadly, however, he was angry with God for the flood. If it was God's final warning, the heart attack victim paid no attention to the Lord.

Paul never allowed this sort of response to undermine his boldness in sharing Christ with the unsaved. Regardless of where the apostle ministered—whether in the city of Philippi or chained to a guard under house arrest in Rome—he wanted to be sure that everyone he encountered was saved.

When the members of your class adopt this way of thinking, they will be better able to overcome impediments they encounter in witnessing for Christ. He will enable them to work together to encourage even the most hardhearted of unbelievers to trust in Jesus for salvation. Even when some refuse, the class members can remain resolute in proclaiming the Gospel to others.

Introduction for Youth

Topic: *Good No Matter What*

During a high school wrestling match, Caleb "the underdog" appeared on the verge of losing. The state champion was about to pin him. But suddenly, in what seemed like a miracle, Caleb threw off his opponent and defeated him. How? Because Caleb never gave up hope in the midst of hardship.

Wrestling is a picture of the Christian life. Paul reminded his readers that they wrestled with powerful spiritual opponents. He himself demonstrated what it was like. Paul never quit, despite physical beatings, abuse, and imprisonment. Rather than succumb to defeat and despair, he came up rejoicing. He refused to be pinned.

The same spiritual principles can work for saved teens. As they pray for one another and the Holy Spirit helps them, good can even come out of their most difficult moments (see Phil. 1:19).

Concepts for Children

Topic: *Stand Firm in Trouble*

1. Paul was in jail in the city of Rome for telling people about Jesus.
2. Paul did not let being in jail stop him from telling people about Jesus.
3. God wanted Paul to be bold in telling people about Jesus.
4. God wants us to be courageous in letting others know about our faith in Jesus.
5. God wants us to live in a way that brings honor to the good news about salvation in Jesus.

Lesson Commentary

I. EXALTING THE MESSIAH: PHILIPPIANS 1:18B-26

A. Anticipating Deliverance: vss. 18b-19

Yes, and I will continue to rejoice, for I know that through your prayers and the help given by the Spirit of Jesus Christ, what has happened to me will turn out for my deliverance.

During Paul's second missionary journey, he planted the first European church in Philippi (see Acts 16:9-40). This probably occurred around A.D. 50. A few of the converts of Philippi, such as Lydia, became some of his dearest friends. The dramatic conversion of a jailer and the exorcism of a slave girl also occurred in this city. Some Bible scholars suggest that the physician Luke was from this town, since it had a prominent school of medicine and because he noted its prominence (vs. 12). In any case, the Philippian church always held a cherished place in Paul's heart. He came back to visit this city on his third missionary journey around A.D. 55–56. In fact, he may have passed through the city twice on this particular trip.

After the Philippian believers sent Paul a generous gift while he was under house arrest in Rome, the apostle wrote this letter to thank them for their kindness and to report on his current situation. At the same time, Paul took this opportunity to urge them to remain strong and united in their faith in Christ though many external and internal elements may have been discouraging them. The apostle was referring to his house arrest when he spoke of himself as being "in chains for Christ" (Phi. 1:13), and not of his later imprisonment in the Mamertine dungeon prior to his execution (see Acts 28:30-31).

Undoubtedly, the Philippian Christians knew that Paul was under house arrest and was awaiting his trial before Caesar on serious charges. The consequences of those charges could be terribly grievous for Paul, at least physically. It was possible that he could be sentenced to either death or a long, harsh imprisonment for sedition against Rome. His friends in Philippi probably prayed fervently that God would comfort and deliver him from his unpleasant and precarious situation. Aware of their concern for his welfare and safety, the apostle wanted to assure them in this letter that God was not only caring for him but also bringing unexpected and marvelous fruit to his ongoing ministry (Phil. 1:12).

Paul was especially excited about the Lord's work among the emperor's guards, for everyone there knew that the apostle was under arrest because of his unswerving faith in Jesus and his courageous defense of the Gospel. Some of them had even received Christ as their Lord and Savior. It was clear to everyone that Paul was not under house arrest because he had violated a civil law or because he was a political agitator. The sentries who were responsible for guarding the apostle probably observed how he lived out his faith in Christ. Some may have listened to Paul's teachings about the Messiah and shared what they learned with other palace guards, noting that the apostle's characteristics were nothing like those of most of the criminals they guarded. Moreover, the Gospel was advanced not only among these guards but to many other people as well (vs. 13).

Furthermore, Paul attributed the proclamation of the Gospel by other Christians in Rome to his being "in chains for Christ." Whether the apostle was describing an actual condition in which he was chained to a guard or was referring to his imprisonment and sufferings in general is not clear. In any case, he was elated that his example encouraged other Christians to be brave and bold in declaring the Word of God (vs. 14). All of Paul's believing readers might also come under the iron fist of the Roman authorities. If the Lord could still bring fabulous fruit to the apostle's ministry while he was under house arrest, they too could be fruitful for the Lord whether in or out of prison.

When Paul said of his imprisonment that he was "put here for the defense of the gospel" (vs. 16), he was specifically saying that God had brought him to Rome for a particular purpose. It was no accident or quirk of fate that the apostle was there. In the approximately 30 years that had passed from Christ's resurrection to Paul's imprisonment, the Gospel had been carried through incredible means from an obscure province of the Empire—Judea—to the court of Caesar himself. The apostle had been chosen to defend the truths of Christ in front of the most powerful and influential leaders of the day. The Roman world could reject the life-giving message Paul brought, but it could no longer ignore it.

Paul was confident that he was securely in God's hands. He believed whatever befell him would bring glory and honor to the Lord because God was in control of his life and the circumstances that affected his well-being. Therefore, though the apostle was under house arrest in Rome, he could rejoice and keep on rejoicing, for the Lord was with him and sustaining him (vs. 18). Furthermore, Paul knew that his Philippian friends were praying for him. A unique intimacy had developed between Paul and the Christians in Philippi, and the apostle naturally cherished their deep concern for him.

Moreover, Paul coveted the prayers of other Christians because he appreciated the distinctive power that believers' prayers had in enlisting God's aid (vs. 19). Paul also valued the strengthening he received from the Spirit of Christ, which supplied him with the courage, determination, and hope to persevere joyfully under his current circumstances. Most certainly the apostle depended on the Lord's Spirit to deliver him from any situation that brought hardship to him. Whatever the Romans decided to do with Paul, God Himself would vindicate the apostle.

B. Living and Dying for Christ: vss. 20-21

I eagerly expect and hope that I will in no way be ashamed, but will have sufficient courage so that now as always Christ will be exalted in my body, whether by life or by death. For to me, to live is Christ and to die is gain.

As Paul awaited his trial, his major concern was not whether the Father would save his life, but whether the apostle would present himself in such a way that the Son would be exalted. In fact, Paul was both eager and hoping to bring glory and not shame to the Lord. The Greek word for "eagerly expect" (Phil. 1:20) provides a vivid picture of one who cranes his or her neck to catch a glimpse of what lies ahead. The apostle was letting his readers know that, while ignoring all other interests, he keenly anticipated the honoring of the Lord during his trial.

Paul realized that the verdict could mean life or death for him physically. That is why he referred to "my body" in verse 20. Throughout the long ministry in which he preached the Gospel, whether to friendly crowds or hostile ones, the apostle always sought to exalt the Messiah in his body. Now, whether the Romans released Paul or executed him, he desired above all else that his Lord still be exalted in him. In a few words the apostle beautifully summed up the no-lose situation of belonging to Jesus: "For to me, to live is Christ and to die is gain" (vs. 21). This immortal affirmation expresses a believer's faith and hope. To Paul the gain meant much more than the eternal benefit of heaven. The profit was that the Gospel of Christ would be further advanced if the apostle was martyred for his faith and hope in Christ.

C. Continuing to Live: vss. 22-24

If I am to go on living in the body, this will mean fruitful labor for me. Yet what shall I choose? I do not know! I am torn between the two: I desire to depart and be with Christ, which is better by far; but it is more necessary for you that I remain in the body.

Paul was confident that he would continue to be fruitful in his ministry if the Romans did not execute him. In fact, even if he was forced to serve more time in prison, he would continue to proclaim the Gospel. He remained certain that nonbelievers would turn to Christ because of his preaching. Indeed, because of the apostle's strategic position in Rome, he would have additional opportunities to be God's instrument in bringing more people into the kingdom (Phil. 1:22a).

Nonetheless, to be with Christ in heaven was also appealing to Paul. In fact, if he were given a choice to continue to minister God's Word or be in the presence of Christ, the apostle confessed that the choice would be difficult to make. Yet Paul stated that he would choose to be with Christ because he would have a much deeper intimacy with Jesus in heaven, though the apostle already enjoyed a close relationship with Christ here on earth (vss. 22b-23). Despite Paul's own inclination to depart, he believed it was more important for him to remain. In fact, his whole reason for staying was for the sake of tending to other people's spiritual welfare, specifically for the pastoral care of his friends in the church at Philippi (vs. 24).

D. Rejoicing in Christ: vss. 25-26

Convinced of this, I know that I will remain, and I will continue with all of you for your progress and joy in the faith, so that through my being with you again your joy in Christ Jesus will overflow on account of me.

With bold confidence Paul told the Philippians that he was certain he would live in order to fulfill his duties in bringing them to spiritual maturity. Perhaps the great responsibility he had in caring for so many young believers throughout the Mediterranean world convinced him that it was too soon for him to die. Perhaps the Lord gave the apostle a premonition or an assurance that he would not be executed. Perhaps word was passed to him that the Roman authorities were looking at his case favorably toward him.

Whatever the reason, Paul was now unmistakably upbeat (Phil. 1:25). Moreover, the apostle thought that the Romans would not only spare his life but also give him his freedom, for he promised the Philippians that he would visit with them once again (vs. 26). We do not know whether this joyous meeting ever occurred. If it did, the Philippian Christians would have been overwhelmed with joy at seeing their friend and mentor. They would have listened carefully to the apostle's thrilling account of how the Lord was glorified through his harrowing yet rewarding experiences in Rome.

II. LIVING AS CITIZENS OF HEAVEN: PHILIPPIANS 1:27-29

A. Standing Firm: vs. 27

Whatever happens, conduct yourselves in a manner worthy of the gospel of Christ. Then, whether I come and see you or only hear about you in my absence, I will know that you stand firm in one spirit, contending as one man for the faith of the gospel.

Having been in Philippi and encountered persecution because of his faith, Paul knew what the believers in the city were up against. Also, since the apostle was deeply concerned for their individual welfare and the welfare of their church, he sought to encourage and instruct them with a love and tenderness unique among his known letters. Whatever difficulties might arise against the Philippians, Paul exhorted them to be faithful to the teachings about the Messiah. This demanded a high standard of godly behavior (Phil. 1:27). Only by maintaining this high calling toward one another would they be worthy examples of the Christian life.

Once again Paul reminded the Philippians of his possible return. Much in the same way as Paul asked Philemon to prepare a guest room for him (Philem. 22), the apostle's mention of going to Philippi was a subtle way of applying pressure on his readers to comply with his instructions. It was also typical of Paul to make it evident to his readers that their obedience would be of tremendous encouragement to him. In this case the Philippians could bring him supreme joy as he endured the ordeal of Roman confinement. By adding that he would hear reports about them even if he was unable to visit them shortly, he was urging them to heed his words immediately (Phil. 1:27).

Paul expected his readers to be united in spirit and be of one mind. Of course, he wasn't insisting that they all have the same personality or share the exact same views about everything when he told them to be "as one man." Nor did he want them to be carbon copies of himself. Different people have different gifts with which to serve God, and all are equally valuable to Him. There is also a wide range of personalities within the Church, each integral to the health of Christ's spiritual body. Even so, Paul was concerned with the rivalry and conflict that were apparently dividing the church in Philippi.

For this reason the apostle emphasized the importance of unity. This is especially important when nonbelievers are attacking a group of Christians. These believers should have a common purpose while contending for the Gospel and be supportive of one another. The Greek phrase rendered "the faith of the gospel" could be understood in either of three ways: (1) "the faith, which is the gospel"; (2) "the faith, which originates from the gospel"; or (3) "faith in the gospel." Regardless of which option is preferred, maintaining Christian unity was vital if the believers in Philippi were to withstand the attacks from the outside.

B. Remaining Fearless: vs. 28

Without being frightened in any way by those who oppose you. This is a sign to them that they will be destroyed, but that you will be saved—and that by God.

There were people in Philippi who were extremely hostile to Christians. Perhaps this animosity was a residual result of the incident in which Paul delivered a slave girl of a spirit that gave her fortune-telling abilities (see Acts 16:16-40). Paul and Silas had angered the owners of the slave girl because the owners were then deprived of this income. Thus they stirred the Philippians to attack Paul and Silas by convincing them that these men with their Christian beliefs were a threat to their Roman customs and religion. Although the evangelists departed at the request of the city's magistrates, the believers in Philippi likely encountered continued abuse because of their association with Paul.

The apostle counseled the Philippians not to be overcome by their adversaries. The Greek word rendered "frightened" (Phil. 1:28) can also be translated "alarmed," "terrified," or "intimidated." For believers in the time of Paul, the term would bring to mind an image of the uncontrollable stampede of startled horses. The apostle certainly did not want to see Philippian church in such disarray. Christian unity would steel the believers against their opponents and prevent any emotional chaos in the fellowship. Remarkably, their calm response in the face of affliction was a sign from God to both the persecutors and the persecuted. To the persecutors, it sealed their destruction as enemies of God and the "gospel of Christ" (vs. 27). To the persecuted, this sign confirmed their certain salvation in the Son as His chosen followers. God Himself would see to it that His enemies are defeated and that His spiritual children are saved. Nothing can stand in the way of God's sovereignty (vs. 28).

C. Suffering for the Savior: vs. 29

For it has been granted to you on behalf of Christ not only to believe on him, but also to suffer for him.

According to Paul, belief and suffering go hand in hand. Indeed, suffering for Christ's sake is another sign of the believer's union with the Redeemer. Suffering is a natural consequence of identifying with the Son (Phil. 1:29). Paul identified the suffering of his friends in Philippi with his own afflictions. They had observed firsthand how he was persecuted in their city. They also had heard about his struggles since then, including those during his house arrest in Rome. Hence they should have been able to realize that their burdens and experiences were no different from his. Since Paul was constantly conveying in his letter to them the joy God had given him, despite these adversities, he likewise wanted them to rejoice with him (vs. 30).

Discussion Questions

1. How was it possible for Paul to continue to rejoice while under house arrest in Rome?
2. Where do you think Paul found the courage to remain bold in telling others about the Savior?
3. What led Paul to believe that for the time being, God wanted him to continue to live and proclaim the Gospel?
4. What are some ways that we, as believers, can live as "citizens of heaven" (Phil. 1:27) while remaining here on earth?
5. Why is it important for us, as Jesus' disciples, to remain calm when we are harassed for our faith in Christ?

Contemporary Application

In Philippians 1:21, Paul said that "to live is Christ and to die is gain." Perhaps the apostle's simple testimony sounds otherworldly to us. He can't be real, we think. How could he possibly rejoice while wearing chains and locked in a prison? How could he be so bold and so confident about his life's purpose and destiny? What a contrast to the aimlessness we see in people's lives all around us.

The church stands as a beacon of brightness to people lost in the fog of meaninglessness. How encouraging it is to hear the testimonies of people who say that the Lord Jesus filled the emptiness in their lives. Perhaps at times we are afraid or ashamed to see this in our own life. It takes faith to recognize that with each passing day, Jesus is making a real difference for us.

Paul faced his imprisonment with courage and creativity. Because of Christ, a situation that could have resulted in the apostle being depressed and benefiting no one resulted in an event that produced much fruit for the Kingdom. This is what the Lord Jesus wants to do in our lives. As believers we need to see every difficulty through His perspective. The world is in the hands of the master designer, who creates each day full of new possibilities and potential to serve Him.

Giving of Oneself

Scripture

Background Scripture: *Philippians 2:1—3:1a*
Scripture Lesson: *Philippians 2:1-13*
Key Verse: *Your attitude should be the same as that of Christ Jesus.* Philippians 2:5.
Scripture Lesson for Children: *Acts 23:12-21, 23; Philippians 2:4*
Key Verses for Children: *Each of you should look not only to your own interests, but also to the interests of others.* Philippians 2:4.

Lesson Aim

To consider the interests of others as important as our own.

Lesson Setting

Time: *About A.D. 61*
Place: *Written from Rome to the church in Philippi*

Lesson Outline

Giving of Oneself

  I. Consider the Needs of Others: Philippians 2:1-4
     A. *Living in Harmony: vss. 1-2*
     B. *Living in Humility: vss. 3-4*
 II. Follow the Example of Christ: Philippians 2:5-11
     A. *Enjoying Equality with the Father and the Spirit: vss. 5-6*
     B. *Enduring the Humiliation of the Cross: vss. 7-8*
     C. *Experiencing Divine Exaltation: vss. 9-11*
     D. *Obeying and Pleasing God: vss. 12-13*

Introduction for Adults

Topic: *Serving Others*

We all need reminding that the Lord Jesus is number one. This remains true regardless of whether we are ministers, deacons, trustees, Sunday school teachers, or other church officers. This knowledge calls for humble servanthood in Christ's name.

Often, however, we are like the woman in a certain congregation who was asked to prepare a snack for her children and others in her church youth group for one evening. She retorted in a scalding tone, "You mean you are asking me to come up to the church and do the work of a servant?"

Exactly!

Introduction for Youth

Topic: *Service with a Smile*

Paul wanted the believers in the Philippian church to change. The apostle did not call for a conference on management. Instead, he called for a fresh look at the suffering Savior. Until His followers took Him seriously, they would not discover genuine and joyful humility.

A Christian pastor said, "A person who profoundly changed my life was not a preacher or the leader of a big organization. She was a cheerful office worker at the local bus company. She never married. She used her home and her slim resources to develop Christian maturity among college students. Many of them—including myself—went into the ministry at home and abroad."

Few of us recognize the power of humble, exuberant, Christian service. But when the books are revealed, we may be surprised to learn that the major influences in God's kingdom come from unselfish, loving servants. Our own lives and our churches are immeasurably enriched when we follow the mind of Christ.

Concepts for Children

Topic: *Looking Out for Others*

1. Jesus came from heaven and suffered so that we might have eternal life.
2. One day Jesus will come back and the whole world will submit to Him.
3. God wants us to live unselfishly with one another.
4. Sometimes it is hard to give up what we want for the sake of others.
5. Even when it feels hard, Jesus still asks us to look for ways to help others.

Lesson Commentary

I. CONSIDER THE NEEDS OF OTHERS: PHILIPPIANS 2:1-4

A. Living in Harmony: vss. 1-2

If you have any encouragement from being united with Christ, if any comfort from his love, if any fellowship with the Spirit, if any tenderness and compassion, then make my joy complete by being likeminded, having the same love, being one in spirit and purpose.

In Philippians 2:1-2, Paul called the recipients of his letter to unity, humility, and obedience. As long as the congregation remained divided, they would not be able to resist the opposition they faced from antagonists (see 1:28). Although the Jewish population in Philippi was small, the problems in the city could have been caused by Jews from other cities who sometimes followed Paul and made trouble for his ministry in the towns he visited (Acts 17:13); however, the opposition referred to in Philippians 1:28 was probably the resistance of the pagan populace in general.

The persecution Paul's readers encountered undermined their Christian unity. Well aware of how this problem was manifesting itself among his friends, the apostle appealed to them in four stirring ways. First, Paul noted the united position of his readers in Christ (2:1). As believers, our starting point is always who we are in Christ—that is, we are all saved sinners because of what He has done for us on the cross. What can be more encouraging to us than being delivered from the condemnation of God? Also, what can be more unifying than for all of us to receive the same mercy? Paul was saying to the Philippians, "We are all in this together."

Second, the apostle reminded his readers about Christ's love. Jesus died for each one of them because He loved each one of them. This knowledge of the Father's love for us in the Son should always give us comfort. Being so loved should naturally prompt us to be loving as well. In fact, Jesus Himself exhorted His followers to love one another and prayed that we be one (see John 15:17; 17:21). Third, Paul stressed the indwelling of the Holy Spirit in each of his readers. Since there is one Spirit, there is one body of believers of which the Philippian believers were a part. Thus the sharing of the one Spirit of God should have compelled them to avoid any action or attitude that would divide the Body of Christ.

Finally, Paul spoke about the tender feelings and deep sympathy his readers were to have for one another (Phil. 2:1). This was prompted by the apostle's strong desire for these believers to be drawn together. Yet, rather than command the Philippians to bury their resentment toward one another and behave as good Christians should, Paul appealed to their hearts in such a way as to motivate them to be loving and forgiving toward one another. Although the apostle had zealously persecuted the earliest followers of Jesus Christ, the Lord still called this passionate Pharisee from Tarsus to be an important messenger to the Gentiles of the Gospel of love and forgiveness. Paul accomplished his God-appointed mission by both personally establishing churches throughout Greece and Asia Minor and writing divinely inspired letters to Christians throughout the Mediterranean world—including those living in Philippi.

Just as the apostle made four appeals to his readers, so he listed four results from such an effort to be united. First, the Philippians would be of the same mind. This does not mean they would always think the exact same thoughts. Instead, Paul meant they would be in agreement about laboring together for the glory of Christ. Second, they would experience the love for one another they each had in the Savior. Third, they would be wholeheartedly of one accord. Finally, they would be of one mind in purpose as a church (vs. 2).

B. Living in Humility: vss. 3-4

Do nothing out of selfish ambition or vain conceit, but in humility consider others better than yourselves. Each of you should look not only to your own interests, but also to the interests of others.

Paul warned his readers not to succumb to those spiritual viruses that damage Christian unity. "Selfish ambition" (Phil. 2:3) and "vain conceit" were evils that had evidently stricken some of the Philippian believers. Perhaps there were some who were engaging in party strife and petty squabbles because of their self-centeredness. Instead, the apostle admonished them to be humble, not like one who cringes before others, but like one who treats others as being more worthy than himself or herself.

In ancient times, the Greeks disdained the quality of humility, regarding it as shameful. It was something to be avoided and overcome with positive thoughts and actions. Believers, however, operated differently. God wanted them to recognize their true sinful condition and need for His grace. This is in keeping with the Greek word rendered "humility," which means to think rightly about one's position in life. Here we see that humility is a continual appreciation of our need for the Savior and of our need to always depend on Him. This was the opposite of the Greek concept of freedom, which called for a person not to be subject to anyone or anything, including God.

For Christ, humility meant a recognition of His role as a servant in becoming human. Since He was sinless, recognition of His true condition did not involve sin. He did, however, demonstrate the need to depend daily on the Father for strength. In light of what has been said, how can we demonstrate such Christlike humility? Paul advised that believers should look to the interests of other Christians as well as their own (vs. 4). Without ignoring what is important to us, we can daily show others that we value and appreciate what is important to them.

II. FOLLOW THE EXAMPLE OF CHRIST: PHILIPPIANS 2:5-11

A. Enjoying Equality with the Father and the Spirit: vss. 5-6

Your attitude should be the same as that of Christ Jesus: Who, being in very nature God, did not consider equality with God something to be grasped.

The supreme example of humility was the attitude that Jesus had when He rescued us from sin. If we truly are to be in Christ, then we should also have this attitude of loving humility in relationship with others and self-sacrificing obedience to God. This was the attitude that Paul wanted the Philippians to embrace. The apostle portrayed Christ's attitude in what some scholars have suggested was originally a hymn sung in the early church. Even then, believers sang songs expressing their devotion and faith in Christ (Col. 3:16). Most of these hymns are now lost to us, but a few are probably preserved in Paul's letters. Besides the possibility of Philippians 2:6-11, parts of other probable hymns may be found in Ephesians 5:14, Colossians 1:15-20, and 1 Timothy 3:16.

Those in favor of the previously mentioned view maintain that Paul quoted the song in Philippians 2:6-11 to provide an example of humility. These experts note the solemn tone of Paul's words, the way they fit together, and the manner in which they were carefully chosen. Read aloud in the Greek, the rhythmical quality of the words provides further evidence that this passage could have easily been sung. There is no problem in seeing these verses as an incorporation of an early hymn. The words definitely reflect Paul's thought and support his point, which would make their inclusion natural. On the other hand, the apostle was capable of writing poetic passages (1 Cor. 13, for example), and he should not be dismissed as the author just because of style. Either way, these verses provide a wonderfully concise theology of the person of Christ and accurately reflect other statements of Scripture regarding the Savior. In particular, we learn about the humility and exaltation of Christ, which Paul wanted to convey to his readers.

In his Letter to the Philippians, Paul wrote some of his most enduring statements about faith and hope and shared his most penetrating insights about the divine nature of Christ. Succinctly put, this letter provides believers in Christ with timely encouragement and godly wisdom. Indeed, the sacred truths revealed in Philippians came from the heart and mind of a man who had learned God's truths through many years of sacrificial service to Christ. Throughout the Philippian letter, Paul's deep affection for the believers who had supported him with their prayers and financial aid is evident. Though these Macedonian Christians were being persecuted for their faith in Christ, they had not abandoned Paul's teachings nor discarded his friendship. Their steadfast devotion to the Lord and to him compelled Paul to pour out his heart to them, confessing his longing to be with them and his special love for them.

With respect to Philippians 2:6, we discover that prior to Jesus' incarnation, He eternally existed as God with the Father and the Spirit. One of the key doctrines of the Christian faith is that Jesus is, always was, and always will be God. In fact, Paul declared in Colossians 2:9 that in the Lord Jesus all the fullness of the Godhead dwelt in bodily form. Philippians 2:6 reveals that Jesus not only is God but also decided not to use His privileges as God to seize His share of divine glory and honor but instead chose the path of lowly obedience.

B. Enduring the Humiliation of the Cross: vss. 7-8

But made himself nothing, taking the very nature of a servant, being made in human likeness. And being found in appearance as a man, he humbled himself and became obedient to death—even death on a cross!

The Son acted upon His decision to be obedient to the Father by emptying Himself, which is the literal meaning of the Greek phrase and which the NIV translates as "made himself nothing" (Phil. 2:7). In this selfless act Jesus did not give up His divinity, but laid aside His kingly privileges as God to become a human being. He also did not choose to be an earthly monarch, a wealthy merchant, a powerful military leader, an idolized athlete or entertainer, or even a renowned philosopher. Jesus became a servant. Once Jesus became fully human through His incarnation, people who knew Him could see that He possessed the full nature of a human being—except that He was without sin. He hungered as any human would. He felt the discomfort of hot and cold weather as any person would. He became tired after a long walk in the same way His fellow travelers became exhausted.

In verse 7, Paul described three steps in Jesus' mission. He "made himself nothing"; He took "the very nature of a servant"; and He was "made in human likeness." From birth to death, Jesus lived in humility. He was born in a stable. His parents were refugees in Egypt. Jesus grew up in obedience to His parents. He worked at a humble trade, as a carpenter. Jesus cried with those who grieved. He washed the feet of His disciples. Paul summarized Christ's self-emptying this way: "Though he was rich, yet for your sakes he became poor, so that you through his poverty might become rich" (2 Cor. 8:9).

Because of His sinlessness, however, Jesus could choose whether to die. All men and women are subject to physical death unless God decrees differently, but Jesus could conceivably have rejected this final conclusion to His earthly life. Jesus, however, chose to die—not to just leave this life peacefully like Enoch, but to die on the cross in anguish and humiliation so that we might live in renewed and eternal communion with God (Phil. 2:8).

C. Experiencing Divine Exaltation: vss. 9-11

Therefore God exalted him to the highest place and gave him the name that is above every name, that at the name of Jesus every knee should bow, in heaven and on earth and under the earth, and every tongue confess that Jesus Christ is Lord, to the glory of God the Father.

Paul could not end his extended illustration with Jesus on the cross. The place of honor that Jesus willingly forsook was given back to Him with the added glory of His triumph over sin and death. In response to Jesus' humility and obedience, the Father supremely exalted the Son to a place where His triumph will eventually be recognized by every living creature (Phil. 2:9).

The apostle emphatically tells us that every person who has ever lived will someday recognize Jesus for who He is. The "name of Jesus" (vs. 10) signifies the position

God gave Him, not His proper name. By bowing their knees, every human being and angel will acknowledge Jesus' deity and sovereignty. Everyone will confess that Jesus is Lord—some with joyful faith, others with hopeless regret and despair (vs. 11). Centuries earlier the prophet Isaiah had announced the words of the Messiah: "Before me every knee will bow; by me every tongue will swear" (Isa. 45:23). Philippians 2:6-11 affirms that this universal acknowledgment of Jesus' lordship will ultimately come to pass.

D. Obeying and Pleasing God: vss. 12-13

Therefore, my dear friends, as you have always obeyed—not only in my presence, but now much more in my absence—continue to work out your salvation with fear and trembling, for it is God who works in you to will and to act according to his good purpose.

Immediately following Paul's description of the supreme humility and obedience of Jesus' servanthood, he charged his friends in Philippi to be as obedient as Christ was. When the apostle labored among them, they obeyed his instructions. Moreover, they had followed Paul's teachings after he had left. Now the apostle told them to maintain their diligence in submitting themselves to God's Word. This was not so that they might earn their salvation, but that they would express their salvation in such a way that the spiritual health of their Christian community would grow in unity.

Paul characterized how he expected them to act by adding the phrase "fear and trembling" (Phil. 2:12). He was not saying they should comply strictly out of fear of what God would do to them if they weren't obedient, but that they should strive to be Christlike while having utmost reverence for the Lord. In fact, it is only God who gives us the desire and power necessary to do His will (vs. 13). As Christians today we must be completely dependent upon God if we are to be faithful to Paul's charge. While salvation is entirely a work of God and a free gift of His grace, it does require a response of obedient faith on the part of the believer. And while God deserves all the glory for our deliverance from sin, we are not totally passive in how the inner change affects our daily activities.

Similar truths are found in Ephesians 2:8-10. Verses 8 and 9 reveal that when it comes to salvation, believers have no room to boast. After all, their redemption is by God's grace through faith in Christ. The grace Paul referred to is the Lord's favor that He shows without regard to the recipient's worth or merit. God bestows His kindness despite what the person deserves. This is possible because of what Jesus did at Calvary.

God's grace is one of His key attributes. For instance, Exodus 34:6 reveals that the Lord is "the compassionate and gracious God." His redemption of His people from Egypt and His establishment of them in Canaan was a superlative example of His grace. He did this despite their unrighteousness (Deut. 7:7-8; 9:5-6). Christ is the supreme revelation of God's grace. Jesus not only appropriated divine grace but also incarnated it (Luke 2:40; John 1:14). Christ died on the cross and rose from the dead so that believing sinners might partake of God's grace (Titus 2:11). Their entrance into God's kingdom is not based on their own merit.

Some mistakenly think that the act of believing mentioned in Ephesians 2:8 is a good work that earns one a place in heaven. Rather, faith is simply putting one's trust in Christ for salvation. Accordingly, God receives all praise for this incredible gift of salvation. He made it possible for us to turn away from our sin and receive Christ by faith. The implication is that God saves all Christians by His grace. This is His free act of doing something good for us, even though we don't deserve it. God's grace is activated in our lives through faith. Paul said that when we put our trust in Christ, we become the recipients of His grace, and so we enjoy salvation.

Discussion Questions

1. What does unity in your congregation look like?
2. How do we develop humility and dispose of selfish ambition?
3. What effects does Jesus' humiliation have on the Christian's outlook on life? On the life of the church?
4. Why is it hard to live by the principle that exaltation follows humiliation?
5. How might your church's business meetings be different if Philippians 2:1-11 was read thoughtfully before the meeting started?

Contemporary Application

Have you ever seen an advertisement for a seminar on humility? There are lots of ads about how to be successful, how to get ahead, and how to be number one. But how to be humble? Forget it.

We need to understand the part humility should play in our daily interactions with people. When we are humble, we will pay closer attention to those around us and regularly ask God such questions as the following: How can I see this person's concerns as being as important as mine? What can I say to this person that would show Your love? How do You want me to use my time to serve his or her needs? Then we wait on the Lord to give us the answers, and we reach out in His name.

Admittedly, when we, as Christians, take seriously the high standards of the Gospel, we run smack into the world's way of thinking. That's why one of our most powerful influences in society is our model of humility. When people see Christians following the humility of the Savior, they cannot deny that Jesus makes a difference.

Our churches would also find larger responses if they were known as communities where people put the interests of others ahead of their own. Too often, it seems, the public sees more fighting than humility among God's people. Having the mind of Christ shapes the church and shakes the world.

Living into the Future

Scripture

Background Scripture: *Philippians 3:1b—4:1*
Scripture Lesson: *Philippians 3:7-16*
Key Verses: *One thing I do: Forgetting what is behind and
straining toward what is ahead, I press on toward the goal to
win the prize for which God has called me heavenward in
Christ Jesus.* Philippians 3:13-14.
Scripture Lesson for Children: *Acts: 27:1-2, 13-14,
18-26; Philippians 3:13*
Key Verse for Children: *I press on toward the goal to win
the prize for which God has called me heavenward in Christ
Jesus.* Philippians 3:14.

Lesson Aim

To decide to leave things behind and move toward
what's ahead.

Lesson Setting

Time: *About A.D. 61*
Place: *Written from Rome to the church in Philippi*

Lesson Outline

Living into the Future

    I. Remaining Focused on Christ: Philippians 3:7-11
        A. *The Incalculable Value of Knowing Christ: vss. 7-8*
        B. *Depending on the Righteousness of Christ: vs. 9*
        C. *Living for Christ Right Now: vss. 10-11*
    II. Following Paul's Godly Example:
       Philippians 3:12-16
        A. *Pressing Toward the Goal: vs. 12*
        B. *Anticipating Future Glory with Christ: vss. 13-14*
        C. *Embracing a Mature Attitude: vss. 15-16*

Introduction for Adults

Topic: *A Focus for Life*

Sadly, when people talk about "church," they often focus on programs, staff, buildings, and denominational differences. There's more than enough criticism to go around, which means outsiders frequently are turned off by what they see and hear.

However, the essence the Christian life is none of these. Indeed, the previously mentioned concerns often get in the way of genuine, saving faith. The reality of the latter is demonstrated by trusting in Jesus and focusing one's life on obeying His will. In the case of Paul, he had to jettison a lot of religious baggage that kept him from knowing and serving the Lord. Saved adults have to do the same.

Striving to be Christlike is more important than anything else. If we find anything in religion that keeps us from knowing the Savior and living for Him, we have to discard it. This may mean radical changes for some people who have been in church for years. If some kinds of church experiences keep your students from living for Christ, they can still make fresh starts. There is no use wasting time arguing about things that may seem important, but are really dangerous, especially if their Christian growth is stunted.

Introduction for Youth

Topic: *Back to the Future*

One of the favorite ways to prove that a diet works is to show before and after pictures. Typically, the photo on the left shows an obese person weighing 300 pounds, but the photo on the right shows the same individual weighing 150 pounds. The ad reminds potential customers that this outcome could be true for them, that is, if they stick to their diet.

In the spiritual realm, Paul never said he had arrived at the place where he could relax. In contrast, many teens start the Christian walk, but fail to keep at it. They do not pursue the present and future goal of Christlikeness as doggedly as they should. Paul's example can motivate them to keep shedding the weight of sin and remaining spiritually trim in order to win their race of faith in the Lord Jesus.

Concepts for Children

Topic: *Look Ahead*

1. Paul was on a ship traveling to the city of Rome when he experienced a violent storm.
2. An angel of God told Paul that all the people on the ship would survive the storm.
3. The people on the ship were calmed by the words and actions of Paul and his trust in God.
4. God's goodness allowed all of the people to reach land safely.
5. Like Paul, we are wise to live for Jesus.

Lesson Commentary

I. REMAINING FOCUSED ON CHRIST: PHILIPPIANS 3:7-11

A. The Incalculable Value of Knowing Christ: vss. 7-8

But whatever was to my profit I now consider loss for the sake of Christ. What is more, I consider every-thing a loss compared to the surpassing greatness of knowing Christ Jesus my Lord, for whose sake I have lost all things. I consider them rubbish, that I may gain Christ.

Philippians 3:1-4 reveals that the faith of Paul's readers was being undermined by the heretical legalism of his doctrinal enemies, the Judaizers. Indeed, they were enemies of the Gospel. The apostle metaphorically referred to them as filthy "dogs," as evildoers, and as those who insisted on mutilating the body through the rite of circumcision in order to be saved. Paul did not attack circumcision itself, but rather the significance that the Judaizers placed upon it, namely, that righteous-ness comes through observing a religious ceremony such as circumcision.

Paul transformed the meaning of circumcision from an external cutting of the body, which could be done only to men, to the internal work of God's Spirit, which marks every believer's union with the Father based on the Son's redemptive work. The latter is the authentic "circumcision" (vs. 3), and this mark of true believers shows that they worship in God's Spirit and glorify the Lord Jesus. These people acknowledge that human effort cannot earn them a right standing before God. If anyone could put confidence in their own fleshly pursuits, it was Paul. Indeed, his antagonists could not accuse him of falling short of any of their own benchmarks of religious attainment (vs. 4).

Verses 5-6 provide us with an exceptional glimpse into the apostle's life and expe-riences prior to his conversion. For instance, he was circumcised on the eighth day. What is implied here is that Paul's parents were devout Jews, who followed the laws of their religion faithfully (see Gen. 17:12) and trained him in his pious duties from the time he was an infant. How many of Paul's detractors could say the same? Next, the apostle stressed his birthright as a Jew. Not only was he a member of God's elect by birth, but also he was from the tribe of Benjamin. As such he could boast that the first king of Israel was a Benjamite (see 1 Sam. 9:1-2; 10:20-21). Interestingly, Paul's birth name was the same as that king's name—Saul. Furthermore, Jerusalem and the temple in the holy city were located within the dis-trict of Benjamin.

The apostle's fourth reference to himself is that he was "a Hebrew of Hebrews" (Phil. 3:5). This means in part that Paul was the Hebrew son of Hebrew parents. The phrase probably also indicates that he was taught Hebrew, the ethnic language of the Jewish people, as well as being schooled in the Jewish traditions (see Acts 22:2-3; Gal. 1:14). To his birth and training as a Jew, Paul added three personal achievements. Foremost, he was a Pharisee. Within the Jewish community, no group of people were more highly esteemed as strict observers of the Torah, the

Law of Moses. In fact, Gamaliel, one of the most highly respected rabbis in the Pharisee party, was the apostle's mentor (see Acts 22:3).

Paul also demonstrated his fervor for the law by zealously persecuting Christians, whom he believed were God's enemies. The apostle not only denounced the followers of Jesus, but also actively hunted them down in order to imprison and execute them (Phil. 3:6; see Acts 8:3). In a way Paul was even more blind to the truth than the Judaizers were. Finally, he said he was blameless when it came to his outward submission to the Jewish laws. If the law could produce righteousness in a person, then he would qualify because he had obeyed the law without fault. Of course, the apostle knew that people cannot become righteous before God in this way.

Paul rejected as inconsequential everything he had accomplished as an upstanding Jew before his dramatic encounter with Jesus the Messiah on the road to Damascus. In light of the Redeemer's work in the apostle's life, Paul considered his birth as a Benjamite Jew, his high standing in the Pharisee party, and even his dedication to the law as worthless. All that had been a profit to Paul (that the Judaizers esteemed), he counted as a loss because of his devotion to Christ (Phil. 3:7). The apostle did not feel that this loss was regrettable. What he had gained in having an intimate relationship with Christ Jesus as his Lord was of supreme worth to Paul. Everything of which he once boasted as a Jew he now considered as worthless refuse to be buried in a landfill (vs. 8).

B. Depending on the Righteousness of Christ: vs. 9

And be found in him, not having a righteousness of my own that comes from the law, but that which is through faith in Christ—the righteousness that comes from God and is by faith.

Paul now knew that true righteousness can come only "through faith in Christ" (Phil. 3:9). The Judaizers had demanded that believers be purified through circumcision. The apostle's argument was that he was circumcised and did far more in his efforts to be justified under the law—and yet none of that was of any value to God. We cannot attain righteousness. Only God can offer it to us, and that takes effect when people place their faith in Jesus Christ. This was the heart of Paul's teaching. The apostle wanted his Philippian friends to permanently establish this truth as the doctrinal cornerstone of their church.

In the New Testament, the Greek word translated "righteousness" comes from a root term that means "straightness" and refers to that which is in accordance with established moral norms. In a legal sense, righteousness means to be vindicated or treated as just. From a biblical perspective, God's character is the definition and source of righteousness. As a result, the righteousness of human beings is defined in terms of God's holiness. Because the Lord solely provides righteousness, it cannot be produced or obtained by human efforts. God makes His righteousness available to all people without distinction. Just as there is no discrimination with Him in universally condemning all people as sinners, so God does not show partiality by offering righteousness to one particular ethnic group. The Lord freely gives it to all people—regardless of their race or gender—when they trust in the Messiah.

In the New Testament, the Greek word translated "justified" signified, in Paul's day, a court setting, with a judge declaring an individual "not guilty." The idea of justification comes from a judge pronouncing someone to be righteous or innocent of a crime. The word had a technical forensic application of a one-time rendering of a positive judicial verdict. Paul used the term to refer to God's declaration that the believing sinner is righteous because of the atoning work of the Messiah on the cross.

C. Living for Christ Right Now: vss. 10-11

I want to know Christ and the power of his resurrection and the fellowship of sharing in his sufferings, becoming like him in his death, and so, somehow, to attain to the resurrection from the dead.

When Paul expressed his desire to "know Christ" (Phil. 3:10), the apostle meant more than learning theological facts about the Savior. Paul desired to "know" Jesus in a personal way, that is, to have an ongoing relationship with Him through which Paul could experience the Messiah working in his life. The Greek word that apostle chose for "know" expresses the idea of understanding and perceiving an object in an intelligent manner. The word implies personal acquaintance, experience, and familiarity.

Paul described the two experiences by which he wanted to grow in his knowledge of the Savior. First, the apostle wanted to know the power that raised Jesus from the dead. Expressed differently, Paul wanted to experience that power working in his life to bring about Jesus' righteousness in the apostle. Second, Paul wanted to have fellowship with Christ in His sufferings. Put another way, through Paul's own apostolic sufferings, he wanted to understand the sufferings Jesus endured on the cross. Paul wanted to conform to Christ's death. This means the apostle wanted to be like Jesus when He defeated sin and death.

While many believers want more of Christ's power, few would crave participation "in his sufferings." Paul, however, saw suffering for the Redeemer as a sought-after privilege (Rom. 8:17; 2 Cor. 12:10). The apostle's ultimate desire was to be raised from the dead along with other believers on the day appointed by God (Phil. 3:11). When that event occurred, Paul would completely know Jesus as supreme Ruler and Redeemer. The apostle had no doubt that this would occur, but was uncertain about the outcome of his current situation. Nevertheless, his confession of faith in the Messiah made it clear that salvation totally and without question depended on the atoning work of the Lord Jesus.

II. FOLLOWING PAUL'S GODLY EXAMPLE: PHILIPPIANS 3:12-16

A. Pressing Toward the Goal: vs. 12

Not that I have already obtained all this, or have already been made perfect, but I press on to take hold of that for which Christ Jesus took hold of me.

Paul had just described the kind of knowledge of Christ he desired. The apostle also wanted to correct any misconceptions the Philippians might have had about what he had just said. He noted that he had not yet acquired a perfect knowledge of the Savior, nor was he in a state of spiritual flawlessness. Instead, Paul was pursuing the redemption that Jesus had attained for him—the redemption that the apostle would fully possess when God raises believers from the dead. Yes, the Messiah had already redeemed Paul, but he needed to "press on" (Phil. 3:12) to the goal Christ had set for him.

Paul used the metaphor of a race to illustrate what it means to follow Christ. Both the Greeks and the Romans were avid fans of sporting contests. Sometimes the Roman games were violent and cruel, but often combatants merely engaged in feats of strength, endurance, and speed. Running was one of the more popular sports. When runners won their races, they might win prizes of wealth. Of far more value to most of them, however, was the honored recognition they received. After each contest, a herald proclaimed the victor and his hometown, and a judge presented him with a palm branch. At the conclusion of the games, each victor received a wreath made of olive or laurel leaves (see Phil. 3:14; 4:2). According to Greek tradition, an oracle from the god Delphi had established this custom.

B. Anticipating Future Glory with Christ: vss. 13-14

Brothers, I do not consider myself yet to have taken hold of it. But one thing I do: Forgetting what is behind and straining toward what is ahead, I press on toward the goal to win the prize for which God has called me heavenward in Christ Jesus.

Paul repeated his statement that he had not yet attained the spiritual faultlessness that comes only with the final resurrection. Moreover, he called his readers "brothers" (Phil. 3:13) to further emphasize his point. If the apostle did not claim to be spiritually complete, surely the Christians in Philippi could not make such a boast. There were two things Paul could do as he strove for the lofty goal he saw before him. First, he could put his past behind him, which might mean either his former life as a Jewish zealot or all his successes up to that point. He was probably thinking about his former life, since he had earlier described his attainments as a pious Jew.

Despite the apostle's outward success and dedication to the Mosaic law, he had failed to acquire God's favor or personal righteousness. Paul was not talking about obliterating the memories of his former life. Instead, he did not want to recall his former achievements with the intention of noting how they had contributed to his spiritual progress. Nor did the apostle want to dwell on his past sins (which may have included the execution of Christians), for God no longer held these sins against him.

Second, Paul could strive for the future. The apostle used specific Greek words to draw a picture in the minds of his readers of an athlete who is participating in a running contest. Just as runners exert all of their efforts to push forward, so Paul used every effort to drive himself forward. The great difference between races in a sporting event and the race Christians are running in is that a sporting event has only one winner. In the case of the Christian life, all who finish the race win.

Paul's utmost effort to win the prize was not to run faster or longer than all other Christians, but to reach a common goal. He was not trying to excel above all other believers, but to win a prize that Jesus will award to all who run for Him (vs. 14). The apostle did not say exactly what the prize would be, but he did indicate that he would receive it in heaven in the presence of his Lord and Savior, Christ Jesus. In any case, God was the one who called Paul to press on toward this goal, and it was God who enabled the apostle to run the race. Thus Paul ran for the glory and honor of God.

C. Embracing a Mature Attitude: vss. 15-16

All of us who are mature should take such a view of things. And if on some point you think different-ly, that too God will make clear to you. Only let us live up to what we have already attained.

Paul apparently was aware of those Philippian Christians who believed they had arrived spiritually. They may have looked down upon those who did not share their belief about themselves. In the apostle's subtle manner of rebuking this group, his statement about maturity was his way of regarding them as spiritually immature (Phil. 3:15). Paul was convinced that if a Christian was sincere in his or her desire to faithfully serve the Lord, in time God would show that believer that everything the apostle said was true. In fact, he was so confident of his teaching that he called upon God to correct those who disagreed with him.

Probably most of the Philippians agreed with Paul's primary teaching on this issue, but questioned, or could not understand, the secondary points of what he had written. Again, the apostle felt that those who truly seek God's truth will be rewarded with the full measure of understanding. Paul recognized that God had imparted varying levels of spiritual insight to the members of the Philippian church. His instruction was that they put into practice the truths they had learned (vs. 16). In other words, he admonished them to walk according to what the Lord had taught them. Neither the apostle nor anyone else can expect more from a Christian. In fact, to demand more is to overstep what the Holy Spirit is doing in that believer's life.

Paul trusted in God's sovereignty. The apostle believed God was in control not only of his life but also of the lives of the Christians in Philippi. Though some of the Philippians might have disagreed with Paul, he was confident that God would enlighten them to the truths he declared and change their behavior accordingly. Nevertheless, Paul's strong belief in God's sovereignty did not silence him. Put another way, the apostle did not think the best solution was to stand back and let the misunderstanding somehow resolve itself. Instead, since Paul knew that he had the gift of communicating God's truth, he voiced his views so these Christians would have the tools to advance in their walk with the Lord. Whether they used these tools was up to them. Thus Paul's plan was to humbly provide direction for God's flock in Philippi while trusting that the Lord would use the apostle's efforts to bear fruit for the Kingdom.

Discussion Questions

1. What sorts of personal attainments in Paul's life did he now consider loss for Christ's sake?
2. What did Paul regard as the basis for a right relationship with God?
3. Why would Paul be willing to endure suffering for the cause of Christ?
4. Why should we, as Jesus' followers, want to know Him more perfectly?
5. How is it possible for us, as Christians, to hold on to the spiritual progress we have already made?

Contemporary Application

Today, when journalists write about Charles Colson, many refer to him as an indicted former member of President Richard Nixon's White House, a man who served time in prison for his role in the Watergate scandal. Watergate, however, was over three decades ago, and Charles Colson has done much in the intervening years.

After becoming a believer in prison, Colson went on to write a string of best-selling books about the Christian life, found the International Prison Fellowship Ministries, become a highly regarded speaker, and receive the prestigious Templeton Prize for Progress in Religion. Those are some incredible achievements. But the media seems stuck in the past.

Sometimes Christians can also remain stuck in the past. Unless we learn to leave the failings of our past behind, we risk overlooking the rewards God has for our future. These are the eternal, heavenly blessings Paul had in mind in the Scripture passage for this week's lesson.

If anyone had a past to dwell on, it was Paul. As a former persecutor of Christians, Paul had dragged believers off to jail and stood by approvingly as Stephen, the first recorded Christian martyr, was stoned to death. Paul once tried to destroy the church he later helped to build. It took an encounter with the risen Lord Jesus to turn Paul's life around. Thankfully, Paul had learned not to dwell on the failings of his past. Instead, he said "I press on," keeping his eyes on heaven and the future.

Likewise, God has called us to run for Him. He wants us to strive for the prize that awaits us in Christ Jesus and to put forth every ounce of effort to attain the goal God has set before us. The Lord will reward us with a prize of far greater worth than anything we could possibly receive on earth.

Growing in Joy and Peace

Scripture

Background Scripture: *Philippians 4:2-14*

Scripture Lesson: *Philippians 4:2-14*

Key Verses: *Whatever you have learned or received or heard from me, or seen in me—put it into practice. And the God of peace will be with you.* Philippians 4:9.

Scripture Lesson for Children: *Acts 27:27, 29, 33-36, 39, 41-44; Philippians 4:6*

Key Verse for Children: *Do not be anxious about anything, but in everything, by prayer and petition, with thanksgiving, present your requests to God.* Philippians 4:6.

Lesson Aim

To replace anxiety and learn contentment through prayer and thanksgiving.

Lesson Setting

Time: *About A.D. 61*

Place: *Written from Rome to the church in Philippi*

Lesson Outline

Growing in Joy and Peace

  I. Important Exhortations: Philippians 4:2-9
     A. *Settling Disagreements: vss. 2-3*
     B. *Being Joyful and Gentle: vss. 4-5*
     C. *Experiencing God's Peace: vss. 6-7*
     D. *Thinking in a Godly Manner: vss. 8-9*
  II. Appreciation for Gifts Given: Philippians 4:10-14
     A. *Faithful Support: vs. 10*
     B. *Contentment in Christ: vss. 11-12*
     C. *Strength in Christ: vs. 13*
     D. *A Desire to Share: vs. 14*

Introduction for Adults

Topic: *Finding Peace*

It's easy to tell someone not to be afraid when everything seems to be going well, but when a friend comes down with a serious illness that's a different matter. Automatically, it seems, fear kicks in. Fear has positive value when it keeps us from taking risky chances. However, fear has negative value when it begins to undermine our ability to find peace.

When the trials of life seem overwhelming, we should fortify our souls, not with wishful thinking, but with truths about God revealed in His Word. We can't promise people that everything will be all right. But we can reassure them that God's love and care will be there when they need it.

Our prayers and our counsel must be rooted in the strong affirmations found in Scripture, such as Philippians 4:6-7. In these two beloved verses we learn that God's peace will guard our hearts and minds as we live in the Lord Jesus.

Introduction for Youth

Topic: *Why Worry?*

What an encouragement it is to be reminded of God's care. In this regard, familiar passages in the Bible help us to recall how God has helped and protected His people. We all can benefit from the spiritual reinforcement these memorable portions of Scripture offer.

That's why it's valuable to take time to recall what the Lord has done down through the centuries. Such accounts need not focus just on hair-raising rescues. Even what seems to be unimportant can help us recognize the hand of God at work in the lives of His people.

When we reflect on these things, we quickly come to understand that God watches over all we do. He will uphold us when we feel spiritually weak and He will guide us when we feel morally confused. There is no reason for us to worry or feel alone when the great God of the universe is ever present to lead and strengthen us in the pilgrim way.

Concepts for Children

Topic: *Praying at All Times*

1. As the ship neared land, Paul told the people not to panic, for they weren't going to die.
2. Every day on the ship, Paul provided encouragement to everyone around him.
3. In the middle of the storm, Paul gave thanks to God in prayer.
4. No one was harmed on the ship and everyone reached land safely.
5. In Philippians 4:6, Paul encourages us not to worry, but give thanks to God.

Lesson Commentary

I. IMPORTANT EXHORTATIONS: PHILIPPIANS 4:2-9

A. Settling Disagreements: vss. 2-3

I plead with Euodia and I plead with Syntyche to agree with each other in the Lord. Yes, and I ask you, loyal yokefellow, help these women who have contended at my side in the cause of the gospel, along with Clement and the rest of my fellow workers, whose names are in the book of life.

Paul addressed his readers in Philippi with several endearing phrases. He called them his "brothers" (Phil. 4:1) and "dear friends." The apostle told them that he loved them and longed to see them. He described them as his joy and crown. Paul could have commanded them to stand firm in the Lord. Instead, he encouraged them with fatherly affection to be strong and faithful in the Lord Jesus, even in the midst of all their troubles and hardships. The way Paul instructed the Philippians is a powerful example of how Christians can build one another up in their unity in the Messiah.

Evidently the Lord's peace was at times absent in the Philippian congregation, which was why Paul urged his readers more than once to strive for unity. One conflict was apparently so intense that Paul had to publicly mention the dispute between Euodia and Syntyche (vs. 2). He pleaded with each woman individually to come to an agreement with the other person, and to do it in the Lord. Perhaps their quarrel was so bitter that the only way they could reconcile was by putting their commitment to the Messiah ahead of their personal grievances.

Paul called upon a third party to assist the two quarreling women in resolving their differences. The identity of this person is difficult to determine. The apostle referred to this Christian brother (the Greek word is in the male gender) as "yokefellow" (vs. 3), and described him as being "loyal." It is possible that the Greek word Paul used was actually the man's name. In any case, the apostle must have trusted the pastoral skills of this individual enough to know that he could succeed as an intermediary between these two estranged women.

Paul's remarks about Euodia and Syntyche demonstrate that apostle's tact in dealing with a potentially volatile situation. He did not address the cause of the conflict, nor did he take sides. Instead, he noted that both women had labored with him in ministering the Word of God. If they could serve side by side with Paul as he proclaimed the Gospel of Jesus Christ, surely they could overlook their differences and stand side by side as sisters in the Lord. Paul also mentioned other believers who participated in his ministry.

Some experts have tried to identify Clement, whom Paul spoke of by name, as the early church father Clement of Rome. However, it is doubtful that these two Clements are the same person, especially since Clement was a common Roman name. Indeed, nothing is known about this man and the other "fellow workers" except that their names are recorded in "the book of life." Evidently, this is a heavenly list of the names of God's people (see Rev. 3:5). What is important is not that the identity and deeds of these believers are made known to us, but that they are known to God as His chosen children.

B. Being Joyful and Gentle: vss. 4-5

Rejoice in the Lord always. I will say it again: Rejoice! Let your gentleness be evident to all. The Lord is near.

After admonishing Euodia and Syntyche to settle their differences in a spirit of Christian love, Paul repeated what he had earlier written, and that was for his readers to "rejoice in the Lord" (Phil. 4:4; see 3:1). He certainly did not want the Philippians to make up grudgingly. That would only place a flimsy bandage on a wound that required deeper healing. By rejoicing in the Messiah they would show that they were truly reconciled. It should be noted that Paul was not simply encouraging the Philippians to be of good cheer while they were enduring persecution from nonbelievers. Rejoicing in the Lord meant that they could lean on the Son to hold them up. He would fill them with joy while in any situation.

After teaching about one fruit of the Holy Spirit (namely, joy), Paul gave instructions about another—gentleness (4:5a; see Gal. 5:22-23). The Philippian believers were not only to rejoice in the Lord but also to be gentle toward others. A Christlike gentleness is a gracious disposition, which is especially powerful in the face of being wronged. Of course, Paul was not advising his readers to be human doormats, nor was he condoning oppression. Like Jesus, Paul could be quite forceful when speaking out against evil and injustice. Instead, Paul was saying we should be considerate of others with a Christlike humility. He was not saying we must be self-effacing, but that we should interact with others with sensitivity and in such a way that we do not manipulate others.

Paul stated that the Messiah's return was near (Phil. 4:5b). This was not so much a statement of fact as an invocation of the Lord's coming. This petition was common among believers in the first century. Quite probably the first and second generations of Christians thought it likely that the Messiah's return was imminent; nevertheless, this invocation was more a call to believers to be alert for the coming of the Lord than a certainty of its immediate occurrence. Evidence of this invocation appears in such ancient Christian documents as the Didache. On the day of the Messiah's return, He will vindicate His people. Meanwhile, we await His coming with great anticipation. Though it seems to us that the wait has been long, the Lord is not slow in regard to His promise. The certain expectation of the Lord's return is the believer's greatest hope.

C. Experiencing God's Peace: vss. 6-7

Do not be anxious about anything, but in everything, by prayer and petition, with thanksgiving, present your requests to God. And the peace of God, which transcends all understanding, will guard your hearts and your minds in Christ Jesus.

Paul told his friends not to worry about any self-centered concerns (Phil. 4:6). Such anxiety can become all-consuming. It takes our minds off what is important to God and focuses attention on ourselves. We can become self-absorbed, which shunts our ability to rejoice during hard times and be gentle with friends and foes alike. So what is the best remedy for anxiousness? Paul's prescription is prayer. When we turn to God and surrender our anxieties to Him, God's peace can reach our inner-most parts. Paul did not imply that our burdens will vanish, nor was he talking about a state of mind. In fact, it is an inner peace that can come only from God and is beyond our comprehension (vs. 7).

In addition, God's peace will guard our hearts and minds in Christ Jesus. The Greek word rendered "guard" is a military term that depicts a sentry maintaining his watch. Since Philippi was a garrison town, the original recipients of Paul's let-ter would have immediately comprehended the meaning of his metaphor. Every day they would have seen Roman sentries standing guard at the gates. In the same way a trained soldier guards a base, God's peace stands guard over our hearts and minds. The peace of God can come only through the Lord Jesus, who made peace between God and us through the blood the Redeemer shed on the cross. Thus we are in the Son's protective custody only when we are yielded to His lordship. And for those who are, He will leave His peace with us, giving us an inner tranquility the world may claim but can never truly know.

D. Thinking in a Godly Manner: vss. 8-9

Finally, brothers, whatever is true, whatever is noble, whatever is right, whatever is pure, whatever is lovely, whatever is admirable—if anything is excellent or praiseworthy—think about such things. Whatever you have learned or received or heard from me, or seen in me—put it into practice. And the God of peace will be with you.

Paul told the Philippians to think upon specific things. The Greek word that is ren-dered to "think" (Phil. 4:8) does not simply mean "call to mind." In addition, it means to reflect deeply upon something and then allow that thing to shape your conduct. It is not enough to have good thoughts; we must also behave according-ly. So Paul offered his readers six ethical expressions upon which a follower of the Messiah should think reflectively and responsively.

The apostle did not intend that the six desired virtues be taken individually or as steps by which to achieve correct thinking. They are actually reflections of a whole way of thinking. Nor are they meant to be comprehensive. That is why Paul quali-fied them with the words "if anything." He could have provided more descriptions of this way of thinking, but his point is that whatever is thought upon be "excellent" and "praiseworthy," that is, esteemed excellent by God and admired as praisewor-thy by other people.

First on Paul's list is "whatever is true." Focusing our minds on what we know to be true frees us from the hemming and hawing that often accompany mere specu-lation. Second, Paul said, "Whatever is noble." The Greek term for "noble" might be better rendered "honorable" or "worthy of honor." It implies that which is dignified. Thus our thoughts should be on things that are distinguished. The third phrase is "whatever is right." That which is right in God's sight is being obedient to His will made known to us through the teachings of the Lord Jesus.

Fourth, Paul often counseled believers to keep themselves pure. For instance, he told the Corinthians, "Dear friends, let us purify ourselves from everything that contaminates body and spirit" (2 Cor. 7:1). "Whatever is lovely" (Phil. 4:8) is fifth. The Greek term for "lovely" is found only here in the New Testament. It means "pleasing" or "attractive." While evil can be pleasing and attractive, that which is "lovely" is delightful to God. These kinds of thoughts are truly beautiful and winsome. Sixth, we are to think upon "whatever is admirable." Paul used a word that means "of good report" or "speaking well of." We are to reflect upon only those thoughts that are commendable before the Lord.

Earlier in the letter Paul had urged the Philippians to follow his example (see 3:17). Paul was not timid in presenting himself as a model for them to exemplify. In fact, what they had "learned," "received," "heard," and "seen" (4:9) shows that Paul had displayed a character and conduct beyond reproach while he was with them. The result of such obedience is being blessed with the peace that accompanies God's presence. Paul might sound somewhat prideful in admonition to the Philippians to use him as a prime example of how they should act as Christians. However, we should remember that few manuscripts, even of the Gospels, were available to the early church, and only letters such as Paul's gave practical advice on Christian living. Most people would have imitated the behavior of whoever told them about Jesus, thinking that the person would surely be a model of godly living. Thus, Paul was being practical in his exhortation to follow his example.

II. APPRECIATION FOR GIFTS GIVEN: PHILIPPIANS 4:10-14

A. Faithful Support: vs. 10

I rejoice greatly in the Lord that at last you have renewed your concern for me. Indeed, you have been concerned, but you had no opportunity to show it.

Paul rejoiced that God had worked through the Philippians to send a gift to him when he needed it most (Phil. 4:10). The apostle did not intend to sound harsh with his readers for waiting so long to send a gift. They had probably lost touch with him during his imprisonment and shipwreck. But now that he had been in Rome for a sustained period of time, the church was able to again show their support for him.

By understanding Paul's reluctance to discuss his financial dependence on others and the prior charity of the Philippians, we have no need to read something negative into the apostle's words "at last." Probably the delay in Paul's receiving their gifts was due to their inability to raise the funds more quickly because of their own poverty. Or the delay may have been due to the difficulty of a courier coming to him sooner because of the long distance between Rome and Philippi. In either case Paul was not expressing resentment. The apostle never doubted the Philippians' concern for him. Indeed, his reaction is more analogous to that of a person who receives a letter from a loved one after a longer-than-anticipated wait. Paul received a great deal of joy from his relationship with this church.

B. Contentment in Christ: vss. 11-12

I am not saying this because I am in need, for I have learned to be content whatever the circumstances. I know what it is to be in need, and I know what it is to have plenty. I have learned the secret of being content in any and every situation, whether well fed or hungry, whether living in plenty or in want.

Paul voiced his contentment with the little he had. He was not indicating that he didn't appreciate the Philippians' gifts, but that God had taught him to be content with whatever had been provided (Phil. 4:11). In the apostle's day, one group of Greek philosophers, the Stoics, also taught the need for contentment in all situations. For the Stoics, however, contentment meant accepting whatever troubles came in life by relying on human strength and denying all emotion. Sufficiency for all circumstances came from within a person.

The Stoic advice would be to "keep a stiff upper lip," especially as a person learned to endure all things. In contrast, Paul depended on Christ, not himself, and rejoiced in the calm assurance that a loving heavenly Father was in control of all things. The apostle consistently maintained this attitude, even though there were times when he was so poor that he went hungry. There were also other times when he was so well off that he had more than enough food to eat (vs. 12).

C. Strength in Christ: vs. 13

I can do everything through him who gives me strength.

In Philippians 4:12, Paul stated that he had learned the "secret" of living contentedly in every circumstance. And what the apostle's secret? Verse 13 says, "I can do everything through him who gives me strength." Put another way, the source for the apostle's contentment was none other than Christ (rather than some inner resource of human strength). In Him, Paul found the strength to meet any and every situation with confidence and joy.

D. A Desire to Share: vs. 14

Yet it was good of you to share in my troubles.

Although God's grace was sufficient in strengthening Paul during his ordeal in Rome, the apostle still welcomed the material support of his readers. He viewed this support as their way of participating not only in his ministry but in his hardship as well (Phil. 4:14). They were true partners with Paul, and their kindness toward him was a mark of their goodness in Christ.

The apostle's mention of "the early days" (vs. 15) refers to the time when he had

415

first preached the Gospel in Philippi, which had been during his second mission-ary journey around A.D. 49–52 (see Acts 16:12-40). After Paul and Silas departed from Philippi, they went westward and stayed in another Macedonian city, Thessalonica, where both Jews and Greeks became Christians (see 17:1-4). As they journeyed from Philippi through Amphipolis and Apollonia to Thessalonica, the only church to provide them with financial aid was the Philippian congregation.

The Philippians gave Paul material support, but also they had received spiritual blessings from the apostle. This is how they shared with him "in the matter of giv-ing and receiving" (Phil. 4:15). Thus they enjoyed a unique relationship with Paul. The generosity of the Philippians never ceased. Time after time they continued to send him monetary gifts to take care of his physical needs and those of his co-work-ers. Moreover, the apostle was also grateful for the quickness with which his friends sent their aid to him while he was in Thessalonica. Their gift was particularly time-ly since Paul and his associates were laboring night and day in Thessalonica to sup-port themselves (Phil. 4:16; see 1 Thess. 2:9).

Discussion Questions

1. What attitudes did Paul ask the Philippians to develop?
2. How can we, as believers, acquire more of God's peace?
3. What concrete steps can we take to learn to be more content?
4. What was so remarkable about the Philippians' support of Paul while he was in Thessalonica?
5. How did the Philippians benefit from the gift they gave Paul?

Contemporary Application

The high calling of God includes peace in the midst of conflict. Personal peace and joy are the priceless privileges of believers. In light of this, we have to ask why so many are troubled, confused, and worried. Anxiety takes a heavy toll.

Perhaps one reason is that we have missed the simplicity of living by faith in Christ. We look for many avenues of relief, without calling on Jesus to do what He has promised. We neglect the practice of prayer. We allow our minds to be filled with unworthy ideas. The world forces us into its way of thinking. We have not learned to be content in Christ. We have not learned how to be sacrificially help-ful to those in need.

While we prosper outwardly with unparalleled abundance, our souls are lean. That's why we need God's reminder to allow His peace and joy to control our lives. It's a matter of faith to believe that Jesus wants to give us His strength for whatever life may bring. The secret of joy and peace is Jesus.

Upheld by God

Scripture

Background Scripture: *Acts 28; Philippians 4:15-23*
Scripture Lesson: *Acts 28:16-25a, 28-31*
Key Verse: *[Paul] welcomed all who came to see him. Boldly and without hindrance he preached the kingdom of God and taught about the Lord Jesus Christ.* Acts 28:30-31.
Scripture Lesson for Children: *Acts 28:1-2, 10-16, 30-31*
Key Verses for Children: *[Paul] welcomed all who came to see him. Boldly and without hindrance he preached the kingdom of God and taught about the Lord Jesus Christ.* Acts 28:30-31.

Lesson Aim

To reflect on the importance of proclaiming the Gospel to the lost.

Lesson Setting

Time: *Between A.D. 59 and 61*
Place: *Rome*

Lesson Outline

Upheld by God

I. Paul's Arrival at Rome: Acts 28:16-20
  A. *Being Placed Under House Arrest: vs. 16*
  B. *Recounting the Episode: vs. 17*
  C. *Requesting to Be Tried by the Emperor: vss. 18-19*
  D. *Desiring to See the Local Jewish Leaders: vs. 20*

II. Paul's Preaching at Rome: Acts 28:21-25a, 28-31
  A. *Expressing Initial Interest: vss. 21-22*
  B. *Presenting the Truth of the Gospel: vs. 23*
  C. *Encountering a Mixed Response: vss. 24-25a*
  D. *Witnessing to the Gentiles: vss. 28-29*
  E. *Proclaiming the Kingdom of God: vss. 30-31*

Introduction for Adults

Topic: *Keeping Commitments*

The Bible itself is our best defense against evildoers, impostors, and deceivers. Therefore, it's our duty to maintain our commitment to study, proclaim, and obey God's Word. At the same time, we must gear our families and churches for instruction in Scripture, both for salvation and for remaining steadfast in the face of various opponents of the Gospel.

Our Christian education programs must center on teaching salvation through faith in Christ. We dare not assume that just because people attend Sunday school and church—even those who come from Christian homes—they have necessarily come to personal faith in Christ.

We hope and pray that every child will respond favorably when they hear the Good News. Parents, teachers, and pastors committedly working together can help to bring salvation and faith to our children.

Introduction for Youth

Topic: *Committed to the End*

We only mislead people when we offer the joys of the Gospel without the hardships. In our culture, however, hardships are not so easy to define. We might face some ridicule, or lose some friends, but we still have many other choices.

Perhaps we look in the wrong place for the battle to maintain our commitment to Christ. Throughout his ministry, Paul warned not just about physical but also spiritual hardships. These arise when people choose contemporary myths and reject God's Word.

In today's culture, hardships could easily consist of rejecting ungodly, unwholesome elements in entertainment, literature, and sports. After all, Satan uses music, television, radio, the Internet, books, and magazines to lure us away from God's truth. For some youths, it's a hardship to let go of these things for the sake of following Jesus. We, teachers of God's Word, can encourage them to remain committed to following the Savior—even when they face hard times—to the very end of their lives.

Concepts for Children

Topic: *Trusting Always*

1. The people who lived on an island called Malta were kind to travelers from a ship that had crashed on the beach.
2. After three months, Paul and the other travelers again set sail for the city of Rome.
3. After arriving in Rome, Paul was allowed to live by himself while a soldier guarded him.
4. Paul welcomed all who came to him and he boldly to them about Jesus.
5. The Father is pleased when we tell others about the Savior.

Lesson Commentary

I. PAUL'S ARRIVAL AT ROME: ACTS 28:16-20

A. Being Placed Under House Arrest: vs. 16

When we got to Rome, Paul was allowed to live by himself, with a soldier to guard him.

After getting saved, Paul worked with the Christians in Damascus (Acts 9:22), the desert regions of Arabia (Gal. 1:17), and Jerusalem. Opposition from the Jewish leaders drove him to Tarsus (Acts 9:26-30). Paul worked with Barnabas to reach Gentiles through the church at Antioch of Syria (11:19-26). On the first missionary tour, Paul visited the island of Cyprus and the cities of Antioch of Pisidia, Iconium, Lystra, and Derbe (chaps. 13—14). On his second missionary tour, Paul carried the Gospel further west to the province of Macedonia and the cities of Philippi, Thessalonica, Berea, Athens, and Corinth (chaps. 16—18). On his third missionary tour, he worked with churches at Ephesus, Troas, and Miletus (chaps. 19—20).

Paul made his way to Jerusalem, where he reported to the church leaders. They, in turn, asked him to disprove the false rumor that he had been teaching Jews to disobey the Mosaic law. Paul agreed to sponsor four men in a religious vow (21:17-26). When some Jews from Asia Minor saw Paul at the temple, they incited a mob to seize and beat him. Roman soldiers quickly intervened by taking the apostle into custody (vss. 27-33). After Paul's arrest in Jerusalem, he was then taken to Caesarea and appealed to Rome for a hearing before the emperor (21:34—26:32). The apostle's journey to the capital of the empire is recounted in chapters 27:1—28:14.

The ship on which Paul was being transported made stops at Syracuse (on the coast of the island of Sicily) and Rhegium (at the toe of Italy's boot). Then the travelers set out for Puteoli, which was one of Rome's main ports, despite that town's being 75 miles from the capital (28:12-13). Some Christians in Puteoli invited Paul and his companions to stay for a week. They had heard of Paul and wanted to host him so they could hear his story and teaching firsthand. The Roman centurion, Julius, who was in charge of Paul, permitted the apostle to visit (vs. 14). Then they headed for Rome along the Appian Way, one of Italy's main roads.

The news of Paul's arrival traveled from Puteoli to Rome ahead of him. The apostle had not founded the church in Rome, but he had written to the Roman Christians and had long wanted to visit them. The Roman church appears to have been an active one, and of course it was in the most strategic city in the empire. A group of believers from Rome set out to meet Paul on the way. Some stopped at the Three Taverns, a town about 33 miles south of Rome. A second group went as far as the Forum of Appius, another town 10 miles farther from Rome. Their welcome, like a red-carpet treatment for a dignitary, encouraged Paul. God used them to minister to him, reassuring him that he would not be alone in Rome. The apostle thanked God for their help (vs. 15).

In Rome, Paul could have been placed in one of the city's civil or military prisons.

That would not have been a pleasant way to await his trial. Instead, he was permitted to rent his own home, to receive visitors, and to preach the gospel (vs. 16). Soldiers of the Praetorian guard, the emperor's bodyguard unit, took turns guarding Paul while chained to him. Paul was able to share the Gospel with these soldiers as well as others associated with his case (Phil. 1:12-14).

B. Recounting the Episode: vs. 17

Three days later he called together the leaders of the Jews. When they had assembled, Paul said to them: "My brothers, although I have done nothing against our people or against the customs of our ancestors, I was arrested in Jerusalem and handed over to the Romans.

The city of Rome—where Paul now found himself under house arrest—was located on the Tiber River on seven hills, about 15 miles inland from the Tyrrhenian Sea. In the first century A.D., Rome was one of the two largest cities in the world (the other being Xian, China), with a population estimated at 1 million people. Rome was a walled city of less than 25 square miles. It boasted the royal palace, ornate fountains, elaborate baths (some of which housed libraries and social clubs), the Circus Maximus, used for chariot racing and other games, and the 50,000-seat Coliseum. The Forum, where citizens engaged in political, religious, and commercial enterprises, was where Paul likely defended himself and the Christian movement. Some 82 temples were built or remodeled in Rome in the first half of the first century.

During Paul's day, Rome was the political capital of an empire that, by the first century A.D., extended from the Atlantic Ocean to the Persian Gulf, and from north Africa to Britain and northern Europe. As a booming metropolis, Rome was connected to other parts of the ancient world by an intricate system of highways. Also, Rome's communications system was unsurpassed at the time. In fact, during the first century A.D., the city was at the hub of trade and commerce. Because of its location and prestige, Rome was a strategic center for the spread of the Gospel. It's no wonder that people remarked concerning the city, "All roads lead to Rome."

Three days after Paul arrived in Rome, he took advantage of his freedom to have visitors by trying to establish relations with the city's Jewish community. He summarized for a group of their leaders the circumstances that brought him as a prisoner to the capital of the empire. He openly acknowledged his trouble with some Jews in Jerusalem. He insisted, however, he never did anything to hurt the Jewish people. Additionally, he said he never violated the "customs of our ancestors" (Acts 28:17). We learn in Romans 3:2 that the Jews had been trusted with the oracles of God (a reference to the Old Testament). A number of privileges are listed in 9:4-5 that belonged to Israel as God's chosen nation. These included worshiping Him in the Jerusalem temple and receiving His wonderful promises. The Jews were the offspring the patriarchs and enjoyed the honor of the Messiah being an Israelite.

It's not by accident that in the early days of Paul's imprisonment in Rome, he first met with the resident Jews. In every place where there Jews lived, the apostle spoke first to them before going to the Gentiles. Previously, most likely toward the end of his third missionary journey, Paul stated in 1:14 that he had a great sense of obligation to communicate the Gospel to as many people as possible. Indeed, as verse 15 indicates, this is the reason why the apostle had been eager to come to Rome. Even though the present circumstances were less than ideal, this did not deter Paul from evangelizing the lost in the capital of the empire.

Verse 16 explains that the apostle was not ashamed to be associated with the good news about Christ, for it represented the power of God that made salvation possible. Moreover, eternal redemption is available to all who believe, first to the Jew, then for the Gentile. Since Jews were the heirs of the promises of Abraham and the people from whom the Messiah came, it was appropriate for the Gospel to be preached first to them. Eventually, when the Jews rejected the Good News, Paul turned to the Gentiles (see Acts 13:44-46; 18:5-6). According to Romans 1:17, the Gospel explains how unrighteous people can receive an upright standing before a holy God. Regardless of whether one was a Jew or a Gentile, they had to appropriate this righteousness by trusting in the Messiah (see Hab. 2:4).

C. Requesting to Be Tried by the Emperor: vss. 18-19

They examined me and wanted to release me, because I was not guilty of any crime deserving death. But when the Jews objected, I was compelled to appeal to Caesar—not that I had any charge to bring against my own people.

Paul told the local Jewish leaders that the Roman government in Palestine had conducted a judicial hearing regarding the apostle's case. After cross-examining him, the officials determined that Paul had not done anything to deserve death or imprisonment (Acts 28:18; see 26:31). In fact, they struggled to delineate the charges being made against the accused (see 25:27). Even so, when the civil authorities sought to release the apostle, his opponents protested the decision. Moreover, when they continued to press their charges against him, Paul was forced to appeal his case to Caesar (which was his right as a Roman citizen). The apostle was careful to emphasize that he was not bringing any countercharge against his "own people" (28:19). He was appearing before the emperor as a defendant only.

D. Desiring to See the Local Jewish Leaders: vs. 20

For this reason I have asked to see you and talk with you. It is because of the hope of Israel that I am bound with this chain.

Paul's final statement demonstrated the link between Judaism and the Christian church. His ministry, which had led to his current predicament, was due to the "hope of Israel" (Acts 28:20). What the Jews had long hoped for was what Paul heralded as an accomplished fact: the advent of the Messiah. This was a consistent theme in the apostle's evangelistic preaching. For instance, while at Pisidian

Antioch, during Paul's first missionary journey, he told about the one in whom God had most fully revealed His grace: Jesus the Savior (13:23).

Jesus was the descendant of David who had been promised in such Old Testament prophecies as Isaiah 11. Paul declared that the promises of Scripture had been fulfilled in the Messiah. The apostle quoted Psalm 2:7 in support of Jesus' divine sonship (Acts 13:32). Paul quoted Isaiah 55:3 and Psalm 16:10 to back up Jesus' resurrection (Acts 13:34-35). Those passages could not have been fulfilled ultimately in David, since the illustrious king died. But Jesus, David's descendant, was raised immortal. In Him the hopes of the prophets were fulfilled (vss. 36-37).

II. PAUL'S PREACHING AT ROME: ACTS 28:21-25A, 28-31

A. Expressing Initial Interest: vss. 21-22

They replied, "We have not received any letters from Judea concerning you, and none of the brothers who have come from there has reported or said anything bad about you. But we want to hear what your views are, for we know that people everywhere are talking against this sect."

In response to Paul, the local Jewish leaders claimed to have heard nothing "bad" (Acts 28:21) about the apostle. This included the absence of any written correspondence from Judea. There weren't even verbal reports against Paul from anyone who had come from there. While claiming not to know anything negative about Paul, the Jewish leaders admitted having heard unfavorable reports about the Christian church. They called the group a "sect" (vs. 22), which indicated that Christianity was still regarded as a splinter group of Judaism.

In all likelihood, the resident Jews had heard that the followers of Jesus held a low view of the law and created disturbances (see 21:20-21). It's also possible that in this exchange with Paul, the Jewish representatives were exercising some diplomatic restraint to avoid trouble with the Roman officials. Some experts think that religious disputes with Christians, involving major disturbances, had caused the Emperor Claudius to order all Jews out of Rome about the year A.D. 49. Jews had returned to Rome sometime after Claudius died in A.D. 54.

B. Presenting the Truth of the Gospel: vs. 23

They arranged to meet Paul on a certain day, and came in even larger numbers to the place where he was staying. From morning till evening he explained and declared to them the kingdom of God and tried to convince them about Jesus from the Law of Moses and from the Prophets.

Despite their suspicions, the local Jewish leaders agreed to return "on a certain day" (Acts 28:23) to hear what Paul had to say about Jesus of Nazareth and the religious movement connected with Him. It appears that on the surface of things, Paul's fellow Jews seemed open-minded. In fact, for an entire day the apostle reasoned with those who came to hear him. He testified from the Old Testament about the rule of God and the promise of the Messiah found in "the Law of Moses" and "the Prophets." Paul used the Jewish sacred writings to show how Jesus had fulfilled the prophecies in numerous ways. The apostle taught that the kingdom of God includes His rule in the hearts of believers. The divine kingdom was not merely limited to the nation of Israel, as the Jews had long believed.

C. Encountering a Mixed Response: vss. 24-25a

Some were convinced by what he said, but others would not believe. They disagreed among themselves and began to leave after Paul had made this final statement.

Paul convinced some in his audience, but many others remained unpersuaded (Acts 28:24). Animated debate continued among the Jews themselves, with some supporting the apostle's views and others denouncing them. The meeting finally broke up when Paul quoted one more unflattering prophecy (vss. 25-27). He quoted from the Septuagint version (an ancient Greek translation) of Isaiah 6:9-10. In doing so, the apostle declared that his listeners heard but did not understand God's truth. Likewise, they saw but did not perceive God's revelation. Their problem was that their hearts were calloused, insensitive, and unfeeling. The result was that they did not turn to God for spiritual healing.

D. Witnessing to the Gentiles: vss. 28-29

"Therefore I want you to know that God's salvation has been sent to the Gentiles, and they will listen!" After he said this, the Jews left, arguing vigorously among themselves.

In response to the local Jews' refusal to believe the Gospel, Paul declared that "God's salvation" (Acts 28:28) was also being offered to the Gentiles. Furthermore, they would hear and heed the Good News. After the apostle had made this statement, his fellow Jews departed. As they left, they heatedly argued with one another about what the apostle had said (vs. 29).

E. Proclaiming the Kingdom of God: vss. 30-31

For two whole years Paul stayed there in his own rented house and welcomed all who came to see him. Boldly and without hindrance he preached the kingdom of God and taught about the Lord Jesus Christ.

Paul remained in detention in his own "rented house" (Acts 28:30) for "two whole years." He was not assigned a place to live by the government. Rather, he paid his own living expenses. Perhaps this indicates that the apostle earned a living by tentmaking even while in custody. In any case, Paul had considerable freedom to see people. Indeed, this "open door" policy enabled many to visit him and discuss the Gospel. He did not hesitate to proclaim the truth about Jesus boldly and triumphantly in the capital of the empire (vs. 31).

Most likely those who guarded the apostle also heard his testimony, and we can imagine a number of Roman soldiers put their faith in the Savior as a result. Because of Paul's presence in Rome, the Gospel penetrated the inner circles of Roman officialdom and affected influential people in the capital (see Phil. 1:13). It was also during this time that the apostle wrote the so-called "prison epistles" of

Ephesians, Philippians, Colossians, and Philemon. Even while chained to a soldier, Paul remained productive.

The two-year period of house arrest is somewhat mystifying. According to one group of historians, Roman law required cases to be heard within 18 months or they had to be dismissed. Paul's two-year wait suggests to some that his prosecutors failed to press charges within the allotted time. With bureaucratic delays, they say, Paul finally stood before Caesar for formal release after being held two years. Others dismiss this conjecture and see Paul's imprisonment ending with a death sentence passed by Nero.

An unresolved issue is the reason why Luke concluded Acts as he did. Some think he wrote as far as the account had gone. Expressed differently, he couldn't tell the end because he was himself waiting to find out what would happen. Others conjecture that Luke had a grander scheme in mind, namely, that he wanted to emphasize that the church's work continues until Jesus returns. The last verse of Acts also has been viewed as a summary of the accomplishments of the early church as the apostles, especially Paul, spread the Gospel from Jerusalem to Rome: "You will be my witnesses in Jerusalem . . . and to the ends of the earth" (1:8).

Discussion Questions

1. What set of circumstances led to Paul being incarcerated in Rome?
2. Why do you think Paul asked the local Jewish leaders to meet with him?
3. What compelled Paul to request to be tried by the emperor?
4. What did Paul say to his Jewish peers when they met with him a second time?
5. What responses have you encountered after sharing the Gospel with others?

Contemporary Application

How do we make the Gospel available to all people? We can use radio, television, films, and books (to name a few things). We have more means available to us than ever before. At the same time we should not forget the important role that each of us serves in proclaiming the Good News. Believers are critical to the success of evangelism because people want to see our love and passion for them as individuals, not just as part of the mass audience. They want to see Jesus in us. They want to ask why our faith works for us. This reminds us that our personal witness for Christ can be just as effective as any other means of spreading the Gospel.

We should be careful not to assume that everyone has heard the message of salvation, despite the media we may use to disseminate the Gospel. We have to think about people from different backgrounds who may be bypassed by the media and by our churches. We dare not give the impression that the Gospel is anyone's private property. Paul made it clear that everyone who calls on the Lord will be saved and that part of the process includes their hearing and understanding the truth. That's where we come in. May we shoulder this awesome responsibility with joy!

Biblical Integrity and Relevance for Your Classroom

The David C. Cook Bible-in-Life adult curriculum provides everything you need to teach the International Sunday School lessons. An easy-to-follow, easy-to-teach format will help you reach every student in your class with comprehensive biblical material, discussion questions, and a variety of activities. Includes the KJV and NIV Scriptures for comparison, a special teacher's devotional, and ways to relate Scripture directly to your adults' daily lives.

Visit **www.RealLifeDownloaded.com** for free teaching tips that tie current events to each week's lesson and connect Scripture to students' lives.

Available David C. Cook Bible-in-Life Teaching Resources:
- *Adult Teacher's Guide*
- *Comprehensive Bible Study* student book (also available in Large Print)
- *Creative Teaching Aid* with full-color Bible maps and posters
- *The Quiet Hour* daily devotional
- *Power for Living* weekly magazine

Deep Truth. Bold Faith. Changed Lives.

David C. Cook
Adult Teacher's Guide
September–November 2009

BIL
Bible-in-Life

Living in Community
Joshua, Gideon, Ezra, Nehemiah,
Mark, 1 & 2 Peter
Special New Feature: *Life Lessons*
Sharing Your Faith to Your Grandchildren